ATLAS
OF OFFICE
INTERIORS

ROCKPORT

ATLAS OF OFFICE INTERIORS

BEVERLY MASSACHUSETTS

ROCKPORT PUBLISHERS

ÀLEX SÁNCHEZ VIDIELLA

Copyright © 2008 by LOFT Publications

First published in the United States of America by
Rockport Publishers, a member of
Quayside Publishing Group
100 Cummings Center
Suite 406-L
Beverly, MA 01915-6101
Telephone: (978) 282-9590
Fax: (978) 283-2742
www.rockpub.com

ISBN-13: 978-1-59253-431-9
ISBN-10: 1-59253-431-7

Publisher: Paco Asensio

Editorial Coordination: Catherine Collin

Project Coordination & Editor: Àlex Sánchez Vidiella

Texts: Àlex Sánchez Vidiella, Begoña Saludes, Sandra Moya

Editorial Assistant: Esther Moreno, Macarena San Martín De Soto, Francesc Zamora Mola

Art Director: Mireia Casanovas Soley

Cover Design: Rockport Publishers

Cover Image: Shania Shegedyn/Gray Puksand, Architect & Designer

Layout: Conxi Papió Cabezas

English translation: Jay Noden

Editorial project:
2006 © LOFT Publications
Via Laietana 32, 4th Of. 92.
08003 Barcelona. Spain
Tel.: +34 932 688 088
Fax: +34 932 687 073
loft@loftpublications.com
www.loftpublications.com

Printed in China

| INTRODUCTION | 9 |

WORKING AT HOME

Studio in Sant Cugat	14
Solar roof Vienna 5	20
Studio in Berga	26
Graphic Design Studio	32
Attic in Andorra La Vella	38
W Loft	44

OFFICES IN SMLL SPACES

Amazon Air Offices	56
Happy Place	64
MK/3-VA	74
Amalgama 7	80
Maritime Intelligence Group Office	90
Bank in Cerreto Guidi, Mill with Bank	98
Afeijón-Fernández Architecture Office	104
Zonabarcelona Office	116
Habitectura Offices	124
Joaquín Gallego Studio	132
9MAR Offices	138

Bordonabe Barcelona	148
Renegade Film Studio	158
Mixed Greens Gallery	164
Bank in La Fontina, Still Life with Bank 1	172
CODECSA Offices	180
Thirdpoint Offices	190
Beauty Lab	198
Lehrer Architects' Office	210
Schröder & Schömbs PR Agency	218
Golden Nugget	226

Medium Size Offices

FTVentures Offices	236
L'aiguana Studio	242
Bourke Place Studio	248
Bank in Pontedera, Bank with Eyes	254
Institut Català de la Dona	262
Harrison & Wolf Offices	272
Metal Office	280
Rios Clementi Hale Studios Office	286
Hidm.Office Vienna	292
Hangar Design Group Headquarter	298
Signes Offices	310
Klangforum House	318
Amec Spie Offices	326
Construcciones Mon Offices	338
Mediaedge	350
Studio DAtrans	360
Ford Models Headquarters	364
Hydraulx	372
Indes Offices	382
Laird + Partners Offices	390

Large Offices

Glocal Law	400
DDB Office Hong Kong	410
GREY Worldwide	420
Krungthai AXA Life Insurance	426
Affinity Offices	436
Vanke Cheugdu Commercial Complex	446
Office Building A. T. Kearney	454
Offices on Mestre Nicolau Street	462
Kropman	470
Momentum St. Louis	478
Clariant Flexible Office	490
Caballero Factory	496
Bendigo Bank Offices	508
Mayo Institute of Technology	516
Indra Offices	524
Rijkswaterstaat Zeeland Head Office	536
Ermenegildo Zegna	544
Mediabank Private	556
Deloitte Head Offices	568
Laakhaven den Haag Complex	580
Agbar Tower Offices	588

Directory 596

Atlas of Office Interiors presents a carefully chosen and extensive selection of offices, which reflect the most up-to-date trends and ideas in designs for work spaces. If we begin with the premise that the office is the quintessential working environment, where employees invest most of their daytime hours, it makes sense that architects, interior designers, and designers dedicate energy and talent to this type of installation. Despite the fact that the technological revolution of the last forty years has changed our notion of the world, the work space remains the same: a table, a chair, office material, natural or artificial lighting, and space for storing information. In a world where economic globalization is already a palpable fact, companies, property developers, public and private administrations, and governments are all in need of aterritorial offices, and are now potential clients for architectural and design studios all over the planet. To satisfy this need, philosophy and efficiency, characteristics of Asian designs, combine with considerations for the workers' well-being and their integration into the company, in line with North American and European designs, to create a variety of projects, which are notable for both their functionality and their aesthetics.

The original and innovative spaces presented in this "atlas" are classified into four groups: large offices, medium-size offices, small offices and work spaces in the home. This compilation, which covers approximately the last six years, includes multi-functional, dynamic and ductile environments designed to be comfortable for the workers and to improve their efficiency. The projects encompass large-scale installations designed by prestigious architects and interior designers, such as Bonetti Kozerski Studio, De Architectengroep, Fermín Vázquez/b720 Arquitectos, Gray Puksand, Murray O'Laire Architects, Paul de Ruitier, Saguez and Partners, etc.; medium-size offices from studios such as Architecten Bureau Van Der Broek en Bakema, Arconiko Architecten, Conrad-Bercah +W Office/West Architecture Workroom, Cossmann de Bruyn, Group A, Shubin + Donaldson, Wirth + Wirth Architekten, among others; smaller projects, carried out by renowned firms like EQUIPxavierclaramunt, Francesc Rifé + Bordonabe, GCA Arquitectes Associats, Héctor Restrepo, Joaquín Gallego, John H. Lee/Workshop For Architecture, José Abeijón Vela, Massimo Marini Architetto, and many more. Finally there are the work spaces integrated into people's homes, designed by the more intrepid of interior designers, such as Agustí Costa, Ignacio Forteza/Forteza Carbonell Associates, Elisabet Faura, Gerhard Veciana/ARTEKS, andLola Lago Interiors.

When designing an office space, architects and interior designers, generally speaking, are looking to create a space with a strong aesthetic character. Somewhere that avoids formal conventions, where technological advances are applied to generate functional and efficient solutions. When considering these installations, factors need to be taken into account like, for example, making efficient use of space, and its adaptation to a single area for a large number of people. On the other hand, solutions are also considered that make life more comfortable for the workers and improve their sense of well-being.

The increase in the demand for work spaces, particularly in large cities, obliges architects and interior designers to carry out feats of ingenuity, which on occasion result in true works of art. The information technology evolution, changes in lifestyles and the development of new materials have had a decisive influence on spatial conception, internal organization and the decoration of interiors. There are also elements that no longer form a part of office design: large spaces to store information on paper, which have disappeared to make way for small mobile structures; closed spaces to preserve intimacy, which are now open and communal areas; shades of gray and dull colors, which have a negative effect on workers and produce a lethargic monotony—replaced instead by striking colors. Also materials are now used that provide unusual textures and finishes, such as aluminum, glass and plastic, among others. The result is a thousand and one ways to conceive a space, such as the offices characterized by large volumes and communal areas (projects from 3XN A/S, Alfredo Arribas, Jordi Torres, Lehrer Architects and Marta Torelló + Marta González, etc); interiors in which the color range is the dominant element (for example Cheeeeese!, IAD_arquitectos, Leven Betts Studio, Massimo Marini Architetto, Rios Clementi Hale Studios, The Lawrence Group, among others); or installations where the materials are the design centerpiece. Projects stand out in this latter group from Ian Ayers (with glass and concrete as the dominant materials), Lichtblau +Wagner (aluminum), Hangar Design Group (wood), Sarah Bitter/Metek Architecture (exposed concrete), Slade Architecture (stainless steel and aluminum), etc. Finally, the Asian interior designers deserve special mention, exemplars of true craftsmen of minimalism in office design, such as, CL3 Architects, Datrans, DWP, Takashi Yamaguchi & Associates, among others.

When projecting the interiors of these eclectic and innovative offices, the architects and designers have sought functionality, but have also considered the company's corporate image. Depending on the needs of the client, the architects project spaces that oscillate between floor plans physically divided by way of private offices, and those without any physical borders, whose designs encourage communication between employees. Another influential factor when considering the design of an office is the increased scarcity of space in large cities. The reduced dimensions of work spaces mean that divisions are often merely insinuated or simplified.

The following pages pay homage to the imagination, skill, and efficiency that characterize design in the twenty first century.

Working at Home

 Studio in Sant Cugat　　　　14

 Solar roof Vienna 5　　　　20

 Studio in Berga　　　　26

 Graphic Design Studio　　　　32

 Attic in Andorra La Vella　　　　38

 W Loft　　　　44

Studio in Sant Cugat

The interior designer accepted the project to create a studio from a 75 sqft bedroom.

The client was already using this room as an office and the brief presented by the designer proposed a double usage: as a studio on a normal basis, and as a guest room when the occasion required the extra space. He also proposed its use as a living room, hence the installation of a television.

Several pieces of furniture have been designed exclusively to fulfill the aims of this project. The sofa without arms, located in front of the worktable, upholstered in orange and crimson is 4.2 feet wide and unfolds to make a double bed. Opposite this, on the other side of the table, is a red armchair on wheels, in the same color range as the sofa. The square top of the worktable is supported on one side by a rail installed in the wall, while the legs on the other side are equipped with wheels. This allows it to be easily moved when the sofa needs to be unfolded or simply to modify the layout of the room. The red retractable table lamp, however, is fixed and serves as task lighting. It has been strategically placed to act as a bedroom light, since it illuminates the head of the bed and shines onto the work table when this occupies its position next to the sofa.

A piece of plastic behind the sofa, in the same orange as the upholstery, acts as a headboard when the sofa is unfolded, and also a small bookshelf thanks to the circular spaces, whose respective diameter forms a shelf, one orange and one white. This establishes a play of form and color with the walls, which are painted bright white with the exception of an enormous two-color circle that occupies two thirds of the wall behind the headboard/bookshelf. A bookshelf attached halfway up the wall, composed of two transparent glass shelves on a metal frame painted white, completes the studio's furnishings.

Architect/Designer:
Lola Lago Interiores,
Estructuras Joan Calaf

Client: Magda R.
Photographer: Eugeni Pons
Location: Sant Cugat del Vallès, Spain
Completion date: 2003
Area: 75 SF

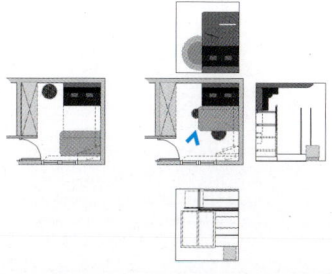

STUDIO IN SANT CUGAT

○ Floor plan

○ Conceptual drawing

Solar roof Vienna 5

This office is characterized by its small size, located within a private home composed of two floors and a loft. The office occupies the highest part of the house, in order to make the most of the natural light and to enjoy the privacy needed to work.

The eye-catching structure of this office is formed by large blocks of wood customized so that they adapt to the space and fit perfectly. Behind these blocks are a small flight of steps, which lead to the main door of the office, where the main worktable has been placed, along with a chest of drawers formed from small drawers for keeping work material. The architects decided to choose these blocks because the space is so small and consequently there was no other choice than to create an entirely functional area, which also had style and its own character. These wooden blocks, which give the space character without making it any less functional, have been covered with fir panels painted yellow, a striking color that gives the composition a modern flavor. This chromatic note also helps to break with the coldness of the concrete walls in this work space.

Sustainability is another one of this project's major features. The roof, made from solar panels, makes this building energy self-sufficient. The storage and use of the energy is controlled constantly by a software, which guarantees its optimum use. Furthermore, the large openings in the façade allow a large amount of sunlight to enter. The interior fir partition walls contribute to the lighting, since they are mobile and can be moved to change the layout, and the temperature control. They are an effective covering for the exposed concrete on the walls.

ARCHITECT/DESIGNER:

LICHTBLAU.WAGNER ARCHITEKTEN

Client: private
Photographer: Bruno Klomfar
Location: Vienna, Austria
Completion date: 2002
Area: 538 SF

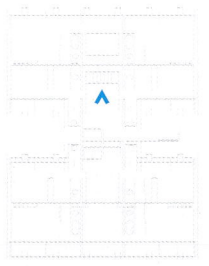

○ The creation of a compartment, through the use of the striking yellow of the panels on the exposed concrete, aims to aesthetically separate the office from the home.

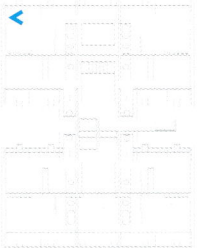

SOLAR ROOF VIENNA 5

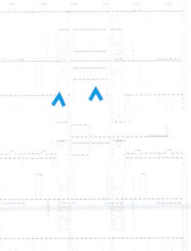

SOLAR ROOF VIENNA 5

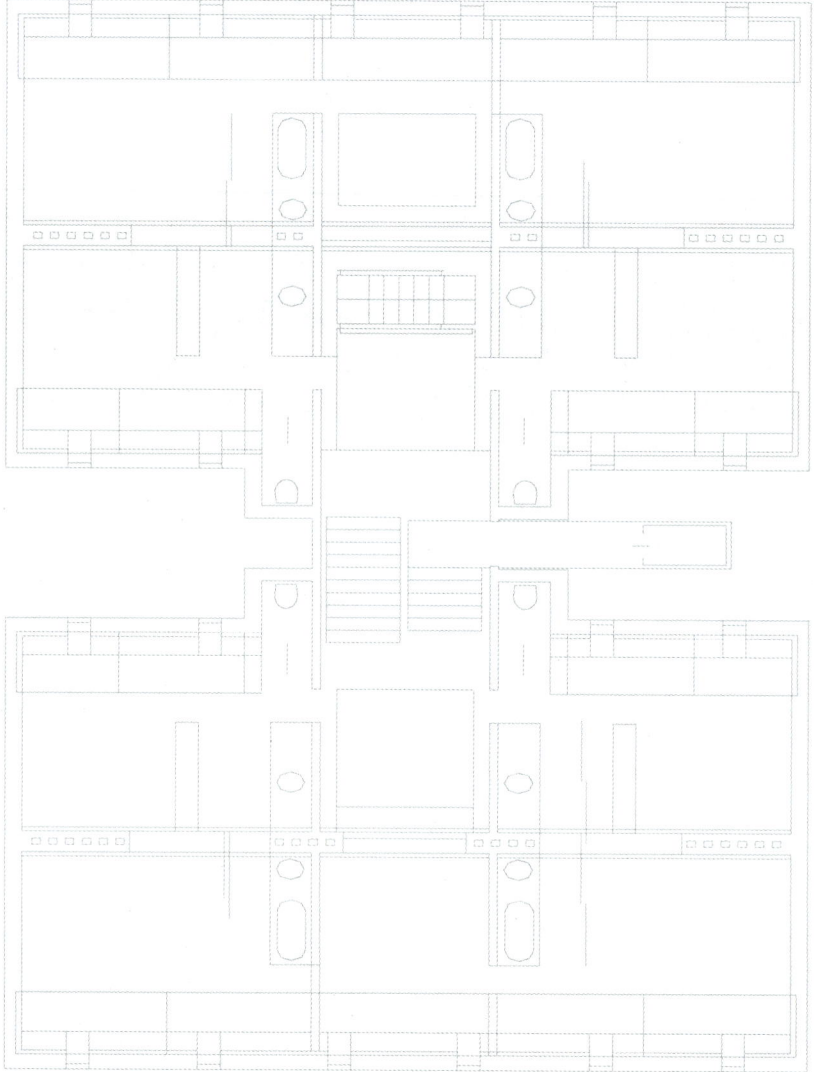

○ Floor plan

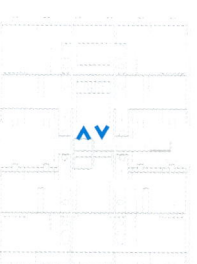

STUDIO IN BERGA

This project required the creation of a studio on the top floor of a home in Berga, a town in the province of Barcelona. The client, a director of a service company, wanted a comfortable space where he could enjoy a certain amount of isolation in which to reflect, read, or simply enjoy the views of the surrounding countryside and the mountains. It also had to serve as a place for receiving visits from friends and family, and be designed to accommodate the 5,000 volumes that compose the client's library.

Because the studio most of the time will be used by just one person, walls were not necessary, increasing the available space and avoiding clear functional differentiations, for example between the lounge area and the work area. The floor plan is organized in a free and fluid way, and the side where the sloping window is located becomes the joining element, embracing the space and providing a global perception of the studio.

The office includes: a worktable; a table for technical equipment: computer, fax, etc.; a space for file storage; a fireplace and a lounge with undefined limits.

Between the general level of the room and the 91-square-foot central space, there is a level difference of 30 inches. The four steps were not enough to integrate both areas, and it was considered necessary to deal with the level change in a way that didn't break up the space, but integrated into its functionality. This is why various functions have been integrated here: a platform, a metal fireplace, indirect lighting, etc.

The floor of the lowest part is the same stoneware as the terrace, with the aim of visually connecting both spaces. In contrast, the highest section is oak with a transparent varnish, preserving the original appearance of the wood.

The library has been distributed around the perimeter, on white, custom-designed shelves with the same wood finishes as the tables.

Architect/Designer:

Agustí Costa

Client: n/a
Photographer: David Cardelús
Location: Berga, Spain
Completion date: 2005
Area: 624 SF

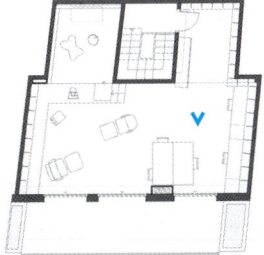

● The general lighting has been carried out with fluorescent lights integrated into the shelves of the library, on the flat roof and in the crooks and crannies of the original structure. It is indirect or semi-indirect and adjustable.

STUDIO IN BERGA
29

STUDIO IN BERGA

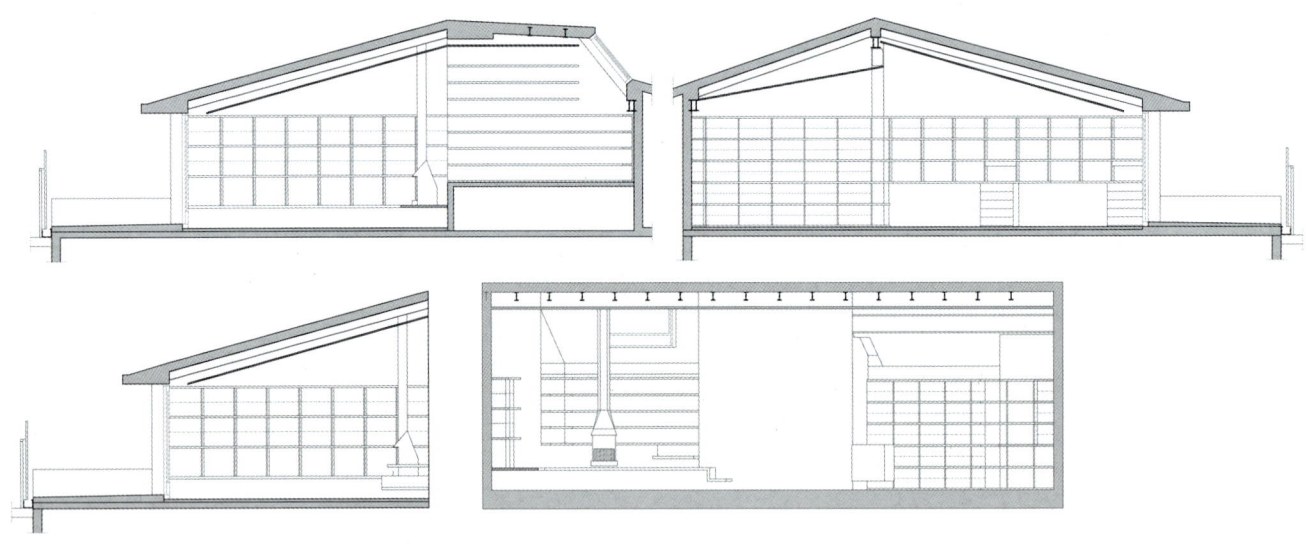

● Sections

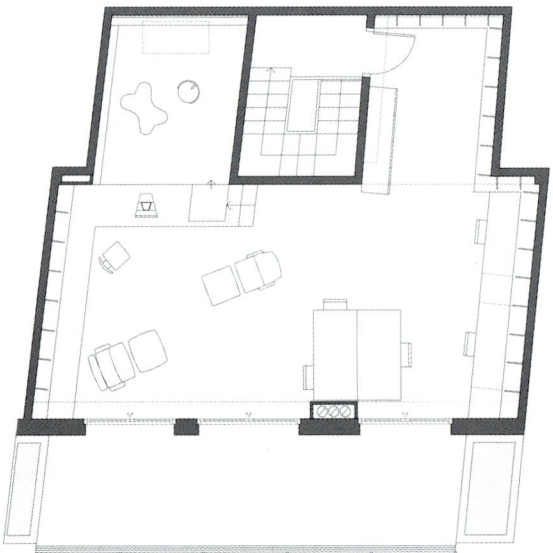

● Floor plan

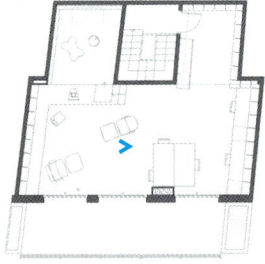

Graphic Design Studio

ARCHITECT/DESIGNER:
FORTEZA CARBONELL ASSOCIATS

Client: Claret Serrahima
Photographer: Eugeni Pons
Location: Barcelona, Spain
Completion date: 2002
Area: 1,184 SF

The client for this project, a graphic design studio, looked for an original building to house their offices and finally opted for the top section of an abandoned palace.

The brief specified the creation of a space with abundant natural light and a balanced environment, fruit of a minimalist intervention, and one which adapted to the pre-existing building.

Two levels have been created beneath the pitched roof of this open floor plan, through the construction of a mezzanine. This new level offers access to the pre-existing 485 sqft terrace, which was previously inaccessible.

The entrance to the studio is connected directly to the reception area, whose left-hand exposed brick wall, belongs to the original structure, while the front wall, made from white plasterboard, hides the rest of the studio space from sight. An L-shaped screen opposite the reception area delineates the meeting room, the exterior of which is adorned with the designs from projects in progress, held in place with magnets.

The work area has direct visual communication with the mezzanine, used as a private office. Beneath this is the library and the service area, composed of a kitchen and the toilets. The mezzanine can be accessed via a light-weight staircase, without a banister, whose iron steps have been painted white.

The most spacious area has been reserved for the work space and has a large modular central table, formed from three tables and a long table situated to one side, where the computers are. This is the same as the reception desk: a glass top resting on stained okoume wood. One end serves as a light table thanks to a fluorescent light installed beneath the glass.

The needs for artificial lighting have been resolved with fluorescent general lighting that hangs from the ceiling and adjustable table lamps for the task lighting. The flooring of the mezzanine above the library has been removed and covered with glass to enhance the natural lighting.

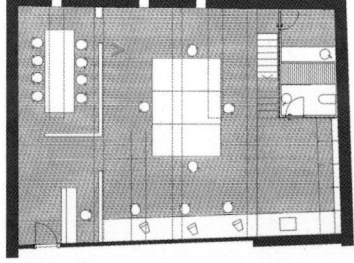

GRAPHIC DESIGN STUDIO

● The architects have taken on the challenge of affording a host of functions to a residential space, whilst also opening access to this large 485 sqft terrace.

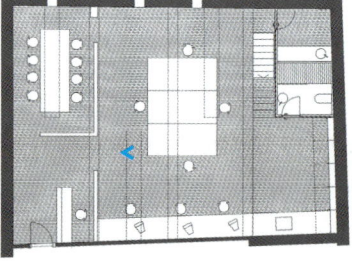

GRAPHIC DESIGN STUDIO

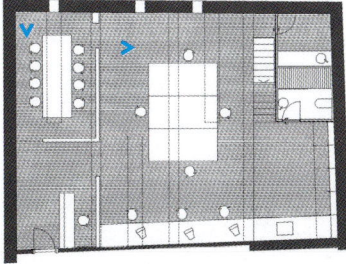

35

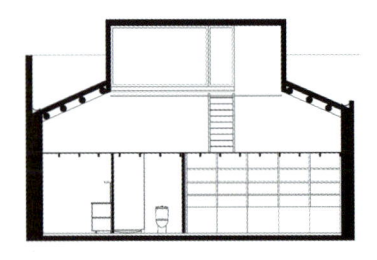

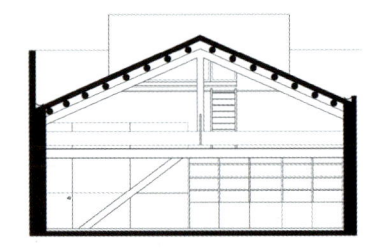

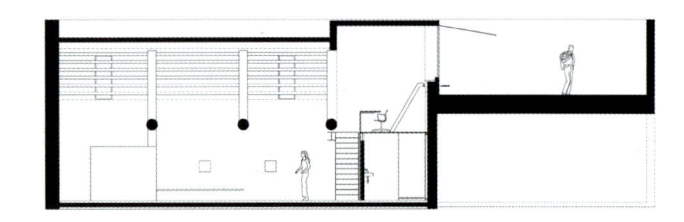

GRAPHIC DESIGN STUDIO

○ Sections

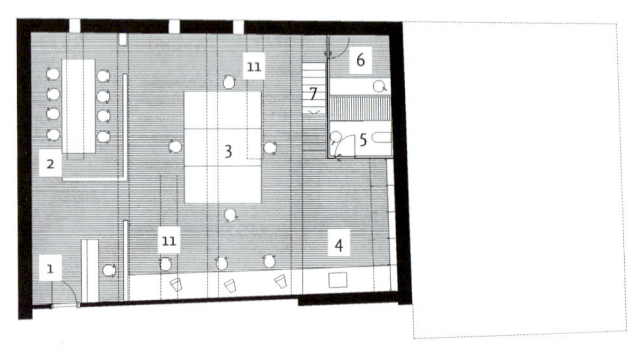

○ Ground floor

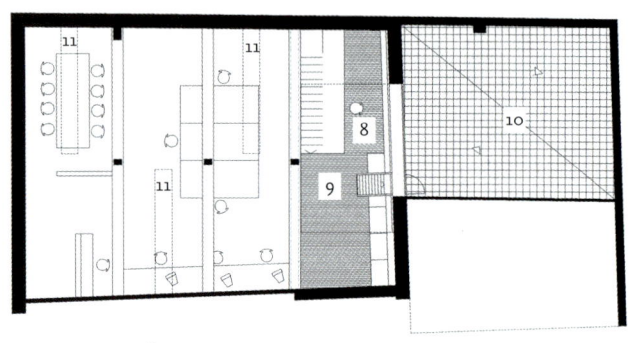

○ Mezzanine floor

1. Reception
2. Meeting room
3. Studio
4. Library
5. Bathroom
6. Kitchen
7. Stair to mezzanine
8. Office
9. Stair to terrace
10. Terrace
11. Skylight

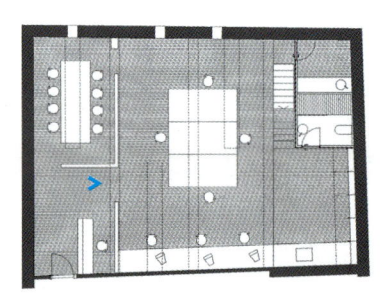

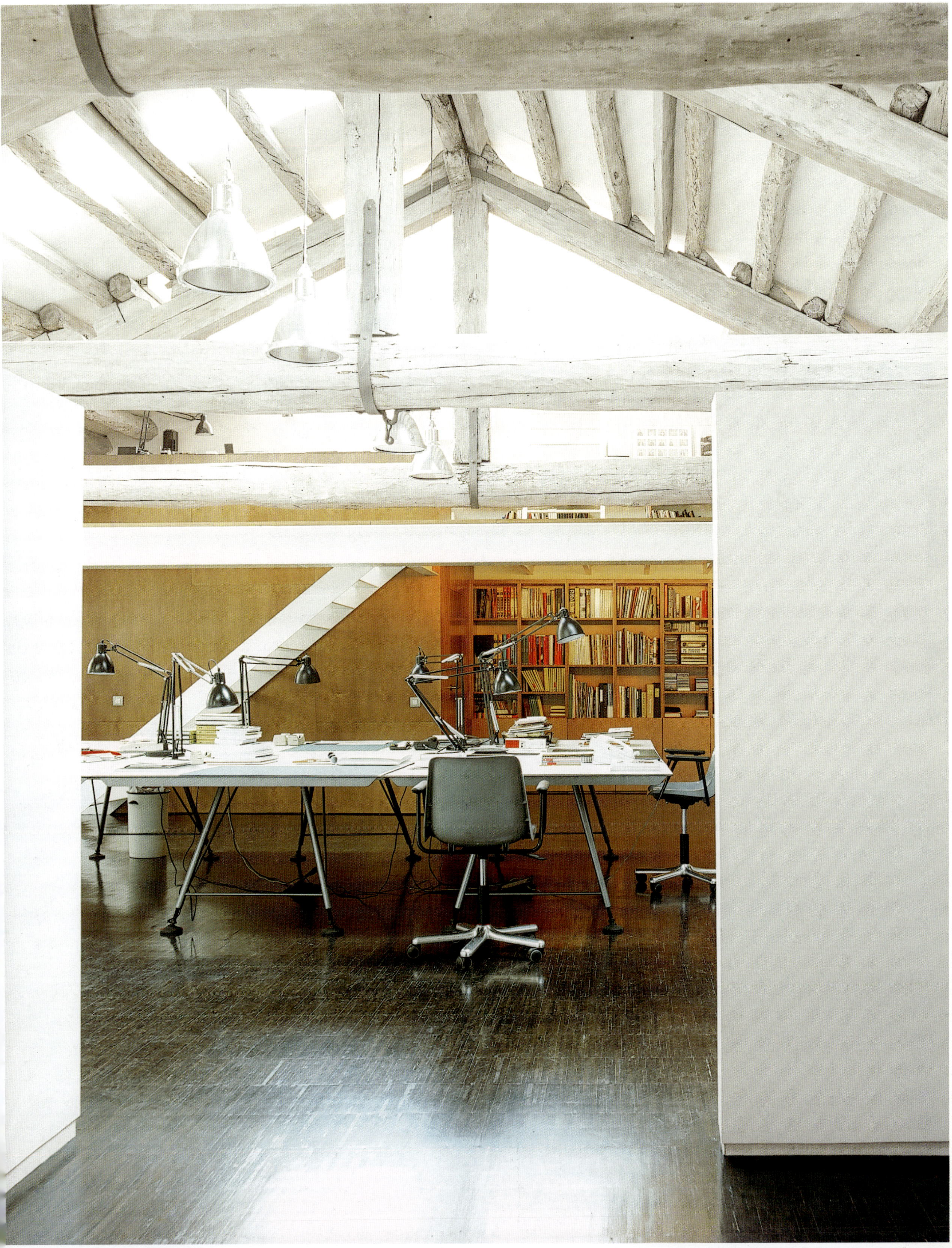

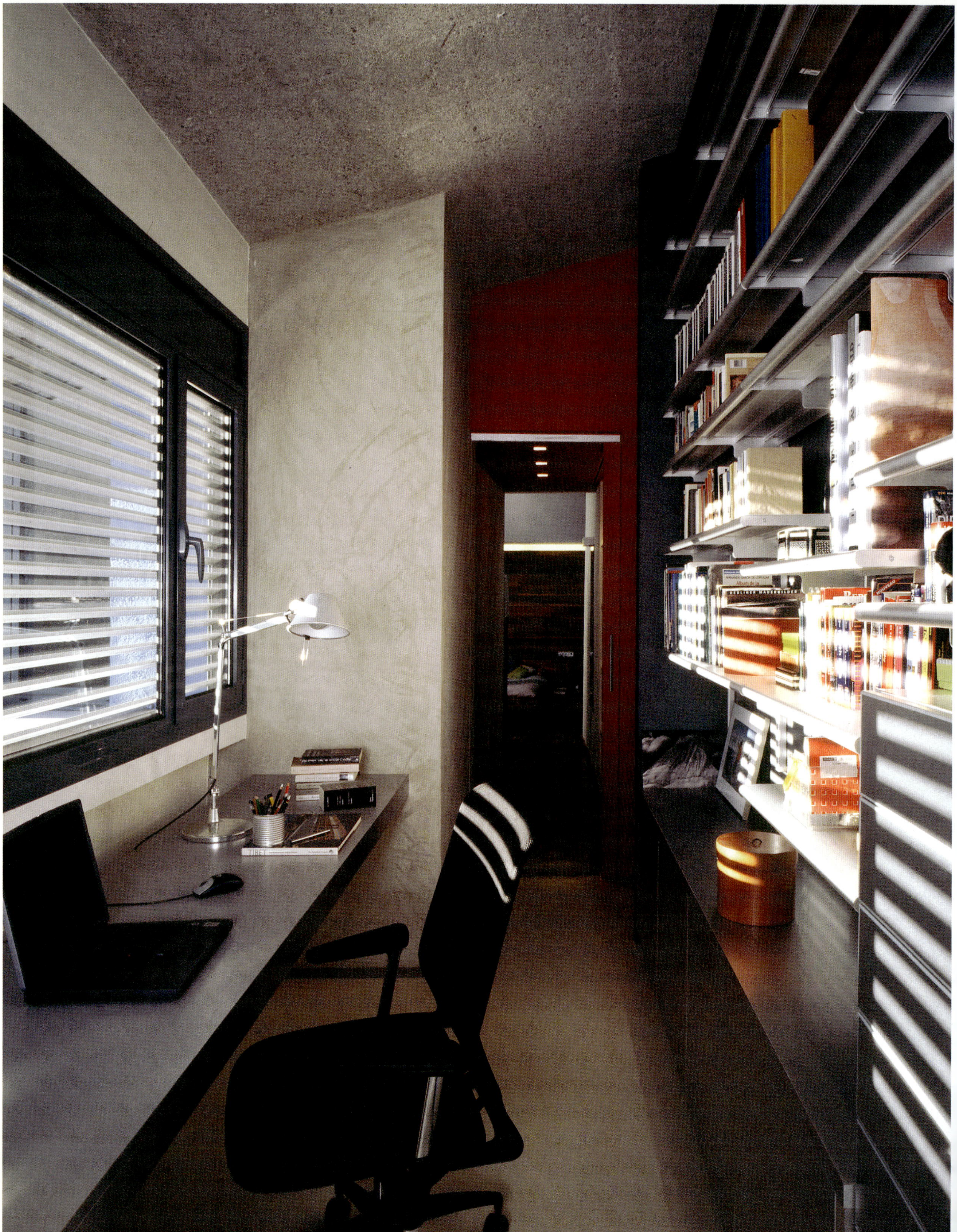

Attic in Andorra La Vella

An entirely remodeled home was the site for the conversion of this space into offices.

One of the main aims stated in the brief was to attain maximum fluidity in the interior. This compensates for the lack of light; a result of two thirds of the building's façade facing an interior courtyard. There is, therefore, visual communication between the office and the other areas of the home, as well as between each of these through the half-height partitions and their strategic positioning, which allows the space to be crossed in different directions.

Strictly speaking therefore the work area in the office is an open space that begins at the entrance. The wall that connects the circulation through the home is located at the entrance to the home. One side of this backs onto the office, which is at once a reading zone and a library.

The worktable is a sheet with a metal finish fixed to the wall, measuring the same length as the window it runs alongside. This opens partially on both sides and includes blinds with adjustable slats.

On the other side, opposite the window, a bookshelf has been installed on the wall, formed by shelves of different lengths and irregularly positioned, as well as closed compartments along the lower section.

The space between the bookshelf and the table is only big enough for the office chair, which is comfortable for working and does not impede circulation.

The fixed furnishings, the worktable and the bookshelf, and the window frame are the same gray color with a metallic finish. The sloping ceiling has also been painted gray, only darker, and the wall next to the window is a lighter shade of the same color. The other walls in the work area are white like the floor, which is made of white concrete and resin, and exists as a single continuous surface without joins.

Architect/Designer:

Elisabet Faura, Gerard Veciana/Arteks Arquitectura

Client: UNIMSA
Photographer: Eugeni Pons
Location: Andorra la Vella, Andorra
Completion date: 2003
Area: 1,270 SF

ATTIC IN ANDORRA LA VELLA

● The open plan compensates for the lack of natural light in the interior. A wall delineates the work area without shutting it off, and a table has been installed by the window.

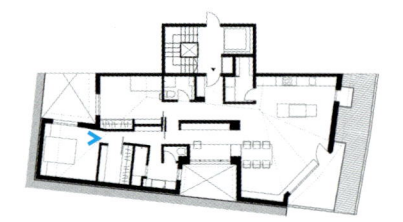

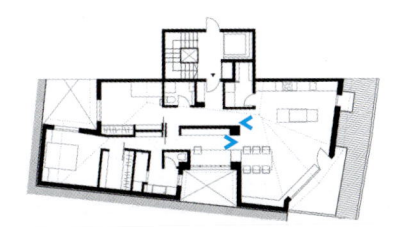

ATTIC IN ANDORRA LA VELLA

41

ATTIC IN ANDORRA LA VELLA

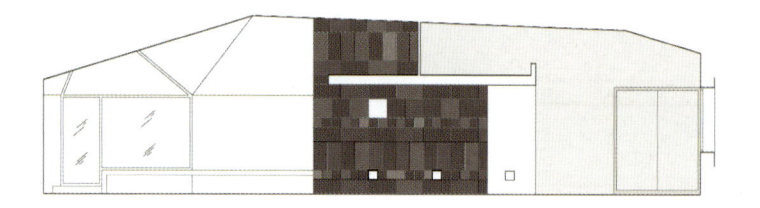

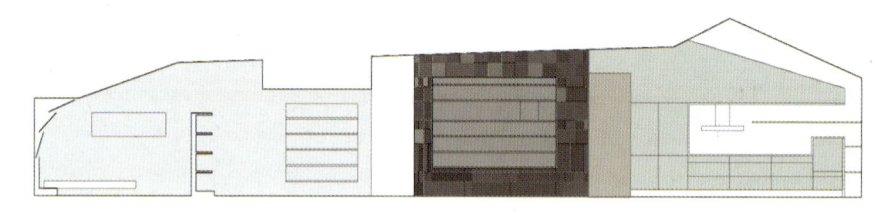

○ Sections

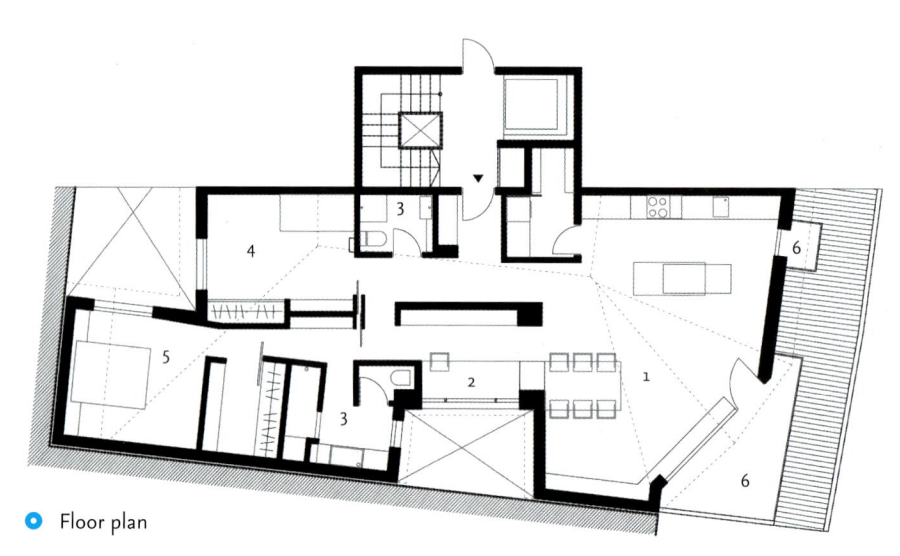

○ Floor plan

1. Kitchen/Dinning room
2. Library
3. Bathroom
4. "Refuge" + room
5. "Suite" + room
6. Terrace

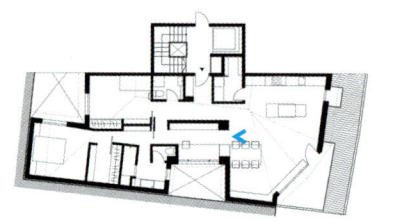

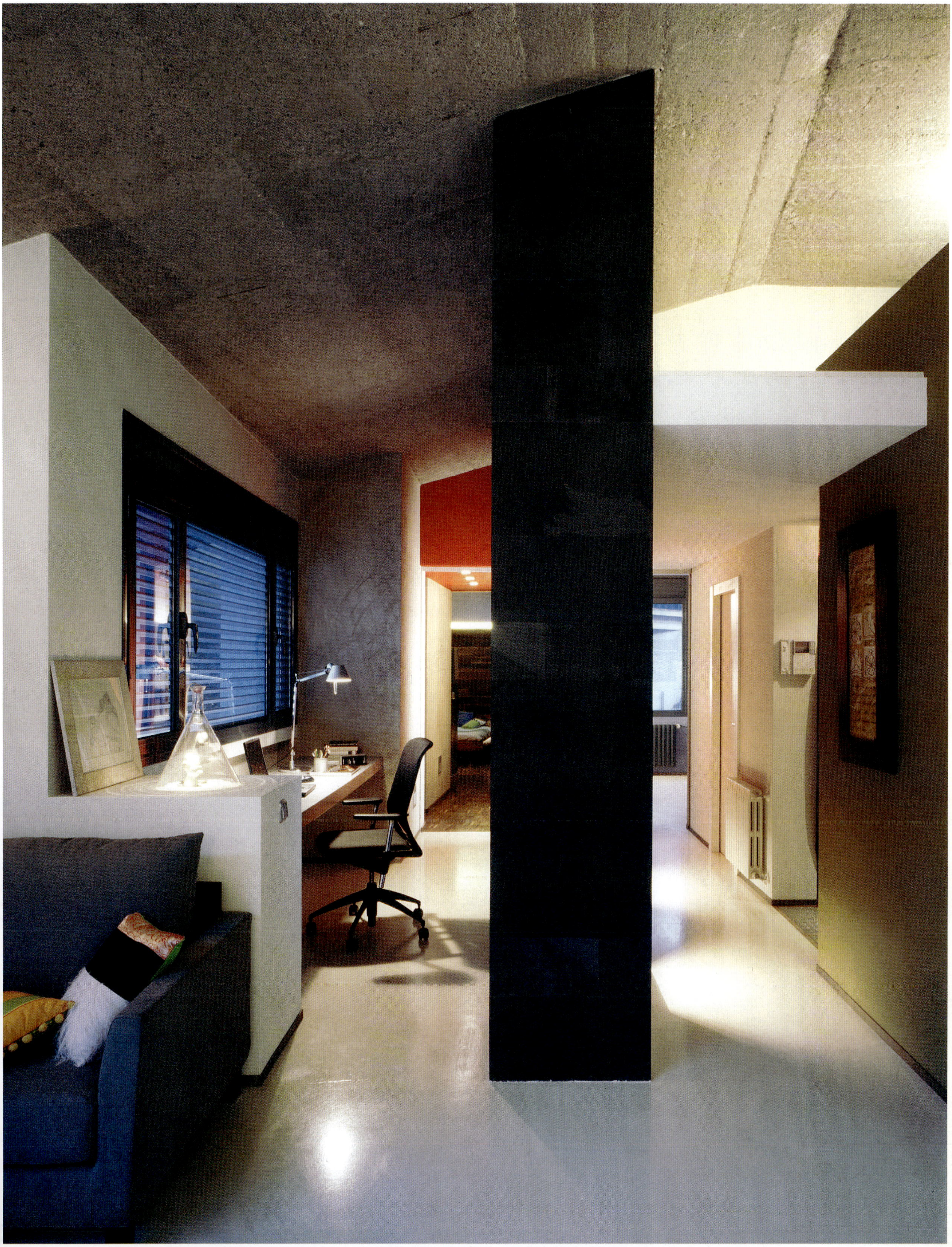

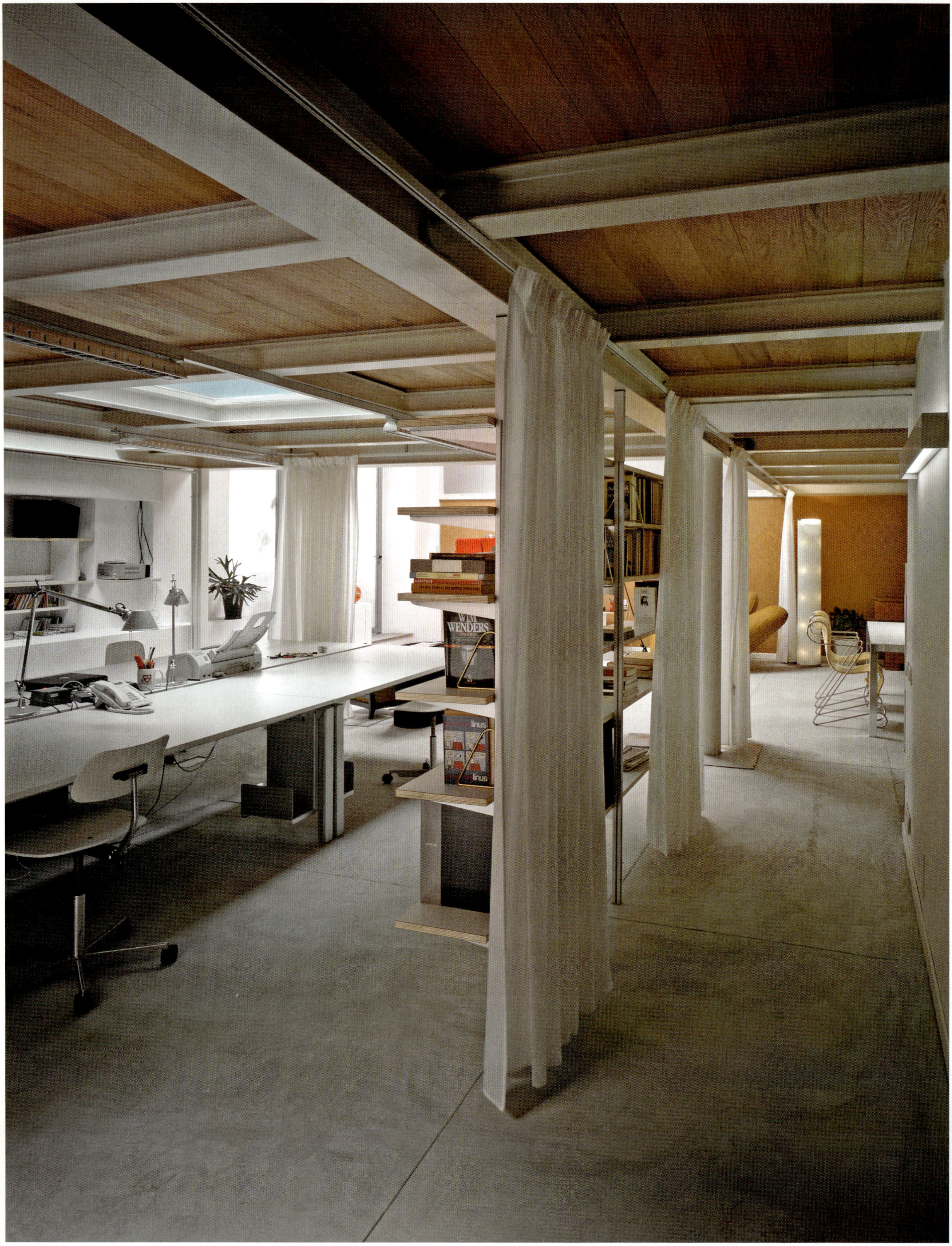
WIM WENDERS
linus
linus

W Loft

This project is located in one of the most run-down neighborhoods of Milan. This abandoned area, previously an industrial area, has slowly been regenerated and transformed. The client dreamed of creating a work space that would also function as a home. The American-born occupant, who adored the city where he grew up, wanted a loft that would remind him of experiences he'd had, people he'd met, landscapes he'd seen and places he'd visited. A space in the style of the Tribeca district in New York. The landscape he was faced with everyday made him feel unstable and ill-at-ease, transforming his longing for the American continent into an anxiety that left him in need of emotional stability.

To minimize this anxiety, the architects used water as a reference for the design, an element that has always been important in Milan's urban landscape. The presence of an old abandoned water deposit, along with the close proximity to the banks of a river, provided the desired nostalgia.

The intervention mainly consisted in exploring the double height of the unused deposit, a distribution that has been used to separate the uses of the space: the work area on the first floor and the home on the top floor. Direct access has been created from the bedroom to the meeting room, by way of a fireman's pole. Materials were used that made reference to the American landscape, like the use of wood in the roof, stairs, and space division; metal H-beams for the dividing beams and columns; and glass allowing for the internal distribution of light. The technology and design is also reminiscent of American society, specifically that of New York. Most striking is the arrangement in the design of different icons from truly American sports: a basketball net, a sofa in the shape of a baseball glove and an American flag. All these elements have been arranged to form an artificial landscape.

Architect/Designer:
Conrad-Bercah/W Office

Client: W Office
Photographer: Alberto Muciaccia
Location: Milan, Italy
Completion date: 2006
Area: 3,229 SF

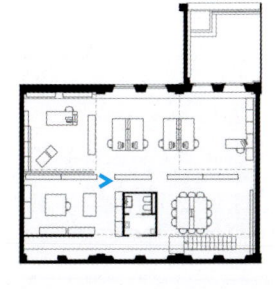

In this loft the architects created a double height to separate the two main uses: the home and the work space. The meeting room is presided over by an Archille Castiglioni light.

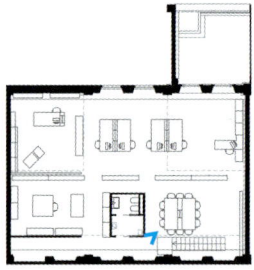

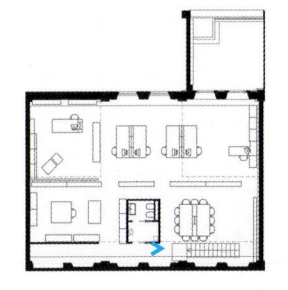

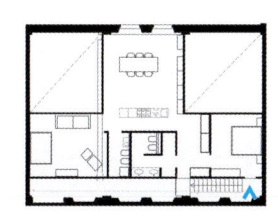

W LOFT

W LOFT
48

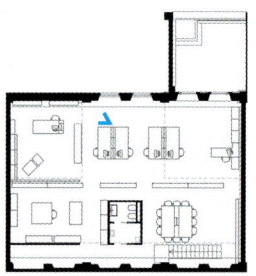

W LOFT
49

W LOFT
50

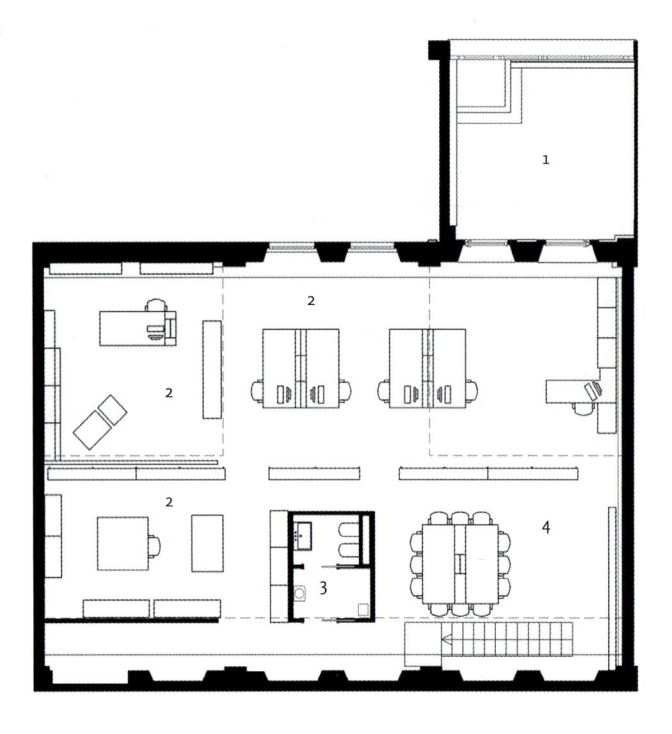

● Gound floor

1. Entrance
2. Work space
3. Bathroom
4. Meeting room

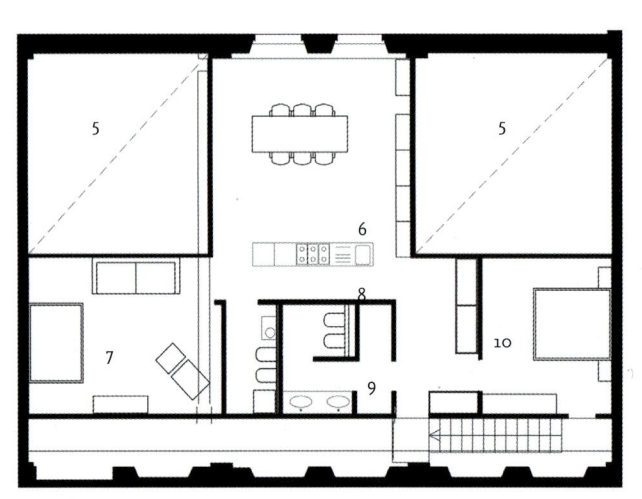

● First floor

5. Void
6. Dining room
7. Living room
8. Kitchen
9. Bathroom
10. Bedroom

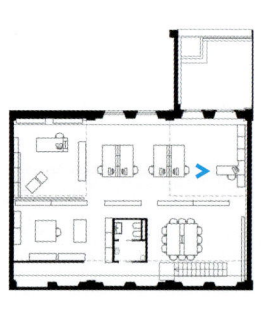

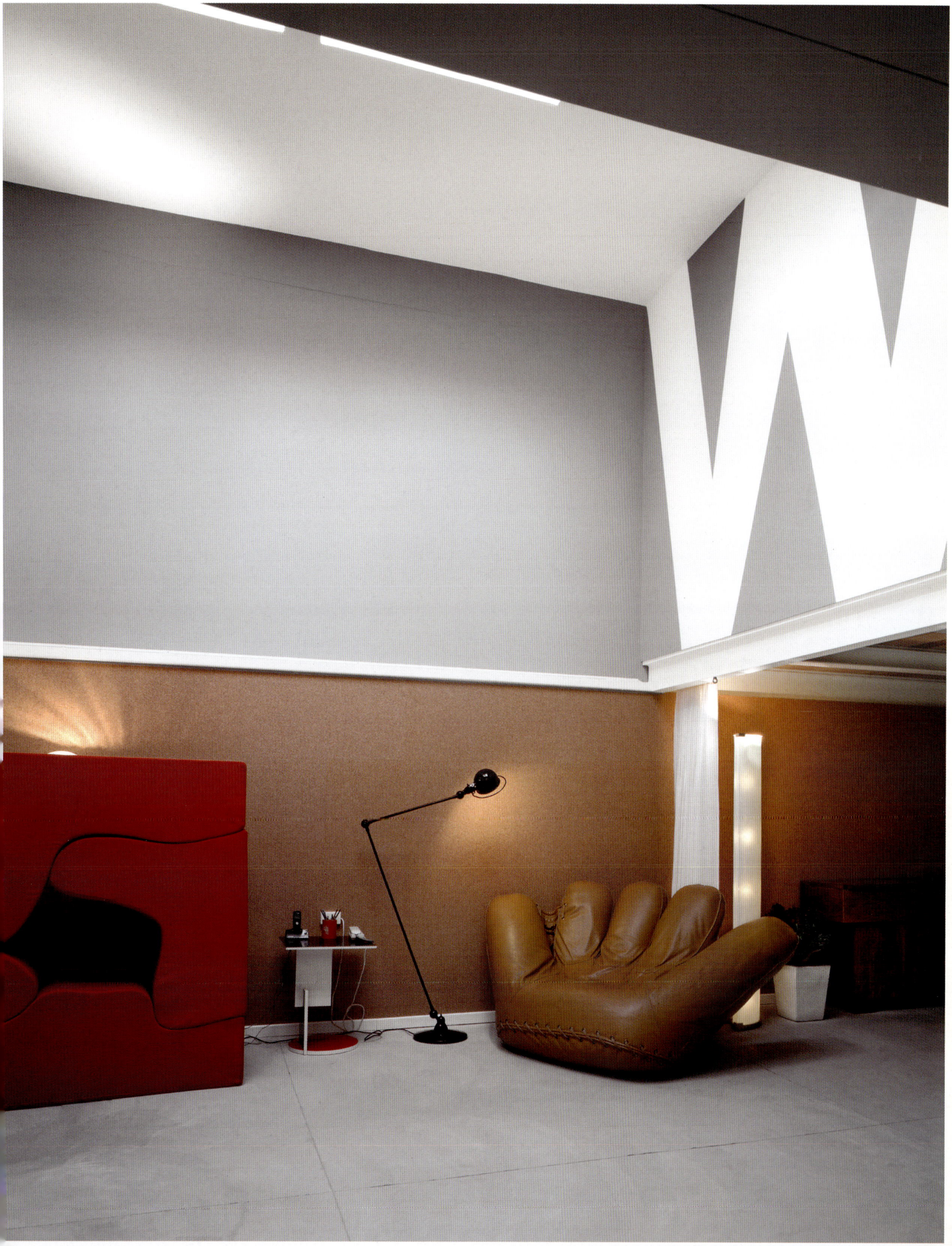

W LOFT

○ Wood, a metal framework and glass, as well as various elements from North American culture (the flag, basketball net, and baseball glove), remind the occupant of the city where he was born.

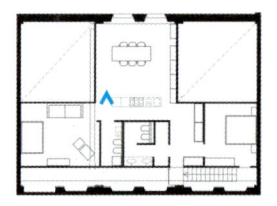

W LOFT
53

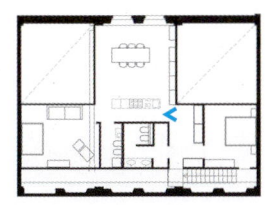

OFFICES IN SMALL SPACES

Amazon Air Offices 56	 Bank in Cerreto Guidi, Mill with Bank 98
Happy Place 64	 Afeijón-Fernández Architecture Office 104
MK/3-VA 74	 Zonabarcelona Office 116
Amalgama 7 80	 Habitectura Offices 124
Maritime Intelligence Group Office 90	 Joaquín Gallego Studio 132

9MAR Offices	138
 Bordonabe Barcelona	148
 Renegade Film Studio	158
 Mixed Greens Gallery	164
 Bank in La Fontina, Still Life with Bank 1	172
 CODECSA Offices	180
 Thirdpoint Offices	190
 Beauty Lab	198
 Lehrer Architects' Office	210
 Schröder & Schömbs PR Agency	218
 Golden Nugget	226

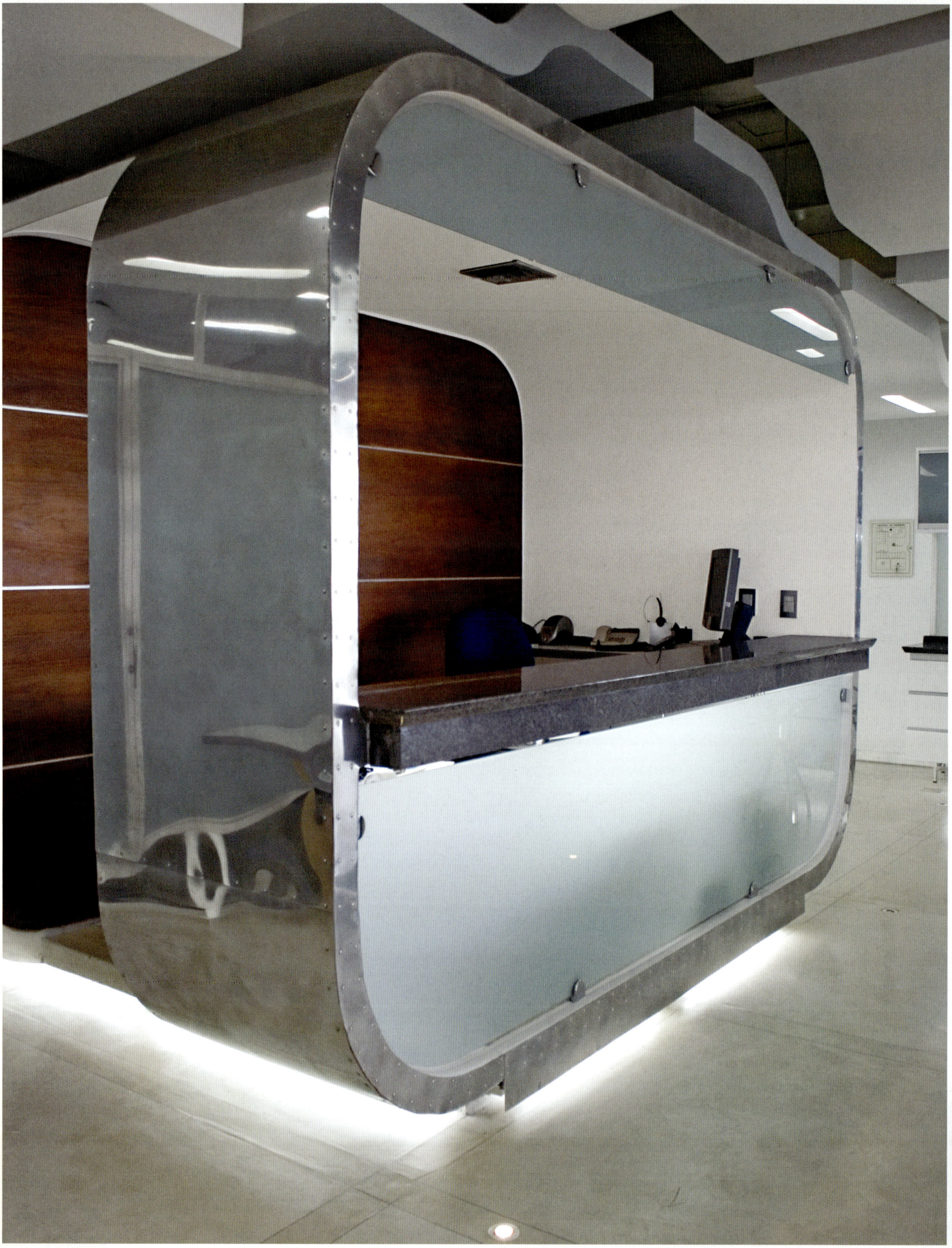

Amazon Air Offices

The client for this project, a large aeronautical company, wanted offices that would respond to their corporate image and transmit a distinct appearance.

The idea was to create an office space that resembled the interior of an airplane. This challenge begins in the reception area, which simulates the departure gate at an airport, thanks to the placement of a large steel block, which imitates the fuselage of a plane, and a translucent glass panel, which evokes the small windows found on a plane.

In the area behind reception is a small executive meeting room, which resembles a cockpit. It is a closed space where privacy is the most characteristic element and whose rigidity is broken only by the door, which is made from opaque glass to separate this room from the rest.

Both the reception area and the meeting room mark the access to the interior via two large translucent glass doors, inscribed with the company logo, whose frame consists of curved metal ribs lined with polished aluminum, with rivets found in the aeronautical industry.

Once passed these doors, there are two clearly defined areas: one contains a mini-bar and a small kitchen, as well as a waiting room for around sixteen people with aluminum cladding on the masonry. In the other area there are two work stations and a small waiting room, comfortably and more informally furnished, which functions as a restrooms for employees.

In keeping with the industrial aesthetic of the space, the round vents for the air conditioning have been left exposed, and on the ceiling cloud-shaped, undulating soffits represent the sky that surrounds this fictitious aircraft.

The lighting throughout the project is characterized by the absence of direct light sources, because all the lighting is indirect and comes from the openings in the plaster that covers the partition walls.

Architect/Designer:

Juan Ignacio Morasso/Morasso Tucker Arquitectos

Client: Amazon Air
Photographer: Julio Armando Estrada
Location: Caracas, Venezuela
Completion date: 2007
Area: 969 SF

AMAZON AIR OFFICES

● Glass, wood and aluminum in a white space help to highlight the pureness of this design. The furniture has been custom designed with a curved aesthetic that underlines the dynamism of the space.

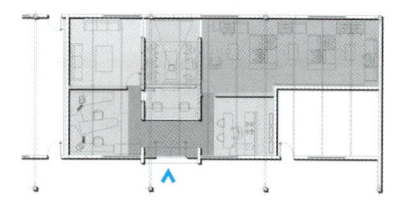

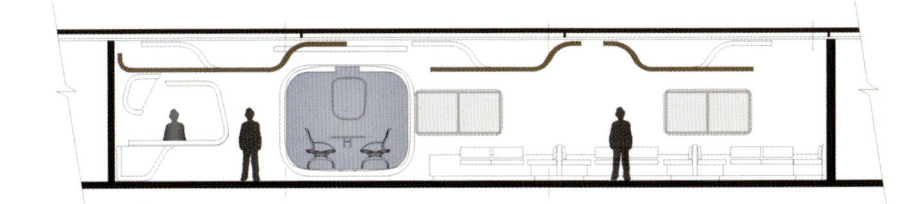

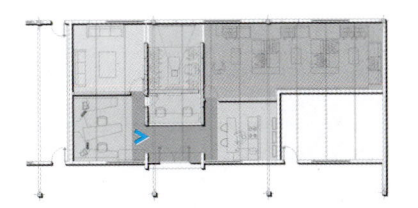

AMAZON AIR OFFICES
59

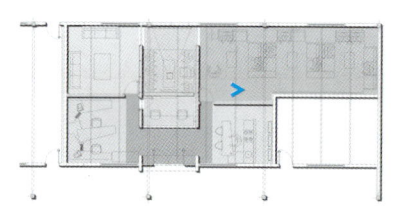

AMAZON AIR OFFICES

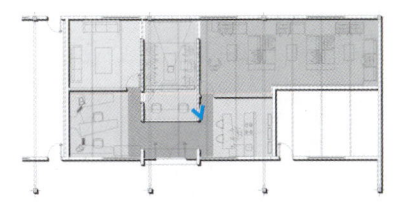

AMAZON AIR OFFICES

61

AMAZON AIR OFFICES

● Sections

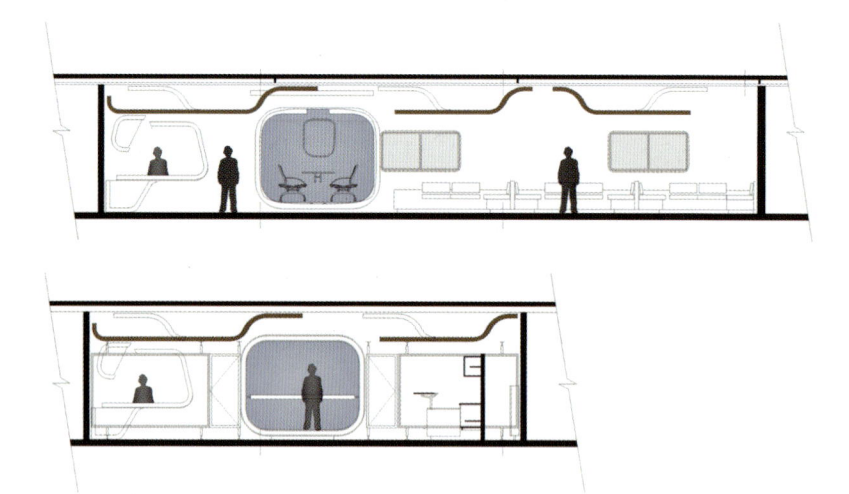

● Floor plan

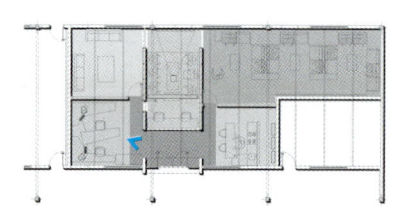

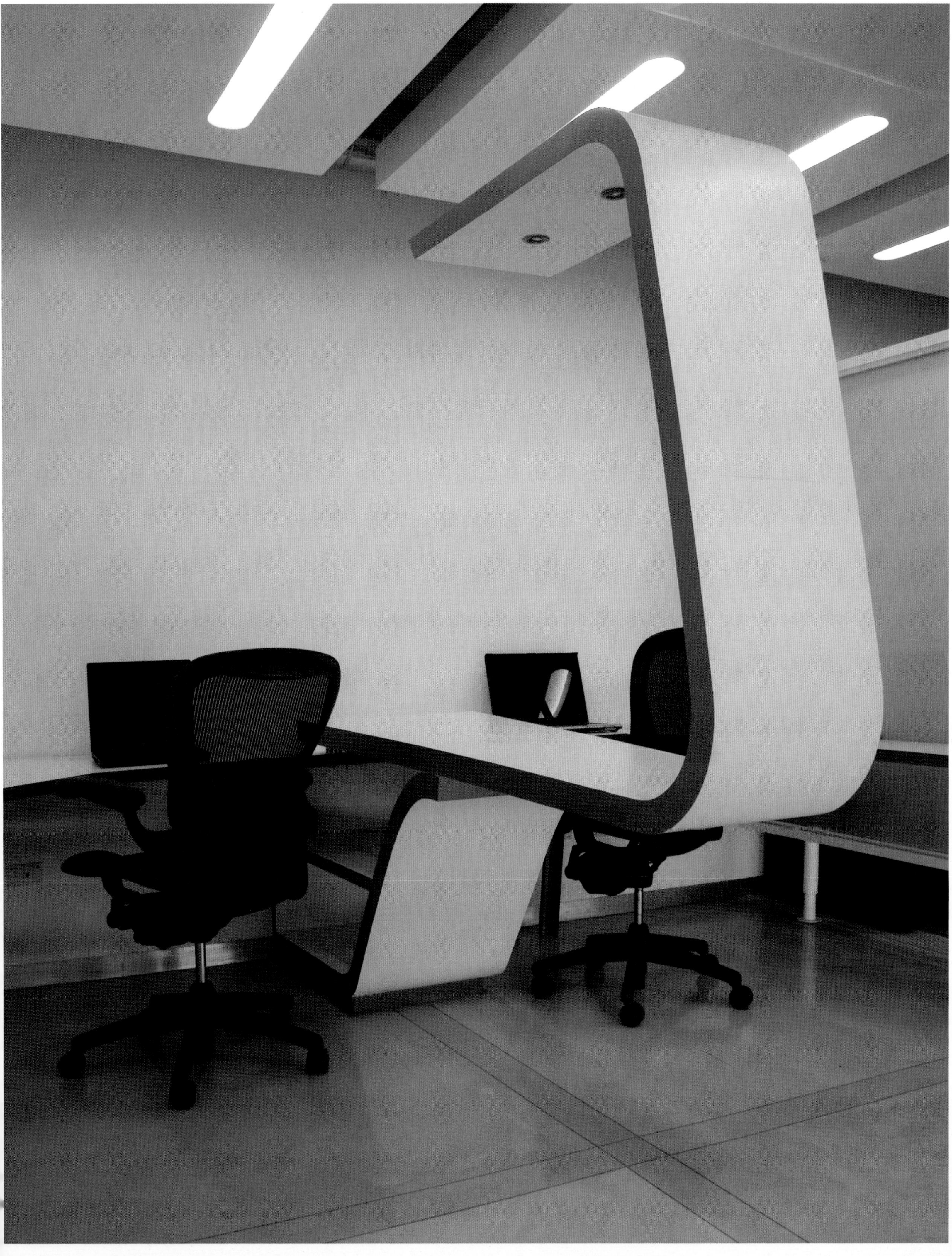

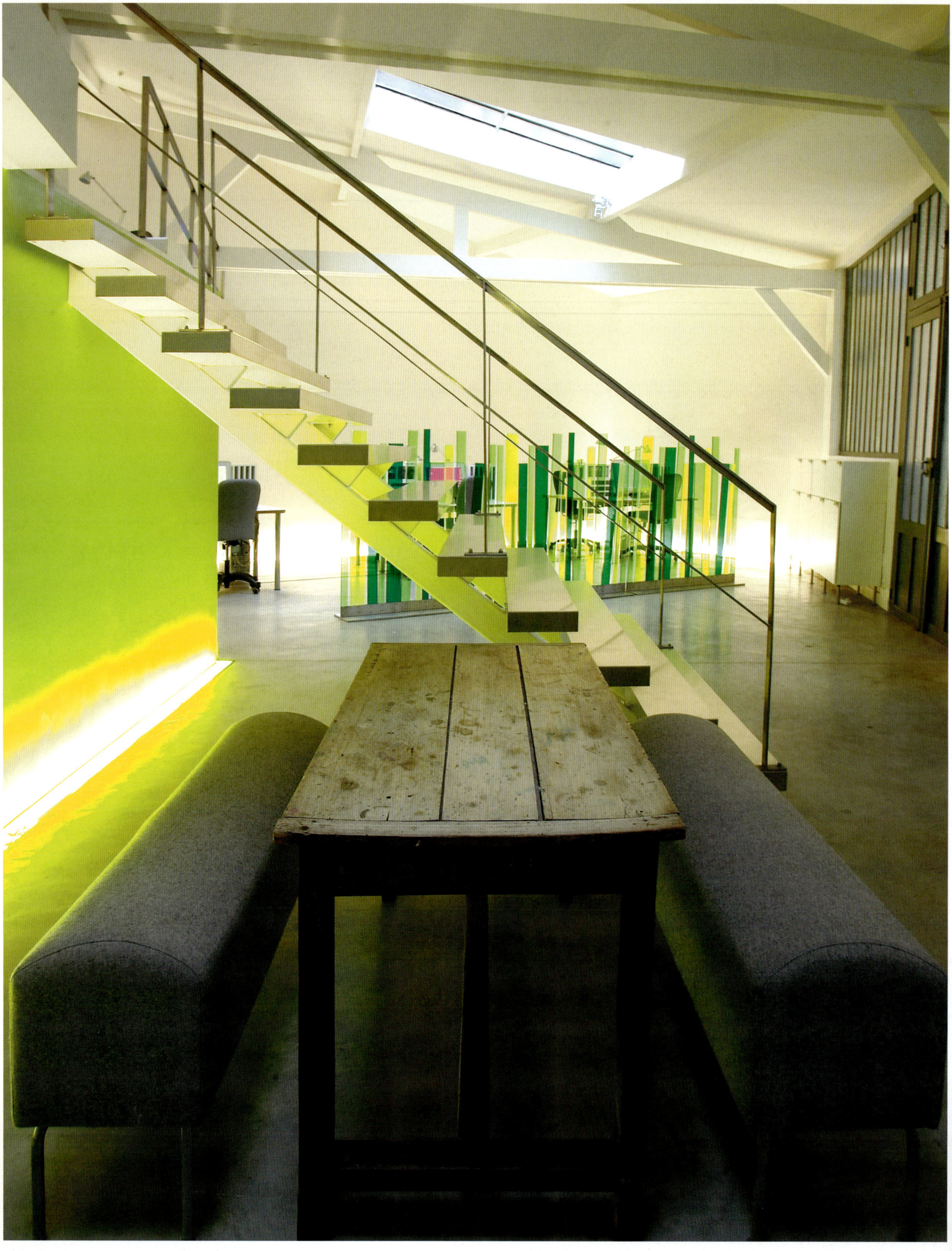

Happy Place

A young advertising agency, located in the Parisian district of Montmartre, commissioned the renovation of 1,400 square feet of floor surface area, spread over two stories, to house their offices. The building dates back to the beginning of the twentieth century and is where photographer Dominique Fontanarosa kept his studio for many years.

The copywriters did not want a standard office, but one that would reflect the emotion of experiencing something for the first time, an emotion that the firm aims for in all of their projects.

The interior was originally divided into three large rooms on the first floor plus the upper floor, characterized by its wooden cladding. The space was a gloomy one, extremely disorganized, with no heating or hot water. In short, a place that could represent the Montmartre of artists like Picasso or Modigliani, according to the clients.

The project sought to preserve the artistic and industrial character that the space originally possessed. This meant maintaining the oak beams, and restoring, or replacing where necessary, the industrial style steel-framed windows.

The natural light has been considerably increased by doubling the number of skylights on the top floor, while on the lower floor the artificial lighting has been intensified by the installation of fluorescent tubes around the perimeter of the exposed concrete floor. To control the temperature, radiant floor heating has been installed.

A stainless steel staircase leads to the top floor, where lime green dominates the decor.

The space has no partitions and between each of the desks used for meeting clients a minimal level of privacy is afforded by the presence of artificial plants. These rest on an aluminum base and are finished in the colors from Manet's *Breakfast on the Grass*.

Architect/Designer:

Cheeeeese! Happy Designers

Client: Cheeeeese! Happy Designers
Photographer: Jean-Marc Perret, Thierry Malty/Cheeeeese!
Location: Paris, France
Completion date: 2004
Area: 1,399 SF

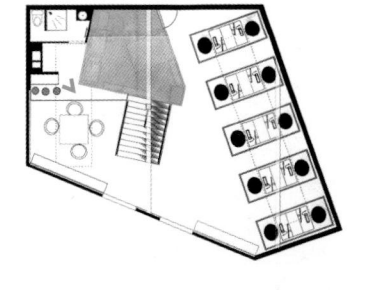

HAPPY PLACE
66

○ The chromatic excitation created by the lime green wraps around the mundane, everyday work tools: a printer, a scanner, a photocopier, and the extractor fan, which removes the smell of glue.

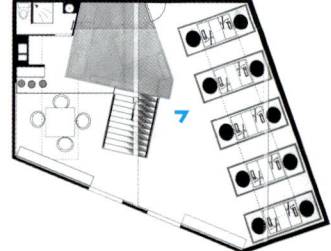

HAPPY PLACE

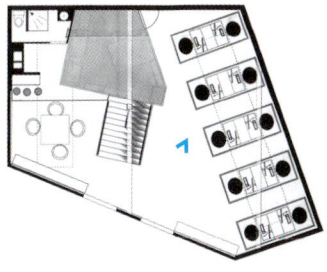

HAPPY PLACE
68

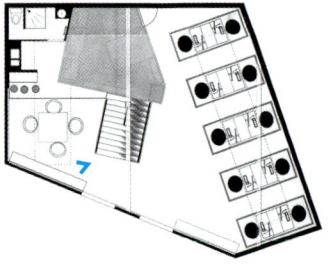

HAPPY PLACE
69

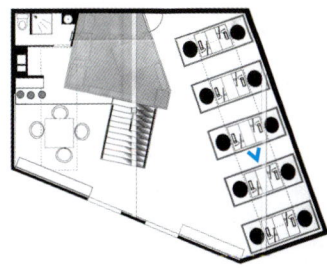

HAPPY PLACE
70

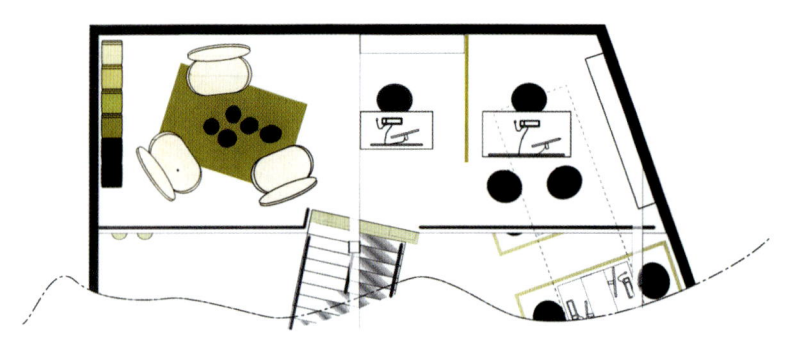

- Mezzanine plan

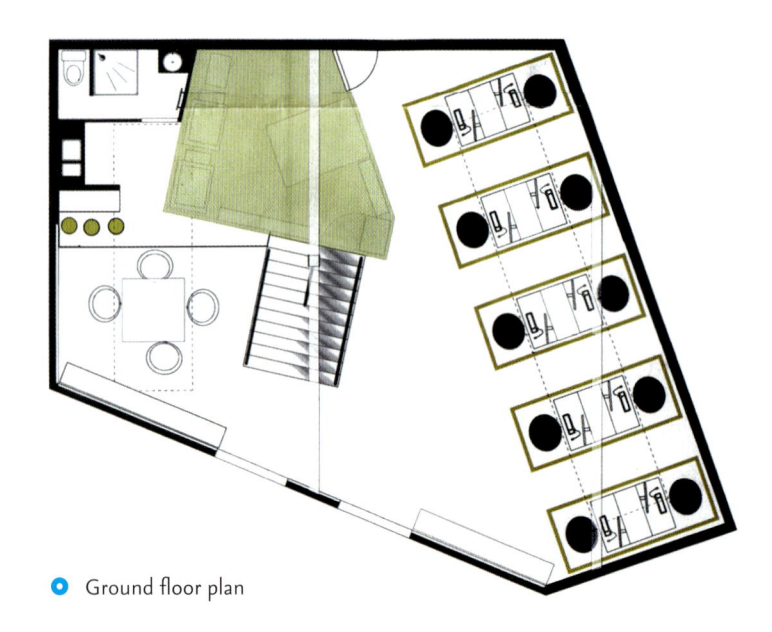

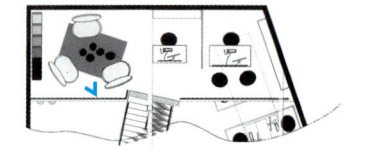

- Ground floor plan

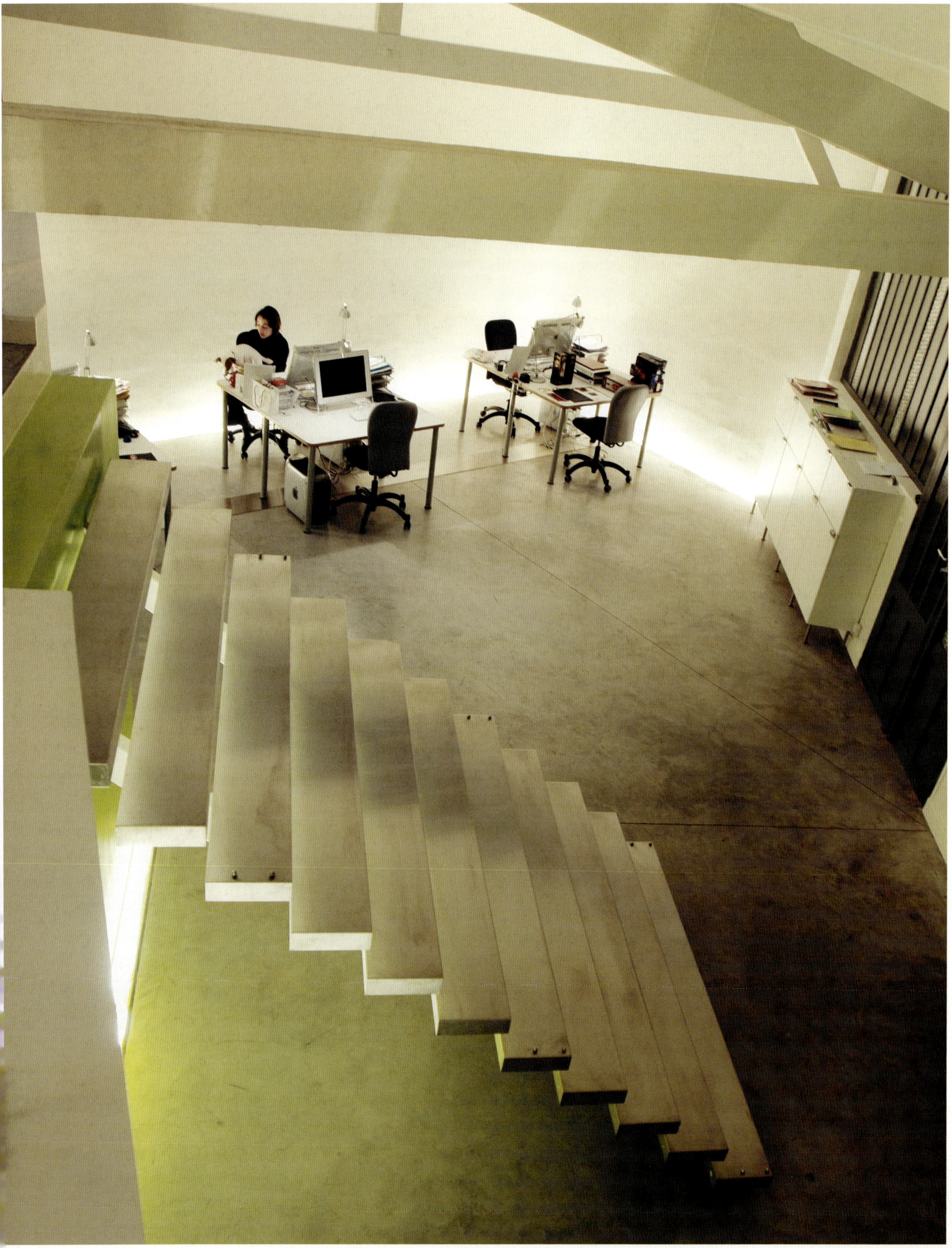

○ Several of the agency's clients come from the cosmetics and luxury products sector. Consequently materials from campaigns for companies like Sephora, L'Oréal, and Veuve-Clicquot have been used as decoration.

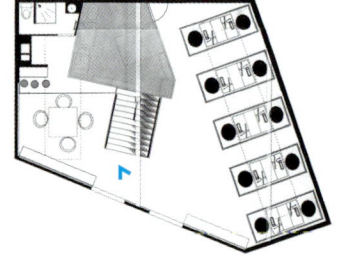

HAPPY PLACE

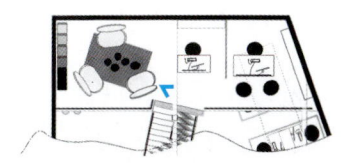

73

Fondation Maeght
3 juillet - 5 novembre 2002
06570 Saint-Paul
Henry

MK/3-VA

A young architectural studio based in Paris were given this commission to design a work space inside of a home. The project reflects the desires of these young architects to create, and the result is a modestly sized but ambitious project.

In the studio, situated on the second floor, both the design and the selection of materials are based on the three elements that characterize the space: the light that enters throughout the day from the north through the skylight, a generous—although variable—ceiling height, and semi-industrial materials. The partition walls on the two longer sides of this floor, which are more or less rectangle, are glass. One faces the street and the other overlooks a Zen inspired garden, surrounded by a brick wall painted white, and feature rounded stones covering the floor and a little vegetation planted next to the wall of the house. Despite its small size, the garden acts as a rest area and there is enough space to comfortably put a hammock here. The other two partition walls are made from exposed concrete.

Because there is not a lot of surface area available inside, 480 square feet, instead of independent functional units the space has been treated as a whole.

Beneath the skylight, at one end, there is a large T-shaped worktable, with room for two people to work. On one side is the garden and the wall is on the other, next to which there is a half-height set of shelves and a plotted plant.

The center is occupied by a table and chairs; near them is a cupboard varnished white, which serves as an office. This area can be used for work meetings, as a waiting room, or a place for relaxing.

At the back there is a filing cabinet and a table light for reading plans.

Architect/Designer:
Sarah Bitter/Metek Architecture

Client: private
Photographer: Pep Escoda
Location: Paris, France
Completion date: 2002
Area: 1,399 SF

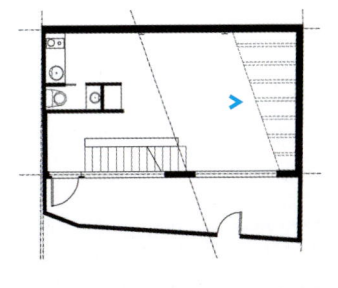

● A stone staircase leads to the home, on the second floor. The right-angle extension of the second step gives way to a bench, which provides extra seating space in the central area of the studio.

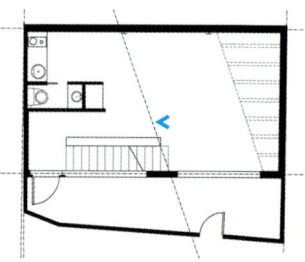

MK/3-VA
77

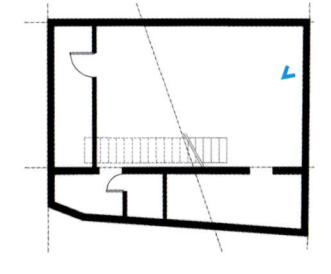

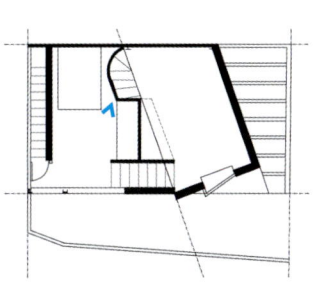

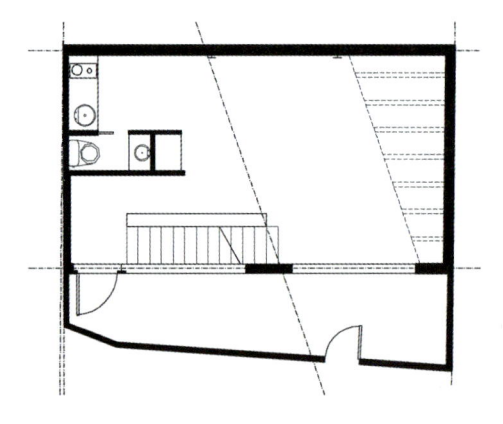

- Ground floor plan 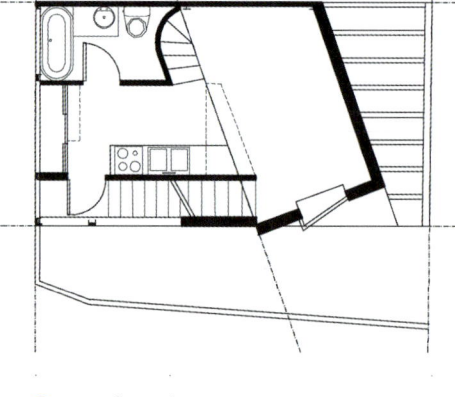
- First floor plan 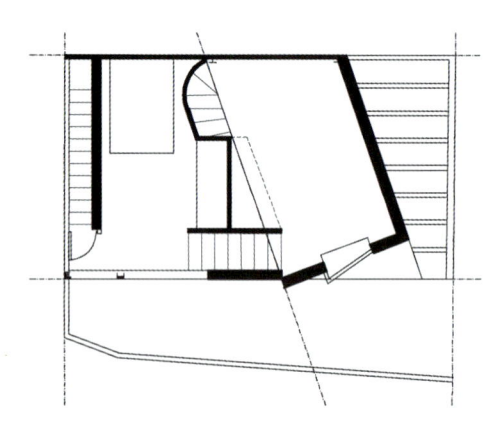
- Second floor plan 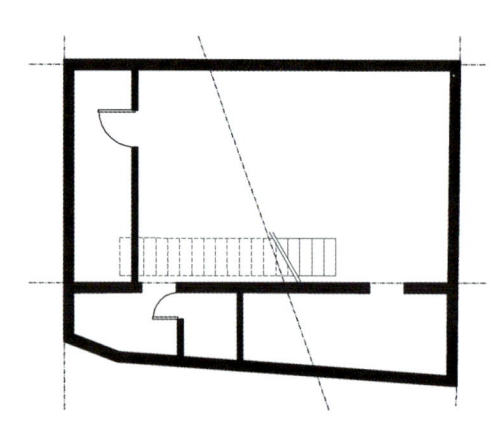
- Basement floor planå

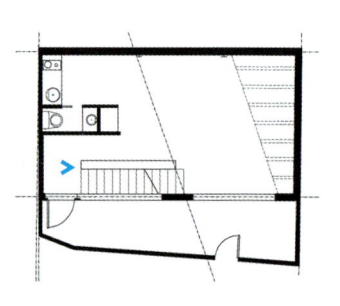

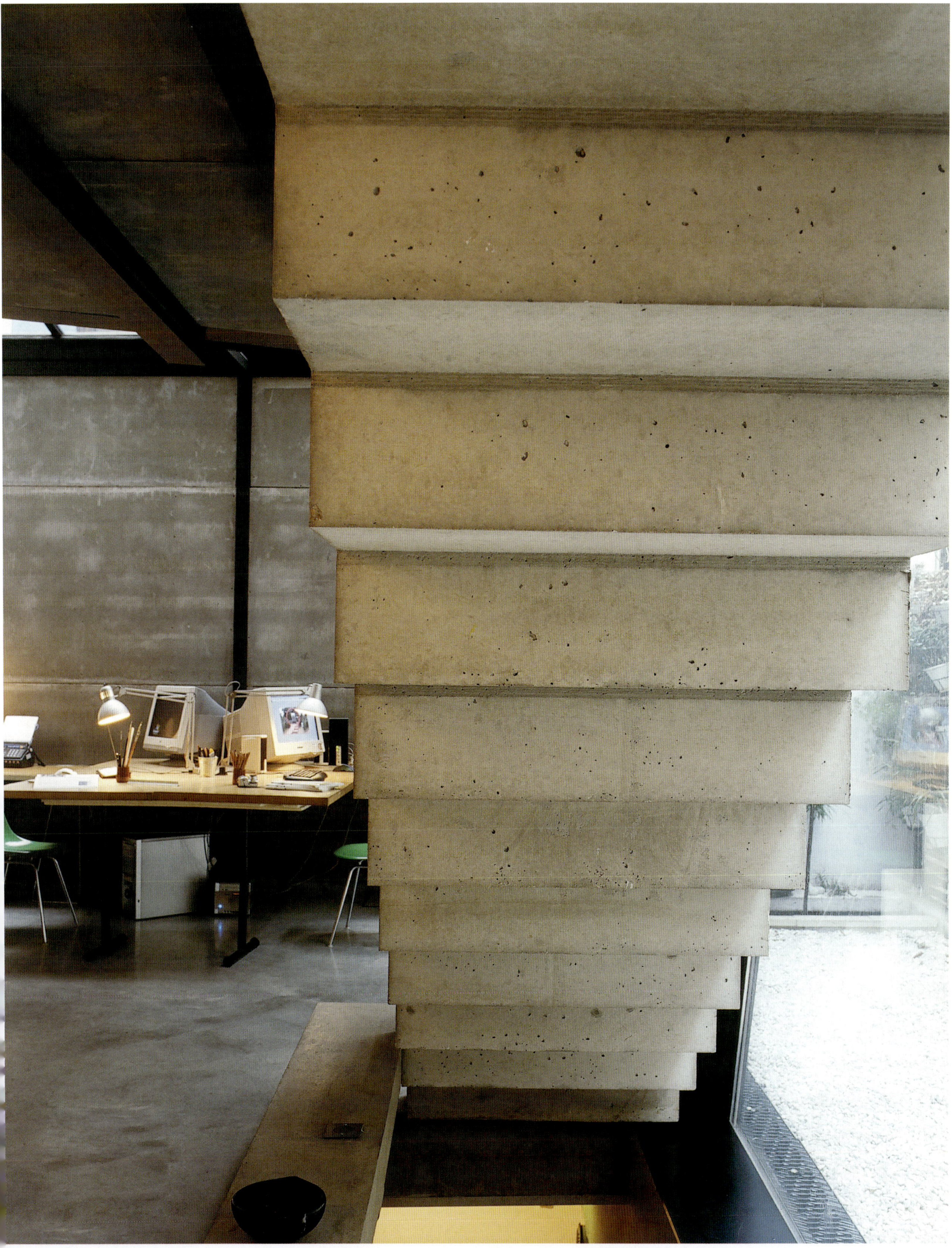

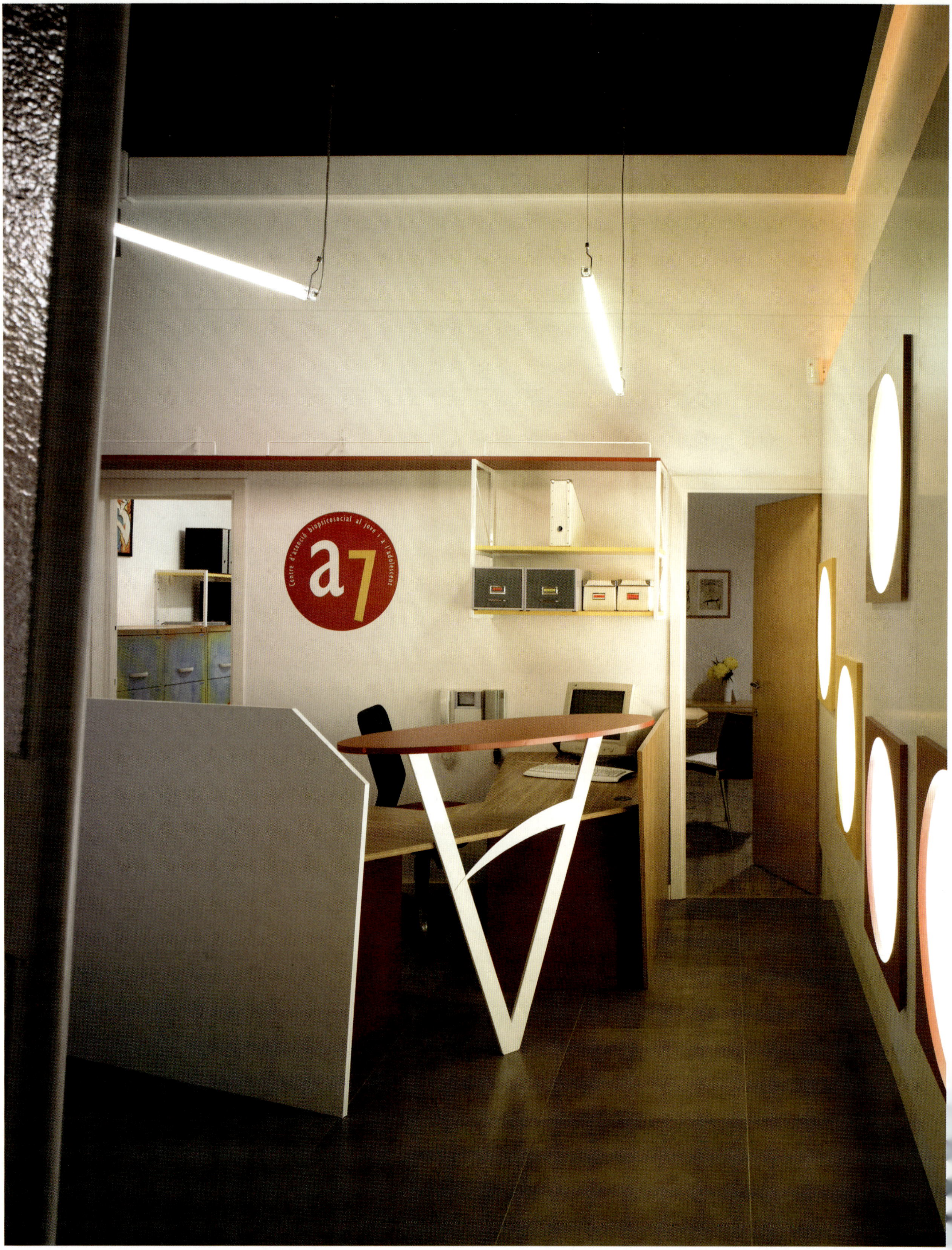
Centre d'atenció biopsicosocial al jove i a l'adolescent
a7

AMALGAMA 7

ARCHITECT/DESIGNER:
LOLA LAGO INTERIORES

Client: Amalgama
Photographer: Eugeni Pons
Location: Barcelona, Spain
Completion date: 2005
Area: 1,830 SF

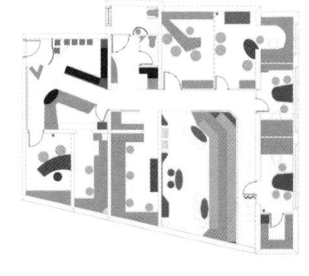

The client asked this interior designer for a design that would be both welcoming and warm, in keeping with Amalgama's role as a company who employs psychologists to help adolescents with behavioral problems or drug addictions. The parents, the visitors, and the teenagers had to identify with the space and feel comfortable there. One of the design solutions to fulfill this objective was to have illuminated openings in the reception area, where photos could be put up of patients who were willing to appear here. This conceptual recourse allows the adolescents to feel integrated on entering the office. The access area also functions as a meeting room through the use of yellow and black stackable cubes.

In the passageway, above the doors, are long shelves that reach the ceiling and are used for storing the numerous reference books owned by the company. This original design makes the most of the space's volume. The same idea has been used in the didactics room, furnished by benches of different heights, improving the visibility and communication for both speakers and listeners.

The corporate image of the company is reflected here in the inscriptions on the walls with words, which start or finish in A, such as AmalgamA. These inscriptions in various languages have not been chosen randomly, but refer to nouns, adjectives, and ideas of kindness and encouragement for the people in attendance.

In one of the areas of the passageways that acts as a generating element for the other spaces is the kitchen and the toilets. On the walls of the bathroom a gloss finish ceramic material has been used where the clients can express their ideas anonymously.

Throughout the project, the lighting is focused and adjustable through spotlights that afford the design intimacy when required.

● The circular illuminated openings, used to show photos of the clients, along with the warm colors of the furnishings and the pastel shades on the walls, create a welcoming and relaxing atmosphere.

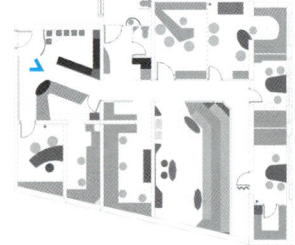

AMALGAMA 7
83

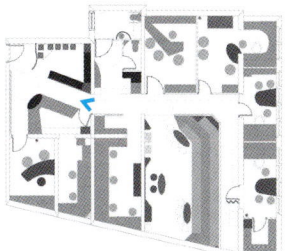

AMALGAMA 7
84

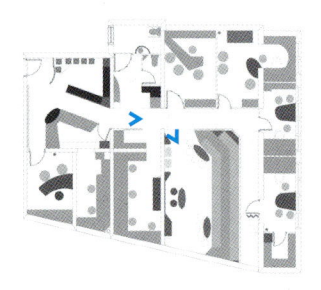

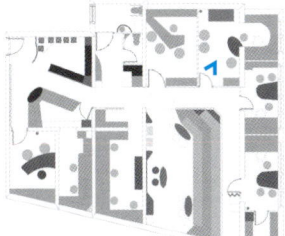

The furniture in the offices has an informal design and presents a hodgepodge of tones and textures of wood in different finishes. Together with the focus lighting, this gives the interiors their homely feeling.

AMALGAMA 7
86

Floor plan

Interior elevations and plan

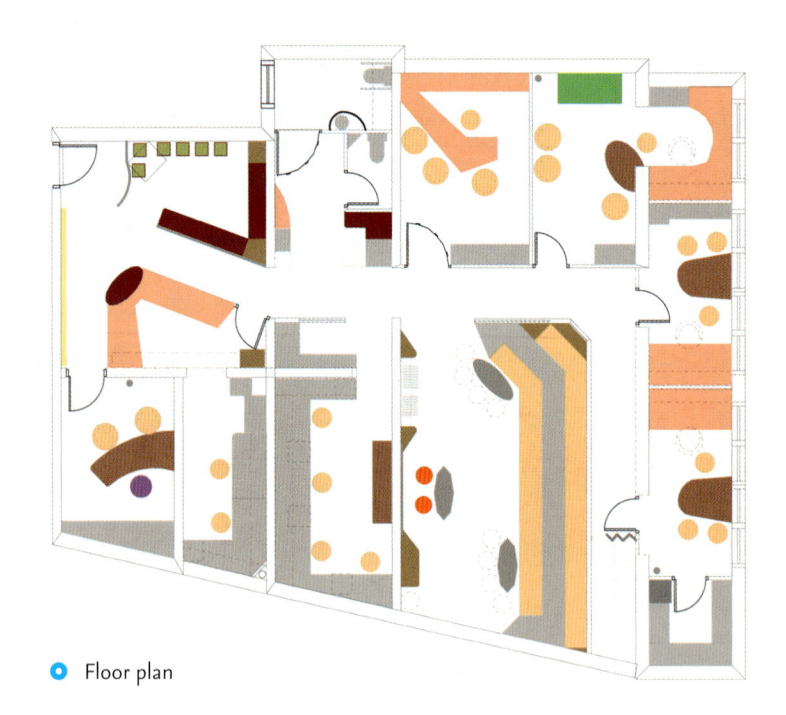

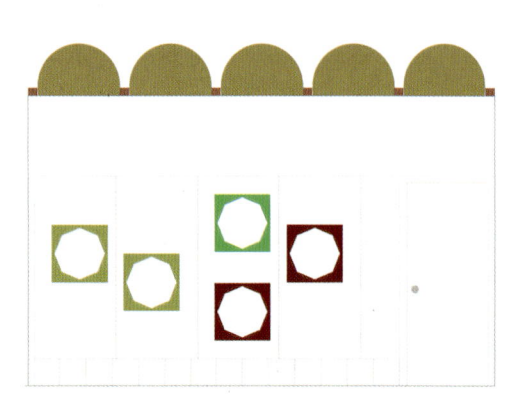

Section

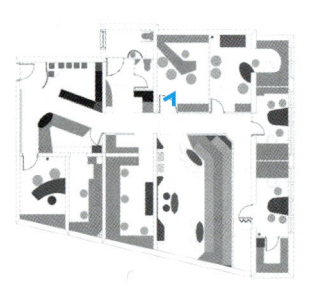

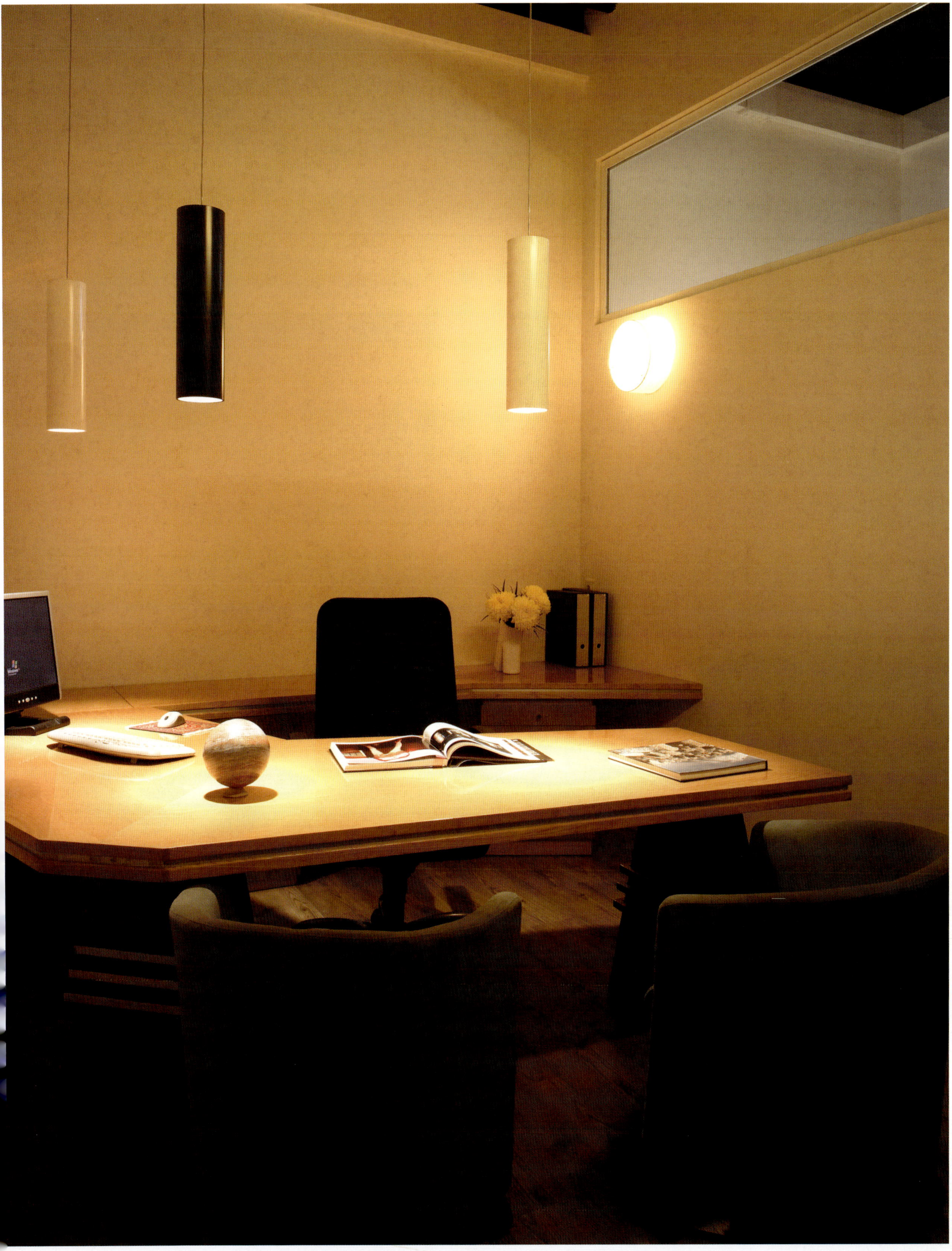

AMALGAMA 7
88

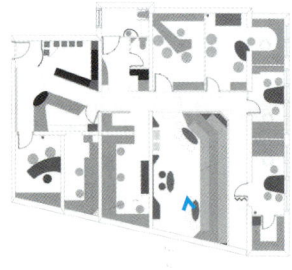

AMALGAMA 7
89

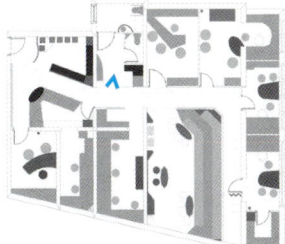

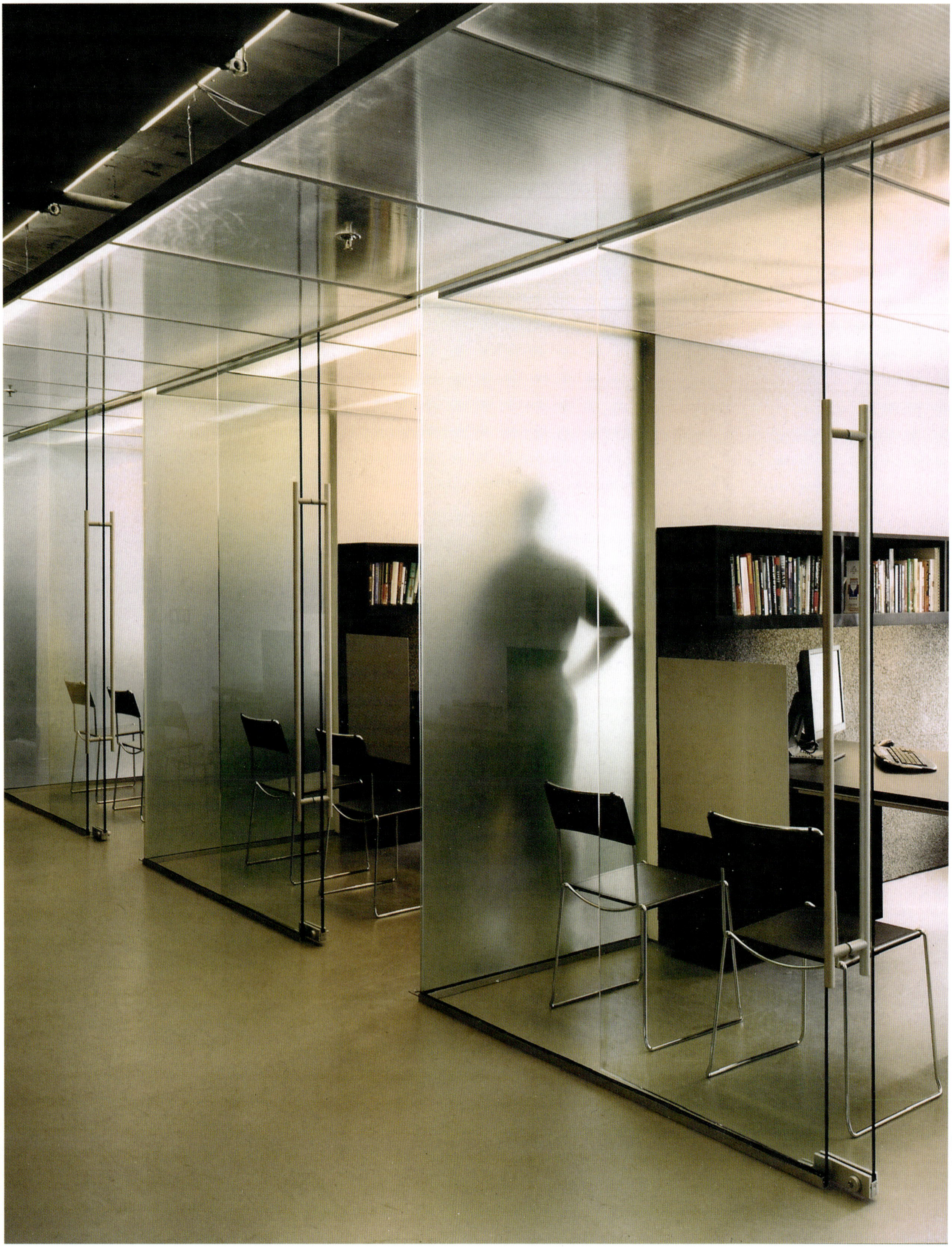

Maritime intelligence Group Office

This project has been carried out for a space, located in one of the city's most central areas, that years ago housed one of the largest and most important factories in Washington, DC. The clients wanted to maintain the original single floor and build several large and comfort-focused offices on it. They also required that it be well-protected to resist both extreme weather conditions and terrorist attacks.

In response to the requirements set out in the brief, the architects decided to create a space that would revolve about two enormous columns located right in the middle of the floor plan. The private offices are situated here, used for meeting clients. The main façade of these offices is entirely glazed from floor to ceiling, with the exception of the aluminum used for the handles. These materials intensify the light in the rooms and break with the rigidity inherent in the two central columns.

The offices have been separated from one another by way of stone and translucent glass partition walls. This helps to integrate all the offices without having to forego the intimacy needed for meeting with clients.

For the floor the architects have sought harmony with the columns, and have chosen marble in a similar color, which also helps it to integrate better with the surroundings.

The ceiling stands out for being installed on two levels. One level is dominated by florescent lights, which illuminate certain areas where natural light does not reach; and the other is presided over by a large plaster plaque covered by a wooden panel that lends continuity to the dominant decorative style throughout the office.

The selection of materials combines coldness, warmth, and richness, such as concrete and industrial felt, which are placed side by side to form contrasts. The space is inspired by Stanley Kubrick's film 2001: A Space Odyssey.

Architect/Designer: John Lee/Workshop For Architecture

Client: Tanner Campbell & Scott Campbell
Photographer: Chuck Choi & John Lee
Location: Washington, D.C, USA
Completion date: 2003
Area: 2,100 SF

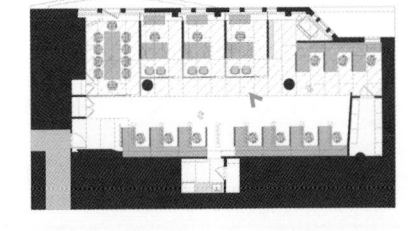

MARITIME INTELLIGENCE GROUP OFFICE

● A row of work stations has been installed in the office area formed by small desks separated from one another by panels, which are half the height and the same length as the desks.

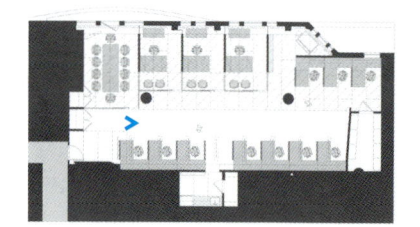

MARITIME INTELLIGENCE GROUP OFFICE

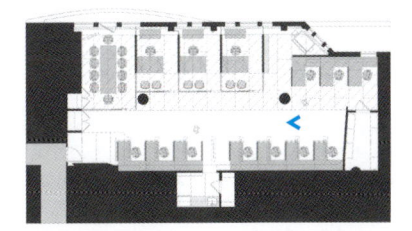

93

MARITIME INTELLIGENCE GROUP OFFICE

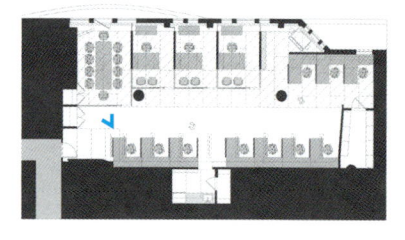

MARITIME INTELLIGENCE GROUP OFFICE

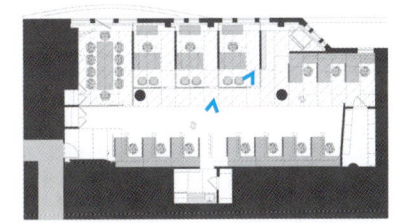

○ The meeting room has three glass partition walls. The fourth is composed of accordion doors in order to be able to extend the space when required. The access is a sliding door made from the same glass as the walls.

MARITIME INTELLIGENCE GROUP OFFICE

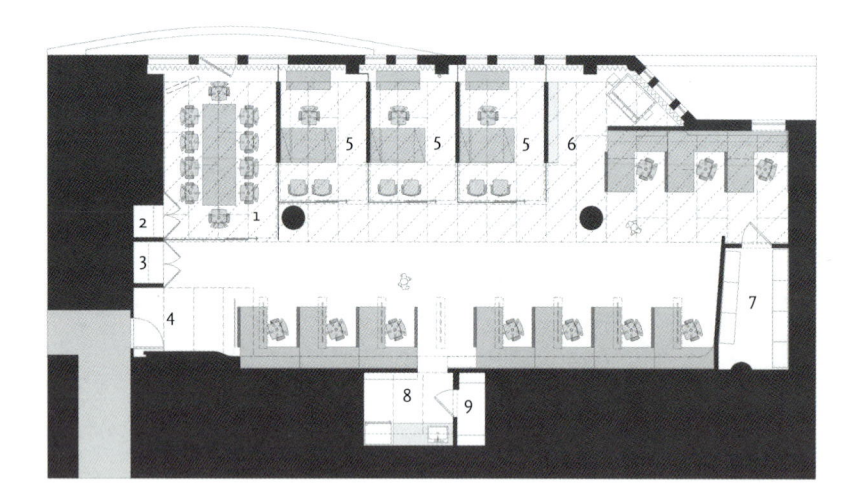

● Floor plan

1. Conference room
2. Audio equipment
3. Coat
4. Entrance
5. Office
6. Copy/Fax
7. Secured storage
8. Pantry
9. Storage

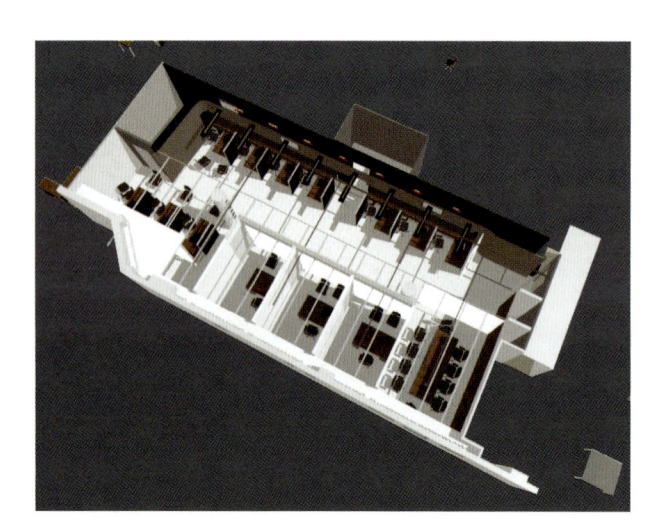

● Rendering

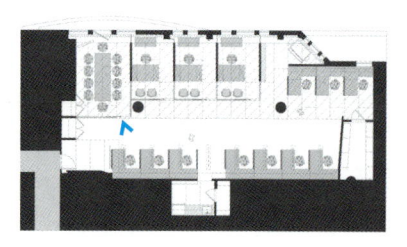

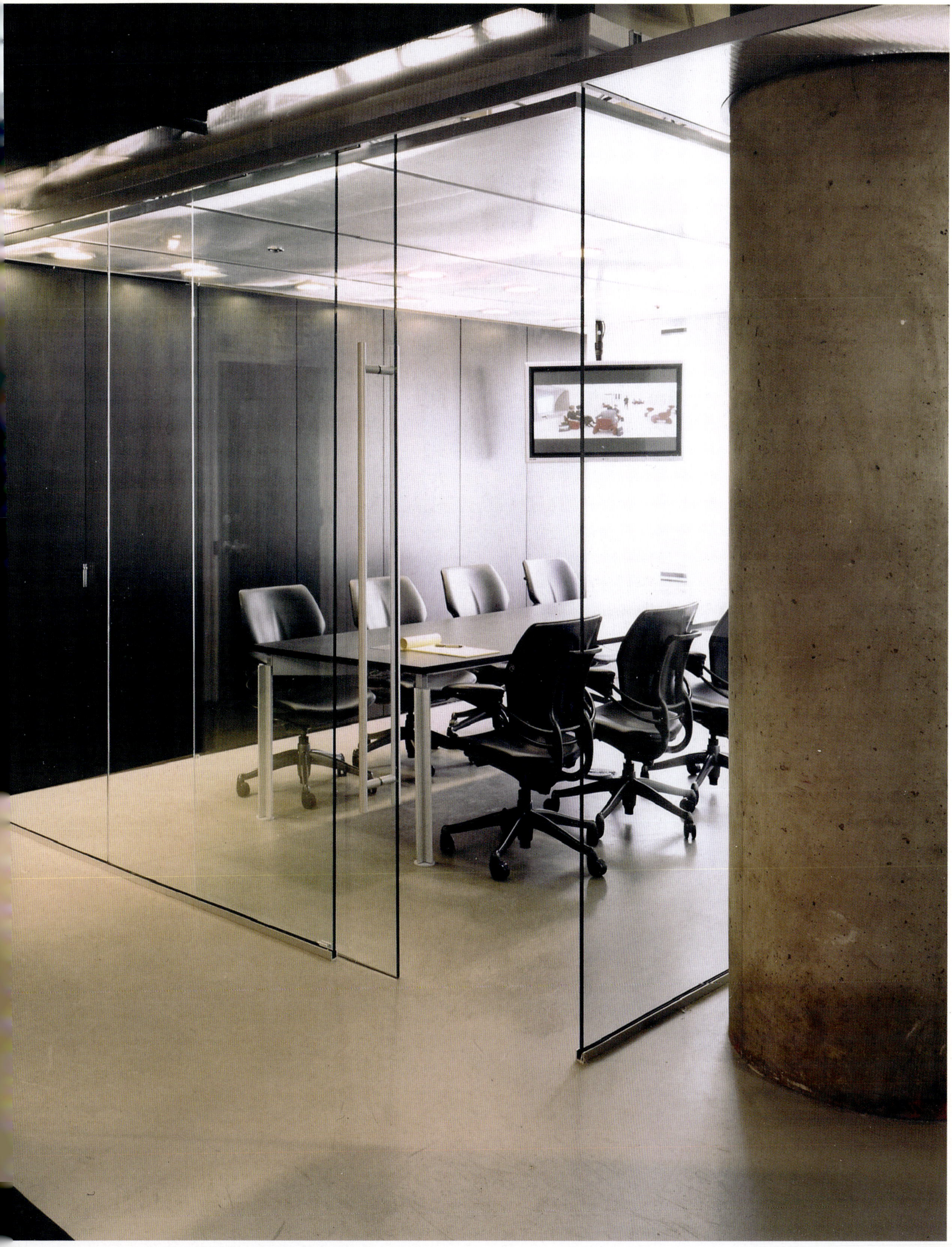

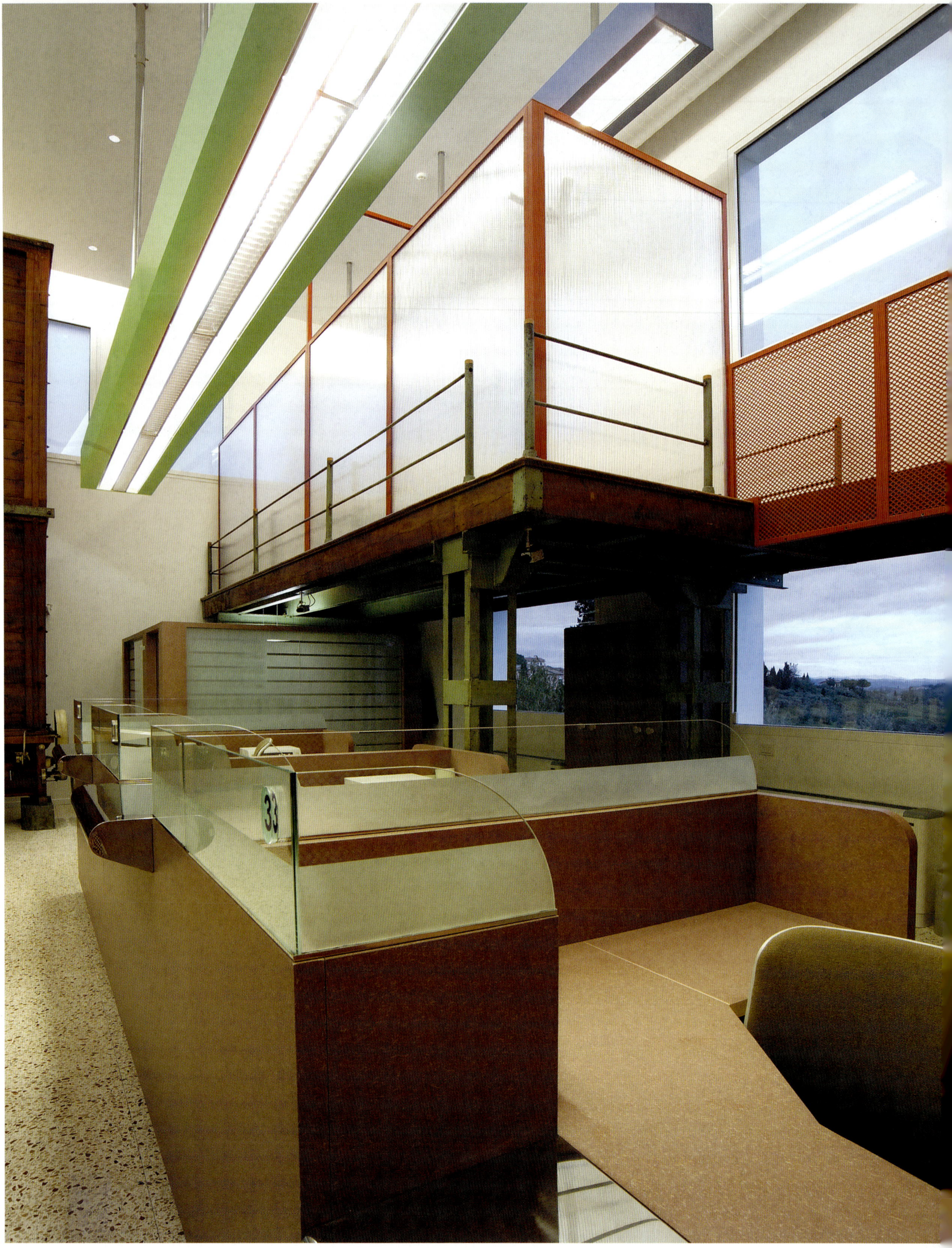
33

Bank in Cerreto Guidi, Mill with Bank

A branch of La Banca di Credito Cooperativo di Cambiano, the oldest banking institution in Italy, is the client for this project. It consists in the remodeling of a former flour mill, which was acquired by the bank to be turned into offices. It is located in the historical center of Cerreto Guidi, a town in the province of Florence.

The architect has preserved some of the original characteristics, such as the machinery and tools from the mill, and has created a modern and practical space, where customers are treated with courtesy, efficiency, and professionalism. In other words, the main aims here were comfort and function.

The first thing that visitors see after entering at street level is the old hopper from the mill, which in this case is a single, large piece. The two levels from the original layout have been maintained, which help make the most of the 2,000 square feet of surface area. The top level is a projecting space, which formerly served as a passageway to reach the opening of the hopper and store the grain. The current project has preserved both its dimensions and its wooden flooring, which has been renovated, and protected the entire length of the hopper with translucent polyvinyl panels. In the widest section, by the hopper, there is a group worktable, which can also be used for informal meetings, and storage space. The access to this floor is a staircase with wooden steps protected by a half-height banister of metal grating, which is similar to that of the old mill.

The program for the lower level encompasses an open area and a closed one. The open area houses the boxes, a counter for seeing clients, and two waiting areas. The closed area is a dead end and is set out on either side of a passageway that starts in the middle of the open area. A display stand has been set up in the passageway where various old farm tools, like pitchforks, scythes, and buckets, etc., are on display.

ARCHITECT/DESIGNER:
MASSIMO MARIANI ARCHITETTO

Client: Banca di Credito Cooperativo di Cambiano
Photographer: Alessandro Ciampi
Location: Florence, Italy
Completion date: 2004
Area: 2,153 SF

BANK IN CERRETO GUIDI, MILL WITH BANK

● The red and the green represent the bank's deep-rooted history in Italy. The other colors in the palette are sober ones, mostly natural browns, in the furnishings, terrazzo, and wood floor.

BANK IN CERRETO GUIDI, MILL WITH BANK
101

BANK IN CERRETO GUIDI, MILL WITH BANK

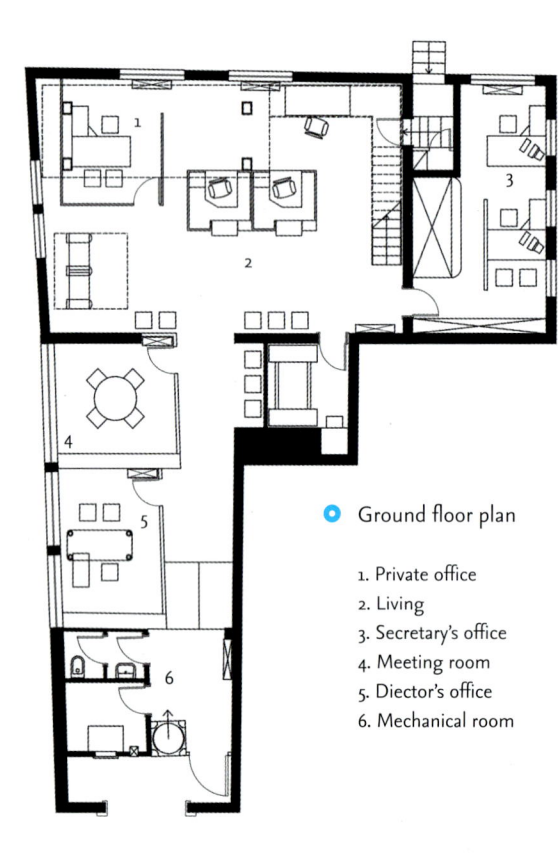

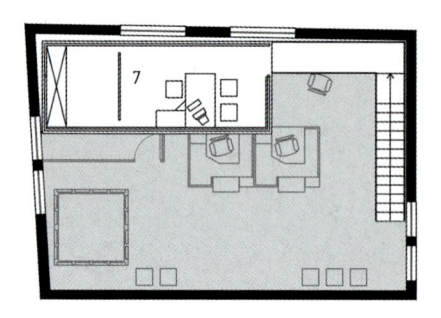

○ Ground floor plan

1. Private office
2. Living
3. Secretary's office
4. Meeting room
5. Diector's office
6. Mechanical room

○ Mezzanine plan

7. Mezzanine's living space

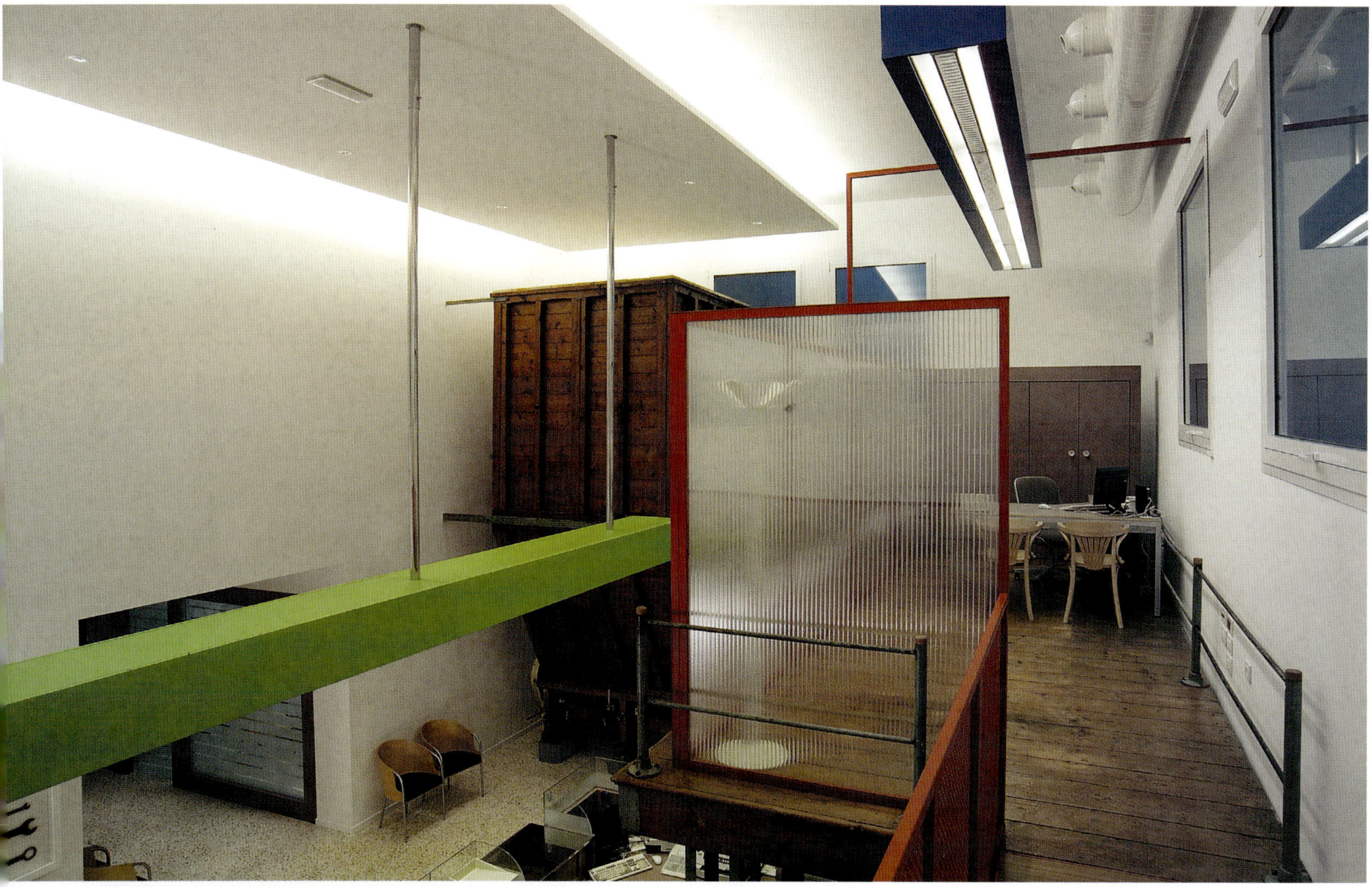

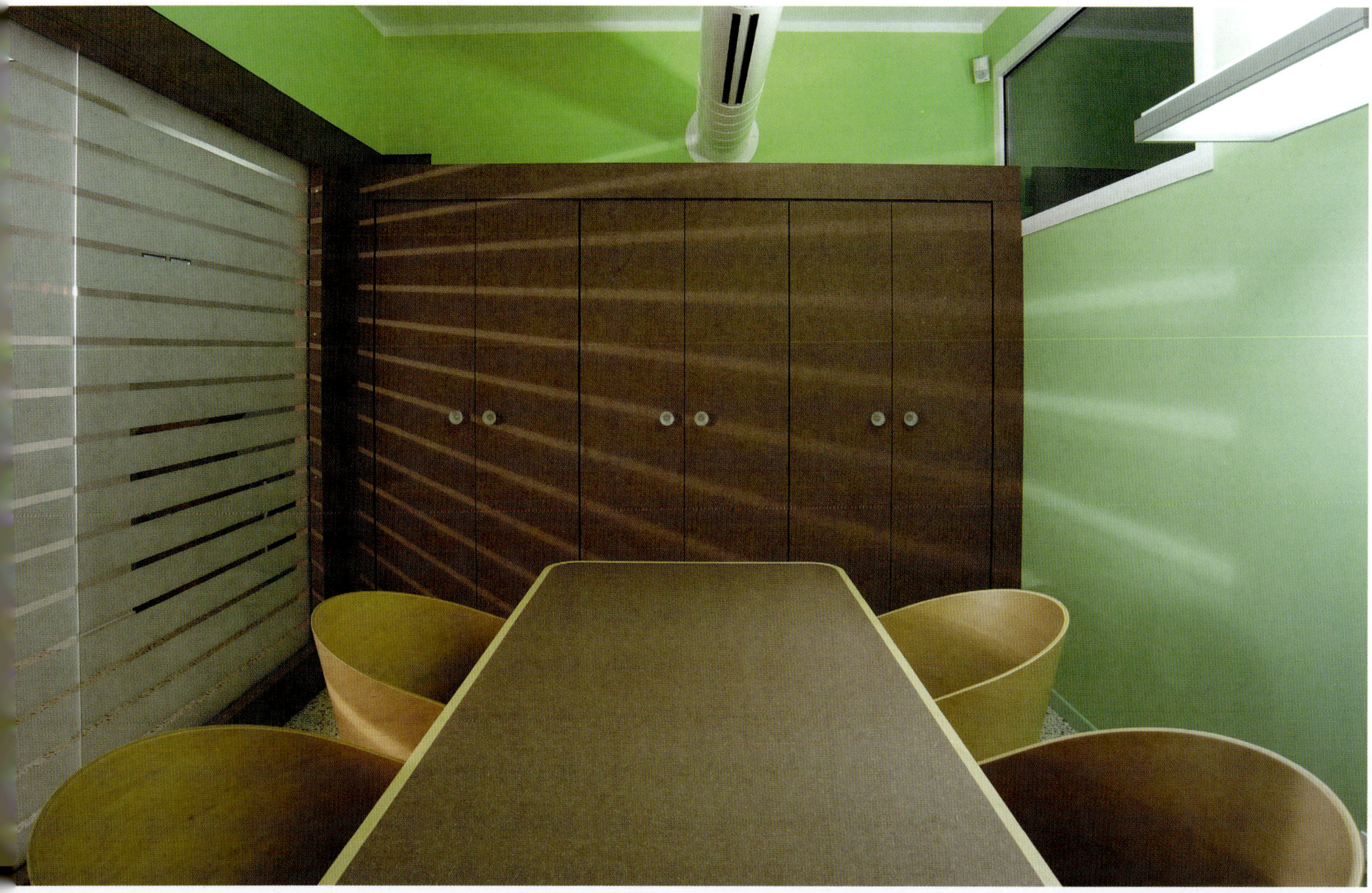

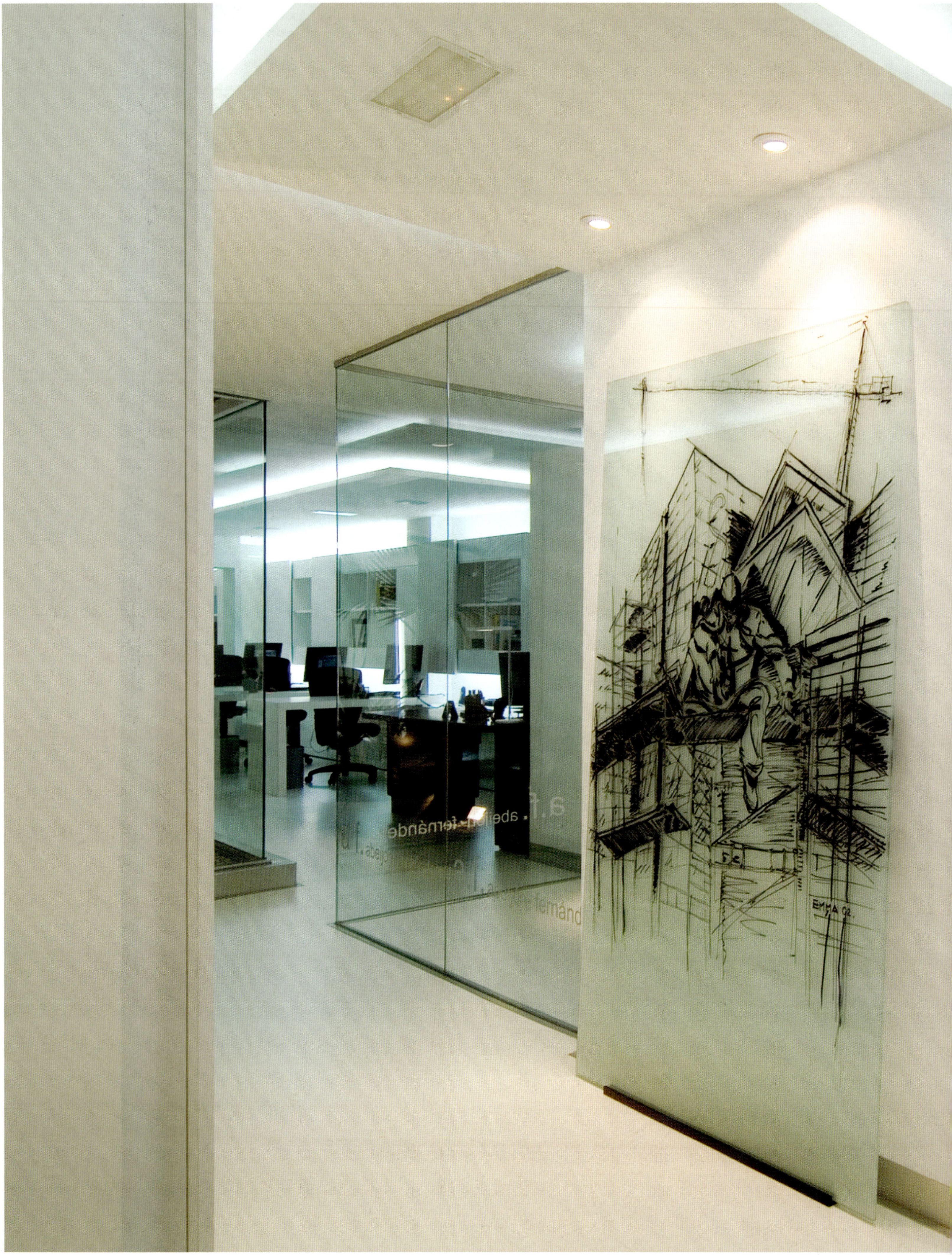
EMMA 02.

Afeijón-Fernández Architecture Office

ARCHITECT/DESIGNER:

José Abeijón, Miguel Fernández
/Abeijón-Fernández Arquitectos

Client: José Abeijón y Miguel Fernández
Photographer: Héctor Fernández-Santos
Location: A Coruña, Spain
Completion date: 2007
Area: 2,185 SF

The architectural studio wanted to renovate their image but maintain their identifying characteristics and adapt to new needs. The architects are also the studio owners and directors.

The project aimed to make the most of the natural light, making this the vertebral element of the spaces, and to use it as a vehicle to express the architects' perception regarding the different components of the composition.

Simplicity has been the guiding principle for the design of the work space, which has been transmitted by way of diverse elements that create a positive, welcoming, and calm atmosphere. The treatment of the furnishings and the walls ascribes to this concept.

The furniture, designed exclusively for this project, with the only exception of the chairs, harmonizes in its whiteness with the ceiling and floor achieving a white envelope that allows light to flow through the space. In the center is an elongated piece of furniture, which is the reference point of this area's configuration.

The project's functional spaces are integrated by three main areas. A hall separates the area for receiving the public from the work area.

The public space comprises a waiting area, two offices, a meeting room, a toilet, and a coatroom.

The work area includes a space with no partitions for general work, an area for printing and working with plans, a filing space, and a room for the installations. These areas are delineated by way of different ceiling heights. The divisions have been reduced to a minimum and those that have been included are made of glass. The result is a continuity and transparency that dominates the relationship between the different areas. Architecturally, the floor plan has been used as a basic element both in the project's geometry and architecture.

AFEIJÓN-FERNÁNDEZ ARCHITECTURE OFFICE

● The aim was to allow the light to flow around the furniture making it appear to float. All of the furniture has been designed exclusively for the project, with the exception of the chairs. Black and white chromatics and the presence of glass dominate the interior.

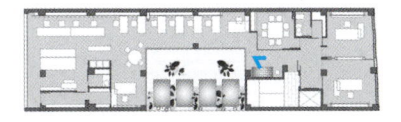

AFEIJÓN-FERNÁNDEZ ARCHITECTURE OFFICE

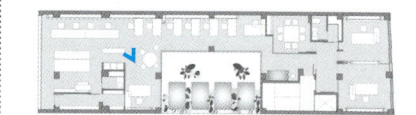

AFEIJÓN-FERNÁNDEZ ARCHITECTURE OFFICE

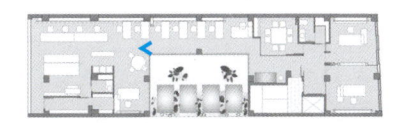

AFEIJÓN-FERNÁNDEZ ARCHITECTURE OFFICE

AFEIJÓN-FERNÁNDEZ ARCHITECTURE OFFICE

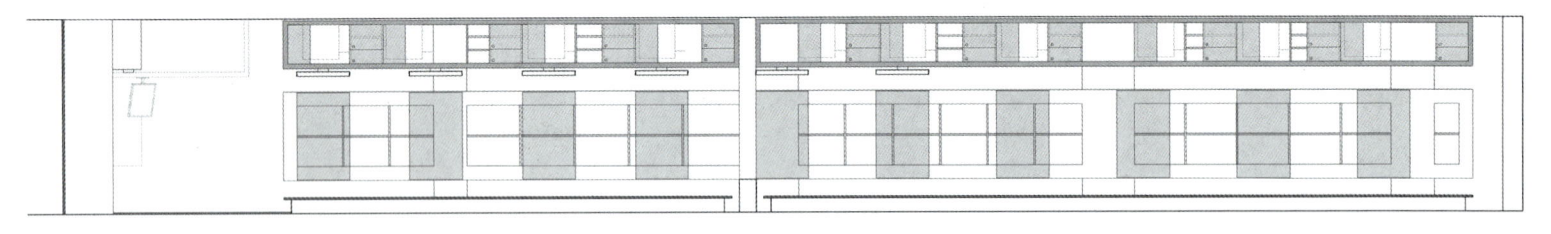

● Section

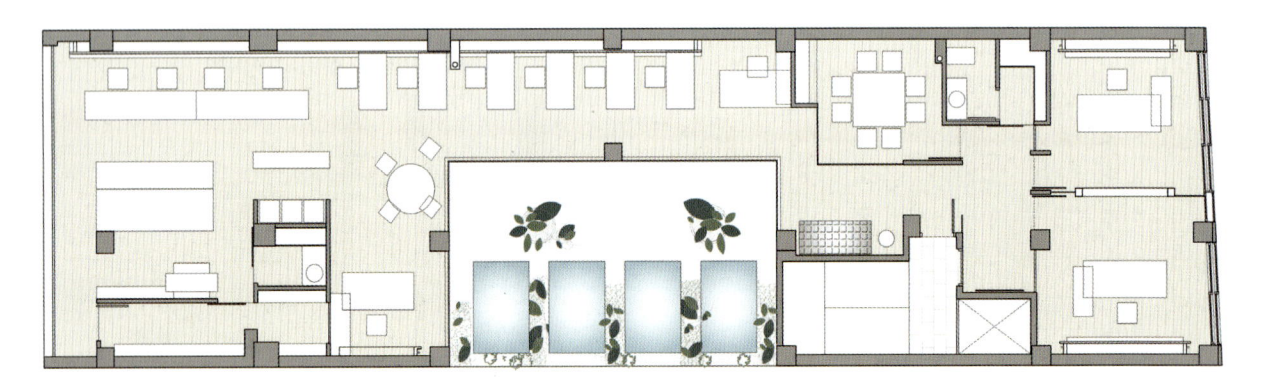

● Floor plan

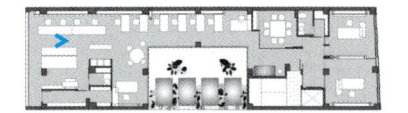

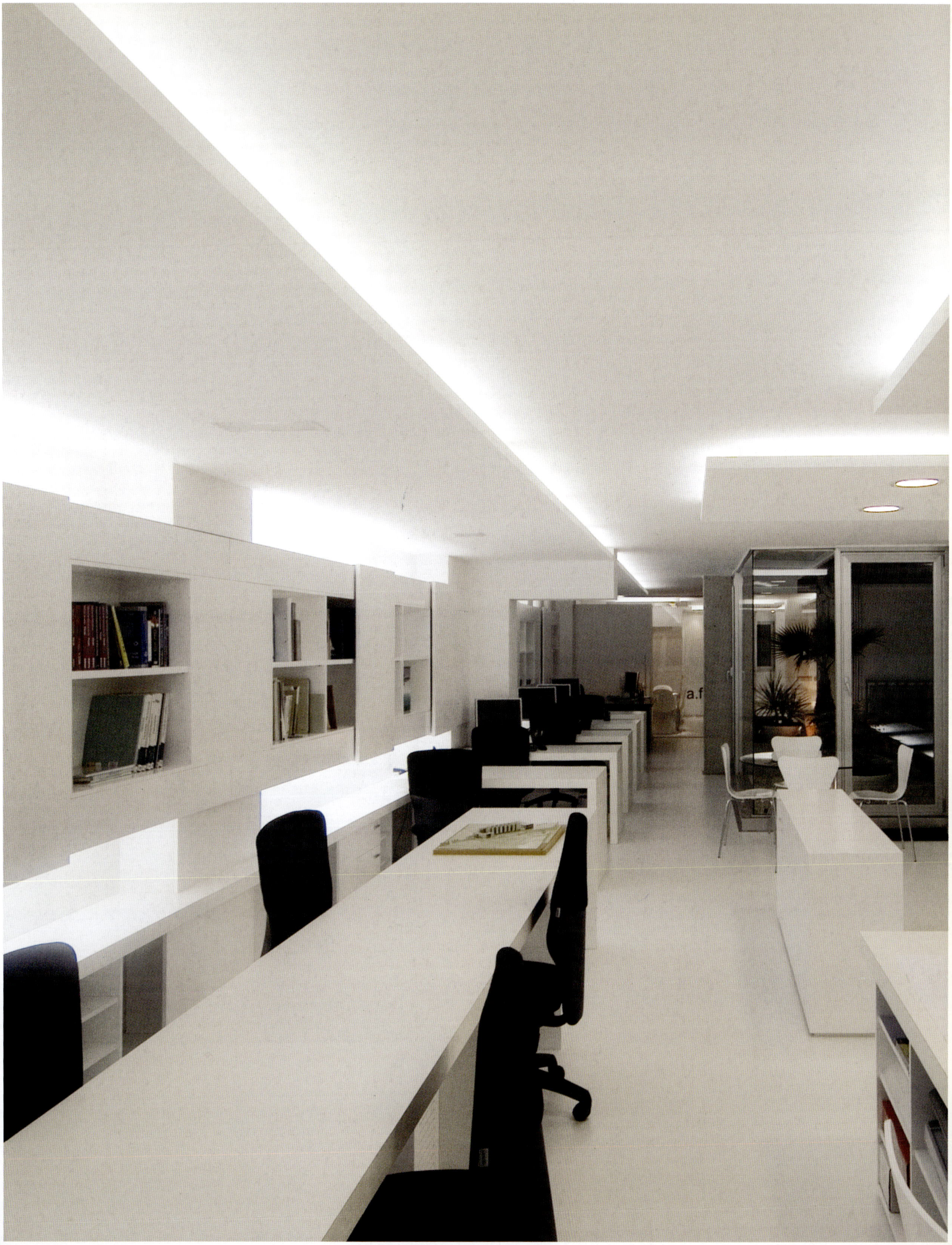

○ The work areas are delineated by changes in ceiling heights and in a few cases by glass partitions. Almost all the lighting is indirect, from halogen lights installed on the ceiling.

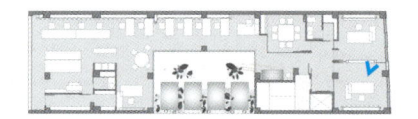

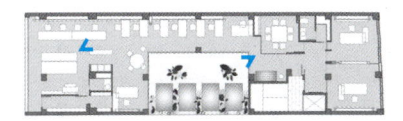

AFEIJÓN-FERNÁNDEZ ARCHITECTURE OFFICE

AFEIJÓN-FERNÁNDEZ ARCHITECTURE OFFICE

AFEIJÓN-FERNÁNDEZ ARCHITECTURE OFFICE

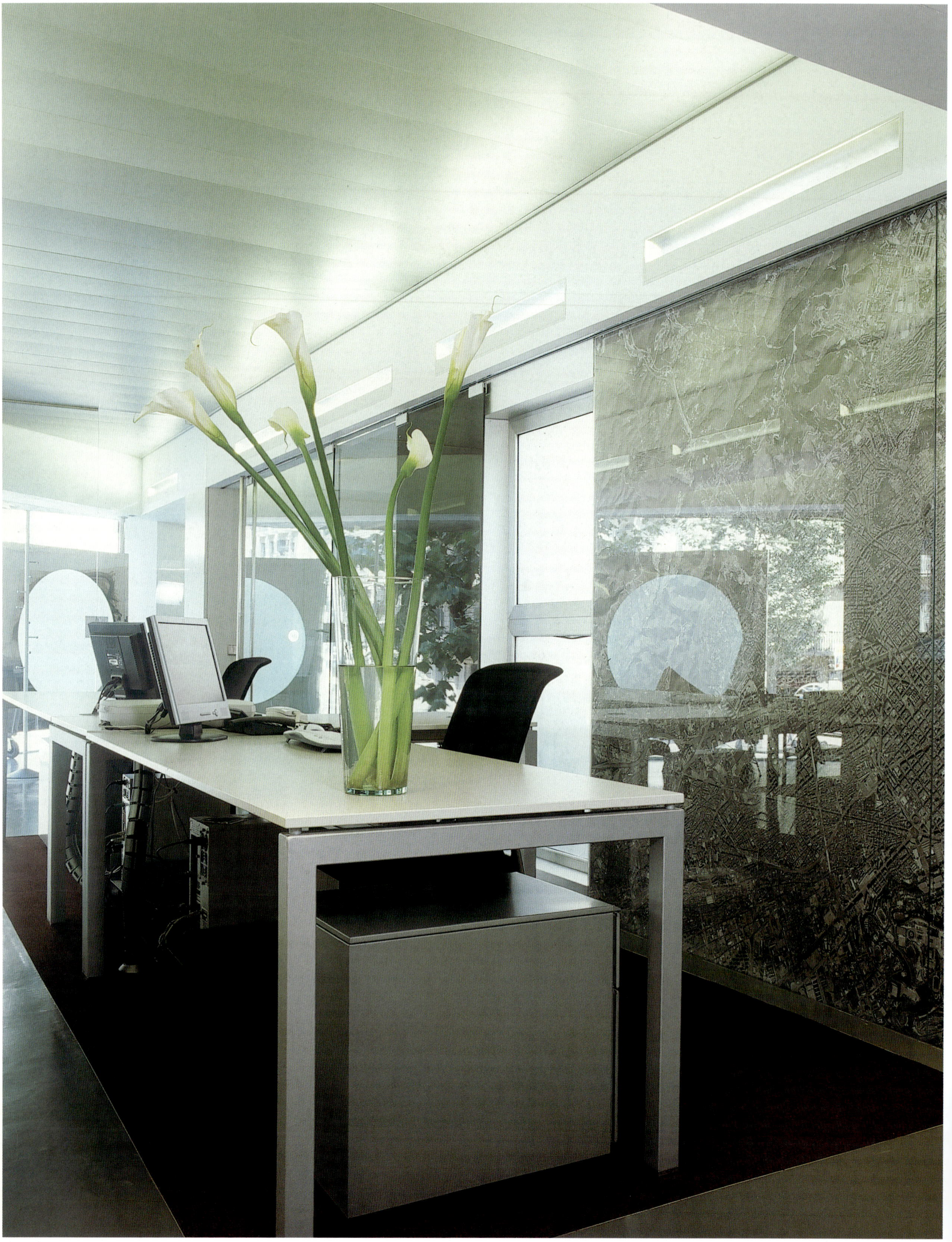

ZONABARCELONA OFFICE

This project consisted of the restoration of an old office space. The starting point of this reorganization was the demolition of the existing partition walls to create the areas the clients requested.

The triangular floor plan of the resulting space, has been divided into two spaces, which related harmoniously with each other and are joined by a shared lobby. A large mural (shown at left), protected by a glass panel, covers the entire wall.

This communal reception area offers access to both spaces, whose main characteristic is that they are openplan, without any opaque divisions to obstruct visual communication between the different areas that comprise them.

The right-hand unit is the headquarters of a local property developer. It is composed of a meeting room, with glass walls and a capacity for around ten people, a toilet beside a small office, which both receive ventilation from the building's interior courtyard and the director's office, located at the vertex of this part of the triangular floor plan.

The left-hand wing accommodates the offices of an architectural studio. This space is totally open, where the only division is a toilet beside the building's other interior courtyard.

To delineate the different work areas, different types of flooring have been used, which link with the ceiling by way of compartments like drawers. Gray linoleum has been laid throughout the work area and carpet in different colors has been used to define the work stations: one piece of carpet for every two work stations. The ceiling has been covered with plasterboard.

The space had floor-to-ceiling openings on the walls, which have been resolved in this project using fixed glass panes without frames. Although these openings allowed a generous amount of natural light to enter, they presented the disadvantage of not protecting the space against the effect of direct sunlight. This problem has been overcome thanks to the installation of revolving stainless steel mullions and with internal lighting used as publicity for the offices.

ARCHITECT/DESIGNER:

HÉCTOR RESTREPO, CRISTINA CUBERES/HERES ARQUITECTURA

Client: Zonabarcelona, s.l.
Photographer: Jordi Miralles
Location: Barcelona, Spain
Completion date: 2004
Area: 2,227 SF

● The wooden furniture and the interior woodwork is all white, the same color as all the walls, with the exception of the toilets, which have been clad in gloss, graphite-color ceramic pieces.

ZONABARCELONA OFFICE
119

ZONABARCELONA OFFICE

ZONABARCELONA OFFICE

ZONABARCELONA OFFICE

Sections

Floor plan

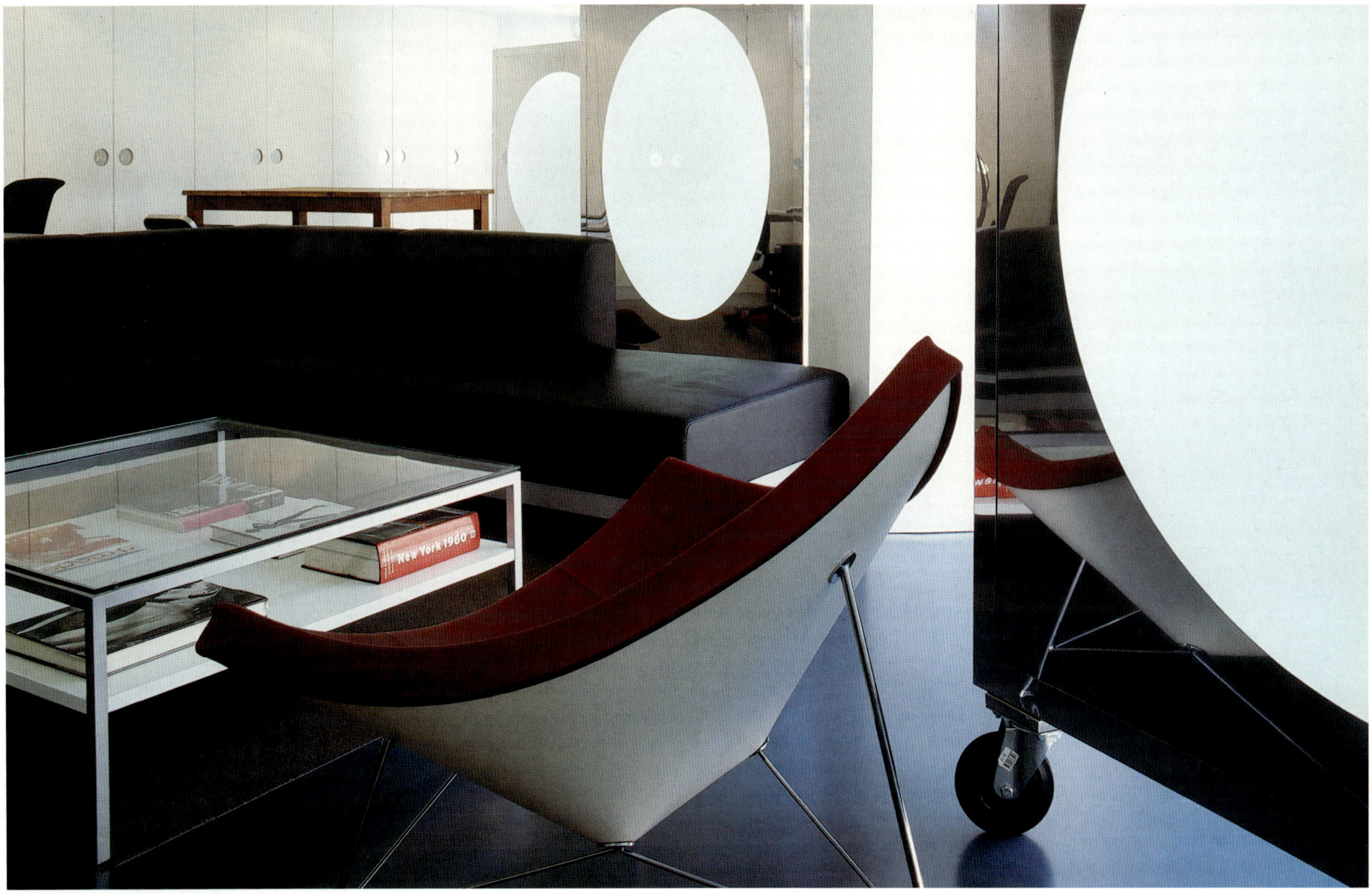
New York 1960

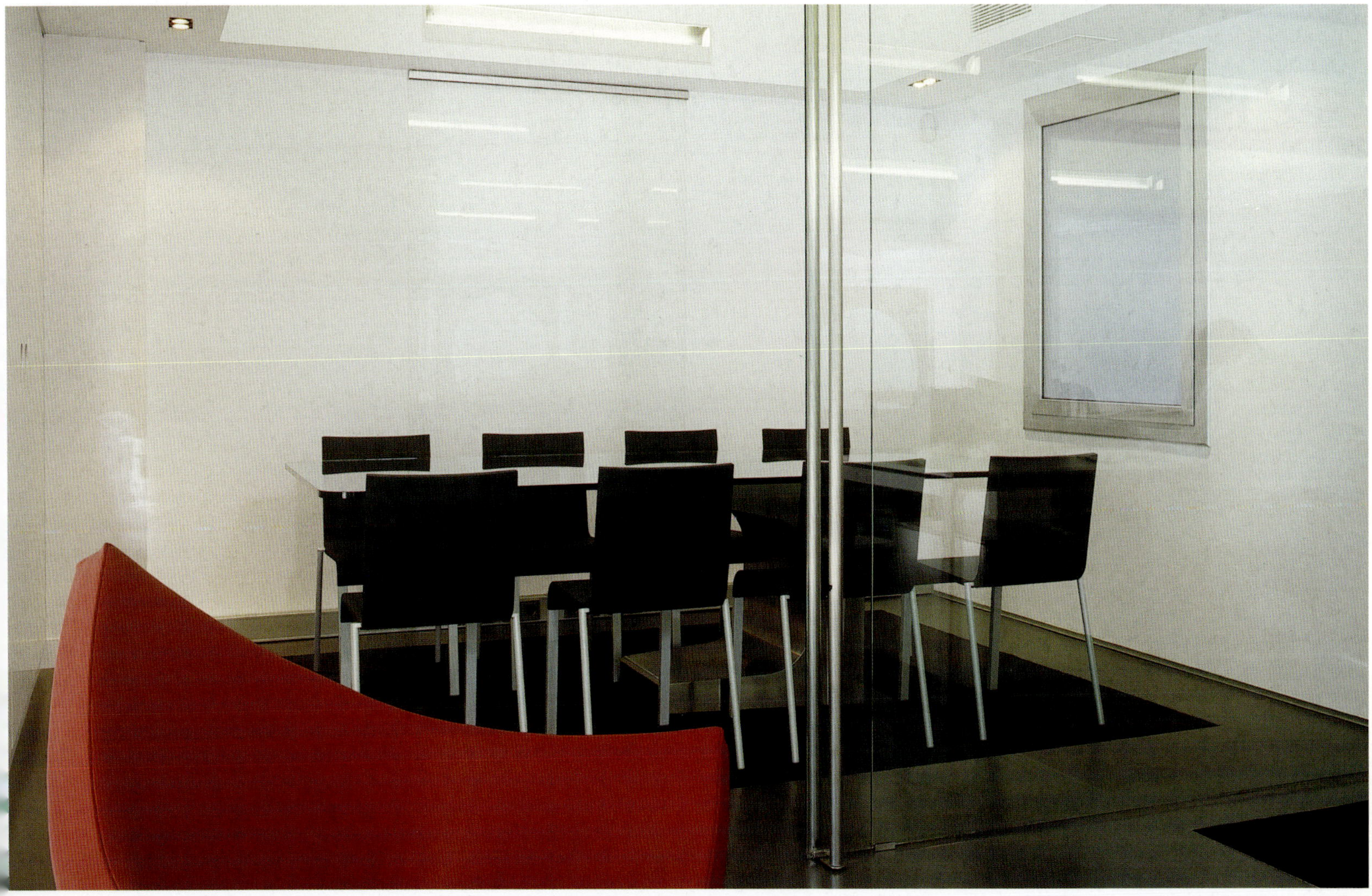

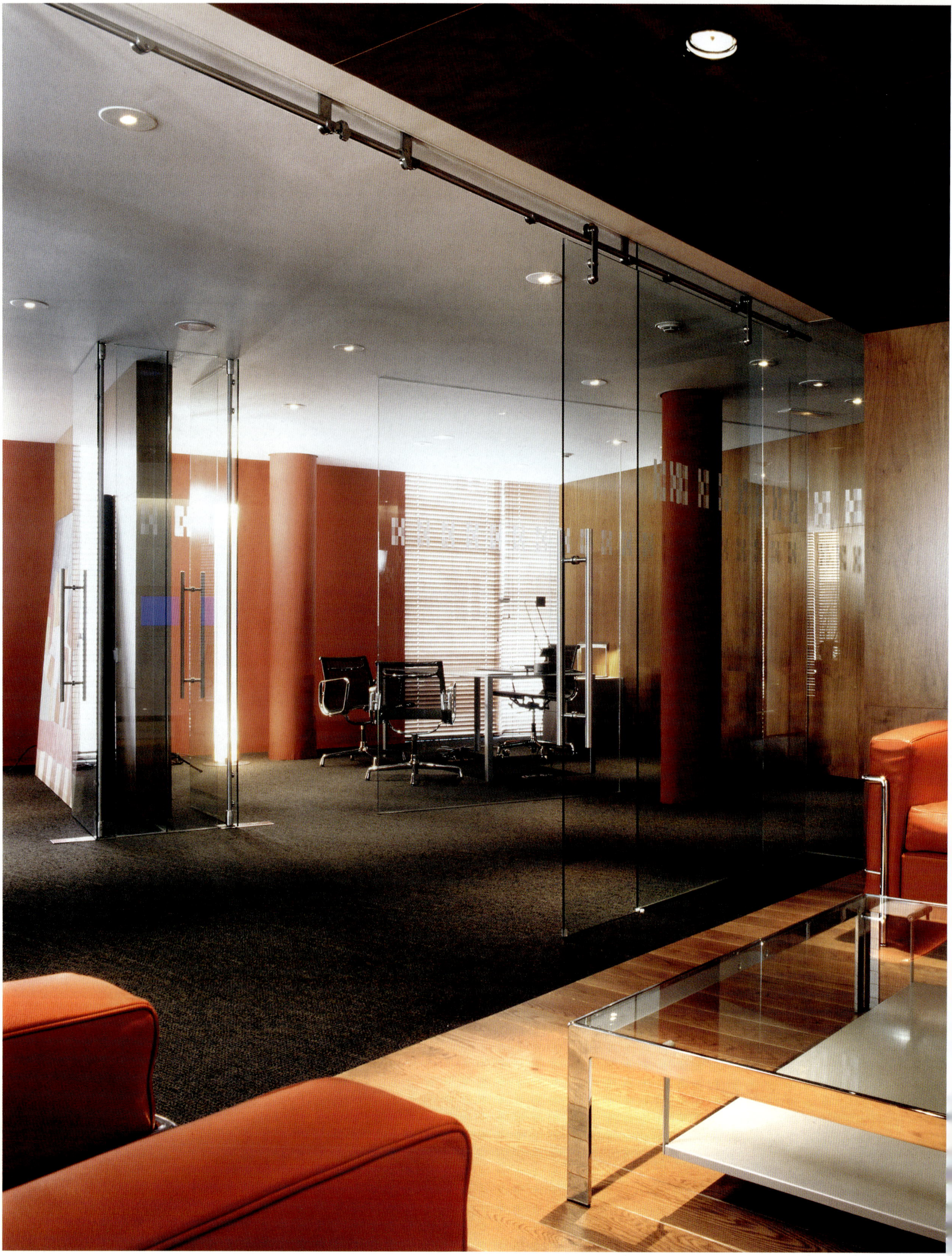

Habitectura Offices

The commission for this project was the renovation of the second floor of a corporate building belonging to property developers in Sabadell, which was to be used as the company's sales department.

The floor plan is trapezoidal shaped and has three façades and a shared wall. On the other side is an office and the toilets, the service core of the floor. Next to this space is the vertical circulation, formed by stairs and elevators.

The layout also includes the reception area, a waiting room, three information rooms for clients, and a signing room. All the work rooms have been positioned next to the façades, while the interior has been reserved for the reception area and the waiting room.

The reception area has been defined by way of oak flooring with a walnut finish, which is different from the rest of the floor. Behind the desk is a mirror with the company logo silk-screened onto it.

The waiting room has been conceived as a box. The two walls, floor, and ceiling are all made from walnut; the other two walls are made of glass and one of them has been installed with three informative monitors. The alternative walnut and glass walls have also been used for the information and signing rooms. All of these rooms have been laid with carpet floor tiles.

The furniture is integrated throughout, in other words built-in or adjoining the partitions, with the exception of the tables and chairs.

The project has attempted to maximize transparency and make this concept compatible with the privacy needed for clients. Facilitating the entry of light also increases the sense of size of the interior. This characteristic extends the façade's morphology, which is mostly made from glass. For this reason the walls that run parallel to each other are glass, thus respecting the façade, and in the perpendicular, opaque wooden walls, the top 12 inches are completed with blocks of glass.

ARCHITECT/DESIGNER:

GCA Arquitectes Associats

Client: Habitectura
Photographer: Jordi Miralles
Location: Sabadell, Spain
Completion date: 2004
Area: 2,368 SF

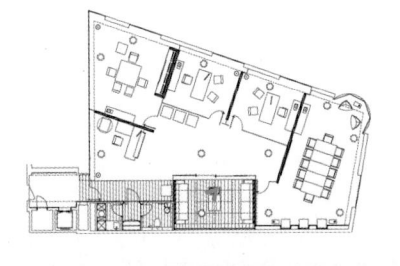

- The furniture has been chosen to be modern, light-weight and functional, in keeping with a timeless aesthetic. Carpet tiles have been laid on the floor throughout the work area.

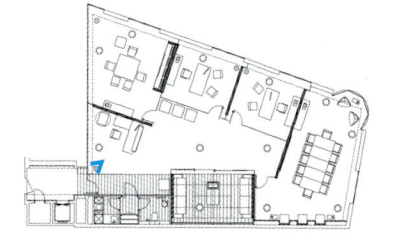

HABITECTURA OFFICES

○ When installing the general lighting, the light fittings were intended to be as discrete as possible, and almost all have been embedded in the false ceiling. The installations have also all been hidden.

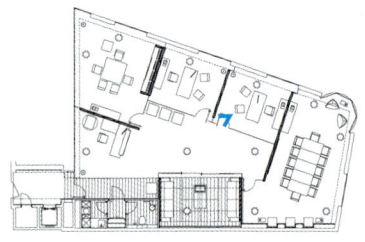

HABITECTURA OFFICES

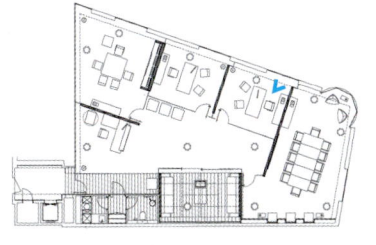

HABITECTURA OFFICES

● Floor plan

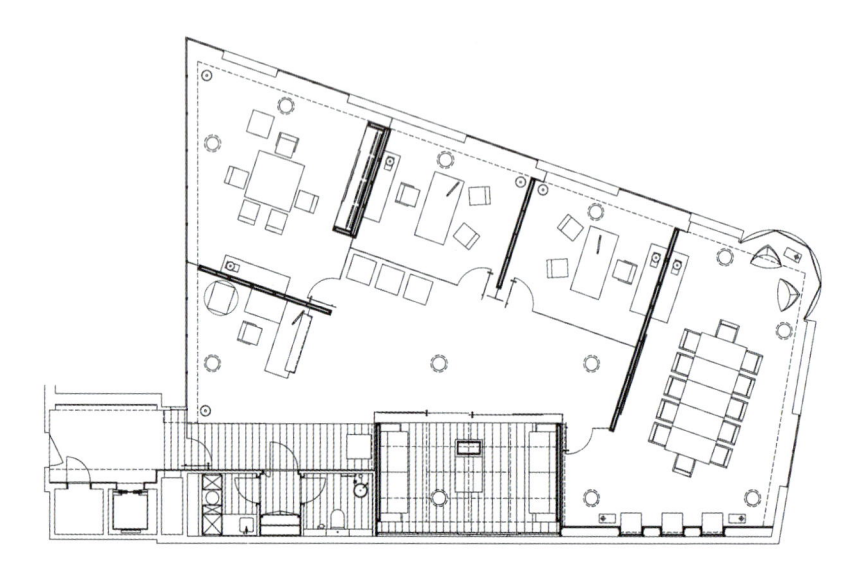

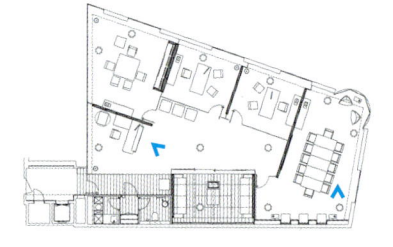

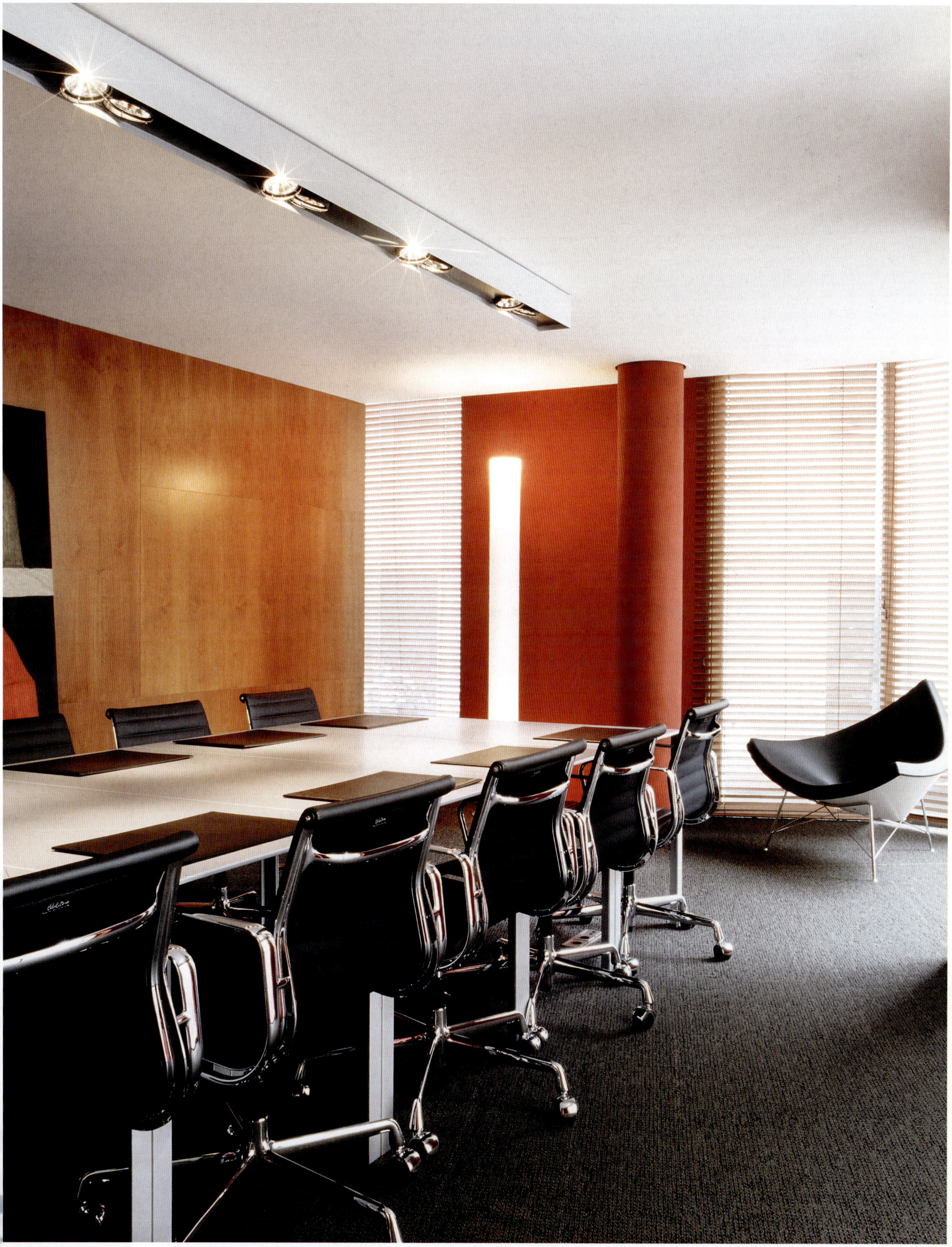

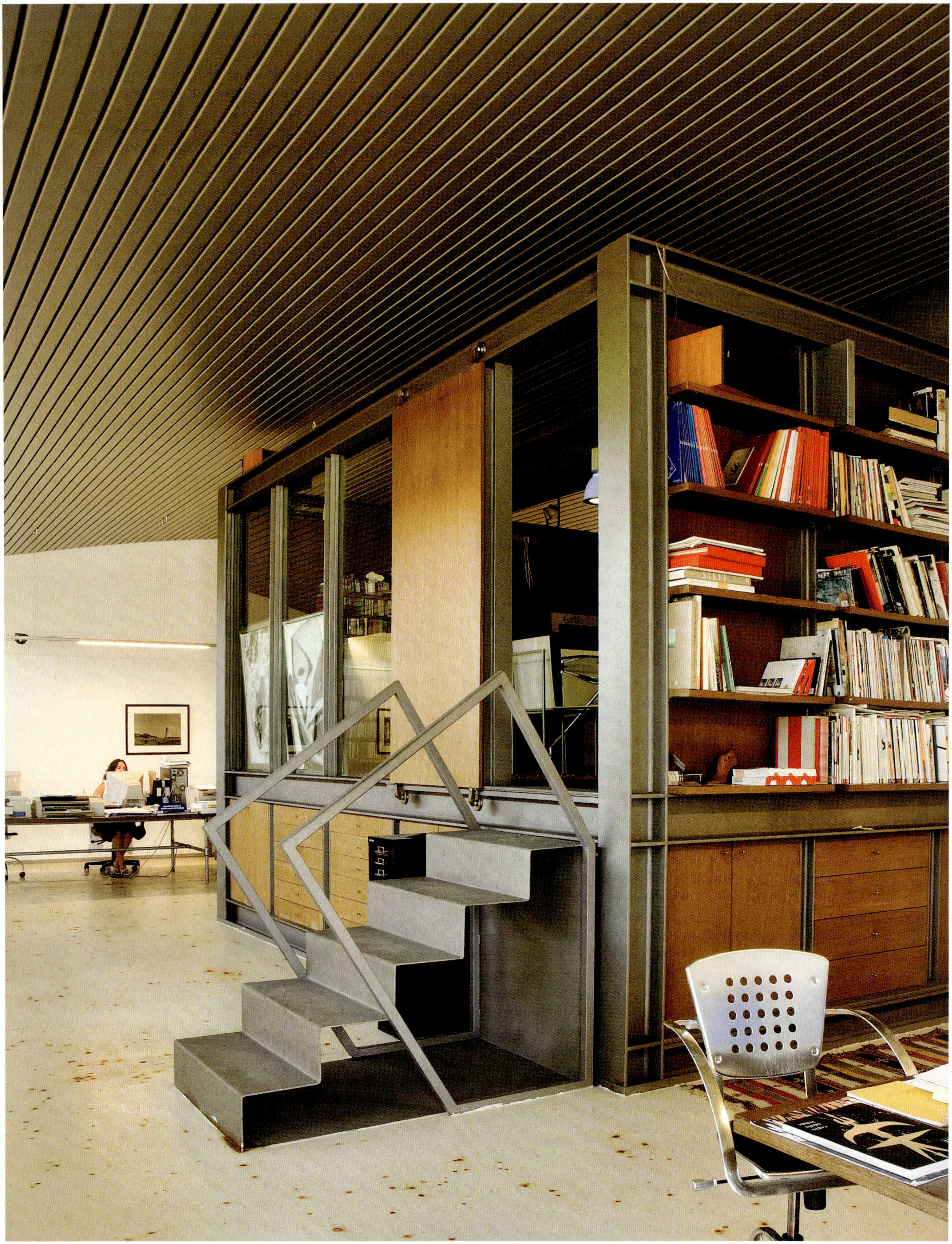

Estudio Joaquín Gallego

ARCHITECT/DESIGNER:

ESTUDIO JOAQUÍN GALLEGO

Client: Estudio Joaquín Gallego
Photographer: Pep Escoda
Location: Elx, Spain
Completion date: 2004
Area: 2,691 SF

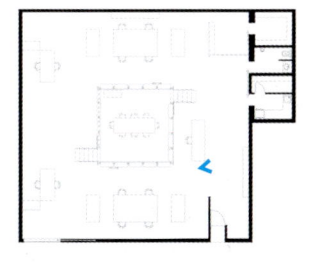

This work space was conceived as an office for between ten and fifteen employees. The interior is distributed in such a way that there are two, which are well-defined yet connected workspaces: the graphic design department and the department of interior architecture. There are also two communal areas: the meeting and conference room, which also serves as an archive for current projects and library, and the services, with toilet, office, storage space and an archive for old projects.

The most notable space is the meeting room, because of its location in the center of the space. It consists of a square independent module, constructed using a structure of 8-inch H-beams, with 4-inch beams in between. The other elements are wooden panels—which on one of the walls have been used to install shelves and consequently create a bookshelf—sliding doors and drawers. The access stairs for this space have been built from folded sheet metal. A long table, made from glass, presides over the interior of this module, accompanied by opaque glass chairs with stainless steel slats.

To give the office a more robust feel, as well as an elegant one, the designer opted to create a false ceiling with the form of a vault, constructed with aluminum laminates, which provide the interior design with continuity and a horizontal aesthetic. Epoxy resin has been used for the floor, a material chosen to reduce costs, since it is cheaper than wood and has the advantage of being a good insulator. Plasterboard panels supported by a steel framework clad the interior walls.

The furnishings are made from wengué wood. The designer opted for a façade clad in corten steel plates that contrasts with the texture of the wood, but harmonizes in the color.

The 2,700-square-foot studio is complemented by an adjacent 540-square foot car park.

ESTUDIO JOAQUÍN GALLEGO

● This central module, made from wooden panels and a structure of metal beams, is an independent volume that serves as a meeting and conference room, as well as a library, with the bookshelf to one side.

ESTUDIO JOAQUÍN GALLEGO

ESTUDIO JOAQUÍN GALLEGO

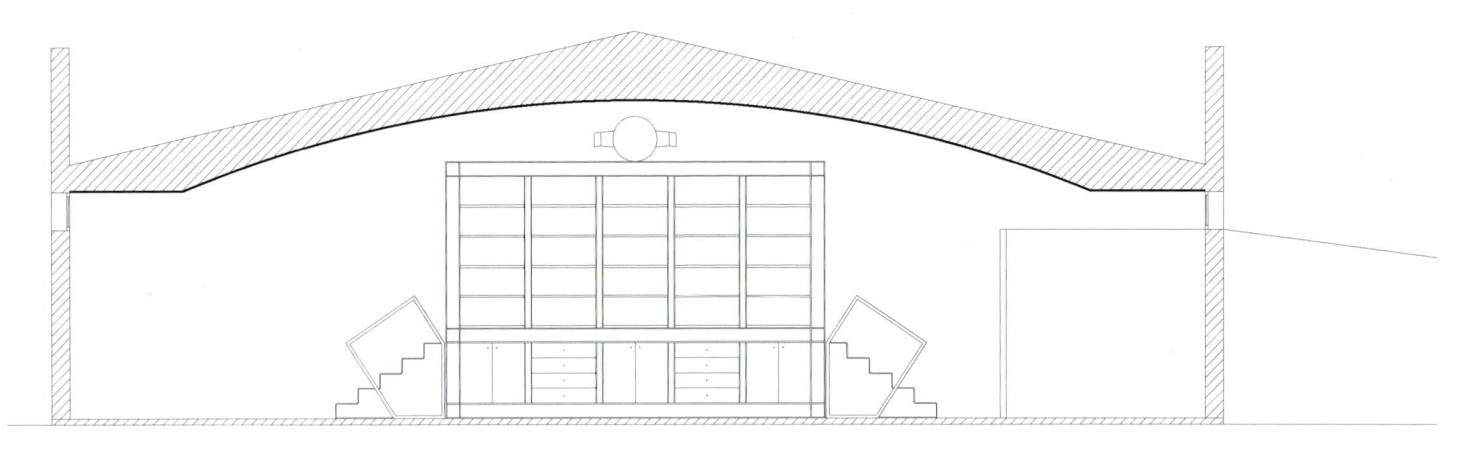

Section

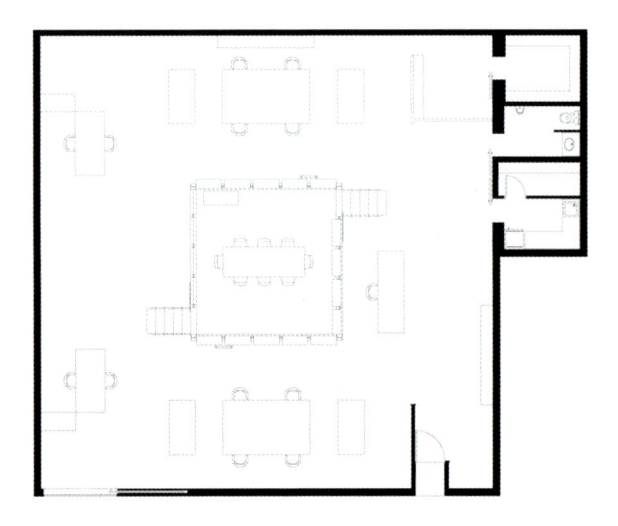

Floor plan

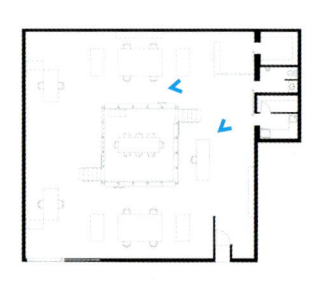

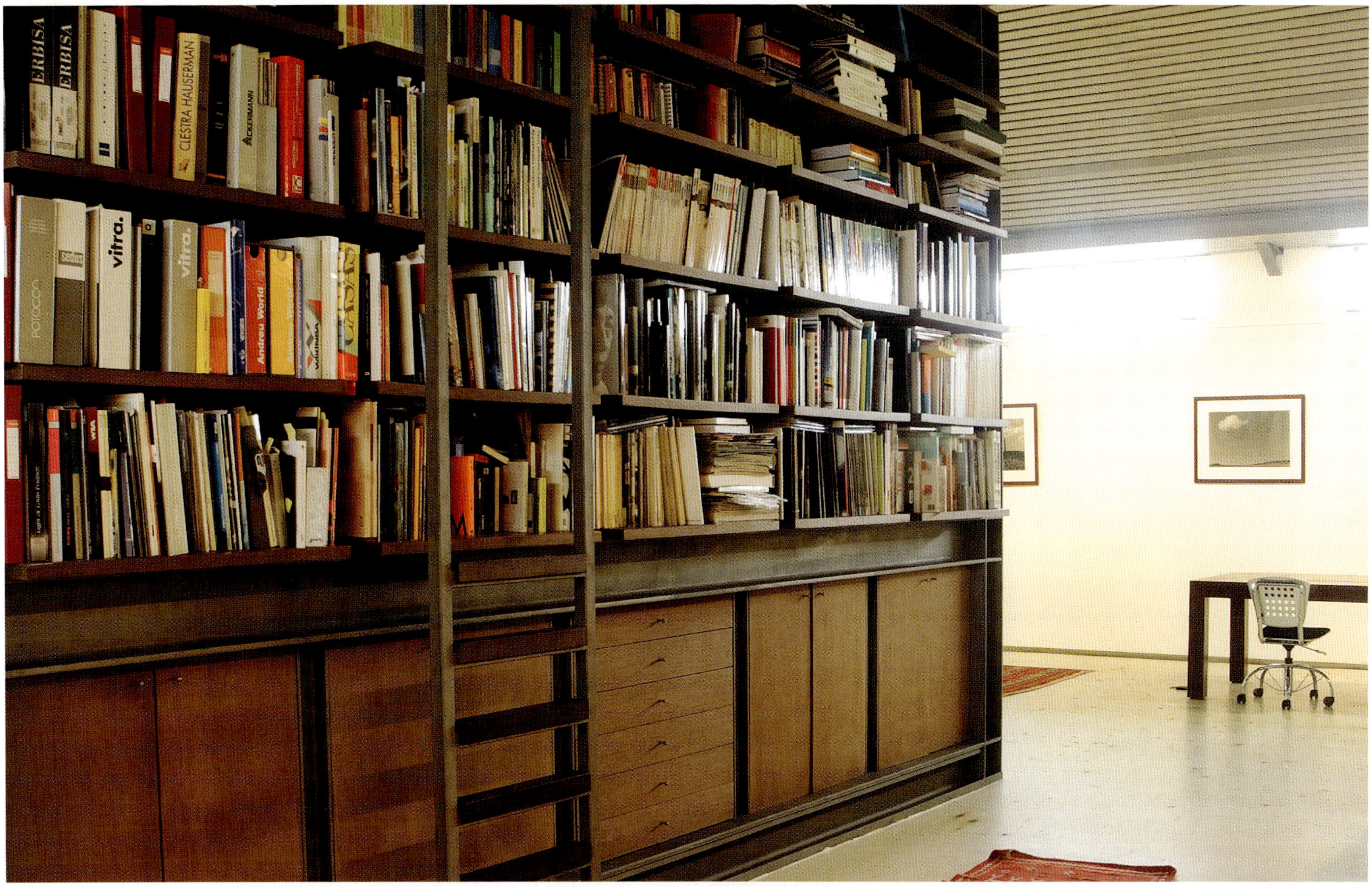
ERBISA
ERBISA
CLESTRA HAUSERMAN
vitra.
vitra.
Andreu World

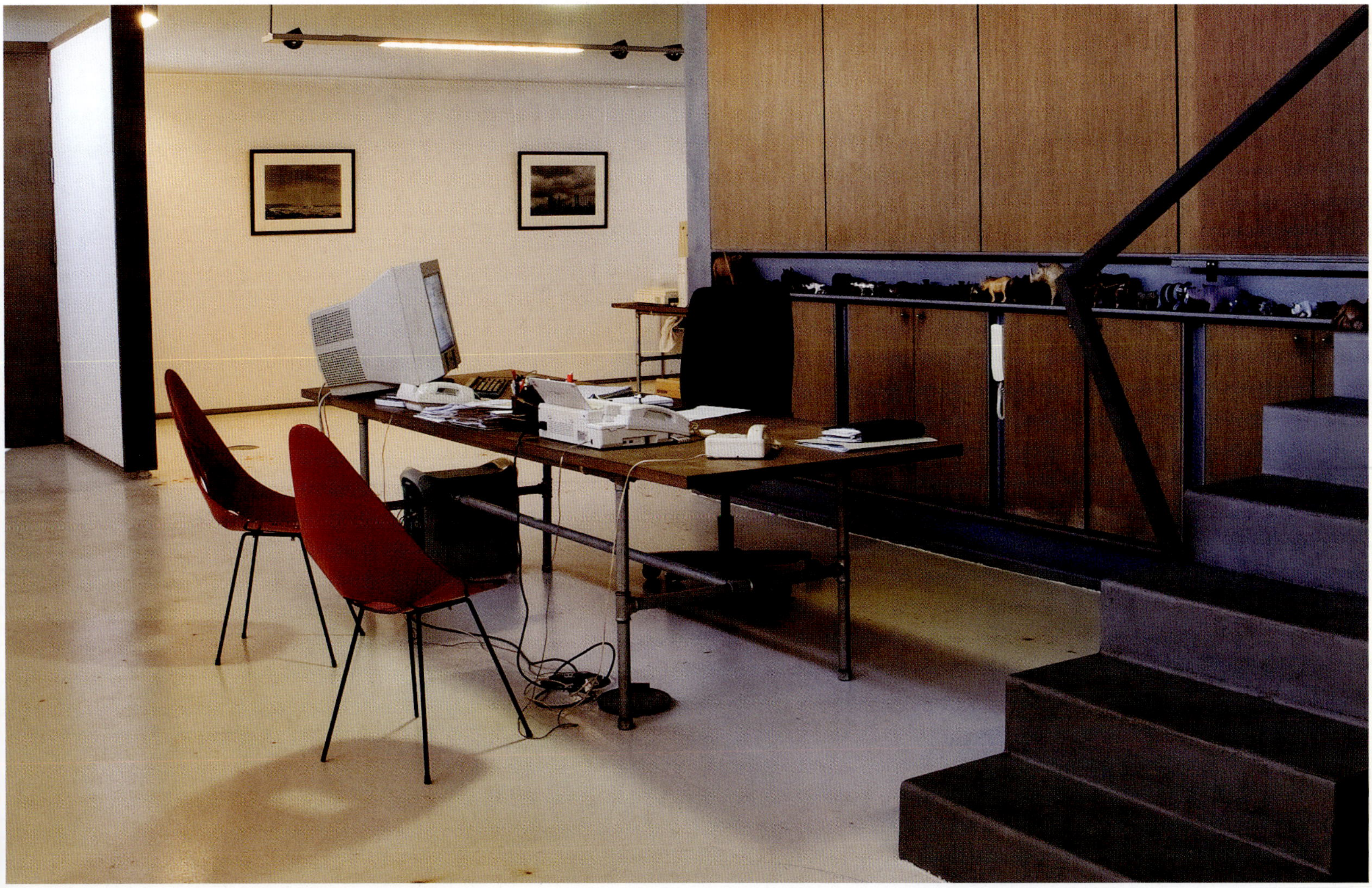

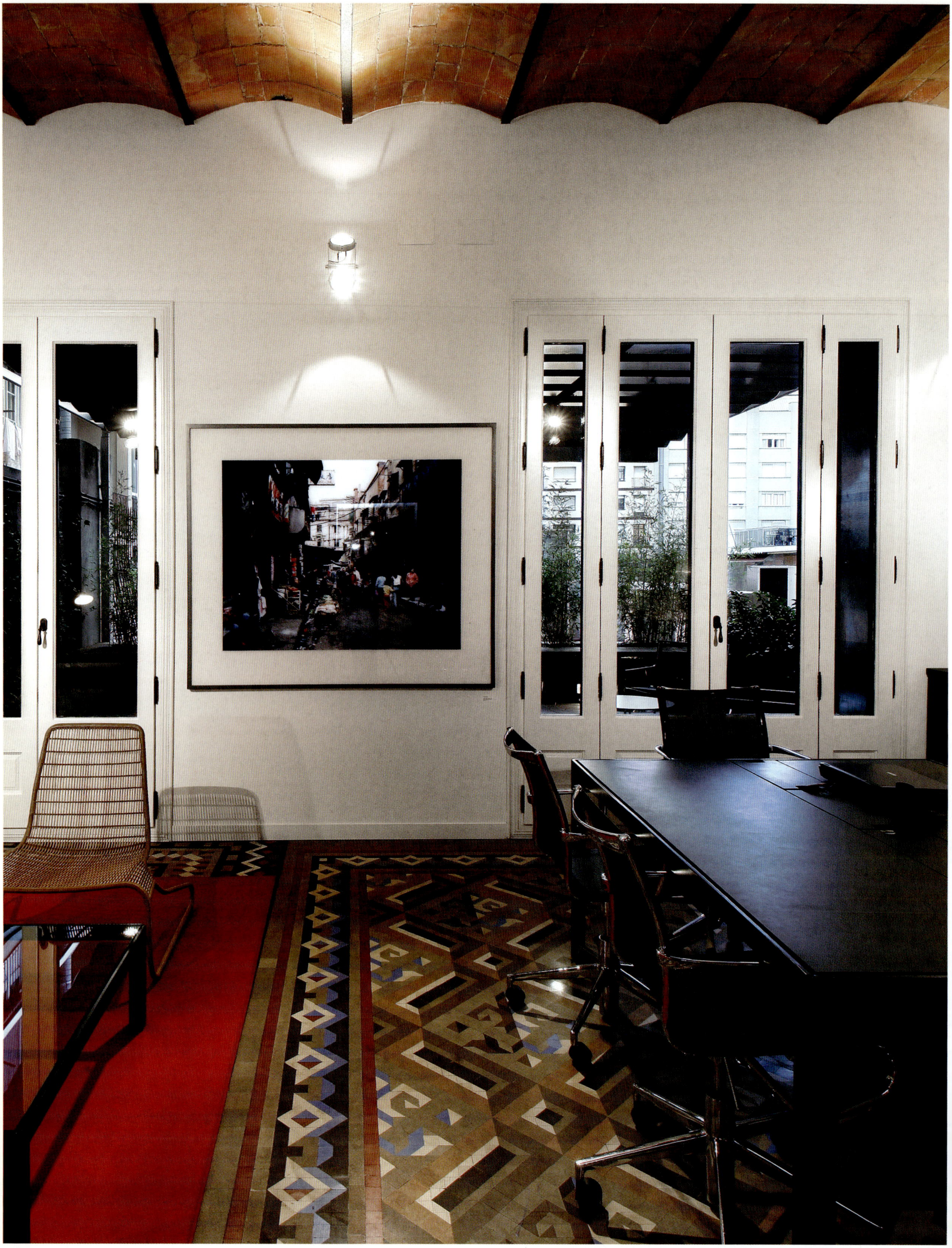

9MAR Offices

The renovation of the offices for a property developer was the aim of this project. On a constructed surface area of 2,800 square feet, the main spaces are the reception area, a management and administration office, a central room for storage and installations, and a large communal work space (but with individual work stations, the result of joining three large rooms). All these areas are multi-purpose: the large room can be used for holding meetings, general work, and seeing clients. The administrative office provides privacy both for administrative tasks and seeing clients. The reception area also serves as an office and kitchen where aperitifs can be prepared for presentations or other similar occasions, thanks to a piece of furniture that conceals a small cupboard and fridge and a small kitchen.

Although the client wanted to preserve the original wattle and daube ceiling, this was only possible in the large multi-purpose room, since in the other spaces previous reforms had left it in an irrecoverable state. The ceiling work was sandblasted and the beams were varnished with fire-resistant paint. The new window and door frames are wood, like the previous ones, but are sealed better and include insulated glass panels.

All installations are hidden behind plasterboard panels, with the exception of the large air-conditioning tube, which has been left exposed throughout the office.

Geometric and simple lines, along with the color white, dominate the design of the furnishings, because the idea was for them to integrate with the project. These were therefore intended to be of neutral design. Most of the furniture is made from matt white medium-density fiberboard (MDF), while the table in the center of the work space is polythene, also white, with the aluminum screws and brackets exposed.

Architect/Designer:

Marta Torelló/Marta Torelló Interiors, Marta González

Client: 9MAR Immobles i Gestió, S.L.
Photographer: Rafael Vargas
Location: Barcelona, Spain
Completion date: 2005
Area: 2,788 SF

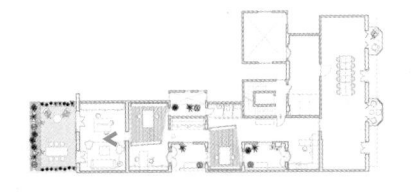

● The original early twentieth-century ceilings and flooring were preserved in the all-purpose hall. Although white is the predominant color throughout, this is the only area where black furniture has been used.

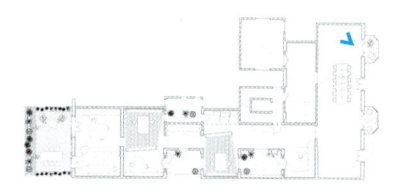

9MAR OFFICES

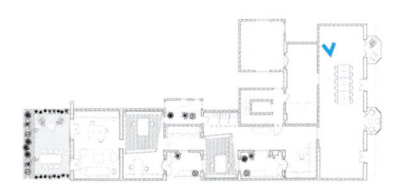

9MAR OFFICES

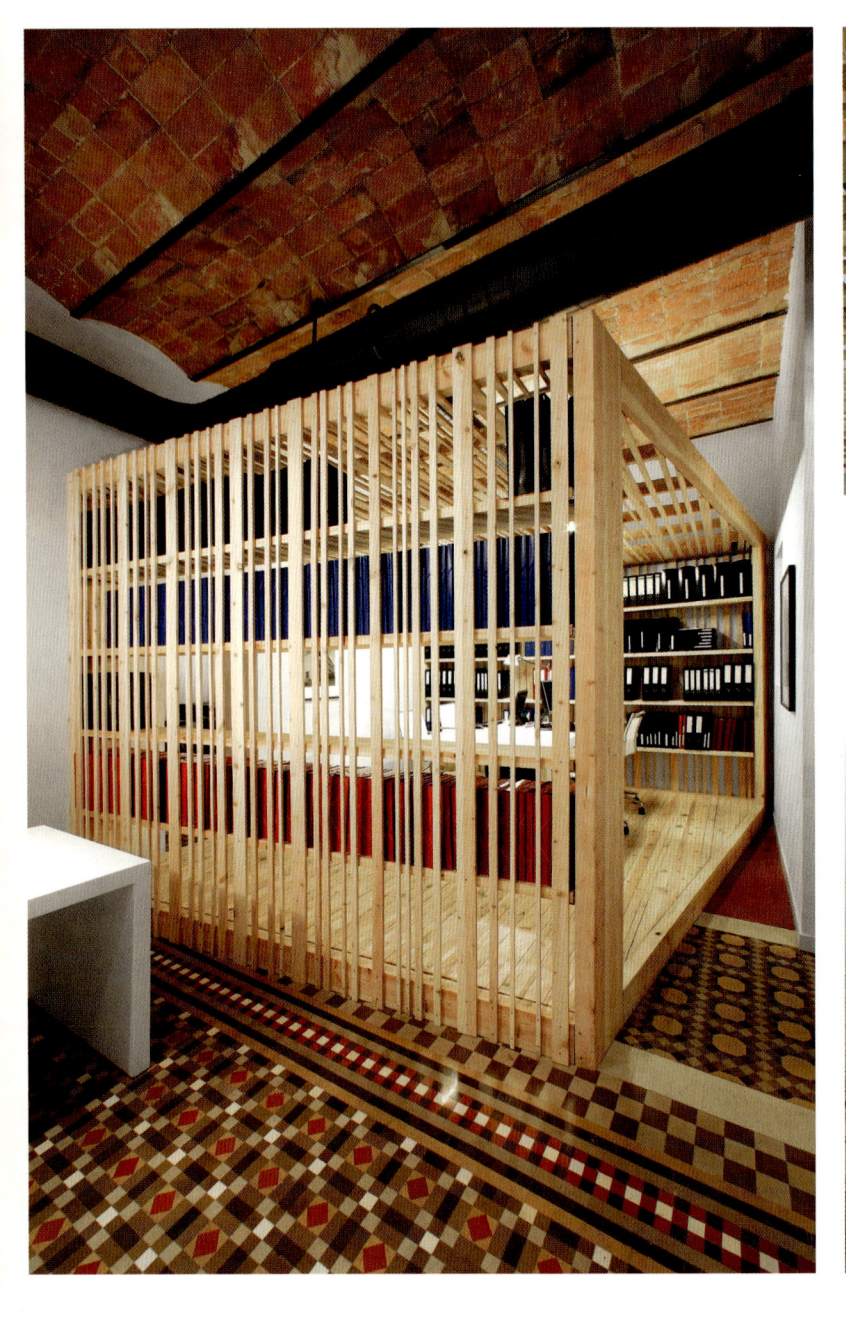

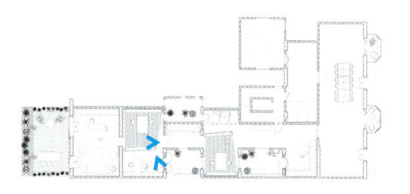

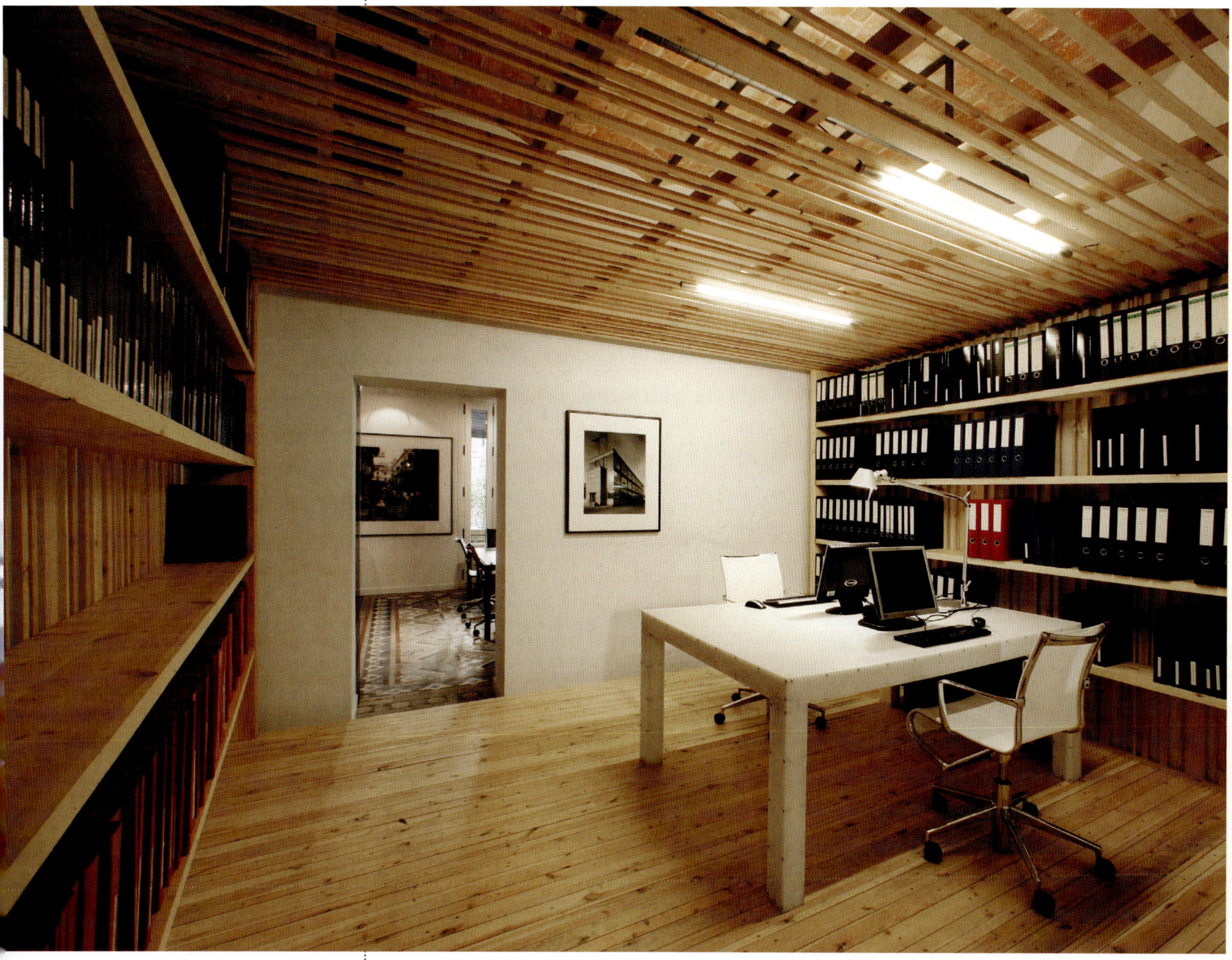

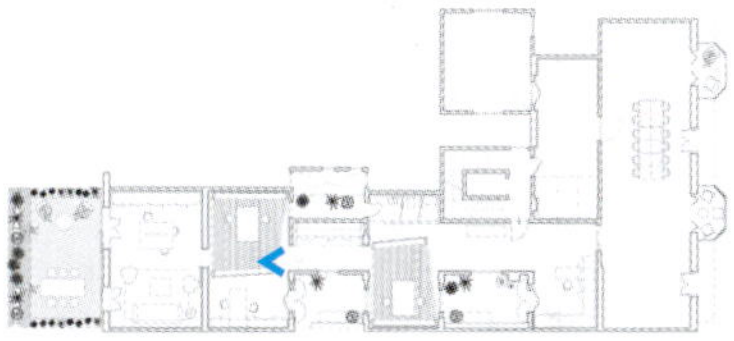

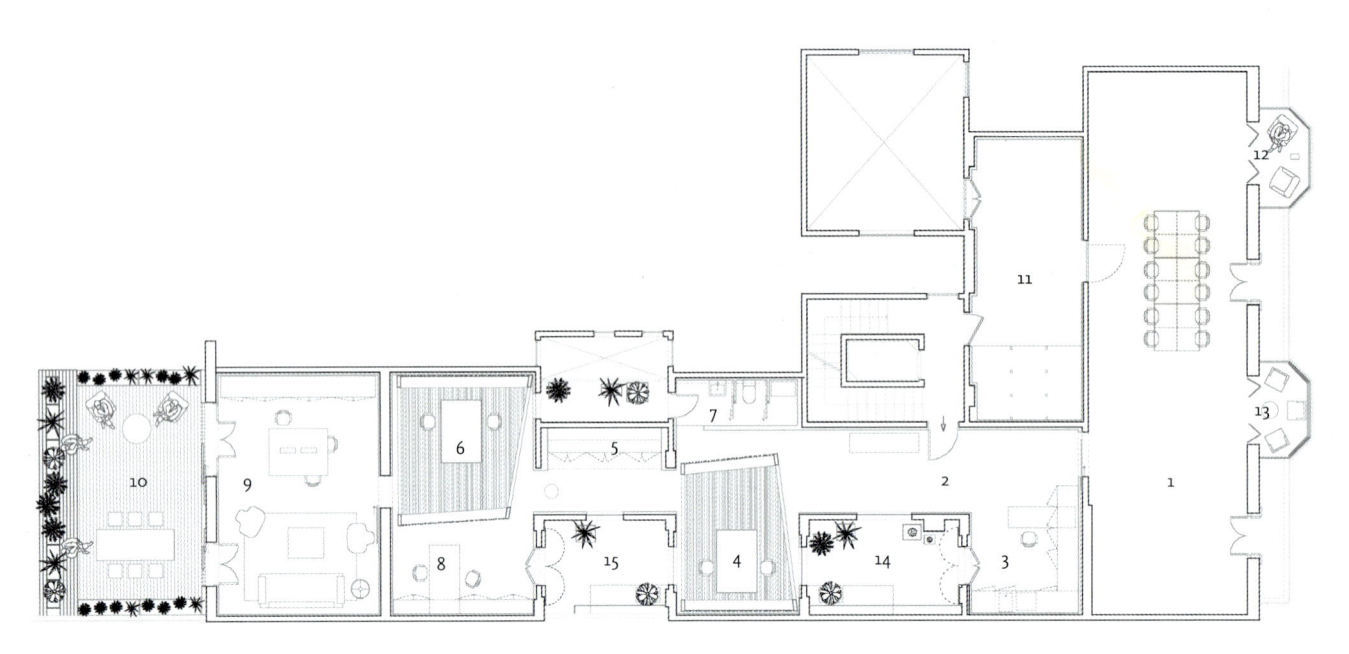

● Floor plan

1. Multipurpose hall
2. Reception
3. Kitchenette and archival
4. Work space 1
5. Office supplies
6. Work space 2
7. Bathrooms
8. Administration office
9. Director's office
10. Terrace
11. Artwork storage
12. Bay window 1
13. Bay window 2
14. Lightwell 1
15. Lightwell 2

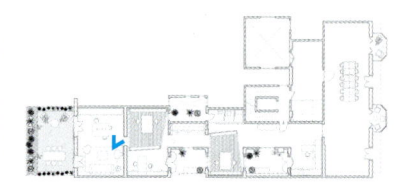

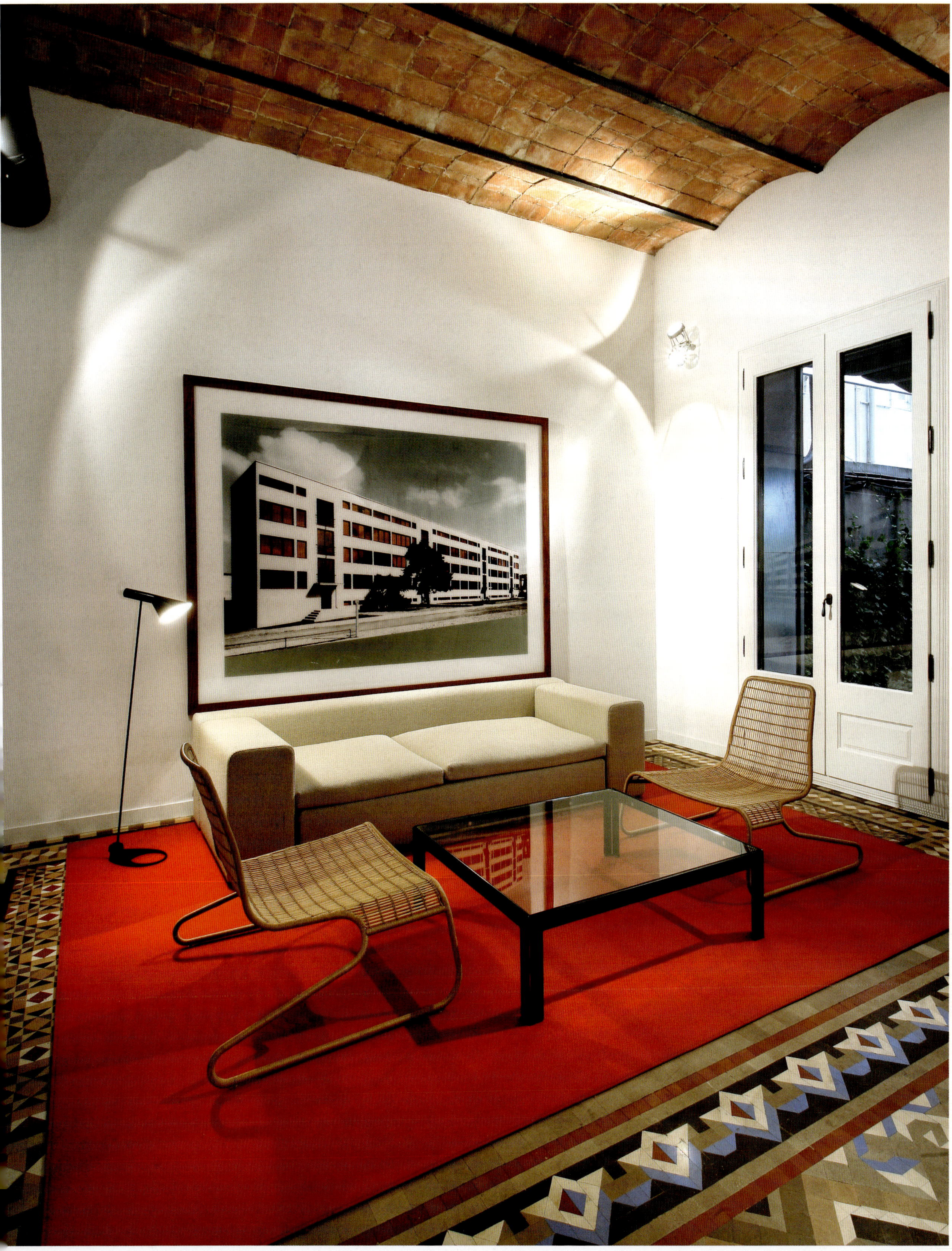

● Polythene, normally used in industrial contexts, has been used as the material for the table in the work area. It is soft to the touch and seems lighter, because of its translucent white color.

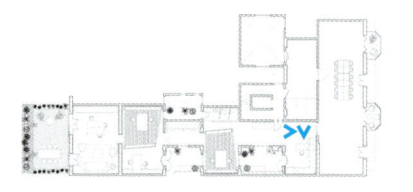

9MAR OFFICES

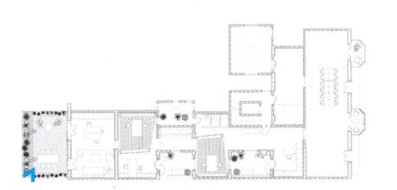

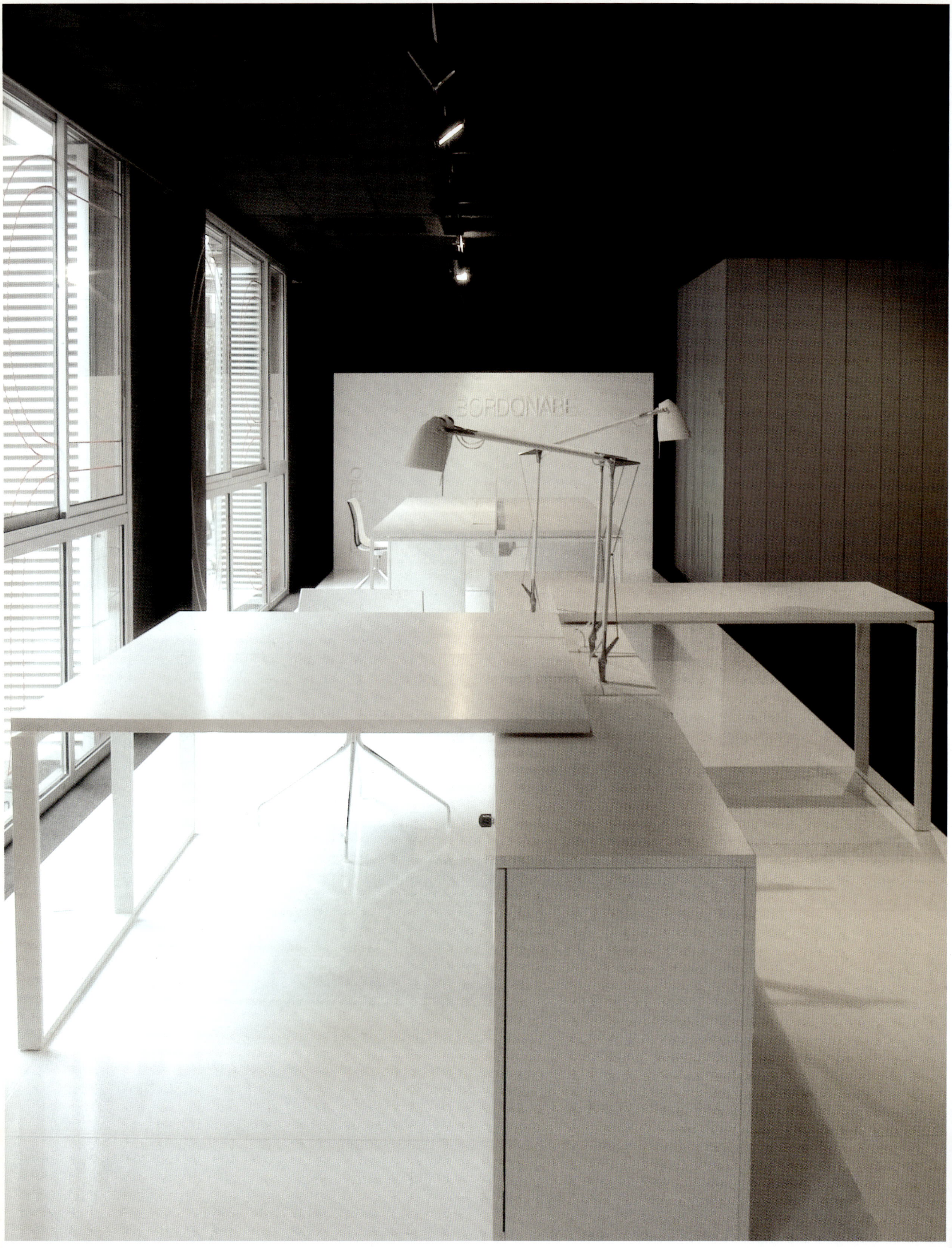
BORDONABE

Bordonabe Barcelona

Architect/Designer:
Francesc Rifé, Bordonabe

Client: Bordonabe
Photographer: Javier Ortega
Location: Barcelona, Spain
Completion date: 2005
Area: 2,906 SF

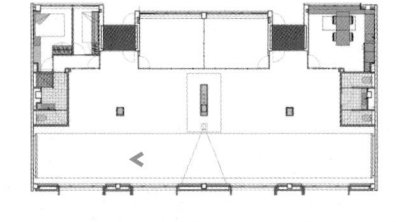

This office space is located on the first floor of a block of buildings located in a central zone of Barcelona. Since it is a recently constructed building, the team of interior designers decided to minimize the intervention on the structure of the narrow, rectangular floor plan. The idea of leaving a light skin differentiated the spaces. The desire of the clients, from Navarra, was to create an office space where the furnishings would stand out above all else.

The project is composed of a showroom, private offices, a meeting room with an office, and a mini-apartment for the exclusive use of the employees working in the different branches of Bordonabe. To favor and emphasize the design of the furniture, as well as the individual spaces, the designers opted to paint the floor, ceiling, and walls black. The result is a clear space in which different atmospheres have been created. On the floor there is white parquet, which helps to differentiate the different modules.

In the middle of this apparent lack of light, a large window acts as a single source of natural light, opening on one of the longer walls. On this glazed façade is the logo of the firm, so that it can be seen both from the outside and the inside.

Glass is another of the materials that divides the different constructive modules, while at the same time leaving the furniture visible. The modular spaces have been conceived as boxes that are raised from the floor and are formed from vertical and horizontal panels, which accentuate the passageway. They have been designed in white to stand out against the black, creating a spectacular contrast, further emphasized by the natural light. The use of these two colors achieves a serene working environment and enhances the firm's product, which is, again, the main feature of the space—the furniture.

BORDONABE BARCELONA

○ Vertical and horizontal lines characterize the interior design of these offices. Glass separates the different spaces and leaves the items of furniture, which are the major features of this space, exposed.

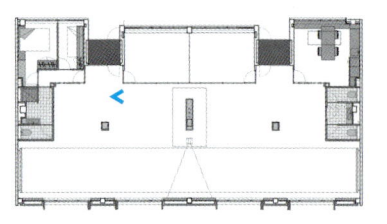

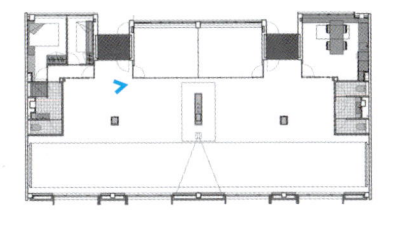

BORDONABE BARCELONA

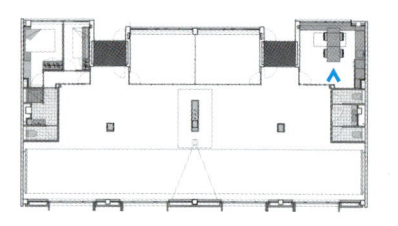

BORDONABE BARCELONA

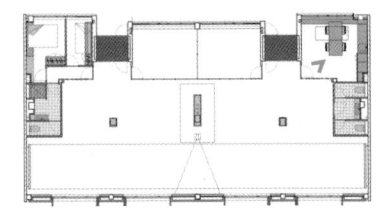

BORDONABE BARCELONA
153

BORDONABE BARCELONA

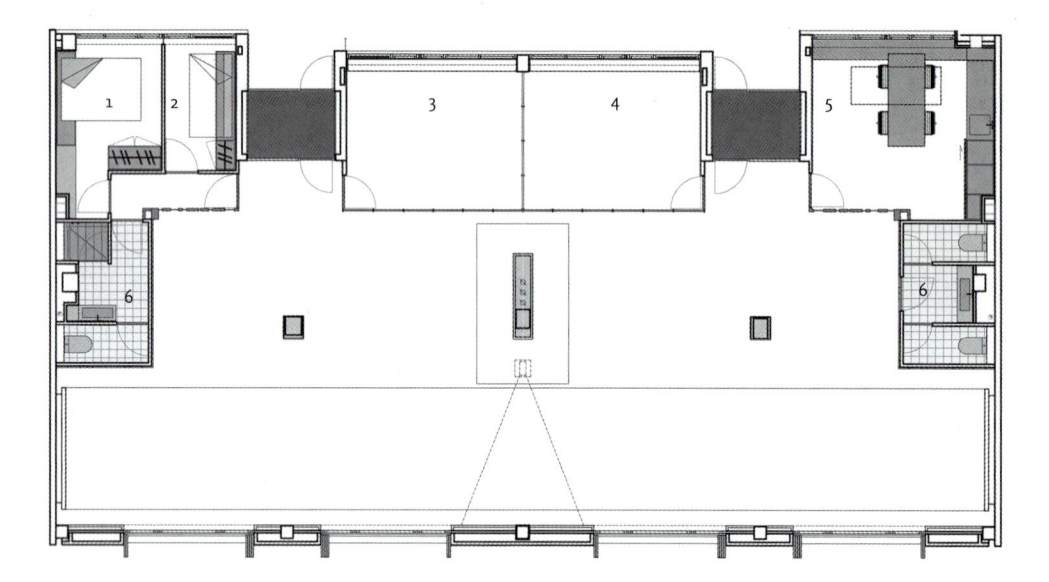

- Floor plan

    1. Room 1
    2. Room 2
    3. Office 1
    4. Office 2
    5. Workroom
    6. Bathroom

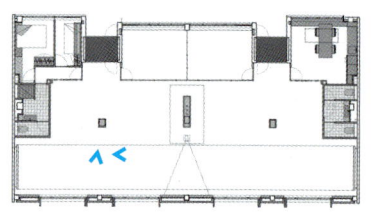

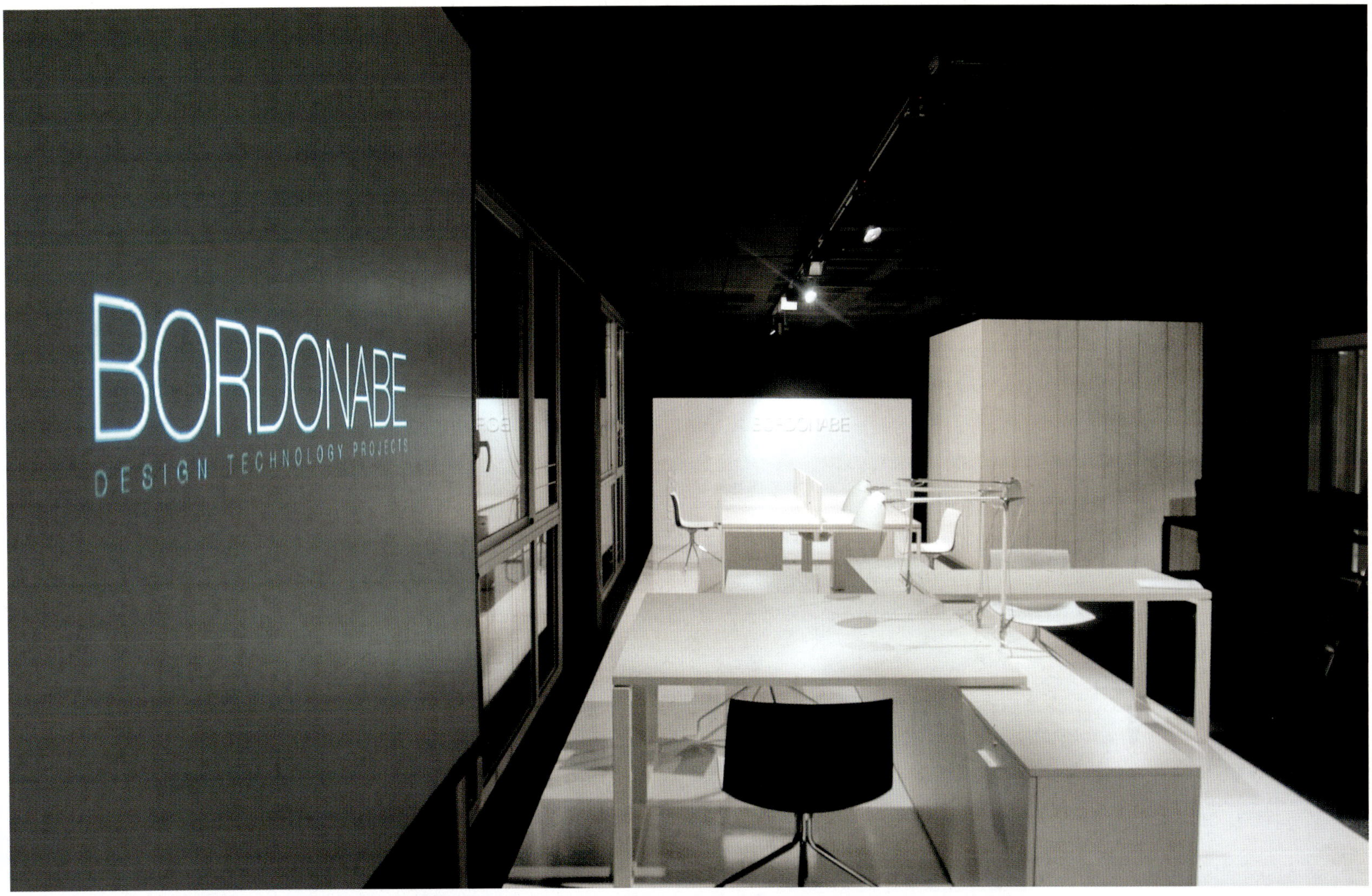
BORDONABE
DESIGN TECHNOLOGY PROJECTS

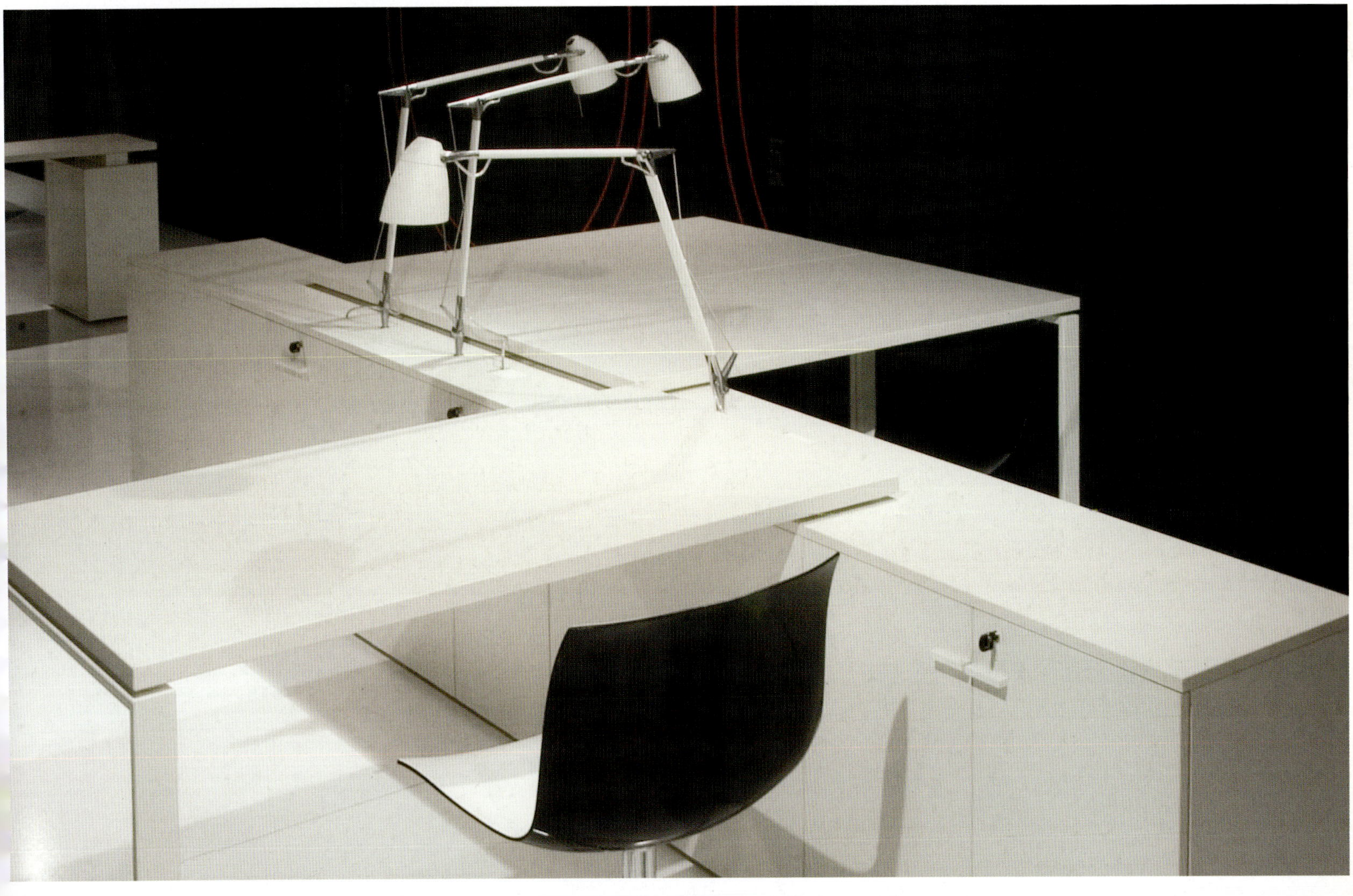

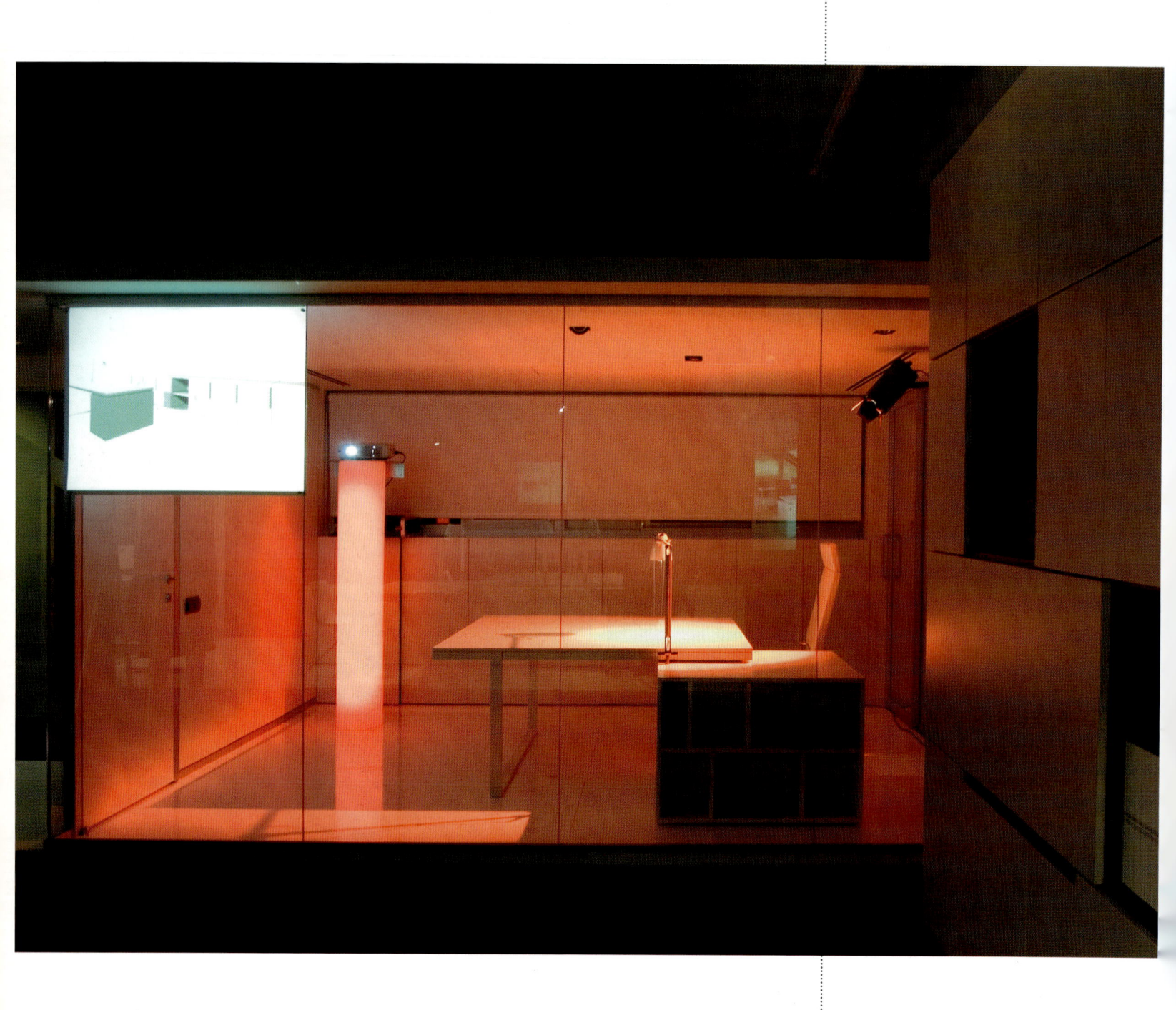

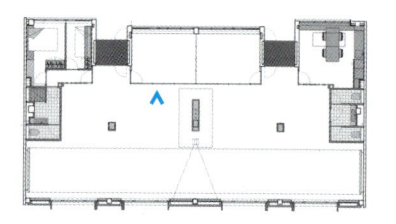

BORDONABE BARCELONA
156

BORDONABE BARCELONA

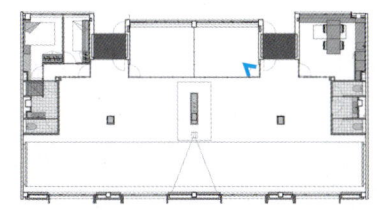

○ The creation of spaces using light sources and the combination of the black floor and the white parquet is in keeping with the clients' and architects' desires to enhance the furniture.

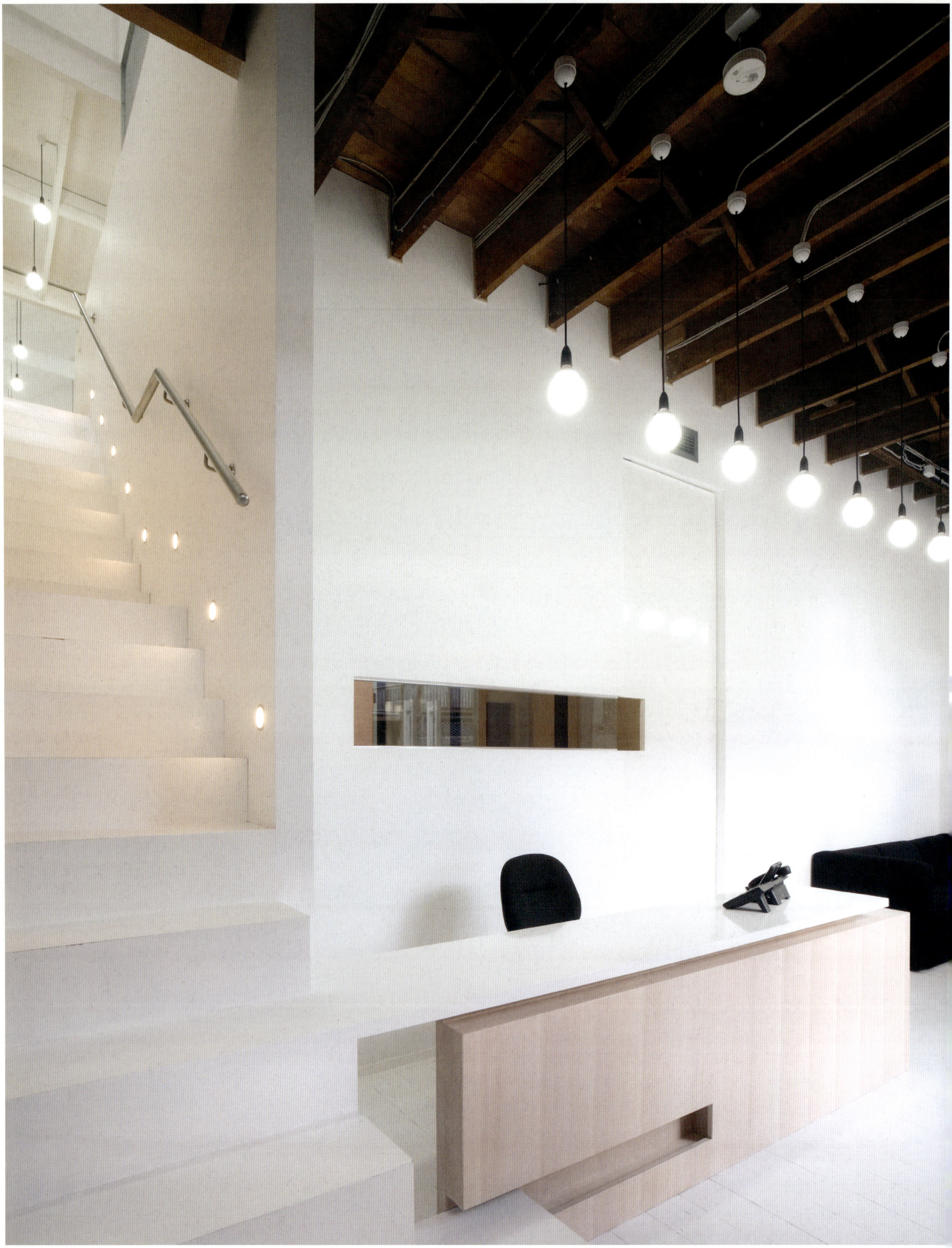

Renegade Film Studio

ARCHITECT/DESIGNER:

ARCHITECTS EAT

Client: Renegade Film Australia
Photographer: Rhiannon Slatter
Location: Prahran, Victoria, Australia
Completion date: 2007
Area: 3,014 SF

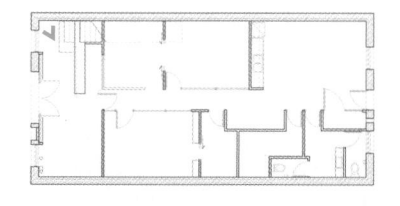

One of Australia's major audiovisual companies, which produces programs and advertisements for television, commissioned this project for office space in a former two-story warehouse. On the first floor is the reception area, waiting room, and some of the offices, while the second floor accommodates the meeting room, more offices, and a rest area for staff.

At street level, a door made entirely from glass is the main access to the building. This leads to the reception area, dominated by the immense ceiling, constructed with beams of laminated fir.

Another of the characteristic elements of the project is the lighting. Throughout the building lights hang from the ceiling providing direct light, with the exception of the main stairway, where downlighters have been installed. The artificial lighting has been positioned to combine with the natural light created by the large openings.

The general strategy was, as defined by the architects, "acorporate-corporate," in other words they avoided the traditional option of creating an interior that strengthens the image of the company in its central headquarters. Their conclusion in this respect is that this strategy is no longer valid or even pleasing to the eye, and that it establishes a monotonous similarity among companies. They sought renovation and found it in three areas: the spatial qualities of the pre-existing structure, the quantitative and qualitative extension of the lighting, and the adaptation of the furniture to the available space.

These principles have lead to the decorative design's limited color palette and few furnishings.

The aim and the result was the creation of a comfortable space for the development of everyday work, in this case, an environment that does not obstruct creativity and one where the occupants feel at home.

RENEGADE FILM STUDIO

○ Instead of imposing the corporate identity onto the pre-existing building, its characteristics have been enhanced and consequently harmonize with its new use. The beams have been left exposed and painted white.

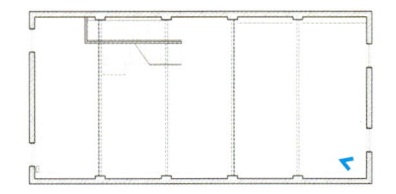

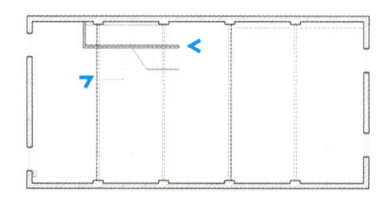

RENEGADE FILM STUDIO
161

RENEGADE FILM STUDIO

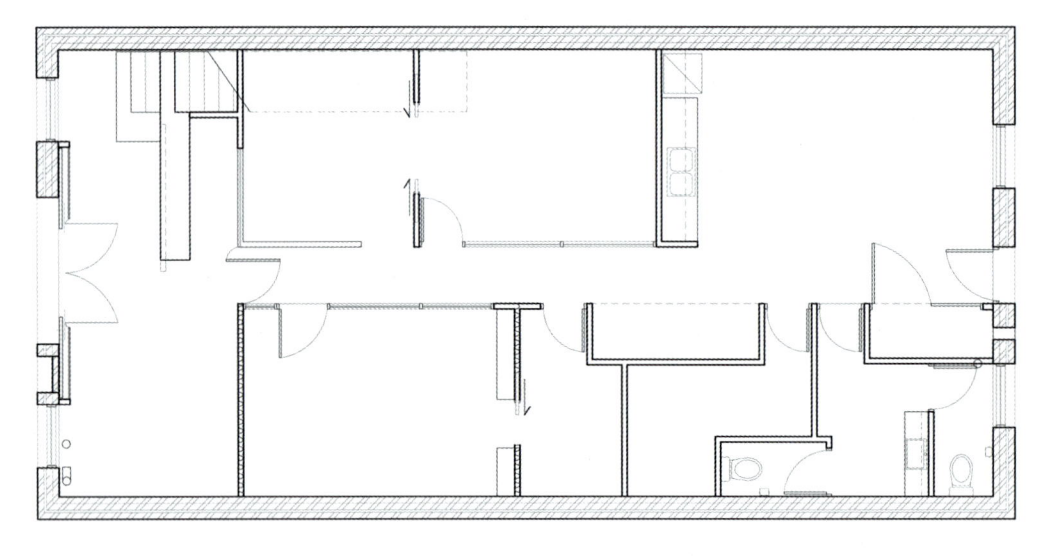

○ Ground floor

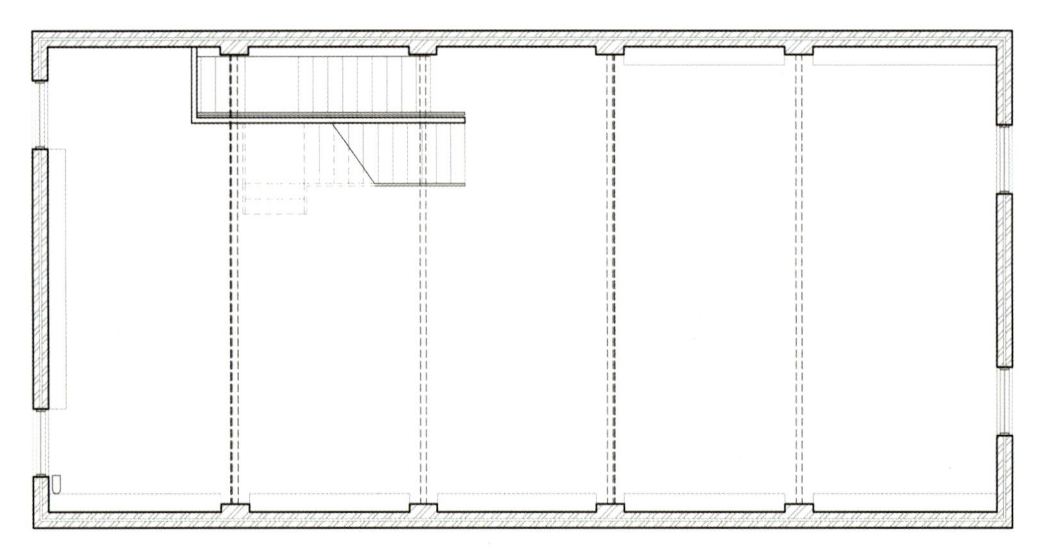

○ First floor and mezzanine

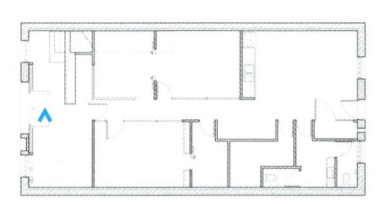

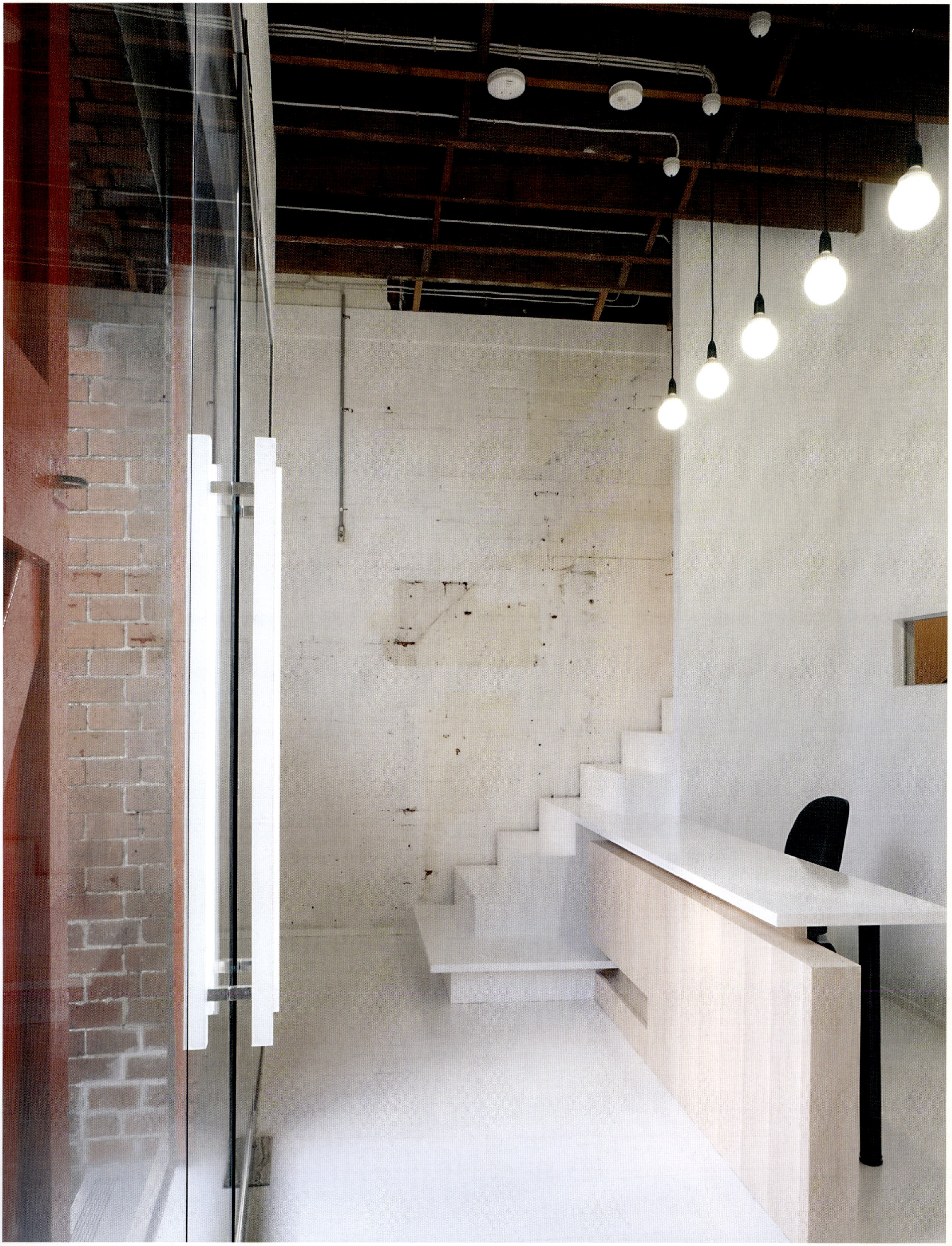

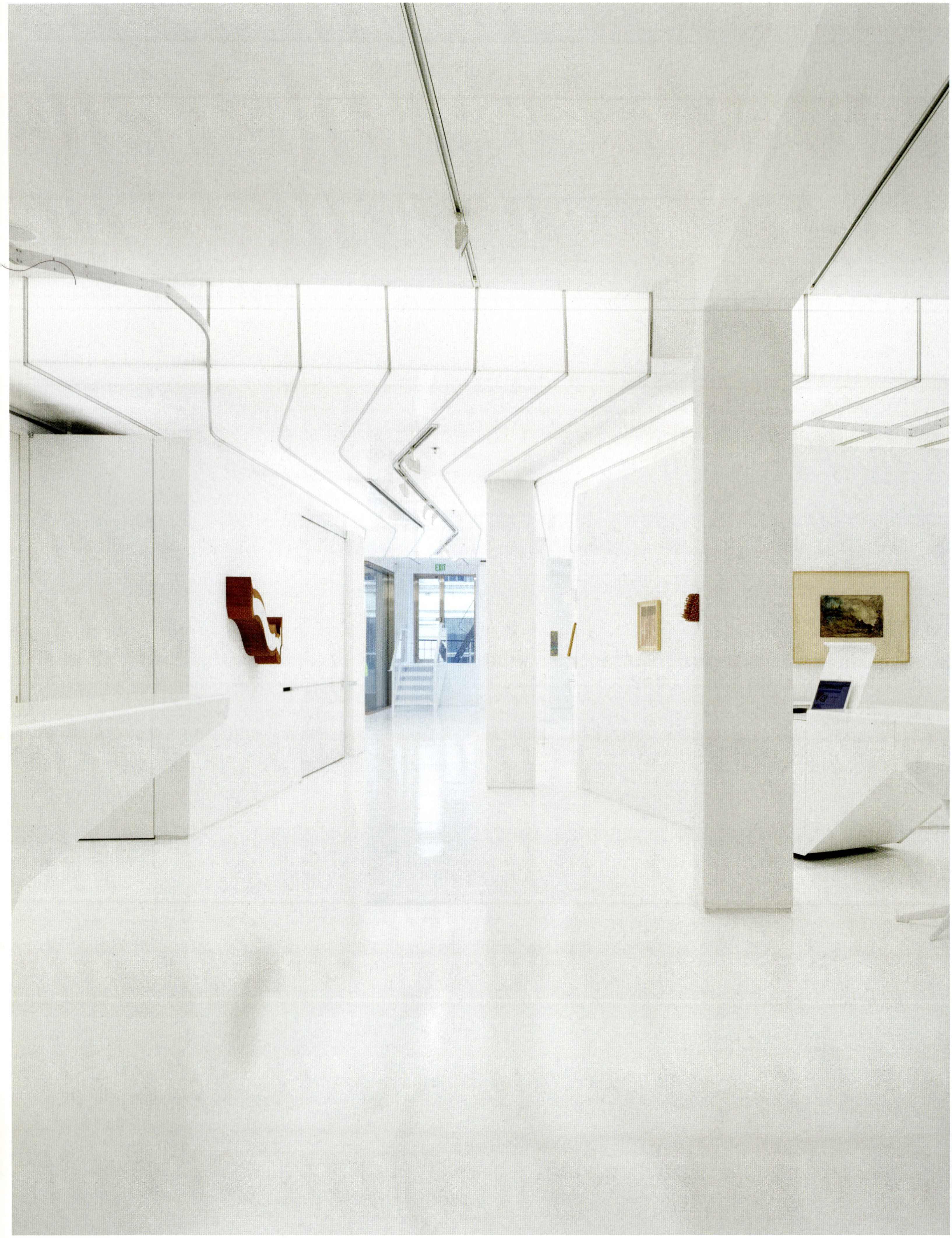
EXIT

MIXED GREENS GALLERY

ARCHITECT/DESIGNER:
LEVEN BETTS STUDIO

Client: Mixed Greens
Photographer: Michael Moran
Location: New York, NY, USA
Completion date: 2005
Area: 3,500 SF

The commission for this project consisted of renovating an old abandoned factory so that it could be used as an art gallery. The result is a space composed of two exhibition rooms, a reception area, private offices, and a bar-restaurant that can also be used as a meeting room.

The architect decided to use the existing structure, making use where possible of the columns and beams, which have been used as separating elements between exhibition rooms and private offices. This has made both elements prominent features of the space.

The luminous ceiling, carried out exclusively for this restoration, which houses the lights for all areas of the gallery, is supported by a series of columns. Two materials have been used for the ceiling: aluminum, which, with fine lines, traces the ceiling's trajectory, and translucent polycarbonate panels, a more modern component which helps to increase light levels.

The aim was to create a large space that was open to the public, so elements that could obstruct the interior circulation were avoided. The inclusion of doors has been limited to where the personal offices are located—sliding doors have been chosen, which are only closed when necessary.

The architects have sought continuity in the design via the application of a single decorative style throughout the spaces. This unity gives emphasis to the works of art on display.

Light colors dominate the palette, in particularly white, both in the walls, floors, pillars, columns, and ceiling. Color has been reserved exclusively for the owner's private office.

There are very few items of furniture, those that were considered essential, and most of them are integrated into the architecture, both spatially and in their appearance. They have been painted white.

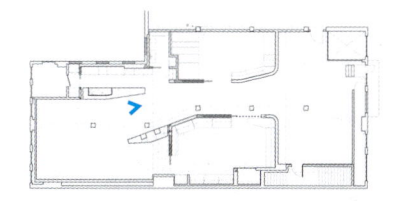

MIXED GREENS GALLERY

● The architect has designed a modern display system for offering complementary information to visitors. White dominates the interior, with just a few exceptions, such as the bowl of the hand basin (see page 169).

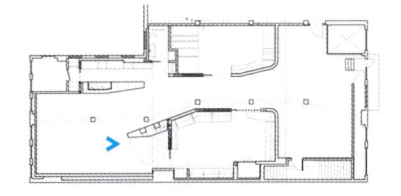

MIXED GREENS GALLERY
167

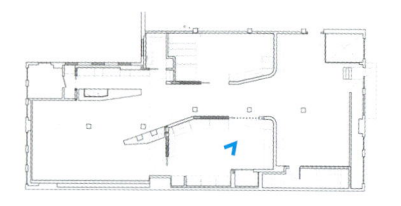

MIXED GREENS GALLERY

MIXED GREENS GALLERY
169

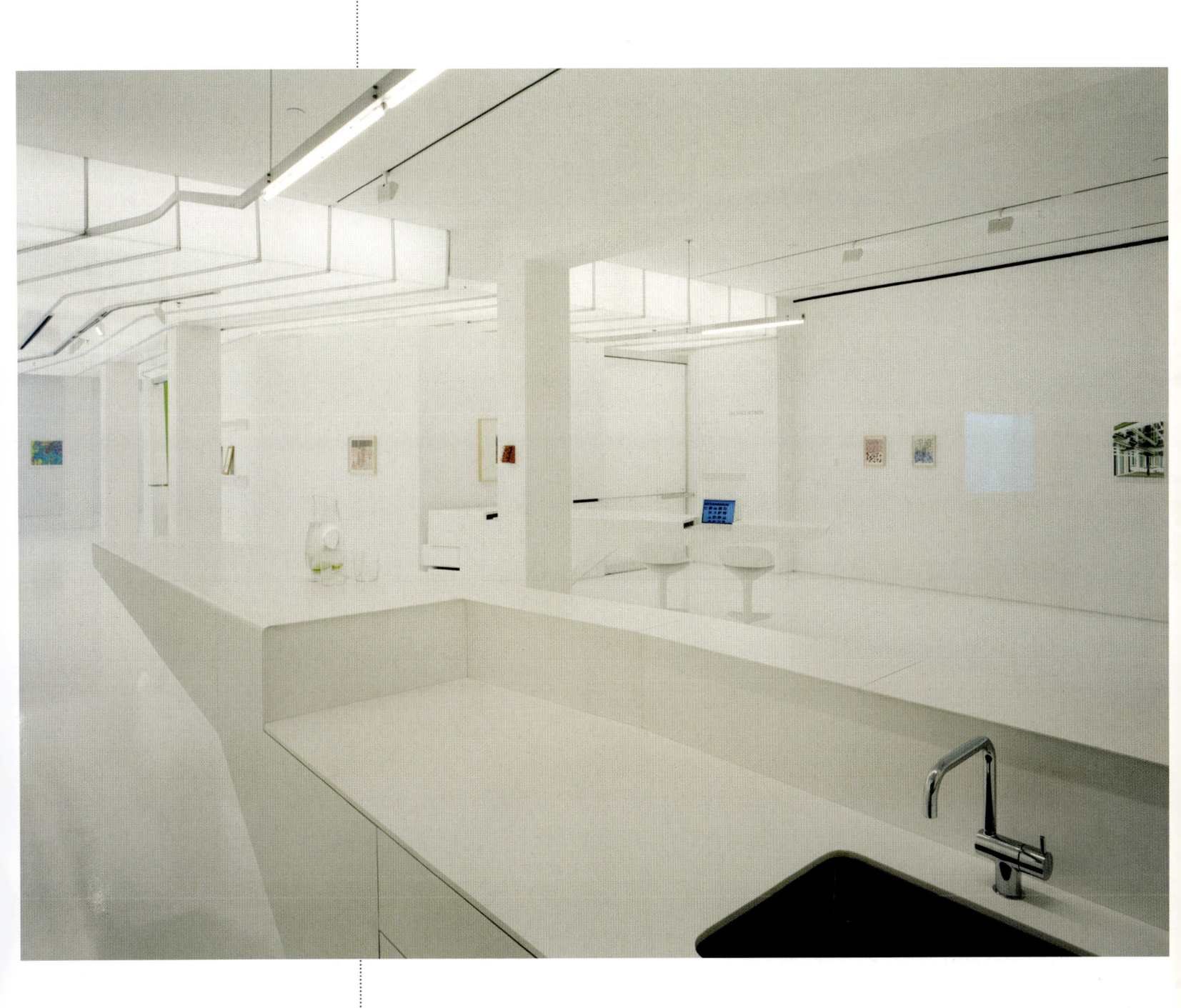

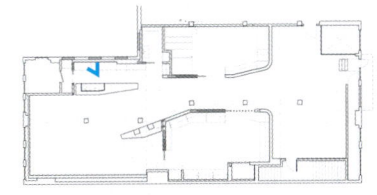

○ The doors have been considered as elements that impede communication within the space and their function has been limited to that of ensuring privacy. They have, therefore, only been used for the toilets and a few offices.

MIXED GREENS GALLERY

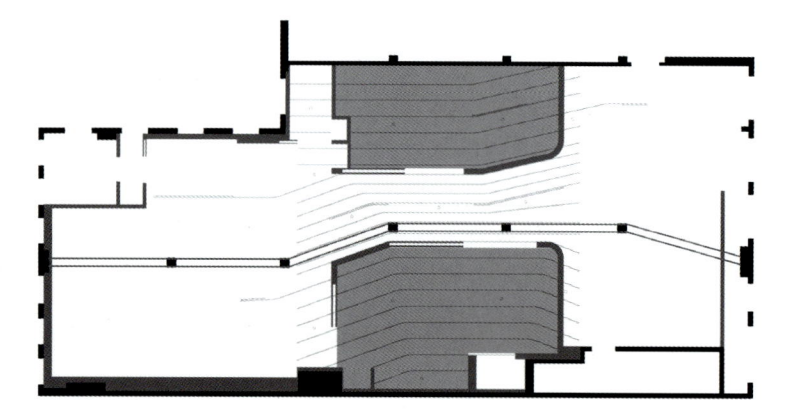

○ Reflected ceiling plan

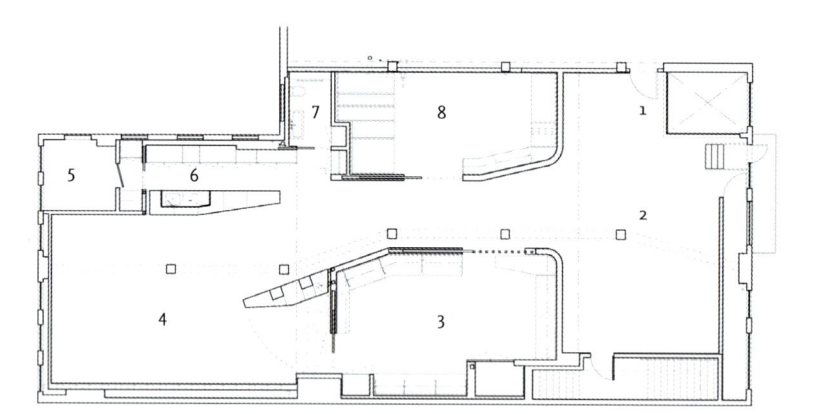

○ Floor plan

1. Entry
2. Gallery 1
3. Office
4. Gallery 2
5. Mechanical room
6. Bar
7. Bothroom
8. Storage room/Packing room
9. Display window

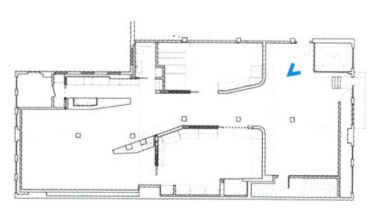

PRINT PORTFOLIO 2005

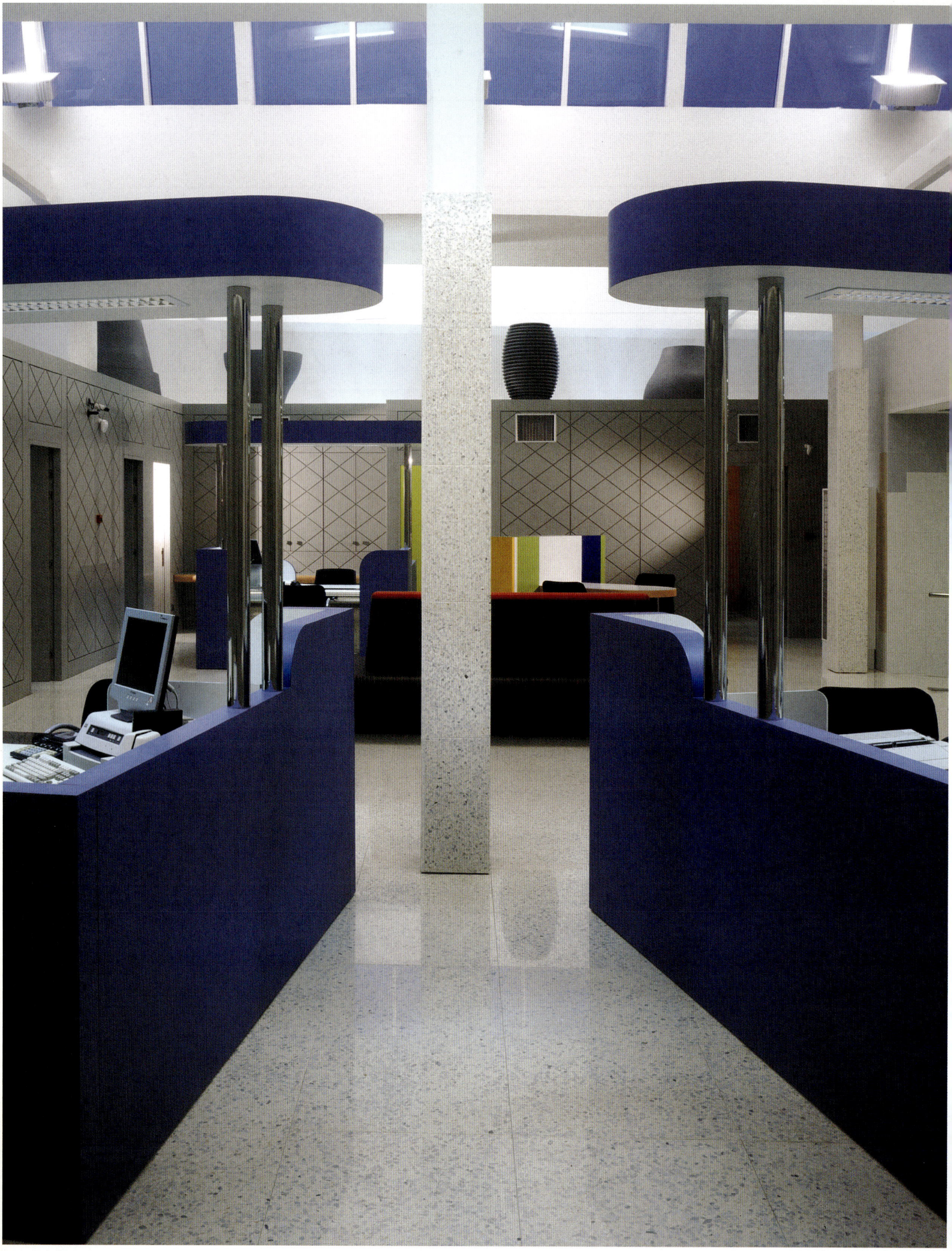

Bank in La Fontina, Still Life with Bank 1

Architect/Designer:

Massimo Mariani Architetto

Client: Banca di Credito Cooperativo di Fornacette
Photographer: Alessandro Ciampi
Location: Pisa, Italy
Completion date: 2003
Area: 3,767 SF

The offices for this bank are located in a recently constructed area in Pisa. They form part of a very large industrial building, of which they occupy a surface area of 3,800 square feet.

The architect intended to break with the conventional image of a banking office, designing this space as a large square in which the spaces where clients can carry out operations are evenly distributed. Only the logo outside identifies it as a bank, since there is nothing that associates the inside with this type of building.

The access, at street level, leads directly to the large space. The counters for attending clients are distributed around the perimeter. The ceiling follows the shape of the roof and presents rows of skylights. Privacy for most of the counters is maintained by way of half-height panels in a bright blue outside and a subtler shade inside, thus creating three-sided compartments. Other counters only have one panel, thus highlighting the colorful furnishings and contributing to the unconventional image, which has been sought.

The closed offices have been situated around the counters used for meeting with the public, which were built as drawers and do not reach the ceiling. The interior of each can be identified by different, bright colors painted on the partitions. From outside the relief of the wall imitates fencing. The service zone and a small rest space complete the layout.

A large sofa occupies the center of the space and enormous vases have been randomly distributed—"as if it were a wine cellar," acc-ording to the architect—mainly on the roofs of the offices, accent-uating the nonconventionalism of this office.

The natural lighting is scarce in this interior, so ample light sources have been distributed throughout to provide general light-ing, in the form of wall lamps, indirect lighting, fluorescent tubes, and so on.

BANK IN LA FONTINA, STILL LIFE WITH BANK 1

● The architect's idea was to make this interior similar to a large square where people spend their free time. The colorful furniture and the variety in the distribution of the work stations enhance this concept.

BANK IN LA FONTINA, STILL LIFE WITH BANK 1

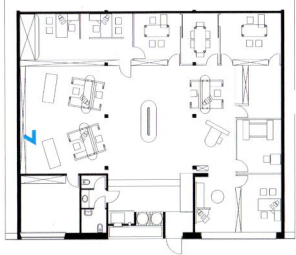

BANK IN LA FONTINA, STILL LIFE WITH BANK 1

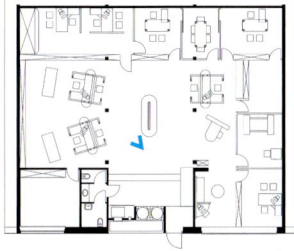

● Many of the surfaces are polycarbonate, which has light-reflecting properties. This is particularly important in a space where there is little natural light, in which bright general lighting has been installed.

○ Floor plan

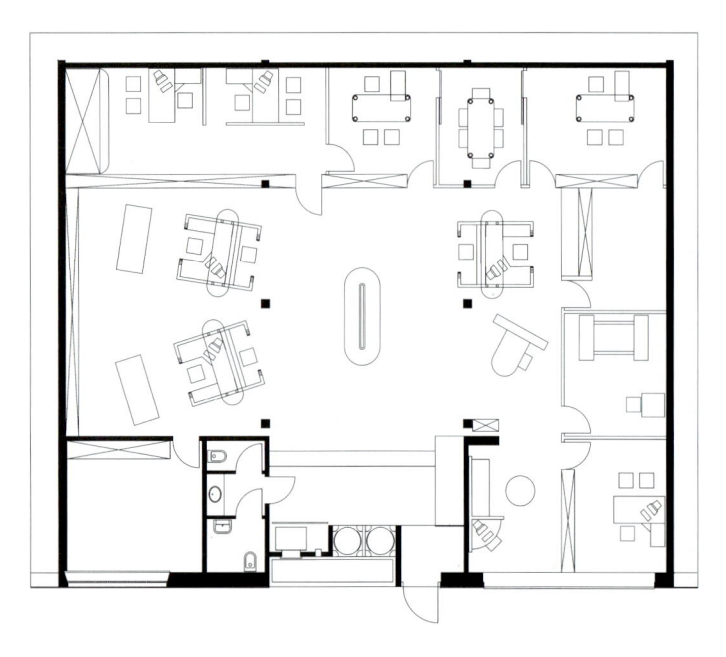

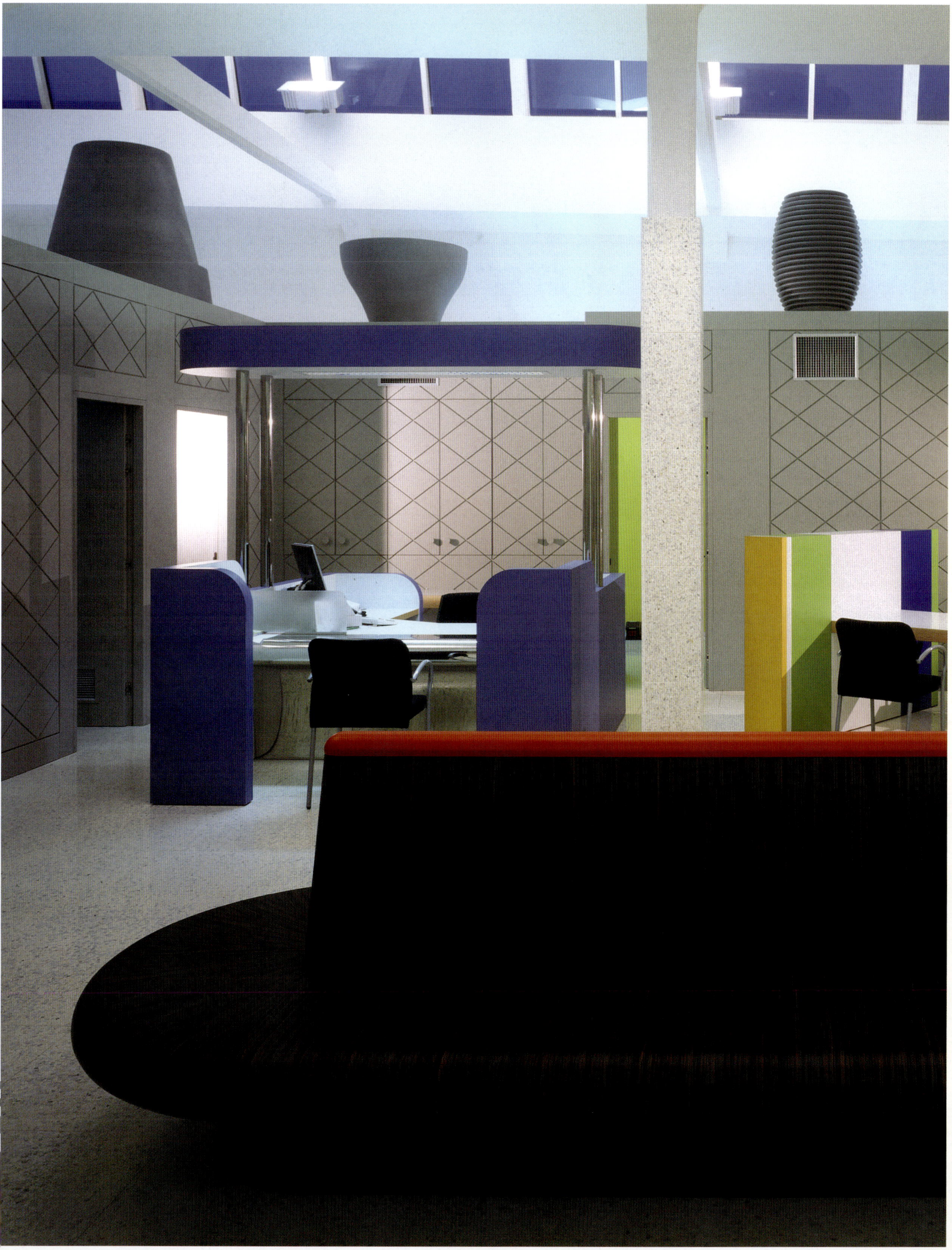

constructora

CODECSA OFFICES

The site of this project was formerly occupied by a ground floor parking lot. The new building preserves the original industrial aesthetic. The construction, raised between common walls, has been ex-clusively designed for office use, on the upper floor there are two apartments and a commercial establishment.

The offices are characterized by their absence of large partition walls. The aim of this layout is to provide more space and facilitate communication among the employees. This is also the reason why the wooden tables are all connected, and why only a small metal panel provides each worker with minimal privacy.

The offices of the company's top executives, located at the entrance, do include partitions, but to avoid the spaces being completely independent of each other, these are made of glass and transparent and opaque panels. The result is two glass boxes, which allow all of the work spaces to be connected as well as being individualized.

The space has a height of 14.4 feet and several skylights have been installed in the ceiling to increase the natural lighting in the interior. Thanks to this and to the fact that the only divisions have been carried out with glass, the interior of these offices results in an open plan space.

The floor is dyed concrete, chosen to represent the client's activity as a construction company, and to provide a solid aesthetic. The upper floor, where the apartments are located, has been clad in a double skin of metal, which acts as a filter to protect privacy from the building opposite. This double skin extends to the ground floor, where the corrugated sheet metal combines with colored glass. This allows the façade, which is other-wise completely plain, to offer an aesthetic in line with a corporate space at ground-floor level.

ARCHITECT/DESIGNER:

GCA ARQUITECTES ASSOCIATES

Client: Constructora CODECSA
Photographer: Jordi Miralles
Location: Barcelona, Spain
Completion date: 2005
Area: 4,306 SF

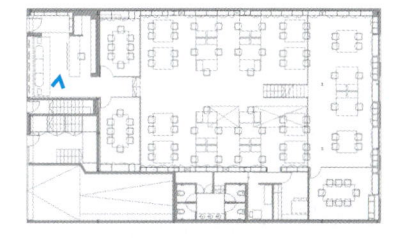

CODECSA OFFICES

● On the floors, the walls and the furniture's light tones increase the luminosity and the sense of the size of the room. The intention was to bring a sense of size to this working environment by choosing light colors for the floor and the furniture. The only partitions in the office are made of glass.

CODECSA OFFICES
183

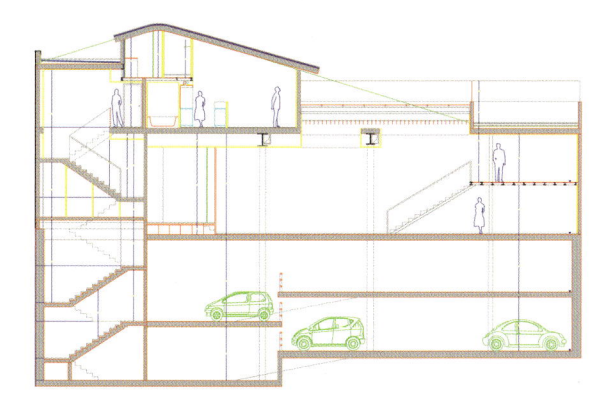

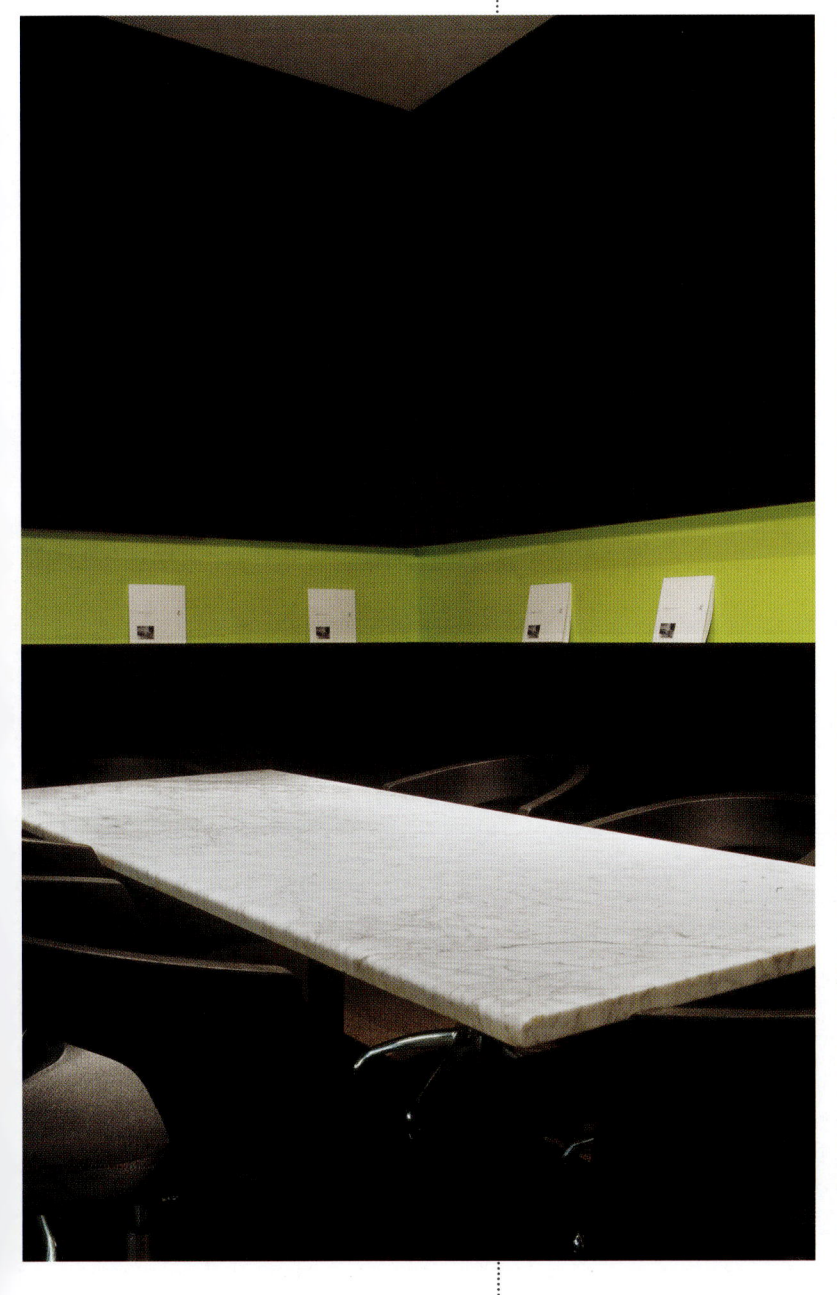

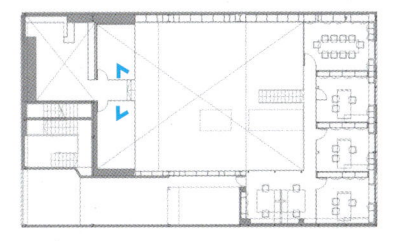

CODECSA OFFICES
184

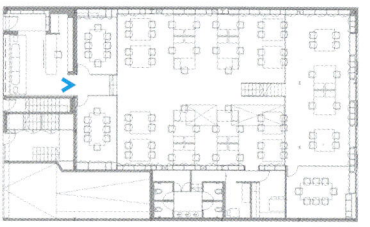

CODECSA OFFICES

CODECSA OFFICES
186

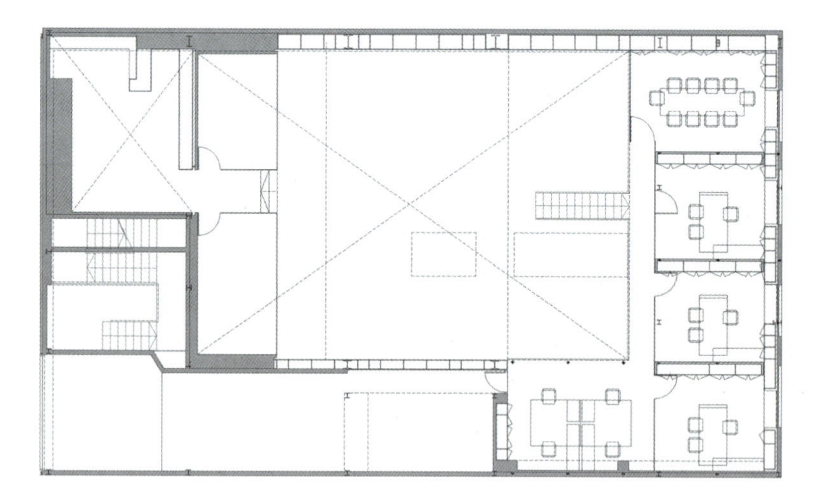

○ Mezzanine floor plan

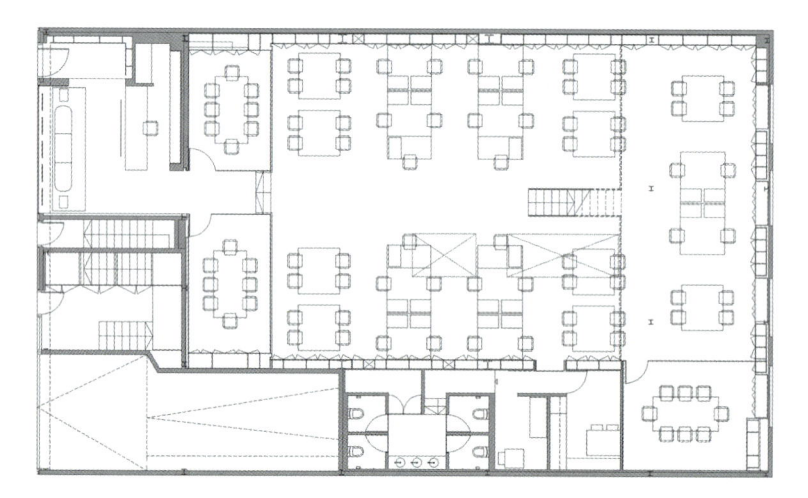

○ Ground floor plan

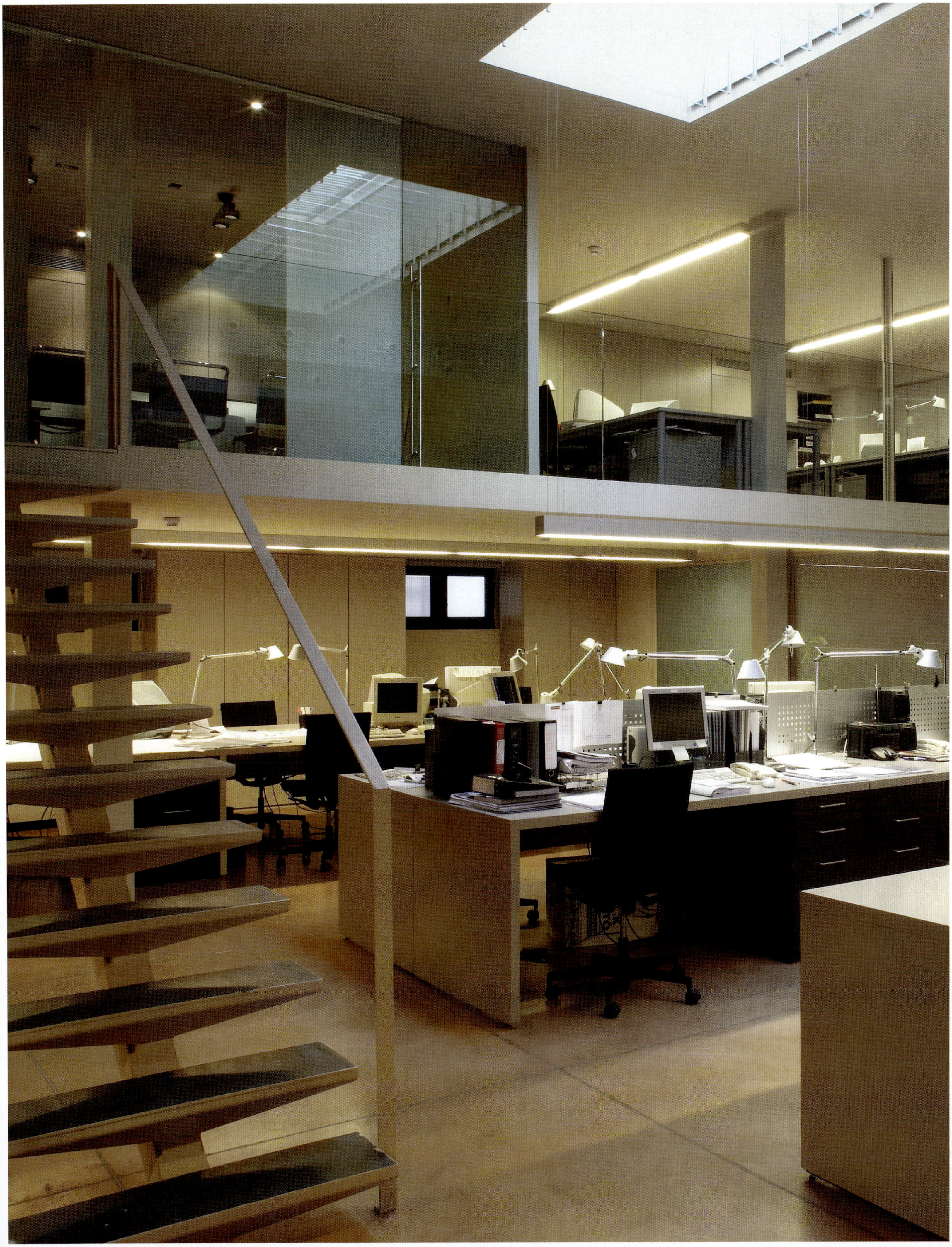

CODECSA OFFICES

● The stairway that connects the two floors is the axis of the office, around which all the different work areas are distributed. It is a simple metal staircase, in keeping with the project's semi-industrial aesthetic.

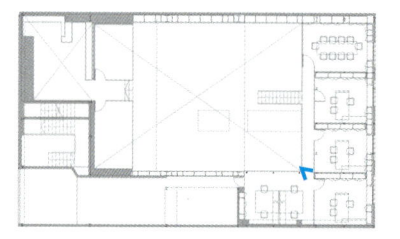

CODECSA OFFICES
189

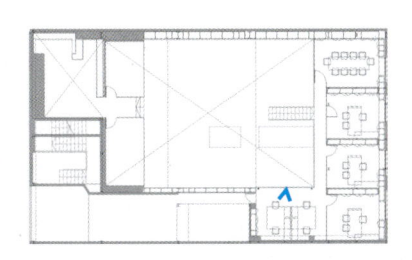

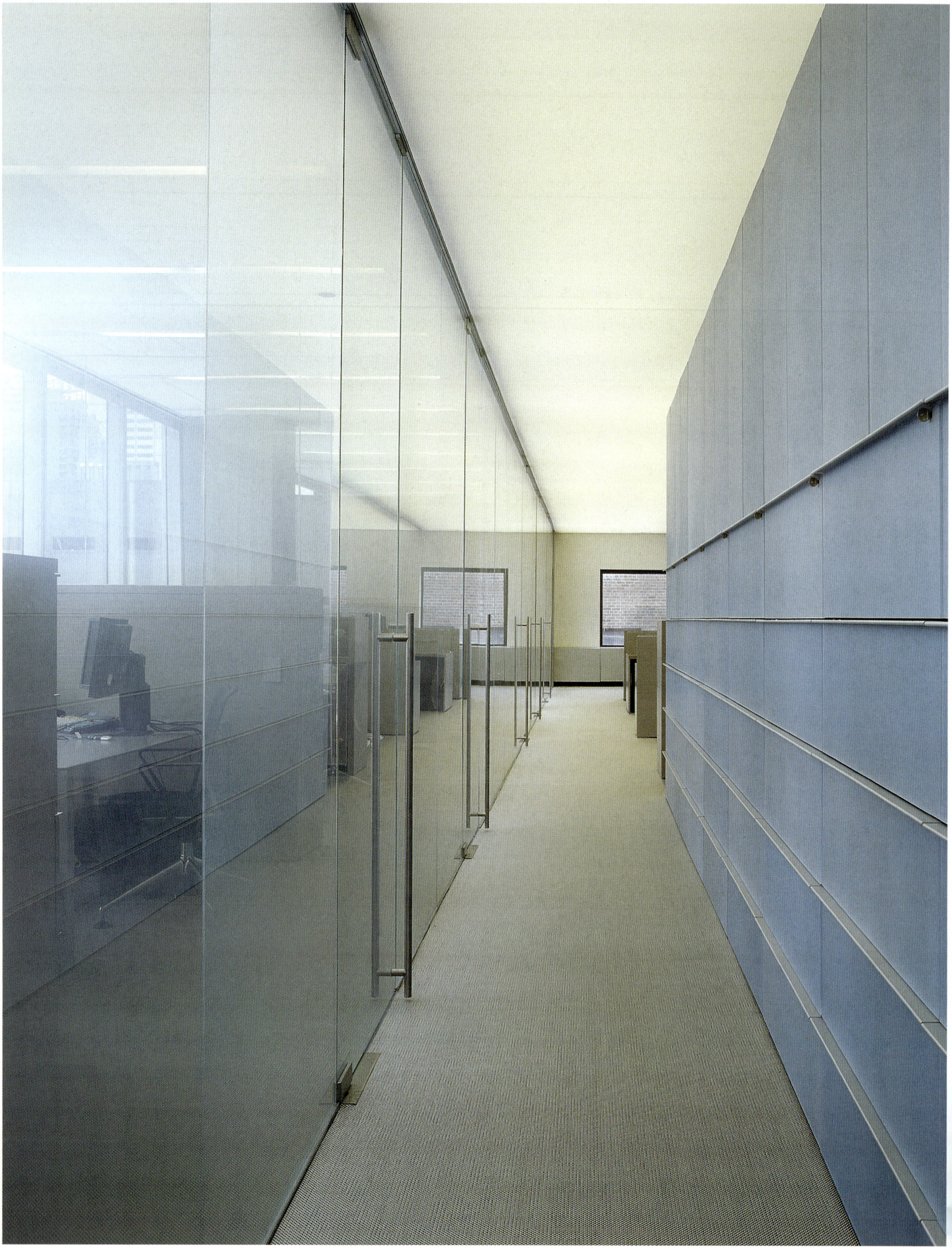

Thirdpoint Offices

The restoration of these offices, located in one of New York's most exclusive districts, was the commission for this project. In addition to asking for the aesthetical integration into the surroundings, the client requested that the architects create a sober atmosphere for working. Bright colors and excessively avant-garde materials have therefore been avoided.

The offices occupy the top floor of the building and are formed by five private and individual offices, a meeting room, and a rest area for the employees.

The natural lighting is one of the most remarkable components of this project. Large windows that stretch from the ceiling down to about two feet from the floor allow the sunlight to reach this floor. This drastically reduces the need for artificial lighting, and, consequently, halogen lights have been installed in just a few specific places away from the windows.

The floor has been carpeted throughout most of the office. The partitions were an important element, since privacy was needed for each of the offices—which feature translucent glass doors.

As the client is an art collector who wished to express his interest for the contemporary world, the architects have designed this space as is if it were floating above the city.

The interior is therefore meant to suggest a cloud and views of the city skyline dominate throughout the space. The façade is a continuous wall almost entirely made of glass, which, to protect the privacy of the offices, has been made from Lumisty, a material that is transparent or opaque depending on the angle of vision. In this case, from an angle of more than 25 degrees the walls are opaque, whereas when entering the offices from the elevator, they are transparent.

The division between the offices runs perpendicular to the façade and was custom made, in stained gray wood with horizontal grain. The result is a series of offices whose appearance evokes the mass of buildings outside.

Architect/Designer:

Slade Architecture Team

Client: Thirdpoint Management Company
Photographer: Jordi Miralles
Location: New York, NY, USA
Completion date: 2001
Area: 5,000 SF

THIRDPOINT OFFICES

○ A shade of gray dominates the interior, which matches that of the mass of buildings outside and therefore helps to integrate the interior with the exterior. This color also helps to express the space as a cloud in the sky.

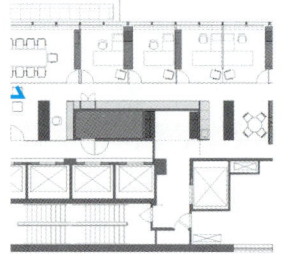

THIRDPOINT OFFICES
193

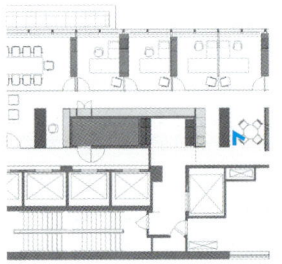

THIRDPOINT OFFICES

THIRDPOINT OFFICES
195

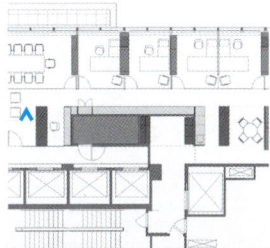

○ The furniture creates depth and a translucent aesthetic via several different elements: a silver rug, aluminum finishes, and the blue, translucent, acrylic wall that delineates the office.

THIRDPOINT OFFICES

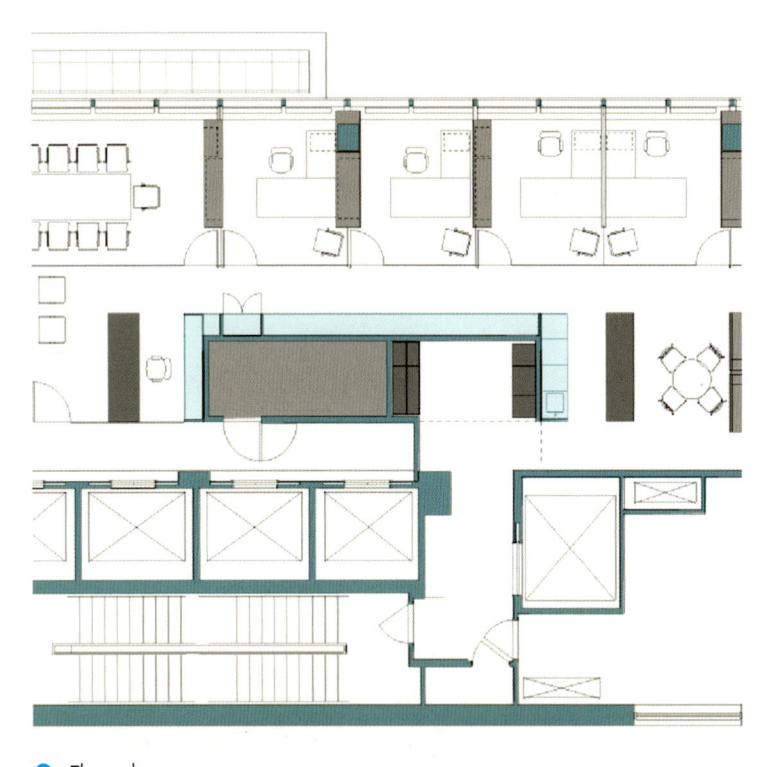

○ Floor plan

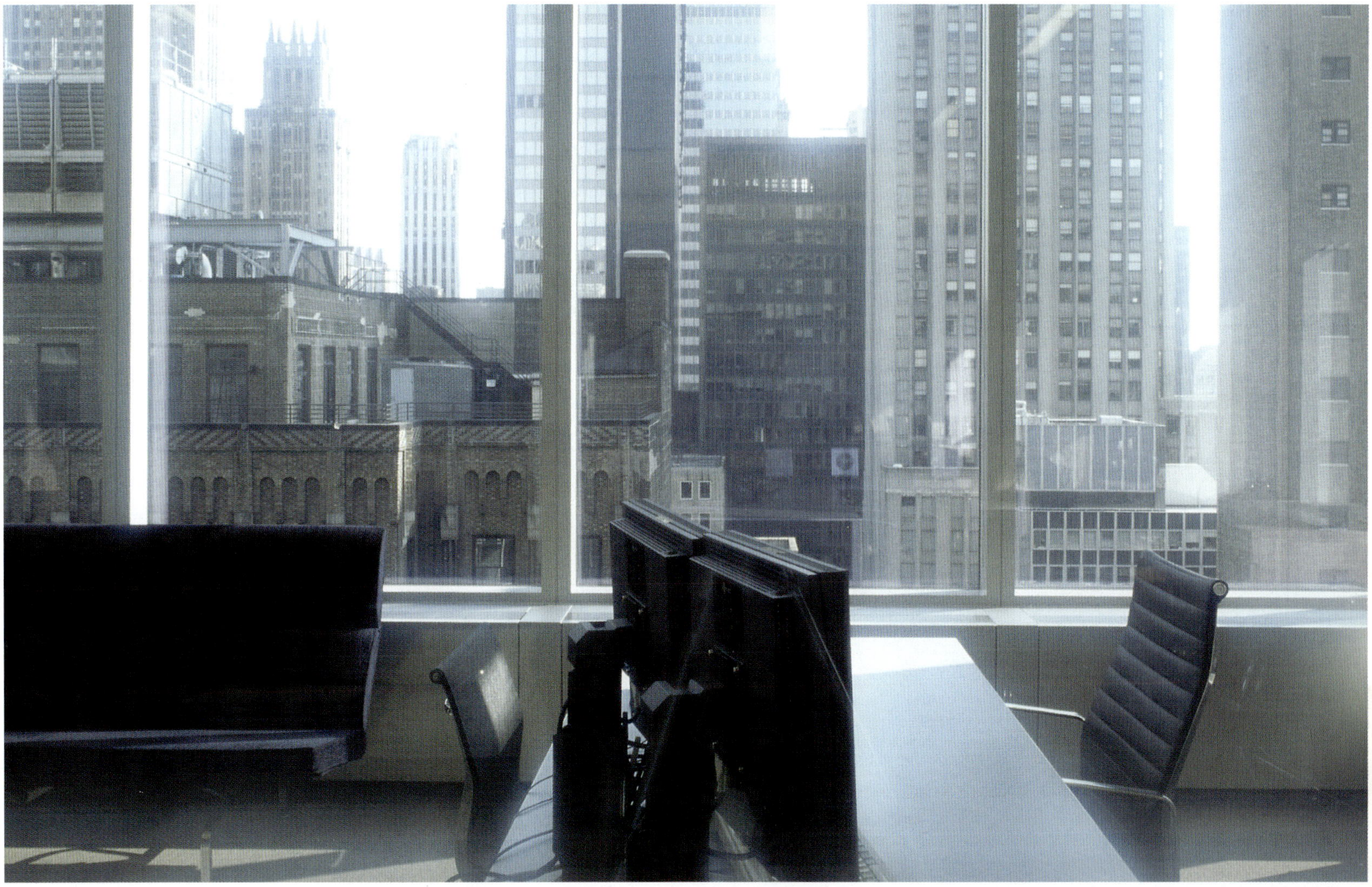

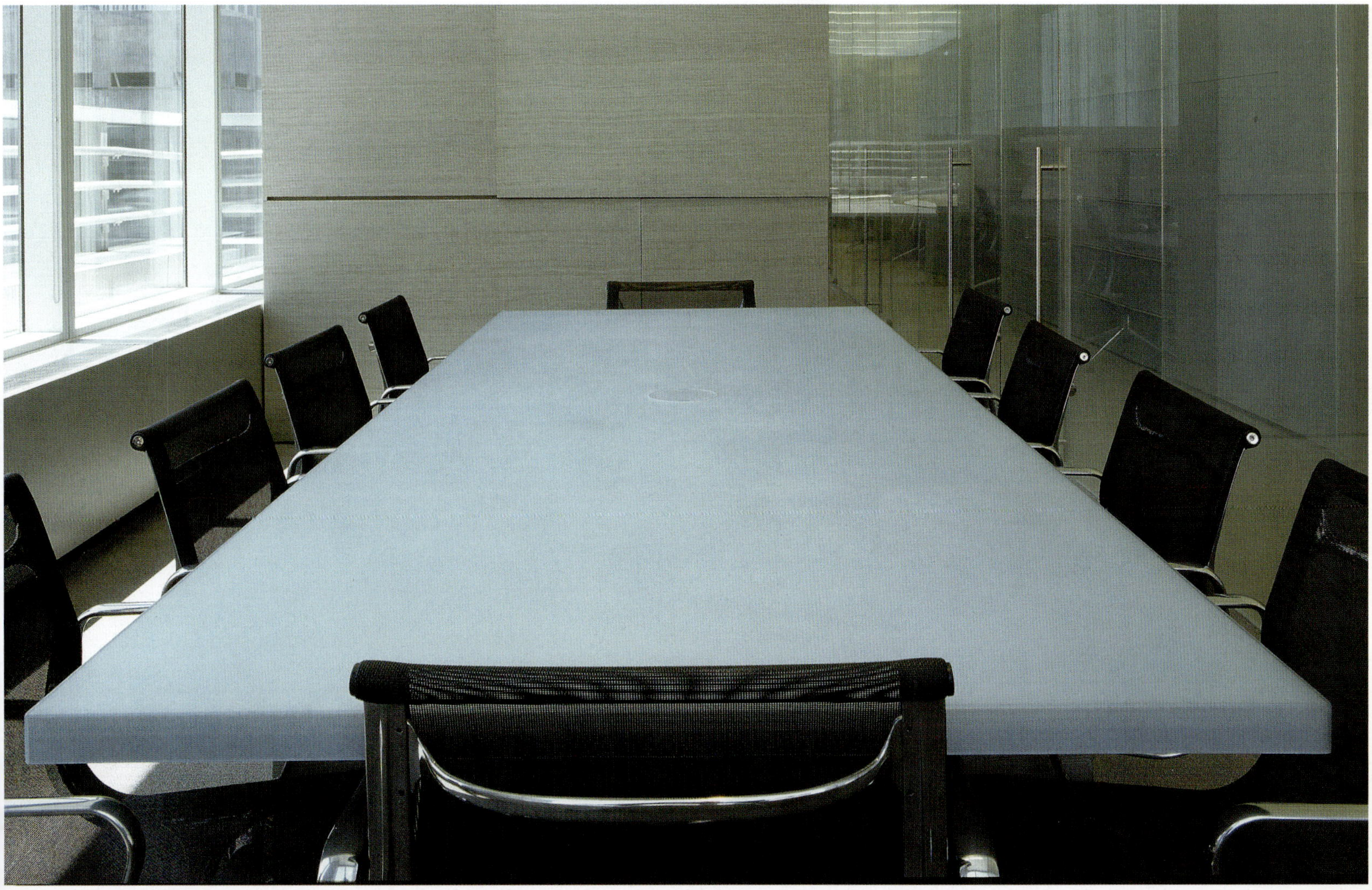

COMME des GARÇONS
*PARFUMS

"... my perfume range is often built around a feeling; scents that will interest the wearer into exploring or..."

...concrete. Smell is ... which is more ...çons..."

COMME des GARÇONS
*PARFUMS

...ng my perfume ... evoke space and ...all..."

Beauty Lab

Beauty Lab, a multinational cosmetics company commissioned this renovation project for the interior of their offices in Barcelona. The total surface area is 5,400 square feet, which occupies a single floor at street level. The L-shaped floor plan is located in one of the corners of the building. The office consists of the reception area, an open work area, several offices, display areas, a project filing and storage section, and a meeting room.

The brief highlighted three main characteristics for the new space: lighting, spatial continuity, and height.

Although the office occupies a corner of a building, one of its façades is interior, which affects the possibilities for natural lighting. This mainly affects the reception area, and to compensate the architects have restored some old skylights that were formerly located in this area: their openings were widened and the glass was replaced. This allows what was previously a dark space to now enjoy bright natural light.

To maintain continuity throughout the space in terms of visual communication, there are no conventional separating walls, and instead plasterboard panels have been used that don't reach the ceiling. As well as dividing space, these have two other roles in the office. First, they house niches that serve as display spaces for the firm's products and for advertising material from some of their campaigns. They also contain the cupboards and files of documentation and materials related to the different projects. With this aim of preserving the unitary character of the space, the individual offices have been enclosed with transparent glass screens.

The height of the ceilings has been resolved by passing the wiring of all the services through the passageway, where it has been encased and hidden. This means the work space could be located where the ceiling is at its highest.

White has been chosen for the ceilings, walls, furniture, and curtains with the aim of using this color's reflective qualities to increase the amount of light in the interior.

Architect/Designer:

GCA Arquitectes Associats

Client: Puig, SA
Photographer: Jordi Miralles
Location: Barcelona, Spain
Completion date: 2005
Area: 5,382 SF

BEAUTY LAB

🔵 All the wiring from the services has been run exclusively through the passageway and has been concealed using runners on the ceiling. These have been used to install light sources, which illuminate the material on display.

BEAUTY LAB
201

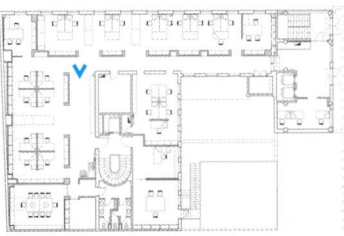

BEAUTY LAB
202

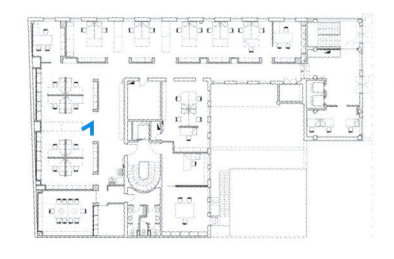

BEAUTY LAB
203

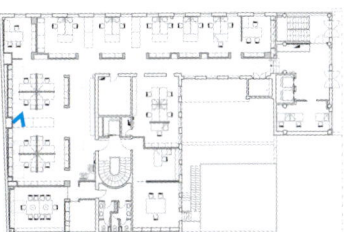

BEAUTY LAB
204

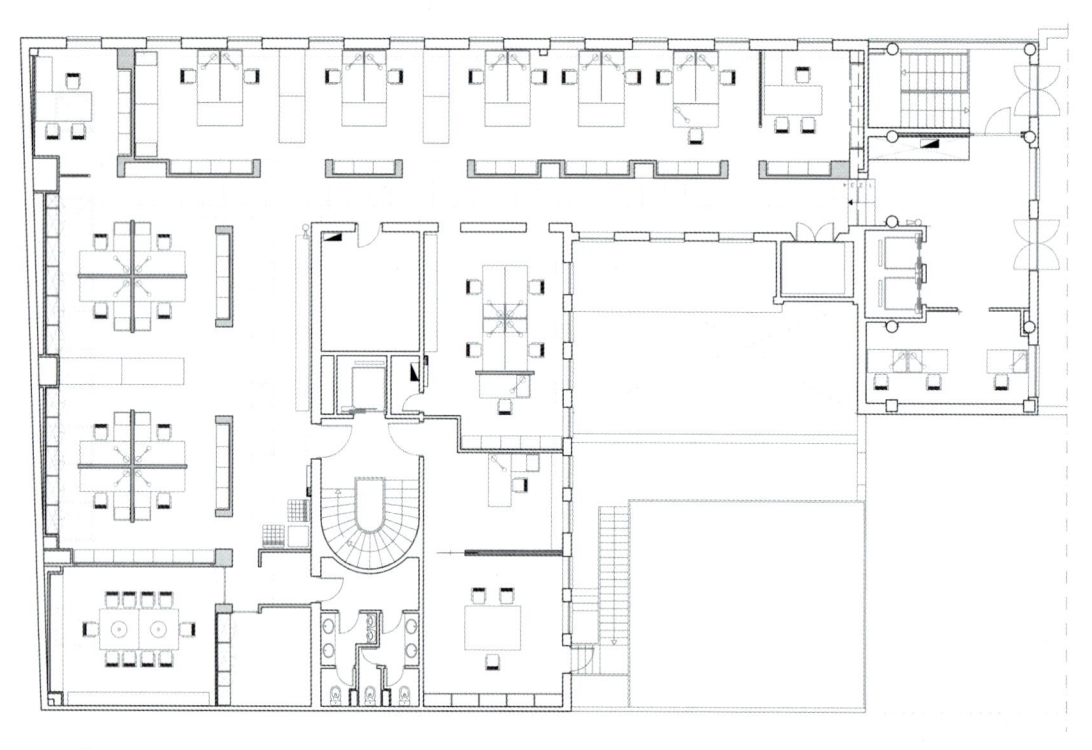

● Floor plan

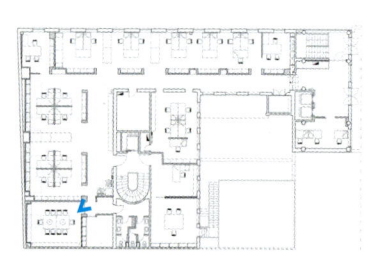

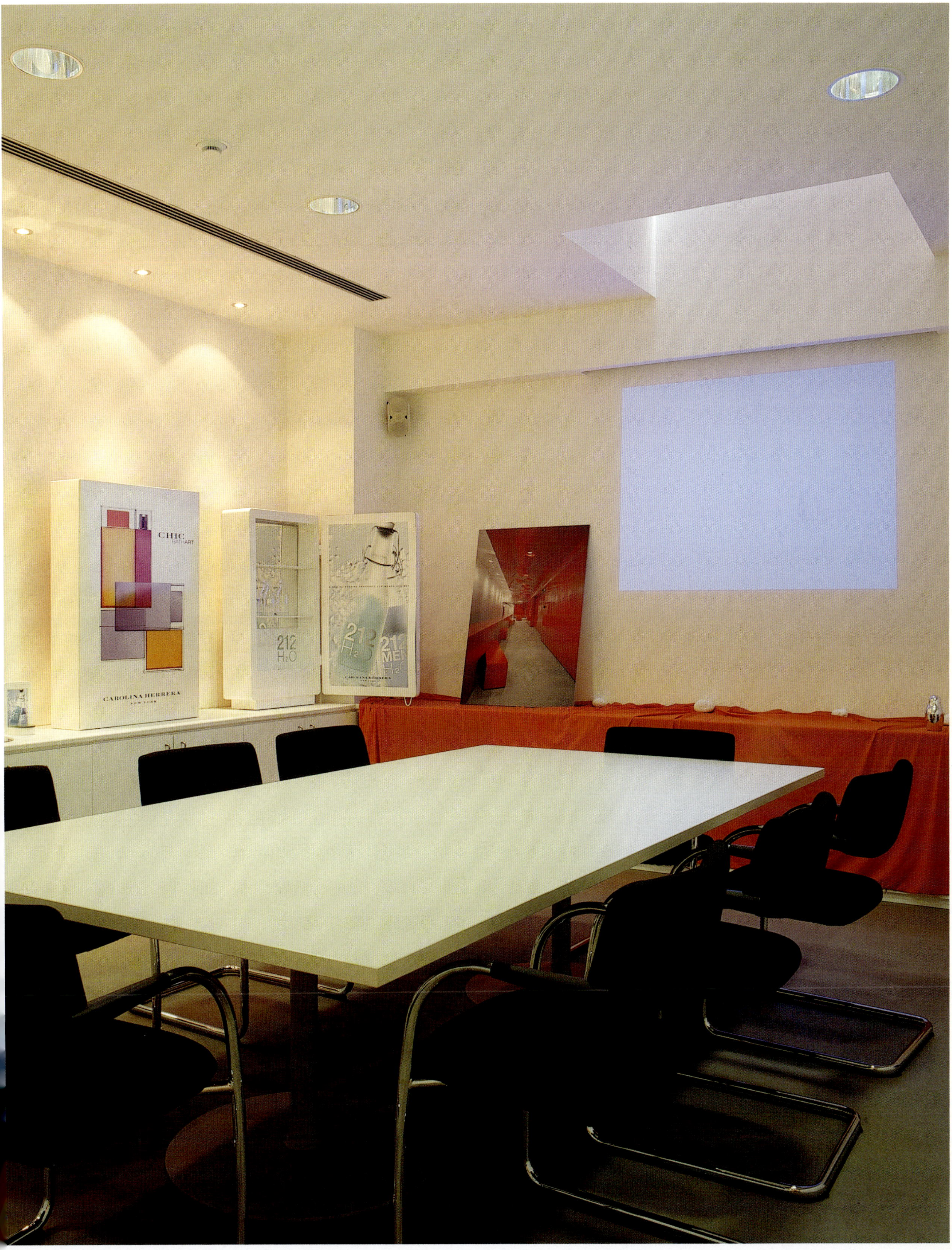
CHIC
CAROLINA HERRERA
212
H2O
212
MEN
CAROLINA HERRERA

BEAUTY LAB
206

BEAUTY LAB

○ The plasterboard partition walls, which do not reach the ceiling, are the only separating elements between the spaces. They have also been used to house filing cupboards and to display products and promotional material.

BEAUTY LAB
208

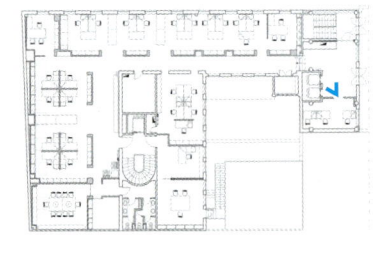

BEAUTY LAB

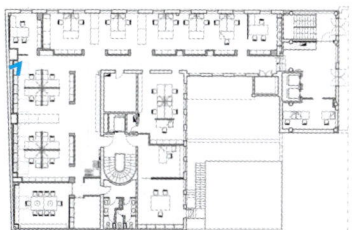

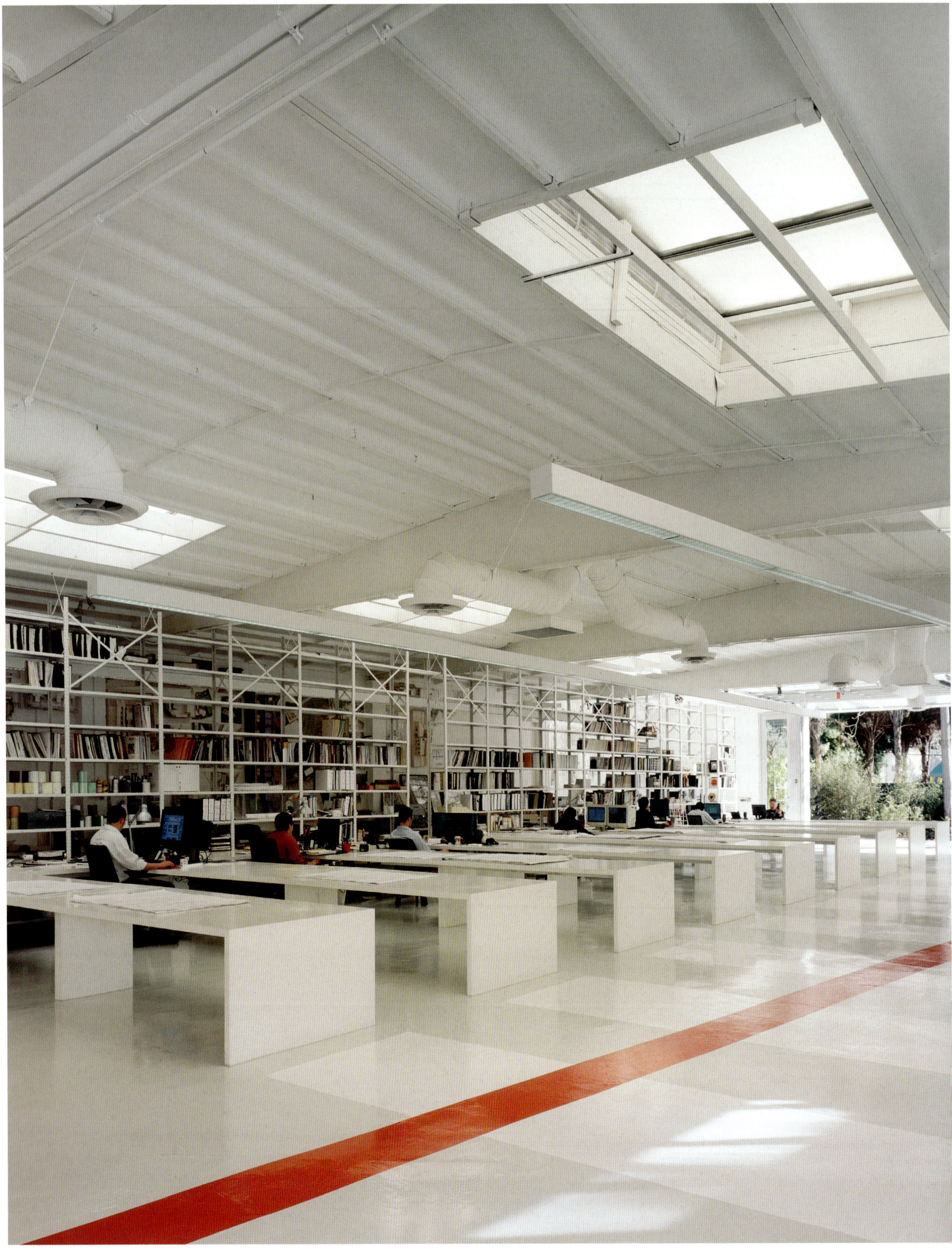

Lehrer Architects' Office

This large-scale project is located in what used to be one of the most important factories in Los Angeles half a century ago.

This prestigious architectural firm wanted to give this space, which would house their central offices, a new look. The building was chosen for its levels of natural lighting, its possibilities regarding temperature control, and its transparency.

All the spaces are located on a single floor, with no partitions to separate them from one another. The result is that the entire floor is one big office where the work develops. There is also a meeting room and an area for rest. Unlike the main space, these two areas are separated via walls and doors to maintain their privacy.

The ceiling is double-height so that skylights could be installed that would make the most of the natural light. The base of the skylights is polyester reinforced with glass fiber. Several square domes have been distributed across the roof, made from high-impact methacrylate. To open these, the architects opted for a manual mechanism with a winch attached to the wall and several feet of steel cable, which creates the most ideal opening for large industrial spaces like these.

Another of the defining elements of the project is the flooring, made entirely from marble, with two dominant colors sandy in one area and white in the other.

The offices feature a garden that surrounds them and establishes visual communication with the interior through the glass used for the front façade and the back of the building. The panels and doors of both partitions have a functional opening system, which improves circulation between the interior and the exterior, so that both spaces are also physically connected. The simplicity of this solution for the building's elongated floor plan aims to integrate the attractive exterior landscape into a working environment, which is bathed in light and has plenty of space for each individual worker.

Architect/Designer:
Lehrer Architects

Client: Lehrer Architects
Photographer: Benny Chan
Location: Los Angeles
Completion date: 2005
Area: 5,400 SF

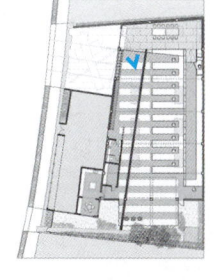

LEHRER ARCHITECTS' OFFICE

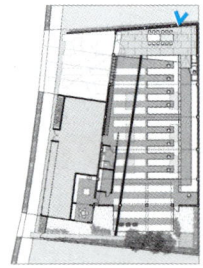

LEHRER ARCHITECTS' OFFICE

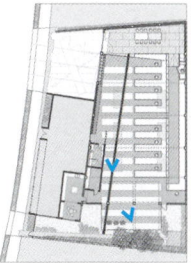

- To encourage communication between staff members, the individual work stations have not been shut off, but instead most are located on the large tables that dominate the office's work area.

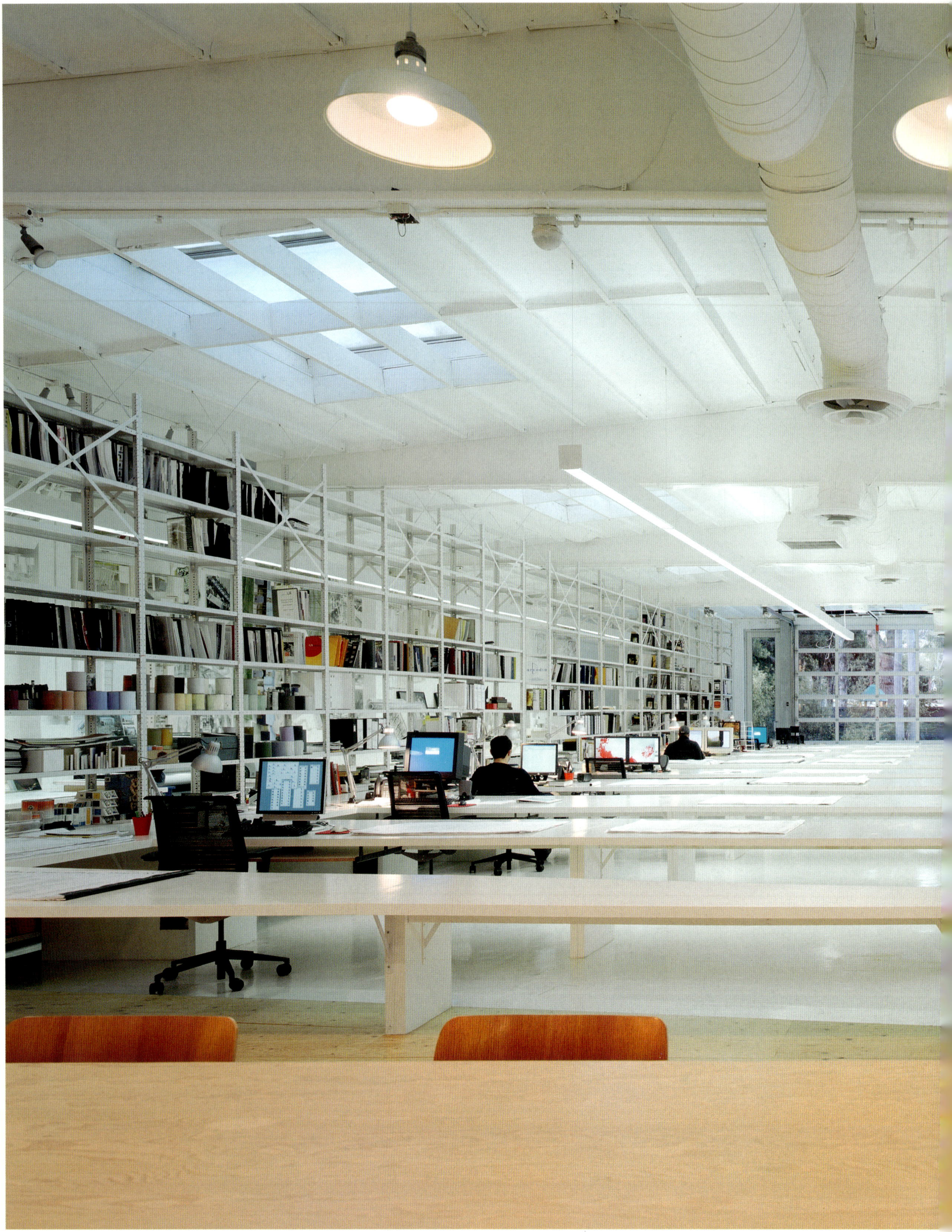

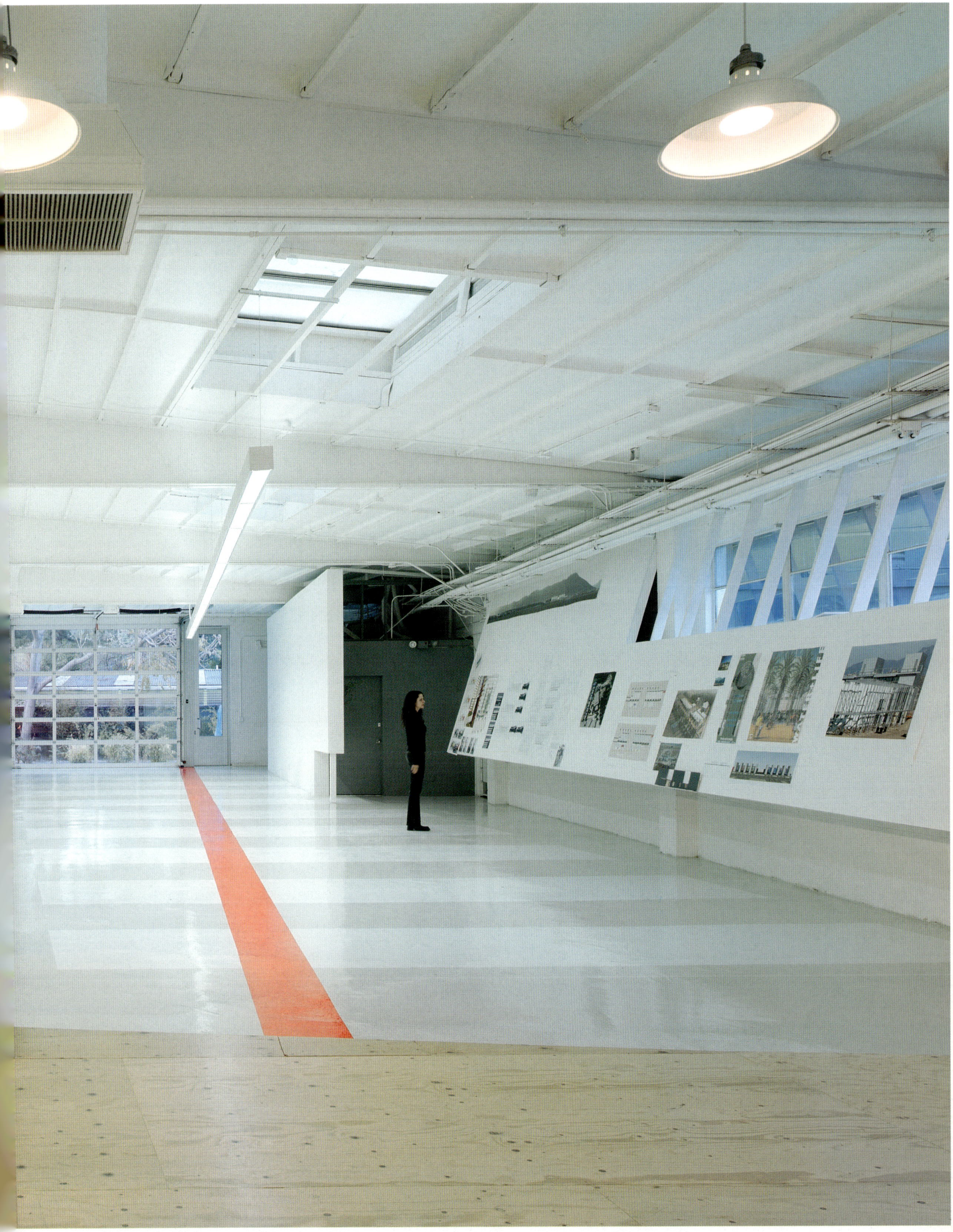

LEHRER ARCHITECTS' OFFICE

● Ground floor plan

1. Entry
2. Meeting space
3. Computer room
4. Work surfaces
5. Storage shelves
6. Office manager
7. Garden
8. Work stations
9. Bathroom
10. Storage
11. Kitchen
12. Work space
13. Display wall
14. Parking

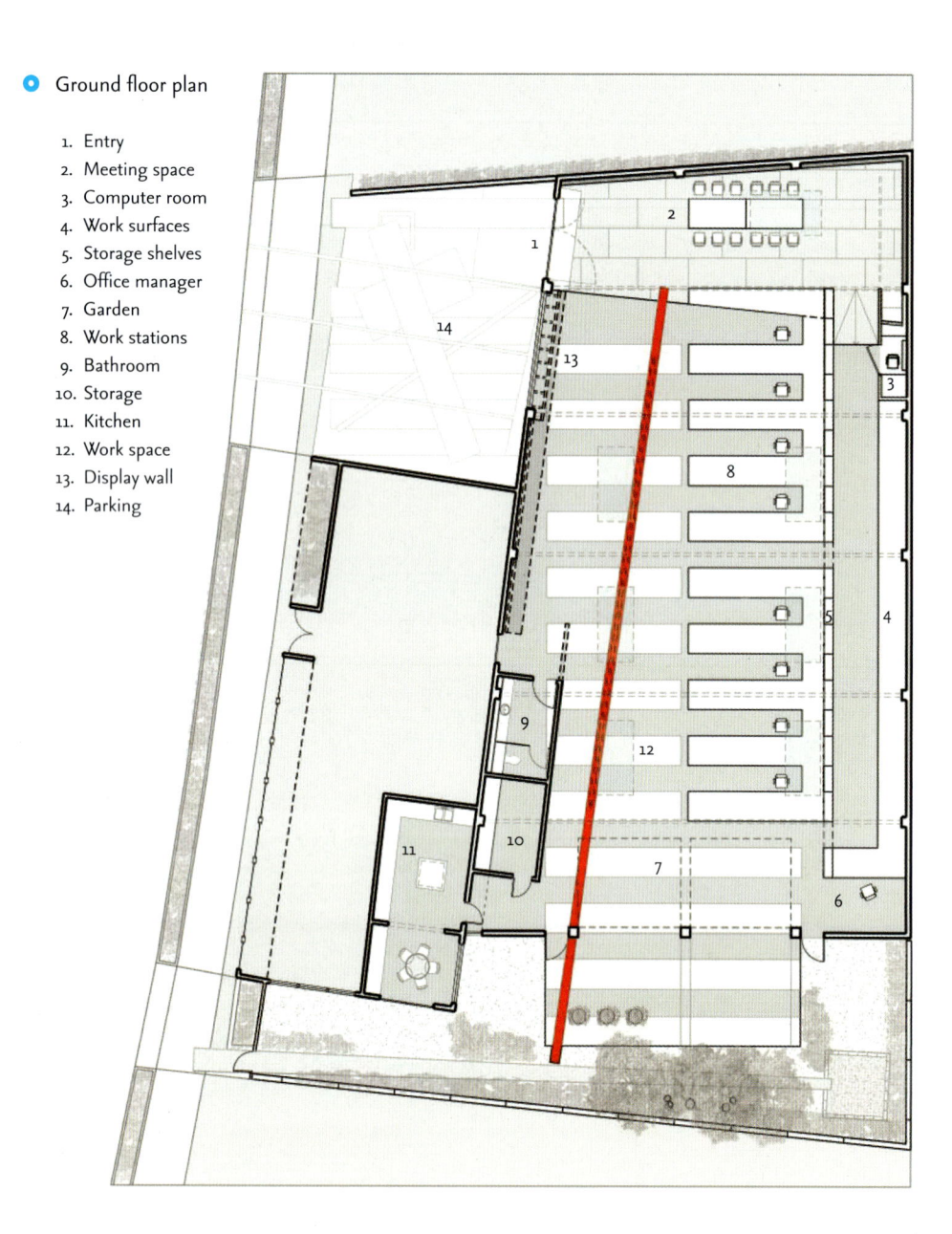

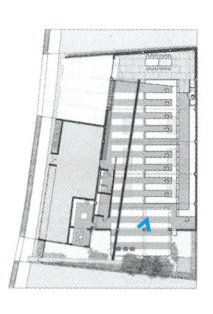

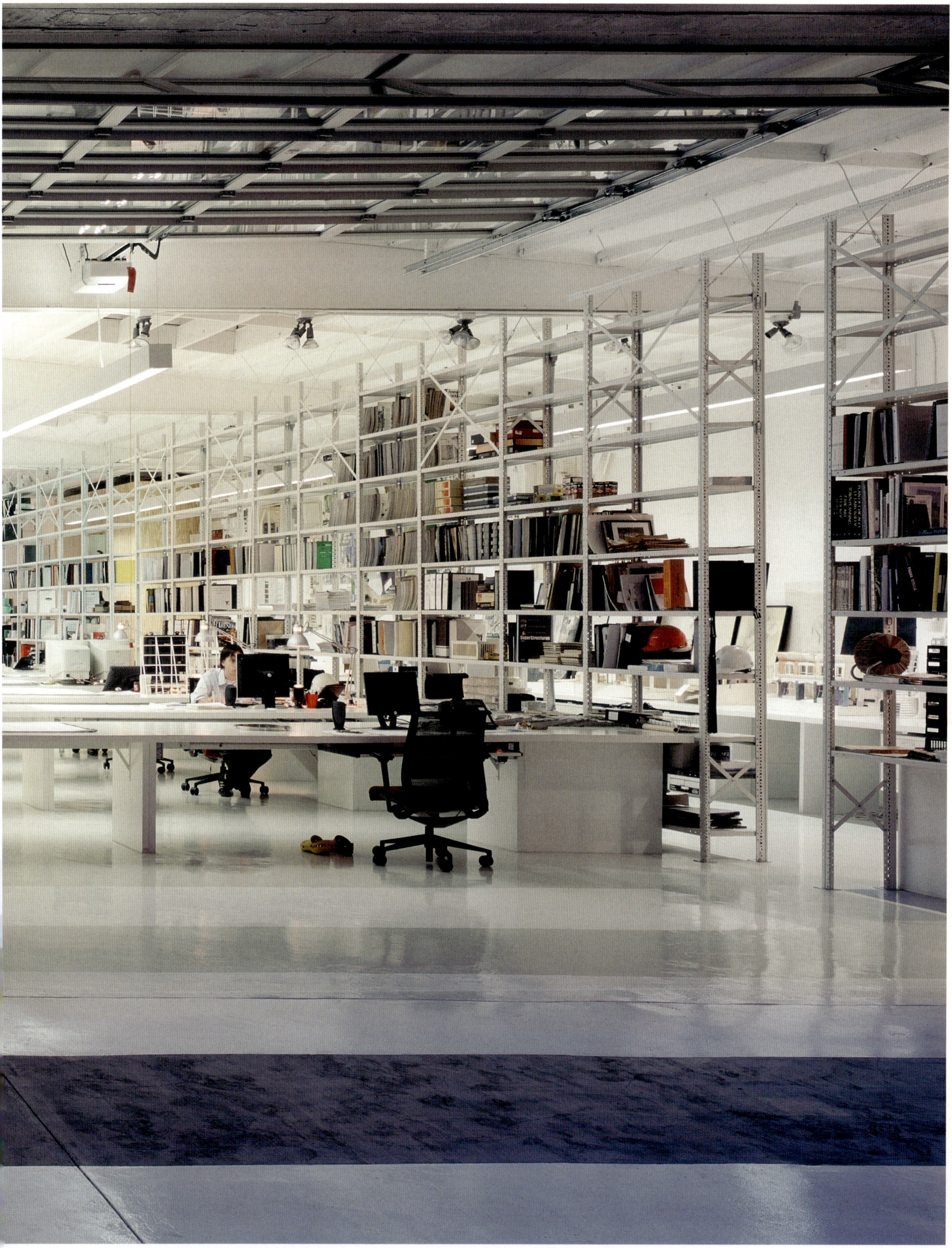

the history of progress
SPEED - EVOLUTION
FAST
FASTER
even FASTER
HIGH LEVEL
THE INTERNET
are YU ready FOR
more+FASTER
BASIC
EXPERT
GET PREPARED

Schröder & Schömbs PR Agency

This project involves the remodeling of an existing advertising agency. The client wanted to adapt the offices to new decorative trends as a strategy to stay in the market and to compete with emerging advertising agencies. The aim was to achieve a modern and up-to-date design that would reflect the style of the company, (i.e. their way of working and the image that they wanted to project to the exterior).

The entire project has been carried out through simple lines on an initial basic structure, which the architects decided to preserve in its entirety. The subtle strategy was to carry out small changes and give the interior a new layout in order to create small individual spaces, each with a strong character.

The agency occupies two floors that consist of a reception area, a waiting room, two meeting rooms, and various individual offices. The main feature of the project resides in the offices, whose limits are not marked by the traditional partition walls, but by sliding curtains. This solution was in response to the clients' desires for all staff members to be able to interact with one another. The curtains hang from the ceiling and reach the floor, offering privacy when needed. These curtains define the different spaces, allow for a large degree of flexibility in the use of the space, and adapt perfectly to the rooms and the lighting possibilities. The curtains, in combination with the parquet on the floor, increase the sense of warmth throughout the office.

The new reception area was designed to also be used as a meeting place for staff and clients, as well as for displaying the publications associated with the agency. As a complement to the textile division of the offices, the three storage volumes have been upholstered in synthetic leather.

Architect/Designer: Angelika Zwingel, Brigitte Feuerer/raum:team92

Client: Schröder + Schömbs PR
Photographer: Stefan Meyer
Location: Berlin, Germany
Completion date: 2007
Area: 5,705 SF

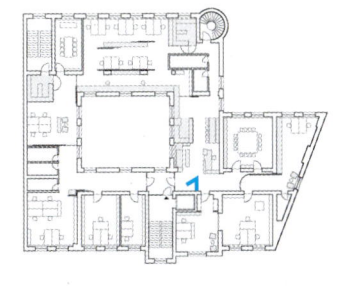

SCHRÖDER & SCHÖMBS PR AGENCY

● White covers the entire space: it is present on the ceilings, the walls, and the curtains that divide the space, which replace partition walls. It is interrupted only by the splashes of orange.

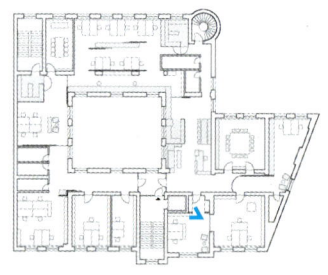

You must *unlearn* what you have *learn*

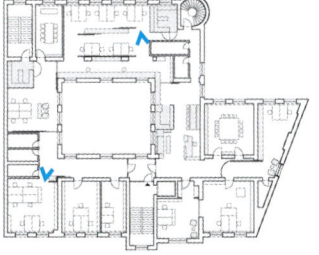

SCHRÖDER & SCHÖMBS PR AGENCY

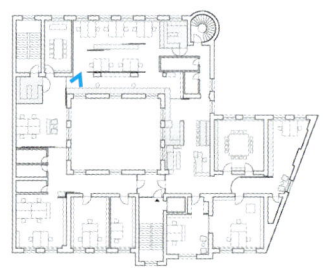

SCHRÖDER & SCHÖMBS PR AGENCY

Tatsachen verdrehen

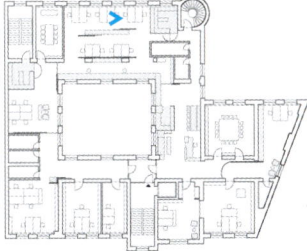

- The furniture is basic and adopts the composition's white-orange combination: white filing cabinets and orange armchairs and other complementary pieces. The tables harmonize with the wood flooring.

SCHRÖDER & SCHÖMBS PR AGENCY

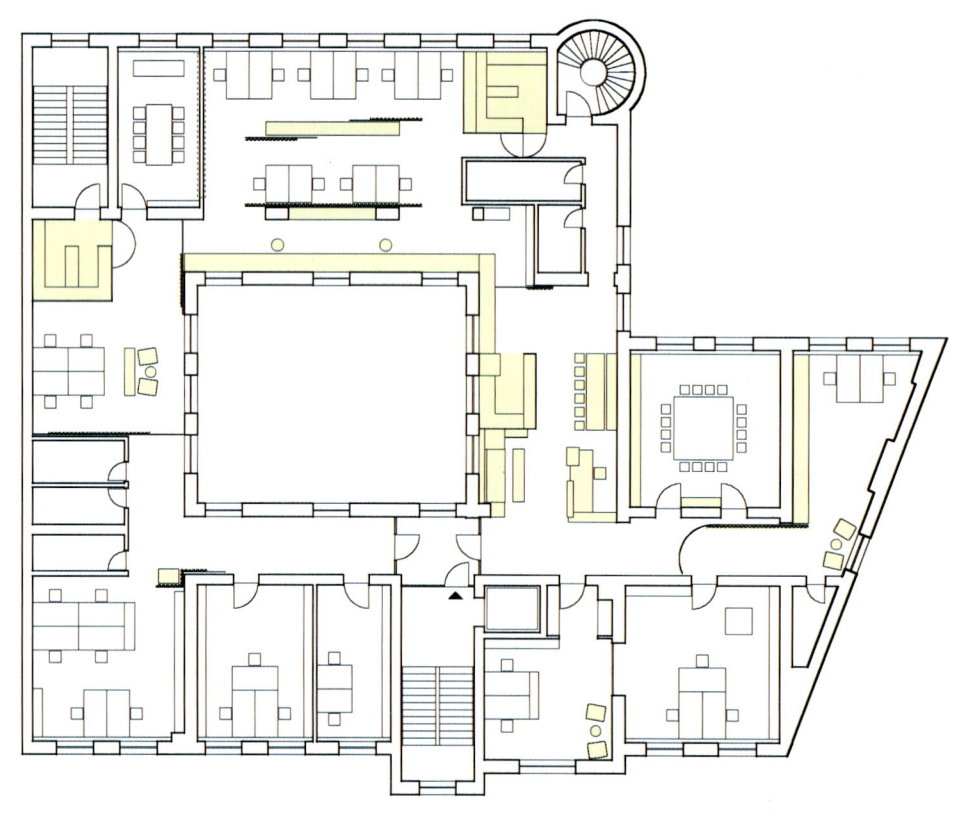

● Floor plan

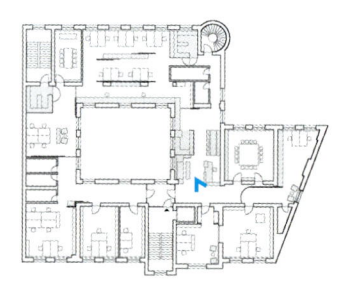

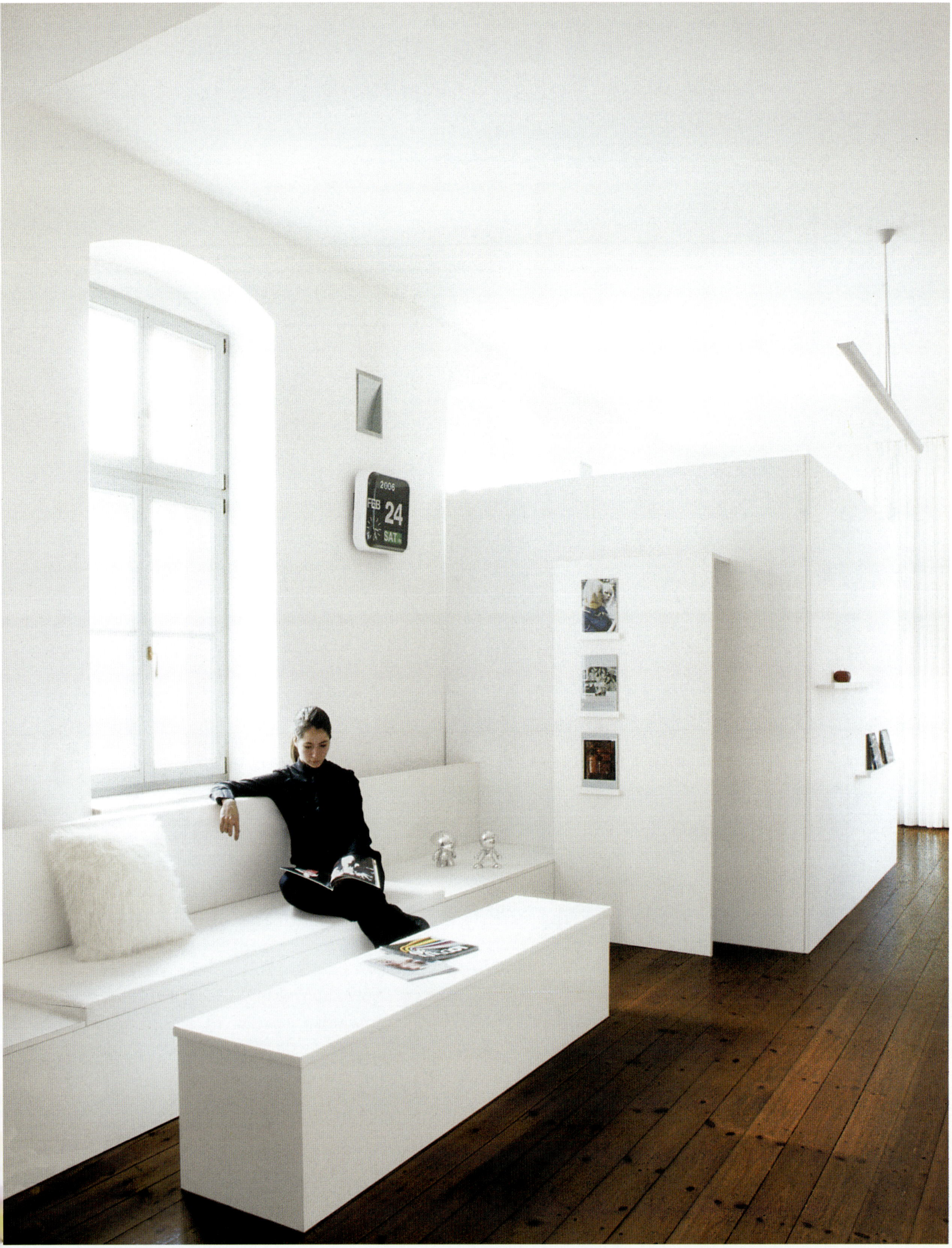
2006
FEB 24
SAT

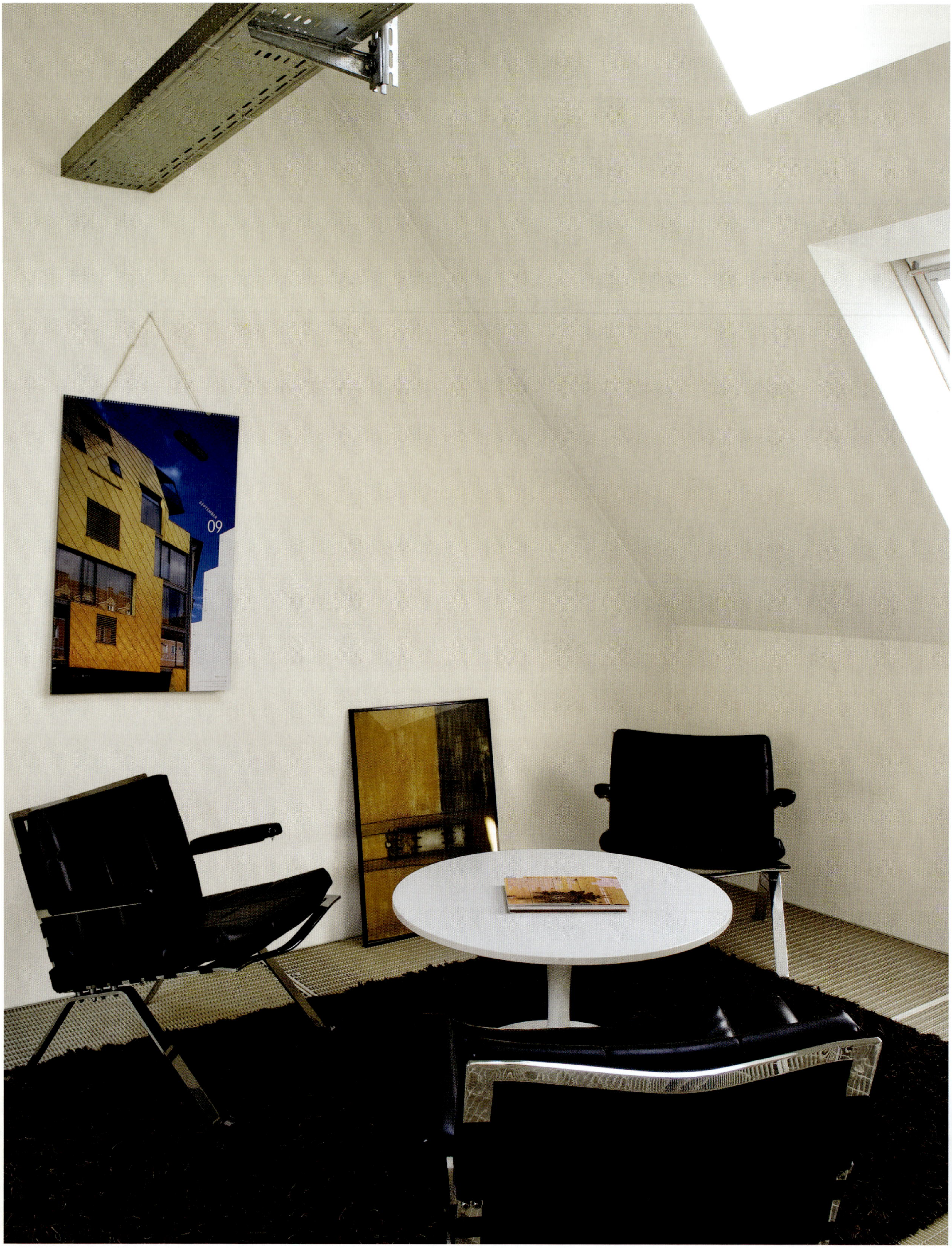
SEPTEMBER
09

Golden Nugget

Architect/Designer:

INNOCAD Planung und Projektmanagement

Client: 99 Plus Projektentwicklung und Bauträger
Photographer: Pep Escoda
Location: Graz, Austria
Completion date: 2005
Area: 5,716 SF

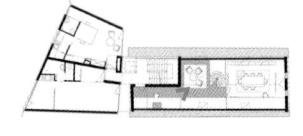

The architects and designers found the best location for this project in the heart of the historical center of Graz. The client asked for a space that would be adequate for people who attach great importance to urban life and to ideals; characteristics that are similar to the work of an architectural studio. It also needed to represent the image of the company.

The project is composed of two buildings: one old, which is located between two historical houses, and the other new, at the back of the site. The connection between both buildings has been carried out through an interior courtyard. The areas are distributed across different floors and gold is the only color used. This is due to the fact that this color forms part of the company's corporate image, whose logo consists of seven golden squares, which continually produce new shapes. This color also harmonizes with the surroundings, which follow a Wilhelminian style. In the design the materials most used are exposed concrete, gold fabric, a cladding of gold panels, and individual surfaces that can be changed. These help to create the urban style requested by the client.

The first floor of the new building and the pre-existing building houses the company's work spaces. The second floor is used by the company as an office for developing projects. While the new building is characterized by its golden surface and the exposed concrete, the building behind it —with the courtyard— has been painted in a pearlescent antiqua white.

The building has been conceived to reflect an appearance of depth and of a temporary space, not as a residential, protective space. The new building has been inserted between two fire-resistant walls and is a homogenous construction, although with a textured surface. The difference between the spaces nearest the street and those closest to the interior courtyard forms part of the urban aesthetic of this interior and also serves to create serenity and encourage relaxation.

GOLDEN NUGGET
228

● The pre-existing house in the back courtyard has been rebuilt and painted antiqua white and connects functionally and formally with the rest of the space. The interior of the new building is characterized by the color gold.

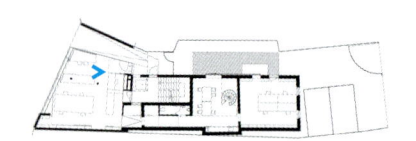

GOLDEN NUGGET
229

GOLDEN NUGGET
230

GOLDEN NUGGET

○ The application of gold to the surfaces with horizontal panels, curtains, metal meshes, etc., responds to the client's desire to reflect the company's corporate identity in their head office.

GOLDEN NUGGET
232

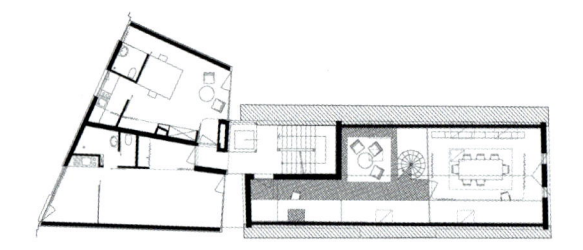

- Second floor

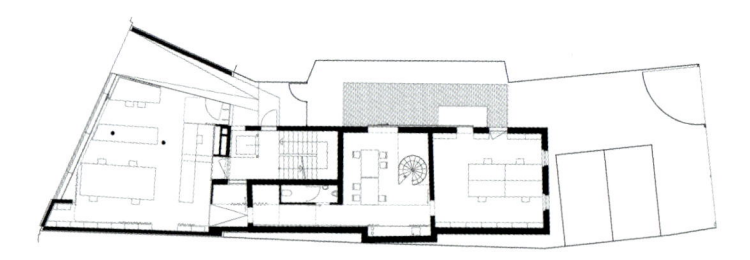

- First floor

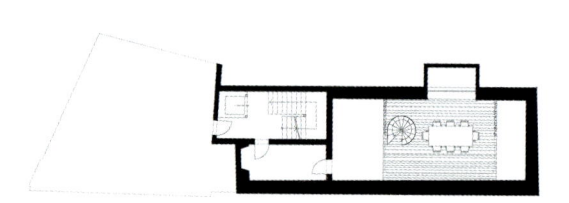

- Basement floor

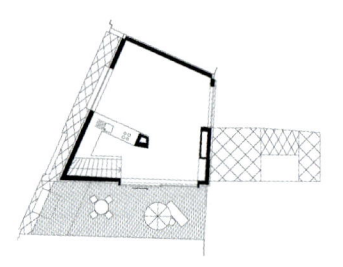

- Sixth floor

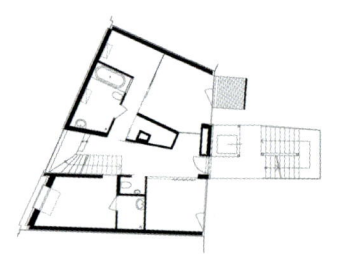

- Fifth floor

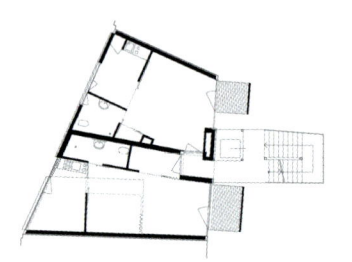

- Fourth floor

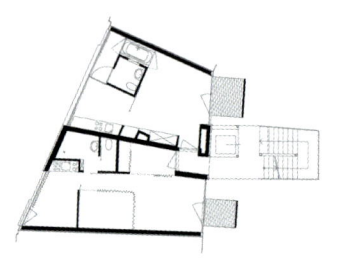

- Third floor

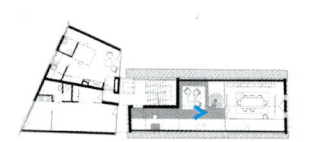

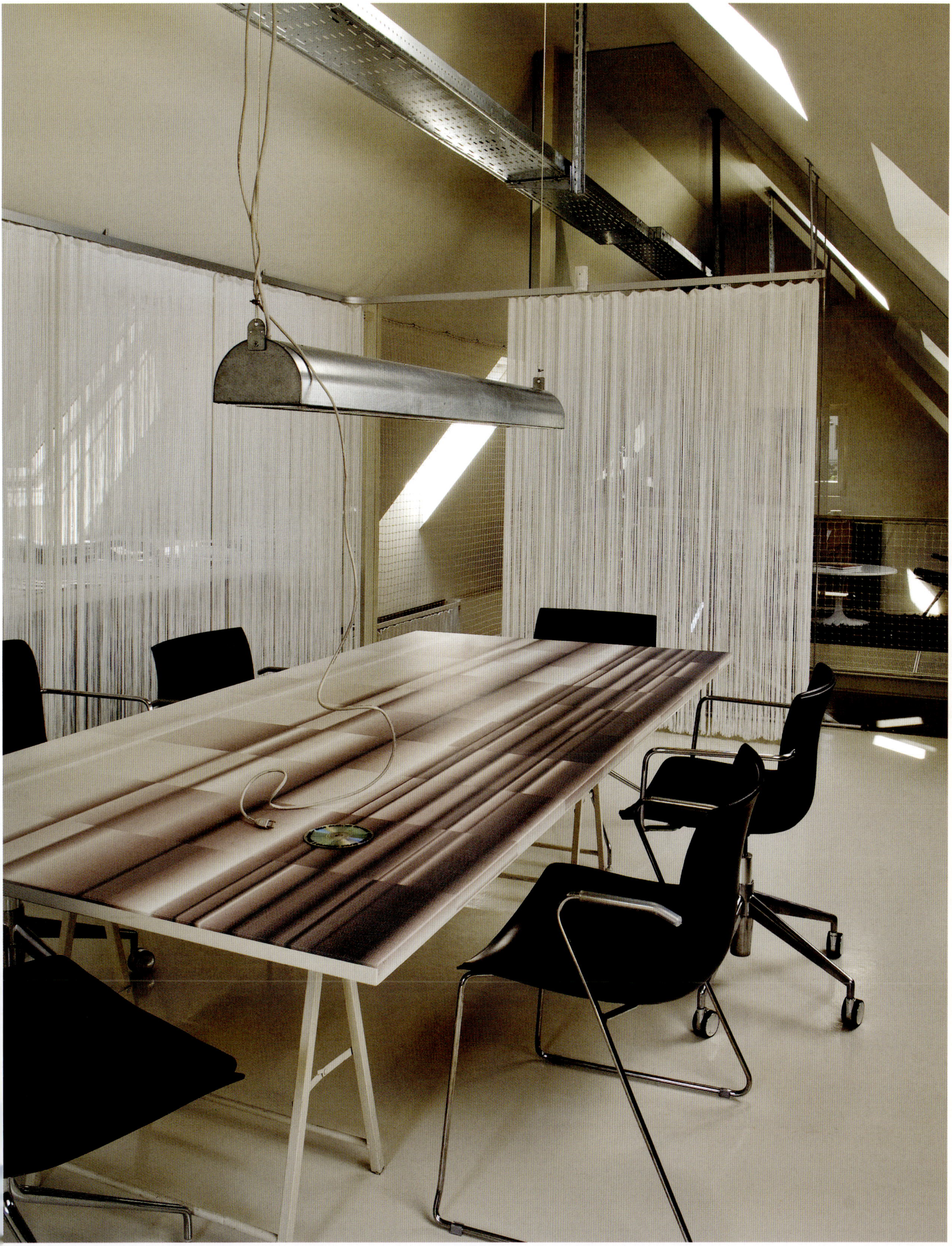

Medium-Size Offices

FTVentures Offices — 236

Laiguana Studio — 242

Bourke Place Studio — 248

Bank in Pontedera, Bank With Eyes — 254

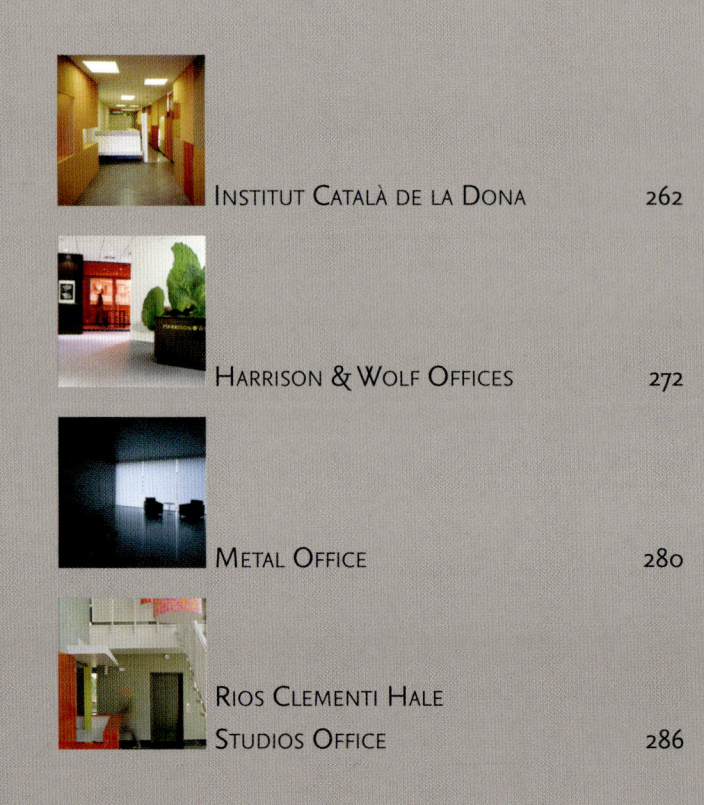

Institut Català de la Dona — 262

Harrison & Wolf Offices — 272

Metal Office — 280

Rios Clementi Hale Studios Office — 286

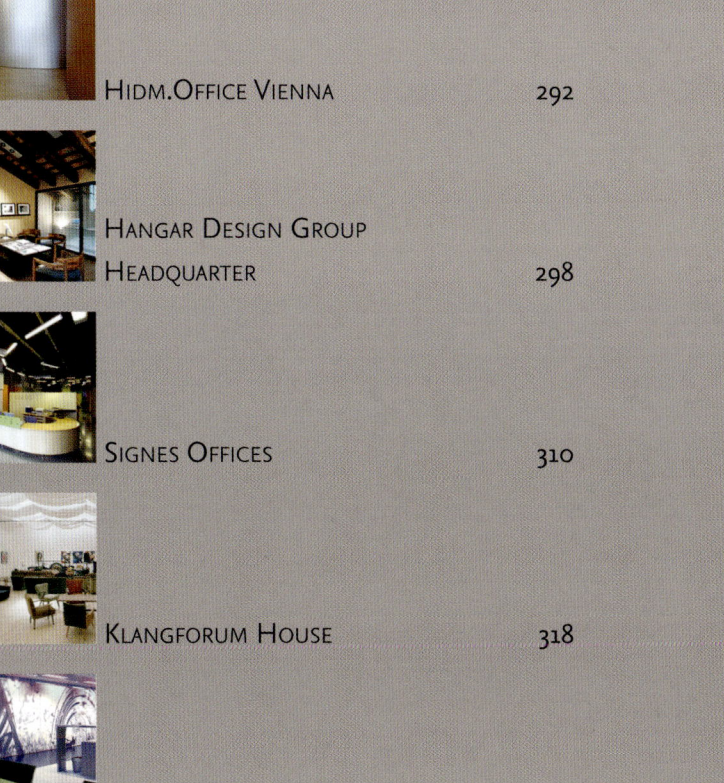

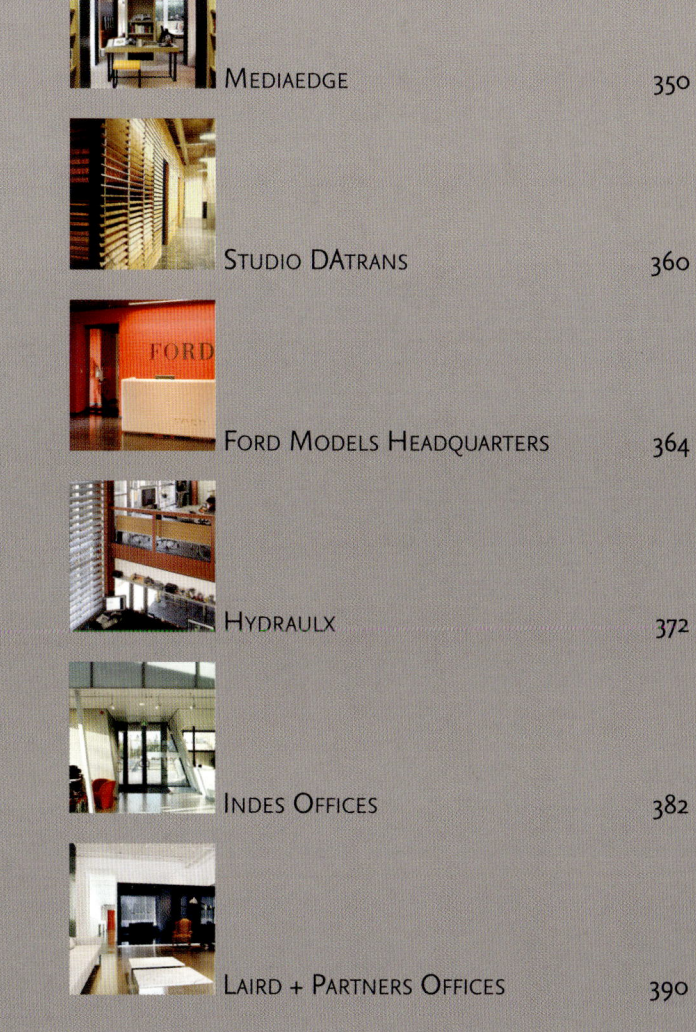

Hidm.Office Vienna	292
Hangar Design Group Headquarter	298
Signes Offices	310
Klangforum House	318
 Amec Spie Offices	326
 Construcciones Mon Offices	338
Mediaedge	350
Studio DAtrans	360
Ford Models Headquarters	364
Hydraulx	372
Indes Offices	382
Laird + Partners Offices	390

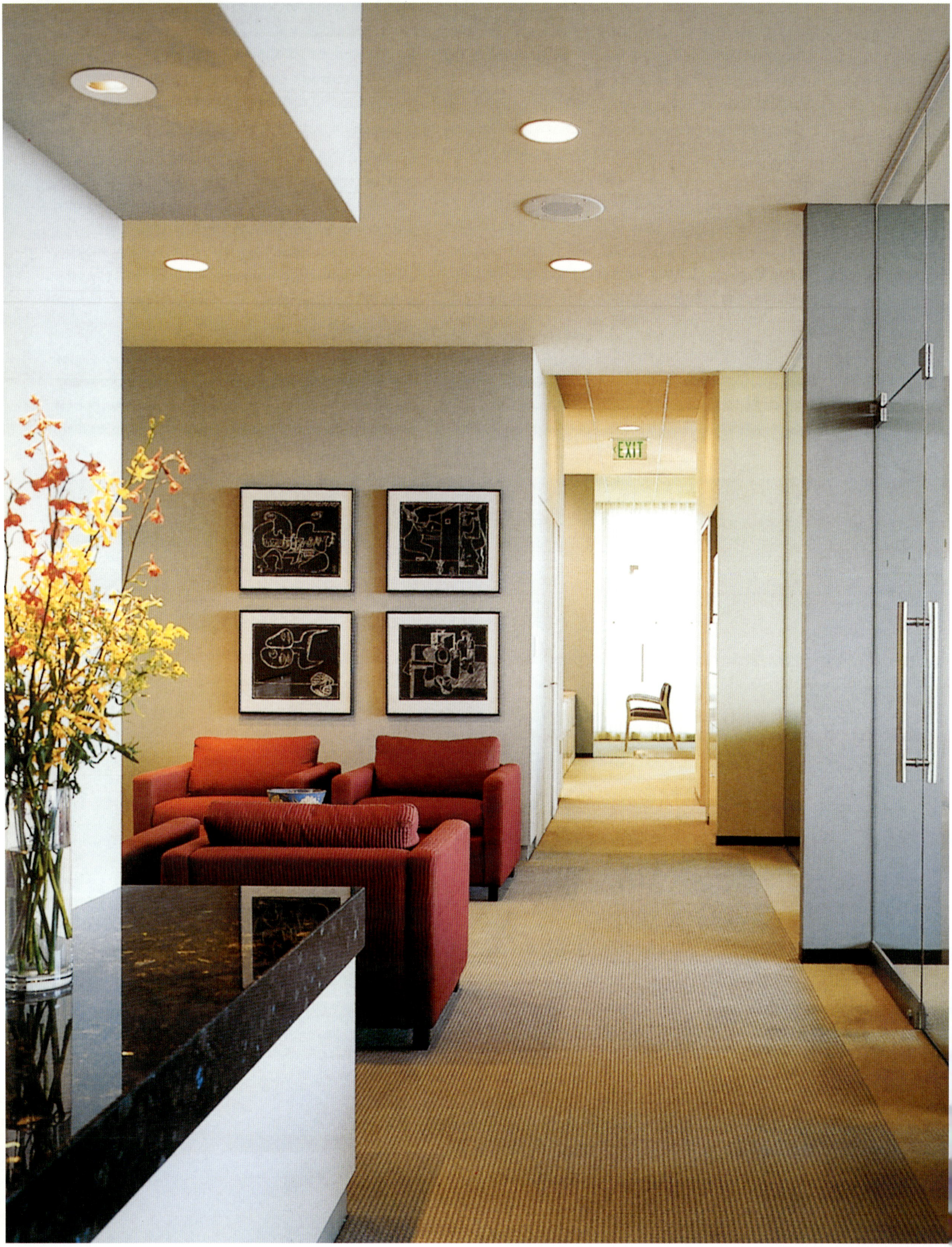
EXIT

FTVentures Offices

ARCHITECT/DESIGNER: IAN AYERS,
JOEL HENDLER/HENDLER DESIGN

Client: Financial Technology Ventures
Photographer: David Wakely
Location: San Francisco
Completion date: 2002
Area: 6,156 SF

These offices are located on the top floor of a building designed in 1962 by Anshen + Allen. The client commissioned an interior that would make the most of the 360 degree views across San Francisco, as well as a design that would reflect simplicity and serenity whilst also being elegant. Both the architect and the designer decided to look for a solution that would capture the international style of the original building and express it through a modern and distinguished space. The interior presents influences from Mies van der Rohe's Pavilion in Barcelona, but updates the modernist concept through its rigorous geometry, precise pieces, and clear composition.

In the center of the space are the elevators, a common architectural solution for a building of this type. Distributed around the elevator shaft are the communal spaces. The exposed concrete wall that encloses the elevators functions as one of the walls that delineate the main conference room, the reception area and the lobby, which accommodates a fireplace. A second spatial ring, houses the individual offices and the balconies that surround the exterior of this floor, which can be accessed via sliding doors.

The renovation consisted of first removing the dark panels that hid the texture of the underlying concrete walls. The concrete has been left exposed and creates an elegant contrast with the elongated structures of the elevator doors. The ceilings are high and all unnecessary decorative elements have been removed from them. The palette includes yellows, of Asian influence, celadon green, and slate gray which lend the space dynamism.

The major feature, despite the striking presence of the exposed concrete, is glass, which has been used extensively. Floor-to-ceiling windows delineate the perimeter of each office, and make the whole space totally transparent, thus creating a visual connection between the offices. This constructive resource allows employees to enjoy natural light during daylight hours, which in turn increases their energy levels and makes them more efficient.

FTVENTURES OFFICES

● Glass has been used extensively to divide the different spaces. This also affords the offices spectacular views over San Francisco. The slate gray of the exposed concrete, wheat yellow of the floor, and the furnishings give the space a simple but elegant appearance.

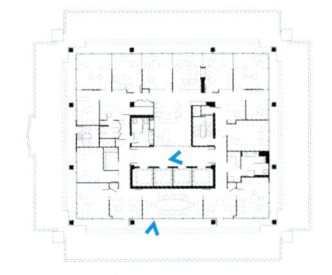

FTVENTURES OFFICES
239

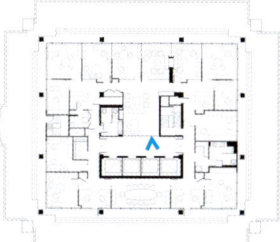

FTVENTURES OFFICES
240

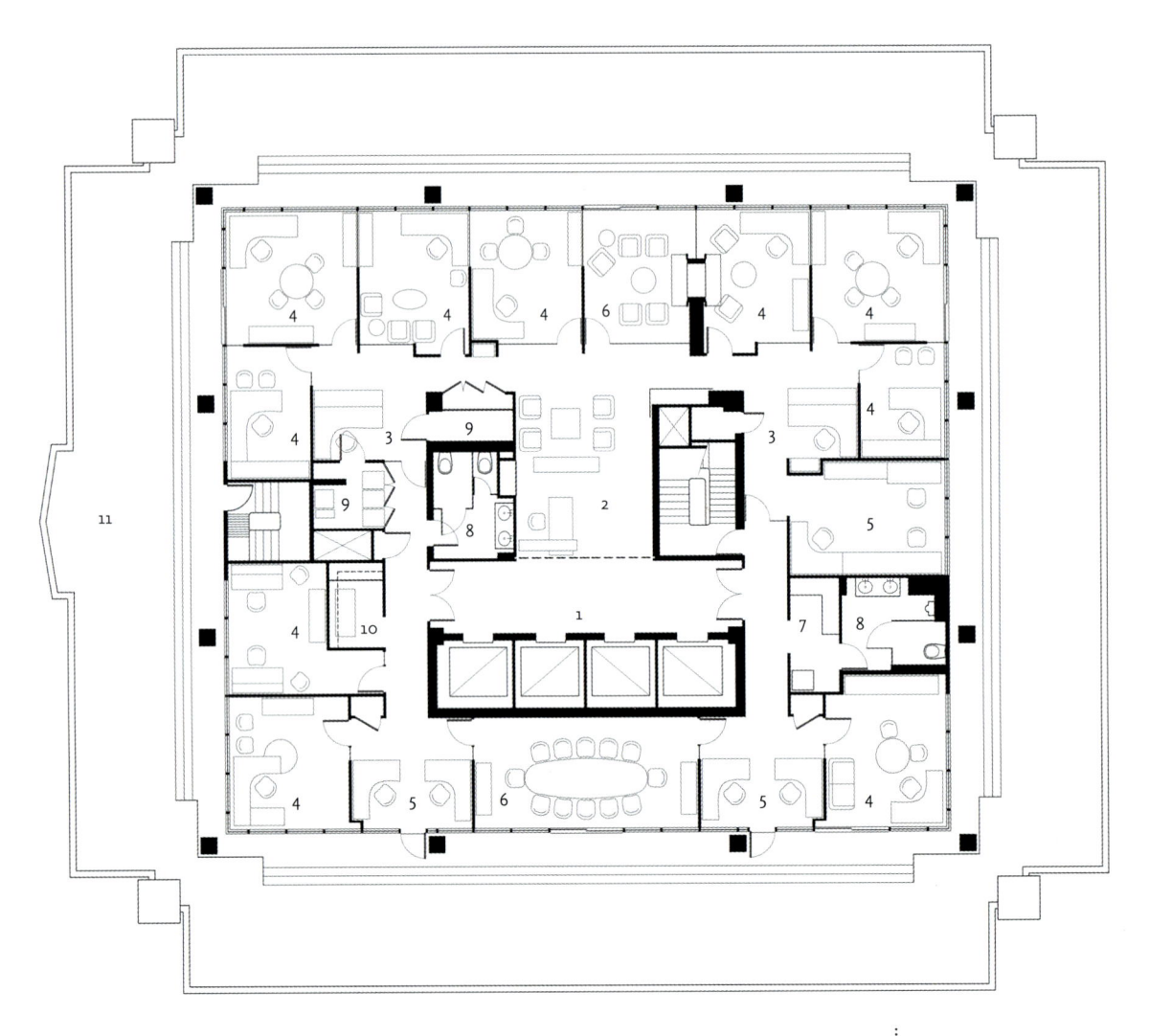

○ Floor plan

1. Elevator lobby
2. Reception and waiting area
3. Assistant
4. Private offices
5. Open offices
6. Conference room
7. Break room
8. Restroom
9. Utility room
10. Copy room
11. Balcony

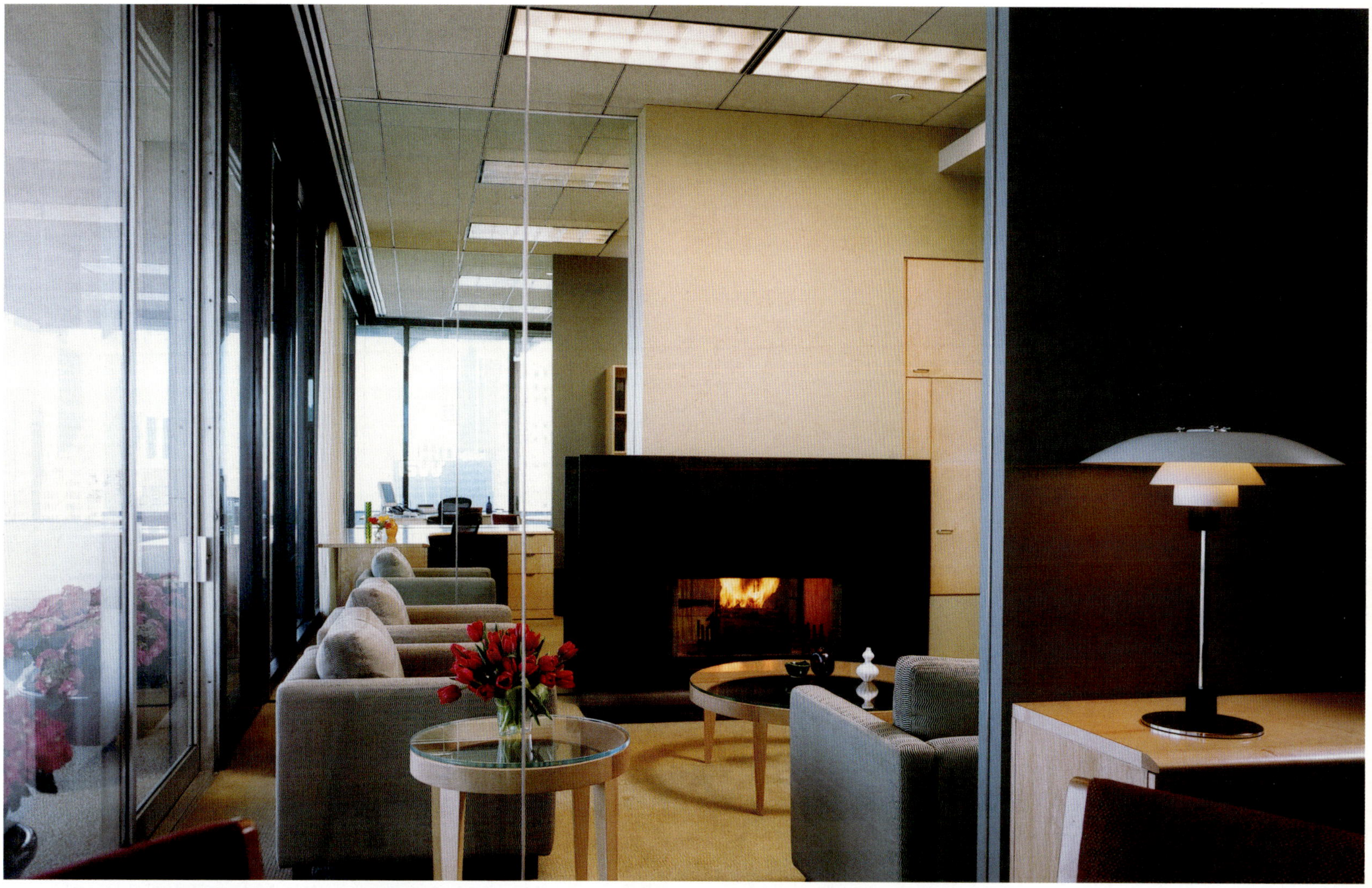

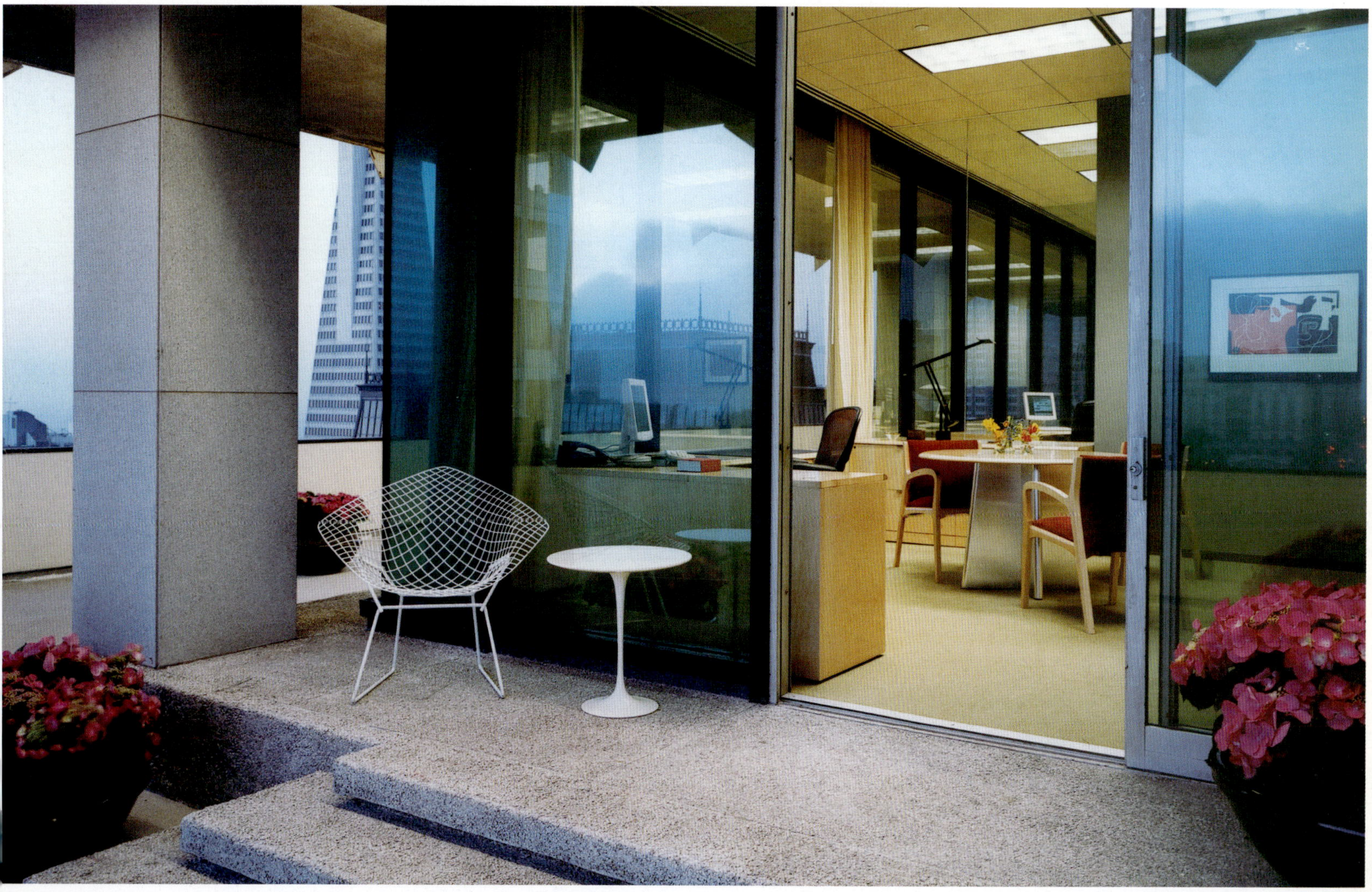

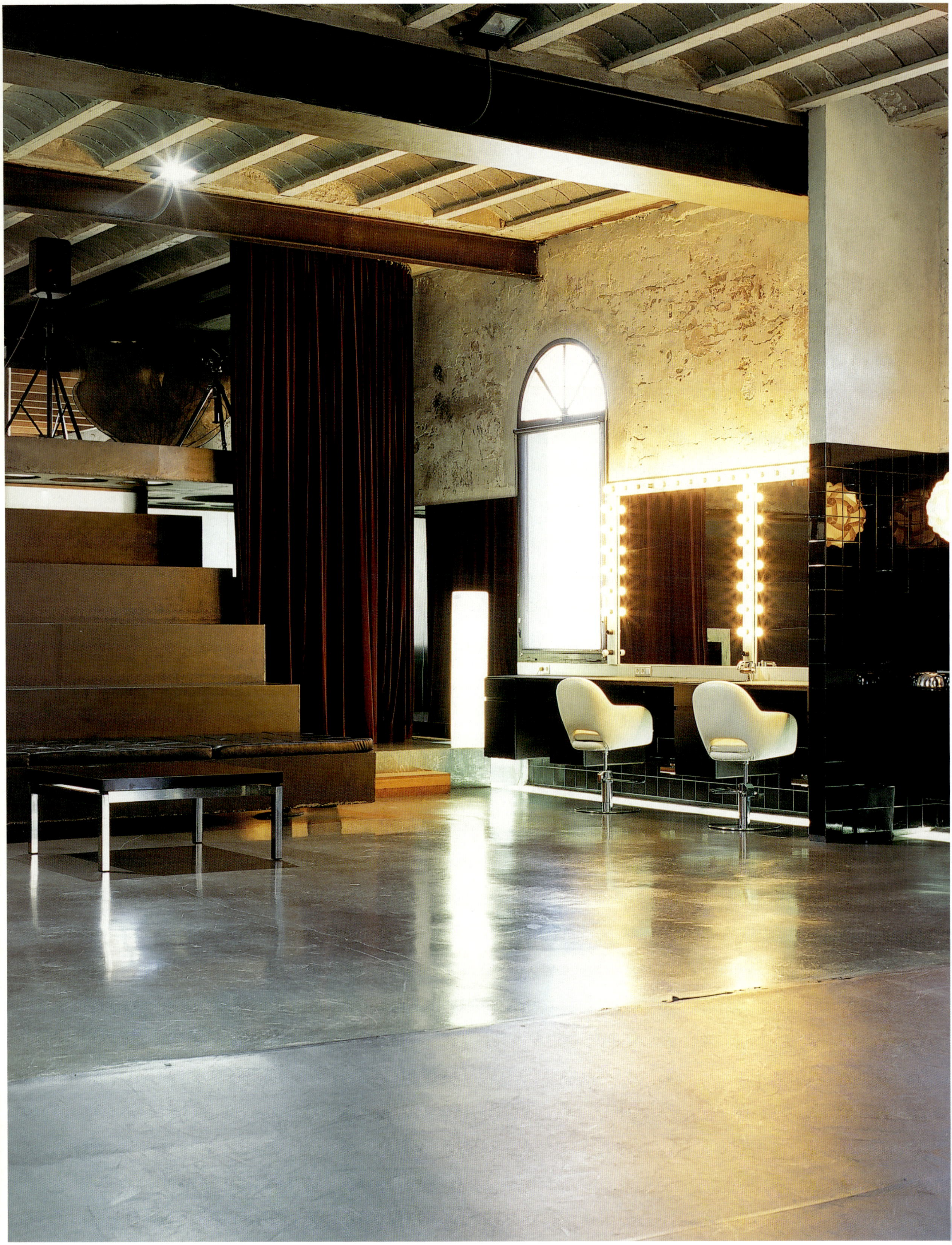

Laiguana Studio

This old factory, dating back to the beginning of last century, is located in Pueblo Nuevo, a known industrial area in Barcelona. The top floor plays host to this project.

In this large L-shaped space the client wanted to install a graphics studio and a set for photo shoots. The studio is composed of several small meeting rooms, offices and amenities, while the photo set is an area without divisions, but which can be subdivided if needed.

To preserve the initial structure of the building, the load-bearing brick walls from the factory and the ceiling have been maintained. The ceiling is the result of a previous renovation and is formed by small vaults and concrete beams, supported by bars from wall to wall, and centrally by a cylindrical metal pillar. The floor, in contrast, was quite uneven and needed to be corrected. New flooring was therefore installed, which floats above the previous floor by way of a metal structure. This maintains the distribution of weight from the original structure.

The access to the graphics studio is located in a wall clad in gloss white, glazed ceramic tiles and is lit by a classic chandelier. After this point is an area defined by a red velvet curtain welcoming the visitor into the studio.

Beyond here is the area for graphics work, the meeting rooms, a few small offices, and two photography sets at the back. The aim is to conserve spaciousness so areas have only been made private where strictly necessary.

The wooden floor establishes spatial continuity, which is broken at one end by a row of seats and another velvet curtain. Behind this, in the shape of an ellipse, are the mirrors and dressing tables where the models prepare themselves for the photo shoots. The seats face away from the first space, which is dedicated to administration and design and are used by spectators watching the photo shoots.

ARCHITECT/DESIGNER:

EQUIPxavierclaramunt

Client: Jaume de Laiguana
Photographer: Jaume de Laiguana, Gogortza & Llorella/Bisou Foto
Location: Barcelona, Spain
Completion date: 2003
Area: 6,405 SF

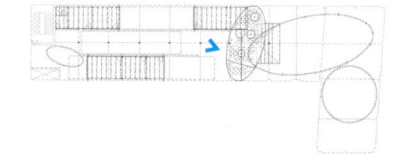

LAIGUANA STUDIO

- To maintain the structure of the factory, the architect has chosen aluminum furnishings. The velvet curtains offer privacy to the dressing area and separate the two work zones: design and photography.

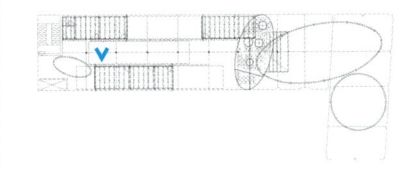

LAIGUANA STUDIO
245

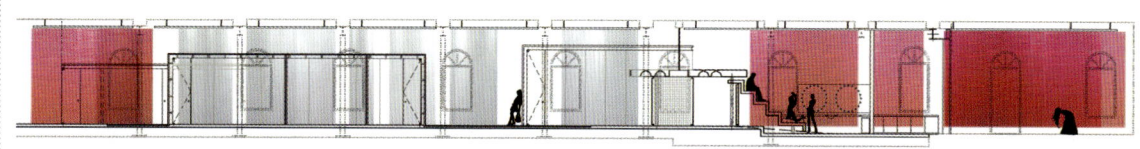

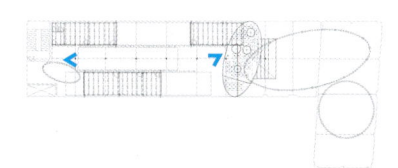

LAIGUANA STUDIO

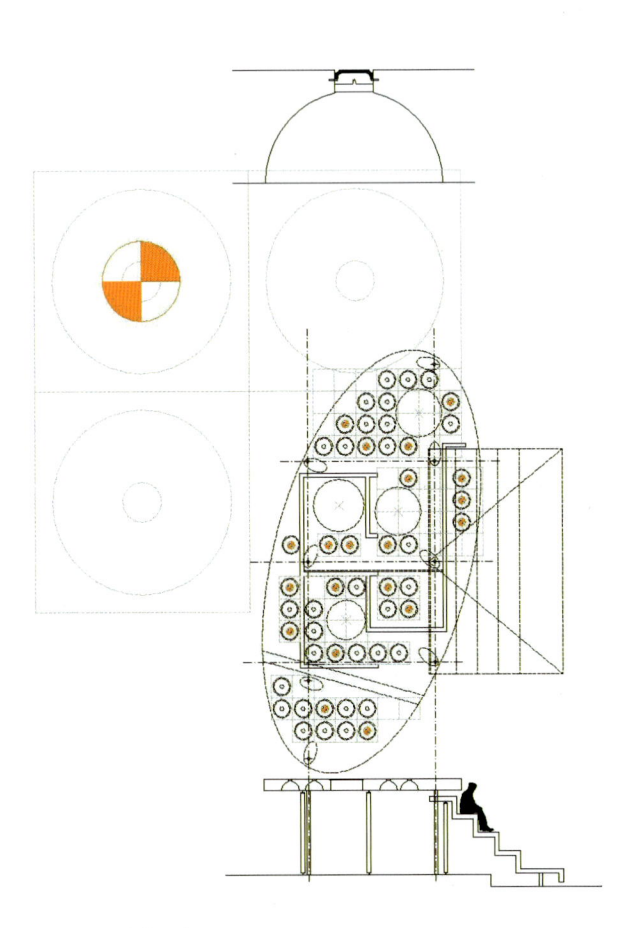

○ Floor plan

1. Studio
2. Photography studio
3. Dressing room
4. Office
5. Bathrooms

○ Stand detail

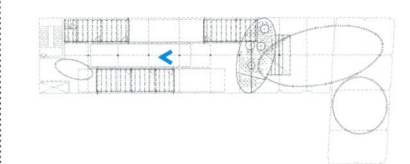

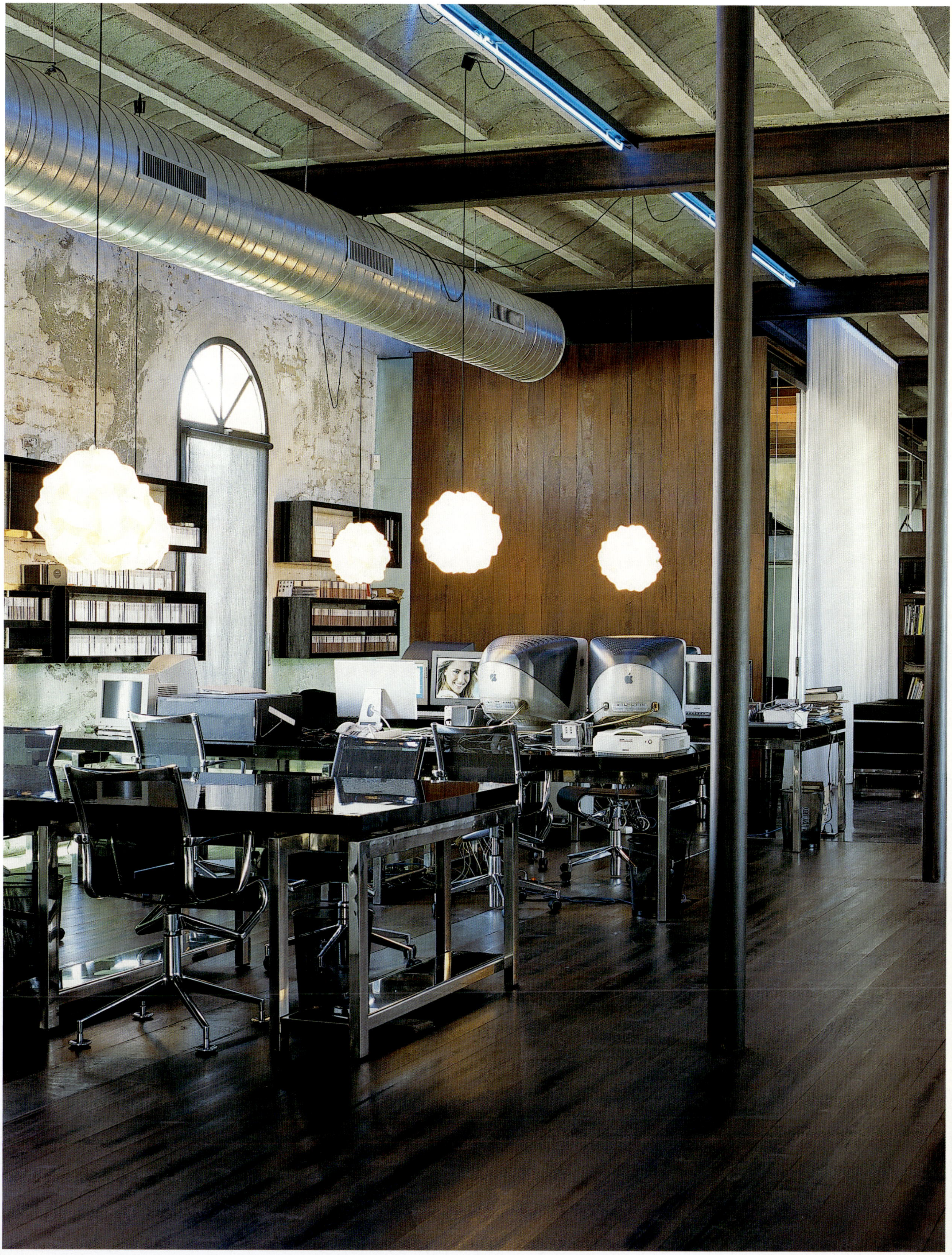

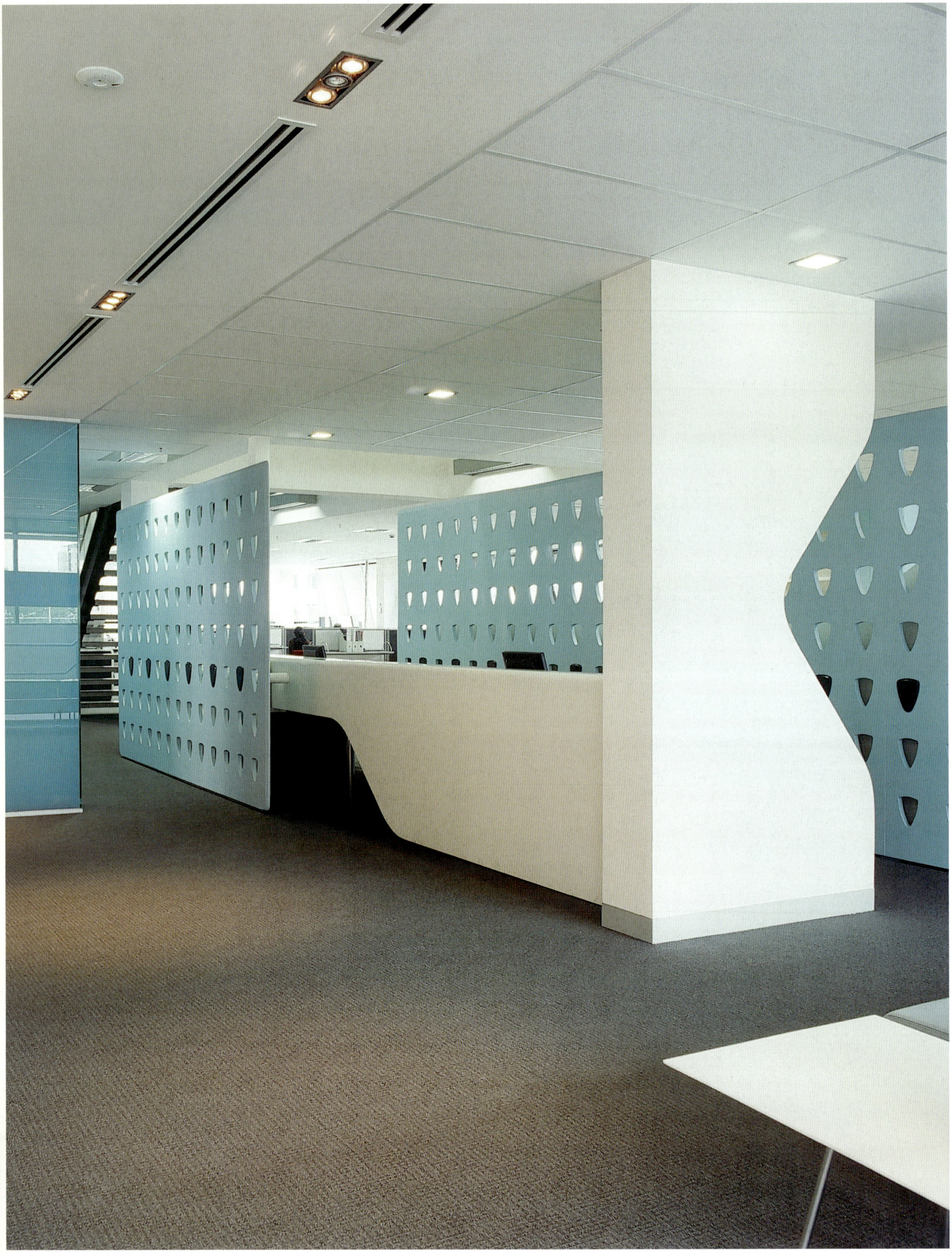

Bourke Place Studio

The company required a complete renovation of their central headquarters, which consisted of a two-story office.

The lower floor, whose access is located at street level, is formed by three meeting rooms, three individual offices, large collective work zones, and a small rest area, which includes the toilets and a small dining room.

On the second floor, accessed by a staircase, there is a terrace next to another large room for communal work. Both have been given a false ceiling made from the plasterboard of the pre-existing ceiling.

Several series of perforated screens throughout the office offer transparency to the interior, project certain zones onto others, and acts as a playful element, as well as delineating the functional areas of the space. These screens have been incorporated into the office using a system of plastic plugs, similar to those used by mobiles or certain toys. Their positions can be modified depending on the activity and they constitute the main element of this renovation, making the work environment interactive and improvised as well as multiplying the space's functional possibilities.

The lobby was not intended to be ostentatious and the budget for all zones was meant to be proportional, so that no area stood out over another. The use of fluorescent lighting brings an aspect of utilitarianism to the project's aesthetics, although the need for artificial lighting has been reduced to a minimum thanks to the large openings in the walls and the open plans of both floors.

The ensemble of furniture does not follow a particular stylistic line. This allowed the architect to underline that the office does not have the global aesthetic of a house, but that each member of staff has to develop a design that is appropriate to their work. The color palette has been limited to pastel blue, which harmonizes with the pre-existing palette.

Architect/Designer:
Gray Puksand

Client: Gray Puksand
Photographer: Shania Shegedyn
Location: Melbourne, Australia
Completion date: 2004
Area: 6,781 SF

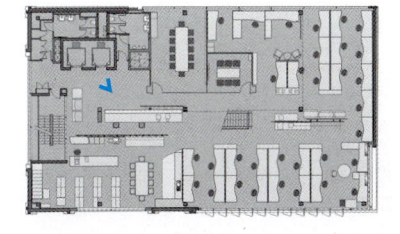

BOURKE PLACE STUDIO
250

○ The architects have attempted to create a space for life, where each person finds his or her own place. Among the various sustainable features, movement-sensitive lights have been installed in the toilets.

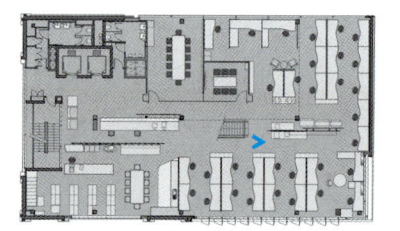

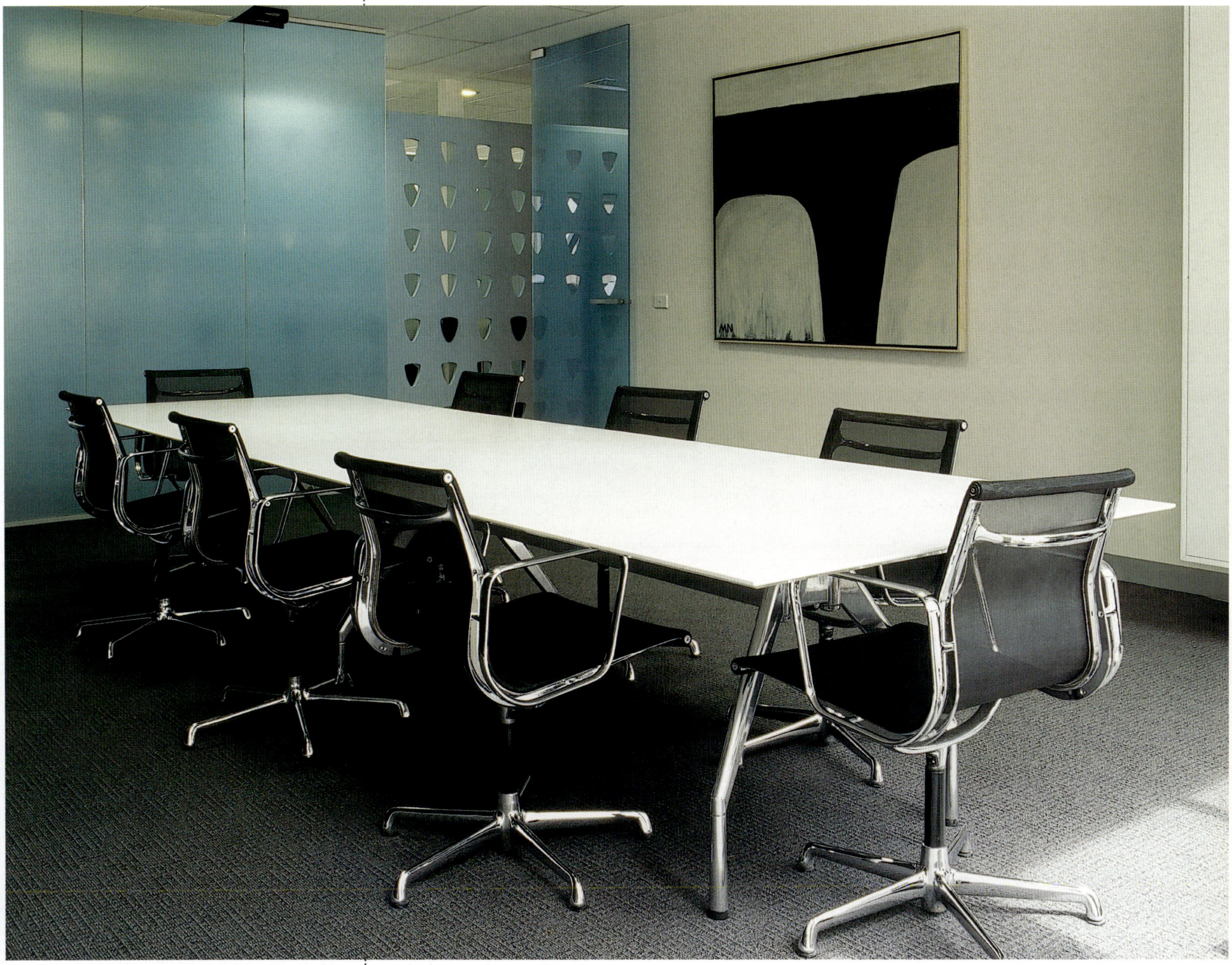

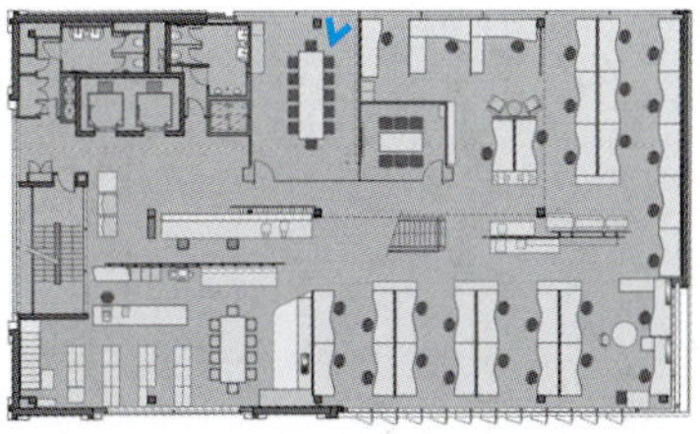

BOURKE PLACE STUDIO

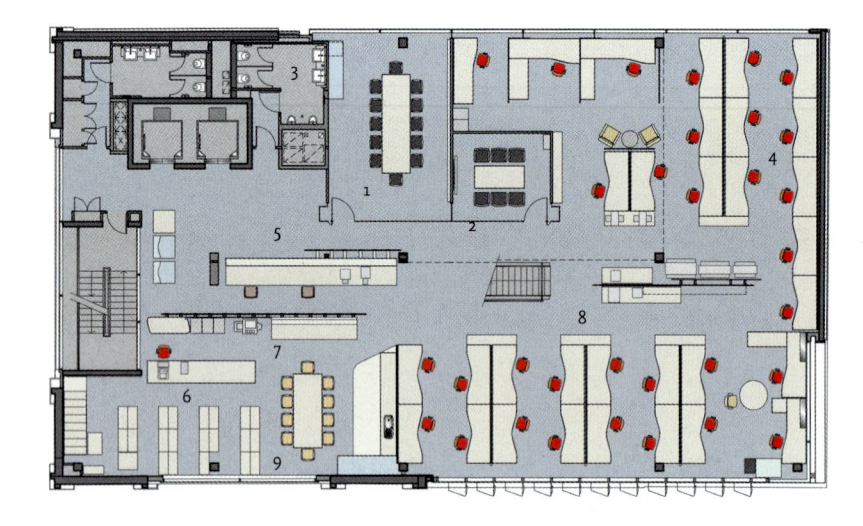

● Floor plan

1. Conference room
2. Meeting room
3. Bathrooms
4. Offices
5. Reception
6. Library
7. Utilities
8. Plotting/Printing
9. Staff

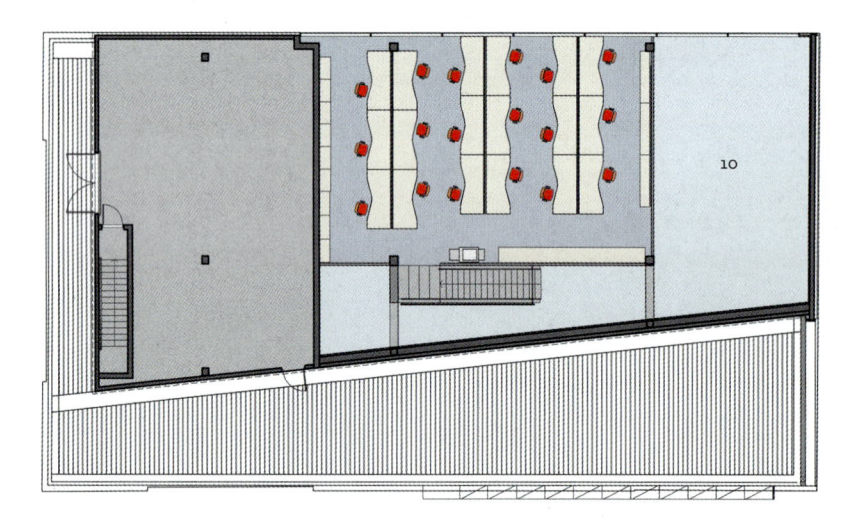

● Mezzanine level

10. Void to below

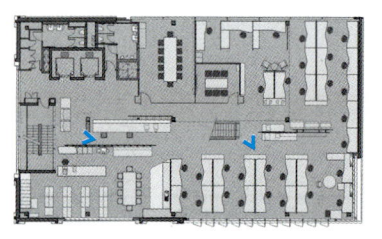

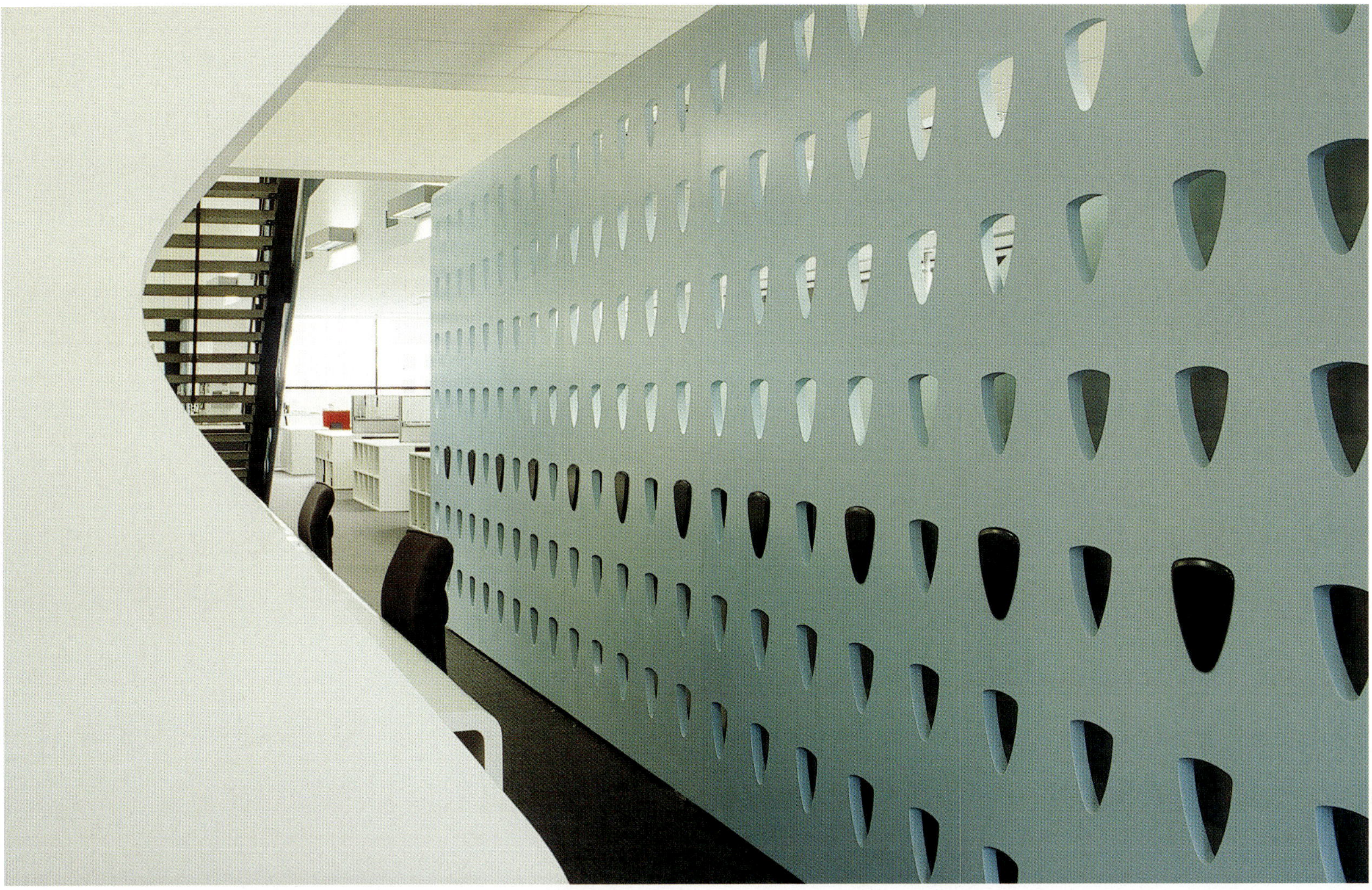

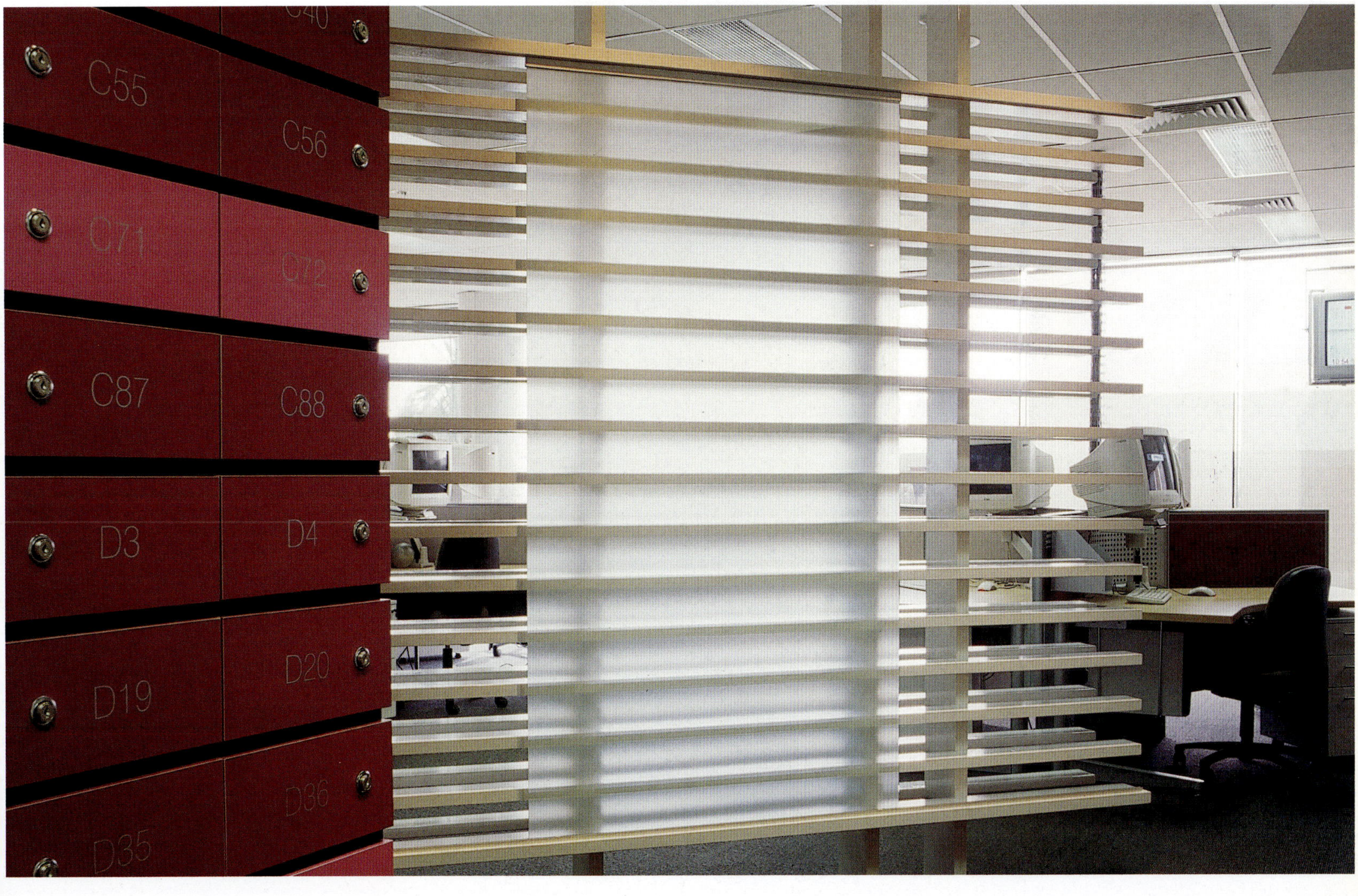
C55
C56
C71
C72
C87
C88
D3
D4
D19
D20
D35
D36

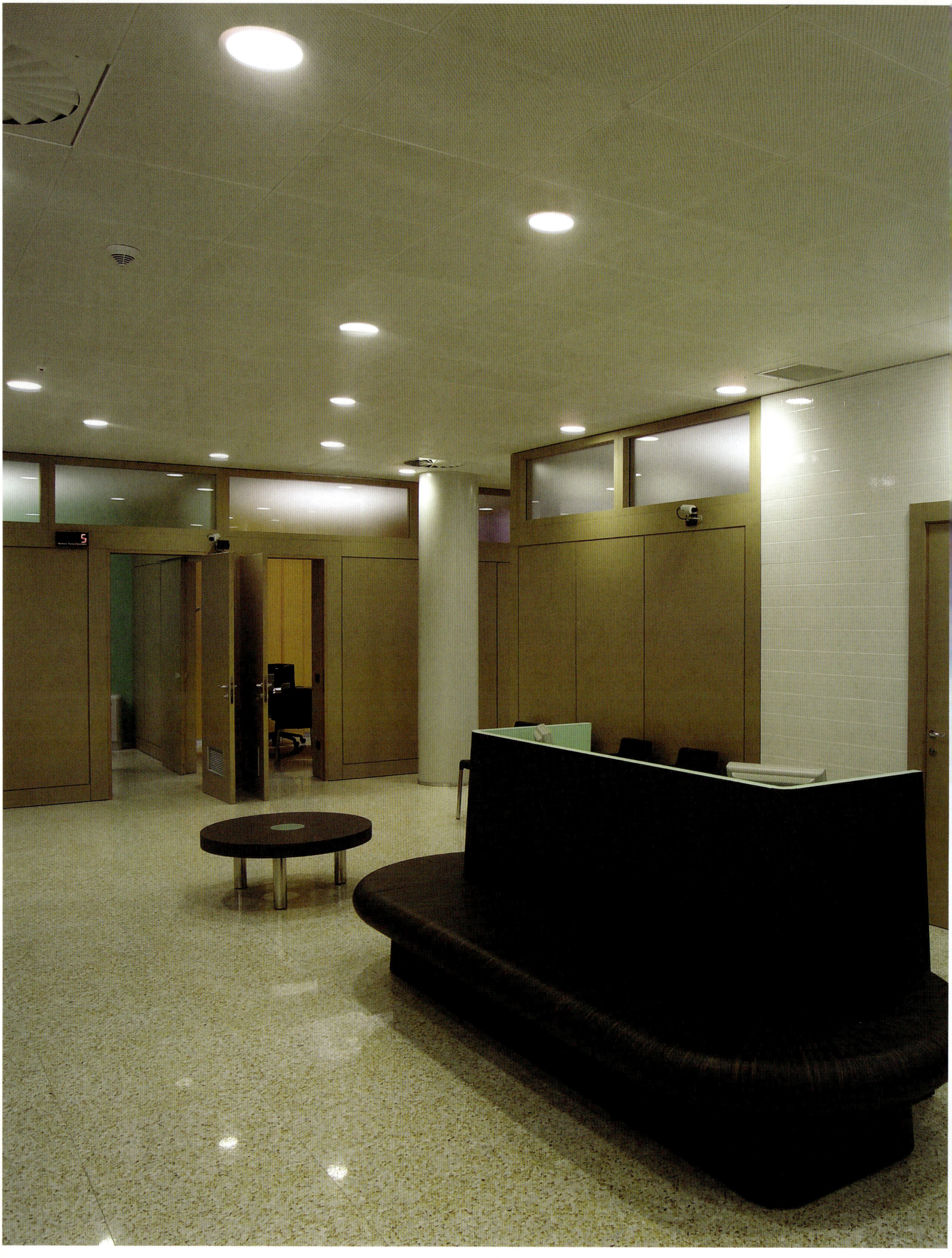

BANK IN PONTEDERA, BANK WITH EYES

ARCHITECT/DESIGNER:
MASSIMO MARIANI ARCHITETTO

Client: Banca di Credito Coperativo di Fornacette
Photographer: Alessandro Ciampi
Location: Pisa, Italy
Completion date: 2003
Area: 6,997 SF

The building that houses the offices for the Banco di Credito Coperativo di Fornacette, is located in the town of Pontedera, which belongs to the province of Pisa and has a population of around 28,000 inhabitants. The project is located at the exit of the Florence-Pisa-Livorno highway, an industrial area under constant transformation.

The construction was originally designed as a private house, whose ground floor in the 1970's accommodated a car dealership. The building then fell into disuse and consequently suffered progressive deterioration. Finally the property was acquired by the bank, which commissioned the Italian architectural studio with its complete renovation.

The exterior work carried out by the architects consisted in the installation of a second aluminum skin, which improved its appearance. They also created elliptical openings arranged to give the impression that the building has eyes. The installations necessary for the workings of the bank were distributed across approximately 7,000 square feet, structured over two floors. This project enriches the architectural studio's characteristic conceptual line, based on the creation of spaces whose designs are not conventional with respect to their use. In this sense, the bank's offices look as if they could be used for another purpose. On the ground floor is the public open space, where the counters and offices for the bank's employees are situated. On the private first floor are the meeting rooms and offices for the bank's administration.

One of the most carefully studied elements is the lighting. Cenital lighting has been chosen, achieved using wall lamps and lights that project both general and task lighting, which is needed for the work. Half-height panels have been used with earthy colors, which provide warmth and transmit a feeling of closeness to the client. In the private offices of both floors, this warm line is continued, bringing comfort and well-being both to workers and users alike.

BANK IN PONTEDERA, BANK WITH EYES

○ The interior design is characterized by the use of warm colors, which help to distinguish the different spaces that comprise the offices. Even the secondary access points have been considered down to the last detail.

BANK IN PONTEDERA, BANK WITH EYES

BANK IN PONTEDERA, BANK WITH EYES

BANK IN PONTEDERA, BANK WITH EYES

259

○ One of the unifying materials of the space is a terrazzo floor. This flooring, formed by a layer of cement with stones or pieces of marble, allows for the creation of massive tiles, which are remarkably durable.

BANK IN PONTEDERA, BANK WITH EYES

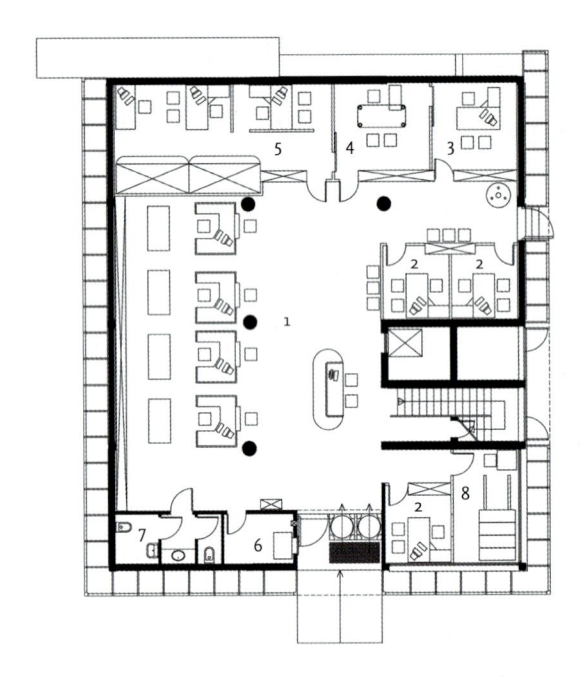

○ Ground floor plan

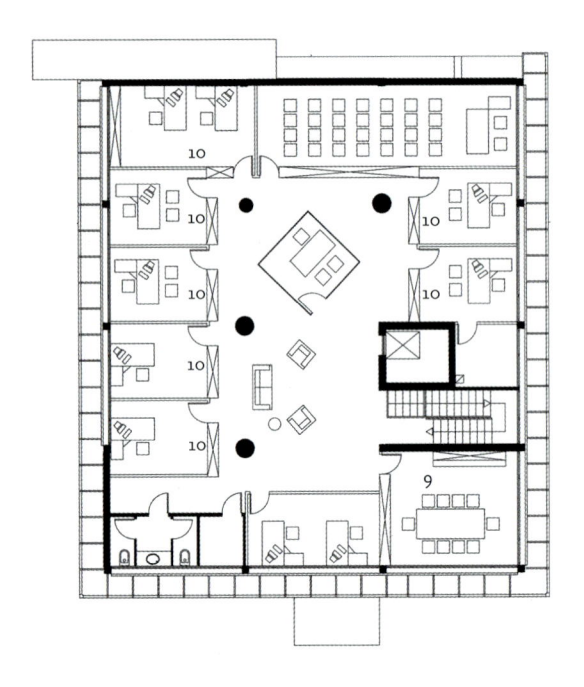

○ First floor plan

1. Living room
2. Offices
3. Vicedirector's office
4. Director's office
5. Secretary
6. Dispenser
7. Bathroom
8. Storage
9. Meeting room
10. Offices

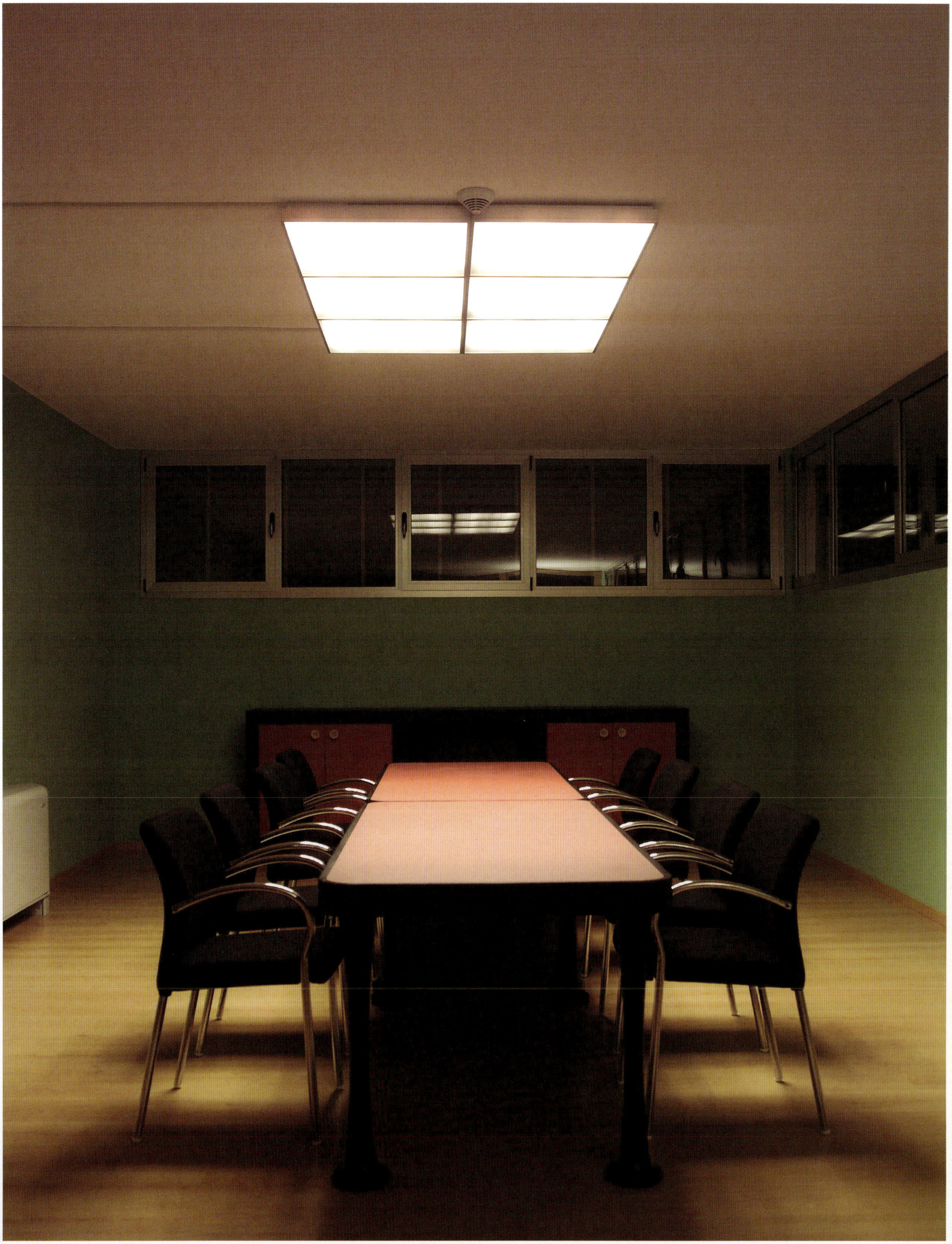

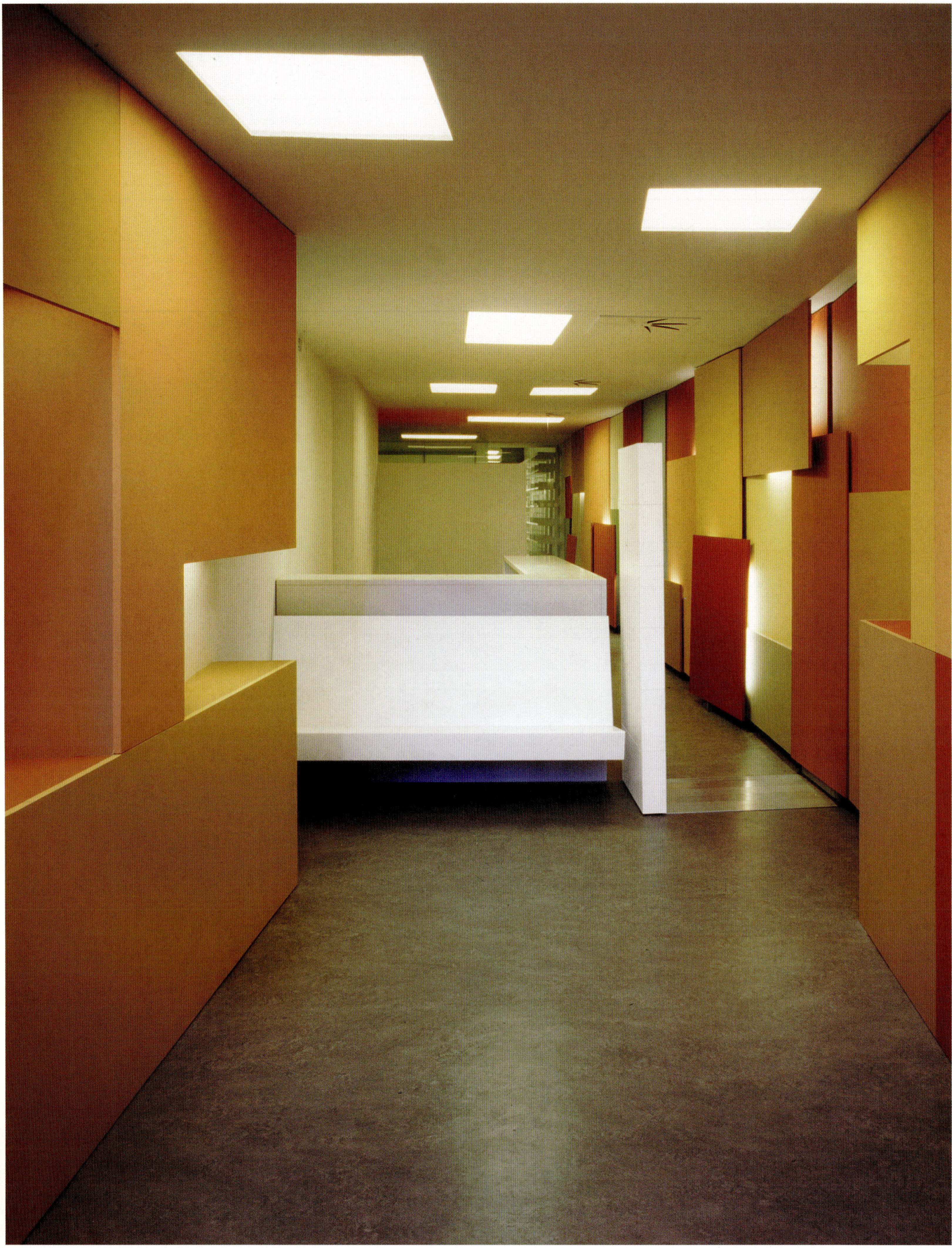

Institut Català de la Dona

A recently constructed building in the historical district of the Raval in Barcelona houses the head offices of the Institut Català de la Dona, which also includes their documentation center and the information office. The clients commissioned this building with the desire to show a unitary and flexible program, a building that is open to the public, is highly accessible, and improves communication. The tight budget for the offices meant specifying strict needs, which maintained the quality of the environment. These premises translated to elementary construction solutions such as linoleum flooring, a false plasterboard ceiling, fluorescent lighting, and mass-produced furniture.

The documentation center is composed of a lobby with a bench, a counter with two work spaces, a consultation and loans room, a reading area, and work zones for the internal personnel. The information office is composed of a lobby with reception desk and waiting room, private offices, and a visitors room.

The neutral work atmosphere in these offices is the result of the natural lighting of most of the interior area of the floor. The installation of various transparent glass walls in the light well— the walls, the library mezzanine, as well as in the information offices, the rest area and the kitchen— facilitates the diffusion of this light to all corners of the floor plan. Artificial lighting then provides different intensities of light, which help to identify the different spaces. Beams of light emerge from the MDF boards distributed irregularly as cladding for the dividing walls, and which form cupboards, storage space, etc.

This neutrality is accentuated through the design's light colors. The entire composition forms an abstract combination, which is visible from all the work stations, whose palette is composed of the basic Mediterranean colors.

Architect/Designer:
Agustí Costa

Client: Generalitat de Catalunya. Departament de la Presidència.
Photographer: Eugeni Pons
Location: Barcelona, Spain
Completion date: 2004
Area: 7,395 SF

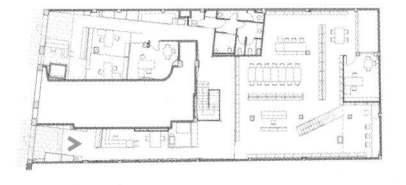

INSTITUT CATALÀ DE LA DONA

● The white tables and shelves are from the Pey collection. The MDF-board counters and benches are finished in a gloss gray-white, which reveals the wood beneath. The chairs are from Jorge Pensi.

INSTITUT CATALÀ DE LA DONA
265

INSTITUT CATALÀ DE LA DONA

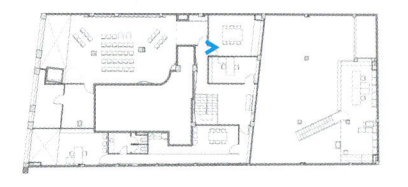

INSTITUT CATALÀ DE LA DONA

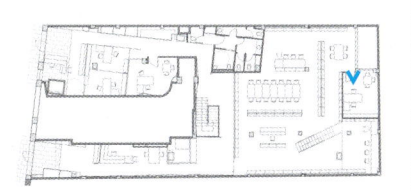

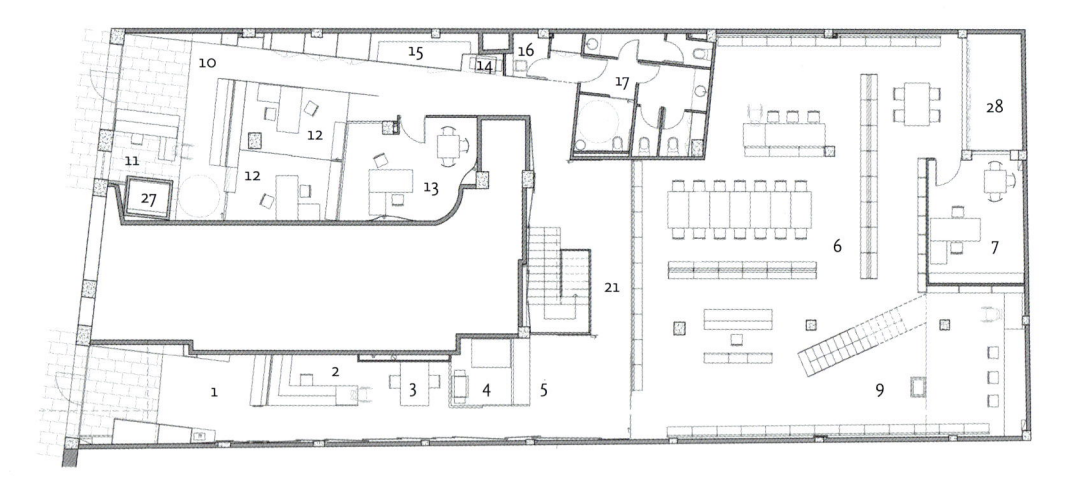

INSTITUT CATALÀ DE LA DONA

Documentation center
1. Vestibule
2. Reception area
3. Information panel
4. Public copier
5. Quick research
6. Library
7. Manager's office
8. Cataloging
9. Book left

Information Office
10. Vestibule
11. Reception area
12. Consultation desk
13. Coordinator's office
14. Copier
15. Storage
16. Utility closet
17. Public services
18. Psychologist's office
19. Legal advisors
20. Visitors room

Common Spaces
21. Vestibule
22. Multi-purpuse room
23. Break room
24. Kitchen
25. Staff services
26. Mechanical room
27. Elevator
28. Lightwell

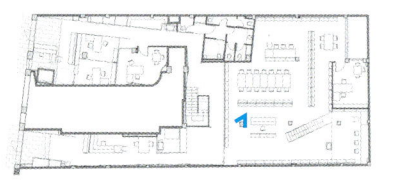

● Grand floor plan

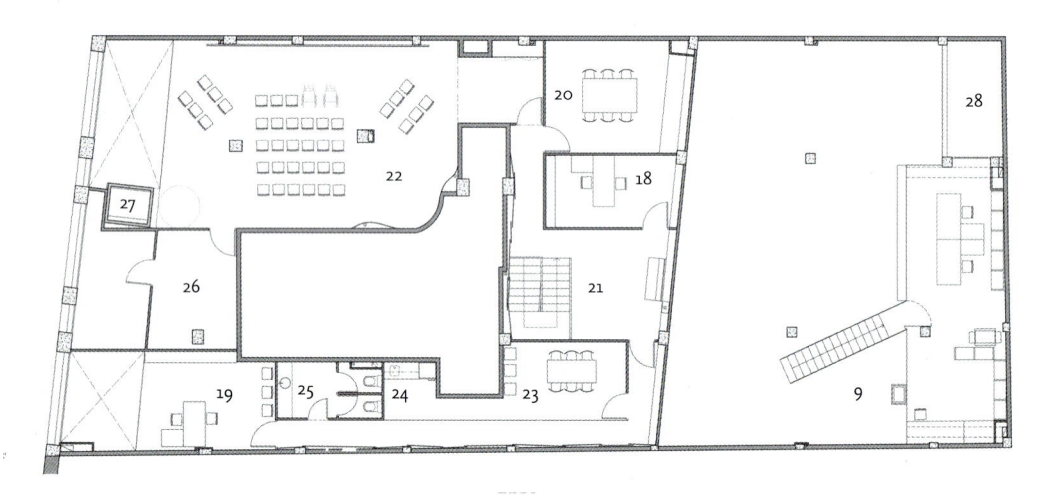

● First floor plan

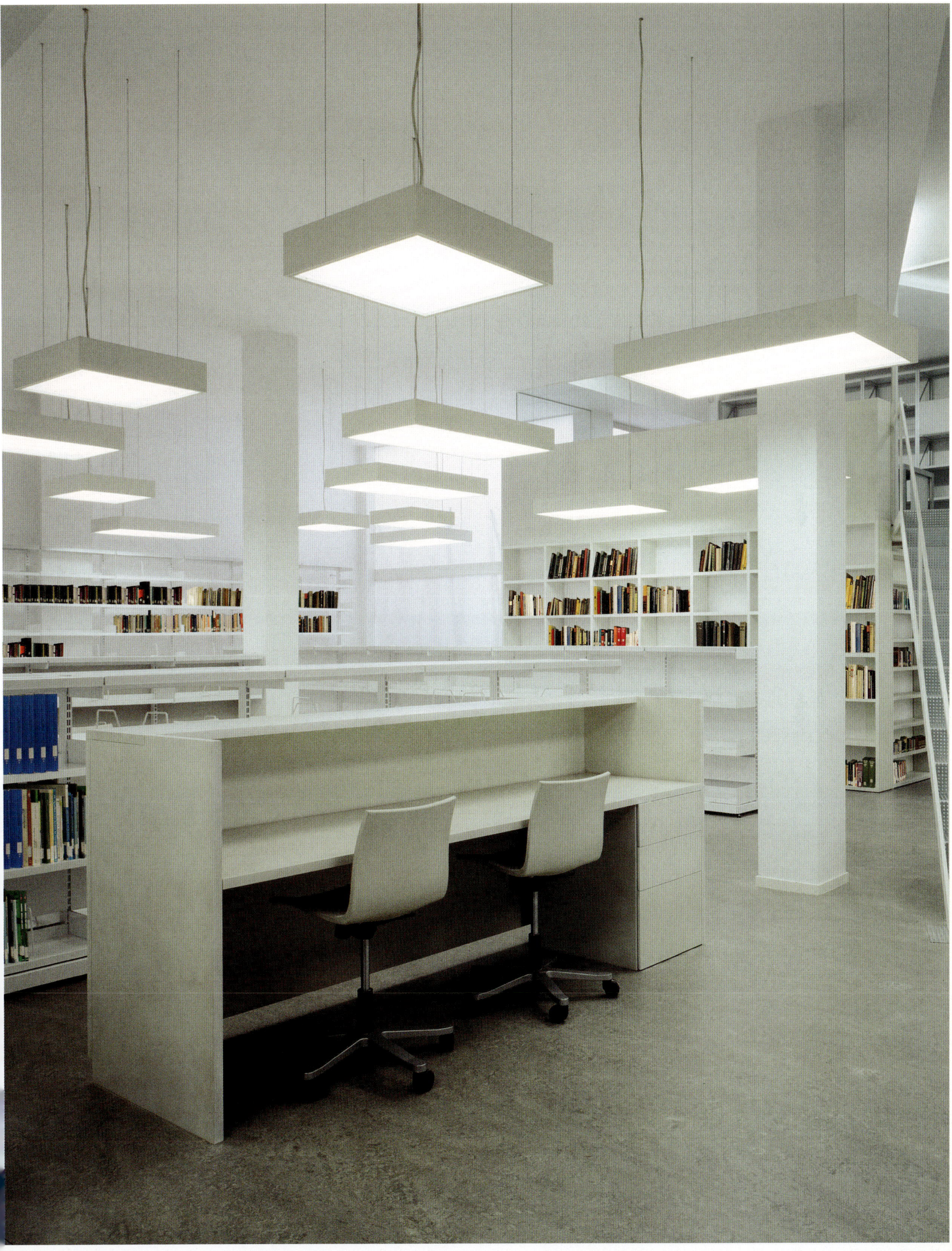

INSTITUT CATALÀ DE LA DONA

- On the shelves of the library, the Gama system has been used, without a wood panel finish and painted white. The false ceiling is made of plasterboard with specially designed light boxes, which lie flush to the ceiling.

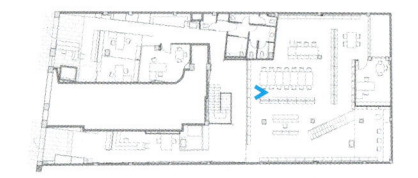

INSTITUT CATALÀ DE LA DONA

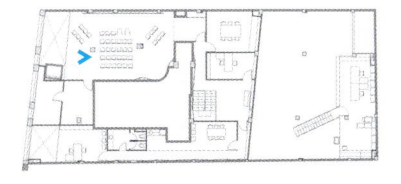

HARRISON & WO

Harrison & Wolf Offices

ARCHITECT/DESIGNER: BERNARD ASTOR/SAGUEZ & PARTNERS

Client: Harrison & Wolf
Photographer: Olivier Seignette, Mikaël Lafrontan
Location: Levallois-Perret, France
Completion date: 2005
Area: 7,428 SF

The client, a communications consultancy founded in 1999, commissioned the agency with the creation of their new offices in this Parisian suburb. The projected has developed from five key ideas. The first of these is to provide a pleasant environment to live and work in, and one which connects with nature. This is why the designers have developed the space as a seed, which grows into a floor plan, offering 'fruits' as it expands.

The second idea was to develop a plan based on the quality of the spaces for the home and on the functionality and organization of the circulation areas. To carry this out the spaces were reorganized in accordance with their uses and the reception was taken as the backbone to the project. The space is divided into two sections: the left-hand side has been reserved for design and the right-hand side for the consultancy and management. Numerous partitions have been designed that serve both as storage space and to separate the different areas. This provides structure and improves the circulation areas.

The third idea was the creation of the different areas through the materials, colors, and plays of light. Lights were hung above the offices to optimize the work environment. Thought is the guiding principle behind the consultancy and has been portrayed with leaves and shoots, and has also lead to the choice of sober colors. The main colors in the offices, however, are raspberry red, lemon yellow and pumpkin orange.

The fourth idea consisted of paying attention to the smallest details by putting up pictures, vases, and plants that personalize the space, maximize comfort, and provide quality of life. The last idea was to stick to budget and make all this compatible with the creation of a tranquil and silent work space that favors concentration.

The spaces allow for multiple functions, which correspond to the activities of the company: creativity, thought, discovery, and communication.

HARRISON & WOLF OFFICES

● The different heights, perspectives, and transparencies result in an open-plan space, where the private areas and spaces for communal activities combine with silent work areas.

HARRISON & WOLF OFFICES

HARRISON & WOLF OFFICES

HARRISON & WOLF OFFICES

● The installation of colored panels offers the space structure, reflects the light from outside, and brings life and color to the place. Some of them reproduce photographic details of vegetation.

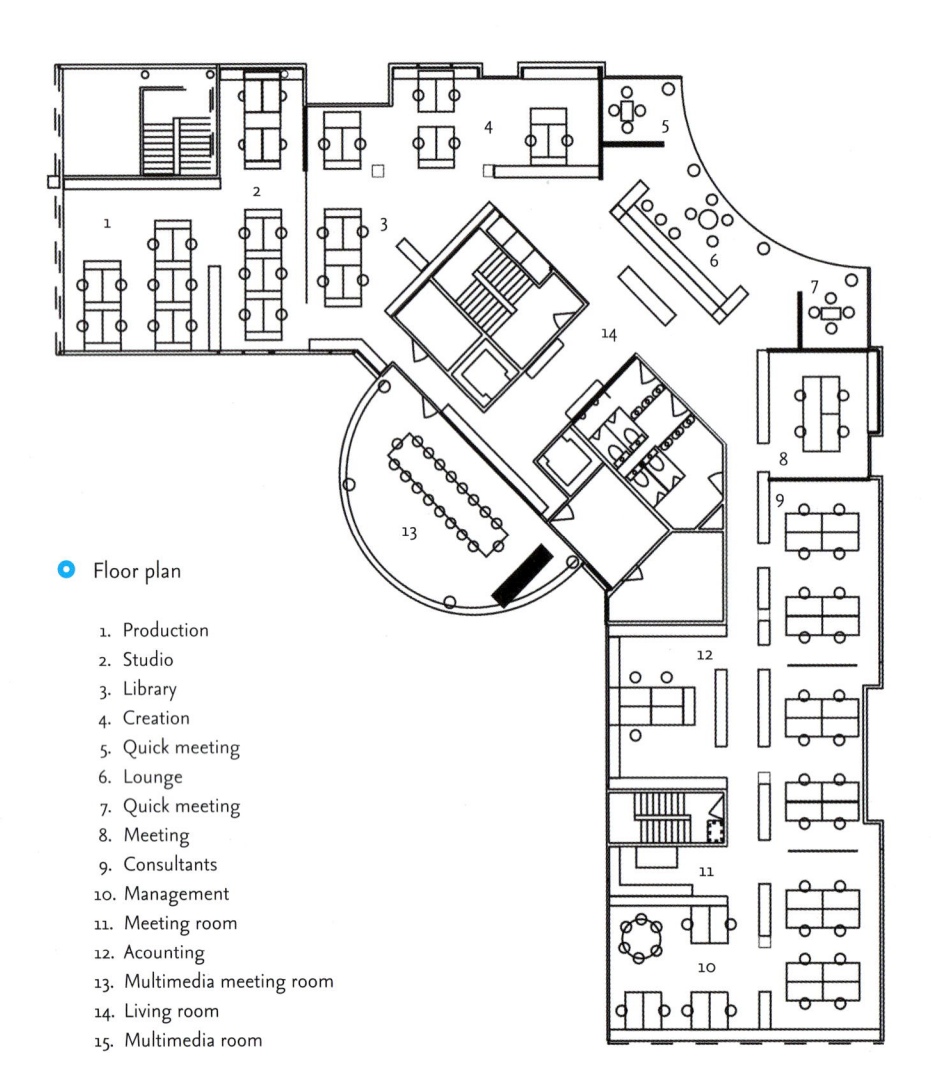

HARRISON & WOLF OFFICES

- Floor plan

    1. Production
    2. Studio
    3. Library
    4. Creation
    5. Quick meeting
    6. Lounge
    7. Quick meeting
    8. Meeting
    9. Consultants
    10. Management
    11. Meeting room
    12. Acounting
    13. Multimedia meeting room
    14. Living room
    15. Multimedia room

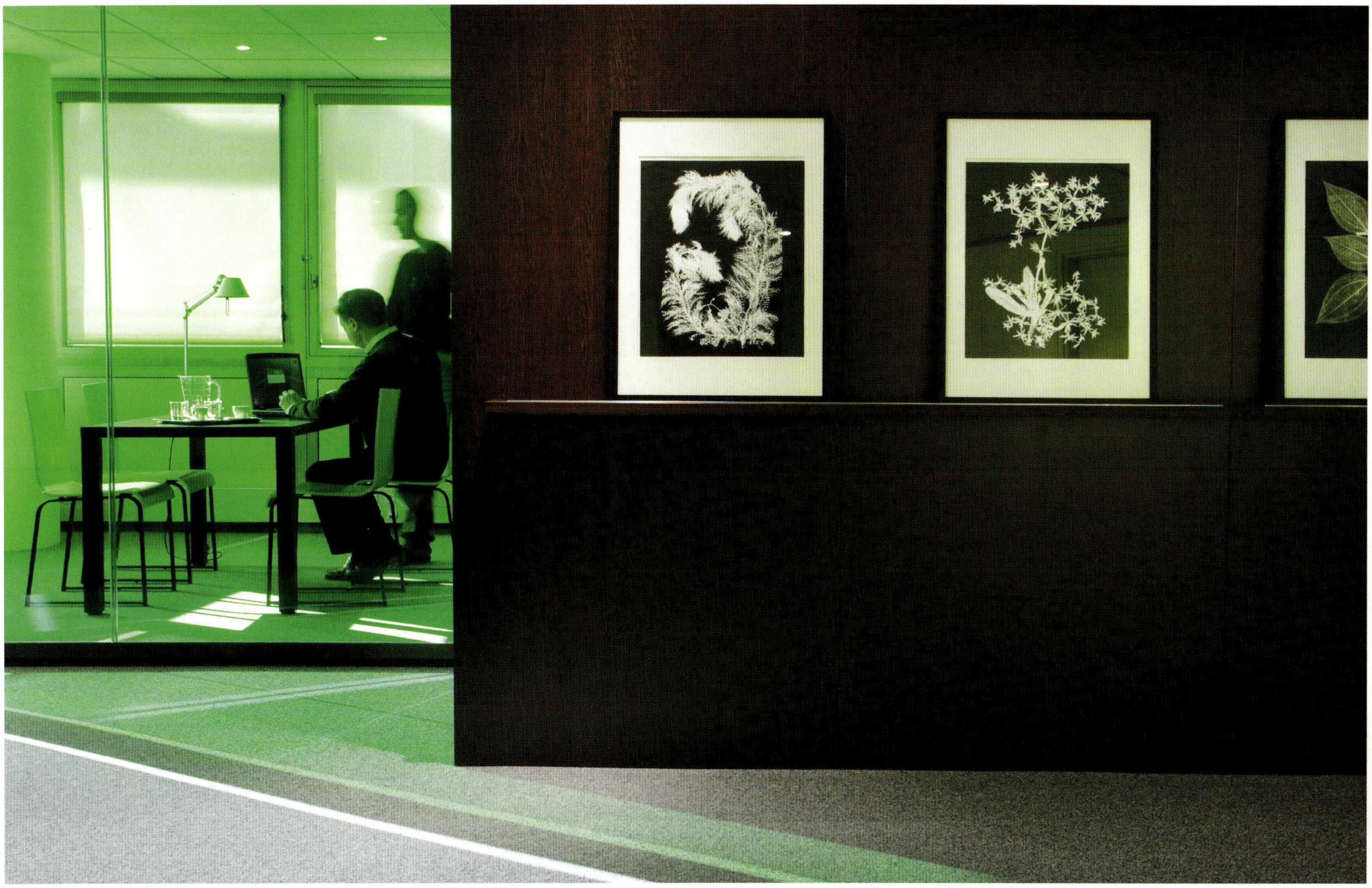

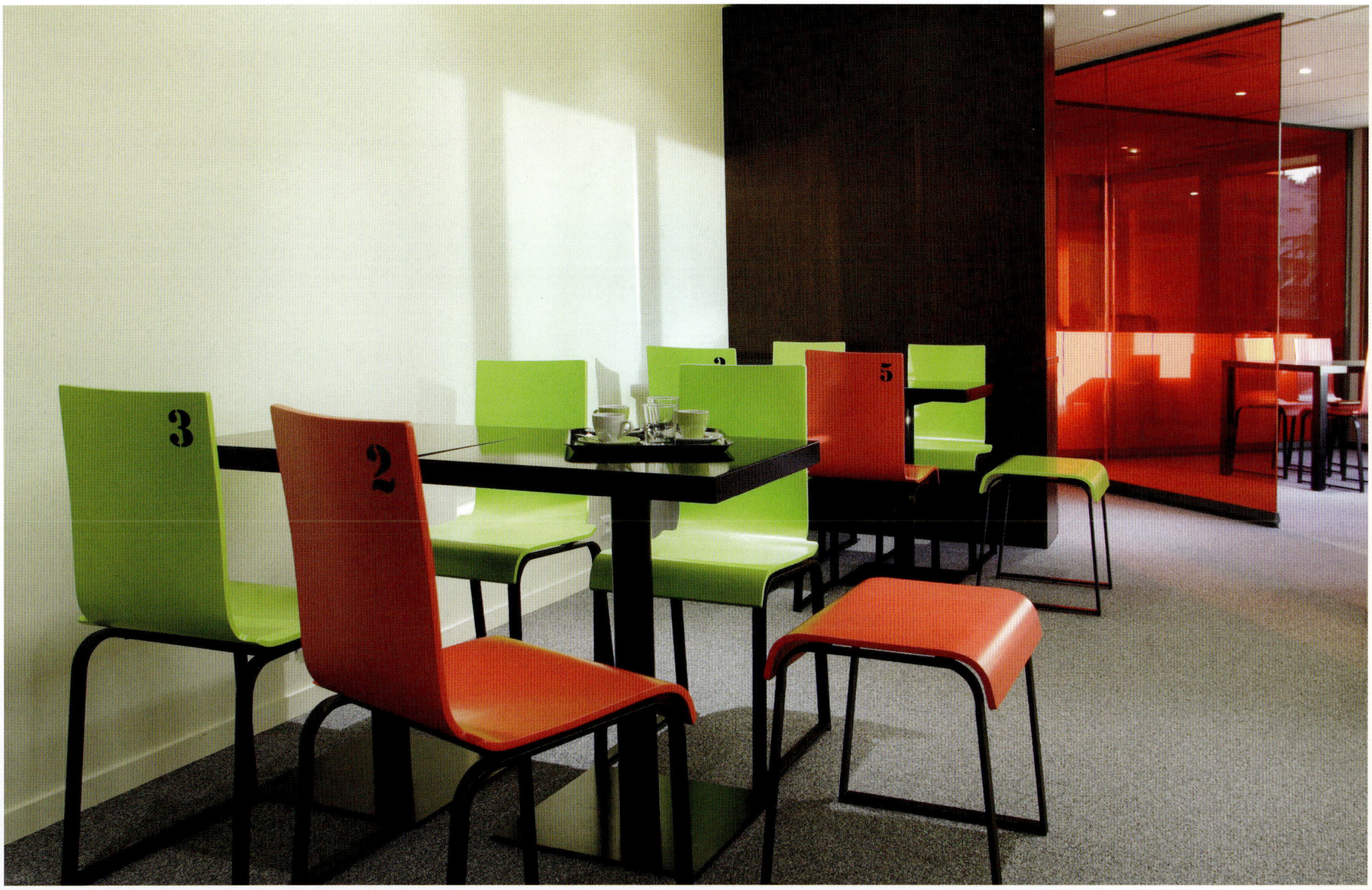
3
2
5

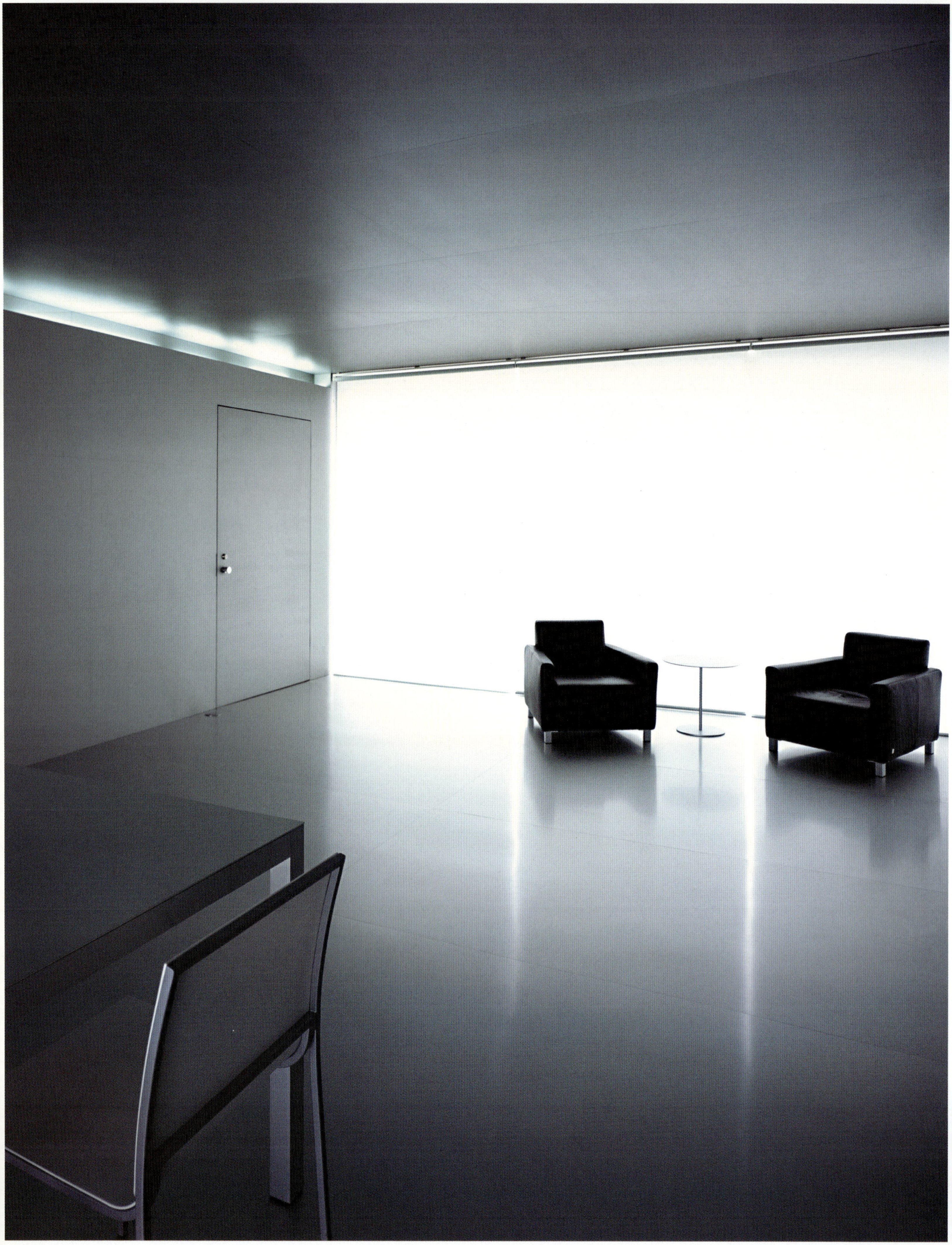

Metal Office

The Kansai Science City aspires to be a complex of gigantic proportions dedicated to research into environmental technology. The site occupied by this project, an office building, is located in the middle of the hills of lush vegetation between Kioto and Osaka, an area rich in history, culture, and natural beauty. A luxurious residential complex has been built nearby.

In the ten feet of height difference on the slope between the access road and the building the architect has designed a garden where bamboo has been planted parallel to the building. This allows the vegetation to act as a boundary to the building's access. A hedge planted at the back establishes a boundary with the adjacent property and hides the parking, located at a lower level.

The company, an importer of precision metal parts, required a building that represented its corporate image and that drew inspiration from the parts it worked with. This is why the architect conceived the building as a mass of metal, with its outer walls, like the floors and ceilings, clad in metal panels. To make the building more noticeable from the road, on its top floor there is a metal block supported by translucent glass so that the block appears to be floating.

The office features the lobby and a showroom at street level; a gallery on the middle level, which serves as a large work area, and two spaces inside the metal block. The lower of the two connects with the route that leads to the parking, and the upper level is a conference room boasting spectacular views.

Together this environment is both functional and comfortable. The aesthetics play with notions of open and closed spaces and the people who work here move between striking contrasts, with the surrounding natural beauty almost constantly on display.

Architect/Designer:

Takashi Yamaguchi & Associates

Client: Dynamic Tools Office
Photographer: Takashi Yamaguchi & Associates
Location: Soraku-gun, Kyoto, Japan
Area: 8,654 SF

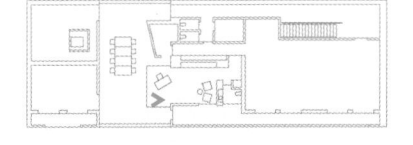

METAL OFFICE
282

● In order to encourage creativity among the people who work in this company, the architect has maximized the visual communication between the interior and the nature outside.

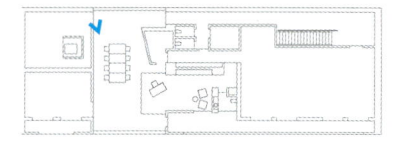

METAL OFFICE
283

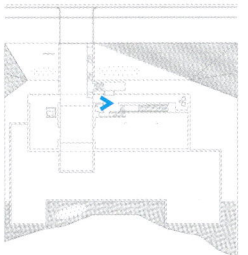

METAL OFFICE

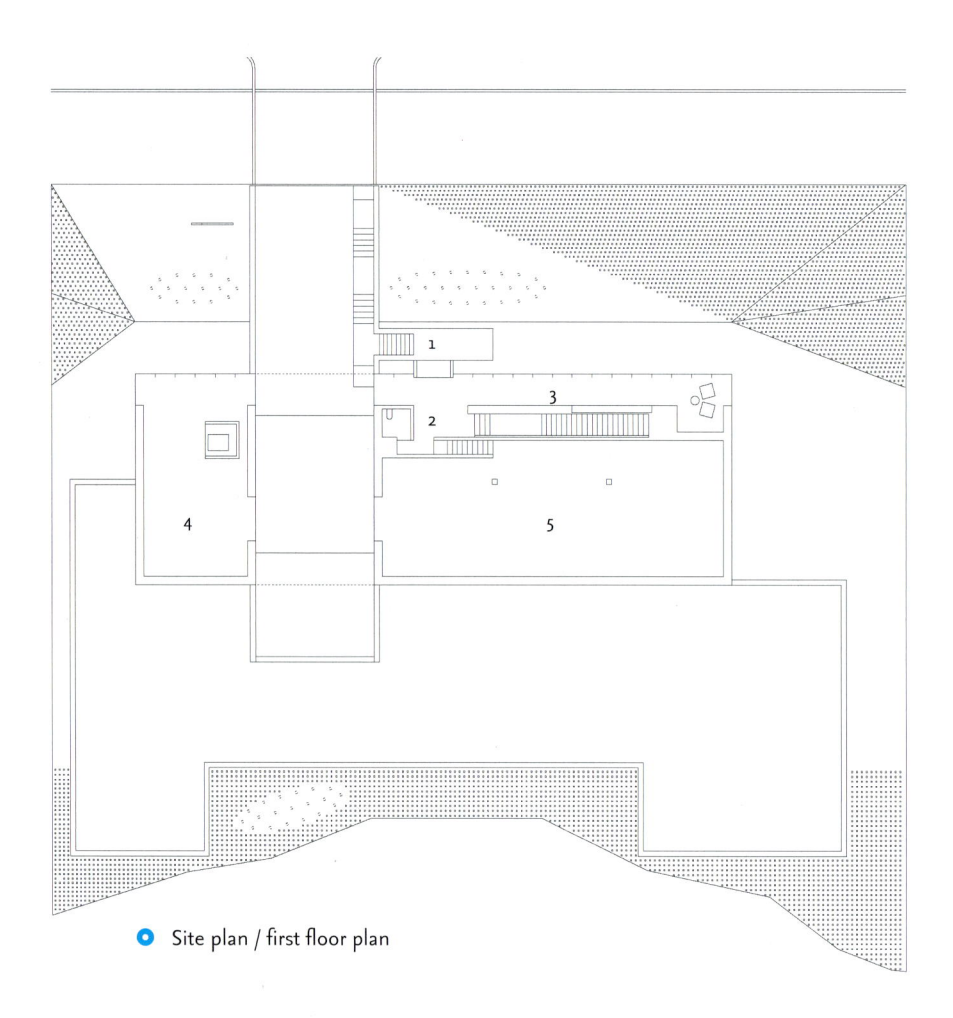

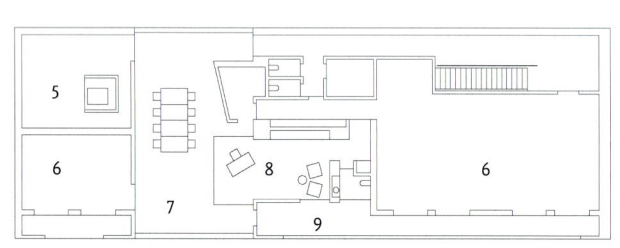

- Site plan / first floor plan

- Second floor plan

1. Entrance
2. Entrance hall
3. Showroom
4. Laboratory
5. Storage
6. Office
7. Conference room
8. President's office
9. Balcony

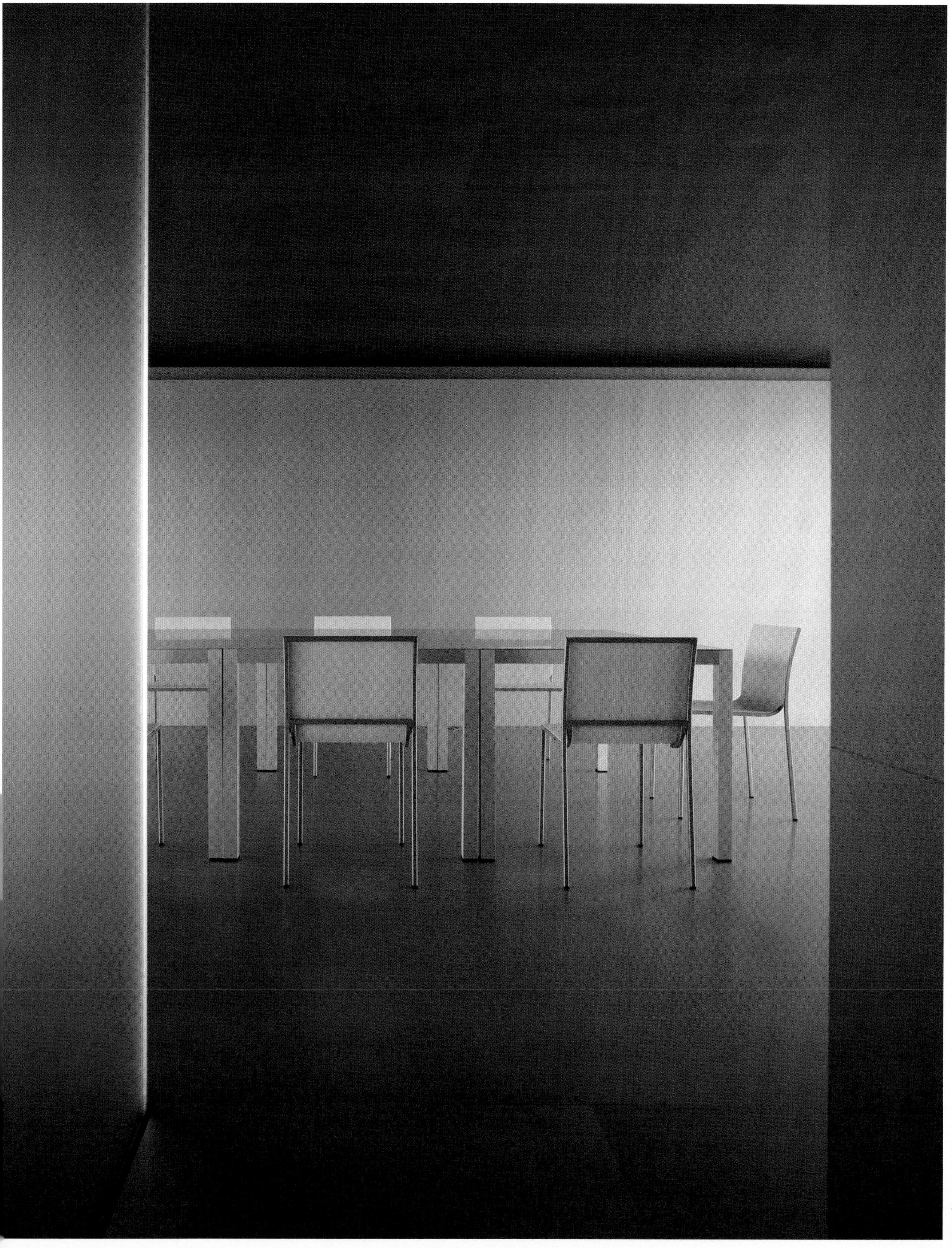

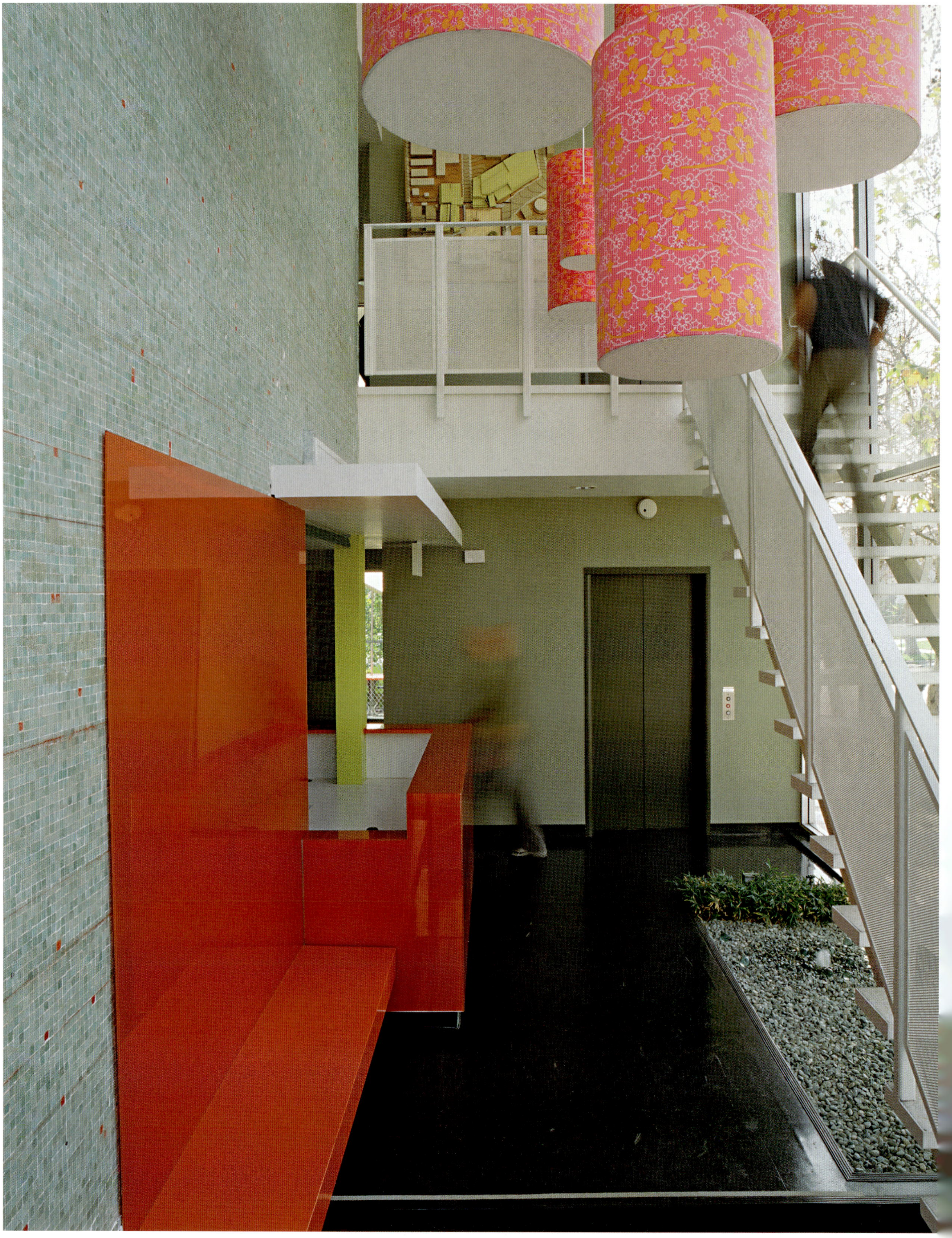

RIOS CLEMENTI HALE STUDIOS OFFICE

ARCHITECT/DESIGNER: RIOS CLEMENTI HALE STUDIOS

Client: Rios Clementi Hale Studios
Photographer: Tom Bonner
Location: Los Angeles
Completion date: 2003
Area: 9,000 SF

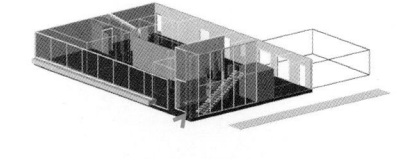

The architect has carried out this project for himself, located in an abandoned industrial building on busy Melrose Avenue in Los Angeles. It is an office custom designed to meet his needs. The layout joins and differentiates the different spaces, relating to the open and multi-disciplinary character of the firm. The resulting, environment is both informal and ideal for teamwork. It is at once open and intimate, a place where ideas can circulate and influence each other.

All this has developed on two floors of the building, a construction from the fifties whose main façade has been restored with glass, as a symbol of the openness towards the surrounding artistic community. A grid of windows, made from four different types of glass, from transparent to opaque, facilitates the natural lighting of the interior and shows the activity that is taking place inside to passers-by.

The keys to the interior design were color and creativity, in keeping with the fifties style of the original structure. Thus, in the lobby the brickwork has been removed that concealed the green and orange mosaic on the side wall, and the white terrazzo on the floor has been exposed. In keeping with these elements, the tabletop for the counter is orange-tinted glass and next to the stairs that lead to the top floor is a fountain with bright green rocks. The adjacent garden, which is visible from the lobby, can be accessed from the meeting room and rare species have been planted there.

The work area, also on this floor, has space for six work stations, delineated as compartments. These offer seclusion to develop the different projects as well as promote communication with the other members of the team. The wall opposite the windows is occupied by a display where images from various works-in-progress are shown.

On the top floor, where there is less available surface area, a library has been installed.

RIOS CLEMENTI HALE STUDIOS OFFICE

- A typical color scheme from the fifties characterizes the interior. The orange of the original wall in the lobby extends into the glass on the reception desk and above into the shelves of the library.

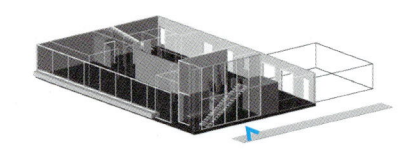

RIOS CLEMENTI HALE STUDIOS OFFICE

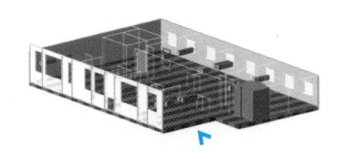

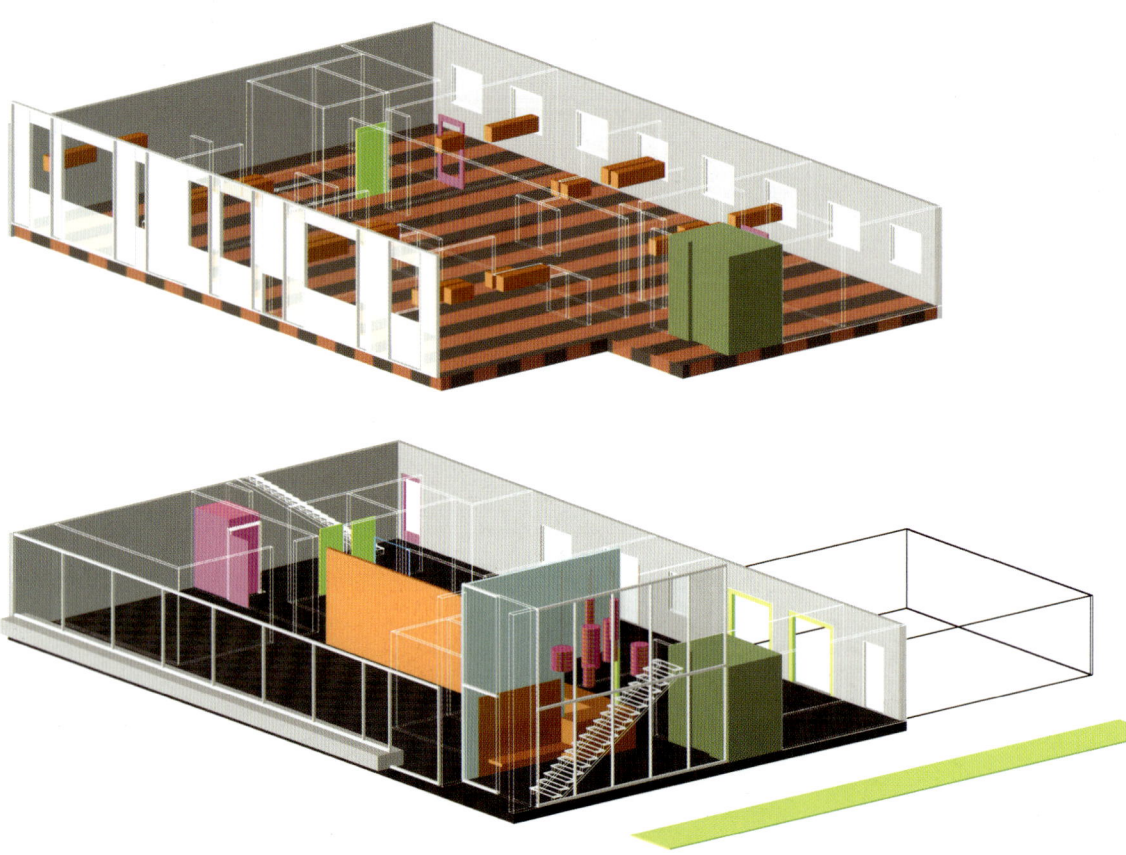

RIOS CLEMENTI HALE STUDIOS OFFICE

● Plans color diagrams

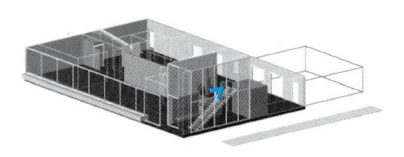

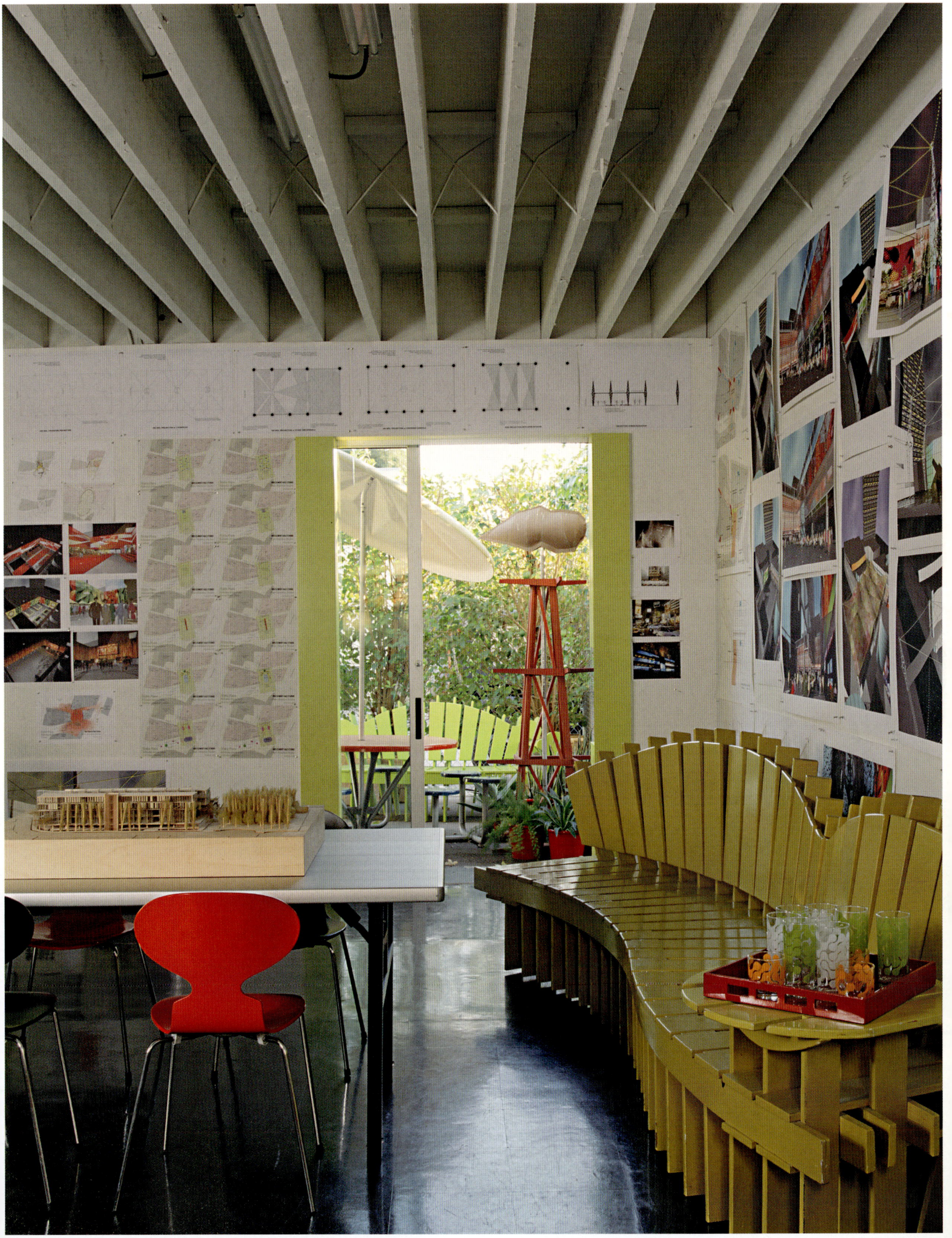

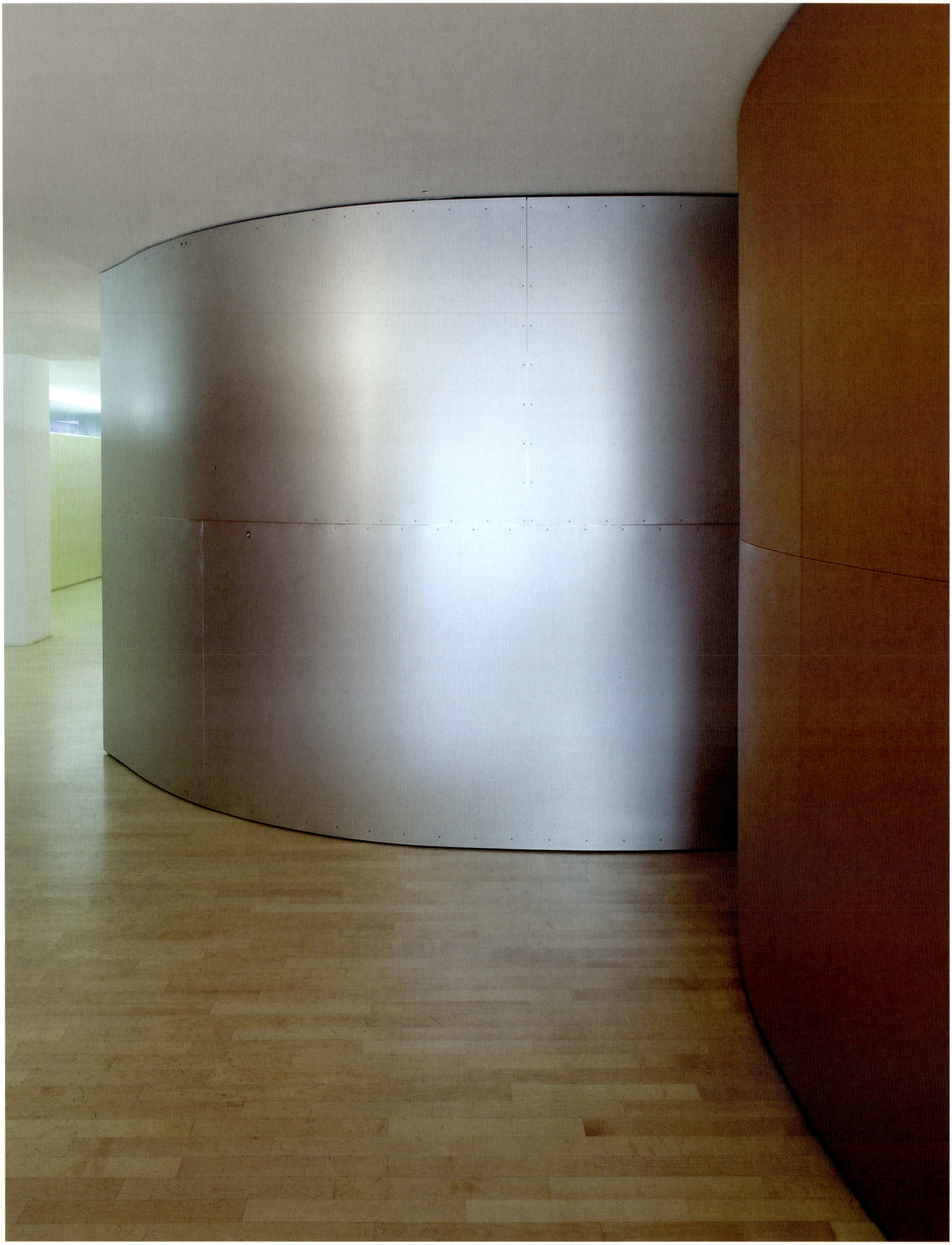

Hidm.Office Vienna

ARCHITECT/DESIGNER:

LICHTBLAU.WAGNER ARCHITEKTEN

Client: Lawyer's office vienna 7
Photographer: Bruno Klomfar
Location: Vienna, Austria
Completion date: 2003
Area: 9,149 SF

A group of young, recently graduated lawyers are the clients for this project for a modern, dynamic, and functional office.

The program consists of the reception area, a small waiting room for clients, two meeting rooms, and eighteen individual offices for the lawyers and other staff. Both the parquet floor and many other components of the project are wooden, which overall is the dominant material.

Curved lines characterize the design in the office's interior. They are present in the partition walls that divide the different spaces. Wood is also found in the large panels that make the partitions, which match the floor thanks to their different shades. The partition that separates the main meeting room is the most striking of all, because of its cladding of aluminum panels.

The columns from the original structure have been preserved and used as an element around which the different offices and other spaces have been distributed.

The original narrow, corner floor plan has become a space that conveys a sense of openness and size, thanks to the juxtaposition of the undulating partitions and the openings, which suggests limits yet does not visibly define them. In the circulation spaces, the undulations of the partitions widen the routes, and therefore the perceived dimensions of the space. The absence of doors in a lot of the rooms also enlarges the interior of these spaces, a goal that has been considered a priority in this project, with respect to privacy.

The artificial lighting has been distributed profusely throughout the interior, which was very dark. Most of the general lighting is from indirect light, which replaces the effect of natural light.

Despite their limitations, these offices enjoy a privileged location in Mariahilfer, the most important commercial street in Vienna.

HIDM.OFFICE VIENNA

○ Wooden partitions separate the work stations while another clad in aluminum panels offers access to the meeting room. Their forms enlarge the space and make the presence of doors unnecessary.

HIDM.OFFICE VIENNA
295

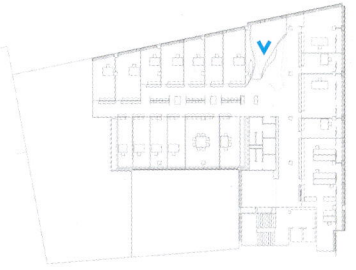

HIDM.OFFICE VIENNA

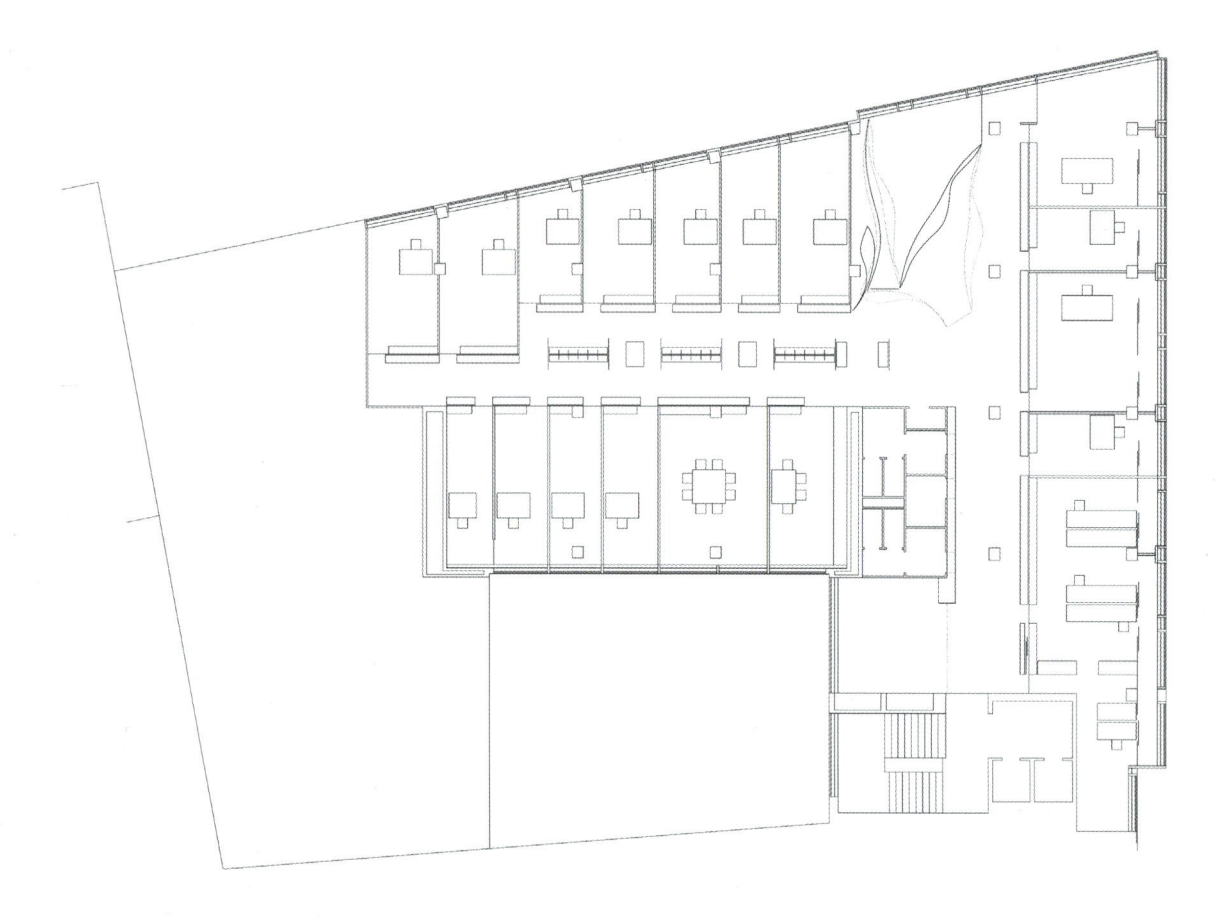

● Floor plan

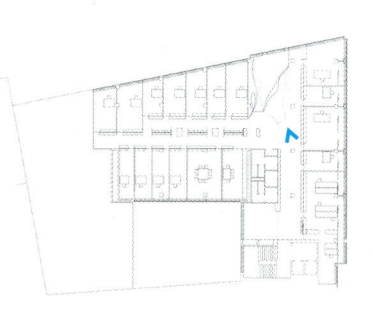

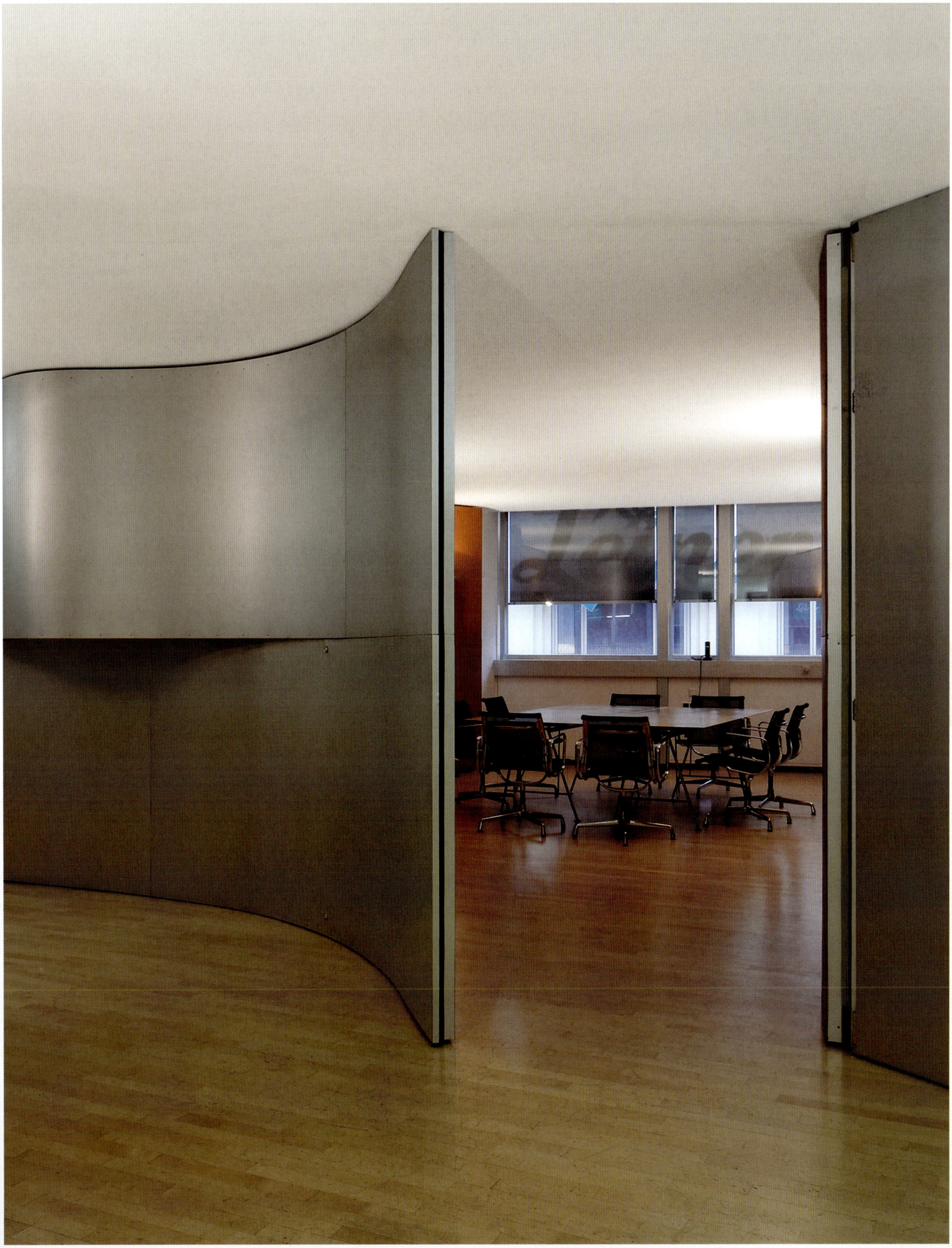

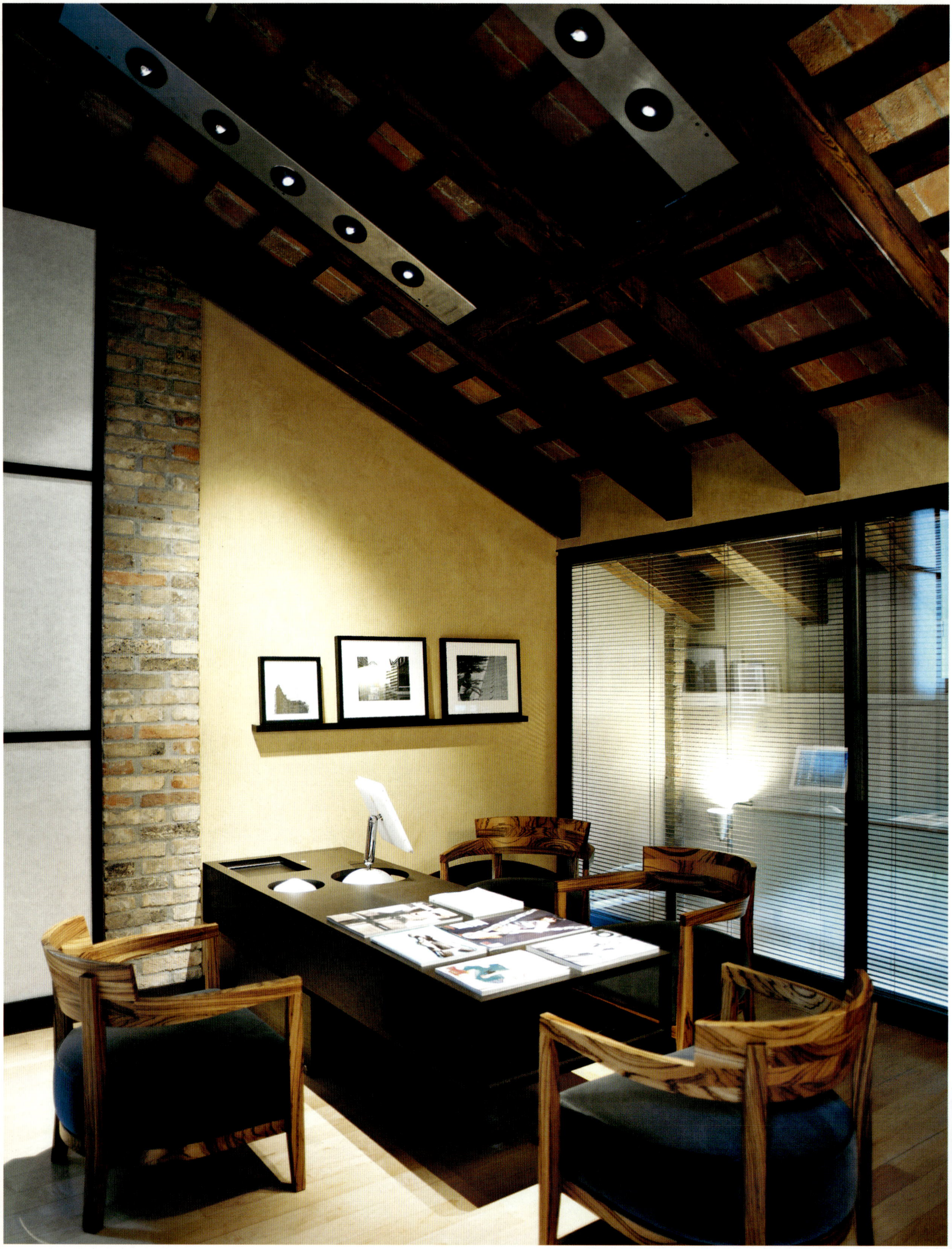

Hangar Design Group Headquarter

Architect/Designer:
Hangar Design Group

Client: Hangar Design Group
Photographer: Alvise Silenzi, Photo Lab HDG
Location: Mogliano Veneto, Italy
Completion date: 2006
Area: 9,688 SF

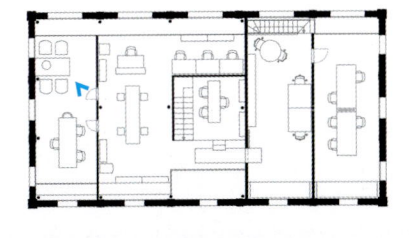

This project is located in the city of Mogliano Veneto, in two twin buildings initially built in the early twentieth century for military use, and subsequently used as a barn and crafts workshop. The building has been renovated to house the offices and production spaces for an advertising and communication agency.

The steel, brick and cement exterior has been maintained, with restoration work carried out where needed; along with the pitched roof with wooden beams, which converts the roof areas of the inserted floor into loft spaces.

The project's starting point was to double the available surface area via the insertion of a floating floor, separated from the original structure, in order to avoid cutting into the large windows on the façade. A staircase connects the two levels.

The layout adheres to a modern space structure in accordance with its creative function, instead of by hierarchies within the organization. Places conceived for interaction have been distributed like capillaries between the individual offices. They include: a library, several rest areas, a room for receiving clients, various meeting rooms, and places for group work around large tables. There is also a flowerbed in the garden, to be used both for group meetings and individual work. All these spaces, designed to facilitate both formal and informal meetings, comprise 40 percent of the available surface area.

Throughout the office, numerous discrete storage and filing spaces have been distributed with the aim of keeping the place in order. The separating walls have been limited to where they are strictly necessary so that the space is as open as possible and the only clearly separate spaces are the reception area and the management office.

On either side of the private road, which leads to the buildings, there are staff parking spaces.

HANGAR DESIGN GROUP HEADQUARTER

- The project revitalizes the building's original aesthetics: it preserves the steel, brick, and cement exterior, and a level has been added that floats in the interior to avoid breaking up the façade windows.

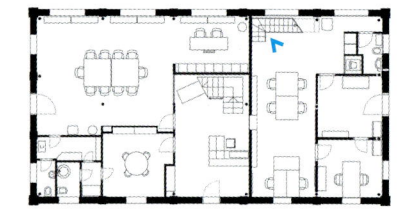

HANGAR DESIGN GROUP HEADQUARTER

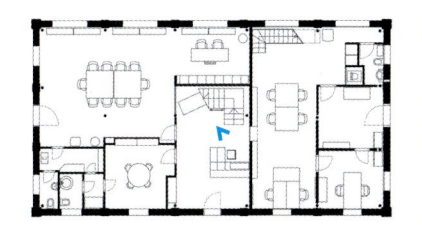

301

HANGAR DESIGN GROUP HEADQUARTER

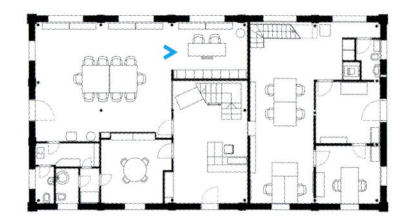

HANGAR DESIGN GROUP HEADQUARTER

HANGAR DESIGN GROUP HEADQUARTER

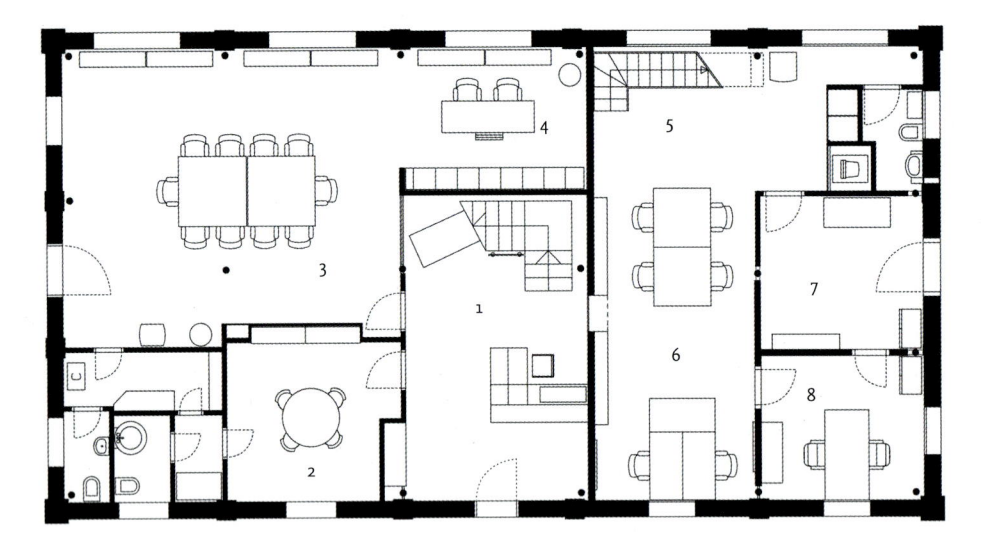

1. Reception area
2. Atelier
3. Meeting room
4. Library
5. Multipurpose area
6. Graphic (creative) area
7. Break area
8. Art direction area

Ground floor plan

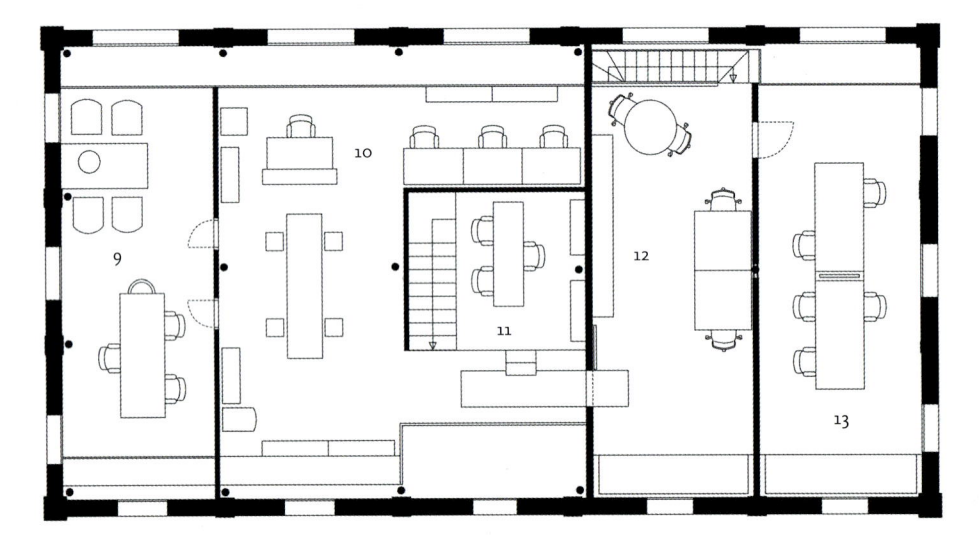

9. Executive area
10. Chairman assistant
11. Account
12. Press office
13. Web & multimedia department

First floor plan

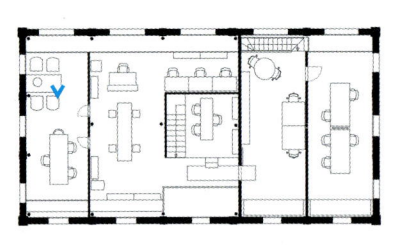

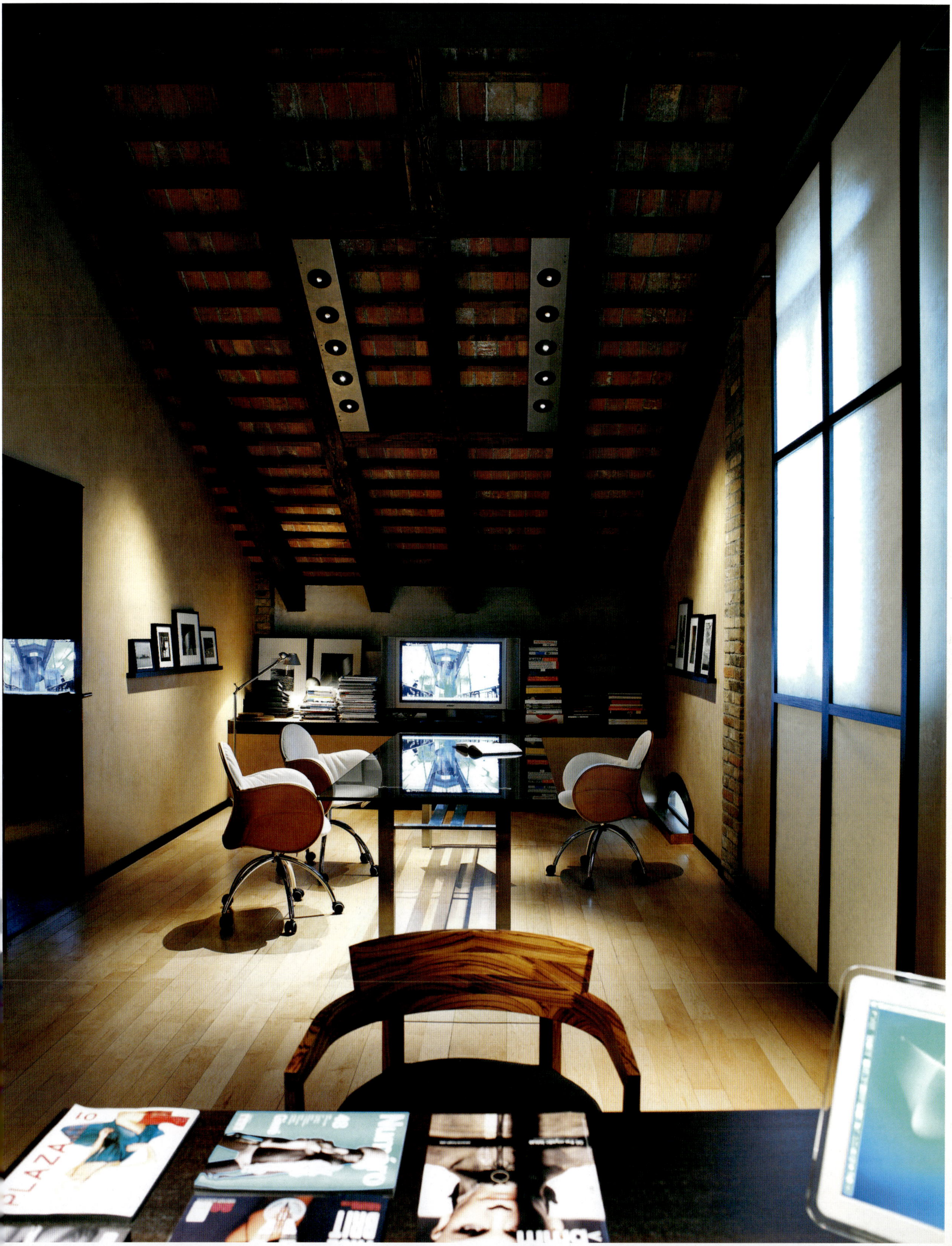
PLAZA

- The wooden beams that support the roof have been left visible. The warmth associated to wood is complemented with large armchairs and coffee tables for informal meetings.

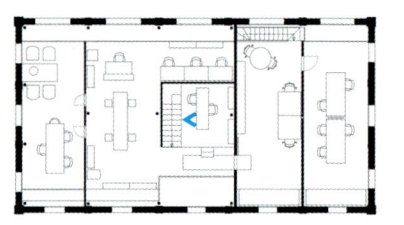

HANGAR DESIGN GROUP HEADQUARTER

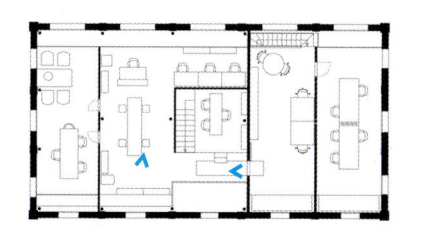

HANGAR DESIGN GROUP HEADQUARTER

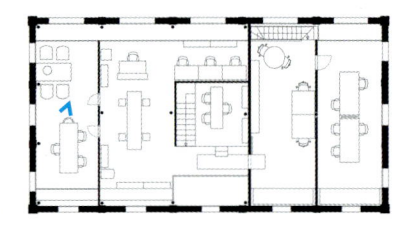

HANGAR DESIGN GROUP HEADQUARTER

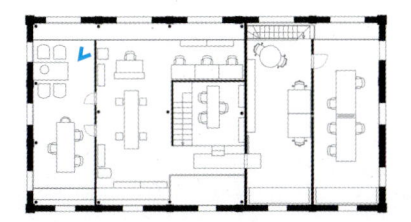

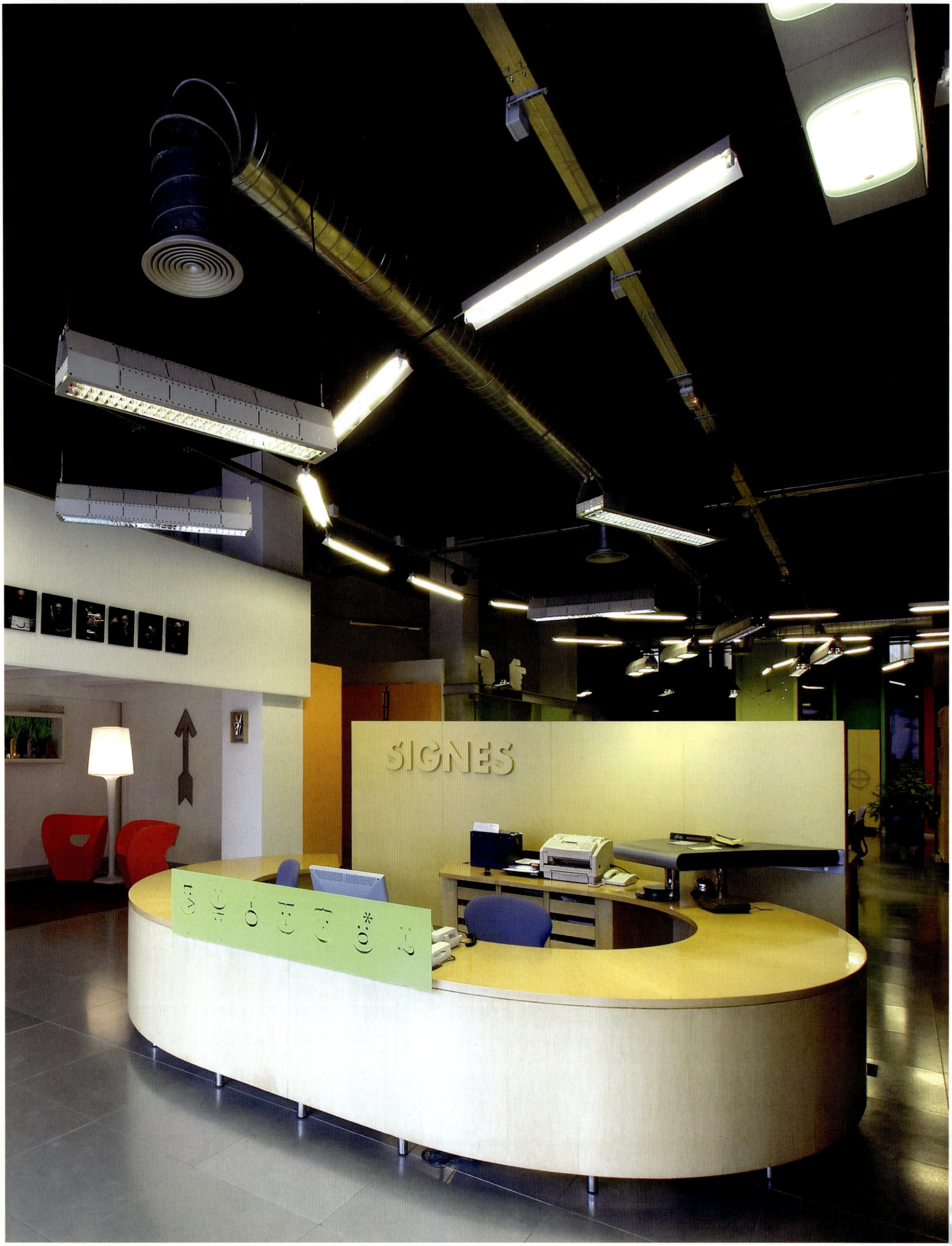
SIGNES

Signes Offices

The clients decided to unite all of the company's different activities, including offices, the studio, storage, the factory, and the vinyl workshop, in this industrial space located in the newest part of Hospitalet. They wanted a space with a homely feel to it, which would be familiar to both workers and visitors alike. As well as the characteristics required by the client, the interior design studio introduced industrialism and toughness for a company looking to the future. A clear combination of art and industry sums up the aesthetics here and demonstrates the firm's activity in graphics and design. The close friendship between the designer and the client was a decisive influence on the final result.

This new space is divided into a basement level for the factory and a ground floor that accommodates the studio, the reception area and the meeting rooms, and finally the large interior space for the offices and the vinyl workshop. Both floors are connected by escalators located between the entrance room and the meeting area.

The materials most used here are glass blocks, which facilitate the access to the offices, and the zinc sheets, which form the flooring of the ground floor. Wood is the dominant material, having been used extensively in the tables, shelving, and frames.

Maximizing the natural light was the prime concern behind this project. Natural light reaches through the interior thanks to the large access from the street and the large windows on the ground floor. The artificial lighting consists of the strategic location of light sources in concentric circles. This generates an idea of continual movement throughout the building. Color has been strategically distributed through the different areas, in order to individualize them.

The most important component of the design is the furniture. The absence of the dividing walls allows the furniture, created by the designer himself, to capture attention and accentuate the idea of dynamism.

ARCHITECT/DESIGNER:

JORDI TORRES

Client: Lluís Morón, Carmen Revilla/Signes
Photographer: Rafael Vargas
Location: Hospitalet de Llobregat, Spain
Completion date: 2005
Area: 10,764 SF

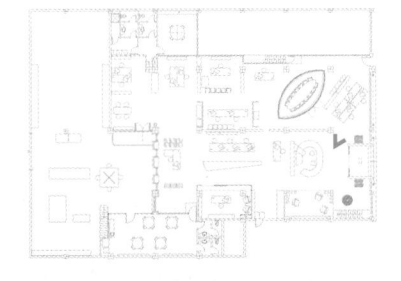

SIGNES OFFICES

- The meeting room is oval shaped and its partitions are made from curved pieces of glass framed in cedar wood. The transparency of the material is supposed to symbolize the transparency of communication.

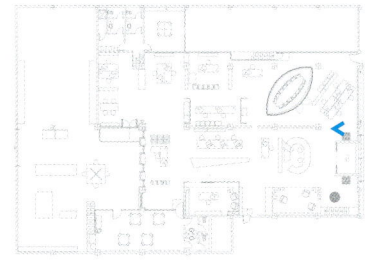

SIGNES OFFICES
313

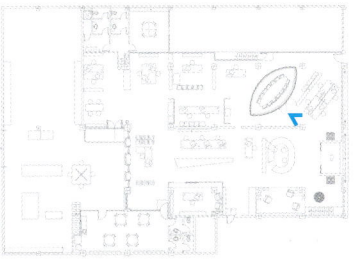

SIGNES OFFICES

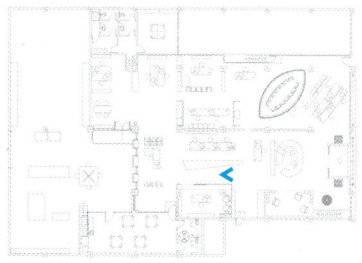

SIGNES OFFICES
315

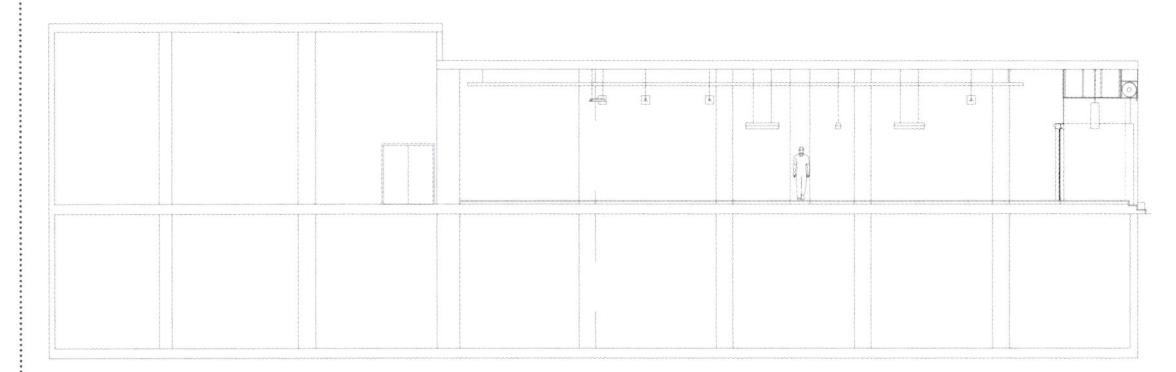

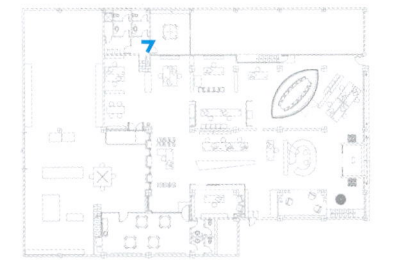

○ The wide palette of colors acts as a dividing element for the spaces. The furniture helps to create a dynamic environment which seeks an urban look without forgetting nature, hence the ornamental plants.

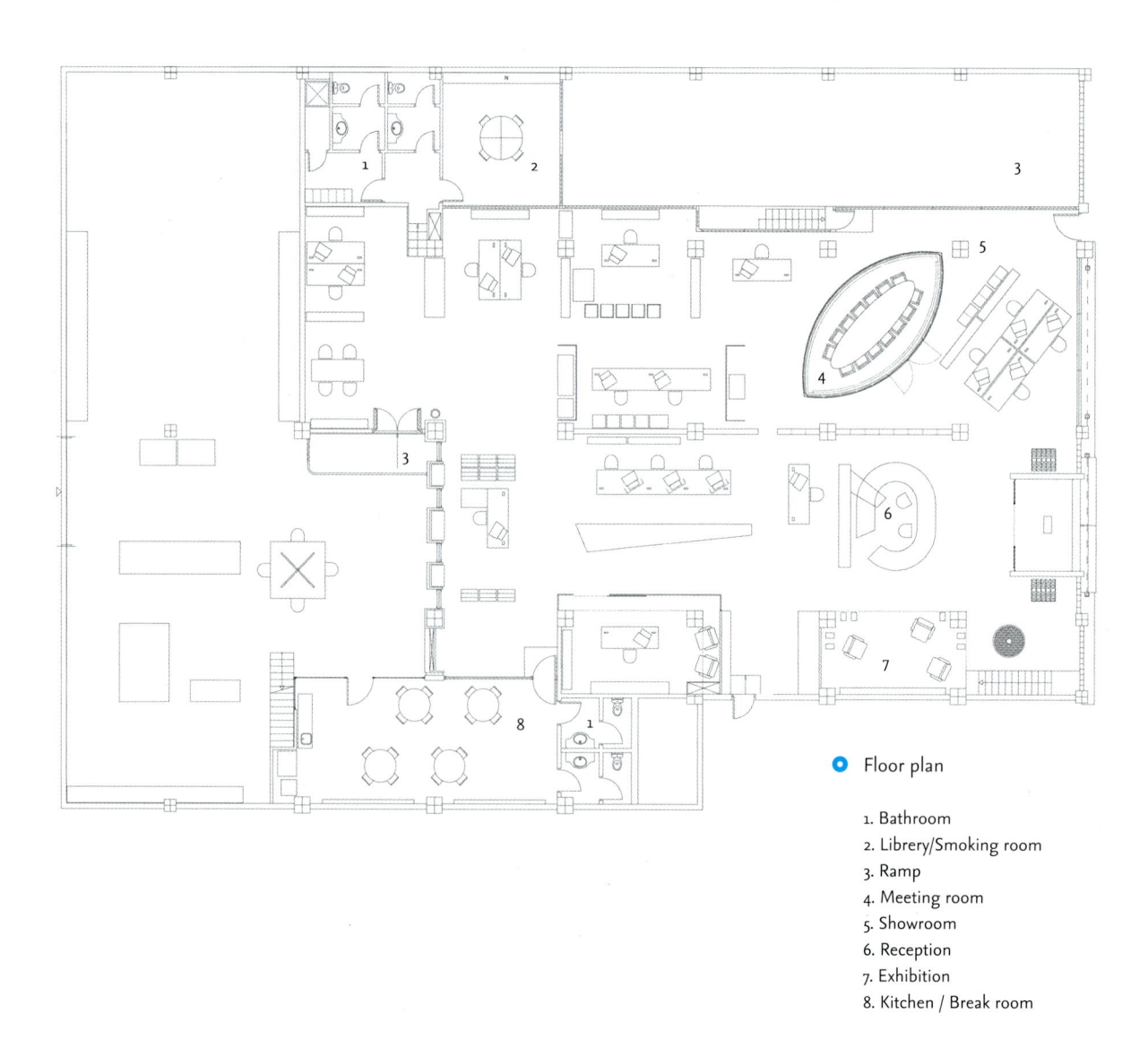

SIGNES OFFICES

● Floor plan

1. Bathroom
2. Librery/Smoking room
3. Ramp
4. Meeting room
5. Showroom
6. Reception
7. Exhibition
8. Kitchen / Break room

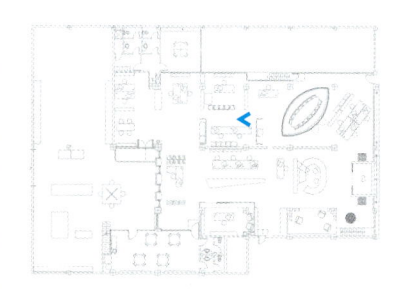

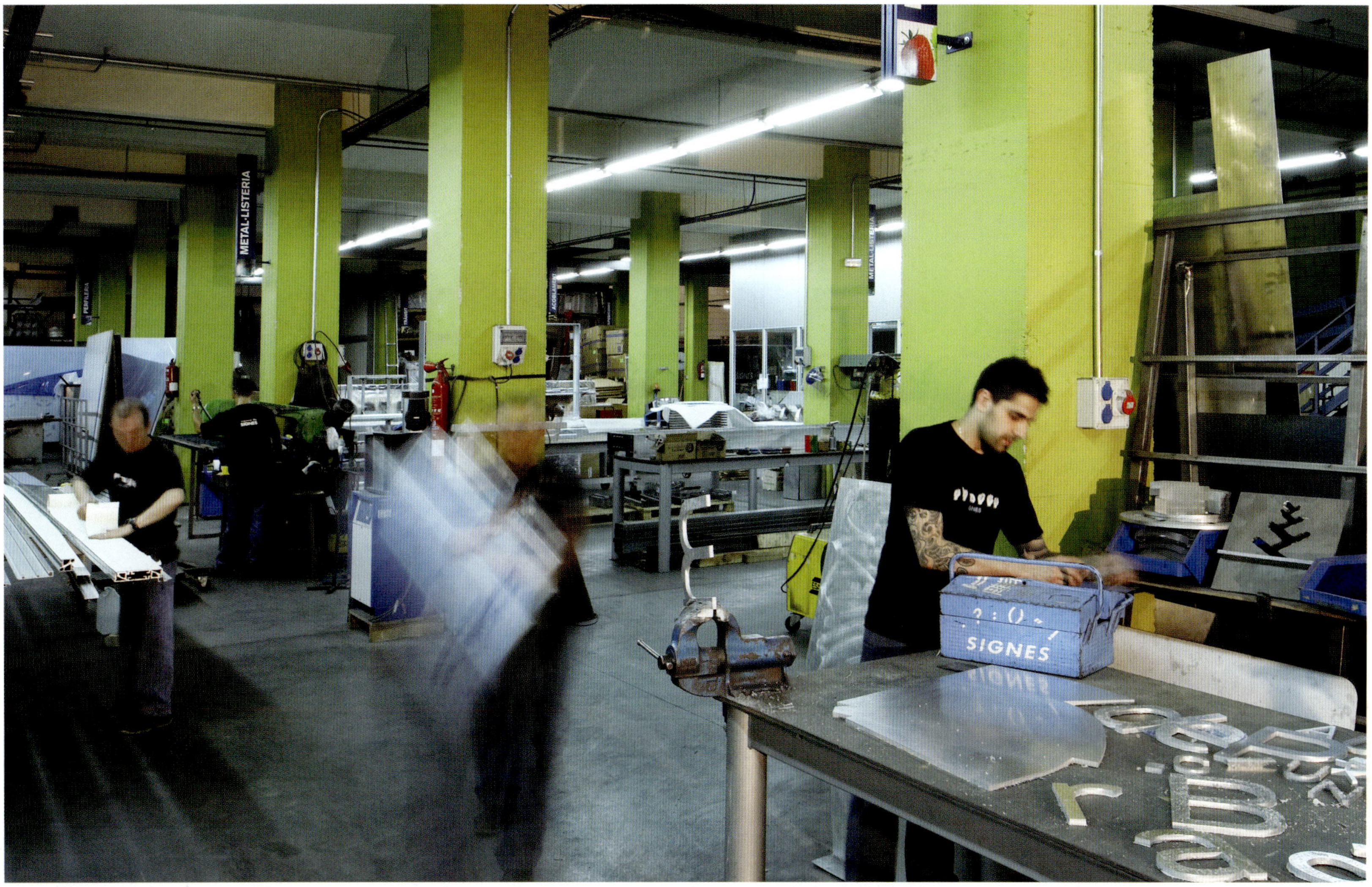
METAL·LISTERIA
SIGNES

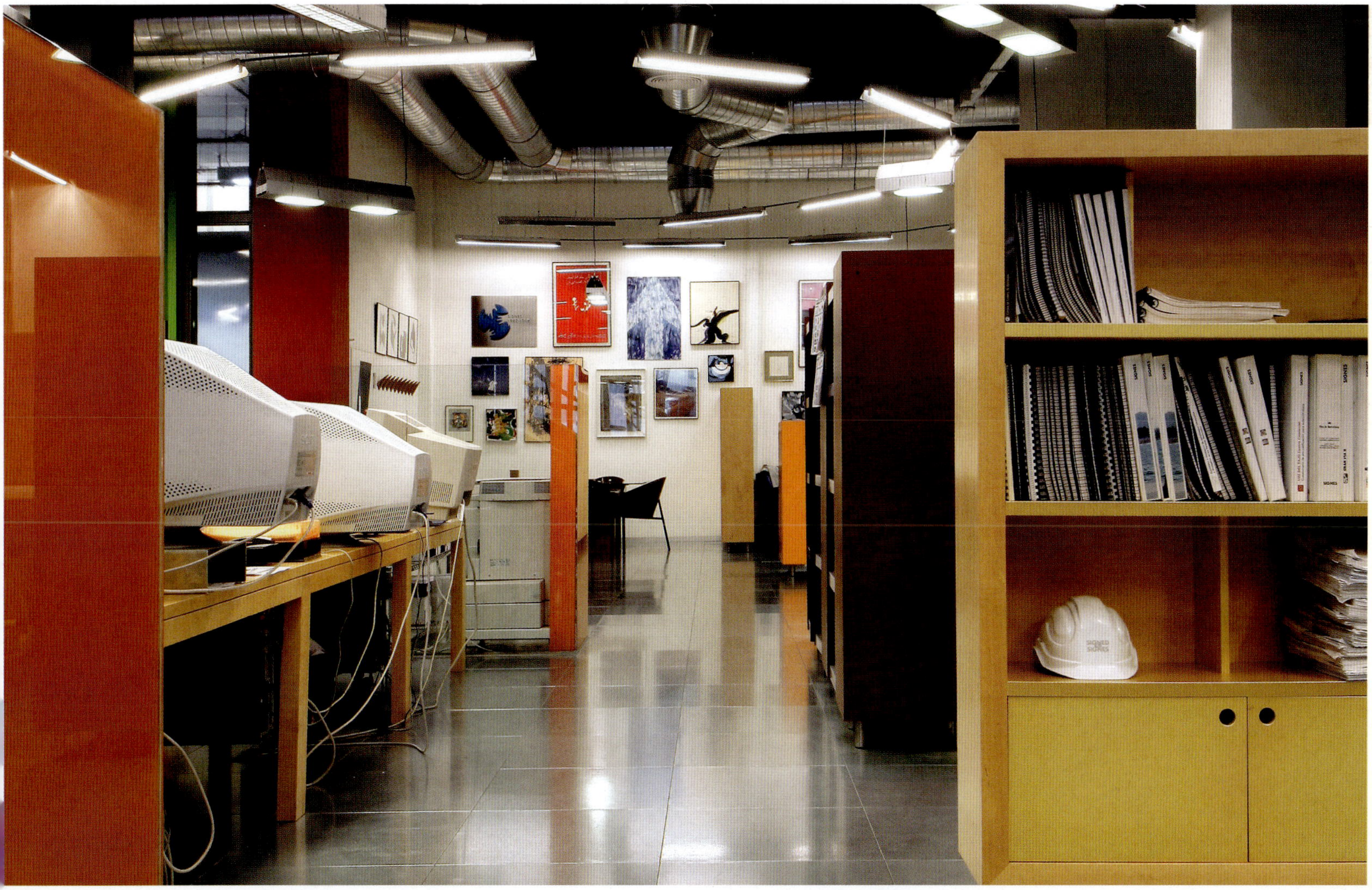

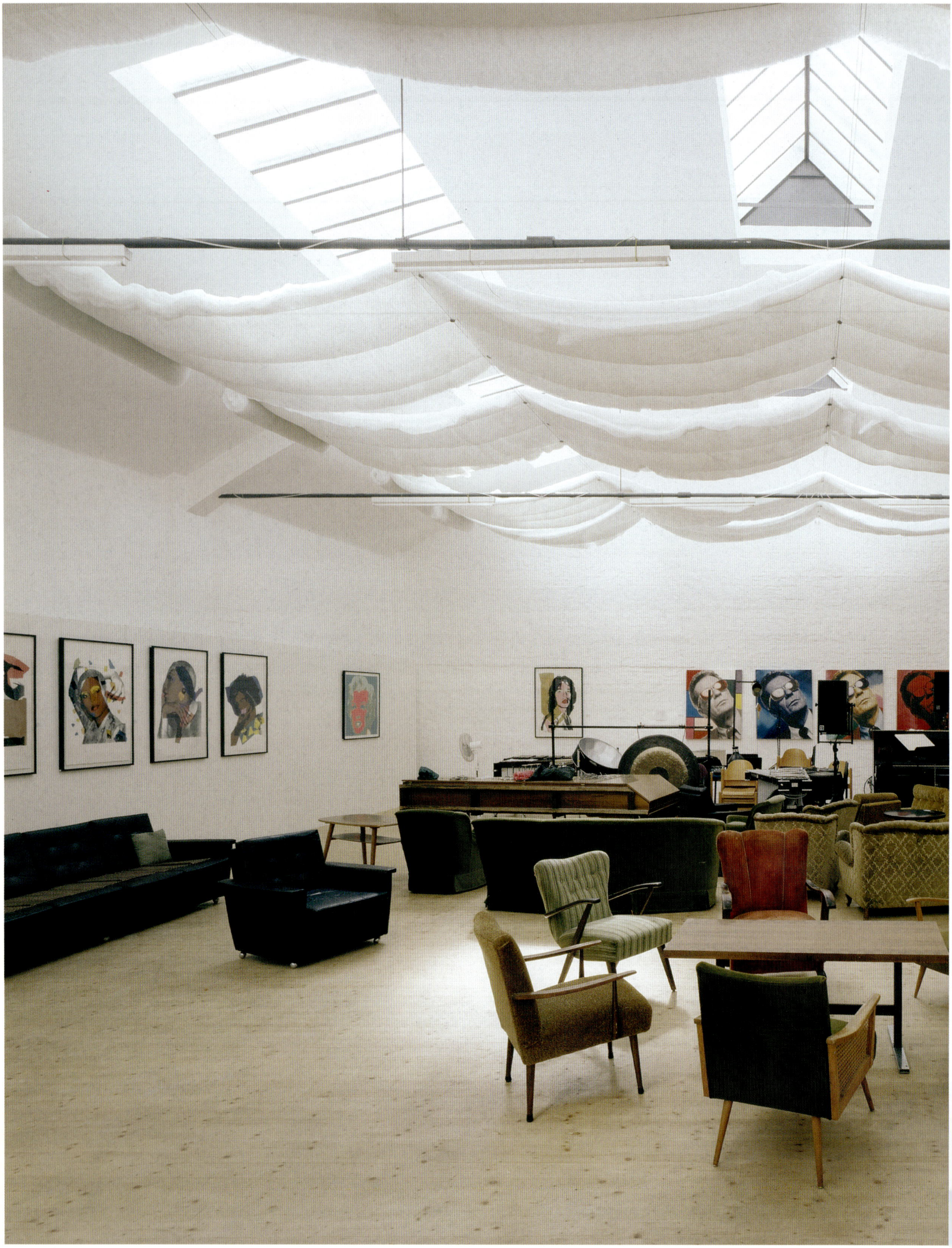

Klangforum House

The architect received a commission to renovate a former residential building and turn it into a large office with classrooms. The clients are the Klangforum, the famous Viennese orchestra of contemporary music. Their aim was to have a spacious place where the school's academic and cultural activities could take place, including concerts, rehearsals, and the management and administrative functions.

Both the administrative offices, designed as small offices, and the classrooms and rooms for rehearsal and teaching music performance have been spread across the building's four floors. Mixed with these are audition and concert rooms as well as other rooms where the musicians, visitors, and other users of the building can meet.

What is most remarkable about this construction is its double-height ceiling, which features small methacrylate panels. This material has been chosen in order to capitalize on the natural light that filters through the skylights located on the roof.

The flooring differentiates the areas designated to music, for which parquet has been chosen, since it breaks with the rigidity of the ceilings and offers a greater feeling of comfort. Granite has been used to differentiate the floor in the office area.

Two rooms are open to the public: on the first floor, the large room for all kinds of meetings, from cocktail parties to conferences, and at street level the bar-restaurant with an annexed garden, which offers a breath of fresh area right in the middle of Vienna. The project here has allowed for direct access to the street in order to facilitate the center's participation, through concerts and other musical performances, in the various celebrations that take place in the streets of the city, such as the Architekturtage or "Days of Architecture."

The lobby of this former steel production plant has been transformed into a work space equipped with the ideal acoustics for rehearsals and recording.

ARCHITECT/DESIGNER:
LICHTBLAU.WAGNER ARCHITEKTEN

Client: Ensemble Klangforum
Photographer: Bruno Klomfar
Location: Vienna, Austria
Completion date: 2004
Area: 10,764 SF

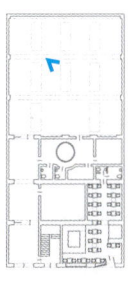

KLANGFORUM HOUSE

● The creation of the ideal acoustic conditions in the spaces for rehearsals and recording was the project's main challenge, especially in the lobby, the musicians' favorite place.

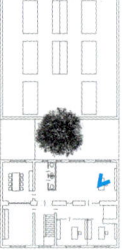

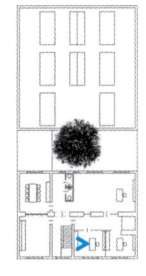

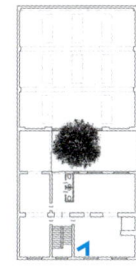

KLANGFORUM HOUSE
321

KLANGFORUM HOUSE

322

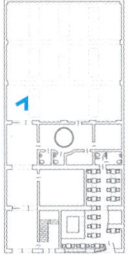

KLANGFORUM HOUSE

323

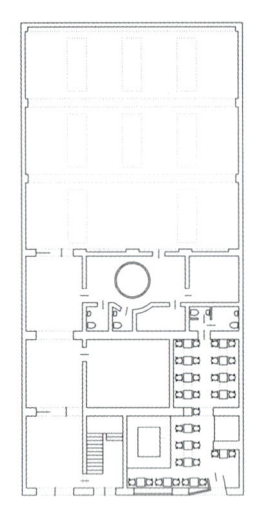

KLANGFORUM HOUSE

● Floor plan 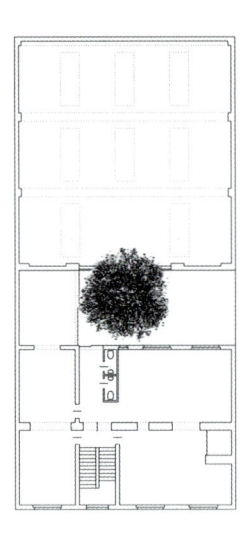   ● First floor plan 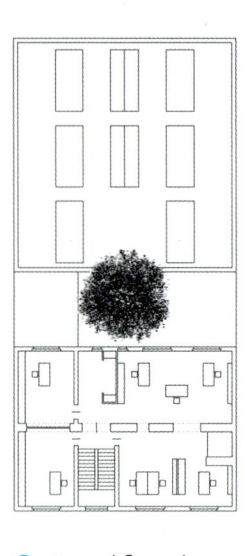   ● Second floor plan 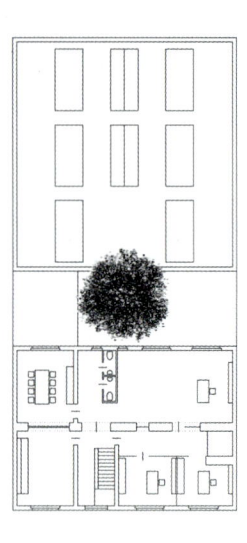   ● Third floor plan

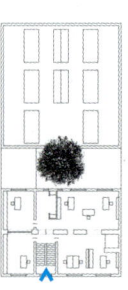

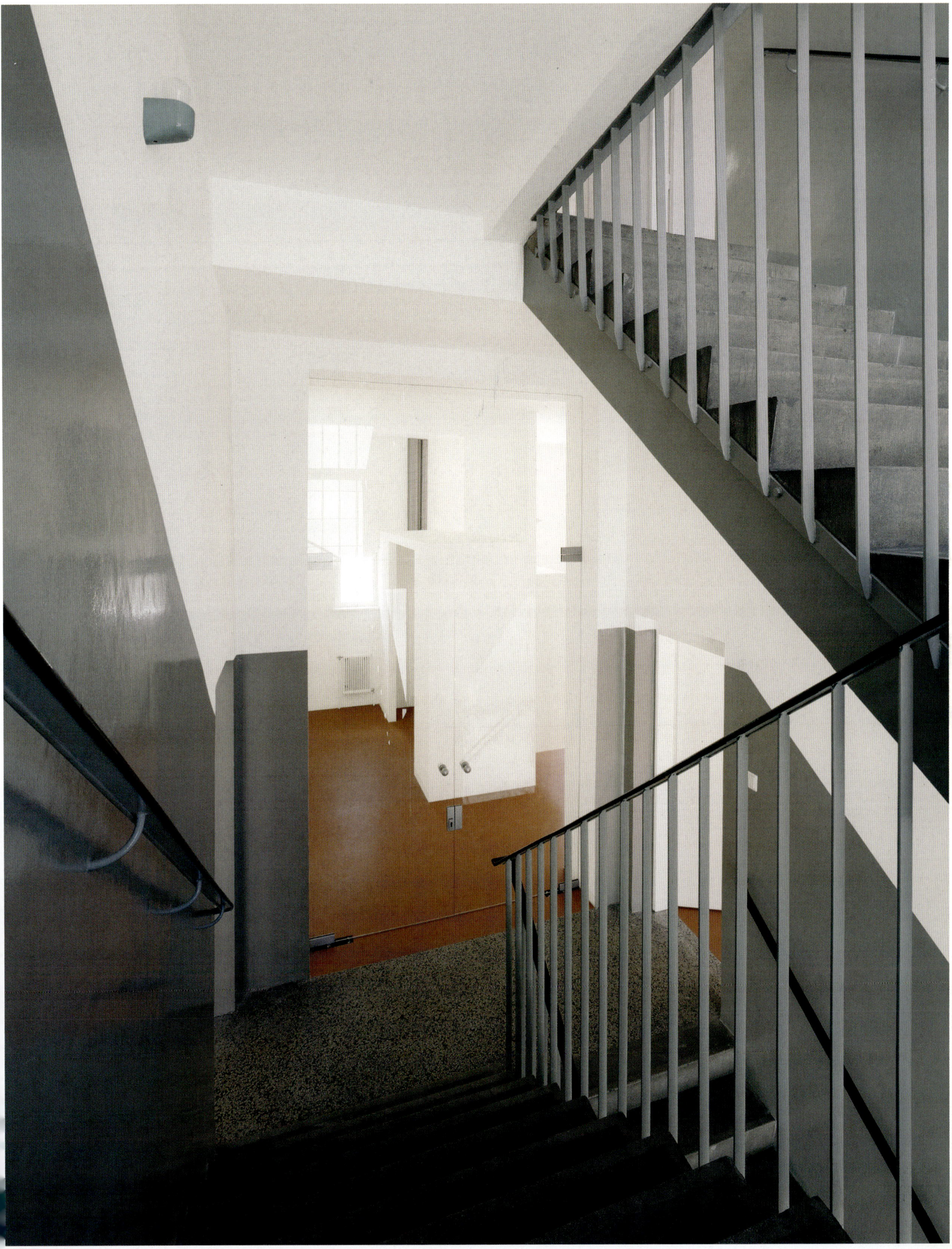

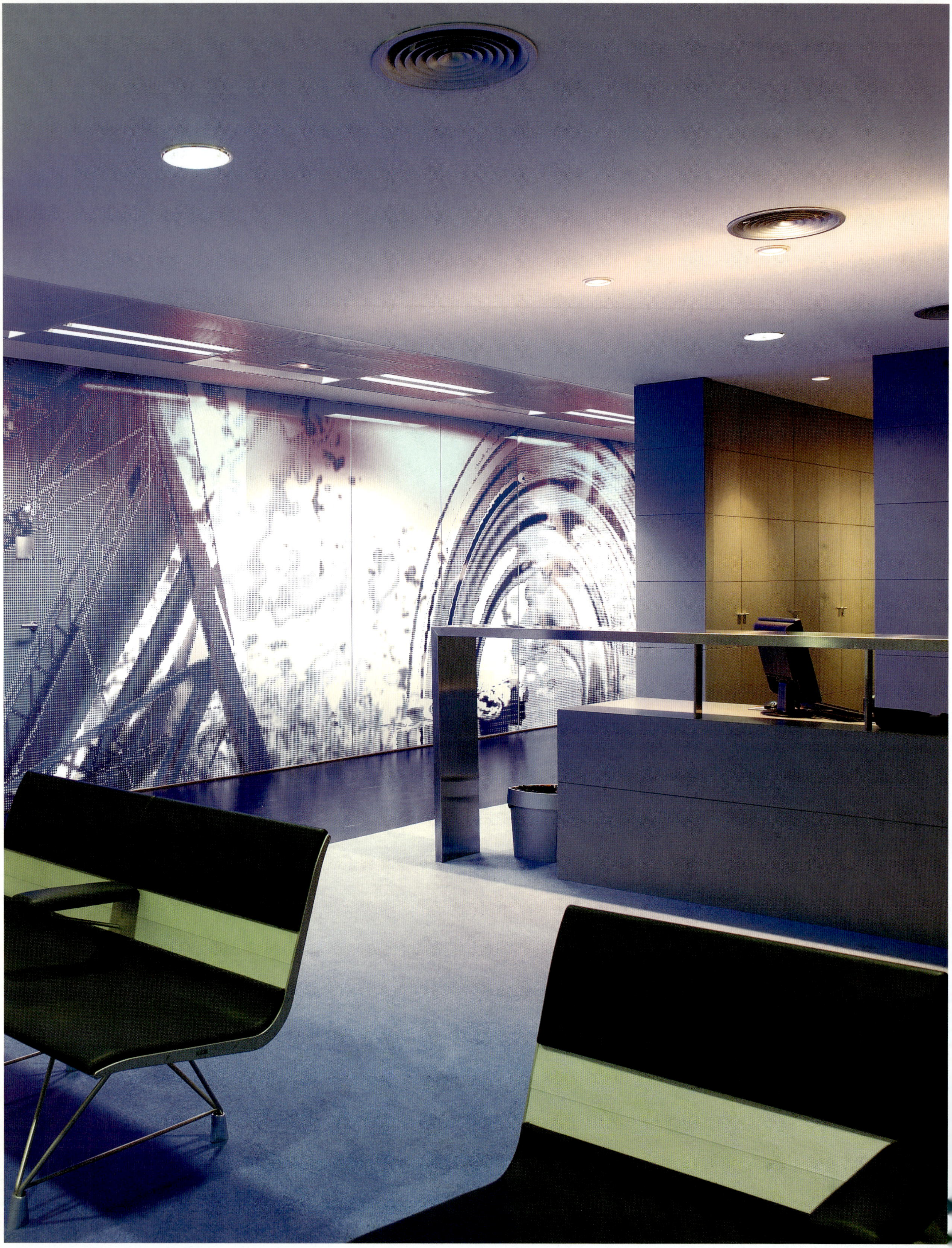

Amec Spie Offices

The client wanted to transform an entire floor of an office building located in the metropolitan town of Hospitalet de Llobregat, so that the engineering company would establish their corporate image on entering the Spanish market. Stéphane Cottrell and Jérome Michelangeli were commissioned with the renovation of the offices around three organizational zones: management, administration, and production. To carry out this project, the architects completely reconsidered the spatial divisions, the flow of movement, the typologies of the offices and, above all, they took into account the well-being of the employees.

The entire floor is organized around what are known as hard points (the toilets, courtyards, and technical rooms) so that these were integrated in two boxes positioned to physically define the three key areas of the project: administration, management and production.

The first box, called the silver box integrates the main meeting room as well as the toilets and a maintenance room. It received its name because it has been lined with wooden paneling and finished in stainless steel. On the perimeter of this structure there is a line of cupboards. This box generates an L-shaped connection, between the management area and administration. Access to the management zone is through a sliding glass door, while the meeting room is accessed via a double door adjusted to the cut of the cupboard doors.

The blue box, lined with glass and with a vinyl cladding is the second box, and integrates the disabled toilets, the cafeteria, the smokers' space, and the I.T. room. A curtain hangs at the back of this space for the reception area, which, in turn, obstructs the views to the production area. This area is organized around long work tables, whose space is divided up into departments. As is the case with the first box, its perimeter is composed of the spaces needed to file all the production documentation.

Architect/Designer:
IADarquitectos

Client: Amec Spie España
Photographer: Jose Luis Hausmman
Location: Hospitalet de Llobregat, Spain
Completion date: 2005
Area: 11,840 SF

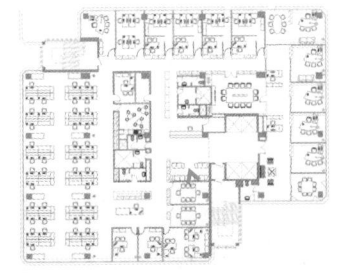

● The architectural studio decided to remove the cupboards from the offices leaving them clutter-free and more useful. This generates a play of geometries and volumes in the administration and management passageways.

AMEC SPIE OFFICES
329

AMEC SPIE OFFICES

AMEC SPIE OFFICES

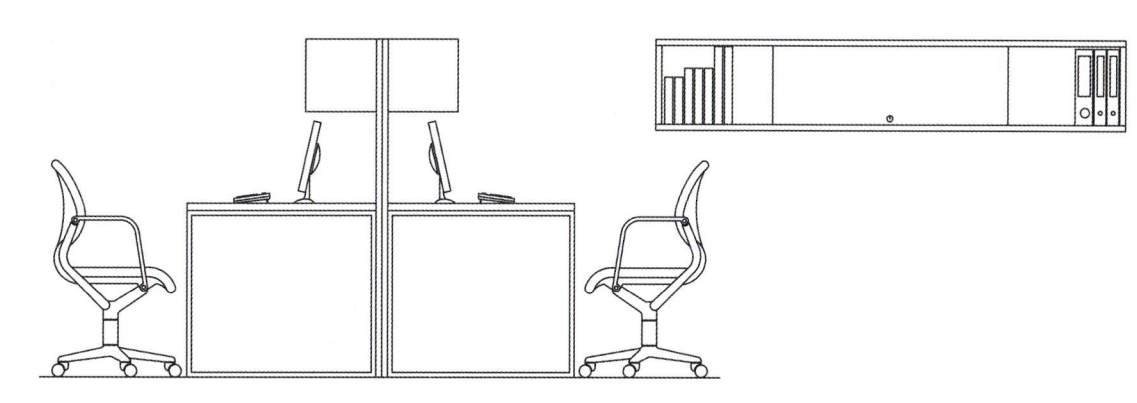

331

AMEC SPIE OFFICES
332

○ The dialogue between cold and warm materials, the colors and the subtle lighting produces a serene atmosphere, which is ideal for working in. The architects sought this effect with the intention of presenting an image that characterizes the company.

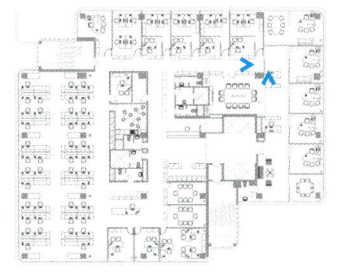

AMEC SPIE OFFICES

AMEC SPIE OFFICES

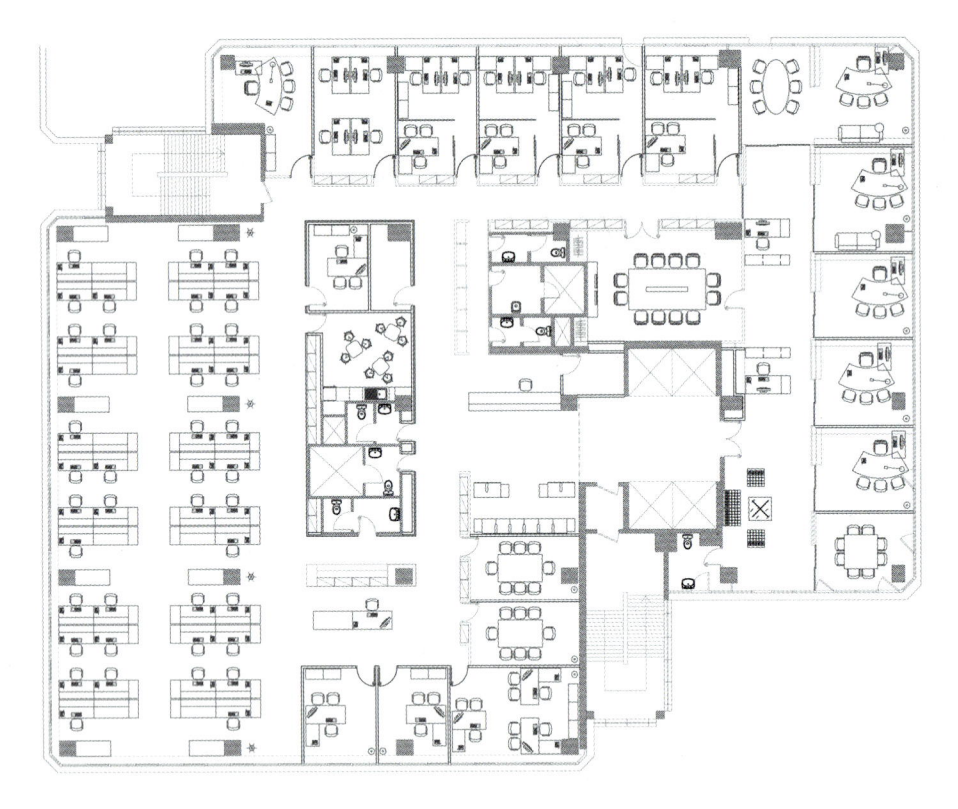

● Floor plan

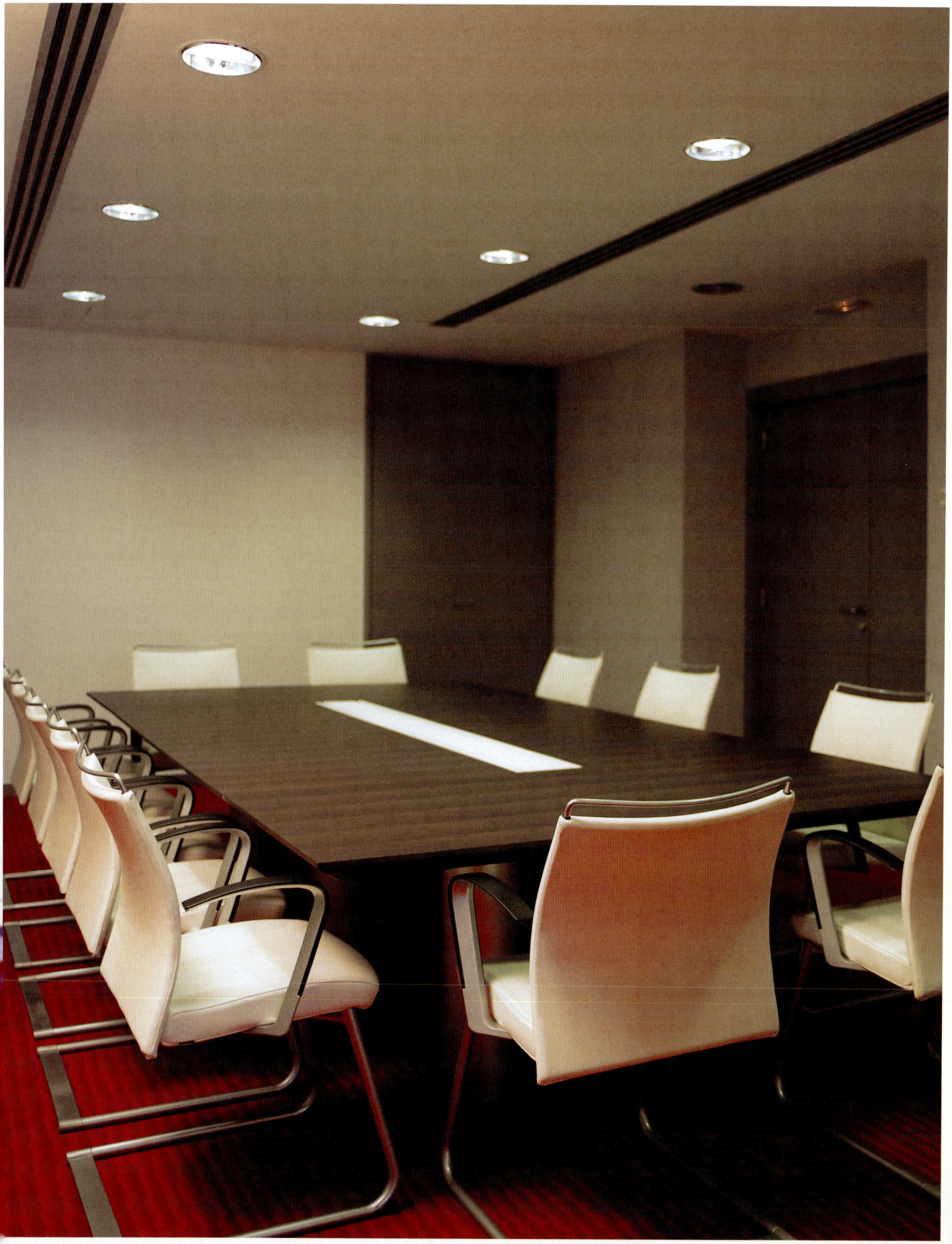

AMEC SPIE OFFICES

AMEC SPIE OFFICES
337

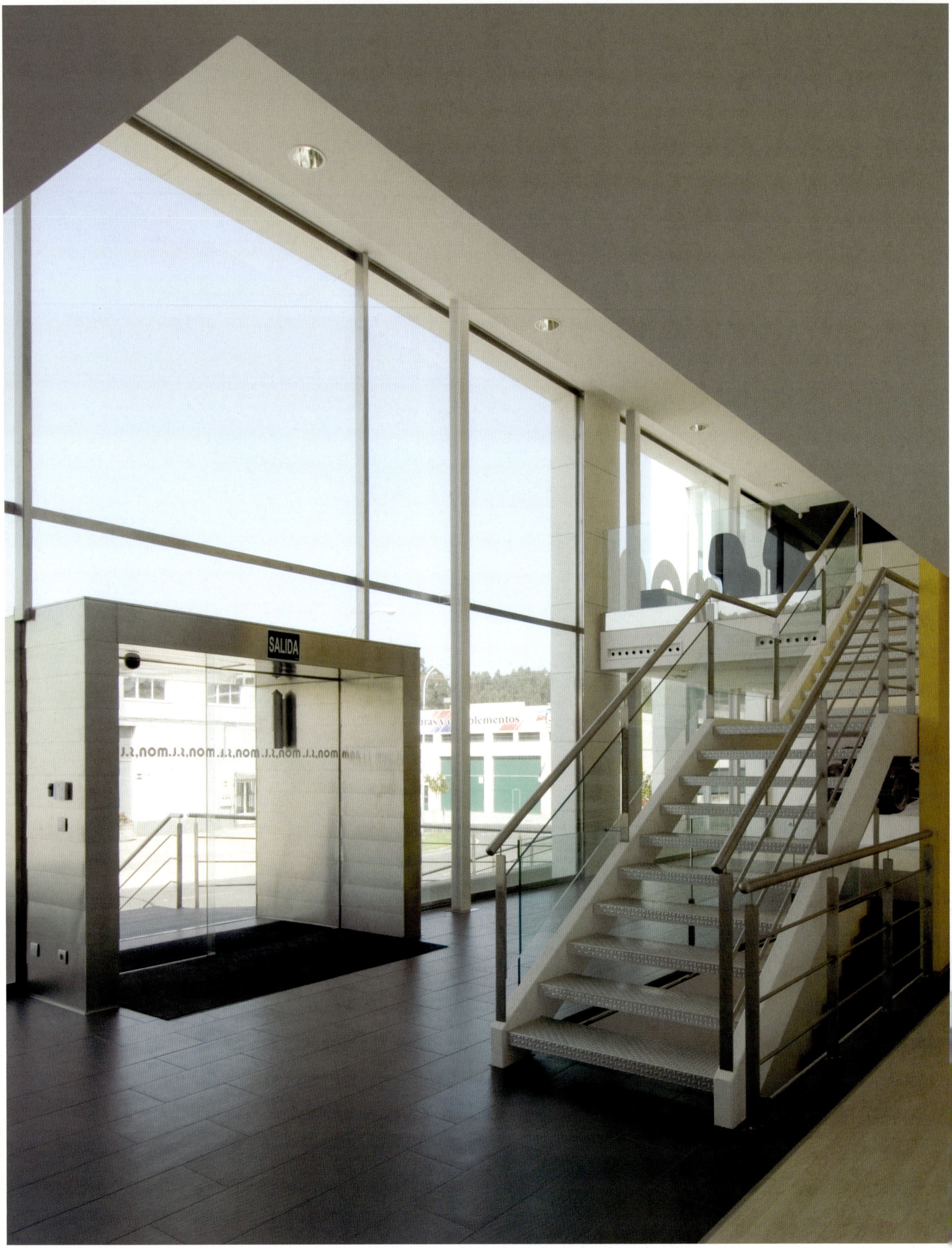
SALIDA

Construcciones Mon Offices

ARCHITECT/DESIGNER:
JOSÉ ABEIJÓN, MIGUEL FERNÁNDEZ/ABEIJÓN-FERNÁNDEZ ARQUITECTOS, ISABEL MON GARCÍA

Client: Construcciones Mon S.L.
Photographer: Héctor Fernández-Santos
Location: A Coruña, Spain
Completion date: 2006
Area: 13,595 SF

The commission for a new headquarters for Construcciones Mon, S.L. required an innovative design that would represent the construction style of the company. This established aesthetic continuity between the building and the streets is thanks to the combination of straight and curved planes. These adapt to the plot's corner location and attract attention as a novel building feature within the setting.

The project has developed in two ways: in the access area there is spatial continuity, while the work area has been compartmentalized, mainly by way of different pieces of furniture.

The building consists of three volumes of descending height, whose point of connection is indicated with glass skylights. Each of these volumes corresponds to a functional area. The first is the most heterogeneous, comprised of the reception area, administration, a technical office, the rest area, the toilets, and a library. The second volume is dedicated to work, with various offices, and the third has been reserved as the management office and a meetings room.

The storage and filing area and the rooms for the installations are all located in the basement. This is accessed directly from the courtyard and is also connected with the upper floors.

The façade has been carried out in glass and forms part of the interior by way of large floor-to-ceiling openings on all floors. The use of glass stretches to some of the partition walls, which are translucent and, in some cases, painted. Although the façade affords the interior a generous amount of natural light, there is also ample general lighting from spotlights and lights that hang from the ceiling. For the task lighting on the desks adjustable tablelamps have been used, and some indirect lighting has been used, such as that found in the kitchen-office.

● Black and white dominate the furnishings, the woodwork and the walls, and offer the space continuity, together with the glass, which has been used for several partition walls and the façade.

CONSTRUCCIONES MON OFFICES

341

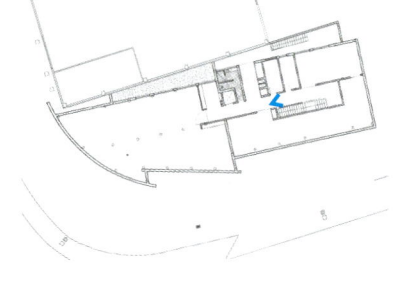

CONSTRUCCIONES MON OFFICES

CONSTRUCCIONES MON OFFICES
343

CONSTRUCCIONES MON OFFICES

- Basement plan

- Floor plan

- First floor plan

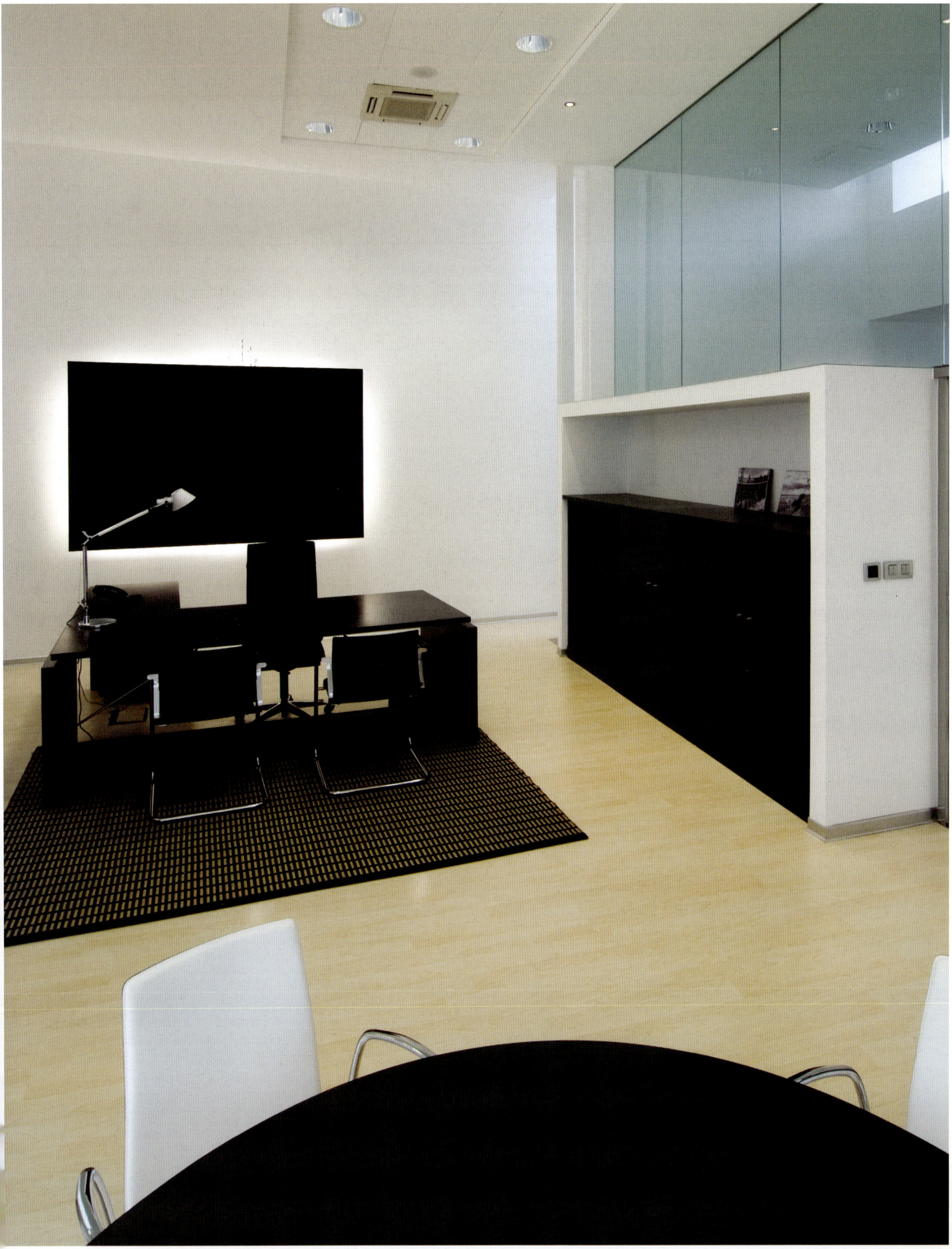

CONSTRUCCIONES MON OFFICES

CONSTRUCCIONES MON OFFICES

● The floor differentiates the access, circulation, and service areas from the work zones. The difference in height between the building's three volumes also identifies the different functional zones.

CONSTRUCCIONES MON OFFICES
348

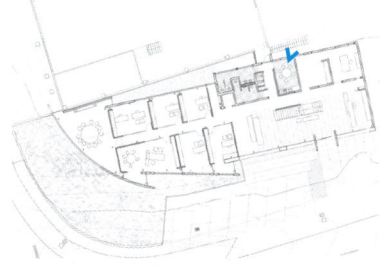

CONSTRUCCIONES MON OFFICES
349

THE SHOP AROUND THE CORNER

Mediaedge

ARCHITECT/DESIGNER:

BERNARD ASTOR/SAGUEZ & PARTNERS

Client: Mediaedge:cia-WWP Group
Photographer: Olivier Seignette, Mikaël Lafontan
Location: Paris, France
Completion date: 2006
Area: 13,810 SF

This company wished to express their corporate values, mainly the fusion between nature and technology, through the renovation of their new head offices. The architects studied the working style of the client before choosing the aesthetics for the interior. The result can be summed up in the phrase: "the office has arrived home," which means that functionality and comfort are the bases to encourage creativity and the exchange of ideas between the members of staff in this company.

The space distribution begins by establishing a clear separation between the access and circulation area and the work area, with the aim of avoiding unnecessary distractions. Communication in this space follows two circulation routes: one goes from the hall and the reception rooms to the management offices and the other connects the work areas.

Since the client gives great importance to the exchange of ideas among the personnel, the number of spaces for informal meetings have been doubled with respect to the previous head office. These have been designed in different sizes, ranging from dimensions suitable for two-person meetings, and they have been carried out at the expense of spaces previously used for work stations. Even the library is a place designed for meetings, as well as for finding inspiration in the different publications.

This building, with an elongated floor plan, has two stories. On the bottom floor is the reception area, meeting spaces, dining room, and a rest area. The top floor has been reserved exclusively for creative work. On entering this area from the elevator a panorama of bright colors unfolds, one for each work department, which infuse both the occupants and the atmosphere with energy.

The visitor contrastingly finds a decoration of birch trunks in the lobby, which infuses calm, along with the enlarged photographs of elements from nature, located on the glass screens that delineate the different areas.

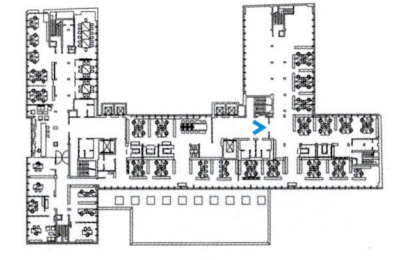

The company's commitment to the environment is represented in the décor and the furniture, such as the birch tree trunks on one of the walls in the hall, the photographs of nature, and a side table that imitates a horned animal.

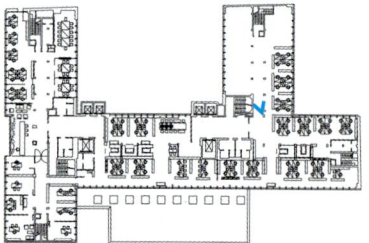

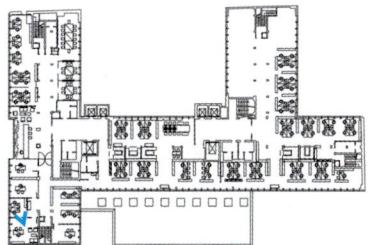

MEDIAEDGE
353

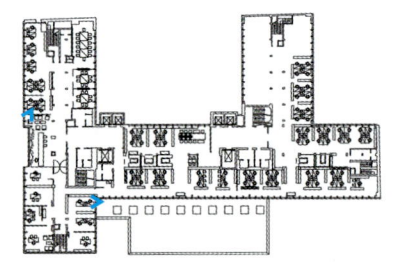

MEDIAEDGE
354

MEDIAEDGE

355

MEDIAEDGE
356

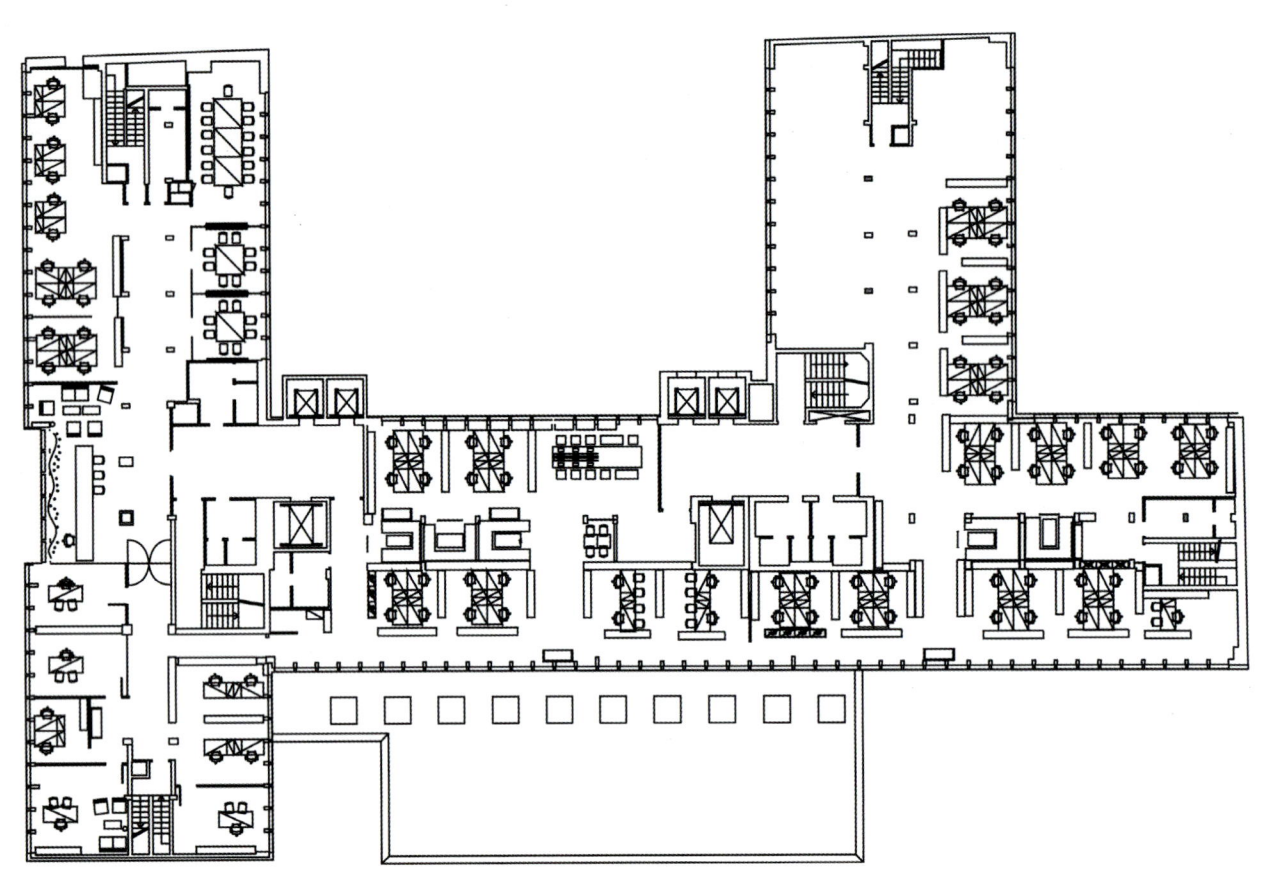

○ Floor plan

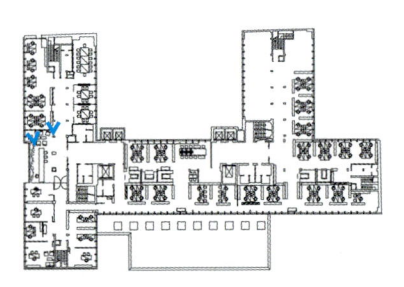

mediaedge:cia

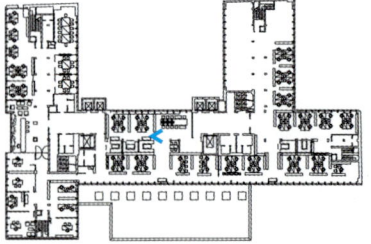

MEDIAEDGE
358

MEDIAEDGE

○ When it comes to color, the Web Bar is one of the most striking areas. This space is equipped with six screens set into a large white table. The design includes photographs that show parts of people´s faces as a reminder that behind the machine there is a human being.

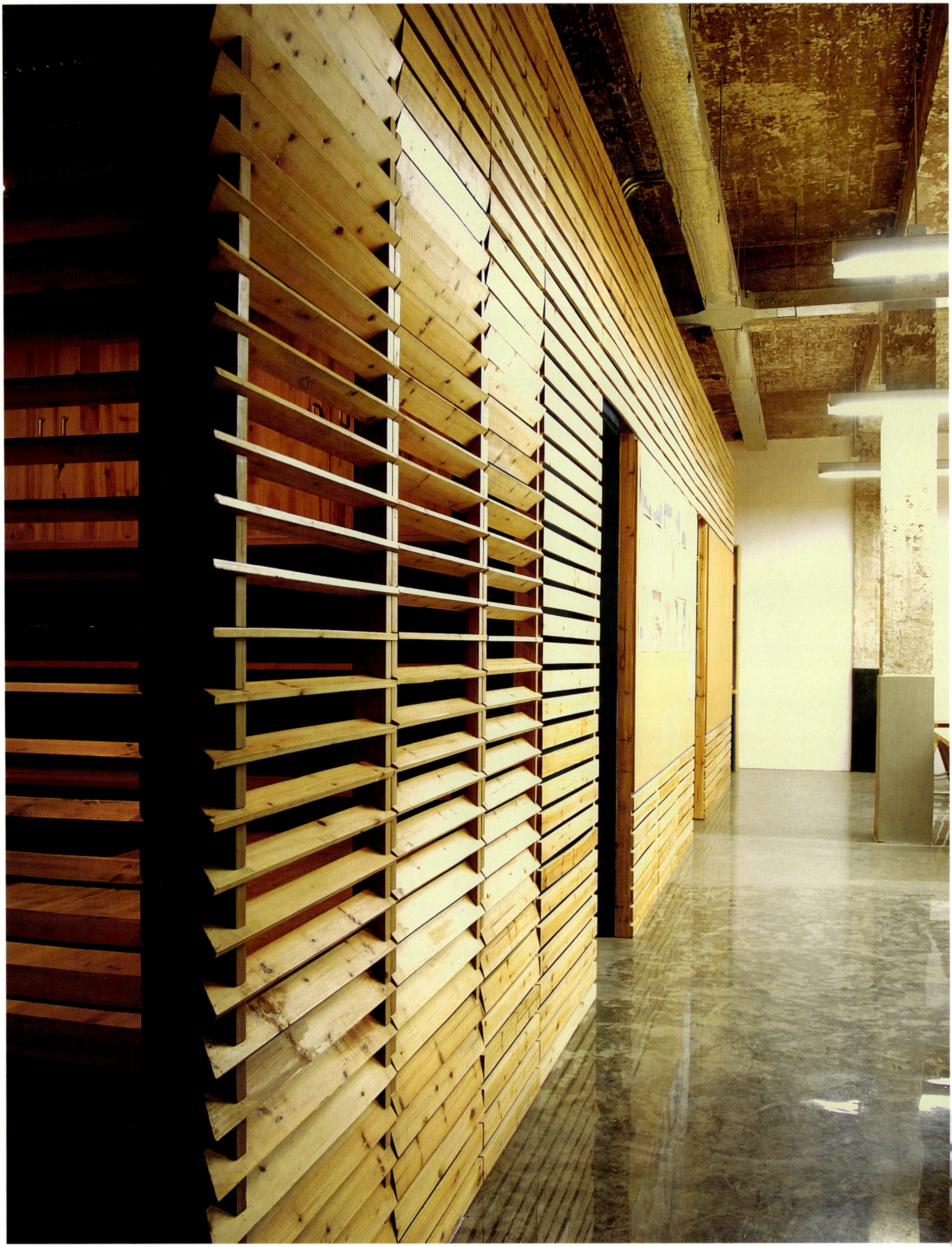

Studio DAtrans

The client for this project, one of the most important architectural studios in China, wanted a modern and functional headquarters. It contains a meeting room, a work area without divisions, six individual offices for each of the managers of the different sections (design, production, layout etc.), and a rest area.

The architects have preserved the original layout of the building and have renovated the interiors through different finishes for the walls, which create different areas.

Thus, a steel box accommodates the meeting room, while the six individual offices have been separated using panels of wooden slats, which also harmonize the interior with the cultural surroundings. The beams on the ceiling have been left visible, an aesthetic option in line with the direct lighting system of tube lights that hang from cables.

The composition of the work areas has developed according to the project's initial philosophy of providing spaces that are both separated and interlinked, where daily activities take place. Consequently, the central area has been left open to favor exchanges among those working in the studio during the projection and production processes, as well as everyday debates and consultations between members of the studio. The idea of "opening up" continues on the walls and floors where the surfaces have been removed leaving the original project's exposed concrete. All of the studio's interior, which was previously used for storage, has been organized with a system of one box inside another, one wooden the other steel. The latter, used as a meeting room, has the double feature of being soundproof and allowing views of its interior, another response to the idea of separation and interrelation.

Architect/Designer:

Chen Xudong, Shen Yirong, Gu Jirong/DAtrans

Client: DAtrans
Photographer: DAtrans
Location: Shanghai, China
Completion date: 2004
Area: 14,521 SF

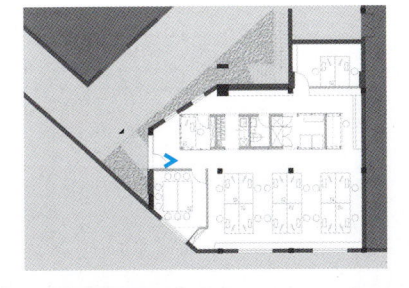

STUDIO DATRANS

● The architectural and decorative design are connected thanks to their common use of wood, which also links them with their surroundings, a former industrial area, now a hub of some of China's top artists.

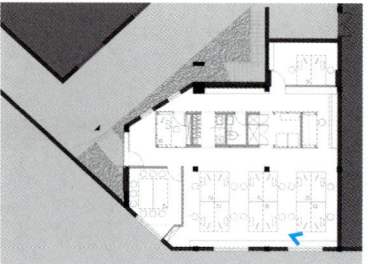

STUDIO DATRANS

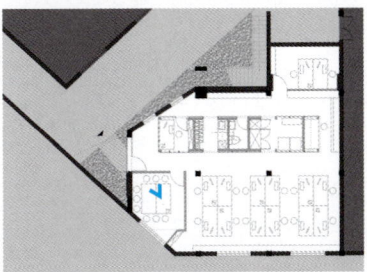

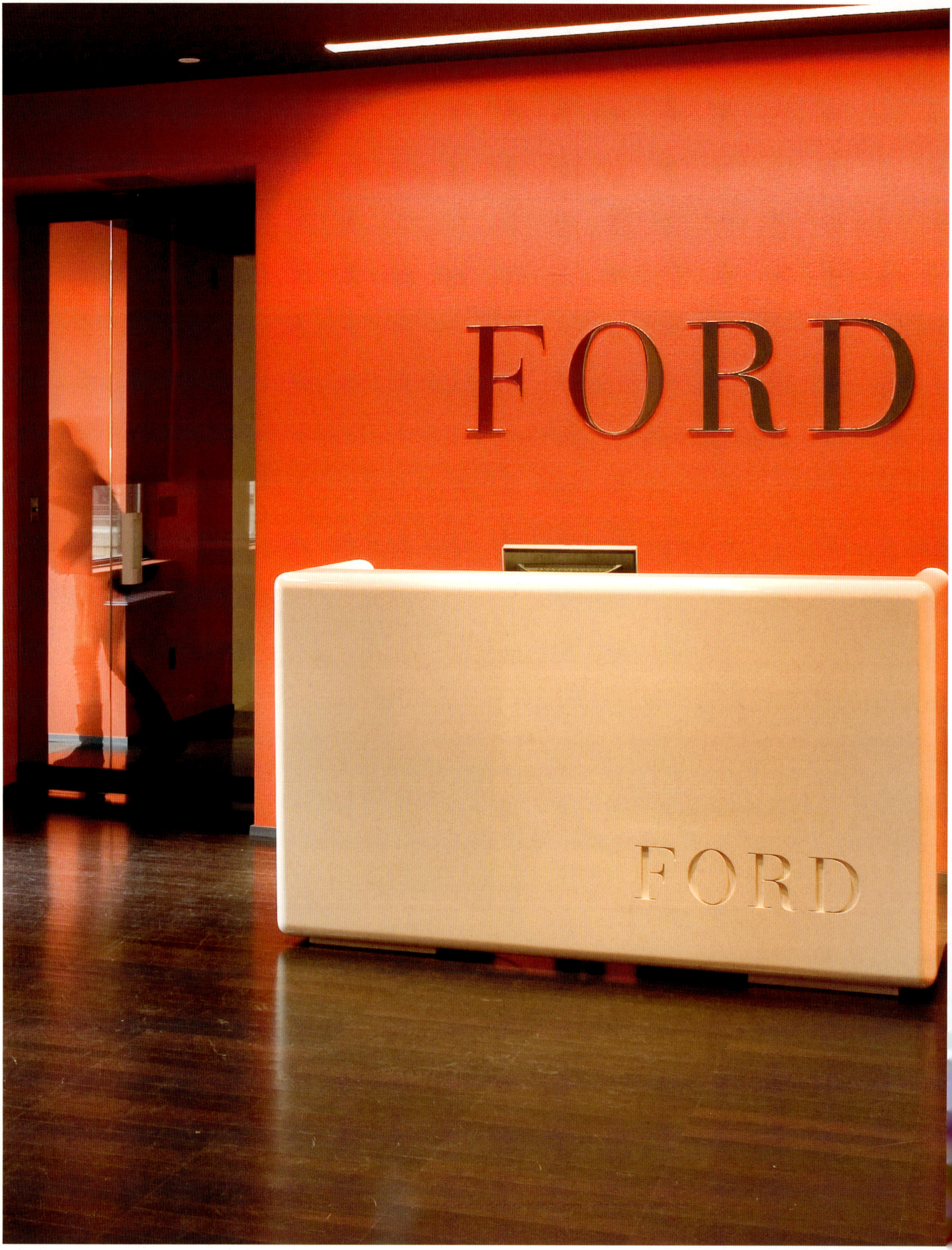
FORD
FORD

Ford Models Headquarters

The model agency that commissioned this project was founded in 1946. The clients understood clearly what they were looking for. They wanted this office to be the agency's headquarters and to create a new corporate image that would reflect functionality and efficiency. An important part of the project was choosing the building that would house the offices. The chosen location was the top floor of a historical building in New York's Flat Iron district.

The nucleus of this design is the area to be used by editors, documentalists, producers, photographers, etc. Large wooden tables have been placed in the central area of the office, where there are no concrete partitions. Each table may be occupied by eight people, who have constant contact with the occupants of the other tables.

In order to separate the different sections, the designers decided to hang large wooden and aluminum panels from the ceiling, which feature photos of the agency's different models. These panels fulfill two functions: they separate the work areas and conveniently display all the photos of the models so that the most appropriate for any given occasion can be chosen. The wood used for the tables, and panels, and the shelves throughout the office is fir, one of the most expensive on the market, in response to the owners' desire to present an image of luxury and quality.

Color appears in the lobby of the office to delineate the two areas. Red and white have been used since they are the colors that give the firm its personality. The wooden module stands out, clad in white plastic panels, which serves as the office reception area.

To access the different spaces, two routes have been created: a wide, well-lit one and another, which is narrower and more isolated.

The space intends to reinforce the image of the prestigious Ford Agency by joining abstract decorative volumes with functional elements.

Architect/Designer:

Bonetti Kozerski Studio

Client: Ford Models
Photographer: Lucca Pioltelli
Location: New York
Completion date: 2006
Area: 15,000 SF

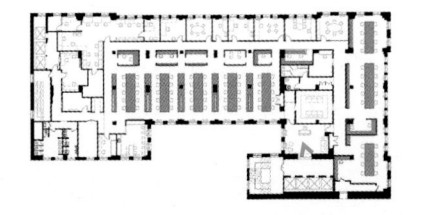

FORD MODELS HEADQUARTERS

● The reception area and lobby have been conceived as the agency's central space. The routes to the other rooms lead from here. The lobby also acts as a casting room as well as a meeting room.

FORD MODELS HEADQUARTERS
367

FORD MODELS HEADQUARTERS
368

FORD MODELS HEADQUARTERS
369

• The work area is divided into two sections: one for the models and the other for seeing clients. At times the agency is very busy, which is why two circulation routes have been created.

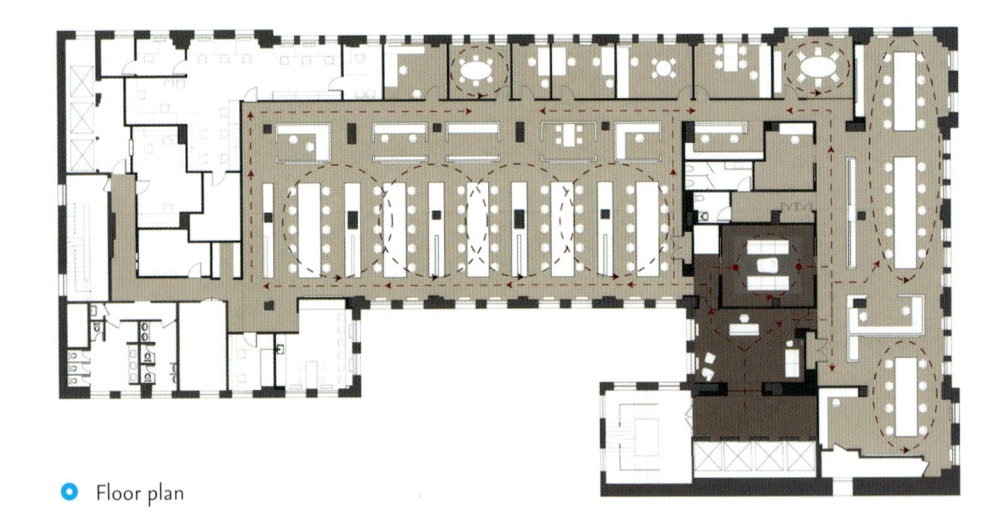

FORD MODELS HEADQUARTERS

Floor plan

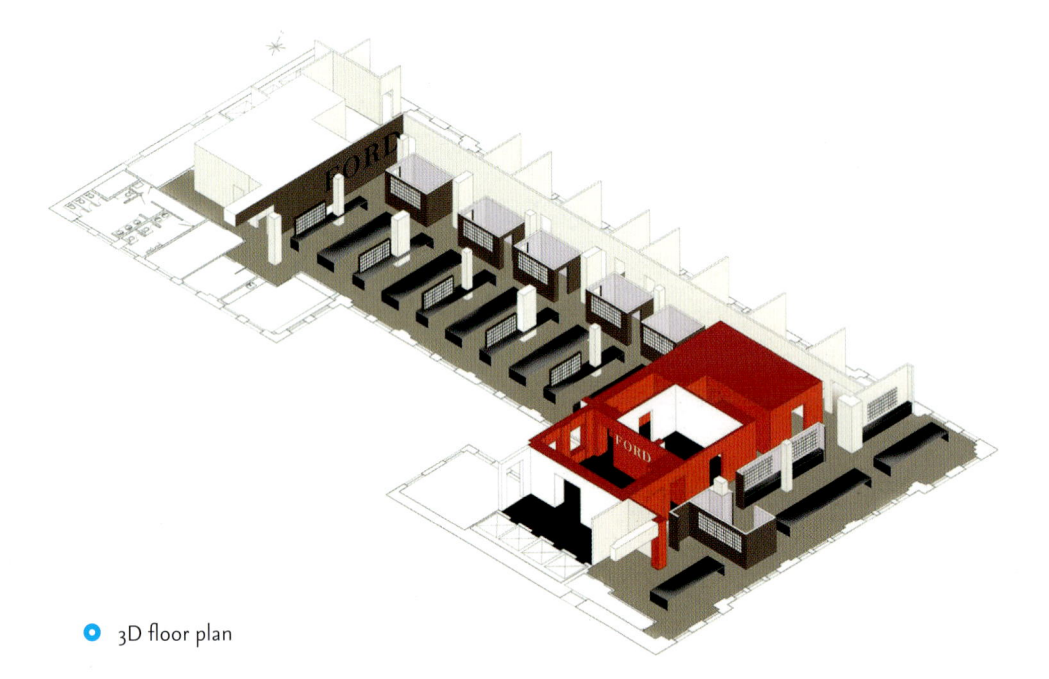

3D floor plan

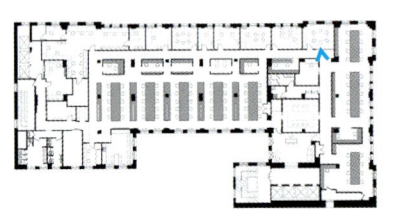

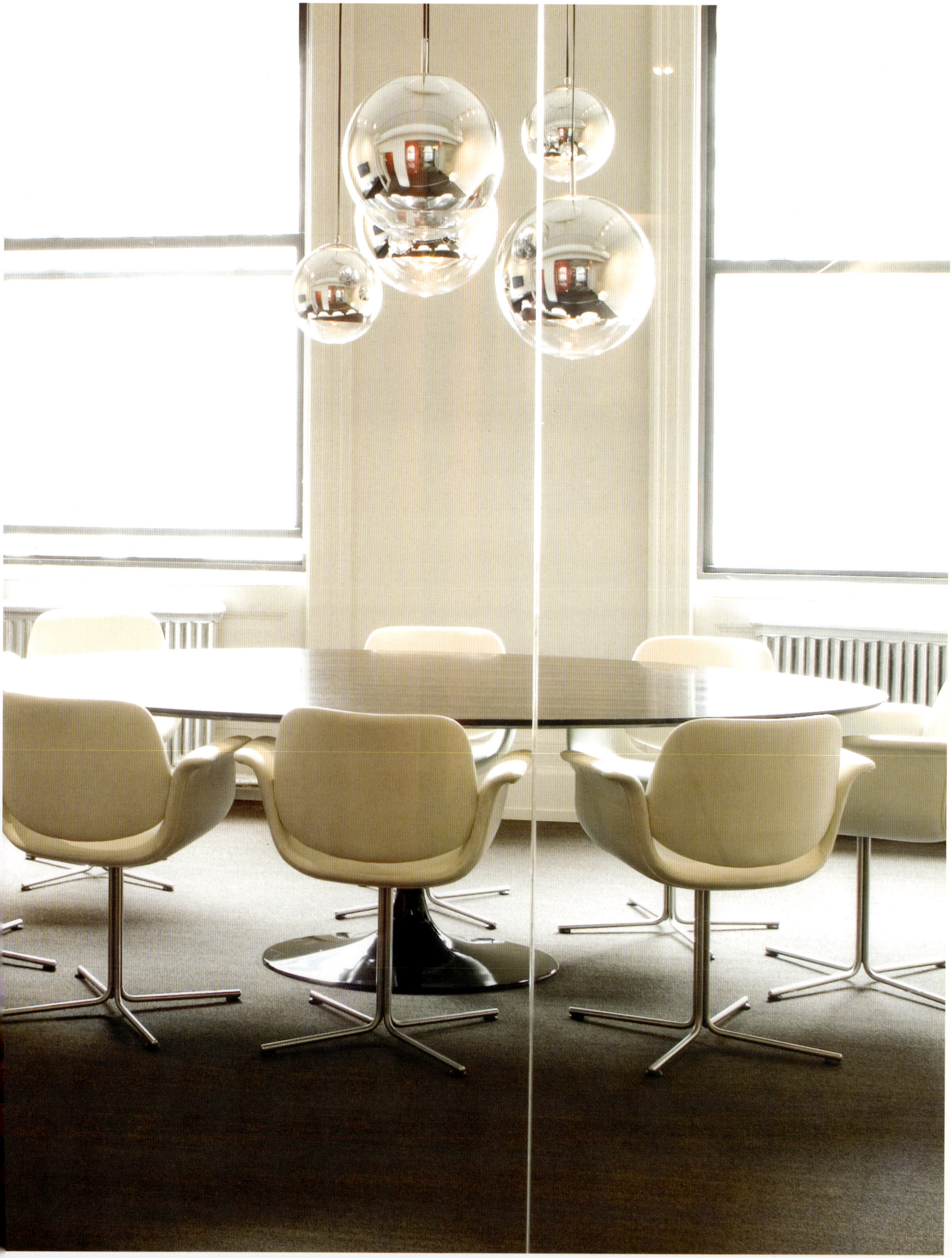

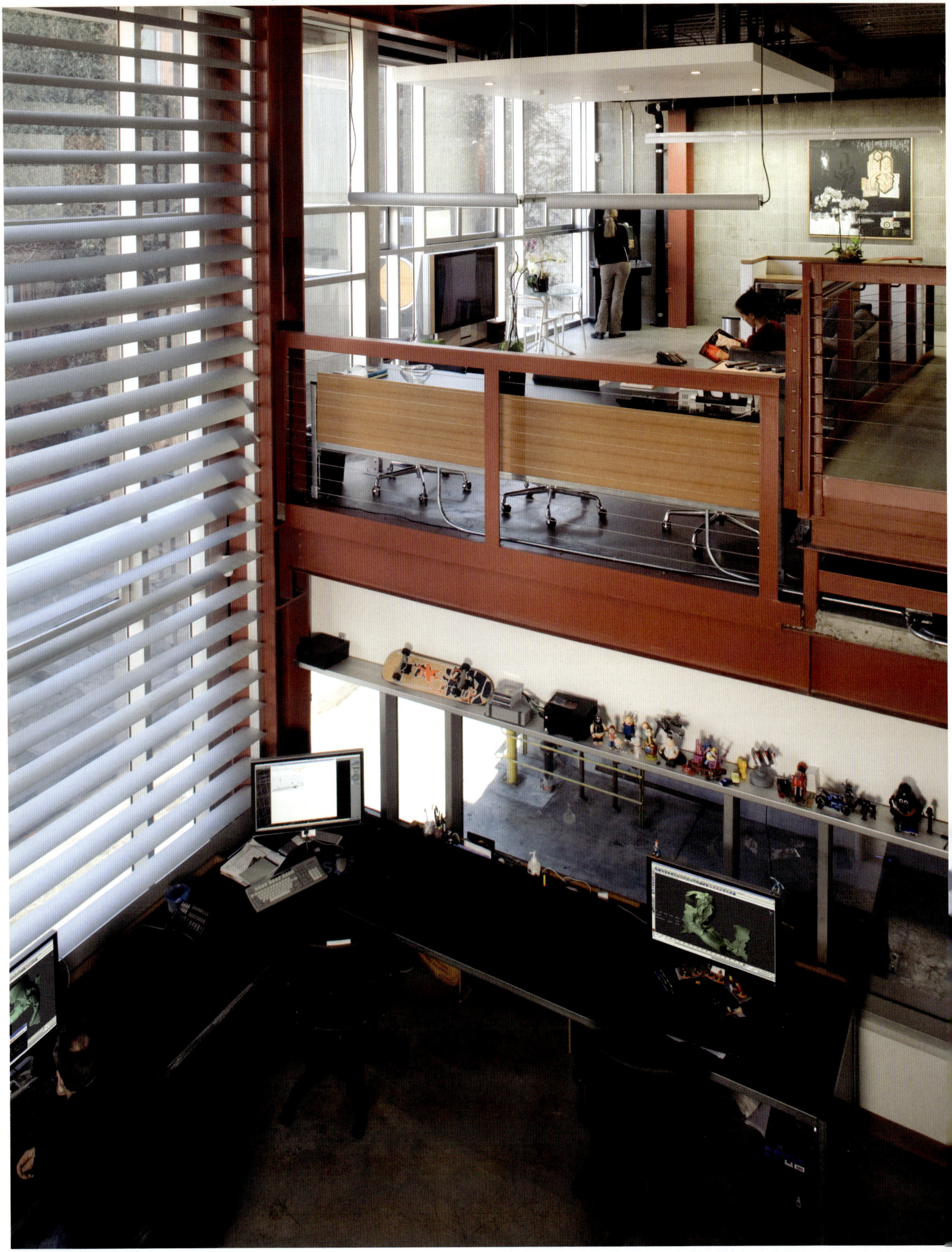

Hydraulx

The owners of a company that creates special effects for films commissioned this office. The four-story building chosen for this ambitious project was previously host to residential apartments. Now, the floor at street level houses a two-story library and an area for meeting with clients. On the first floor is the meeting room, the dressing rooms, the editing studios, the private administration offices, and the main kitchen. The second floor is entirely dedicated to computer installations, since the company makes use of a sophisticated hardware and software to create their productions. On the top floor are the projection rooms, the owners' offices, another kitchen, and the terrace.

The aim of the project was to create the ideal environment for the clients and the artists, a place that would provide privacy and independence, as well as an atmosphere for group work. Most of the spaces are multi-functional in order to best respond to the changing and unpredictable post-production needs.

The interior architecture has adopted a machinelike aesthetic, with various materials from the construction left on sight, as if the interior of the building were the interior of a mechanical device. Thus, for example, the building's iron structure can be seen next to the central staircase that joins the different floors, and both have been painted dark red in order to establish continuity between the construction and the functional elements. For the items of furniture and the finishes, materials like glass, steel, aluminum, perforated sheet metal, and MDF boards have been used. The warmth here comes from various wooden details made from Douglas fir.

On the ground floor the lengths of aerial cable have been turned into a design opportunity and left visible. The shades for the lights are all transparent acrylic plastic.

ARCHITECT/DESIGNER:

SHUBIN + DONALDSON ARCHITECTS

Client: Greg and Colin Strause
Photographer: Tom Bonner
Location: Santa Monica, CA
Completion date: 2006
Area: 15,000 SF

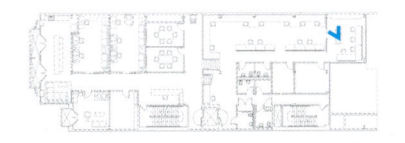

HYDRAULX
374

○ The ground floor is a large extension without partitions housing the library and the area for meeting with clients. The height of the ceiling has been lowered here to make it more welcoming.

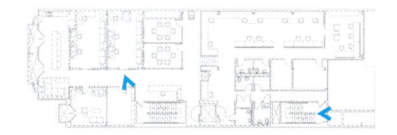

HYDRAULX

375

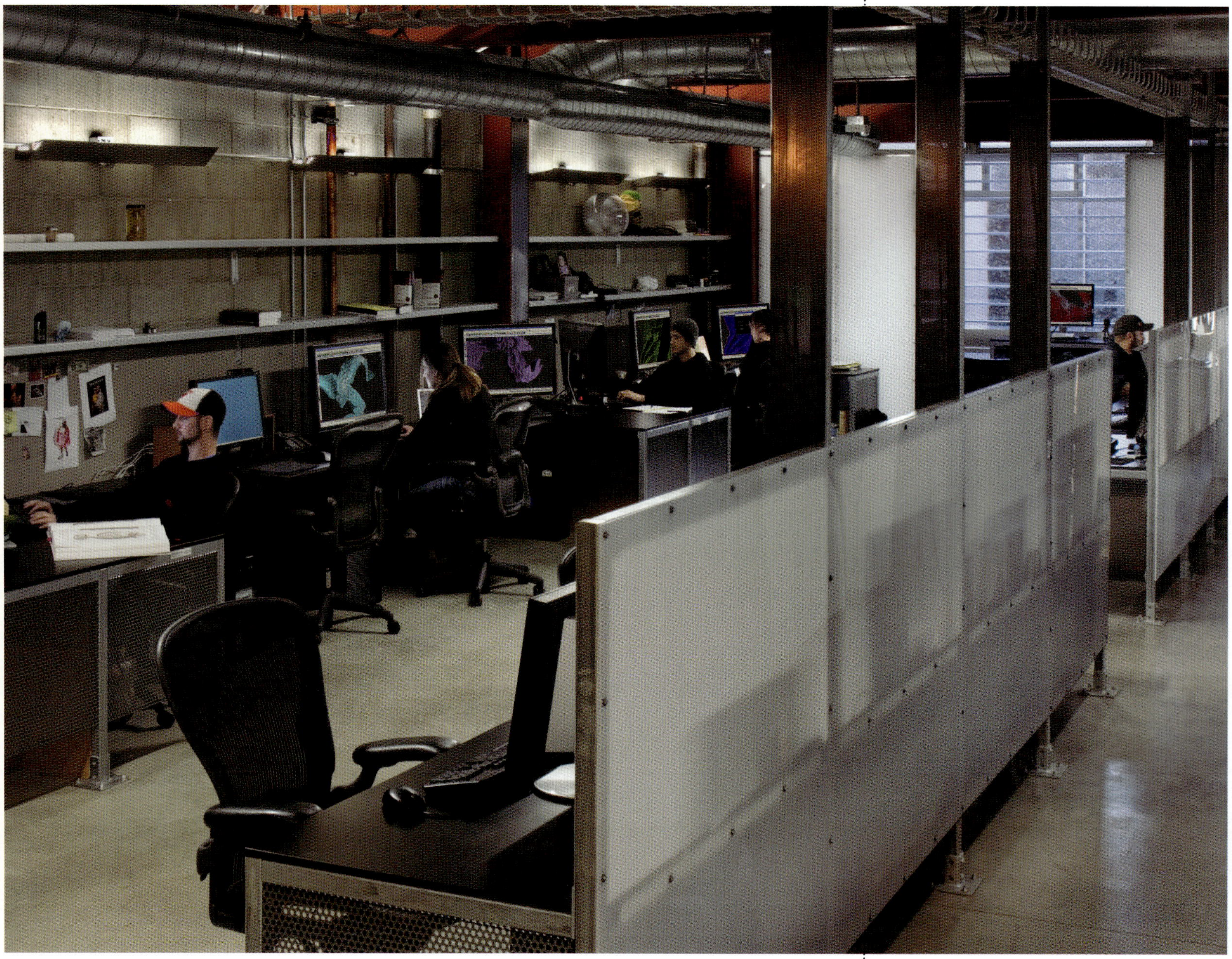

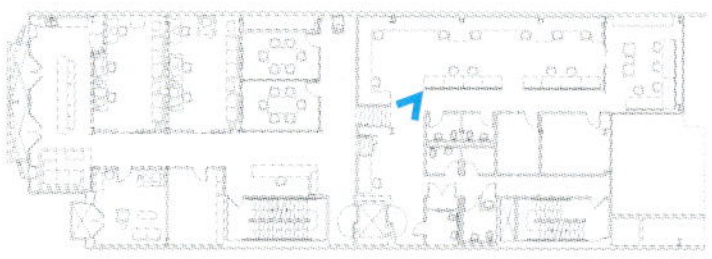

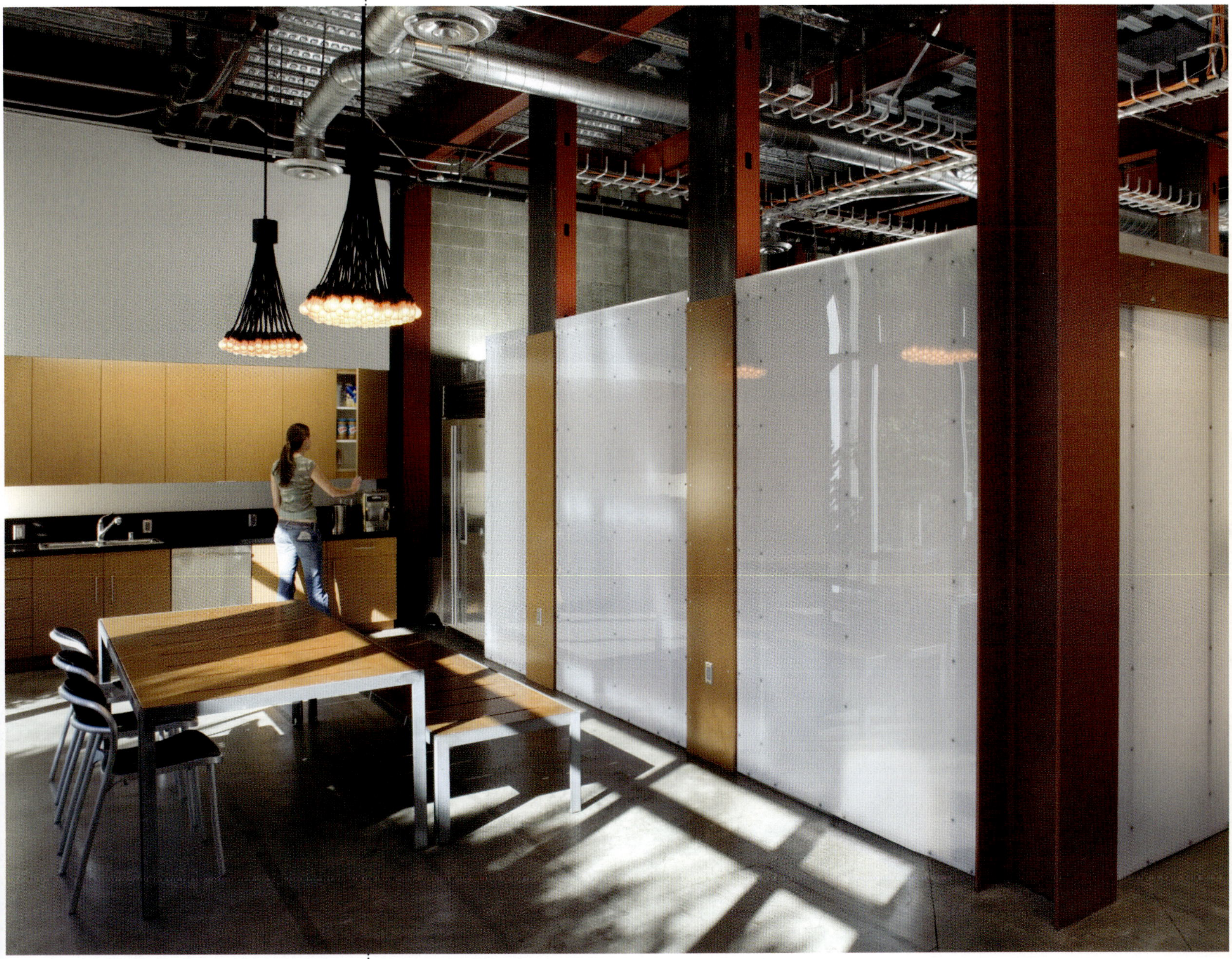

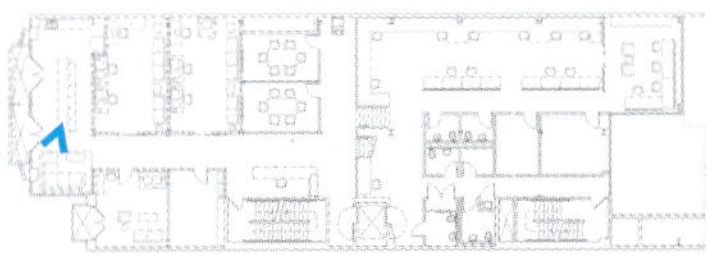

HYDRAULX

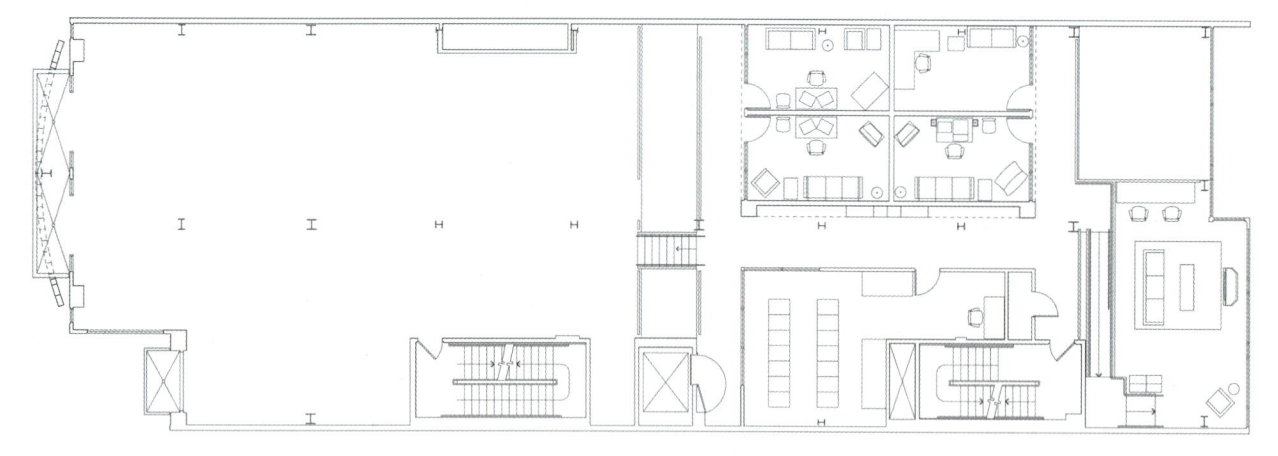

○ Floor plan

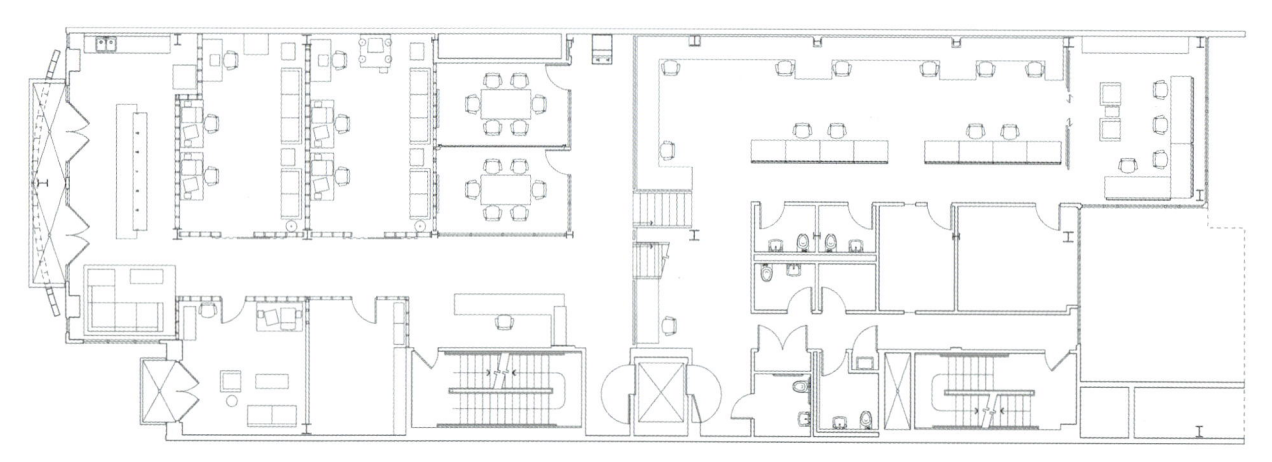

○ First floor plan

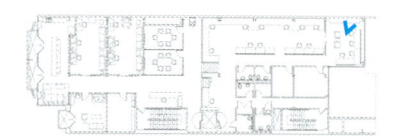

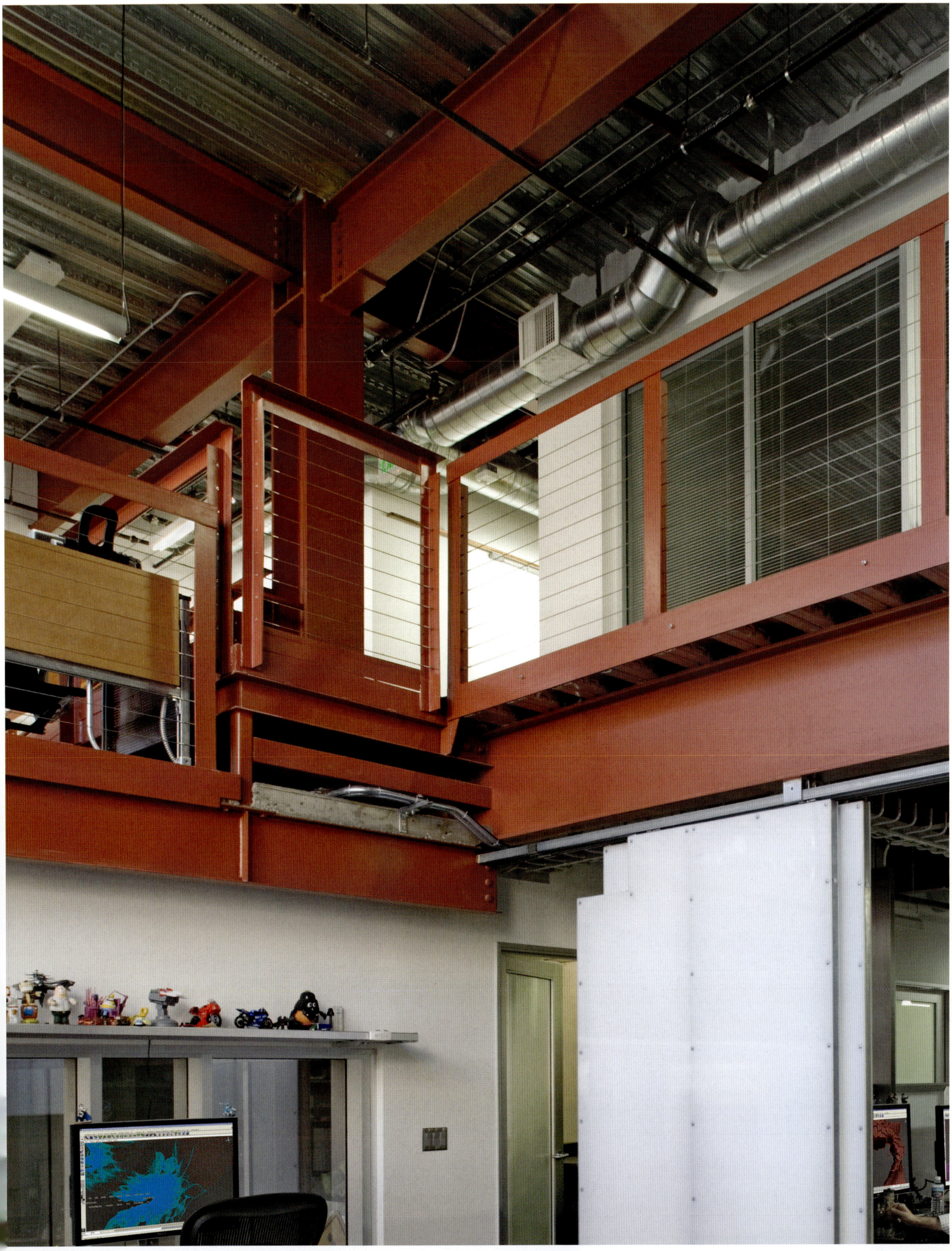

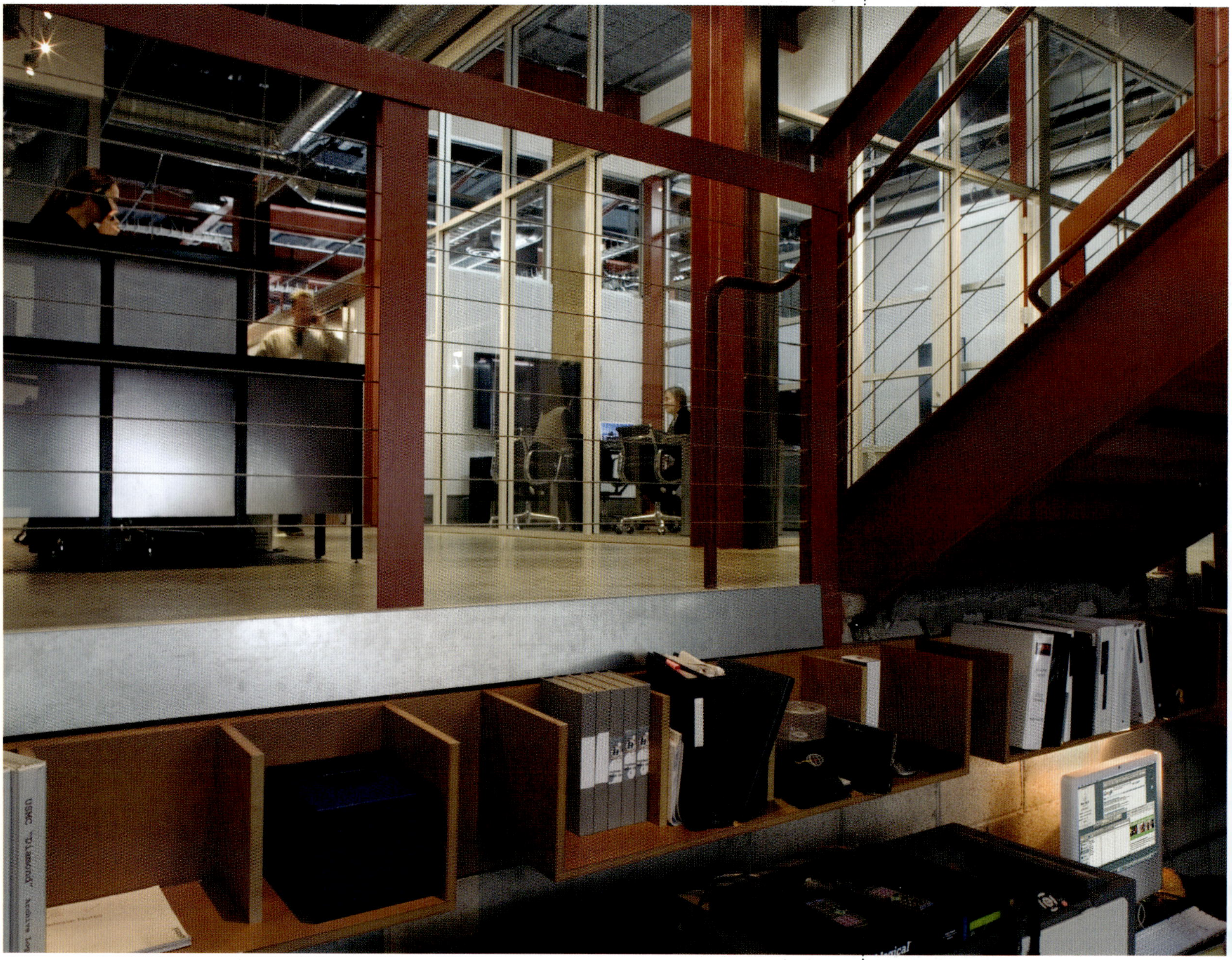
USMC "Diamond"

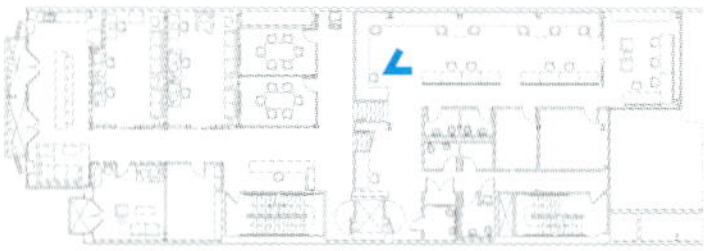

○ The metal constructive structure of the building has been left visible and painted dark red. The steps and banister of the stairs that connect the floors have also been painted this color.

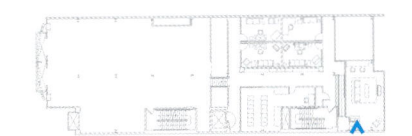

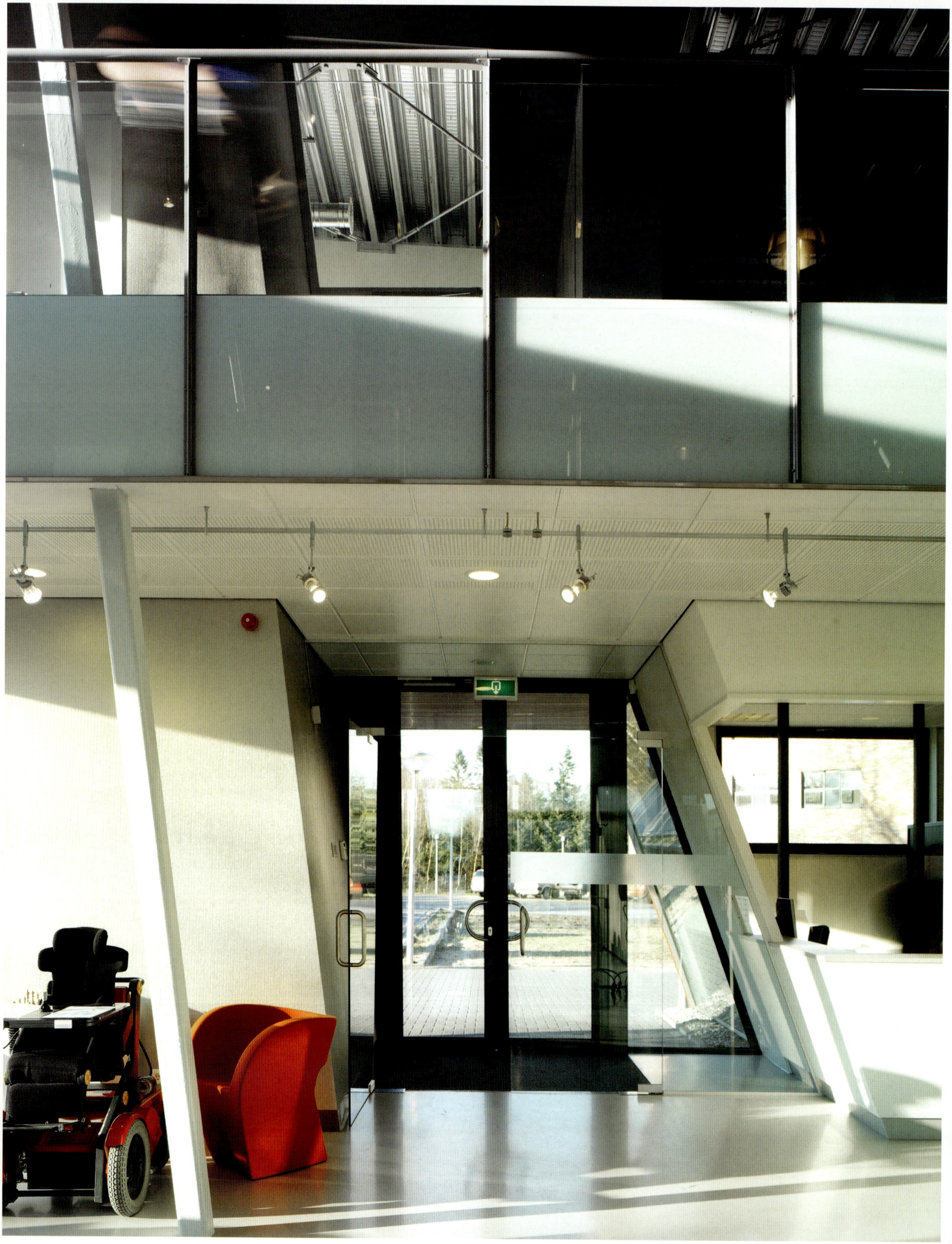

Indes Offices

A park next to a train station, where almost all the buildings have an anodyne and conventional appearance, is the setting for these offices. The initial aim to create an attractive space here did not originally seem like an appropriate solution.

The commission for the project came from a company dedicated to the industrial design of sophisticated technical applications. They wanted their installations, which occupy a three-story building, to be pleasant, practical, and to strengthen their corporate image. The design has brought this idea to life with a view of making this place a symbol of the company.

The major feature of the program is the teamwork area, which has no partitions and is located on the top floor. All the designers' offices are connected to this large space, located in the wing of the building that looks over the train tracks, on the top floor. On the middle floor are the toilets, archives, and storage, while the ground floor contains the reception area and areas for seeing clients.

Many of the pieces that comprise the furniture are movable, a characteristic that responds to the desire for space flexibility stated in the brief.

This also favors the dynamism created by the project, which can be seen in the large façade windows that present the outside with different projections of the activity inside, under different combinations of lights. These windows also serve as viewing points for occupants of the offices.

Another aspect that distinguishes these offices is there sustainability. Although the three-story building attempts to make the company as visible as possible, the vertical volume also favors natural ventilation. In addition, a pump has been installed that extracts energy from the earth to control the interior temperature with hot and cold air.

ARCHITECT/DESIGNER:
ARCONIKO ARCHITECTEN

Client: Indes Design
Photographer: Luuk Kramer
Location: Enschede, The Netherlands
Completion date: 2005
Area: 15,608 SF

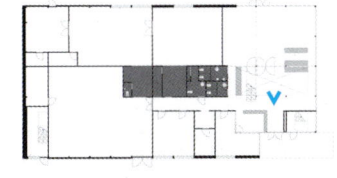

○ A geothermal pump supplies warmth in the winter and cold air in summer by way of a radiant air-conditioning and heating system installed in the floor. Another sustainable feature is the building's verticality.

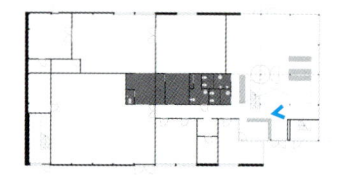

INDES OFFICES
385

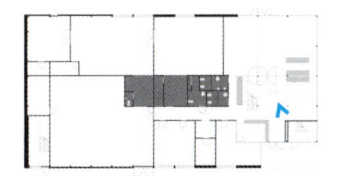

INDES OFFICES
386

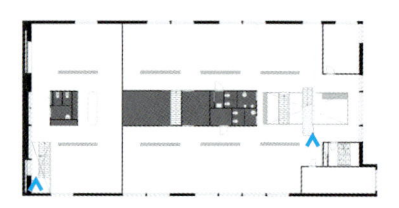

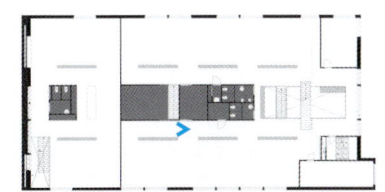

● Although the surrounding, more conventional buildings do not favor creativity, the project has achieved a pleasant space, which is open to the exterior via large windows, and flexible thanks to the movable furniture.

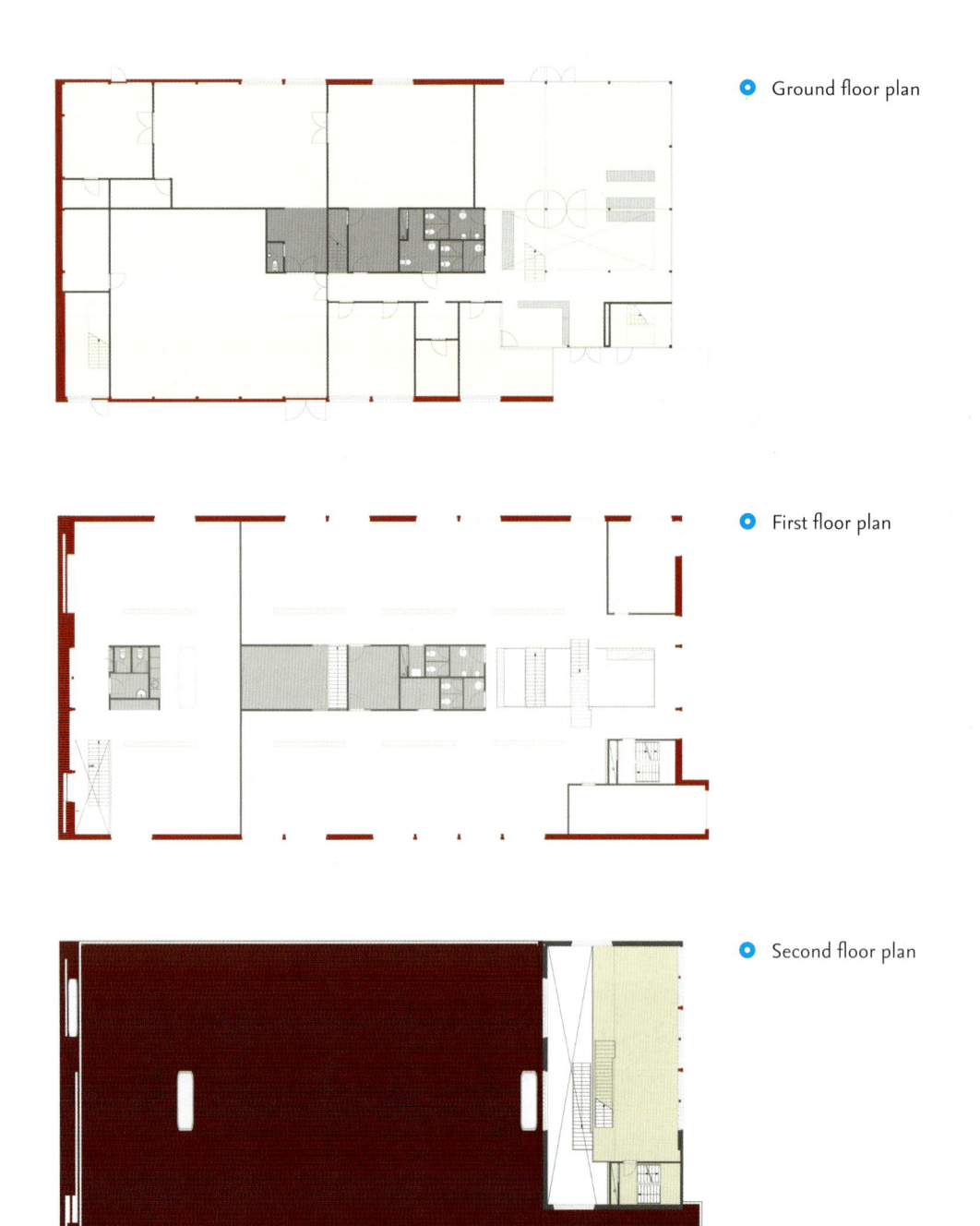

INDES OFFICES

Ground floor plan

First floor plan

Second floor plan

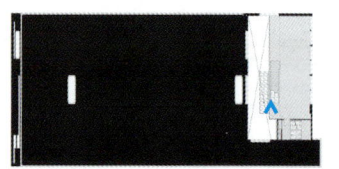

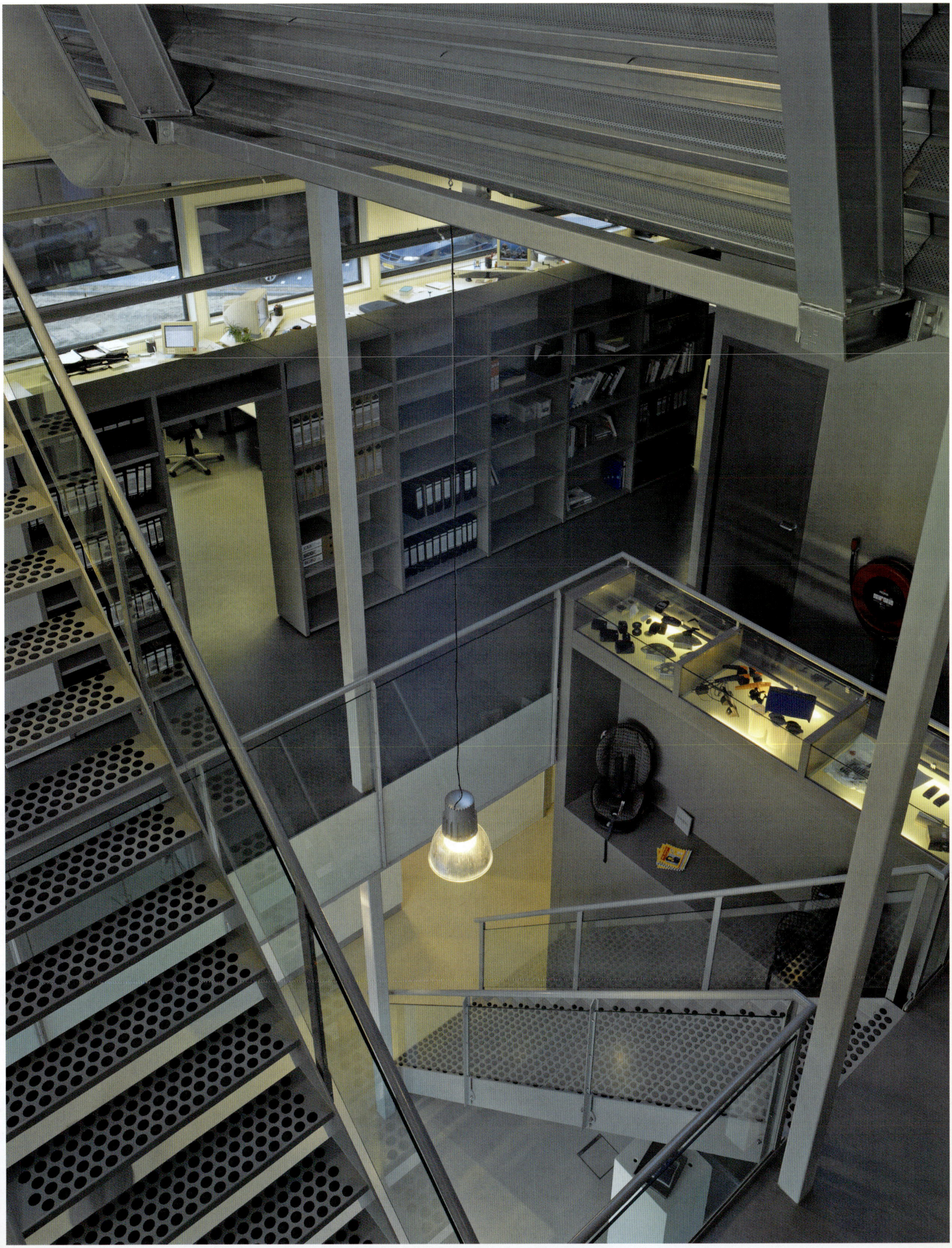

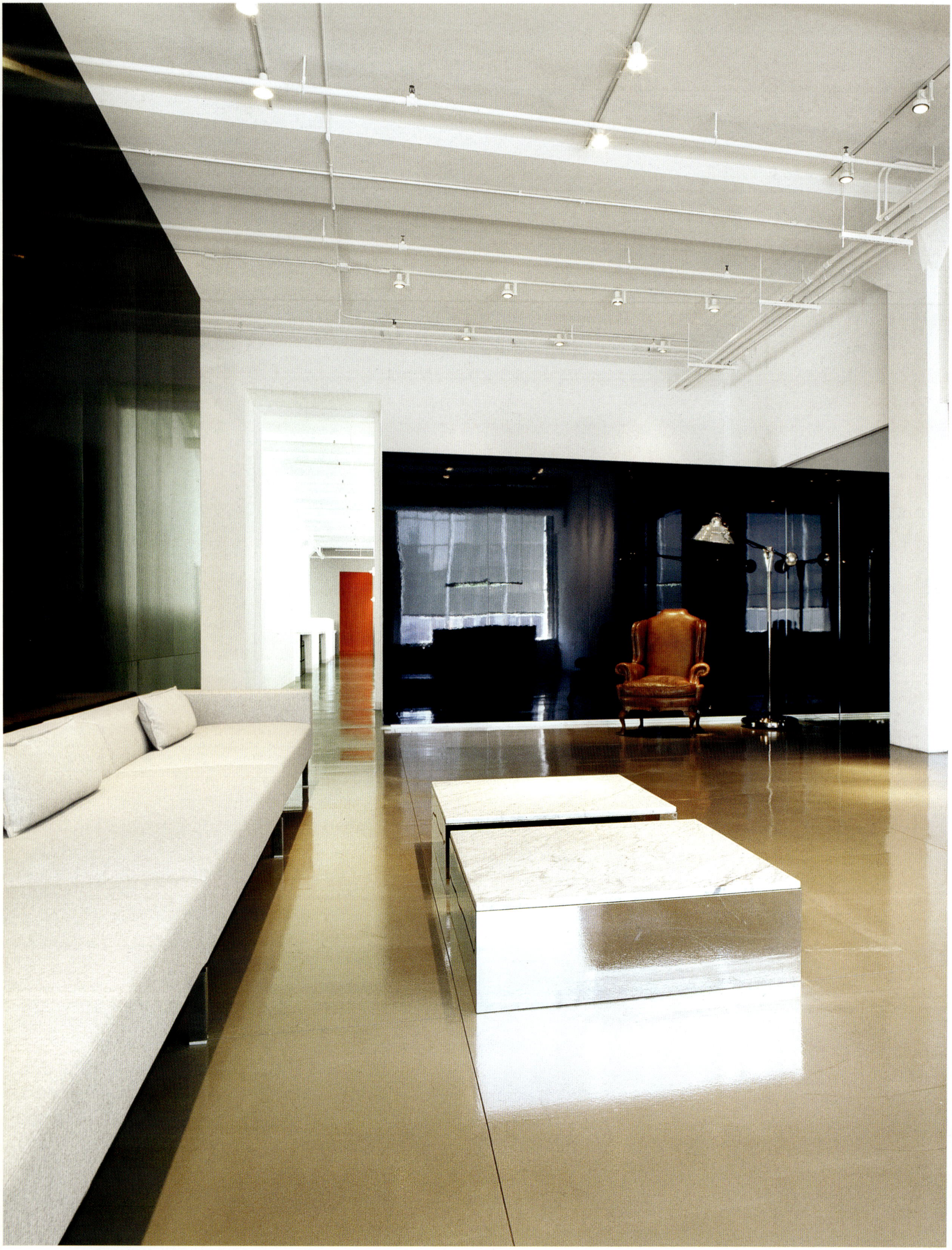

Laird + Partners Offices

ARCHITECT/DESIGNER:
BONETTI/KOZERSKI STUDIO

Client: Laird + Partners, advertising and brand imaging
Photographer: Matteo Piazza
Location: New York, NY
Completion date: 2003
Area: 18,000 SF

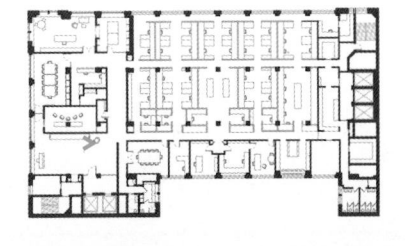

Number 475, 10th avenue in New York is the highest building on the street and is the location of these offices belonging to a major advertising and branding company. The architect received the commission for creating a space with elegance and distinction, in keeping with its location, one of New York's major business districts—and with the other offices in the building—occupied by companies such as designer Massimo Vignelli, architect Richard Meier, architects Gwathmey and Siegel and the hotel company Ian Schrager Group.

Originally, the space for this project housed the printing press for a multinational publishing company.

The program begins with the blue lacquered lobby, which is followed by a large waiting and lounge area, apt for use as both a hall and an informal meeting place. A large office structure, molded from black bakelite, dominates this space, which attracts attention as soon as one enters.

Inside the bakelite volume are the main work areas: the large meeting room, the offices for technical personnel, and a room for presenting campaigns to clients. At the back, in the south-facing section are the management offices and the library.

Old oak has been chosen for the furnishings, varnished in different colors ranging from silver for the tables in the hall to red for the chairs in the library, and a natural tone for a set of stool-chairs.

The sliding doors inside the bakelite office and in the library are lacquered wood, while those in the management offices are made from sheet glass.

The space enjoys the inherited advantage of high ceilings, which are typical of luxurious buildings of this age, as well as large windows that allow abundant natural light to enter. Halogen lights constitute the artificial lighting, installed on rails around the perimeter of the rooms and also as task lighting.

LAIRD + PARTNERS OFFICES
392

● The sofas and tables have been distributed to enhance the sense of size in this space. The shelves in the library, made from dark varnished oak, enrich this area of the office (see page 397).

LAIRD + PARTNERS OFFICES
393

LAIRD + PARTNERS OFFICES
394

LAIRD + PARTNERS OFFICES

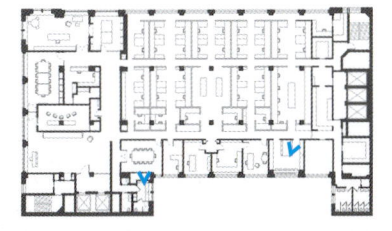

● The materials have been chosen for their richness and their sensorial attraction, another factor the company hopes will strengthen relations with clients, most of who come from major businesses.

LAIRD + PARTNERS OFFICES

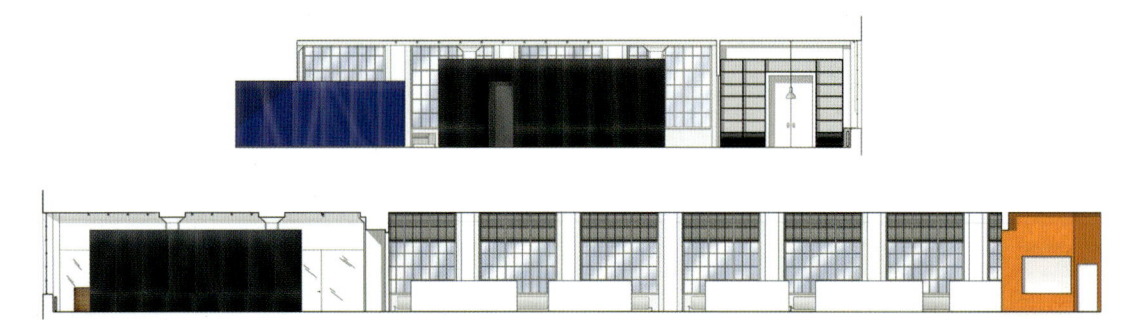

○ Elevation

○ Floor plan

1. Elevator lobby
2. Mechanical room
3. Reception area
4. Coat closet
5. Showroom/Conference room 1
6. Showroom/Conference room 2
7. Conference room
8. Pantry
9. Executive assistance office
10. Assistance office
11. Executive office
12. Library
13. Handicap-accessible restroom
14. Private bathroom
15. Meeting room
16. Office
17. Mechanical room
18. Stock room
19. Men's restroom
20. Women's restroom
21. Cutting/Mark-up area
22. Layout area
23. Open office
24. Fax/Copy room
25. Stock room

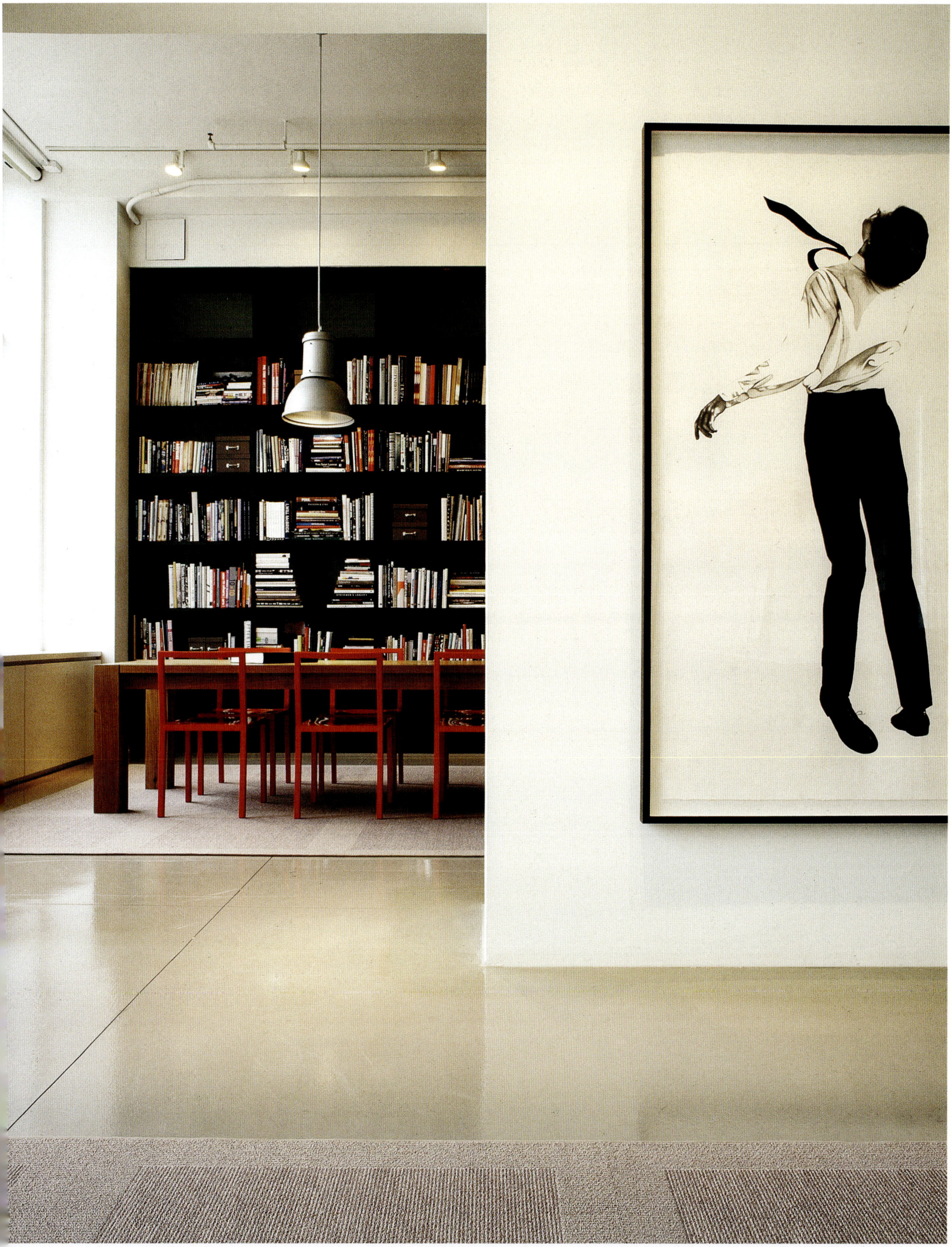

Large Offices

Glocal Law	400
 DDB Office Hong Kong	410
 GREY Worldwide	420
 Krungthai AXA Life Insurance	426
 Affinity Offices	436
 Vanke Cheugdu Commercial Complex	446
 Office Building A. T. Kearney	454
 Offices on Mestre Nicolau Street	462
 Kropman	470
 Momentum St. Louis	478

Clariant Flexible Office	490
 Caballero Factory	496
 Bendigo Bank Offices	508
 Mayo Institute of Technology	516
 Indra Offices	524
 Rijkswaterstaat Zeeland Head Office	536
 Ermenegildo Zegna	544
 Mediabank Private	556
 Deloitte Head Offices	568
 Laakhaven den Haag Complex	580
 Agbar Tower Offices	588

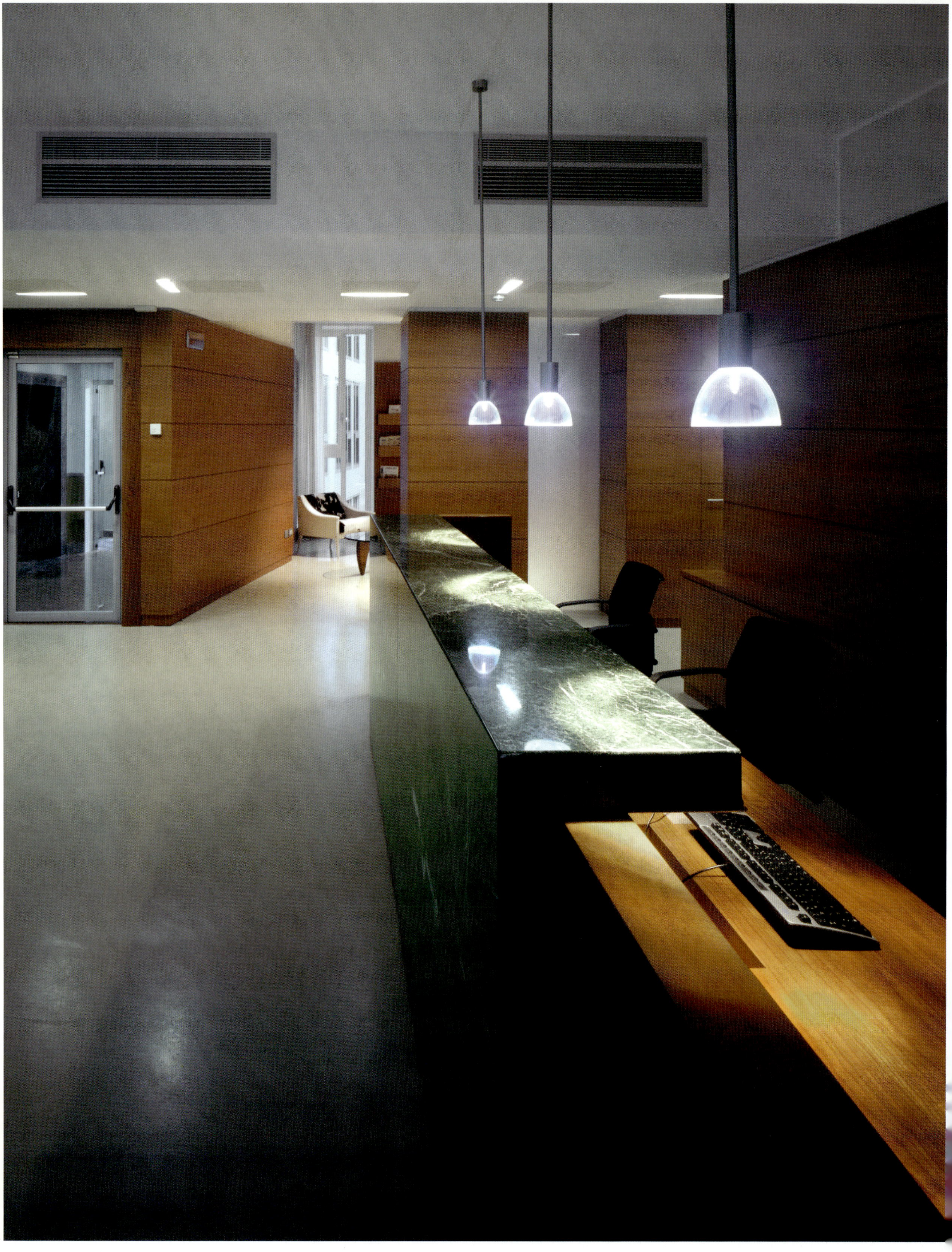

GLOCAL LAW

These offices are located in a building designed by Gio Ponti in 1963, located in the business district of this Italian city. The client who commissioned the project is one of the most famous and prestigious law firms in the world.

The first area on which the designers focused was the *lawyer's cell*. In this space, two spaces were created for two different uses: one zone called *day* and the other *night*. The *night* zone is characterized by cupboards finished in cherry wood for storing the least frequently used documents. The *day* zone has shelves of the same material to make room for materials used on a daily basis, as well as a work table and the equipment needed for the activity in this office, like printers, computers, etc.

Due to the large number of clients and the volume of work that the company has on a constant basis, various meeting rooms have been created. The main room pays homage to architect Ponti with a table that can sit up to twenty-six people and which makes reference to the Pirelli tower, the Italian architect's most famous building. The wall between the main meeting room and the passageway has been clad in cherrywood panels, some of which are mobile. The corridor functions as a gallery, where openings in the wall correspond to cupboards on the opposite side, which are projected toward the corridor.

These offices are distinguished by the materials used to clad the horizontal and vertical surfaces. The cherrywood, glass, and acrylic resin together present an aesthetic of order and transparency, two values that represent the firm's culture. However, the main goal of the project was to win the daily battle against paperwork, with the aim of creating a serene environment to work in.

ARCHITECT/DESIGNER:
CONRAD-BERCAH/W OFFICE

Client: Cleary Gottlieb Steen & Hamilton LLP
Photographer: Alberto Muciaccia
Location: Milan, Italy
Completion date: 2006
Area: 21,528 SF

● The design combines three main colors: white, black, and brown, which have been applied to the furniture, the floor and the decor. The chromatic austerity strengthens the serenity of the environment.

GLOCAL LAW

GLOCAL LAW
404

GLOCAL LAW
405

GLOCAL LAW
406

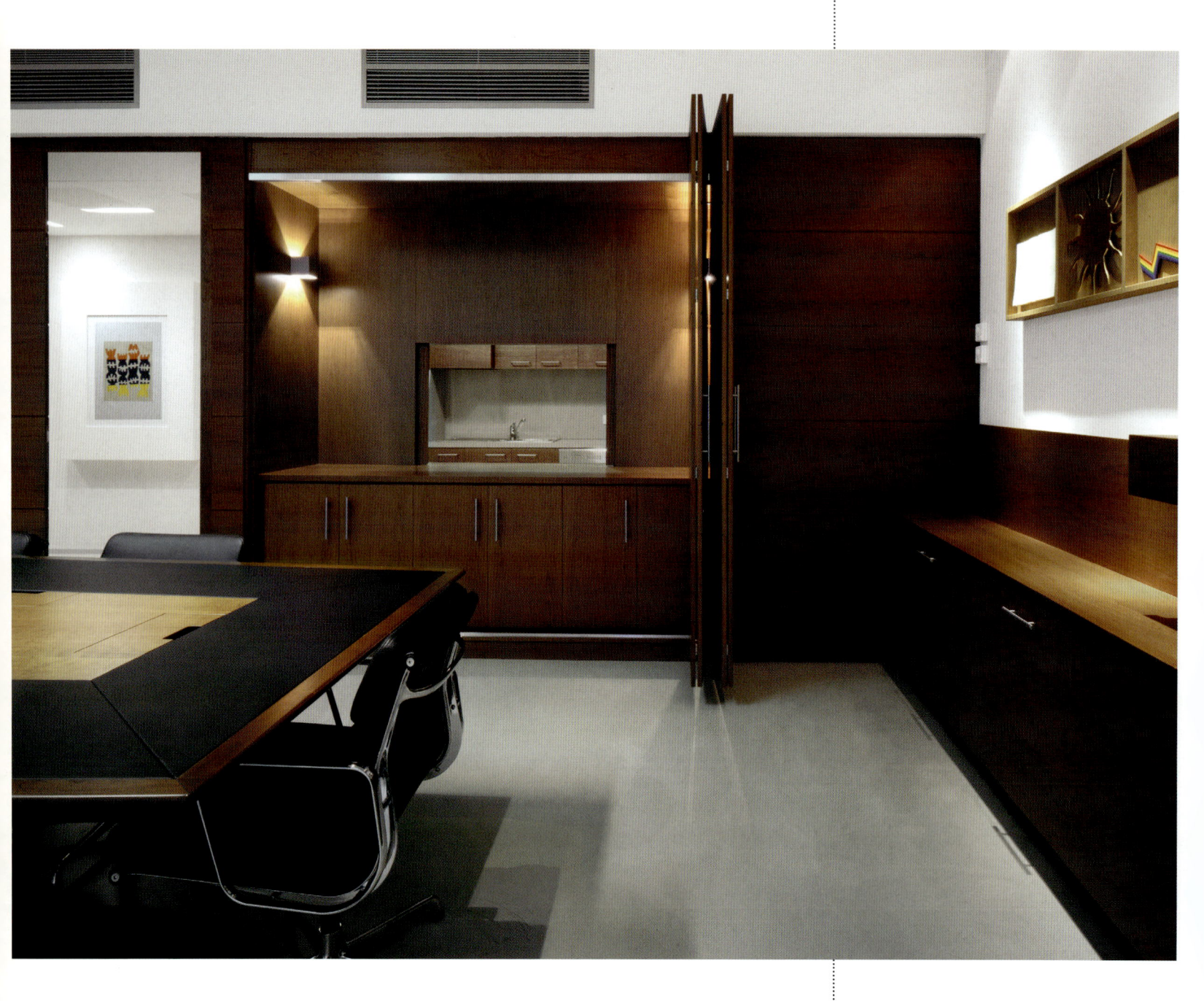

GLOCAL LAW
407

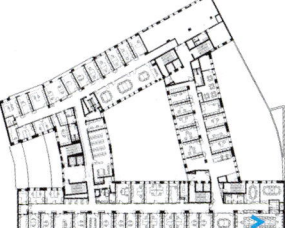

○ The meeting room and the day work area are the spaces that benefit most from the scarce natural light in the offices, due to their location in this busy financial district in Milan.

GLOCAL LAW
408

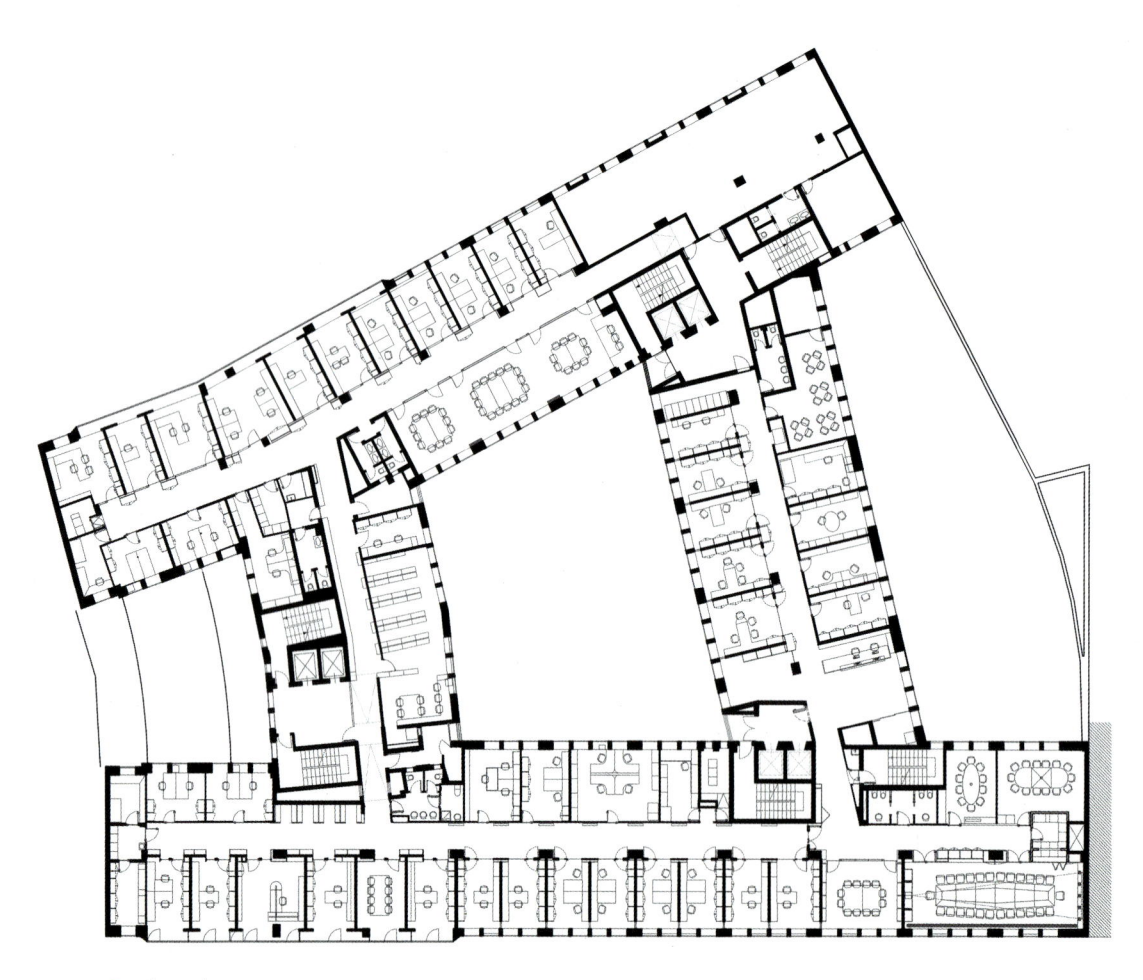

○ Floor plan

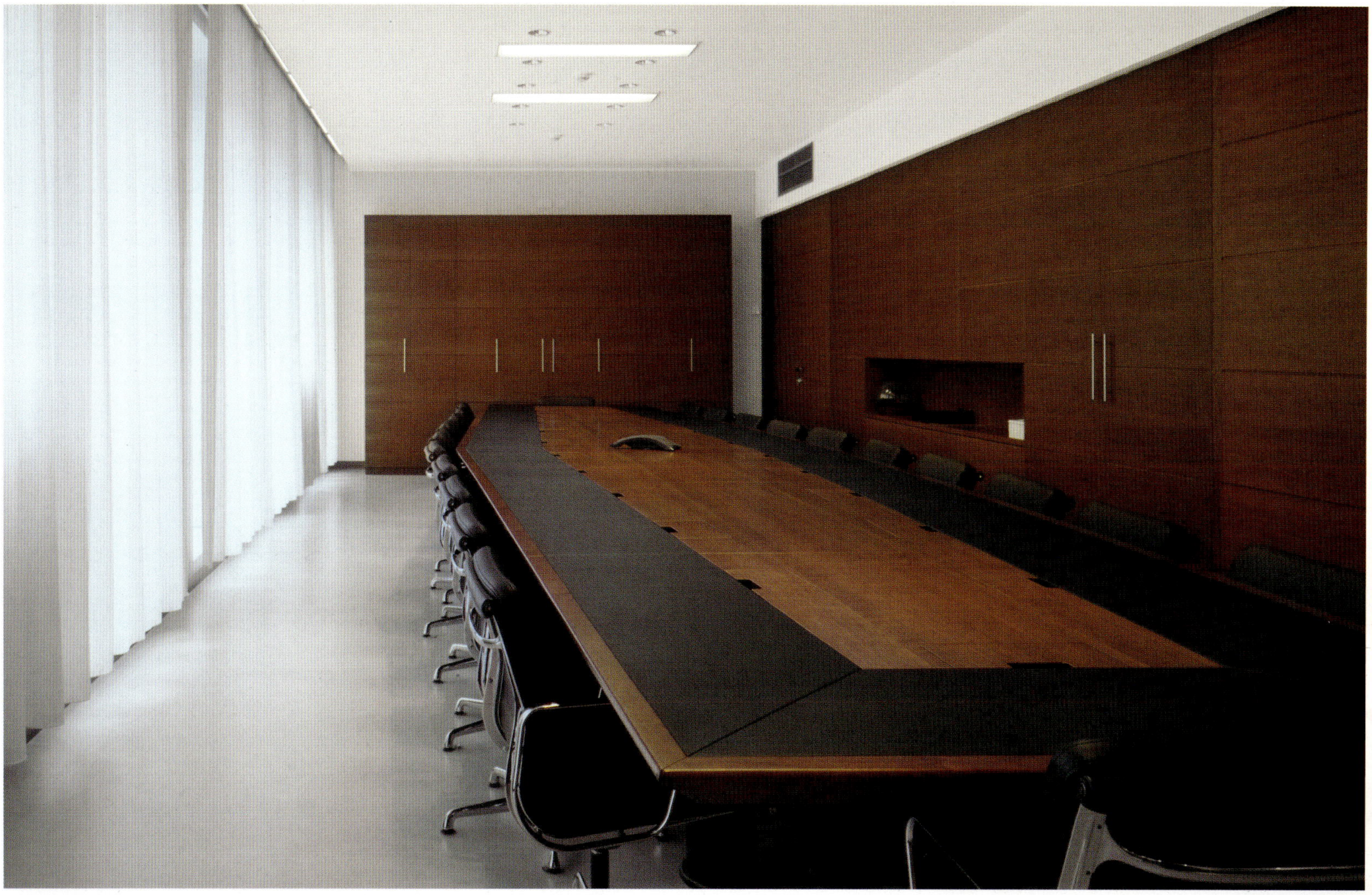

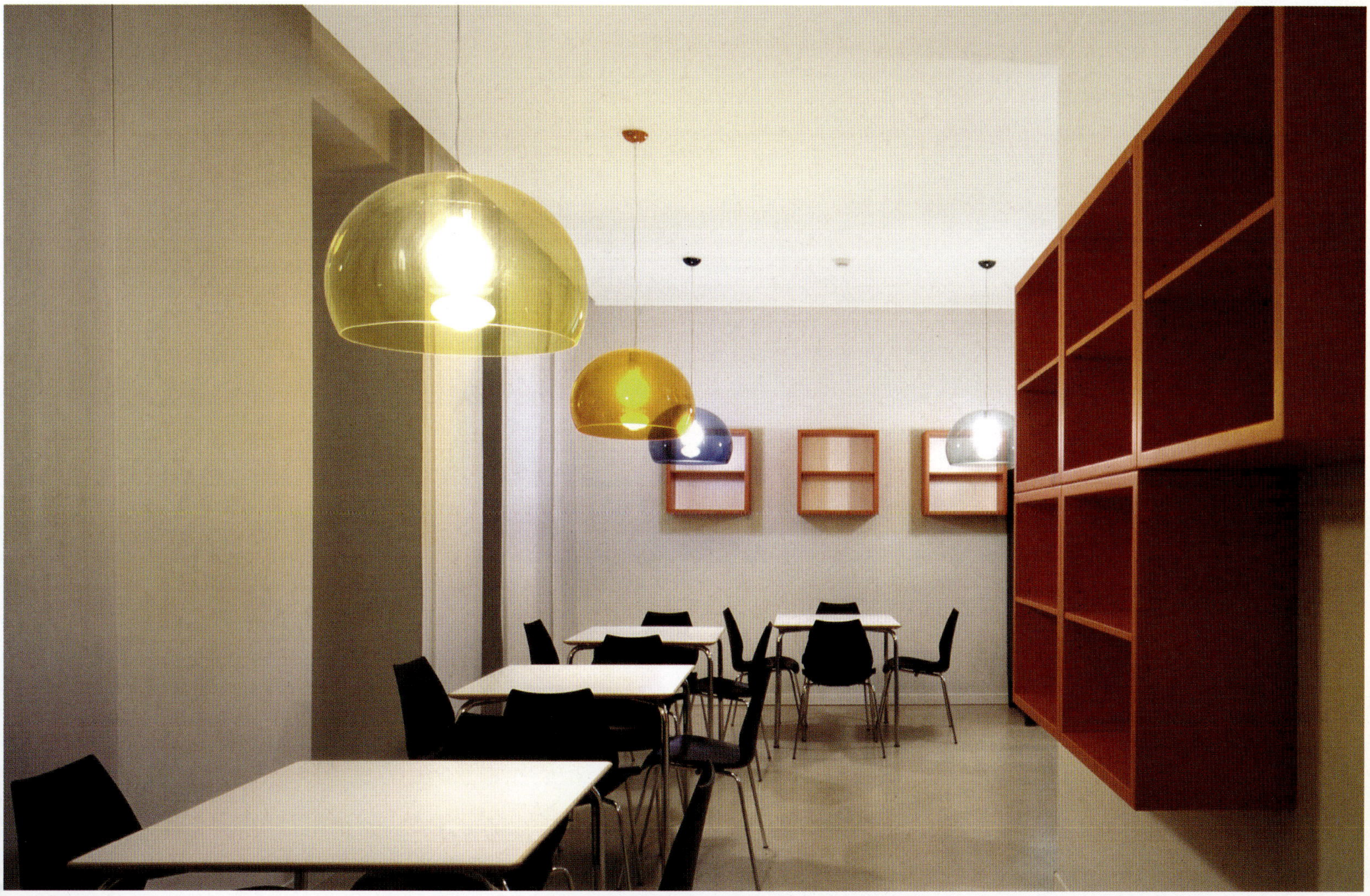

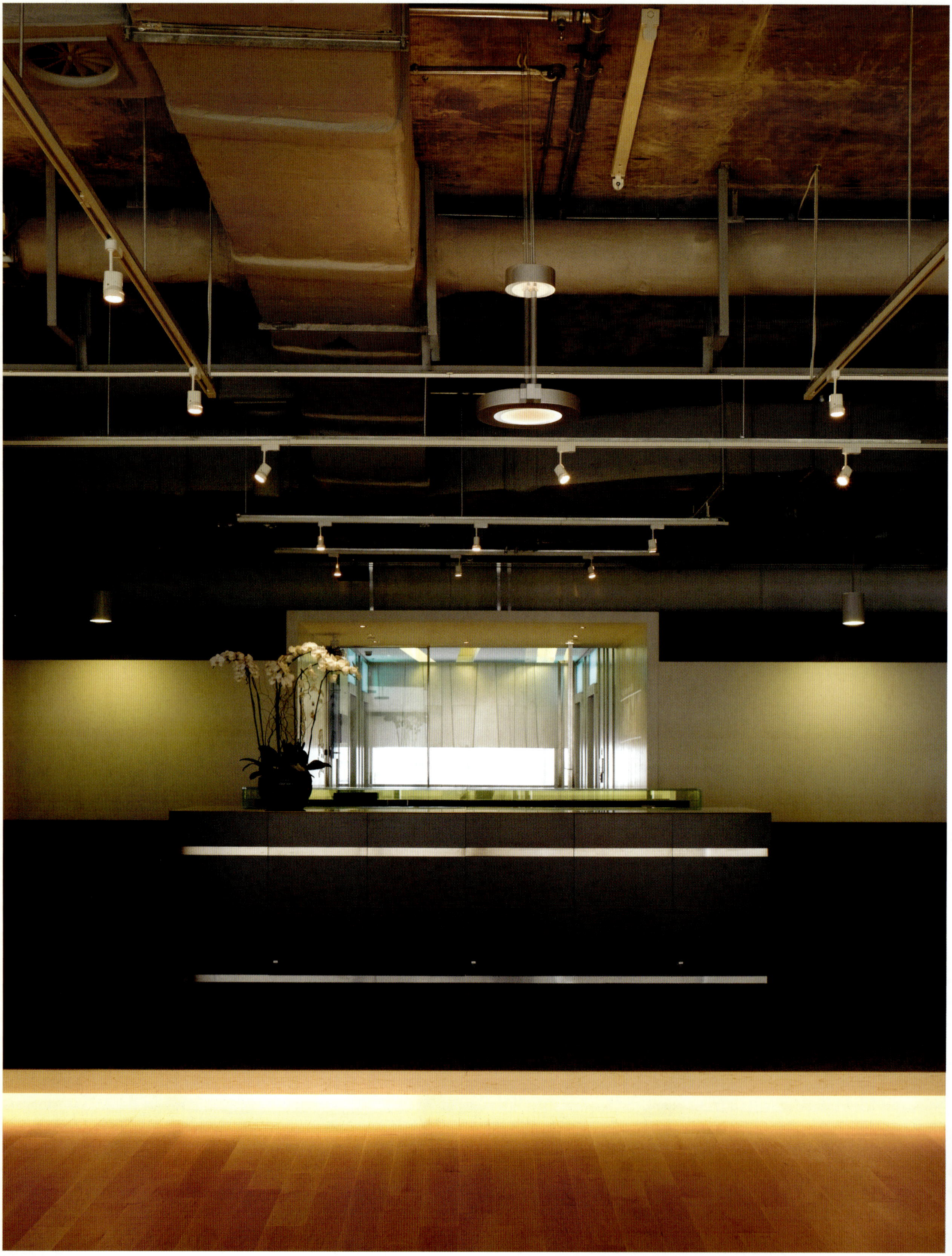

DDB Office Hong Kong

The multi-national advertising agency DDB commissioned this project for its Hong Kong offices. The brief required the creation of a working environment that would stimulate artistic creativity in the young minds of the accounts executives. The surface area covers a single floor of 23,412 square feet.

The company wanted the offices to reaffirm their corporate identity at the same time as allowing each member of staff to express their personality individually. This is reflected in the opening of the spaces, the distribution of the furniture—composed only of items considered to be essential—and the color scheme.

The work areas and meeting zones area all large spaces where visual communication is uninterrupted thanks to the absence of partitions or, in the closed rooms, with partitions and doors made from glass. A combination of levels throughout the floor creates different functional spaces, from those designated for brainstorming to places of meditation. Some are designed to carry out these activities in a formal way and others are more informal. Thus, while the formal meeting room has individual armchairs, its informal counterpart features benches that run down either side of the table. In contrast to the conventional desks, there are places for meditation such as a bubble chair suspended from the ceiling, stairs from a swimming pool, or a seating tier by the large windows of the façade.

As well as using the yellow and black from the company's corporate identity, the color schememainly includes the colors of the construction materials: silver from the aluminum, the different shades of the parquet on the floor—from light tones to almost black—and white from some of the pieces of furniture.

When entering the offices, the visitor is greeted by a white lobby where a display window presents the projects in progress, a prologue to the communication and openness found inside this office.

ARCHITECT/DESIGNER:

CL3 ARCHITECTS LIMITED

Client: DDB Worldwide Limited
Photographer: CL3 Architects Limited
Location: Hong Kong, China
Completion date: 2006
Area: 23,412 SF

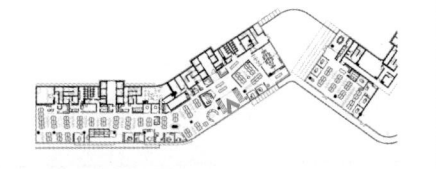

DDB OFFICE HONG KONG

● The executive offices are divided on three sides with wooden panels and on the fourth with glass, where the access is located. They are private yet visually communicate with their surroundings.

DDB OFFICE HONG KONG

413

DDB OFFICE HONG KONG

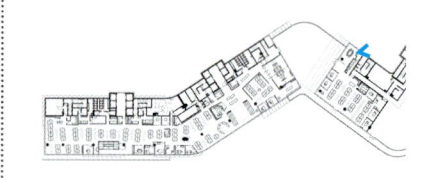

DDB OFFICE HONG KONG
415

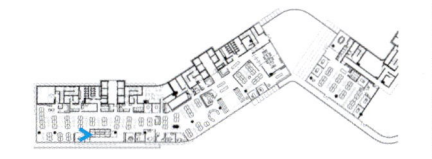

DDB OFFICE HONG KONG

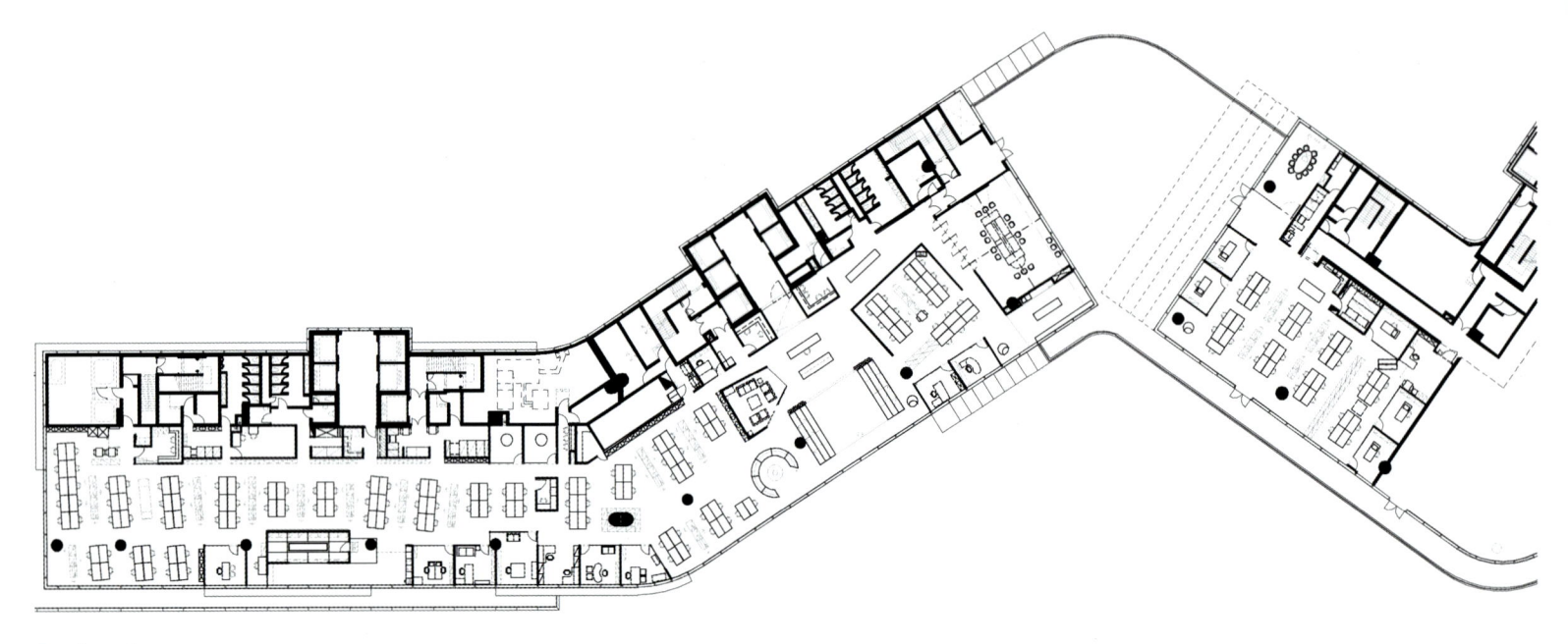

- Floor plan

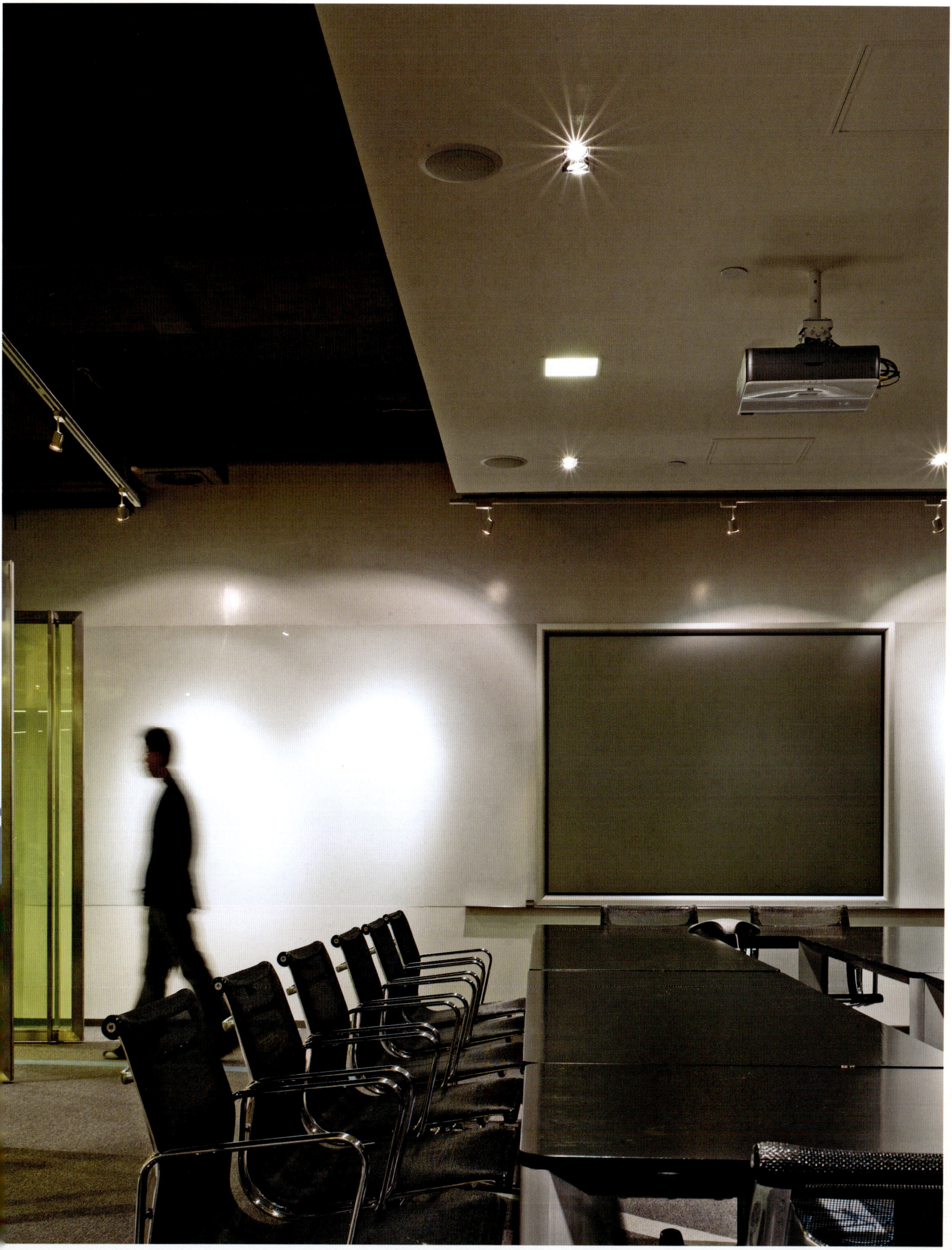

● Places for individual meditation have been distributed throughout the office, such as a transparent plastic armchair, suspending from the ceiling, the seating tier next to the large windows of the façade, and the swimming pool stairs.

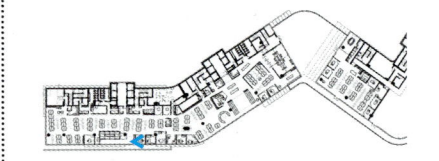

DDB OFFICE HONG KONG
419

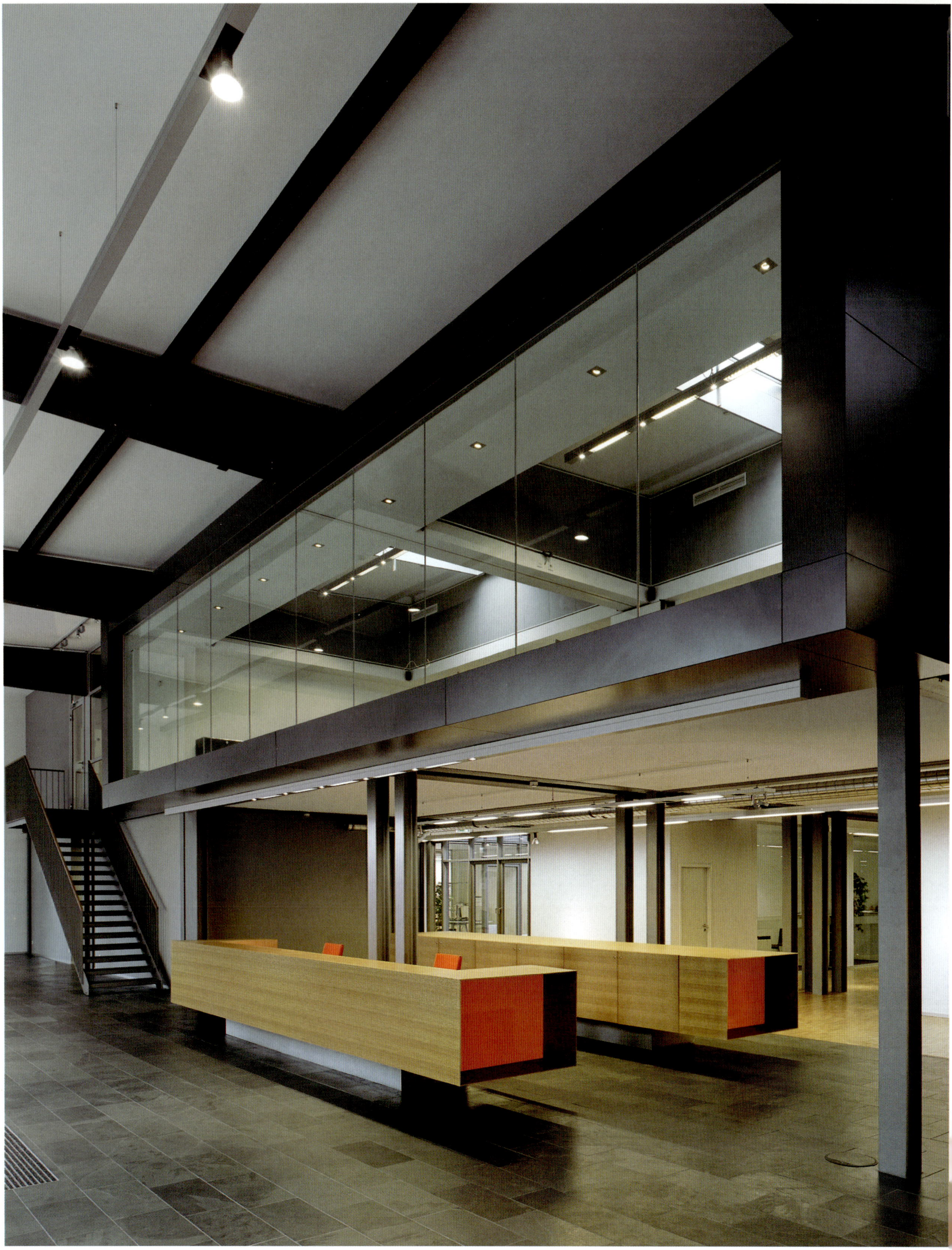

GREY WORLDWIDE

The project for the offices of this major advertising and communication agency is located in a listed building that used to be a warehouse, located in the German city of Hamburg.

The layout has been developed on the base of the original structure, so the space distribution follows a two-story loft scheme.

The design of the interior responds to the notion of openness and transparency between the individual offices and the work stations. These are grouped together in an area without partitions, generating a floor plan that is at once functional and decorative. The same aesthetic can be found in the glazed courtyards, the rest areas, and the rooms for meeting the public, and creates a motivating working environment. The surprising details, the selection of materials, which enhance the characteristics of the building, and the use of the corporate colors in the design all serve to generate an atmosphere which is at once inspirational and full of life.

The iron beams and infastructure have been left visible and restored with a dark gray varnish. The chromatic result of this design option has iinspired the use of this dark gray, the silver from the aluminum, and white for the walls, etc.

On the ground floor, at street level, the access is located in front of a long reception desk; a cubic volume resting on a smaller plinth base with an MDF board tabletop and gloss red sides, which match the upholstery of the chairs. The same materials, cubic volumes and colors have been used for the long table and stools, which have been placed in an area next to the reception area. This was conceived to be used for informal meetings or as an unusual waiting room. The top floor contains the offices, located on either side of a corridor and separated by transparent glass partitions.

ARCHITECT/DESIGNER:

COSSMAN_DE BRUYN ARCHITEKTUR INNENARCHITEKTUR DESIGN

Client: GREY Worldwide Deutschland
Photographer: ArtDoku
Location: Düsseldorf, Germany
Completion date: 2005
Area: 32,938 SF

GREY WORLDWIDE

● The natural lighting comes from the large windows on the ground floor and the skylights on the top floor. This has been complemented by halogen lights, installed as downlighters and on light rails.

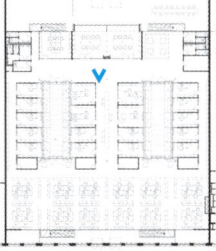

GREY WORLDWIDE

423

GREY WORLDWIDE
424

Floor plan

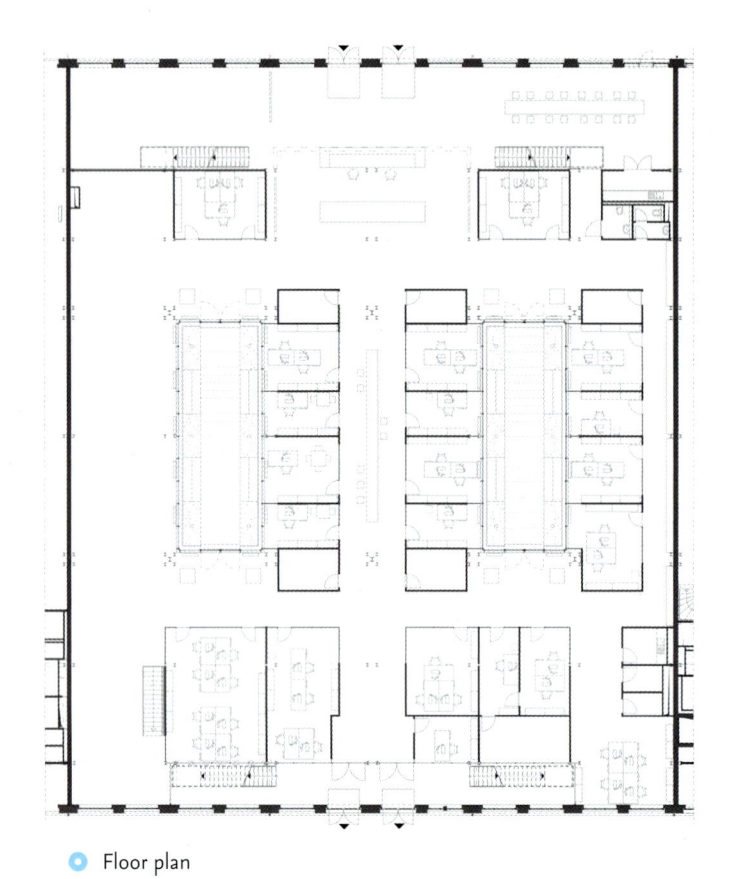

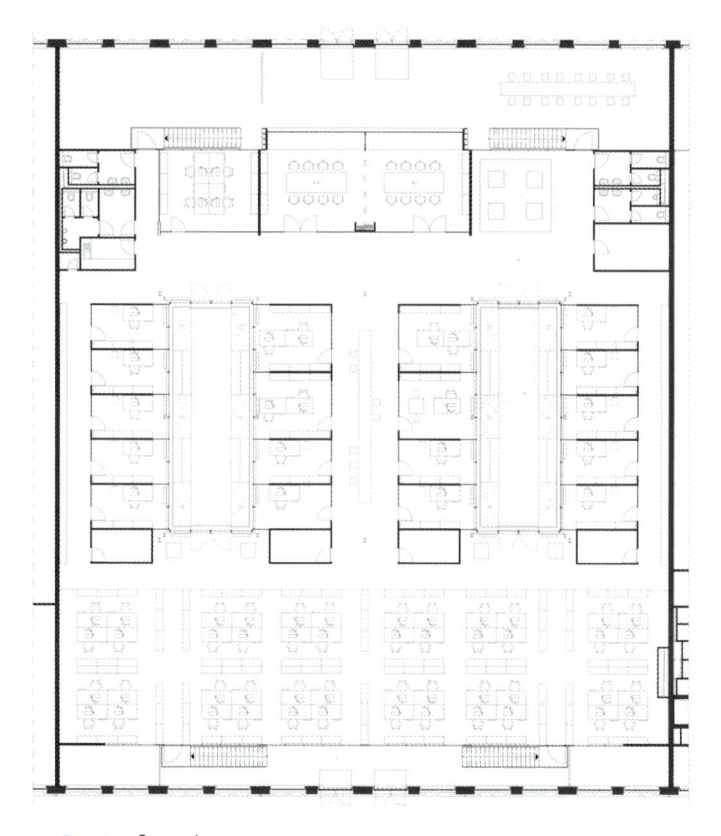

First floor plan

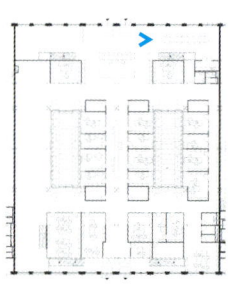

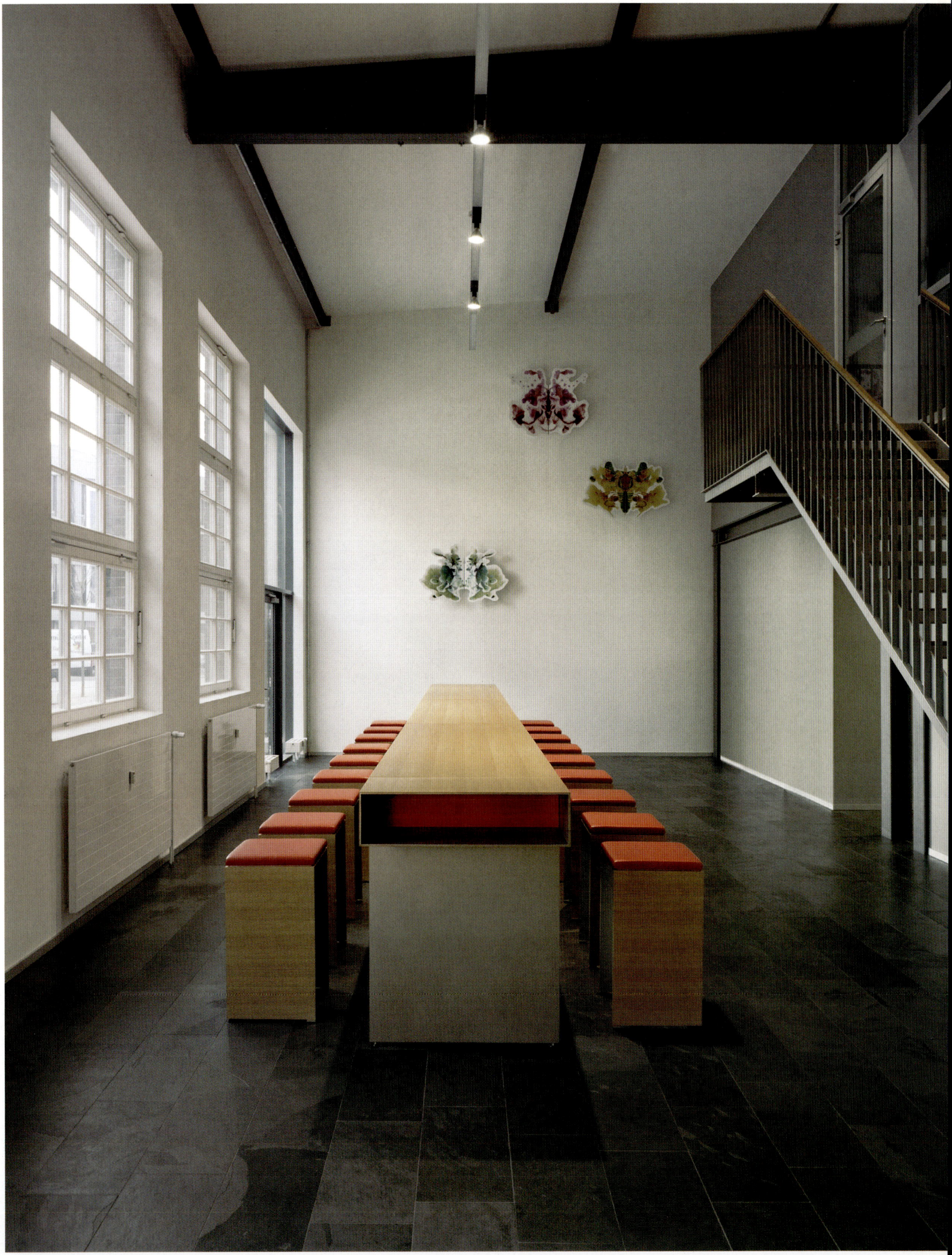

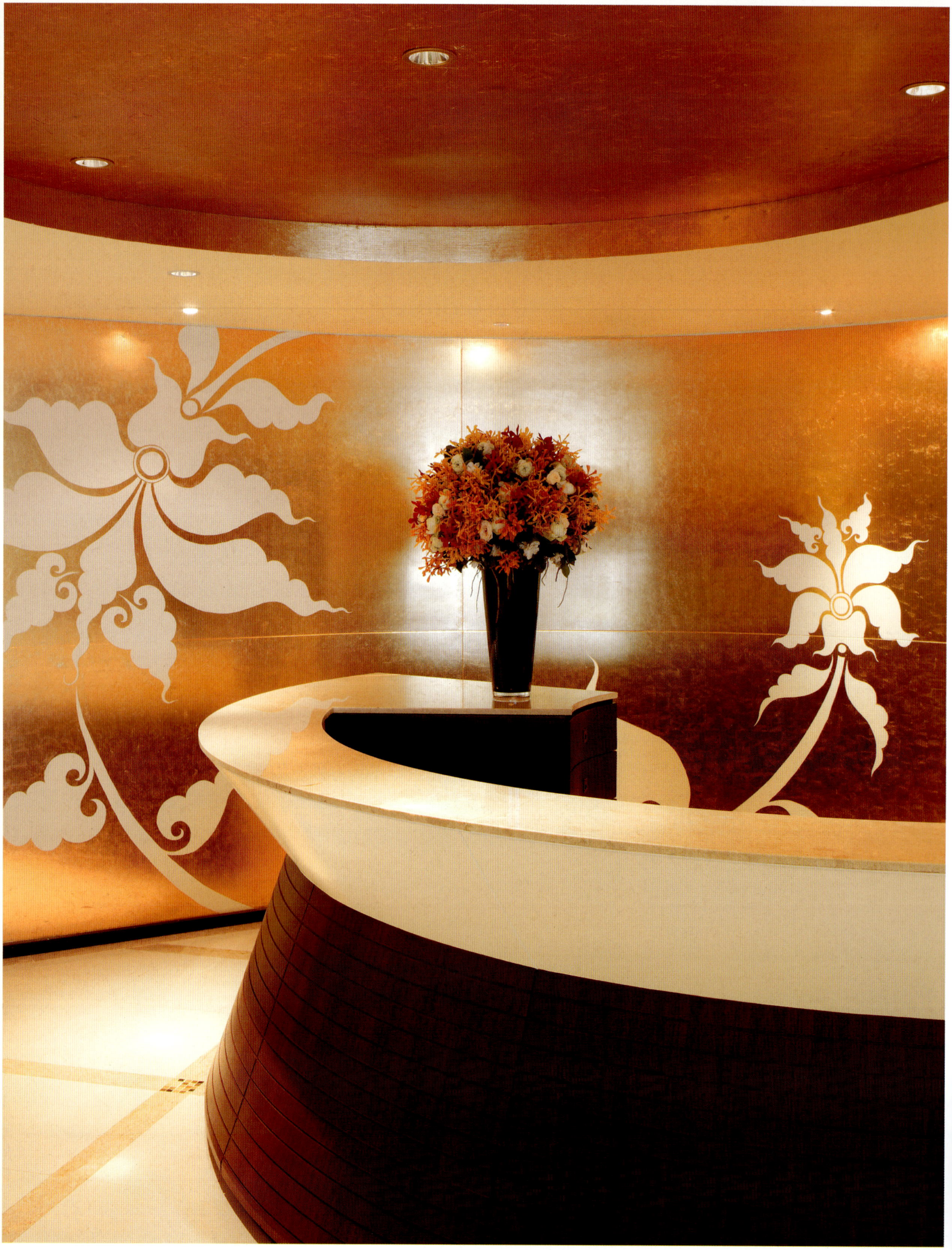

Krungthai AXA Life Insurance

The international insurance company AXA commissioned this project for their offices in Bangkok and the unusual brief required that the design reflect a modern-Thai style. The company wanted the interior to transmit the same relaxing sensation as a spa and, at the same time, reveal the local culture, adopt its warmth, and transmit it to clients who come to the office.

The design project was given to dwp, a studio that normally works in Asia, India, and the Middle East, and has offices in several cities in the area, including Bangkok. The designers chose four regional styles: *sukhothai*, *ayutthaya*, *issan*, and *lana*, one for each space, which also helped to define the different areas. All the styles and spaces share the common element of a huge rug designed as a river, which flows through the space and symbolizes togetherness.

The key elements to the design belong to Thai tradition: doors, organic finishes—almost all with organic motifs—golden leaves, Thai silk, fabric from tribes living in the mountains, decorated ceilings, rattan columns, and paintings in vaulted niches on the walls.

The lavish decor also includes religious objects inspired in traditional art, like bells and gongs, both on the walls and as medium-size objects distributed about the space.

Some of these elements have been adapted to a more modern aesthetic, such as the doors, into which glass panels have been incorporated. However, with the exception of the desks for administrative staff, which are arranged in a peninsula shape, and their respective modern and conventional chairs, the other items of furniture are Thai.

There are no divisions in this space and from the reception desk to the administrative and meetings area and through to the customer waiting areas, it is all contained within a single room, separated into functional zones.

Architect/Designer:
DWP Cityspace

Client: K. Saifon Sutchasila
Photographer: Robert McLeod
Location: Bangkok, Thailand
Completion date: 2006
Area: 33,906 SF

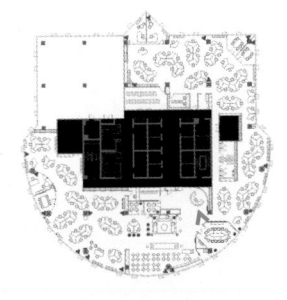

KRUNGTHAI AXA LIFE INSURANCE

○ Rattan can be found everywhere, in the chairs, the table bases, and the columns. The large pots contribute to the multi-colored decor, characteristic of Thai style.

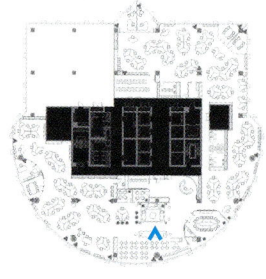

KRUNGTHAI AXA LIFE INSURANCE

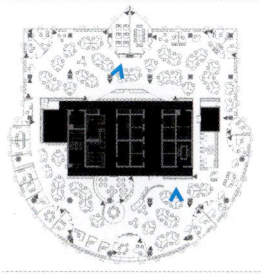

429

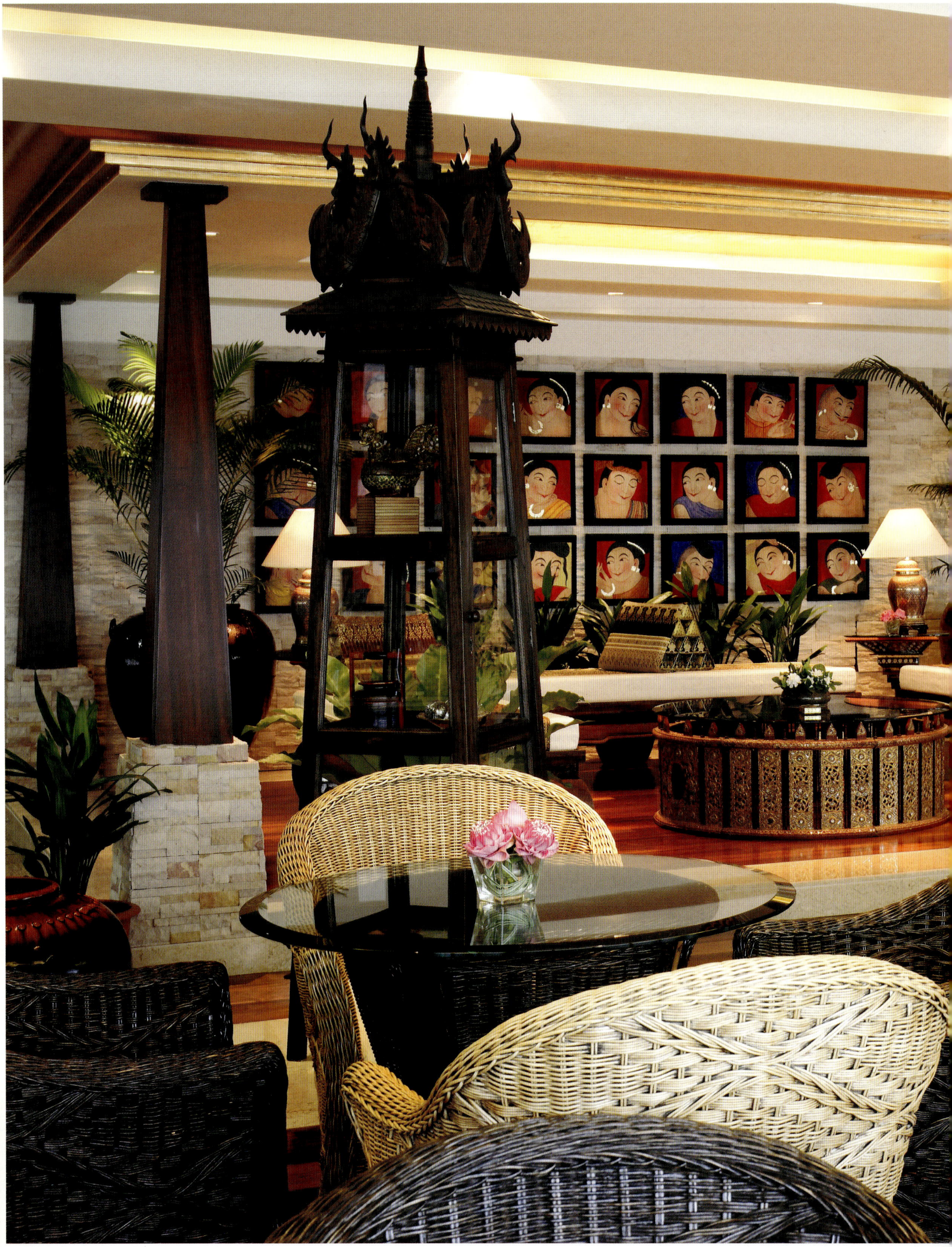

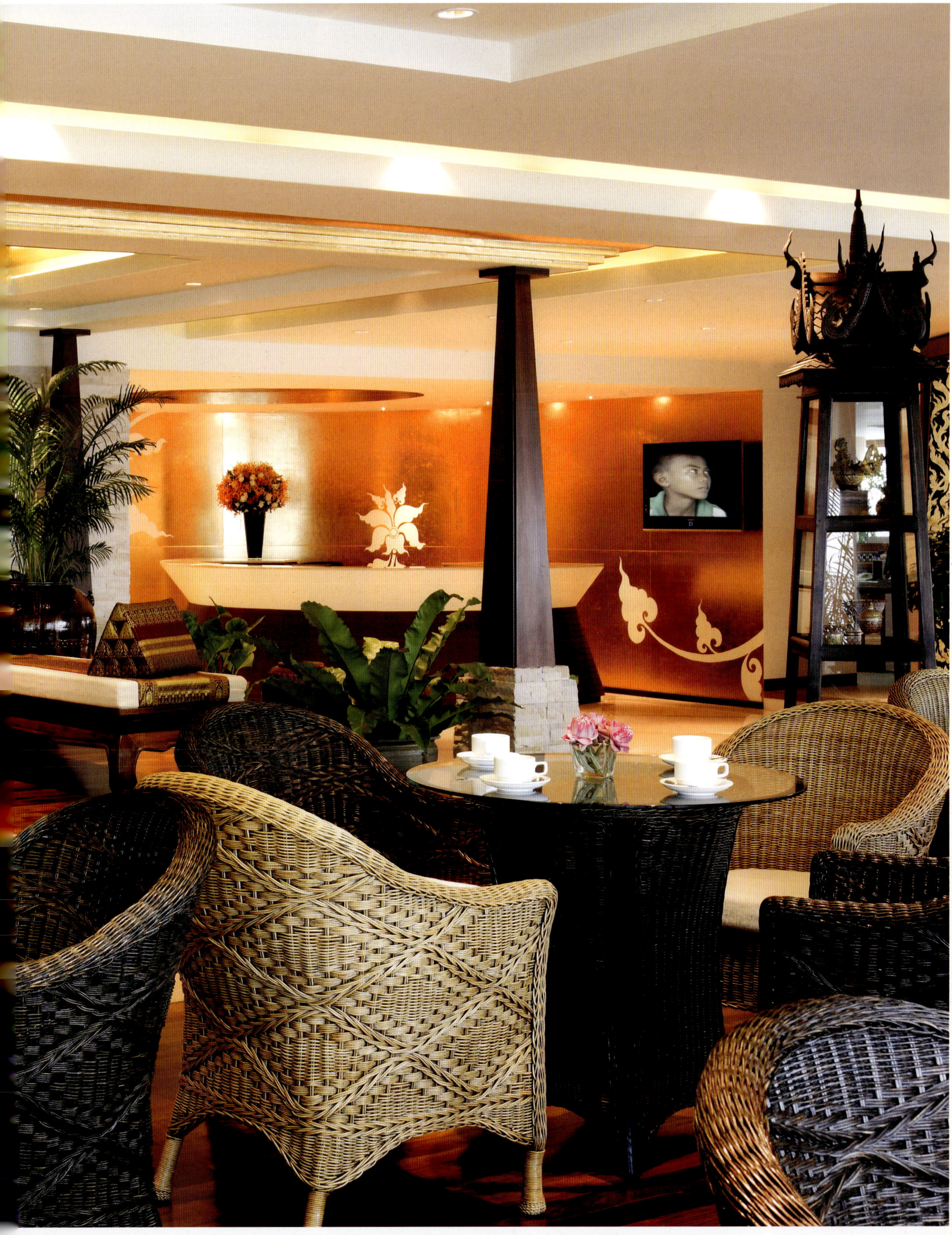

KRUNGTHAI AXA LIFE INSURANCE

432

○ Floor plan

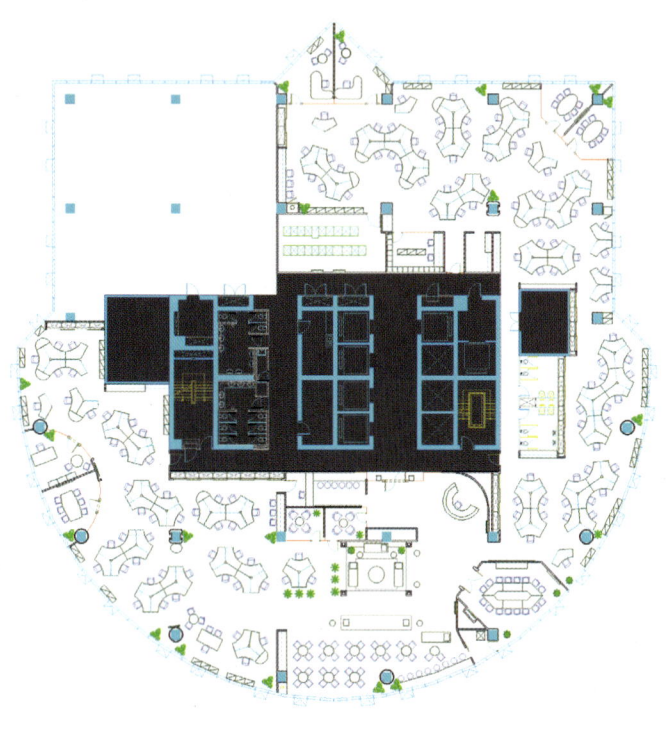

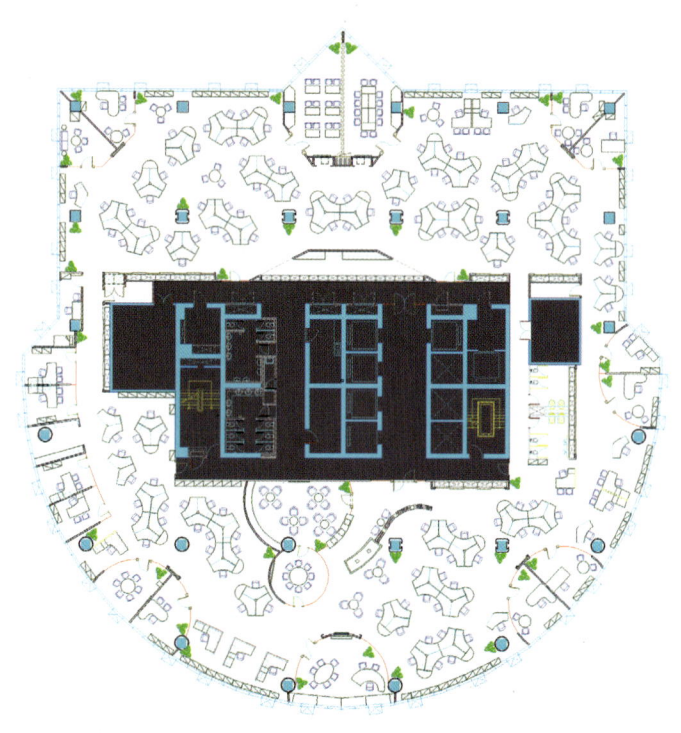

○ First floor plan

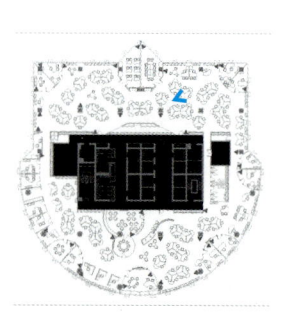

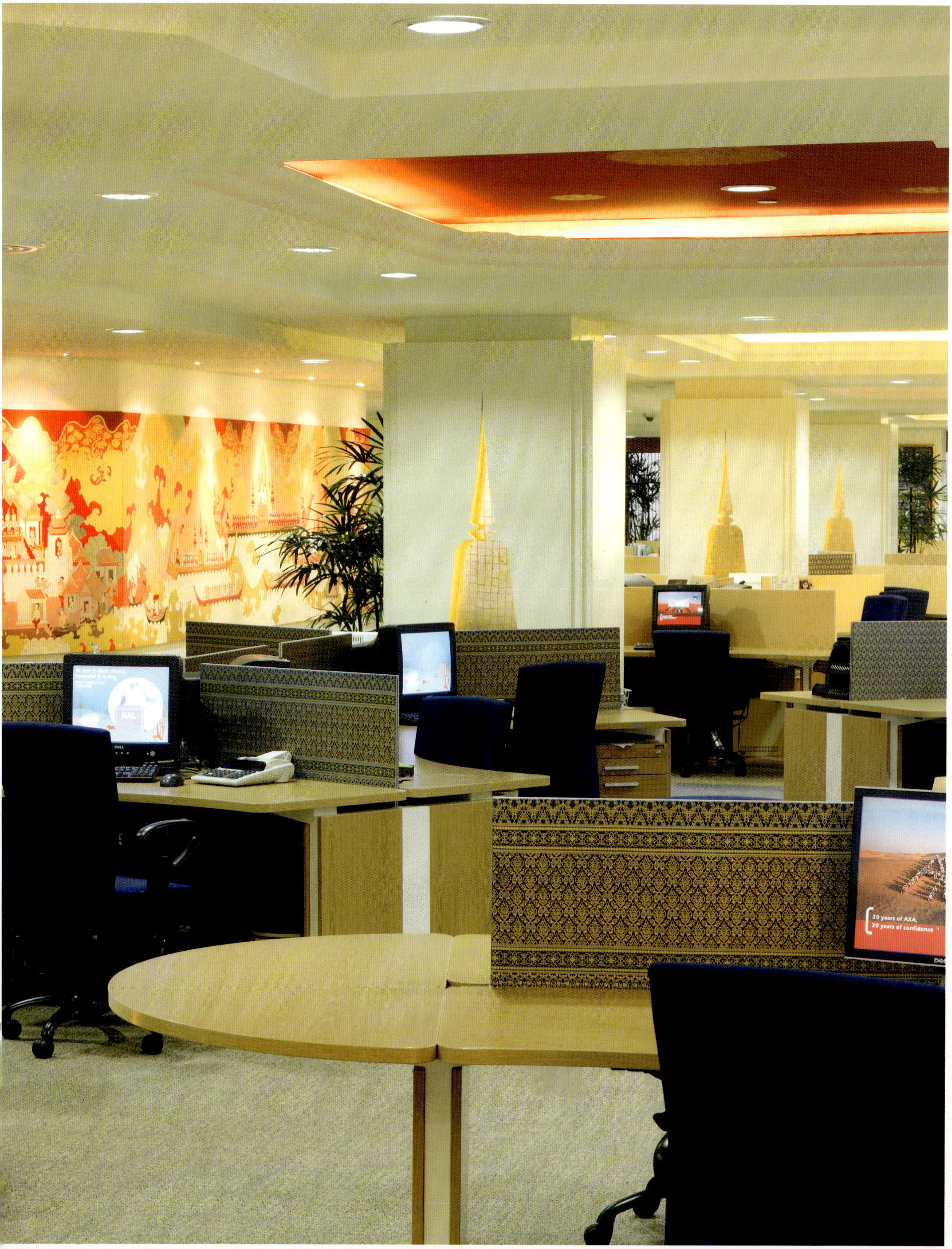
20 years of AXA,
20 years of confidence

KRUNGTHAI AXA LIFE INSURANCE

● Human and geometrical images can be seen on the walls: in the niches, where classical Hindu texts have been painted, and on the television screens, where publicity videos from the firm are shown.

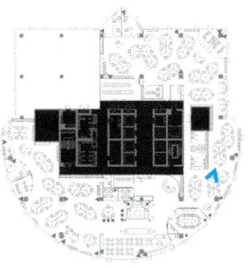

KRUNGTHAI AXA LIFE INSURANCE

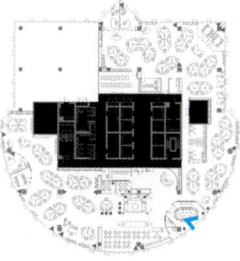

agile, ágil, alerte, confident, seguro de sí mismo, confiante, imaginati e, imaginativo, imaginative, knowledgable competente, compétente, passionate, apasionado, passionnée, professional, profesional, professionnelle, trustworthy, fiable, loyale uplifting, estimulante, vivifiante

AFFINITY OFFICES

ARCHITECT/DESIGNER:

AGUIRRE & NEWMAN ARQUITECTURA,
EDUARDO GASCÓN, WOLFF OLLINS

Client: Affinity Petcare
Photographer: Jordi Miralles
Location: Sant Cugat del Vallès, Spain
Completion date: 2003
Area: 37,674 SF

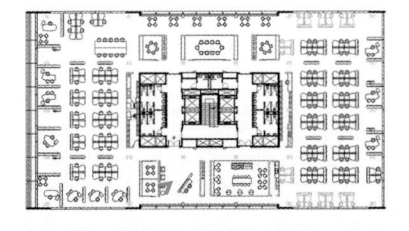

The architects were commissioned to design a functional office that would reflect the exclusiveness and elegance that dominates in the Sant Cugat area where the building is located. At the same time the brief indicated that the interior design and layout of the space should be comfortable and practical, like someone's home. The client wanted to reflect their corporate identity, formed from two components: nature and well-being through the consumption of the product. Although the company's headquarters are located here, the logo and the name are only visible in a large photograph behind the reception desk, in order to create a subtler corporate image.

The office is composed of two rectangular floors, with a central communication and service nucleus. The same concept has been developed on both floors: a spacious and open work area at each end and two more communal service areas on the sides where the access points are. The aim of this layout is to promote communication i.e., formal and informal meetings and connections between people working in the offices. Closed spaces have, therefore, also been reduced to a minimum and use light materials, like aluminum and glass. The formal meeting rooms have been set up as independent bubbles of different sizes with two transparent partition walls; when the meetings require privacy, screens can be unrolled. The informal meeting area is located next to the windows and is afforded warmth thanks to a lamp designed by Álvaro Siza.

The floor has been used as an element to delimit the different areas. It is different in the communal areas, where wood similar to parquet is used. In the cafeteria, recycled rubber witih a smooth texture is used. And in the meeting rooms, carpet is used. The absence of walls allows the light to diffuse freely through the interior and provides views to the exterior from all points.

AFFINITY OFFICES

- The stripes of colors on the wall opposite the reception desk are composed of tiny photographs of bottles used by Affinity. Next to this, a step and a change in flooring mark the transition to the cafeteria.

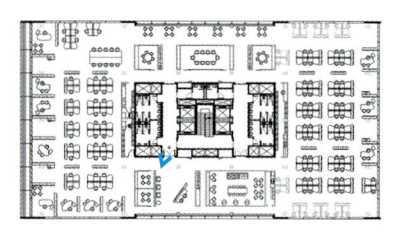

AFFINITY OFFICES

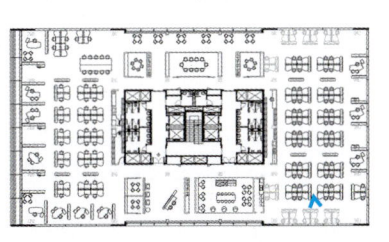

AFFINITY OFFICES
440

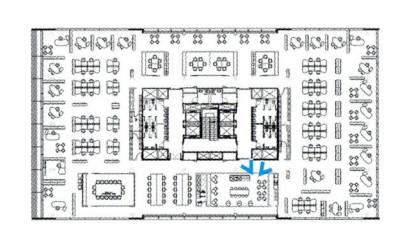

AFFINITY OFFICES
441

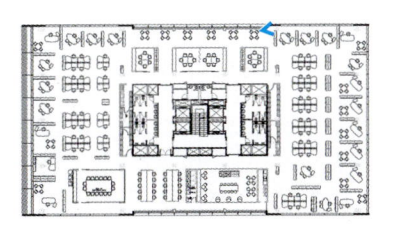

AFFINITY OFFICES
442

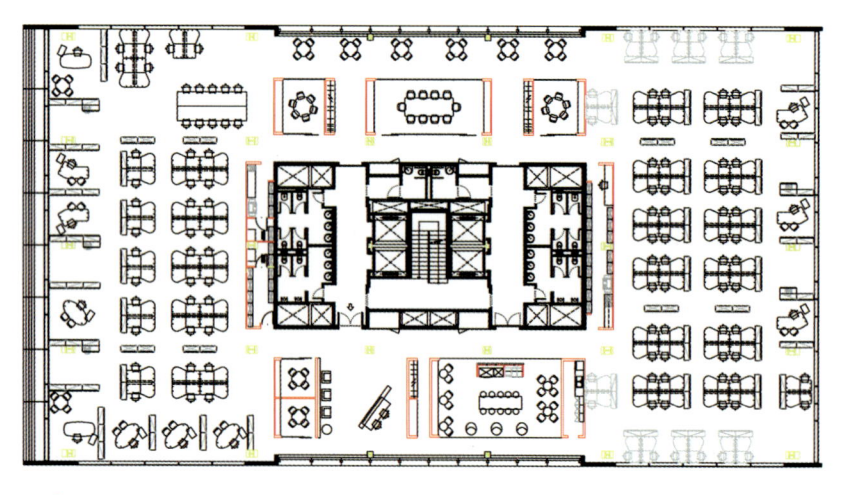

Floor plan

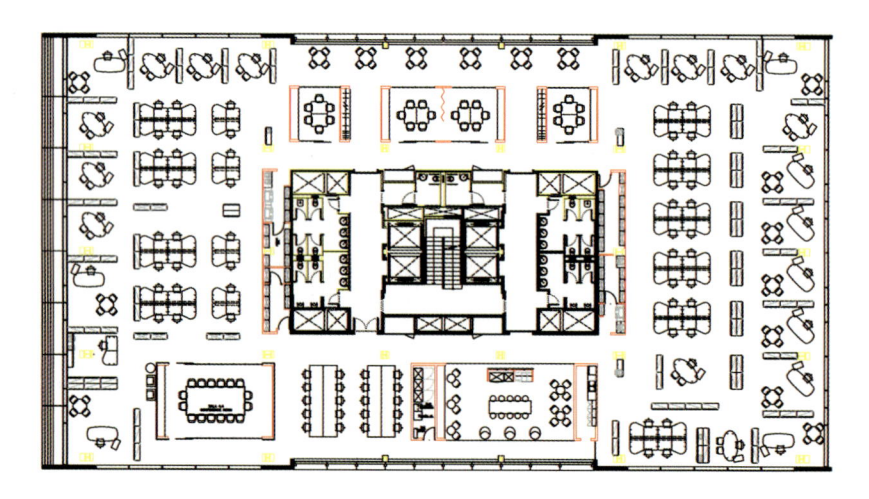

First floor plan

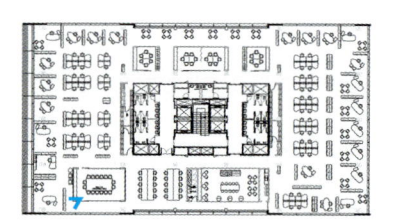

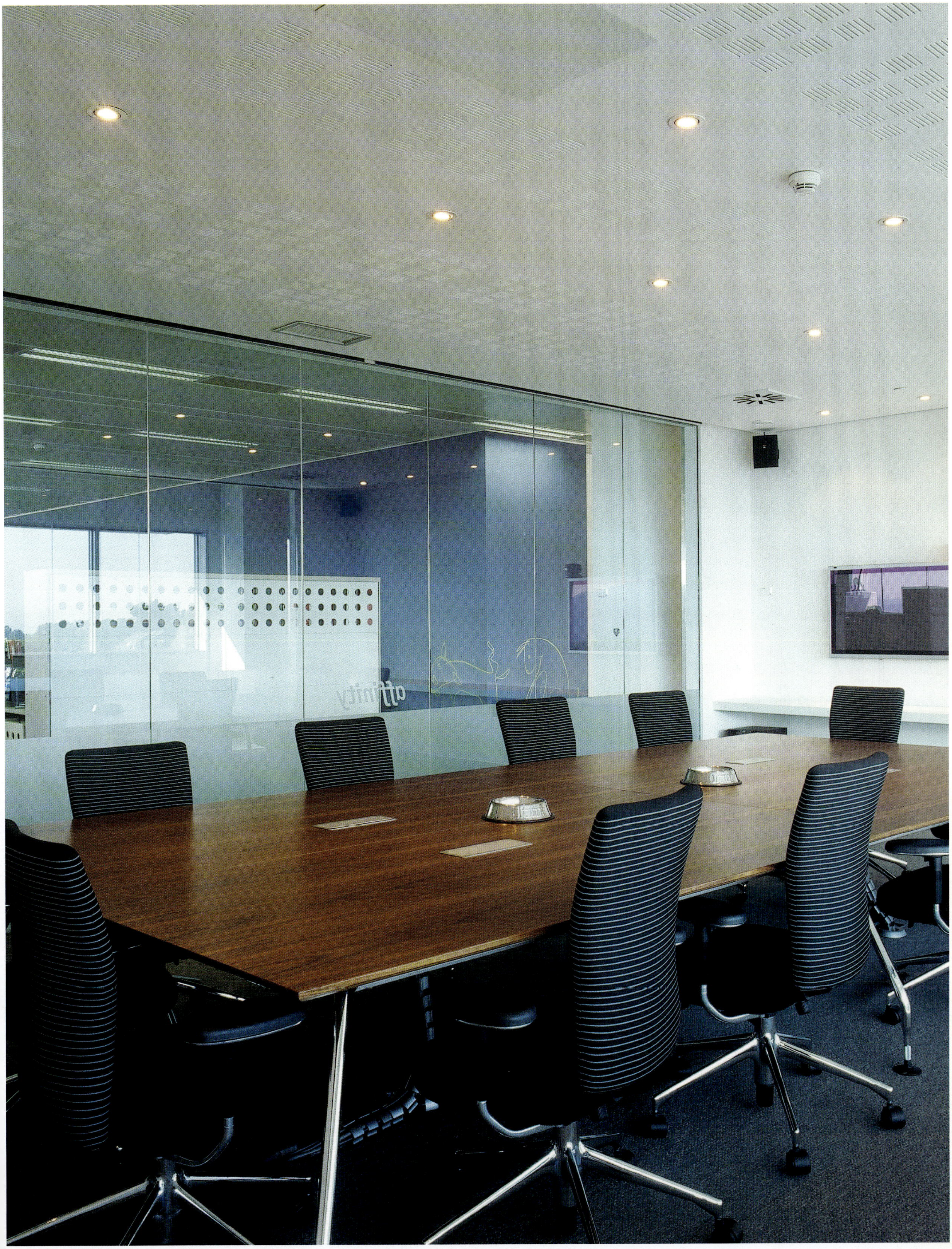

AFFINITY OFFICES

○ Throughout the communal area the same flooring has been used: wooden floorboards, similar to industrial parquet, made from beech. A lamp designed by Álvaro Siza adorns the space for informal meetings.

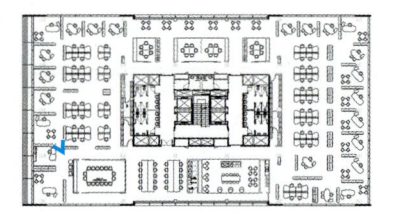

AFFINITY OFFICES
445

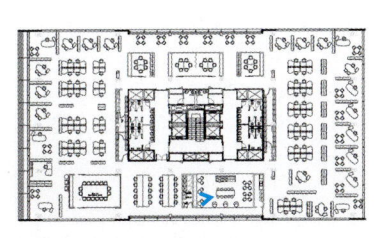

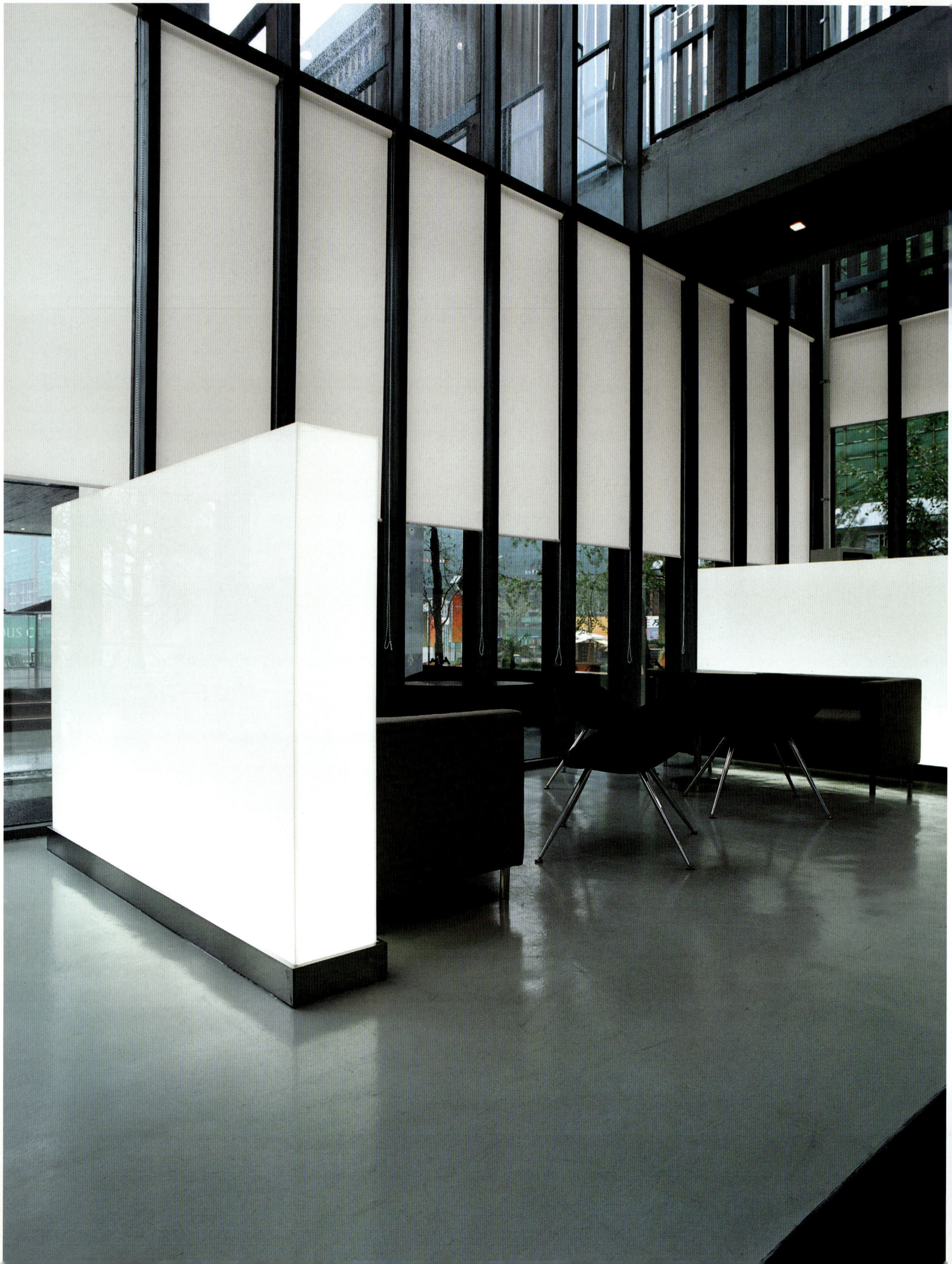

Vanke Cheugdu Commercial Complex

ARCHITECT/DESIGNER:

CL3 ARCHITECTS LIMITED

Client: Chengdu Vanke
Real Estate Co. Ltd
Photographer: CL3 Architects Limited
Location: Chengdu, China
Completion date: 200
Area: 40,655 SF

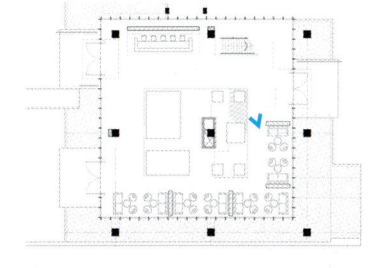

This project won its architects, the CL3 studio, two important awards in 2006: the Asian Pacific Interior Design Award and an award from the delegation of the AIA (America Institute of Architects) in Hong Kong. These are commercial offices for a large financial corporation in China, Vanke, located in the city of Chengdu, in the Sichuan province. The architectural firm was responsible both for the exterior and the interior of the three floors, whose surface area measures 21,500 square feet. The aim was simplicity in design and aesthetic value. Functionally this space has been designed as a residential environment, which is apt for commercial use.

The project makes use of the original construction of exposed concrete, formed by two blocks developed from a square structure composed of units with 26-foot sides. A central glass and steel pavilion with a wooden mullion has been built on top of this. The pavilion, which accommodates the main commercial activities, is connected by way of a concrete bridge with a rest area situated on the building's top level.

The exterior of the construction is also transparent glass with wood finishes. The main access is preceded by a rectangular-based fountain, flanked on either side by low-level jets of water.

A system of spotlights using LEDs embedded into the ceiling is distributed across the three levels, which form a map of light points giving the space a bright and modern appearance. The LEDs have also been used inside of illuminated boxes, which have various uses: for example, in the reception lobby the mullion of the structure and illuminated boxes combine to create a clear space and in the work area they serve to delineate the individual work stations.

During the day, natural light dominates the interior thanks to the glass on the façade and the internal partition walls.

VANKE CHEUGDU COMMERCIAL COMPLEX

- The transparent glass floor-to-ceiling windows allow abundant light to enter the interior. On the exterior the pre-existing façade combines glass with wood finishes.

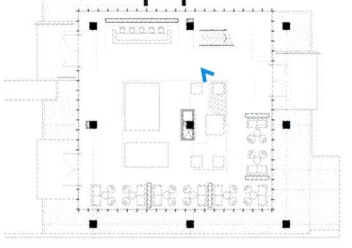

VANKE CHEUGDU COMMERCIAL COMPLEX

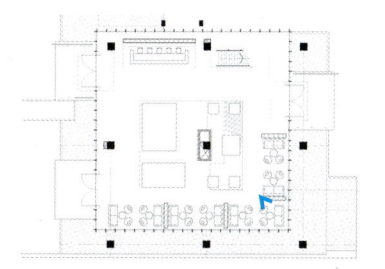

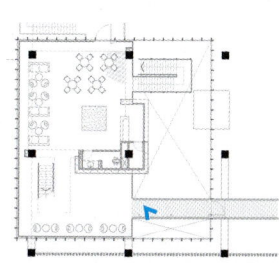

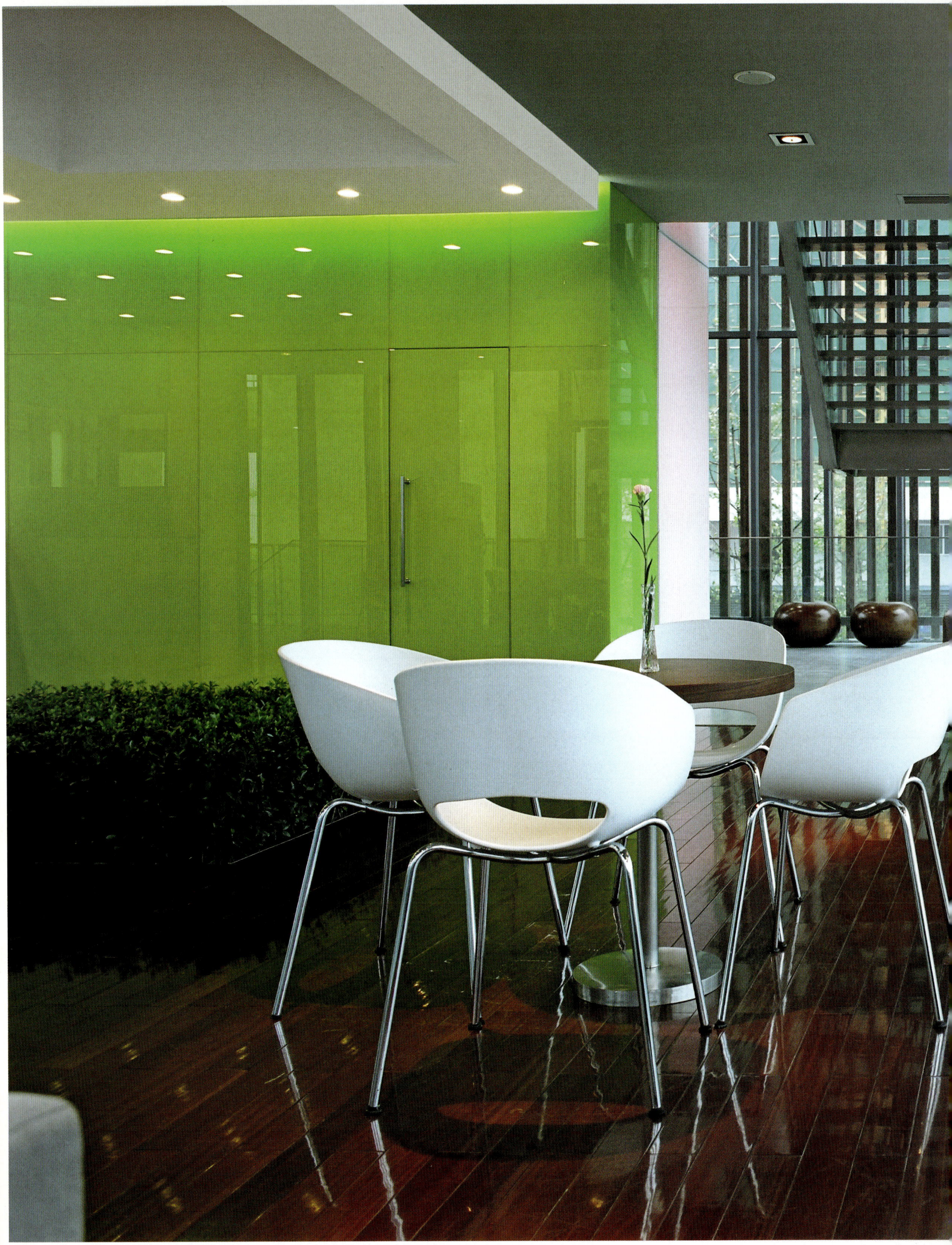

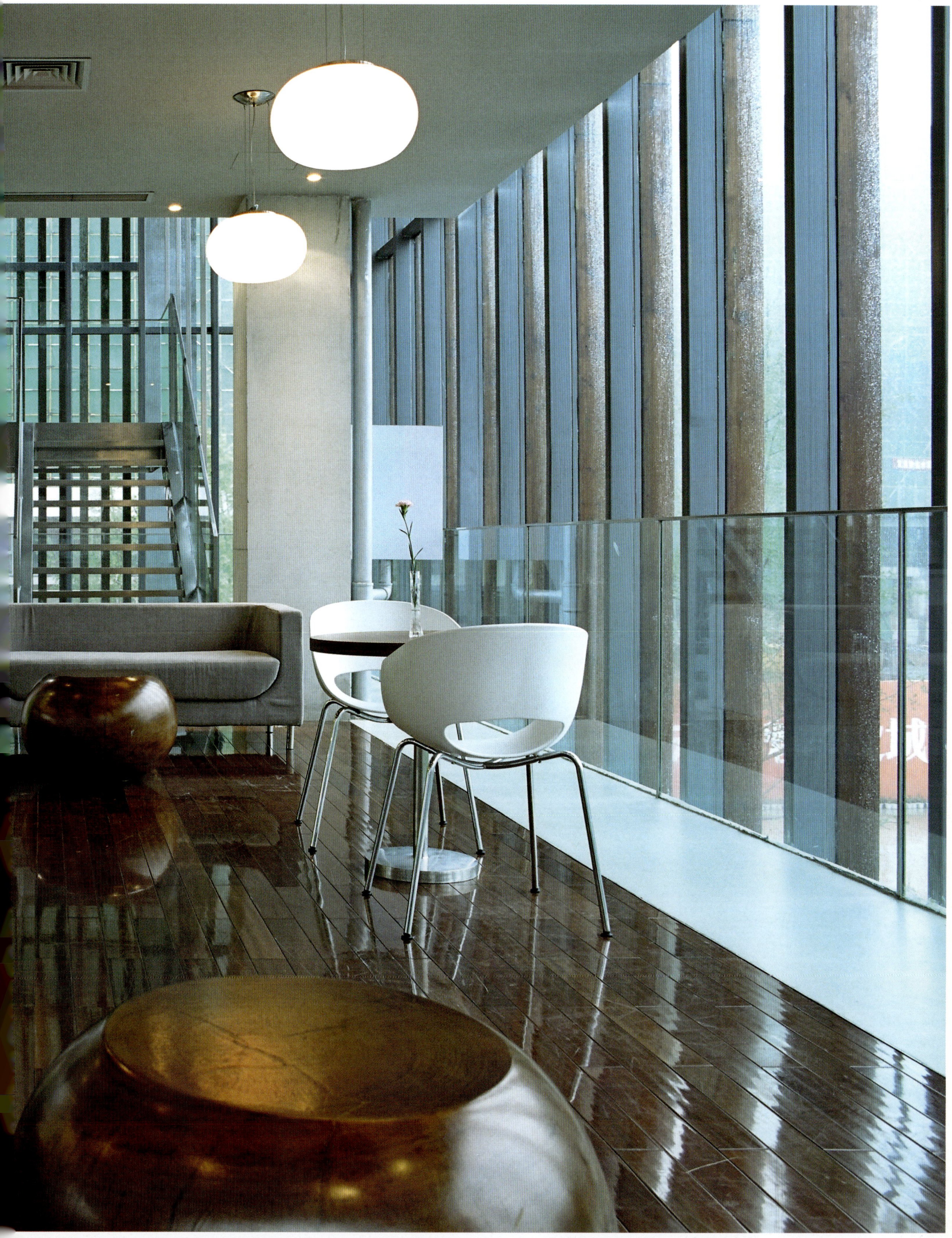

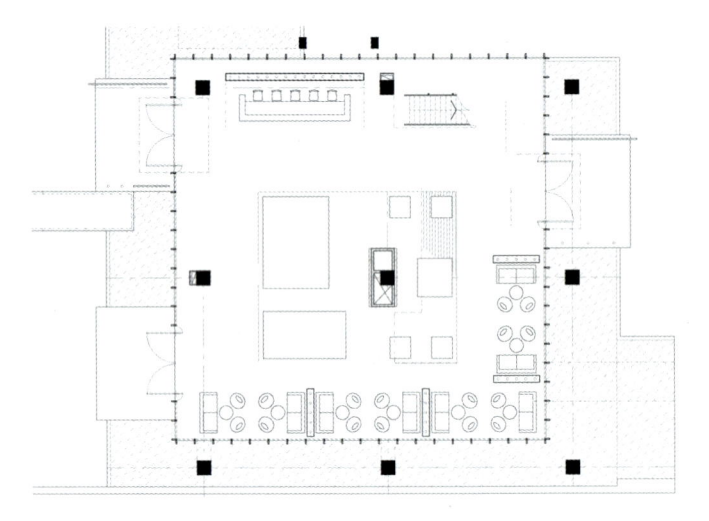

VANKE CHEUGDU COMMERCIAL COMPLEX

○ Floor plan

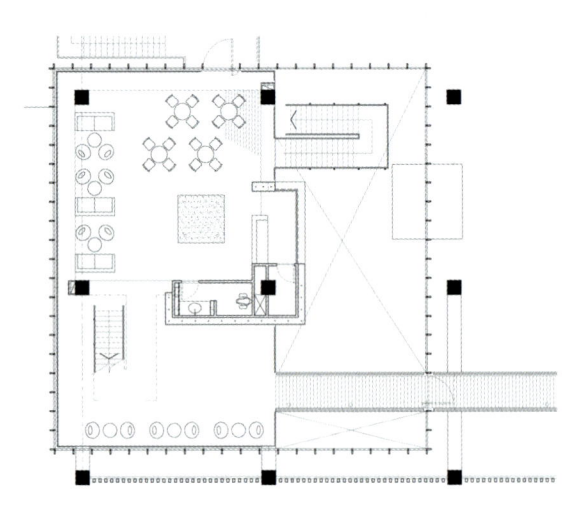

○ First floor plan

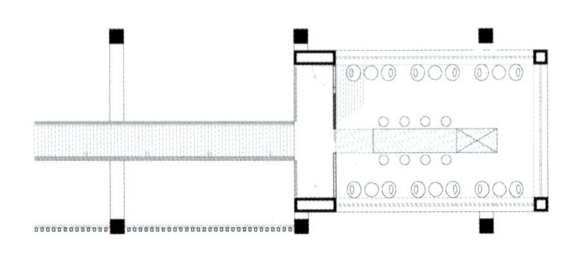

○ Second floor plan

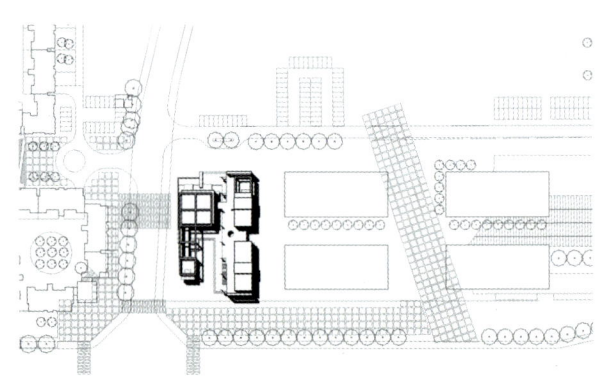

○ Site floor plan

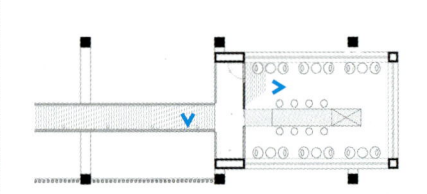

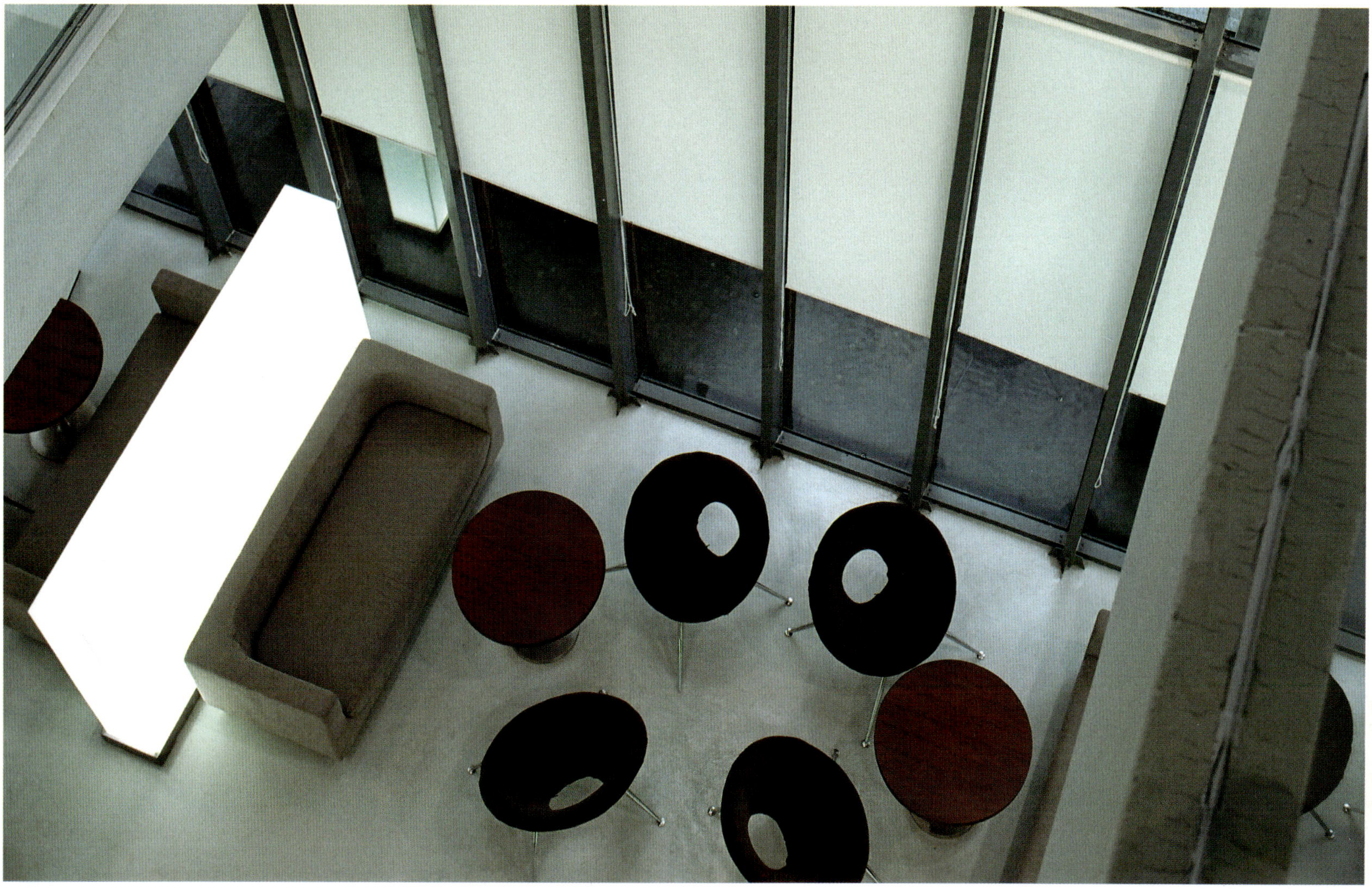

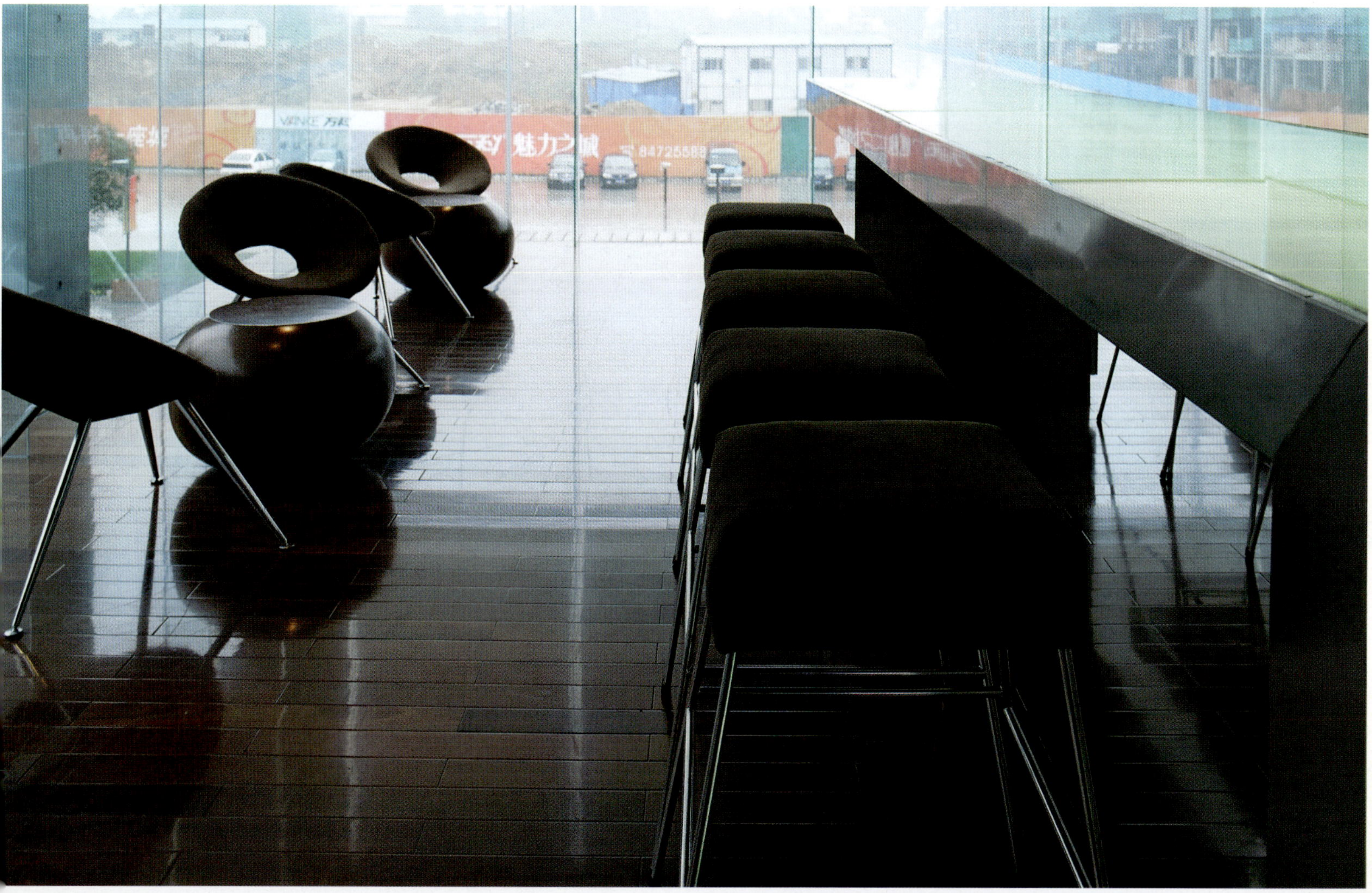
VANKE 万科
魅力之城
84725583

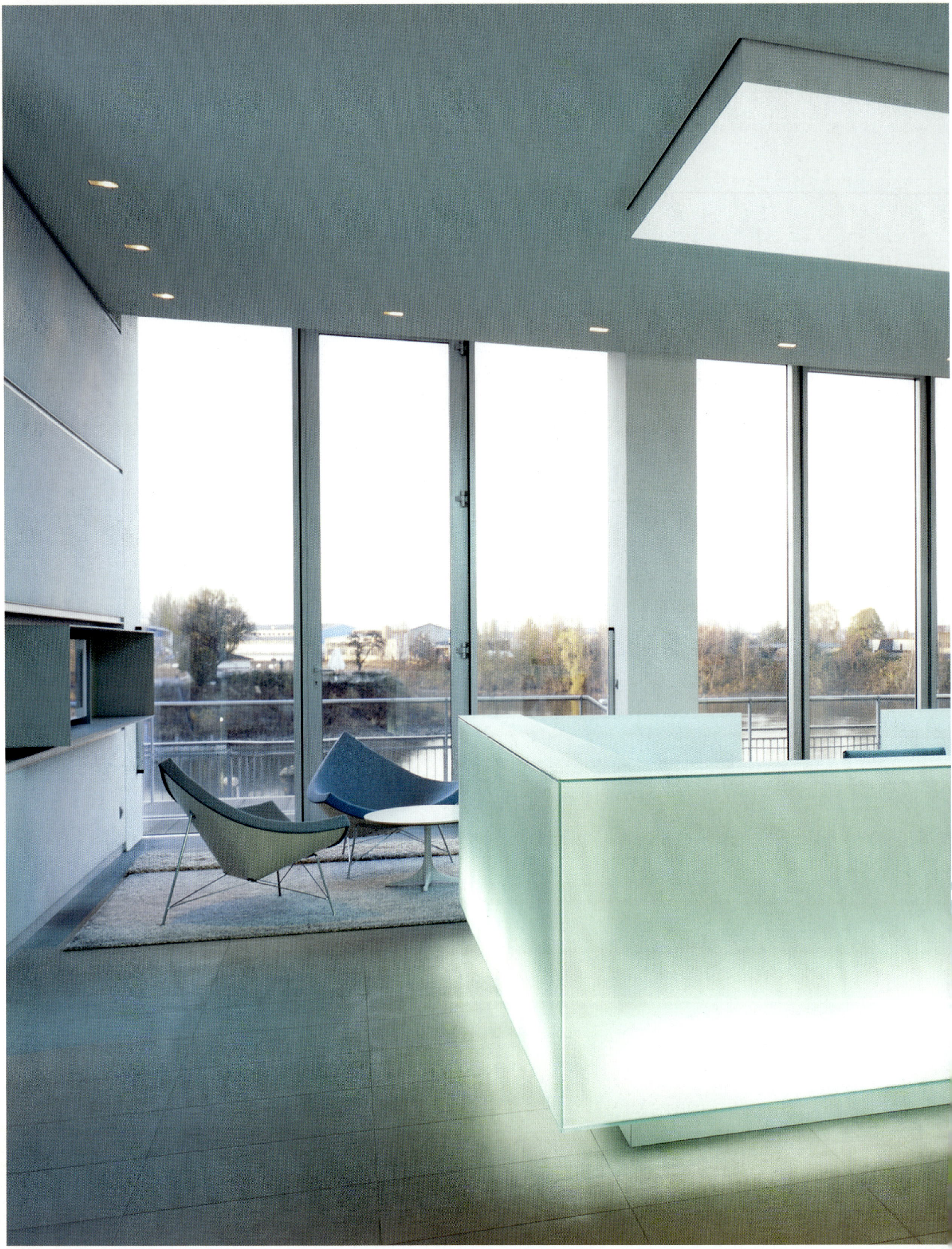

Office Building
A. T. Kearney

The remarkable aspect of this project is its size, since the architect was commissioned to renovate a former six-story warehouse.

The most striking element of the building is its main façade, which is constructed entirely from glass. As well as maximizing the possibilities of natural lighting, this feature has been considered by the architect as an element that generates a positive atmosphere inside the offices. His aim, therefore, was to keep it.

The light, luminous tones that dominate the interiors, both on the walls and ceilings, range from white to aquamarine and match and contrast perfectly with the glass walls that dominate the corridors, which connect the different offices.

On the ground floor, where the most important offices and meeting rooms are located, this choice of light colors goes unnoticed thanks to the strong presence of the pre-existing oak parquet. This has been laid throughout the floor.

On the other floors, homogeneity is the main characteristic. The sides and fronts of the furniture, upholstered in synthetic fabric, contrast with the wall surfaces, which are almost all plain. Functionally, this option improves the acoustics throughout the space, creates new optical and tactile combinations, and provides stimuli for the workers.

The design is based on straight lines, which establish continuity between the different areas and increase the sense of size of the interior. The choice of furniture for this office aims at homogeneity and functionality. The pieces strengthen the effect of transparency and continuity, which the architect proposed as one of the objectives for the project.

The environment created by this composition is discrete and sober, not particularly different from other offices at first sight. However, the difference is perceived by the user of each office, as they have the opportunity to identify with the work space and appreciate a sense of well-being.

ARCHITECT/DESIGNER:

COSSMAN_DE BRUYN ARCHITEKTUR
INNENARCHITEKTUR DESIGN

Client: A. T. Kearney
Photographer: Nicole Zimmermann
Location: Düsseldorf, Germany
Completion date: 2004
Area: 41,075 SF

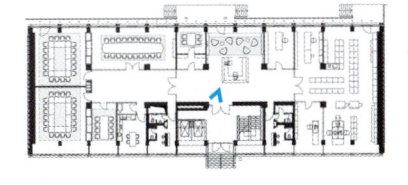

OFFICE BUILDING A. T. KEARNEY
456

○ For the furniture for this project the architect has gone for originality and opted for curved lines. As well as providing a modern aesthetic, the pieces are functional and homogenous.

OFFICE BUILDING A. T. KEARNEY
457

OFFICE BUILDING A. T. KEARNEY

OFFICE BUILDING A. T. KEARNEY

● The project is based on straight lines in order to make efficient use of the space. This avoids setting boundaries and affords transparency to the interior. A greater sense of space is also provided by the light color palette, which ranges from white to aquamarine.

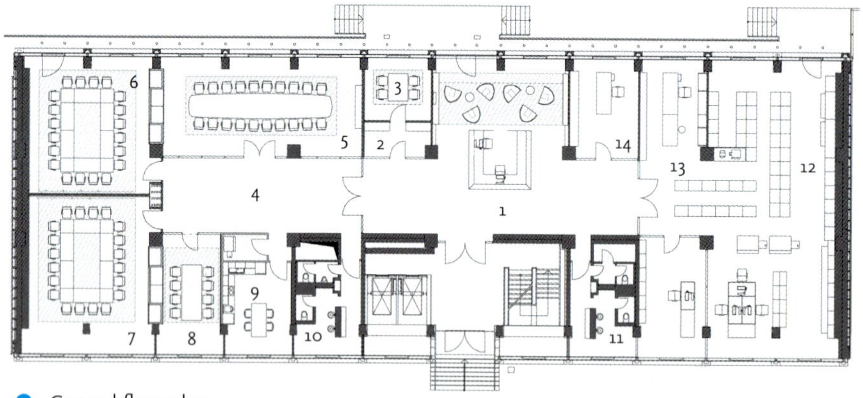

OFFICE BUILDING A. T. KEARNEY

- Ground floor plan
- 1st-4th floorplan
- 5th-6th floor plan

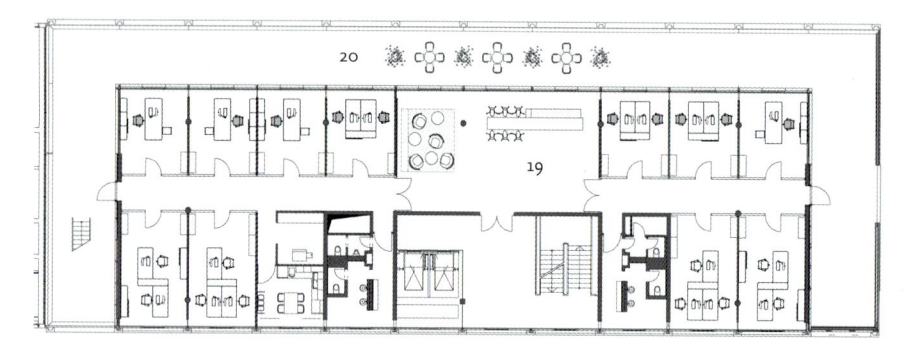

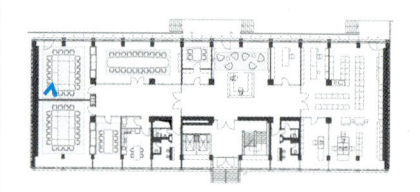

1. Reception area
2. Wardrobe
3. Conference
4. Foyer
5. Boardroom
6. Training room 1
7. Training room 2
8. Training room 3
9. Kitchen
10. Men's Room
11. Ladies Room
12. Office-Support
13. Mail room
14. Back office
15. Conference
16. DTP
17. Copying
18. Restroom
19. Meeting point
20. Patio

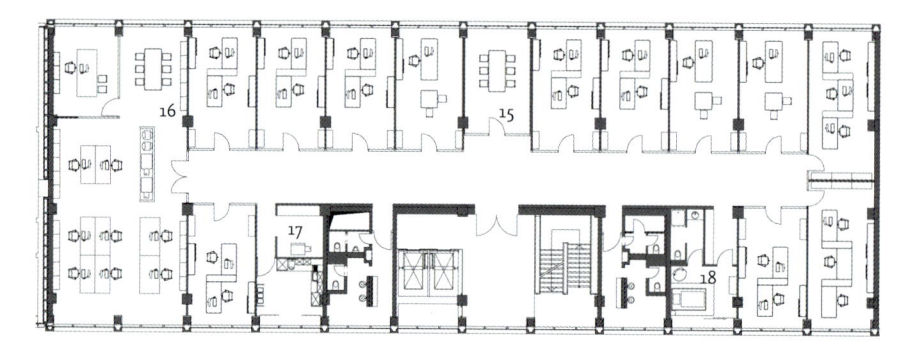

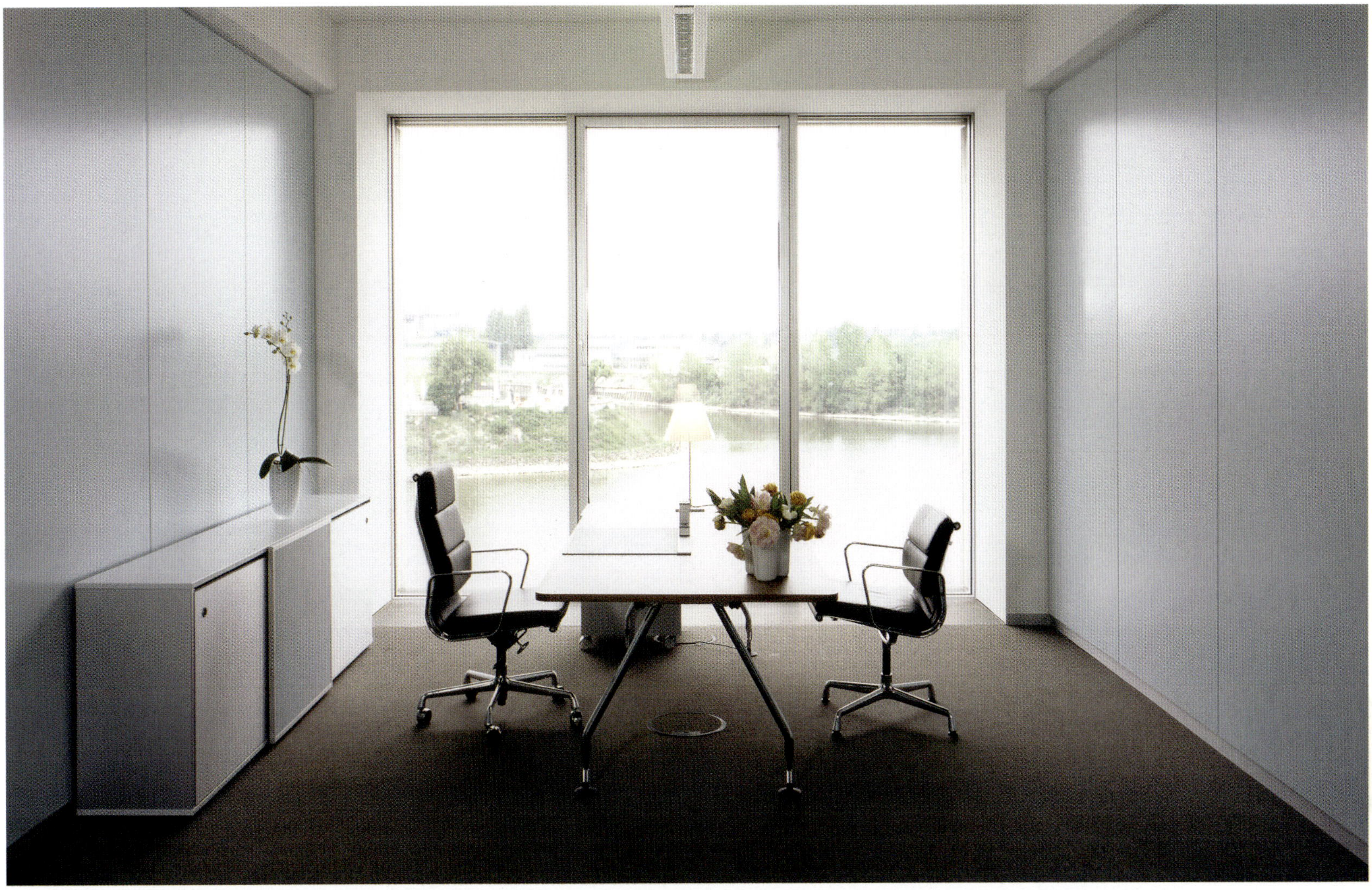

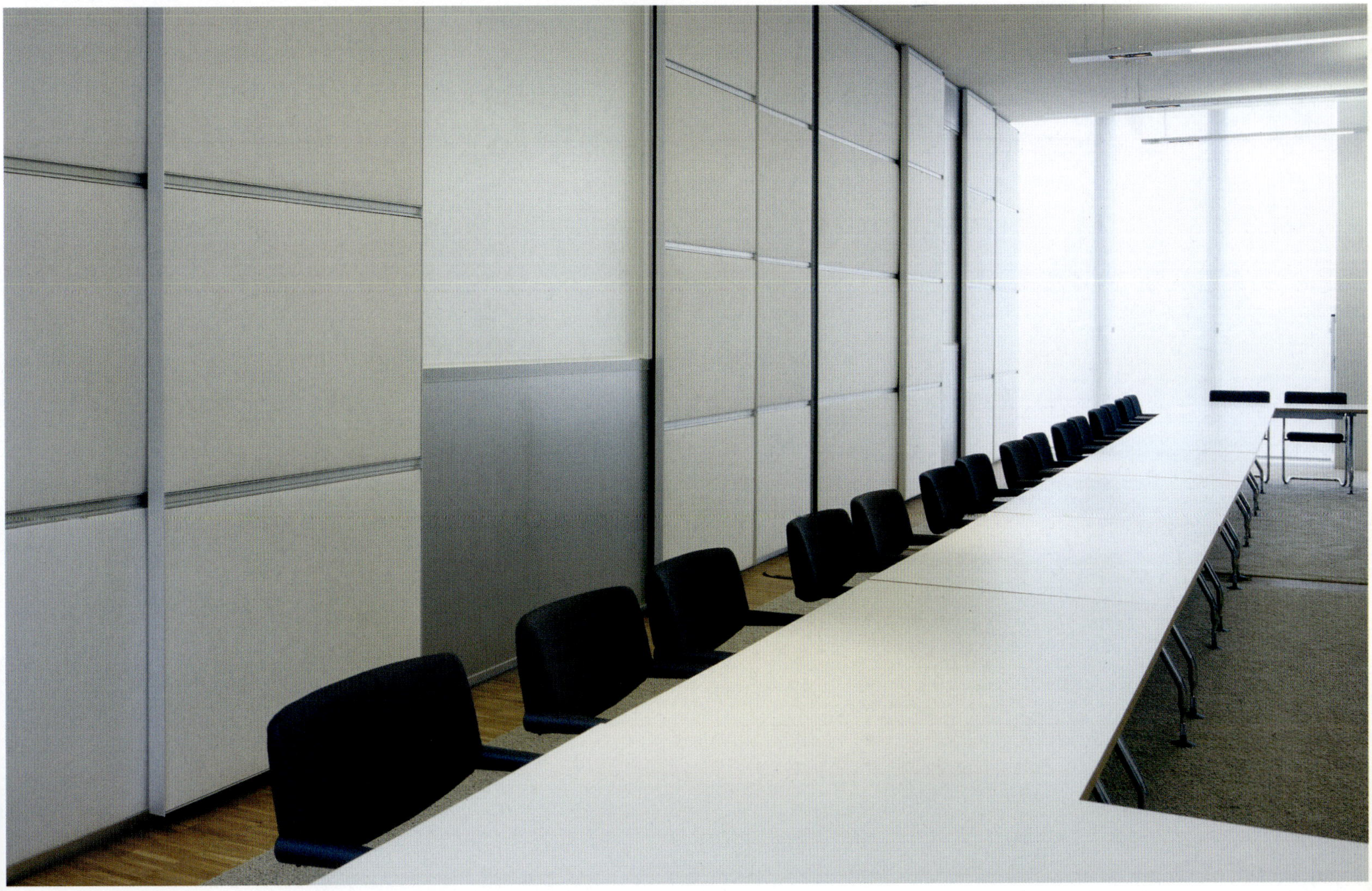

8	FRESHFIELDS BRUCKHAUS DERINGER
7	FRESHFIELDS BRUCKHAUS DERINGER
6	FRESHFIELDS BRUCKHAUS DERINGER
5	Layetana
4	Layetana
3	DOMInus
2	GassóAuditores / Moores Rowland International
1	Layetana / noosAGENCY
B	GRUPASSA

Offices on Mestre Nicolau Street

This old administrative building has been renovated and adapted for use as an office block. The original project consisted of a large number of private offices, reception area, lobby, waiting room, and three meeting rooms.

The façade has been preserved and inside the architects have applied innovative decorative techniques that play an important role.

On the lower floor, located at street level, are the accesses to the offices, the access ramp to the parking lot and a small commercial establishment. There is also a light well here, which is the most important element of the building, around which the small offices are distributed. A wall made exclusively of glass that makes the most of the natural light for as much time as possible has been erected in the well. This entire wall is formed by slats in shades of yellow and orange, which are thicker on the higher floors due to the greater need for protection against heat from the sun.

On the top floor are the meeting rooms and the company owners' offices. These areas can be distinguished by their use of yellow and orange, colors that integrate the building's interior with its exterior.

A new core of access points occupies the central space of the building, previously a light well. Space has been gained here by removing a projection from the interior façade. The work area is therefore composed of two wings of offices, which adjoin the exterior and interior façades, with a central zone in between that acts as an open office. The access to the office area is located at ground level, as well as the access to the staff parking, located beneath the building. Both on the ground floor and in the basement the architect has modified the position of some of the pillars to make this space more functional in its new use as an office.

Architect/Designer:
Fermín Vázquez/B720 Arquitectos

Client: Lucky Town/Layetana Inmuebles, S.L.
Photographer: Rafael Vargas
Location: Barcelona, Spain
Completion date: 2002
Area: 47,846 SF

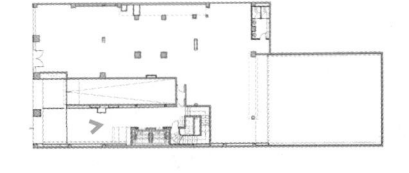

OFFICES IN MESTRE NICOLAU STREET

● The aluminum that has been used to cover some of the wall, and the bright colors around the signboard form part of the corporate image created by this project.

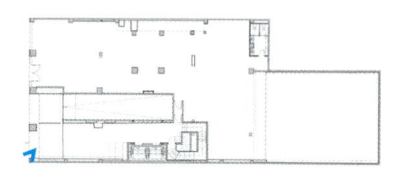

OFFICES IN MESTRE NICOLAU STREET
465

OFFICES IN MESTRE NICOLAU STREET
466

OFFICES IN MESTRE NICOLAU STREET
467

○ Halogen lights have been installed throughout the building, which in some areas have been reinforced by lamps with modern designs. Some walls are at an angle in order to create slits of light.

OFFICES IN MESTRE NICOLAU STREET
468

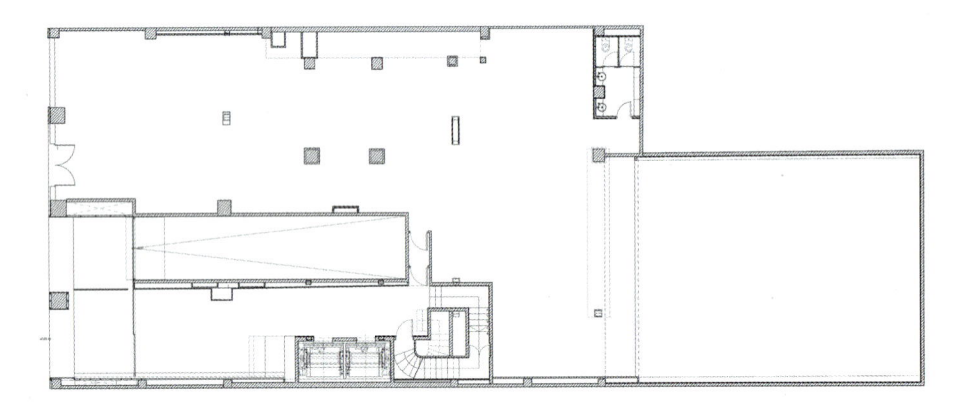

● Floor plan

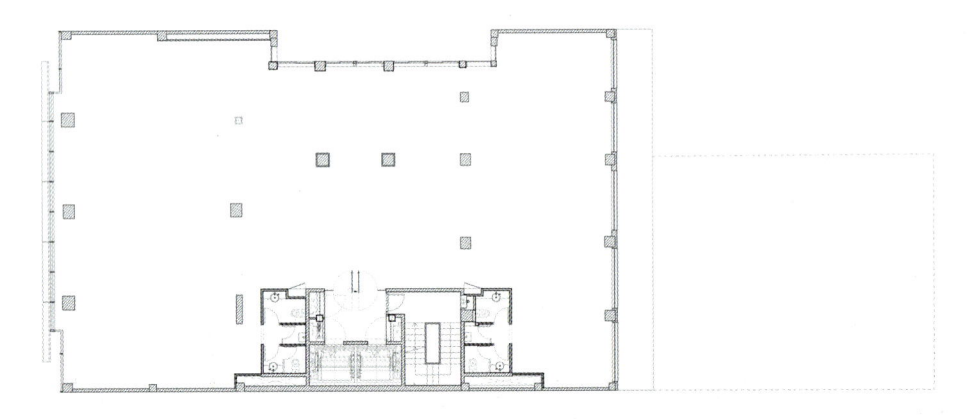

● Typcal floor plan

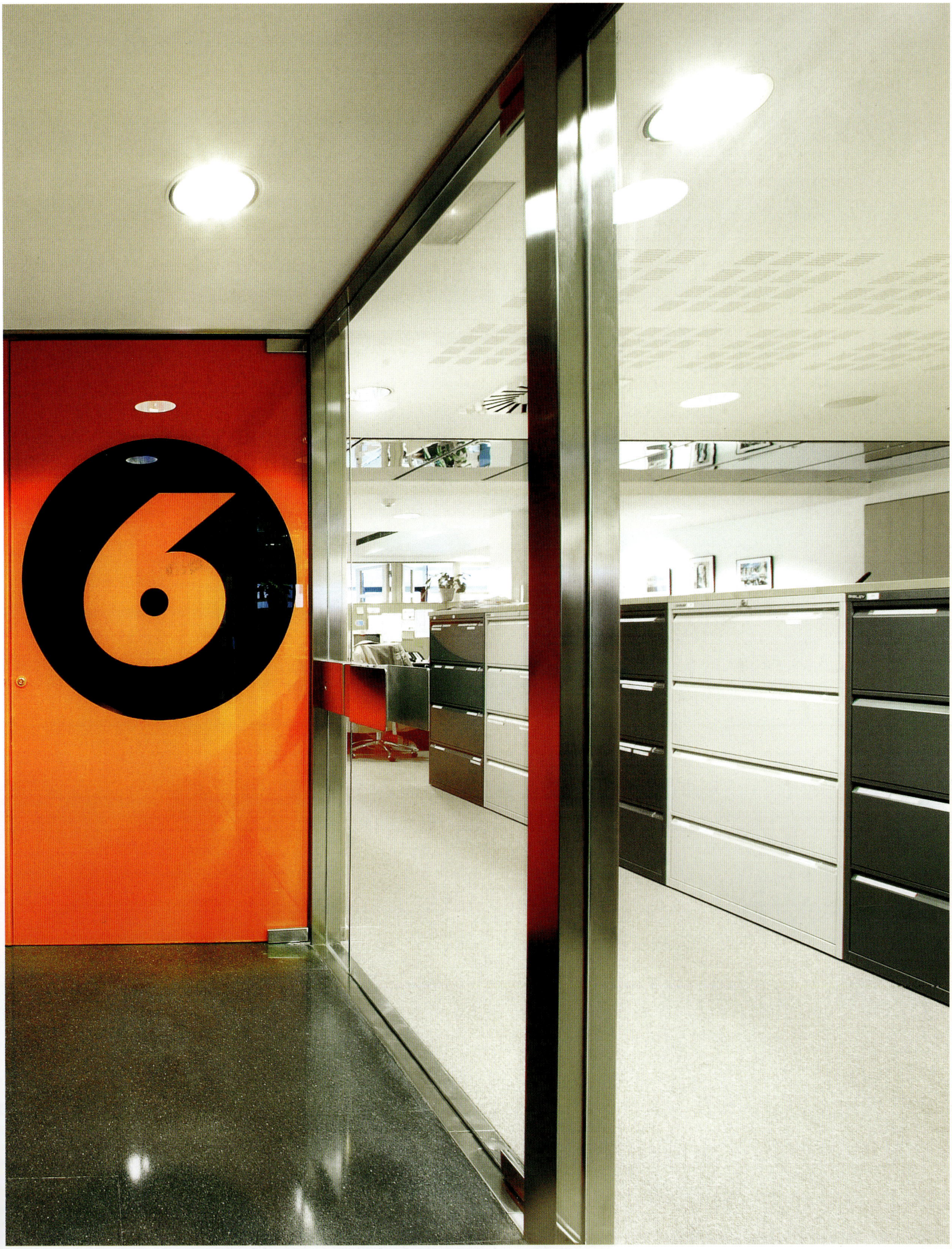
6

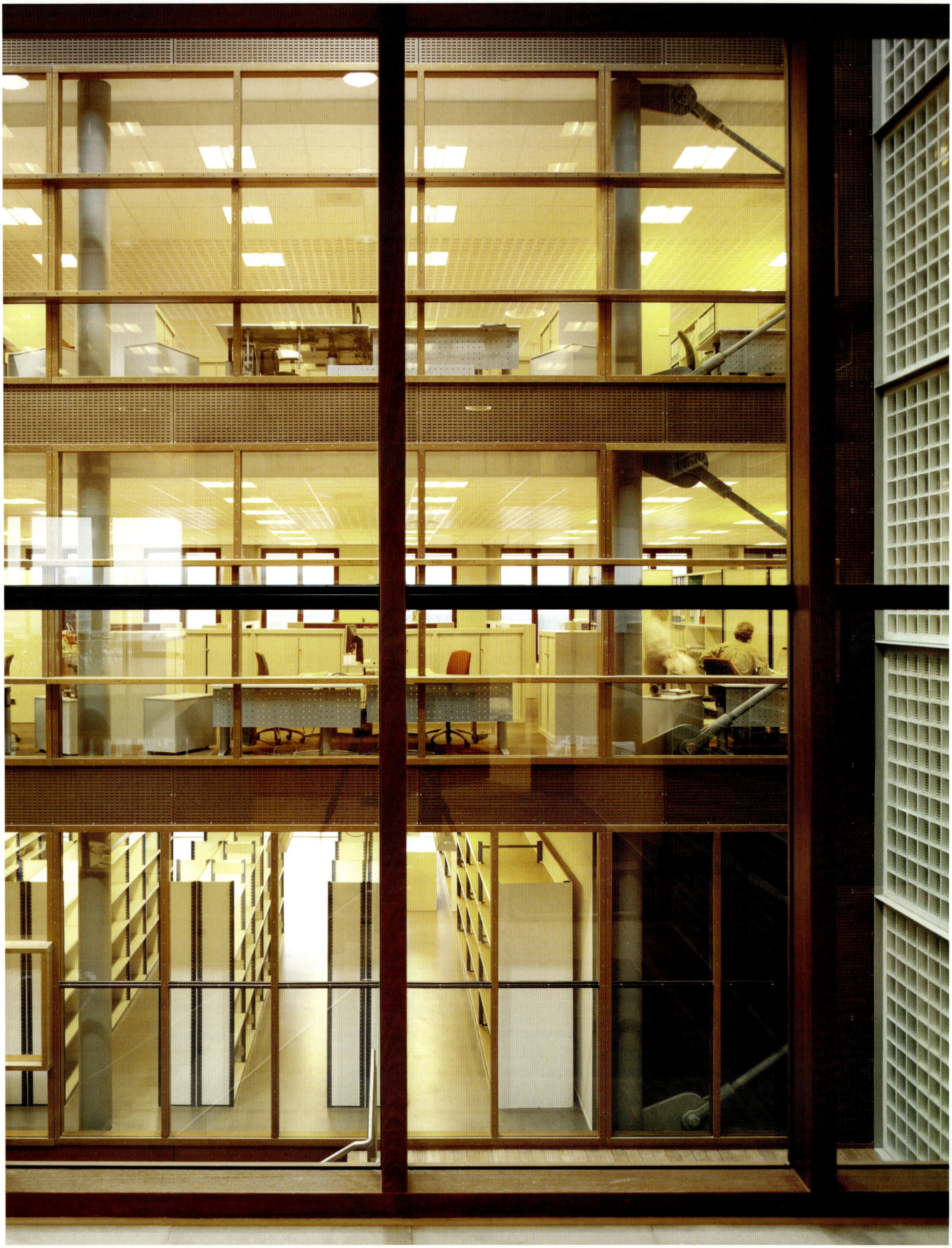

Kropman

Since the site chosen for this project is an industrial park formed solely by office buildings, as well as having to integrate with the surroundings, this project needed to offer something innovative—with personality—a place that would not go unnoticed.

The project began with the idea of creating an industrial, flexible and demountable construction. The resulting building fuses with its environment by way of a glass façade, which reflects the landscape, and with the creation of an open space on the ground floor. This gives the impression that the plot carries the building, which in turn is shown as a lightweight structure, mostly supported by columns. The building consists of a ground floor and three floors above, each of which accommodates private offices, communal work areas, meeting rooms, toilets, coat closets, and rest areas. This means that the stairway that connects the three stories is a major component throughout the building. Both the steps and landings are limestone and the banister is wooden. To form the balustrade, wide wooden panels have been emplaced whose color integrates with the stone floor making the two appear to form a single object.

The main structure of the building consists of an aluminum mesh. The beams are also an aluminum alloy and replace the traditional steel beams.

The four stories share an atrium, which makes the center of the building an open, pleasant space, which affords elegance to the composition. The interior walls are made of glass, which allows visual contact between the offices and the atrium, and also acts as soundproofing. The functional areas, like the toilets and rooms for technical and logistic control, are located in the areas furthest from the center, while the offices enjoy the spacious area next to the atrium. The partitions of the spaces are moveable so that the building can be adapted to future uses, and renovated as the needs arise.

ARCHITECT/DESIGNER:

ERIC VAN ECK/ARCHITECTENBUREAU VAN DEN BROEK EN BAKEMA

Client: Kropman bv Installatietechniek
Photographer: Luuk Kramer
Location: Utrech, The Netherlands
Completion date: 2003
Area: 57,049 SF

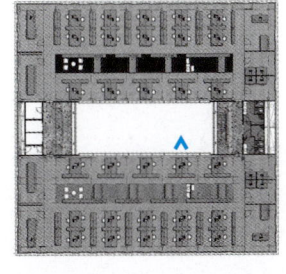

● The construction integrates with its surroundings thanks to the main façade of glass. The reflection of the surroundings in the building's surface helps to fuse the two.

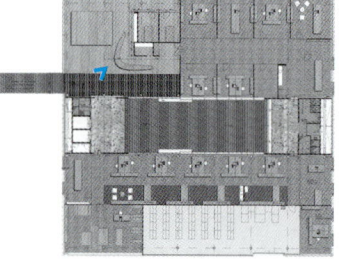

KROPMAN
473

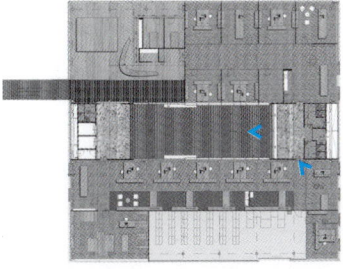

KROPMAN
474

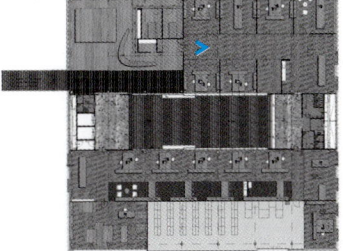

The offices are private areas, separated by glass walls. This system maintains visual communication and soundproofs these rooms. The only sign of color can be found in the doors.

KROPMAN

○ Floor plan

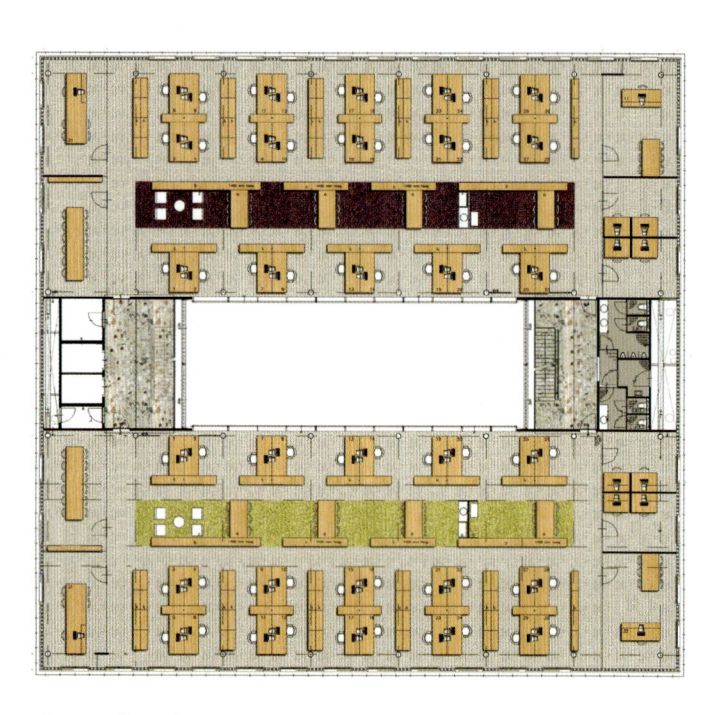

○ First floor plan

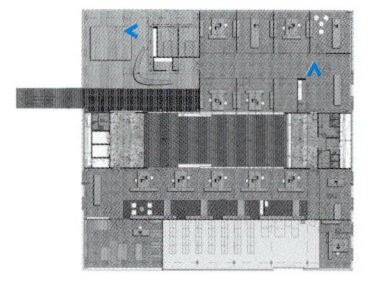

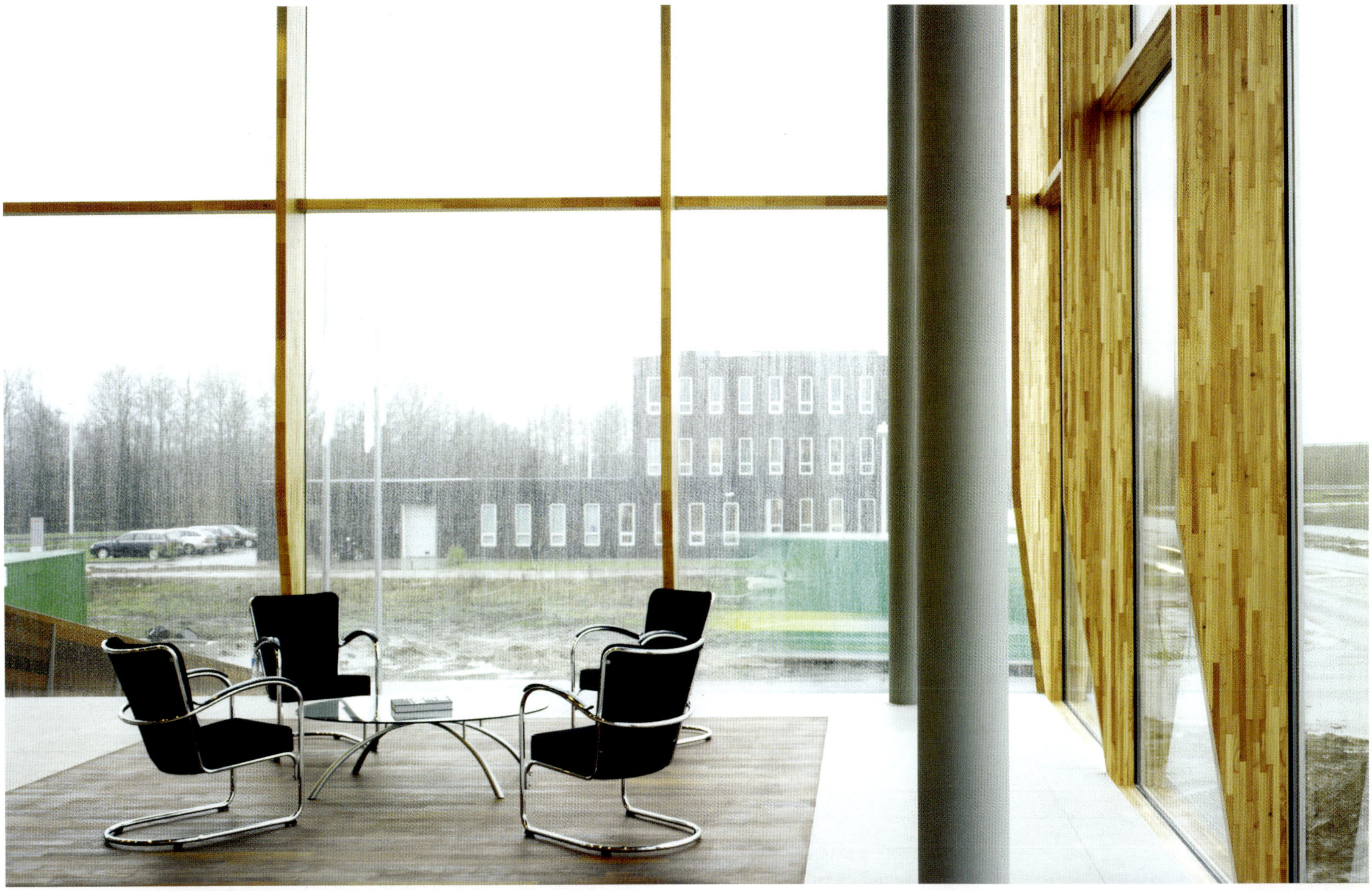

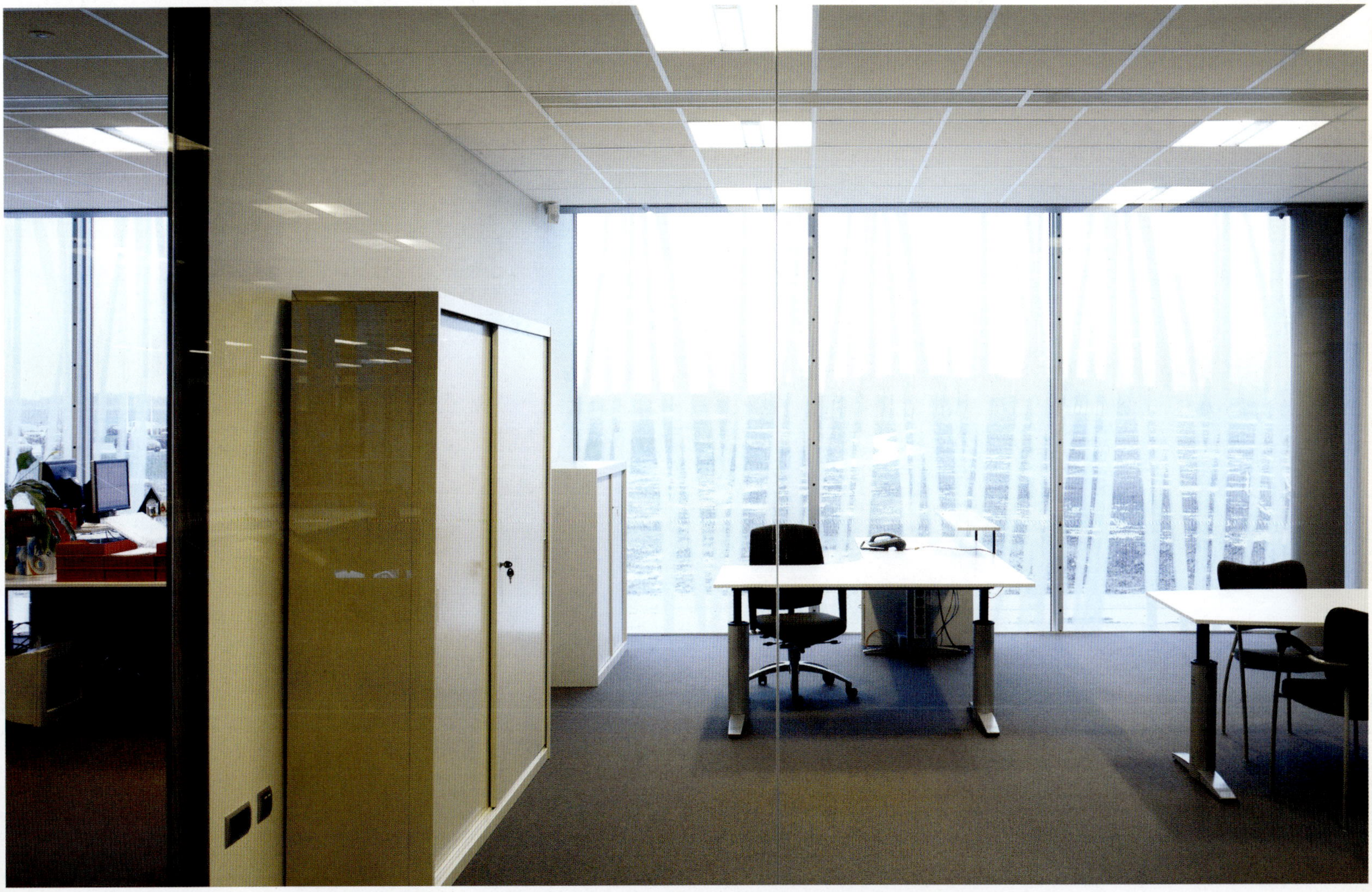

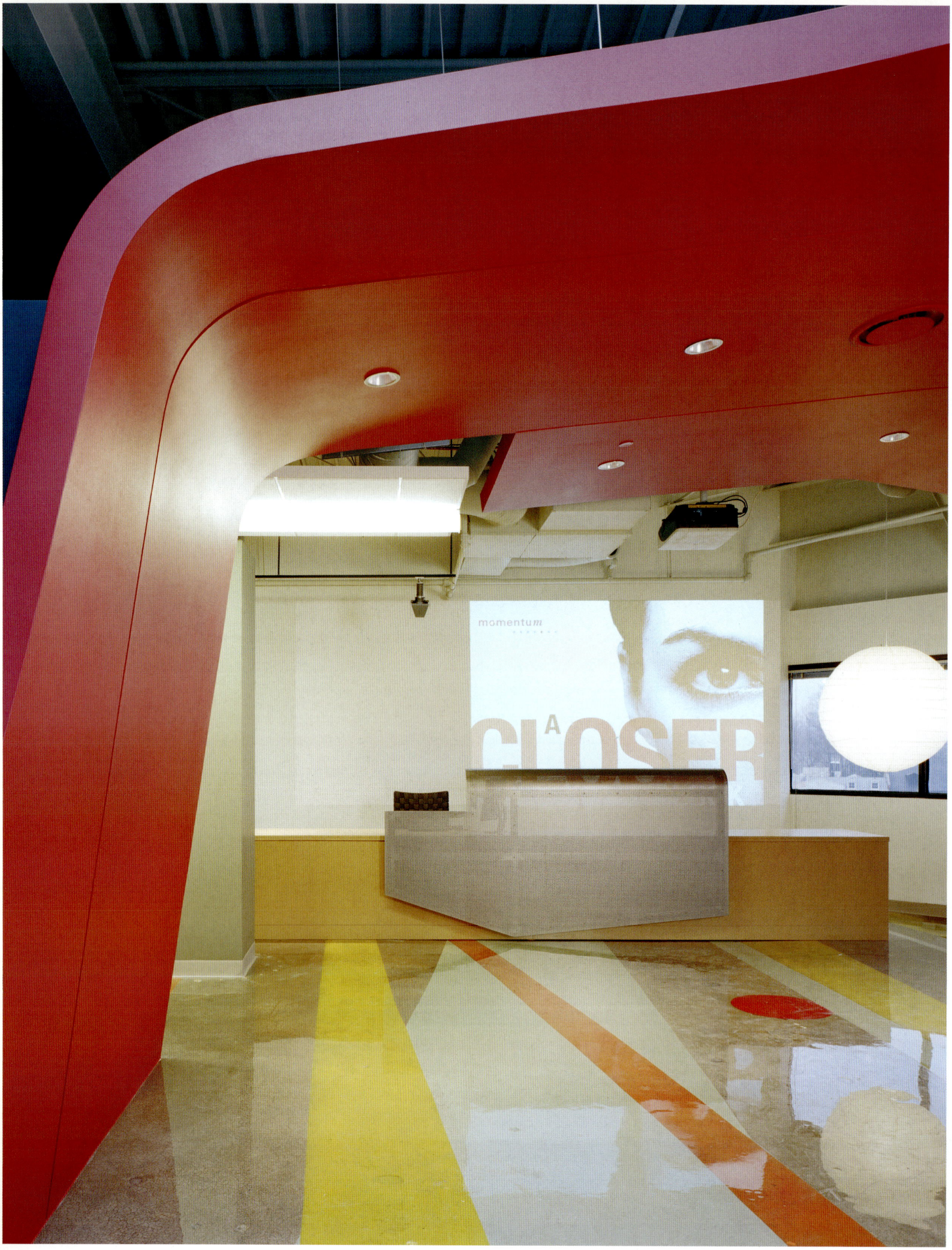
momentum
A
CLOSER

Momentum St. Louis

This project was commissioned as the new St. Louis headquarters for the multinational advertising and communication company, Momentum. Due to its growth, the company decided to move to a larger site, where it could accommodate all of its staff. The brief required the creation of a space that would avoid conventions, provide good vibrations and stimulate creativity for the diverse needs of this agency.

One of the main aims of the project was to strengthen the relationship between the departments and their respective staff. This has lead to the creation of various meeting rooms, designed for both formal and informal meetings, and the opening up of the main work area, where the stations have not been separated and just a few small rooms have been shut off, for use when privacy is needed. The spacious circulation zone connects easily with the rest of the space along its length and breadth. Furthermore, the traditional office for meeting with clients has been replaced by an open area that offers a perspective of activity in the agency. Visual as well as spatial communication has been considered throughout the space, by avoiding partition walls for the most part of the surface area. Interaction is, therefore, the central principle of the design.

For individual work there are various closed offices on one side of the space, next to the spacious executive offices. However, to access this zone, one needs to cross the large collective work area, which serves as a reminder that work is best done in groups. The program is completed by an area for editing and printing.

The combination of marble and concrete stands out on the floors, the hallways and the different functional areas, where strips of bright colors have been applied.

Architect/Designer:

The Lawrence Group Architects

Client: Momentum World Wide
Photographer: Frank Oudeman
Location: St. Louis, MO
Completion date: 2007
Area: 57,900 SF

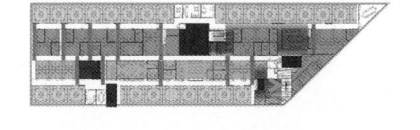

○ The general lighting is provided by groups of four light sources, whether downlighters, fluorescent tubes, or lights that hand from the ceiling, like those installed in the meeting rooms.

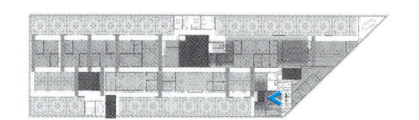

MOMENTUM ST. LOUIS
481

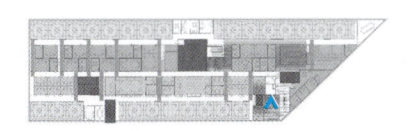

MOMENTUM ST. LOUIS
482

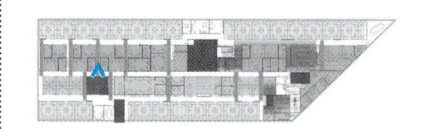

MOMENTUM ST. LOUIS
483

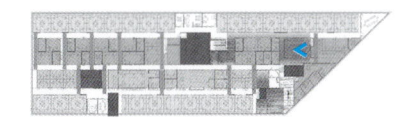

○ Third floor finish plan

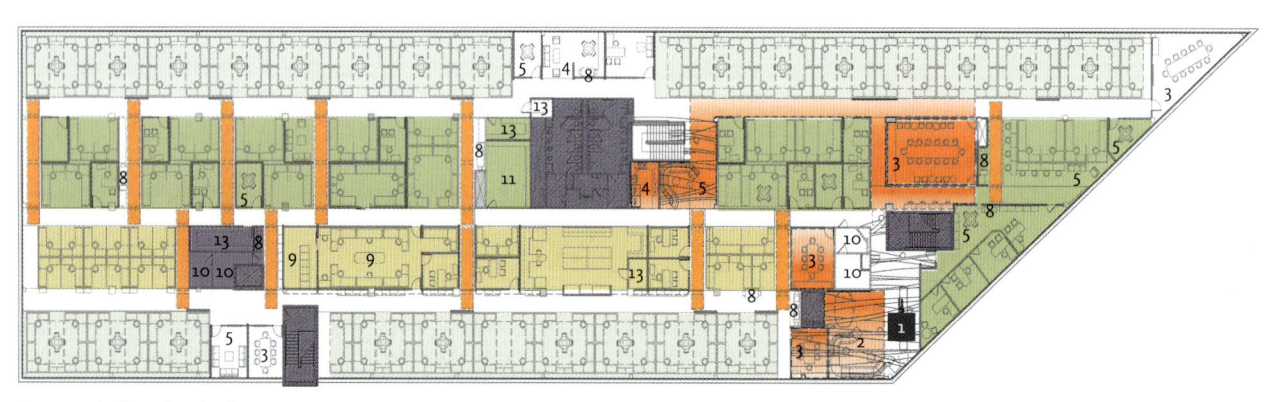

○ Fourth floor finish plan

1. Reception area
2. Wating area
3. Conference
4. Soft conference
5. Meeting
6. Kitchenette
7. Lunchroom
8. C/P/F
9. IT
10. Electrical
11. Library
12. Mail room
13. Storage
14. Fitness
15. Mother's room
16. Male showers
17. Female showers

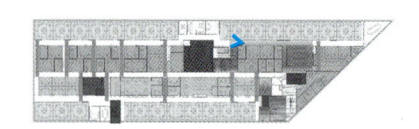

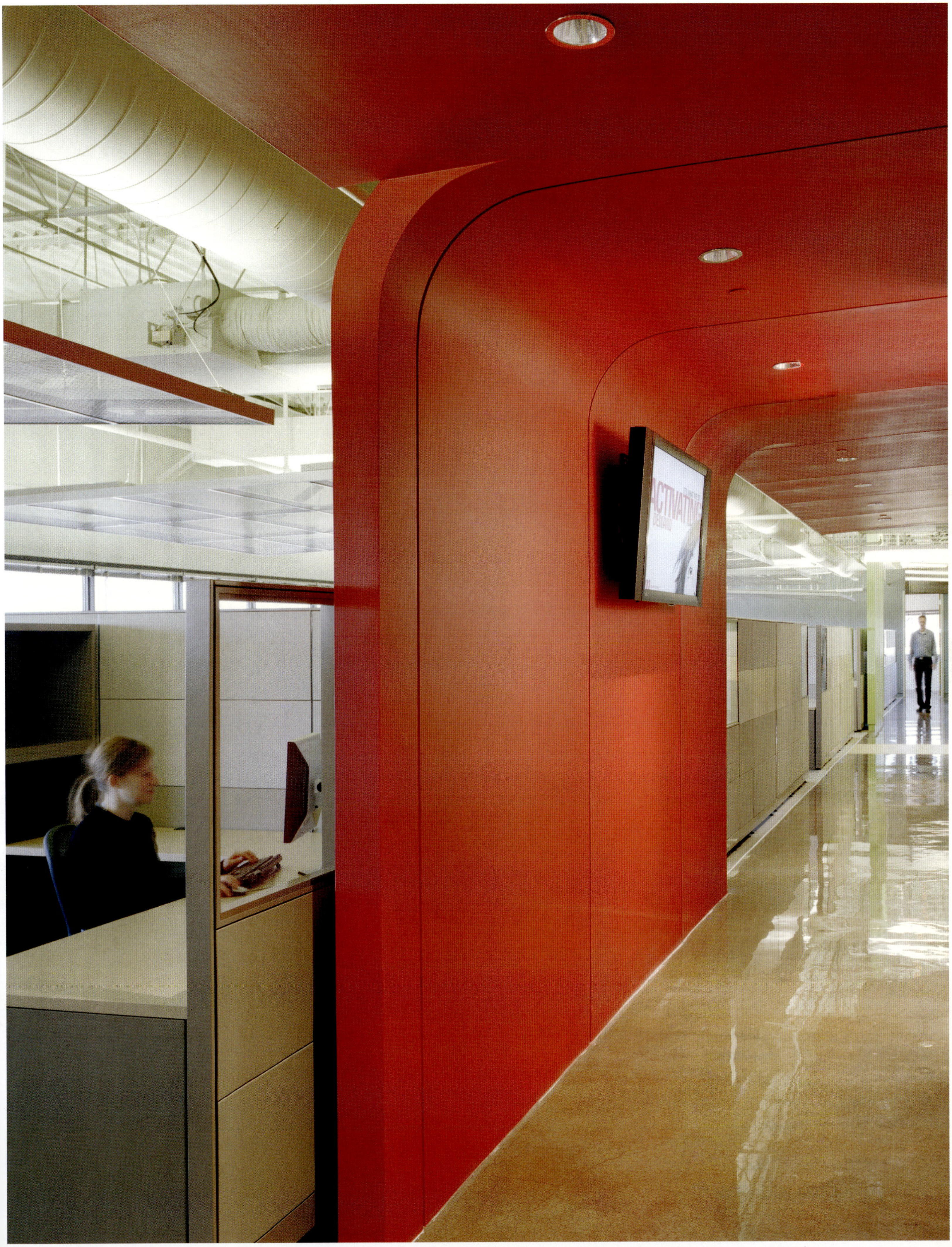

MOMENTUM ST. LOUIS
486

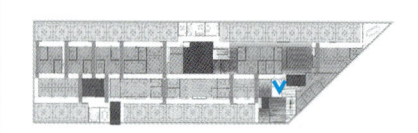

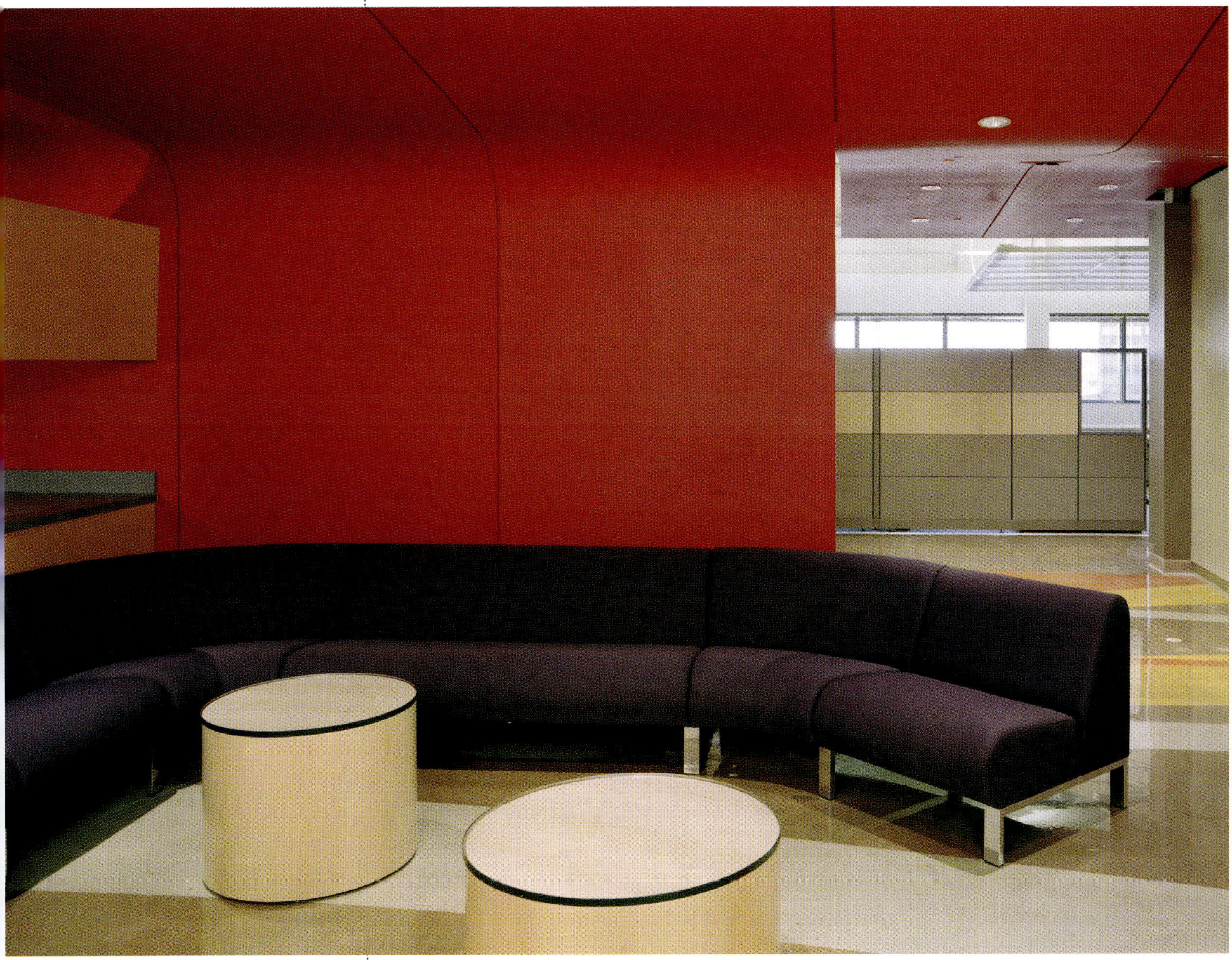

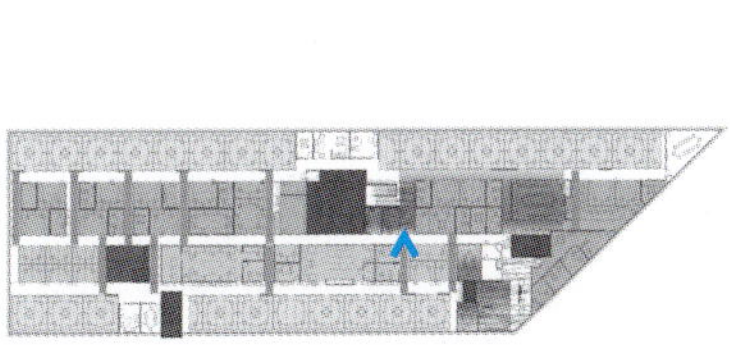

MOMENTUM ST. LOUIS

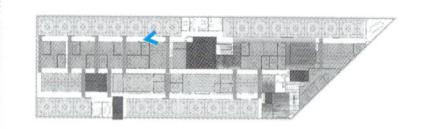

MOMENTUM ST. LOUIS

489

○ The interaction among the staff, which has been the guiding principle behind this project, continues in the closed offices, thanks to the glass screen access and their proximity to the communal work space.

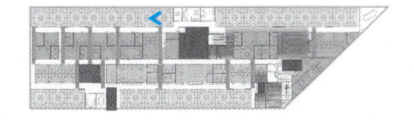

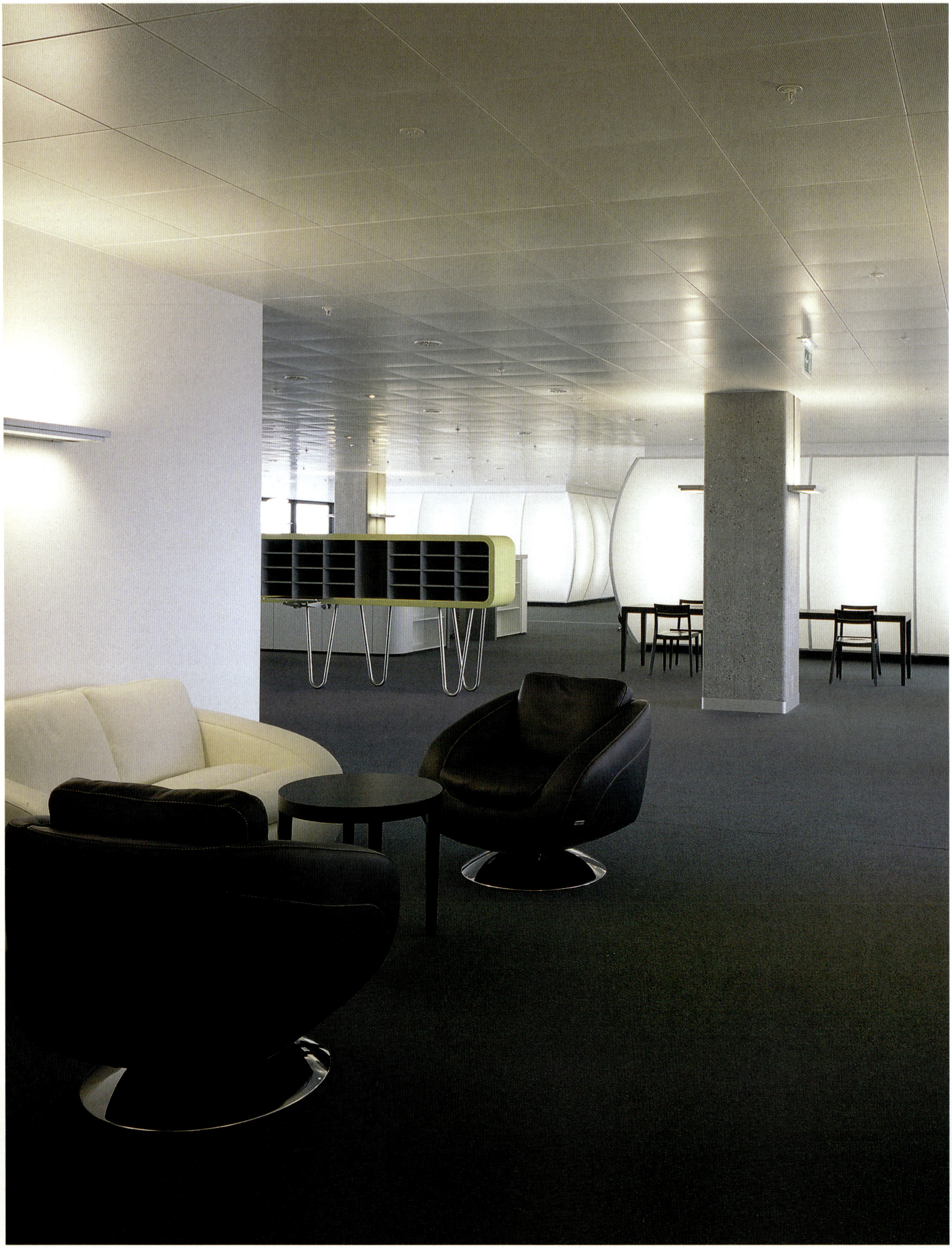

Clariant Flexible Office

The clients of this project are aware that a comfortable space favors efficient work. This is why they asked for their offices to be installed on a single floor, which houses the private and individual offices, as well as the communal and technical support areas.

The main feature of this office are the four modules located in the center of the floor plan. Two of these modules are used as meeting rooms while the other two house the private offices of the company directors. These blocks have been built from white polycarbonate panels. This material affords more light to the interior of the blocks as well as ensuring their necessary privacy.

The common work areas are situated close to the large windows that dominate the office, with the aim of making most efficient use of the natural light. Another feature of this area is the small cupboards, which as well as their storage function, serve to separate the different work tables.

One of the project's main features is its versatility in responding to the changing needs of the work, which occur on a regular basis. This is mainly reflected in the absence of clear separations between the spaces. Instead, color has been used to identify the different borders and functions. This means that any of these areas can be extended at any given moment by using their adjoining areas, and allows for uninterrupted communication throughout the work space. However for the communal rooms (i.e., the cafeteria, lounge, and meeting rooms for the work teams) a central area has been provided that cannot be modified or be given any other use.

As well as the communal area, known as *the active zone*, there is a private work area, with several offices, more meeting rooms, and another for the service points, technical installations, waiting area, etc.

ARCHITECT/DESIGNER:

WIRTH + WIRTH ARCHITEKTEN

Client: Clariant AG
Photographer: Architekturfotografie Kehl Lilli
Location: Münchenstein BL, Switzerland
Completion date: 2005
Area: 59,740 SF

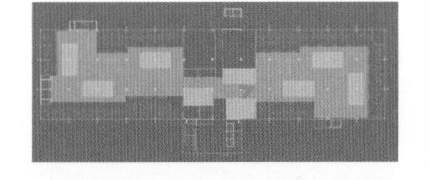

CLARIANT FLEXIBLE OFFICE

- The polycarbonate modules were chosen by the architects to integrate closed offices and meeting rooms in the work area. They have glass doors so as not to be entirely isolated.

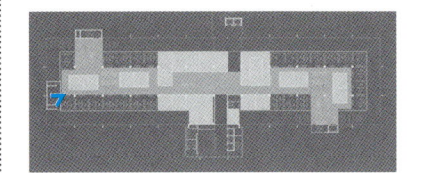

CLARIANT FLEXIBLE OFFICE
493

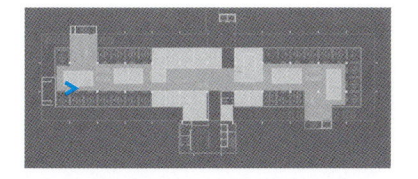

CLARIANT FLEXIBLE OFFICE
494

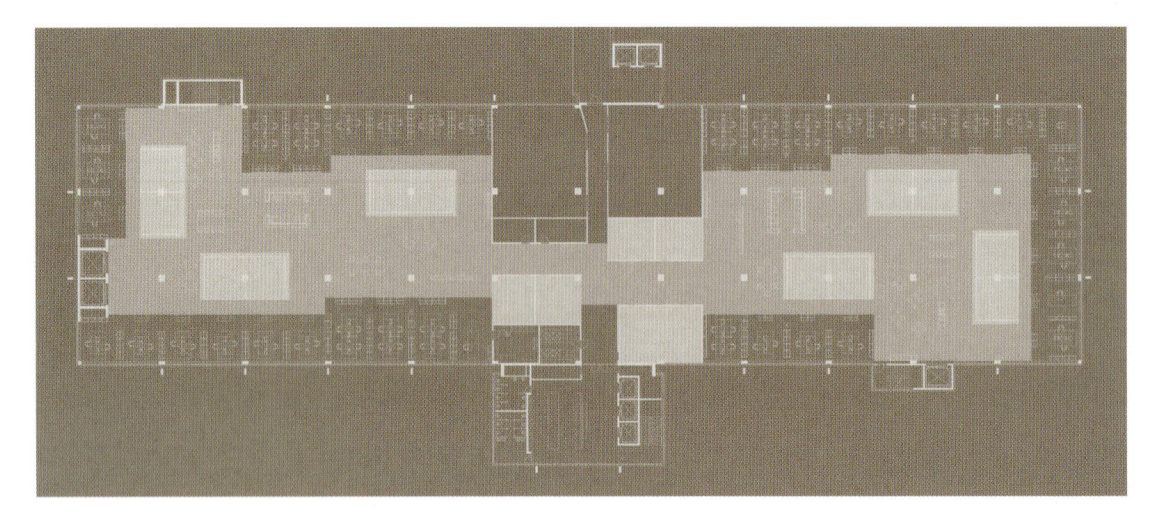

○ Floor plan

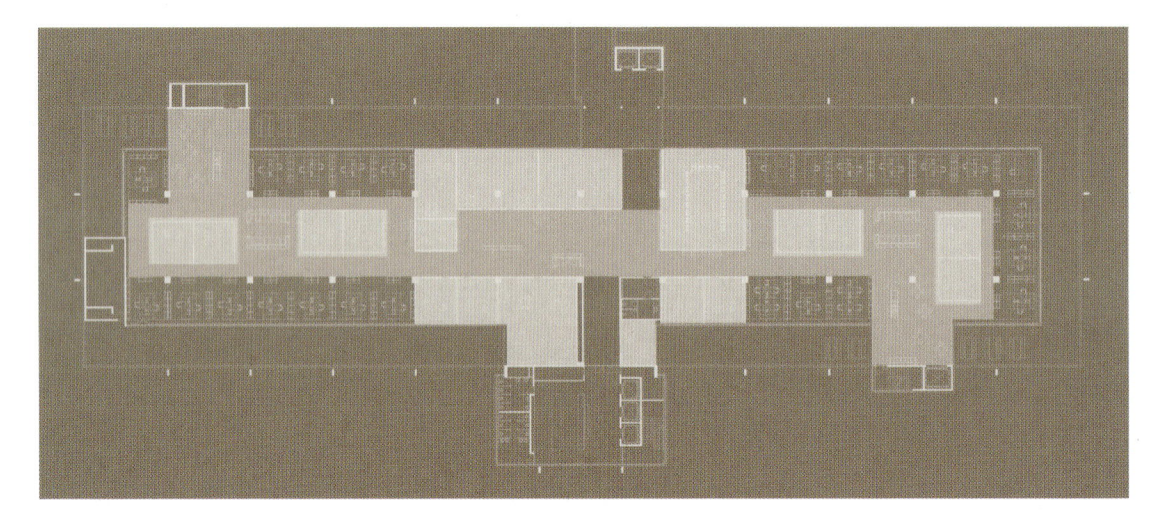

○ First floor plan

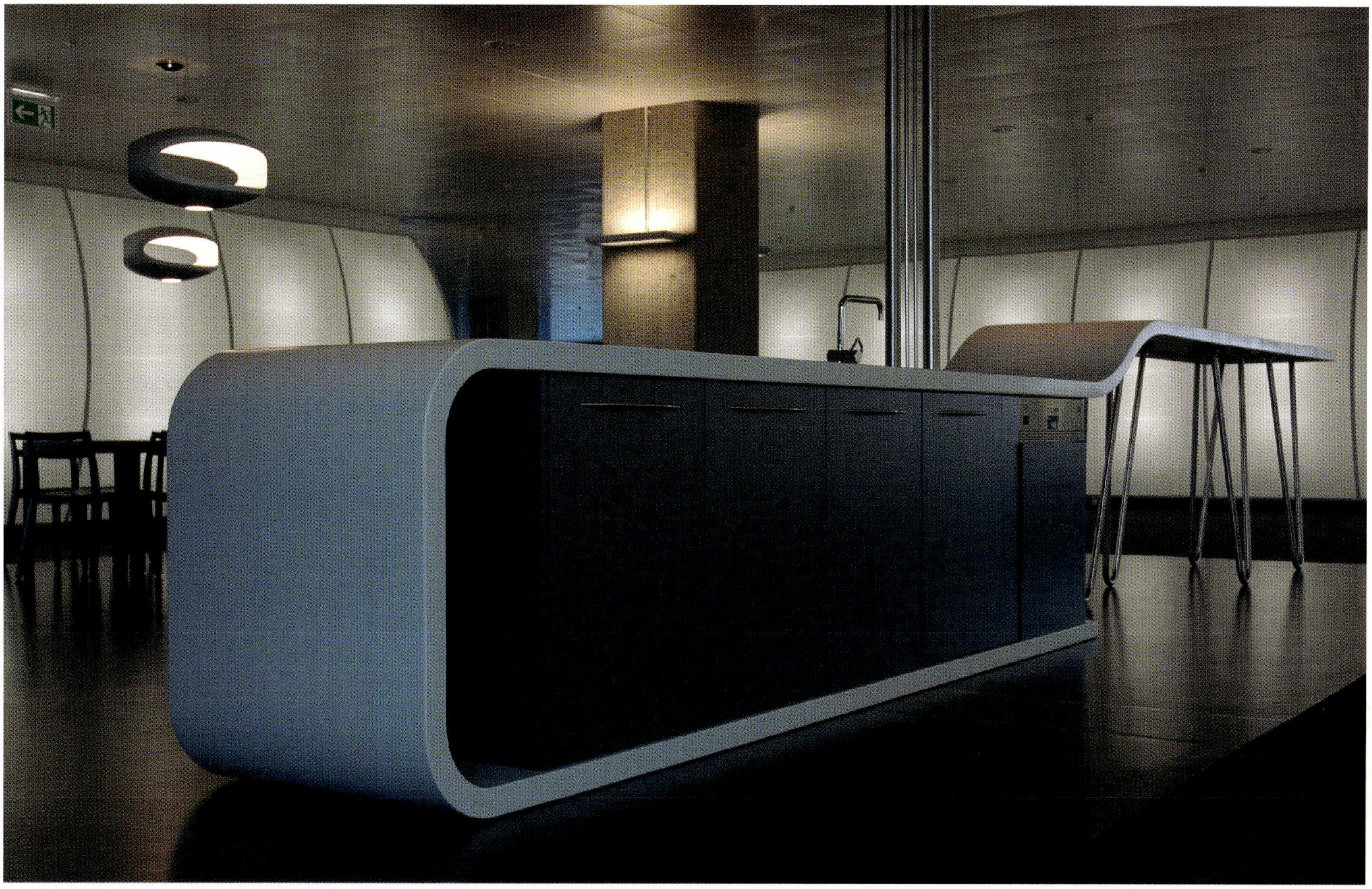

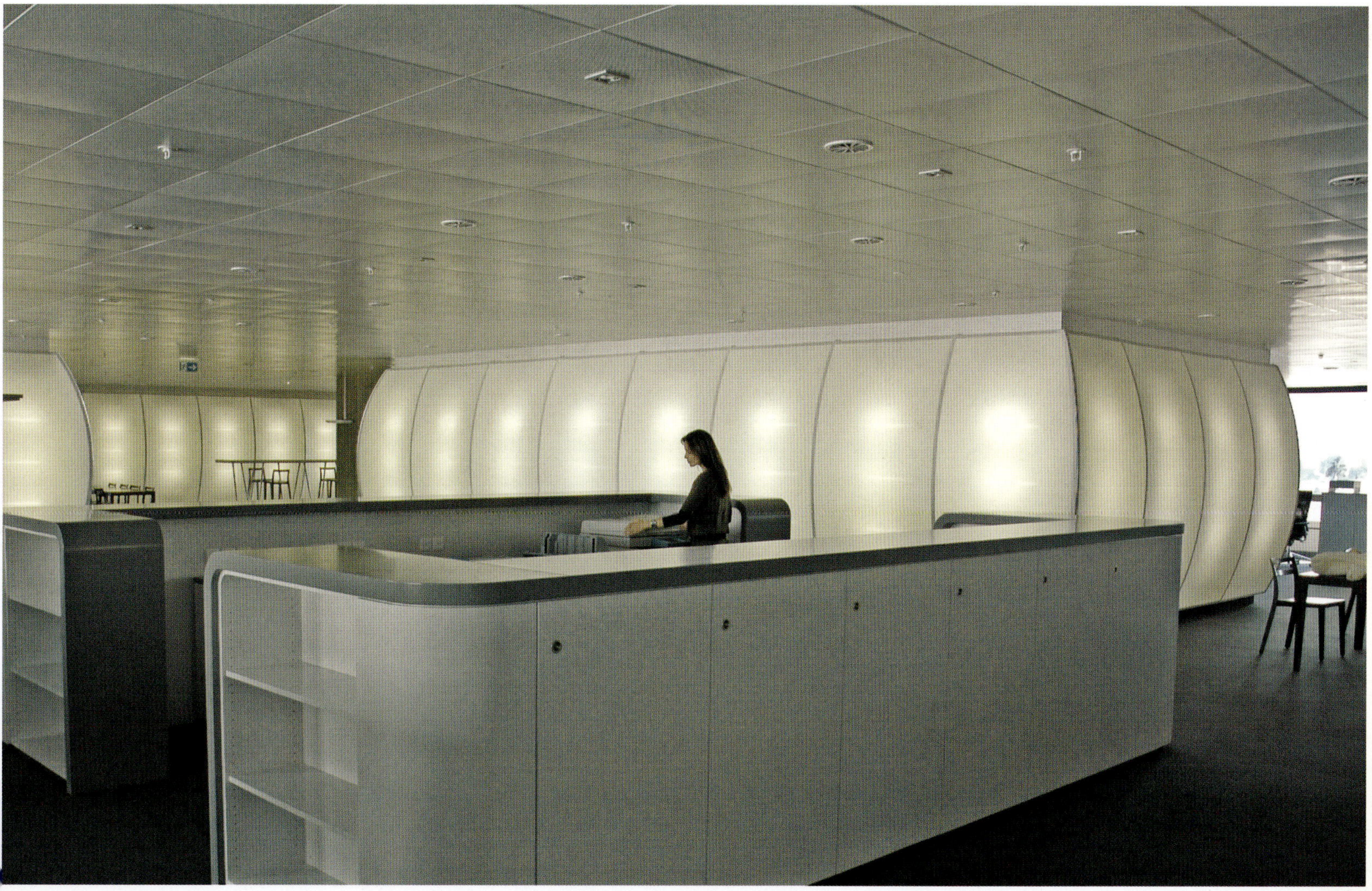

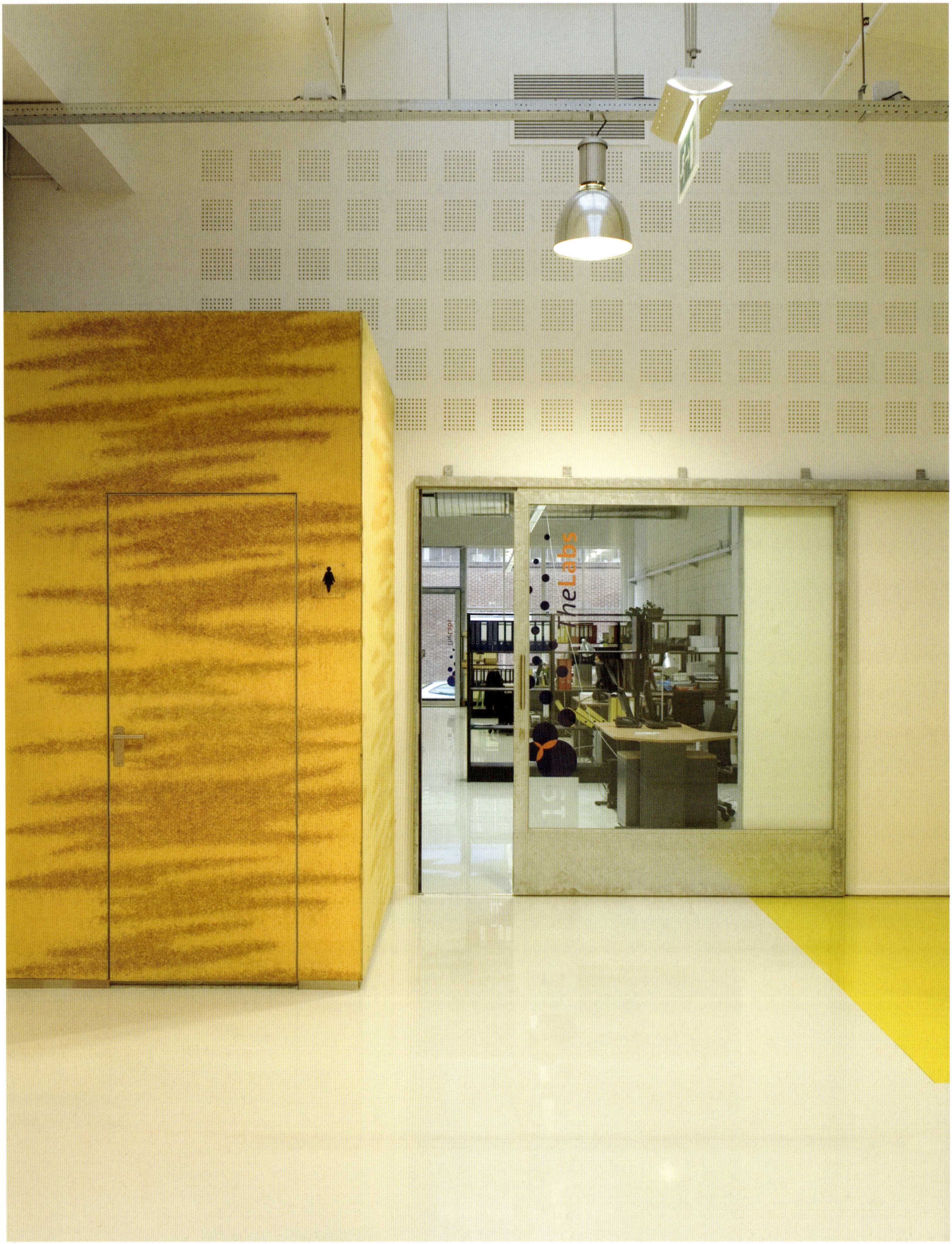
TheLabs

Caballero Factory

Architect/Designer:

Group A

Client: Caballero Factory
Photographer: Luuk Kramer
Location: Den Haag, The Netherlands
Completion date: 2006
Area: 85,035 SF

The town council of The Hague owns the property where this office project is located, with the aim of offering a location to small, young businesses in the cultural sector, namely the media and new technologies.

The building was built by a tobacco company to house their factory. Extensions were later added, which were demolished, and in 1953 the building fell into disuse. The project maintains the industrial character of the place and the new functions have been given a different style. The aim, specified in the brief, has been translated into the creation of an environment that stimulates innovation and creativity, as well encouraging cross-pollination between companies.

The communal areas and the spaces for meetings are the main element of this renovation. The building's backbone consists of the newly built, spacious passageway, which as well as a circulation area, serves as a space for meetings. A bar, several lounge areas and the central reception have all been located here. It also serves as a nexus that connects fifty-six different rooms.

To make efficient use of the surface area and create an open, well lit space, the different conference rooms have been built as boxes suspended from the ceiling, featuring partition walls in wood and translucent glass. The screw heads from the assembly have been left visible in order to establish a similar aesthetic to the original industrial style. For this reason the air vents and other services have also been left in full view.

The lighting plays an important part as a unifying element of the space. Natural light extends through the interior, mainly from the building's skylights, which have been restored in the renovation. The sliding doors, made from the same transparent glass as the partition walls, allow the light to reach throughout the space providing light, openness, and homogeneity.

● Although the style in which the new functions has been designed is modern, it connects with the building's original industrial character in different aspects, such as, for example, the exposed joins of the wooden partitions.

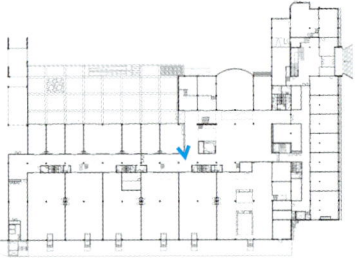

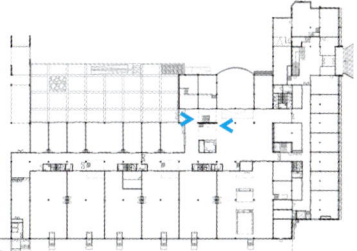

CABALLERO FACTORY

499

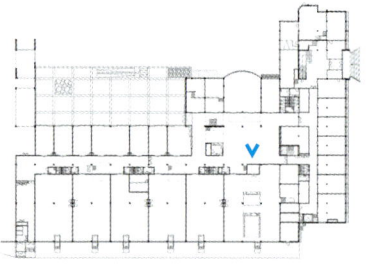

CABALLERO FACTORY

500

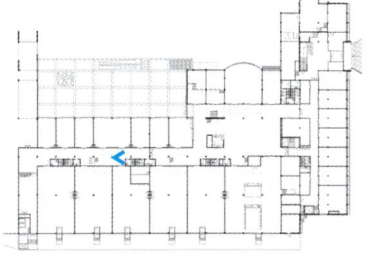

CABALLERO FACTORY

CABALLERO FACTORY
502

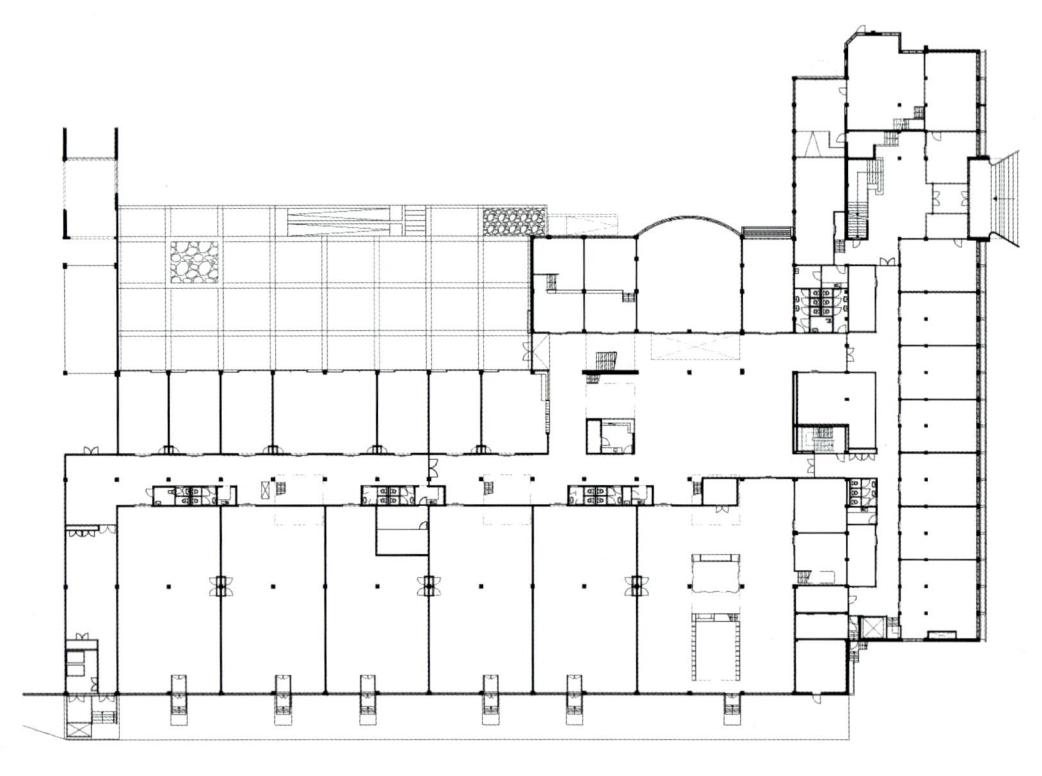

Floor plan

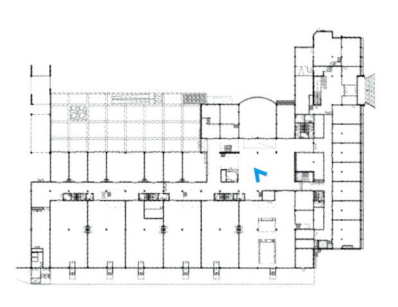

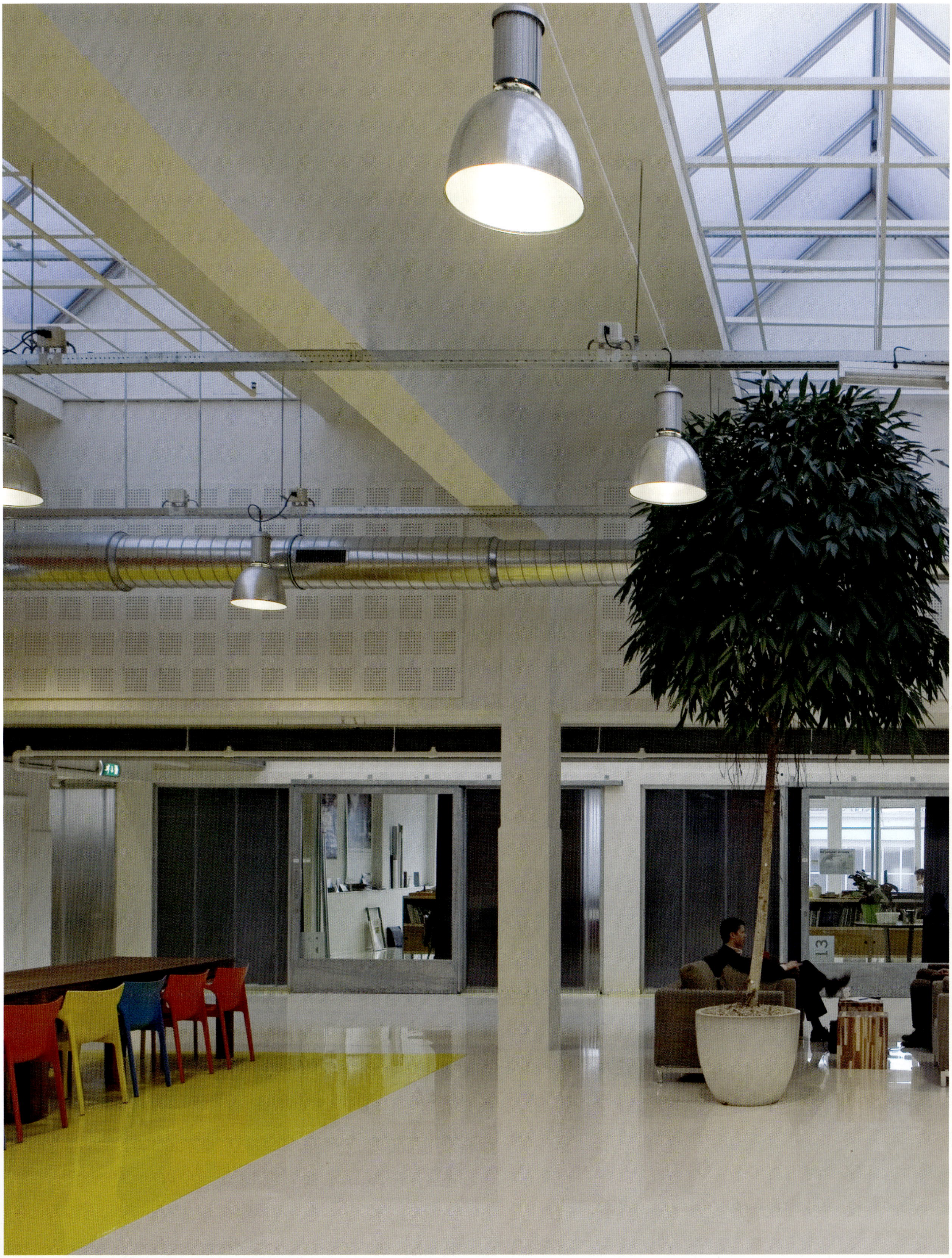

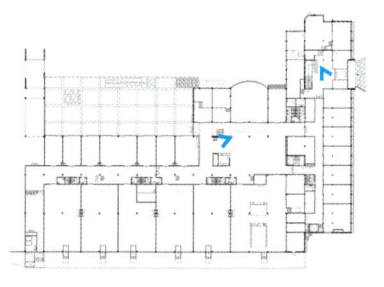

CABALLERO FACTORY
504

● The lighting has been conceived as a unifying element of this work place. The natural light, which comes from the skylights, flows unobstructed through the interior thanks to the transparent glass partitions and doors.

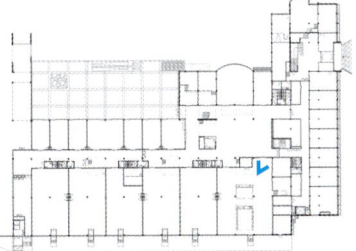

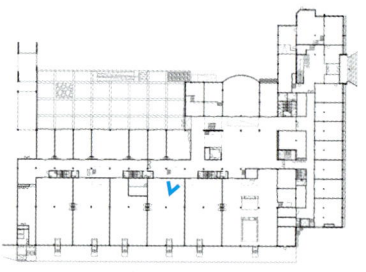

CABALLERO FACTORY
506

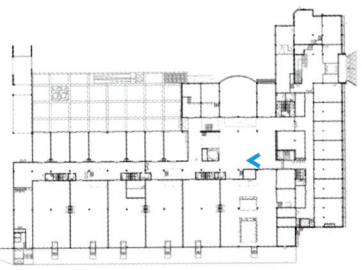

CABALLERO FACTORY
507

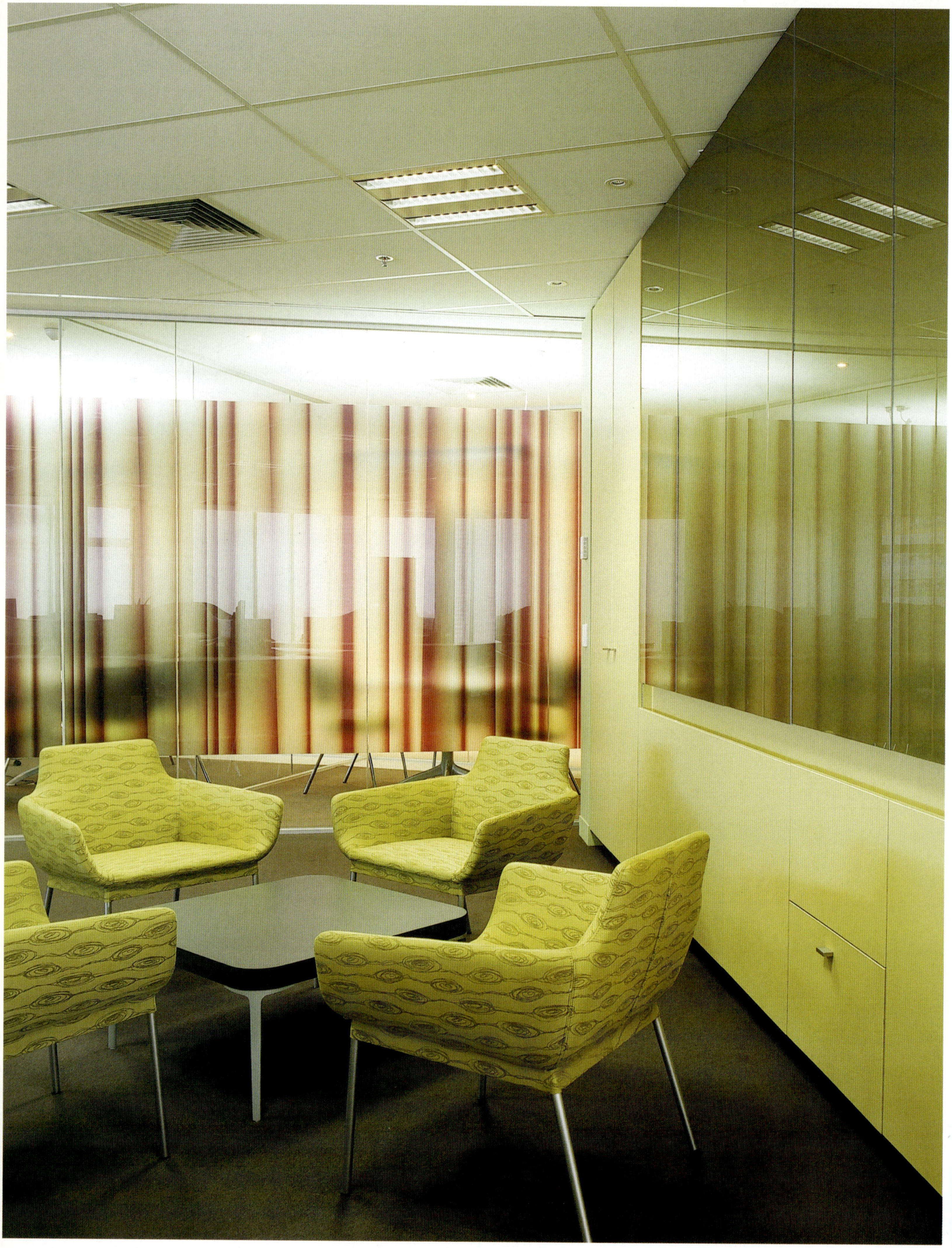

Bendigo Bank Offices

Architect/Designer:
Gray Puksand

Client: Bendigo Bank
Photographer: Shania Shegedyn
Location: Docklands, Melbourne, Australia
Completion date: 2005
Area: 86,111 SF

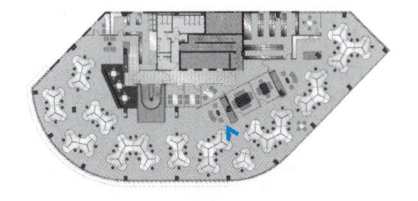

The headquarters for this project's client, Bendigo Bank, are located in Bendigo, a provincial Australian city. The company has a modern organizational focus and wanted to extend their business strategy through the creation of their new offices. The working environment, stated in the brief, required contemporary solutions that would establish a culture in the work place.

Thus Bendigo Bank is one of the first buildings in Australia to incorporate their air-conditioning system into the floor, so all temperature control is done via ‚radiant flooring‚. Another modern feature is the colorful north and east façades, which use double-glazed panels in browns, reds, yellows, greens, and pinks. These control the reflection of the sunlight to provide the interior with both the lighting and the heating required at any given moment. Color is also a factor in the interior, which has been given great importance and has been used to delineate areas; users therefore have a resource they can familiarize themselves with and easily relate to within the space.

On the three large interior levels the program combines open work areas with work stations, which have separating panels integrated into the tables; meeting rooms; a service area, which includes the toilets and the office; lounge areas and offices for meeting with clients. The walls are made from transparent glass so that the light penetrates the façade and diffuses through the interior unobstructed. This opening also connects the business units and facilitates social exchange.

To accentuate the culture of a single space, the central circulation core has been left open, formed by a staircase. Also, the security screens, which delineate the two floors, are made from transparent glass, leaving activity on all floors visible. The stairs thus become an element of physical and visual communication.

BENDIGO BANK OFFICES

● The vertical development is one of the original features of the project, since in Australia it is more common to develop interiors horizontally. The center staircase visually and physically connects the three floors.

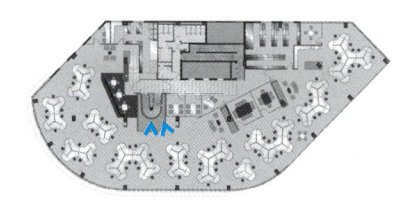

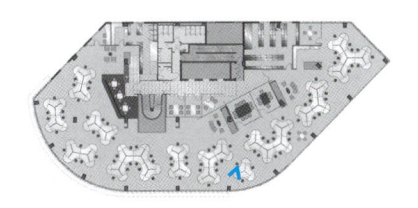

BENDIGO BANK OFFICES
511

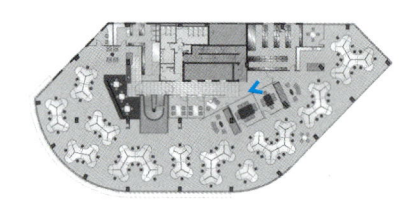

BENDIGO BANK OFFICES
512

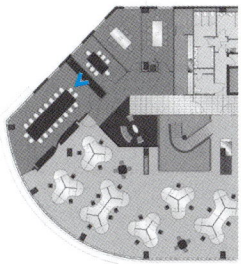

BENDIGO BANK OFFICES

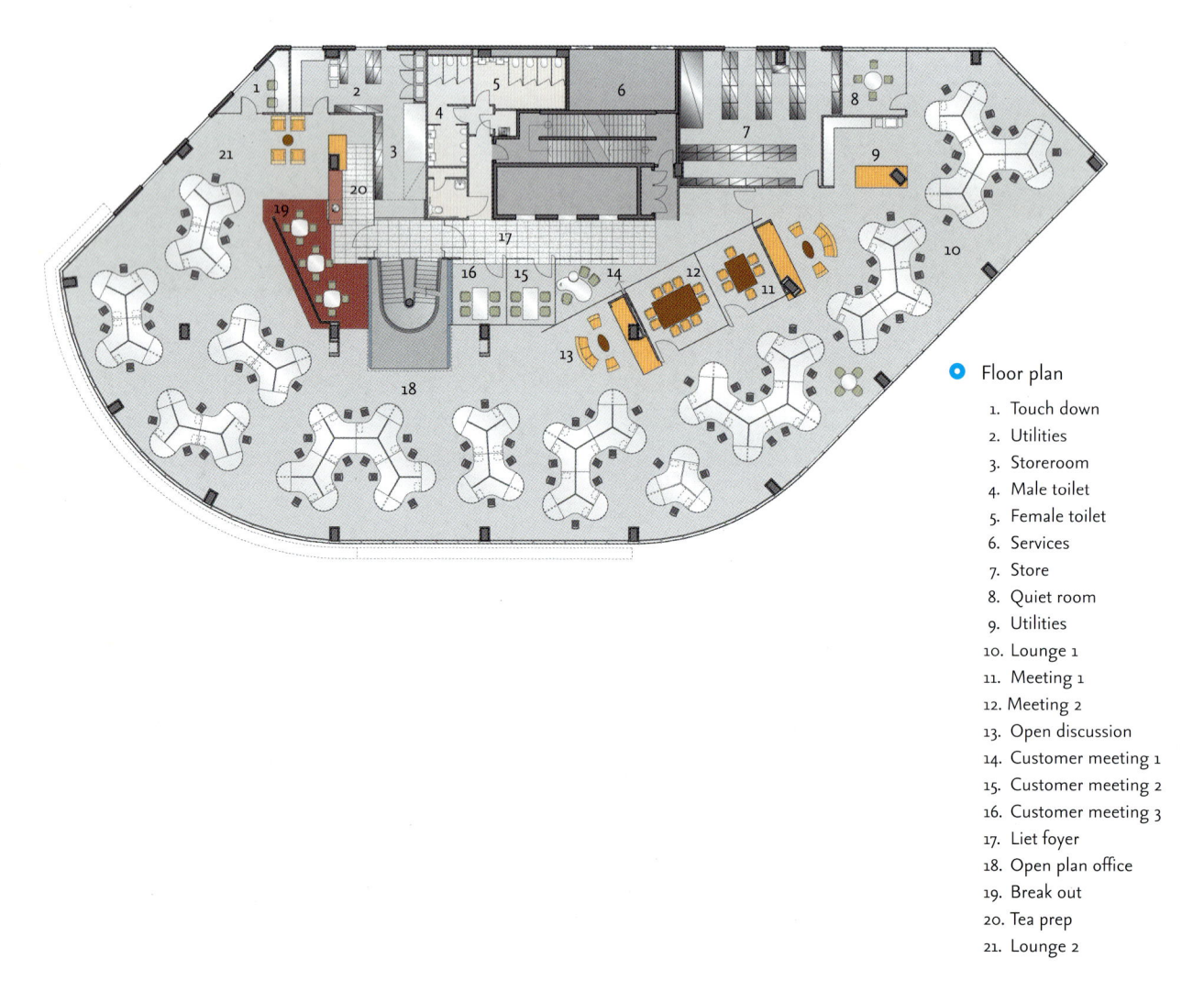

BENDIGO BANK OFFICES

- Floor plan
    1. Touch down
    2. Utilities
    3. Storeroom
    4. Male toilet
    5. Female toilet
    6. Services
    7. Store
    8. Quiet room
    9. Utilities
    10. Lounge 1
    11. Meeting 1
    12. Meeting 2
    13. Open discussion
    14. Customer meeting 1
    15. Customer meeting 2
    16. Customer meeting 3
    17. Liet foyer
    18. Open plan office
    19. Break out
    20. Tea prep
    21. Lounge 2

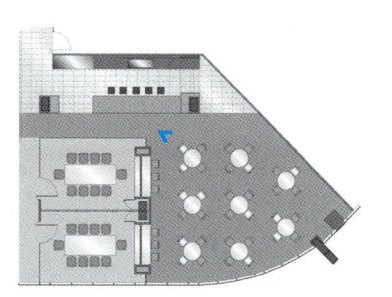

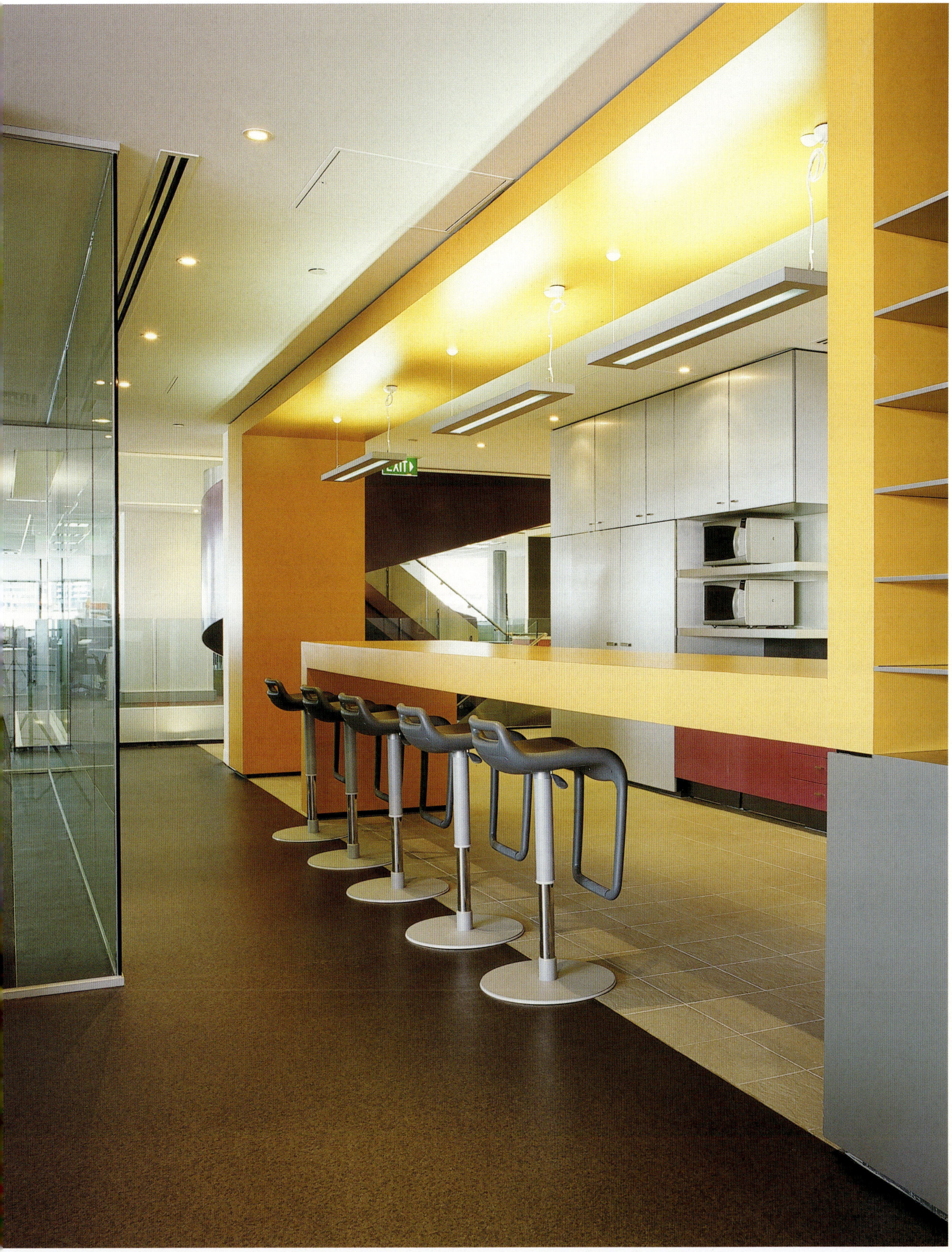
EXIT

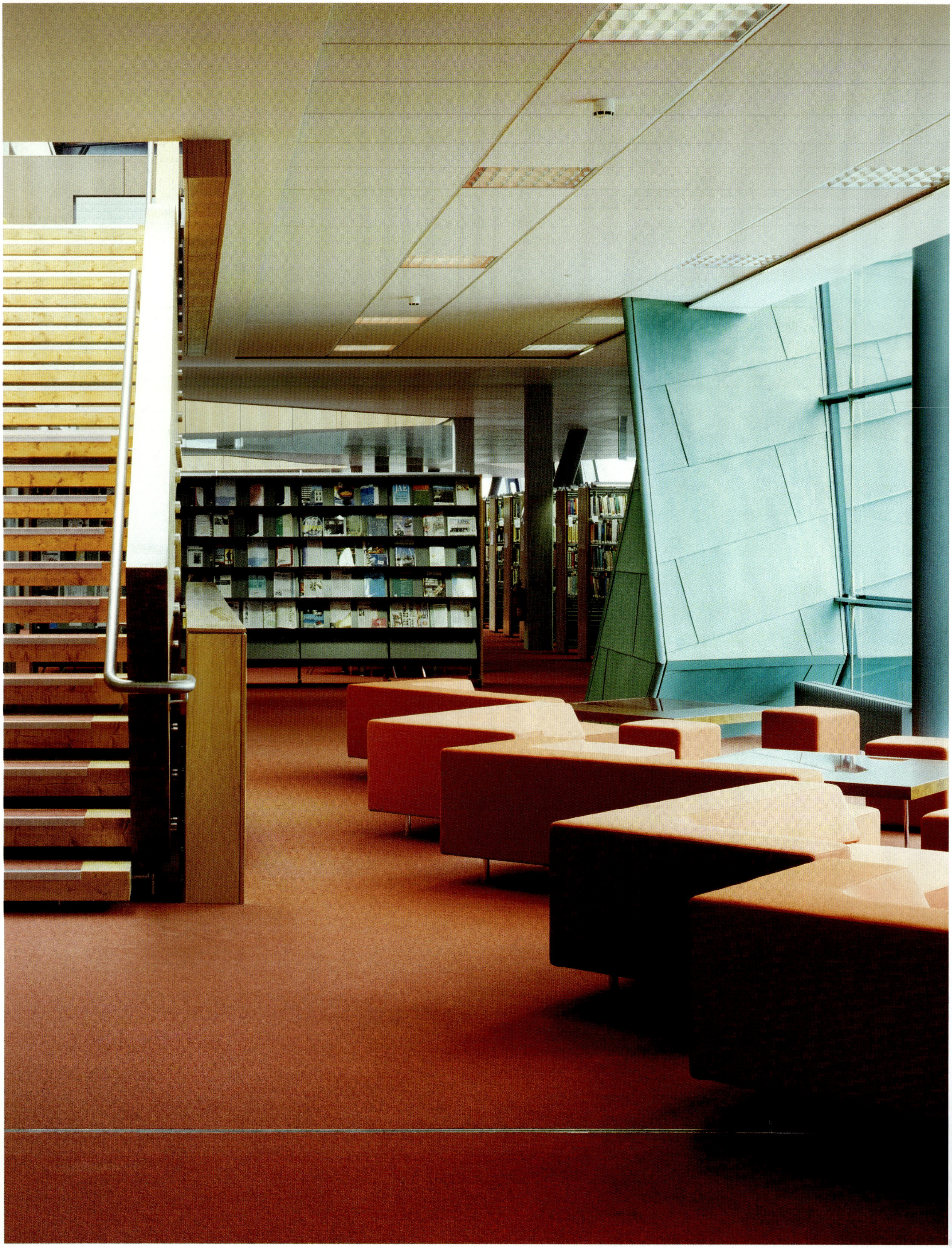

Mayo Institute of Technology

The prestigious academic institution the Galway-Mayo Institute of Technology, in Ireland, is the client for this project. The brief requested the construction of an annex to the institution's main building, which was split into two adjacent volumes: one for the auditorium and the other for the library and information services. The main entrance has been positioned at the point where both blocks meet, where their axis marks the circulation route for the pre-existing building.

The auditorium volume consists of four floors: the first three house the sixteen conference rooms and performance halls, with different capacities, while the top floor has been reserved for the administrative offices.

The block for the library houses 200 work stations spread across two levels, which have a capacity for 670 students and are connected by a central staircase, plus sixteen work rooms and different auxiliary spaces. The interior of the library contains several trapezoidal spaces, which is the same shape as the volume's exterior. Their walls are slightly inclined and the top floor is surrounded by half-height glass walls to give the impression that it is a floating platform.

The main construction materials are local limestone, Connemara marble, and polished copper. The latter has been chosen for its malleability, as a contrast to the rigid trapezoidal geometry.

On the library's exterior, three large copper sheets overlap like screens, which as well as being decorative, generate a cross-ventilation system that provides the interior with fresh air in the summer and warm air in the winter. Air is heated in pipes with a capacity of 1 million cubic feet before being released into the interior. This system was one of the project's biggest challenges.

ARCHITECT/DESIGNER:
MURRAY O'LAOIRE ARCHITECTS

Client: Galway Mayo Institute of Technology
Photographer: Ros Kavanagh
Location: Galway, Ireland
Completion date: 2003
Area: 110,481 SF

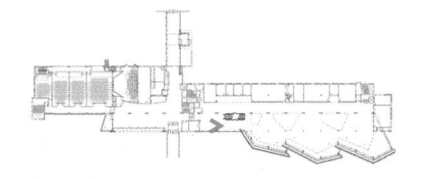

● In the building that houses the library a cross-ventilation system, created thanks to the three copper sheets installed on the building's exterior, generates the interior air-conditioning, both in the summer and winter.

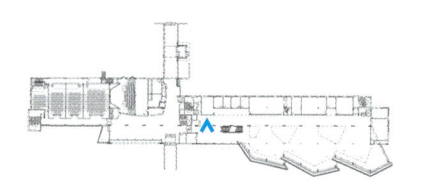

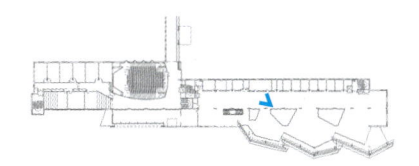

MAYO INSTITUTE OF TECHNOLOGY

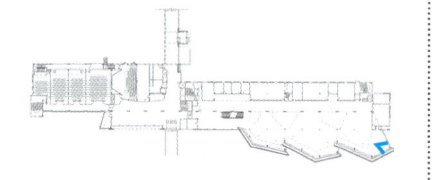

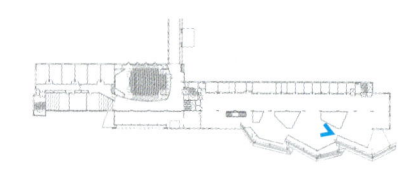

MAYO INSTITUTE OF TECHNOLOGY

MAYO INSTITUTE OF TECHNOLOGY

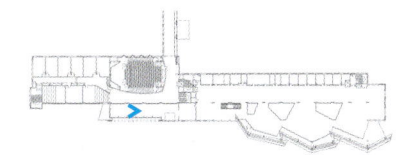

● The auditorium block contains sixteen performance rooms with different capacities. Plaster, local limestone, Connemara marble, and polished copper are the project's main materials.

MAYO INSTITUTE OF TECHNOLOGY

● Directory

● First floor plan

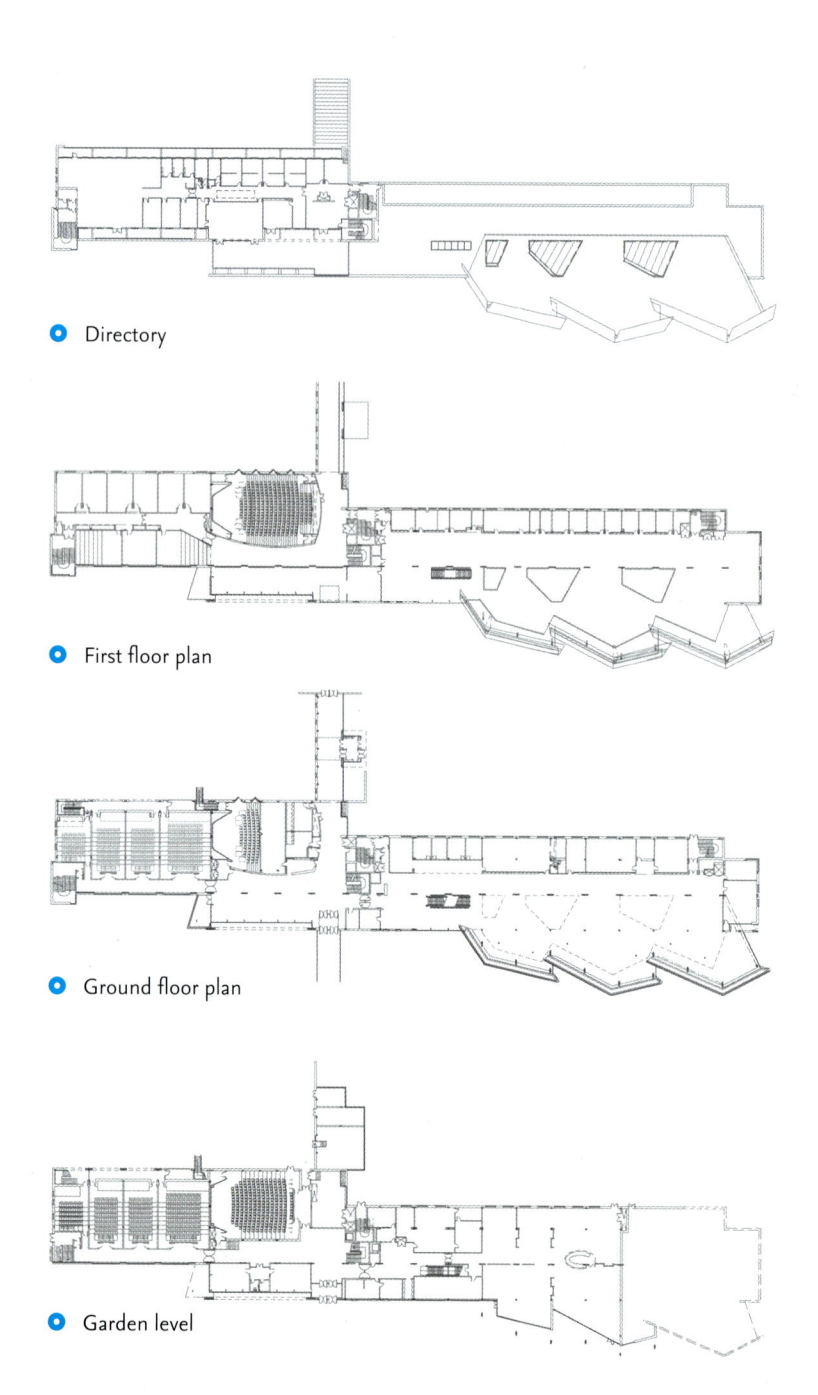

● Ground floor plan

● Garden level

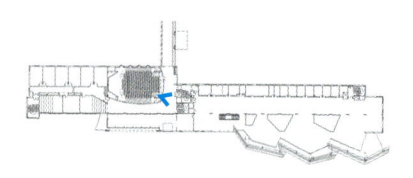

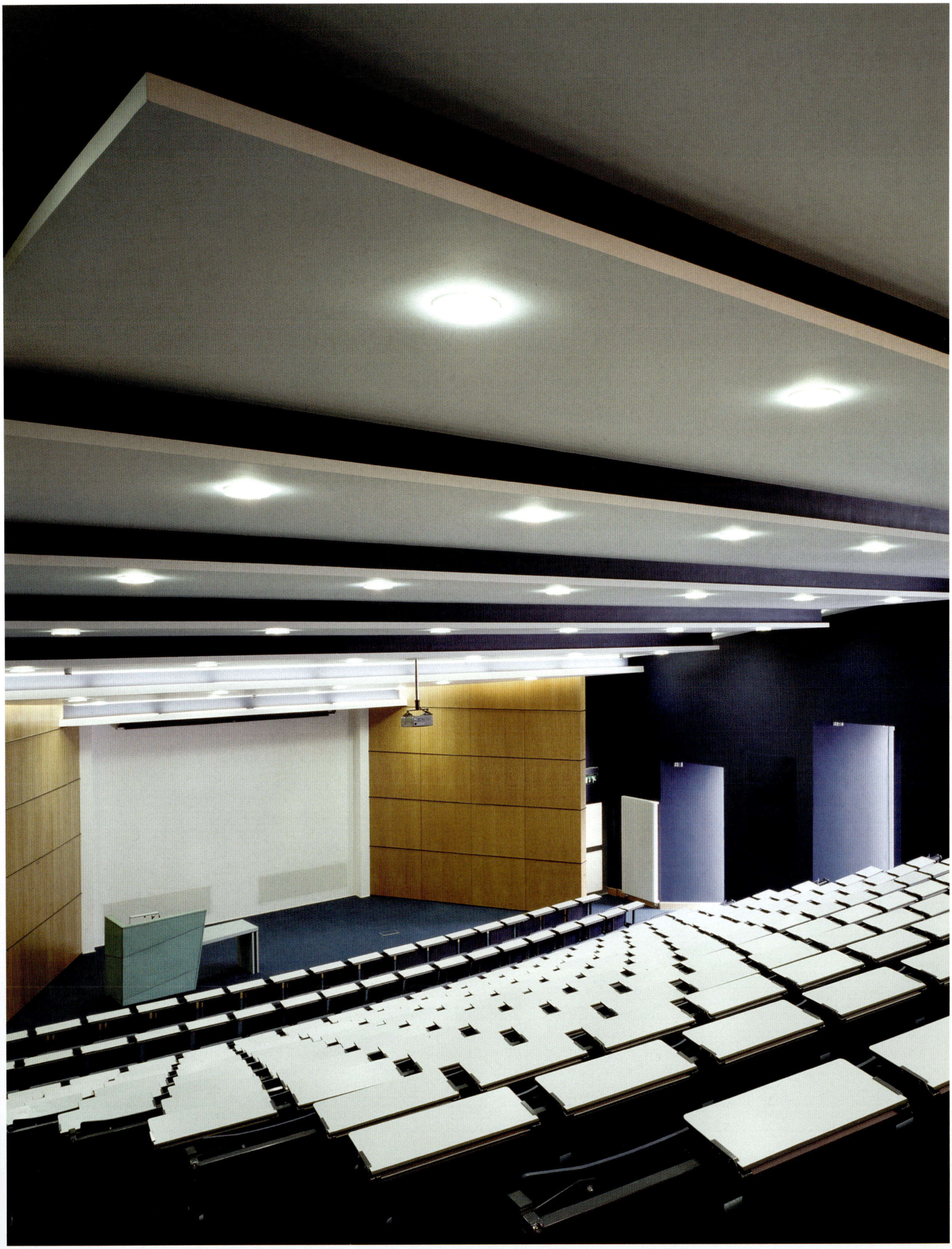

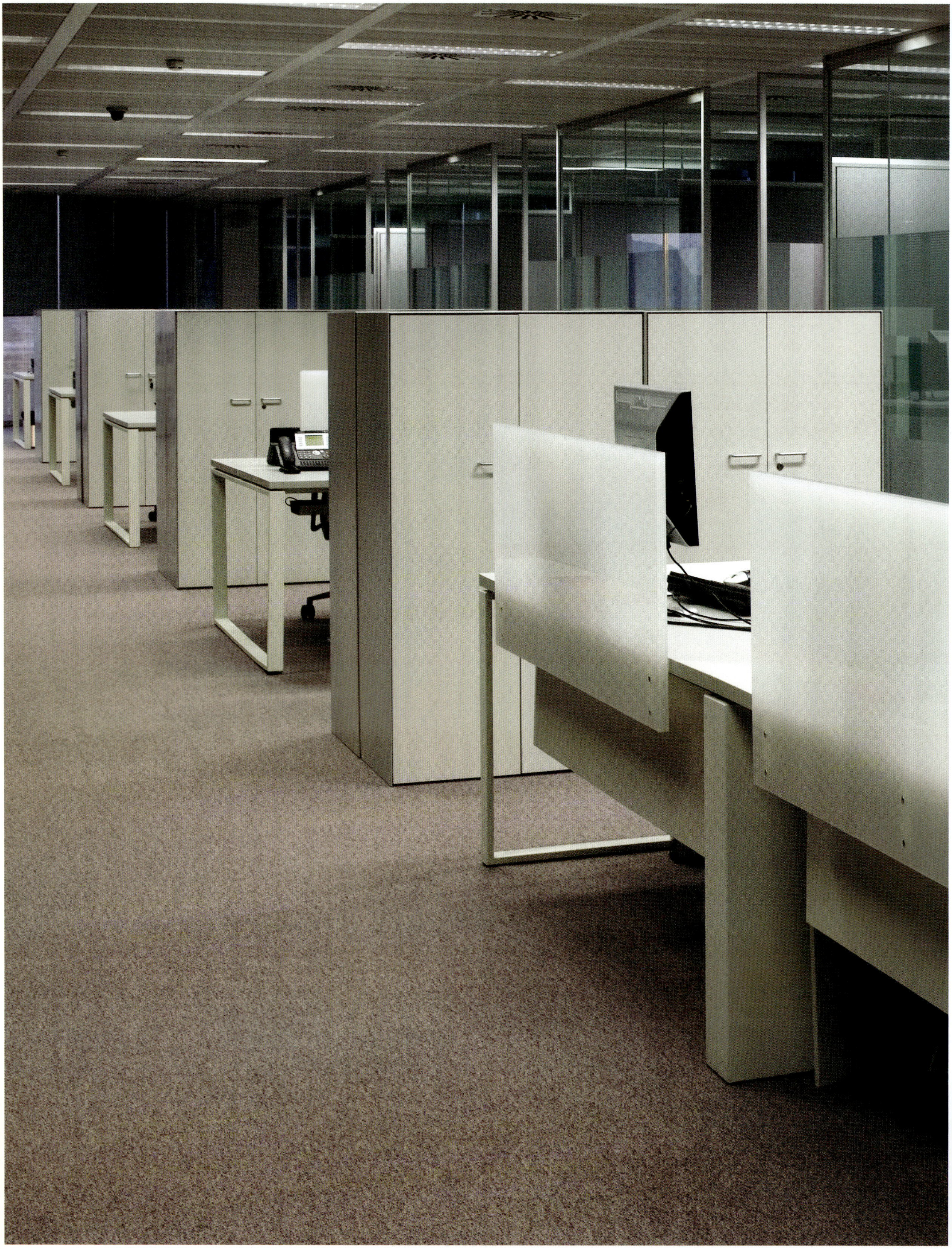

Indra Offices

The construction of a new district in the cosmopolitan city of Barcelona, the 22@, has lead to the appearance of a number of new office buildings, which have modified the urban landscape. It was decided to locate this technological company within this context. Together with a local property developer they decided to unite their headquarters in a single building, which until then had been spread across five different centers. The corporate offices consist of a ground floor, twelve floors above this, a technical floor, and two basement levels. The offices are located in the floors above ground level, while the two basement levels have been used as a parking lot for cars and motorbikes. The technical rooms have been reserved for exclusive and private use only.

A solid and compact base has been built in line with the street, which corresponds to the ground floor and the two floors above it. This piece draws a rhomboidal shape, which follows the street corner, strengthening the slender appearance of the resulting volume. The ten-floor tower is separated from the base via the technical floor, installed as if it were floating above the base, giving the composition a lightweight appearance.

The interior has been conceived so that the different floors can be reinterpreted depending on their use or the desires of the users. For the office furniture there is particular emphasis on an avant-garde and modern design, which represents technology and functionality. The distribution of the work tops, which rest on the buc structures with drawers or cupboards, allows for the presence of the work table alongside the meetings table. The wood and steel furniture is a single color: grayish white. The different work areas are delineated by way of the shelving units, which thus have the role of both ensuring privacy and providing storage space. Smoked glass has been used in the private offices and the meeting rooms to delineate their space with respect to the other areas. The result is spatial order, geometric balance, and formal sobriety.

Architect/Designer:

Fermín Vázquez/b720 Arquitectos, Mercedes Isasa/Estudio TBC, Bordonabe

Client: Indra, Grup Castellví
Photographer: José María Molinos
Location: Barcelona, Spain
Completion date: 2006
Area: 111,676 SF

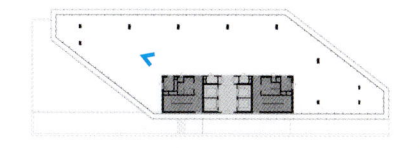

● The option of using a single color creates a neutrality, which typifies this open-plan working environment. The furniture is made exclusively of wood and steel.

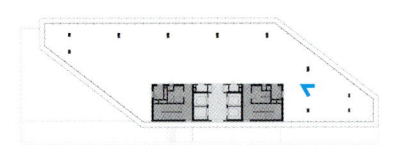

INDRA OFFICES
527

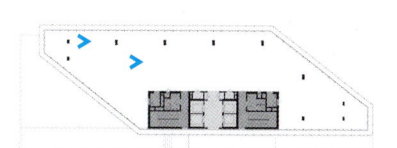

INDRA OFFICES
528

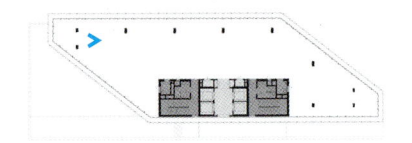

INDRA OFFICES
529

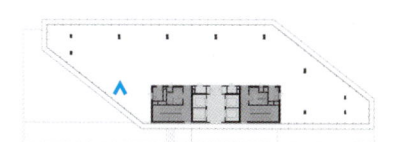

INDRA OFFICES
530

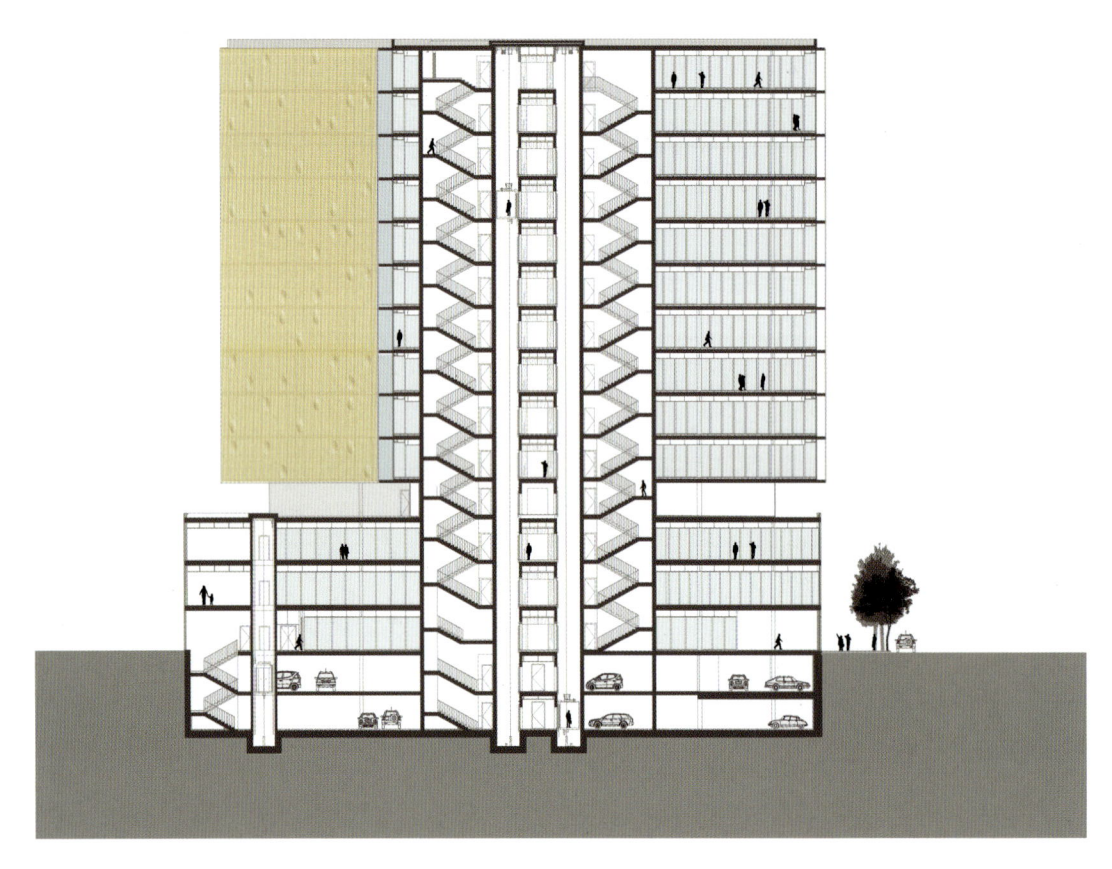

Section

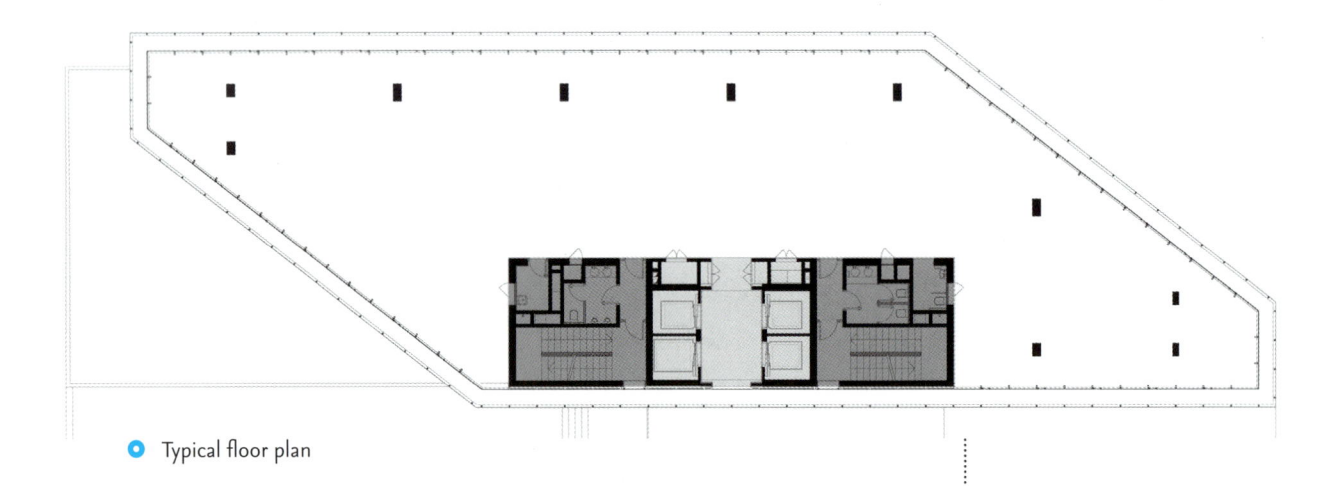

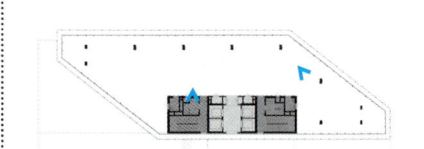

Typical floor plan

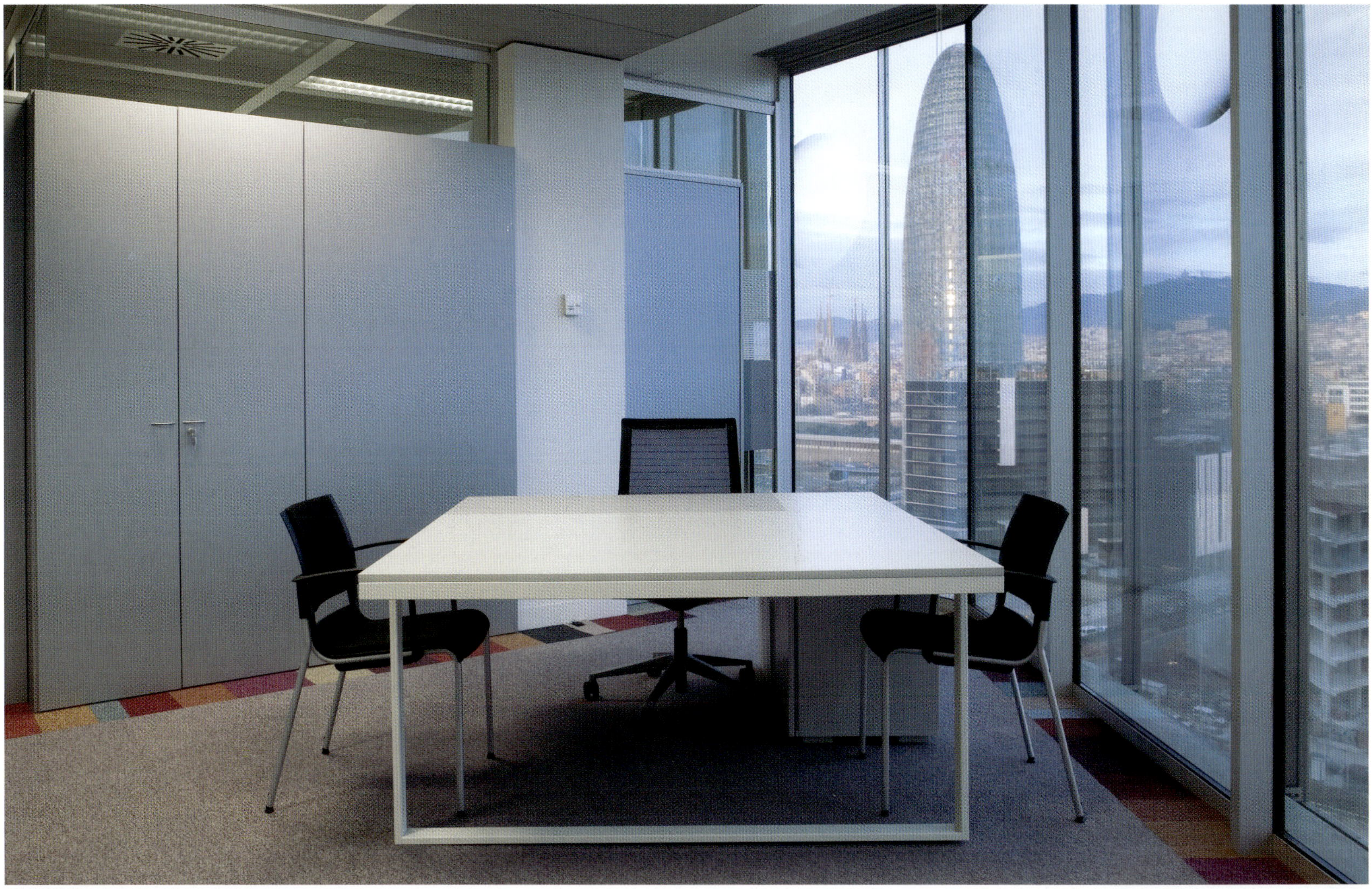

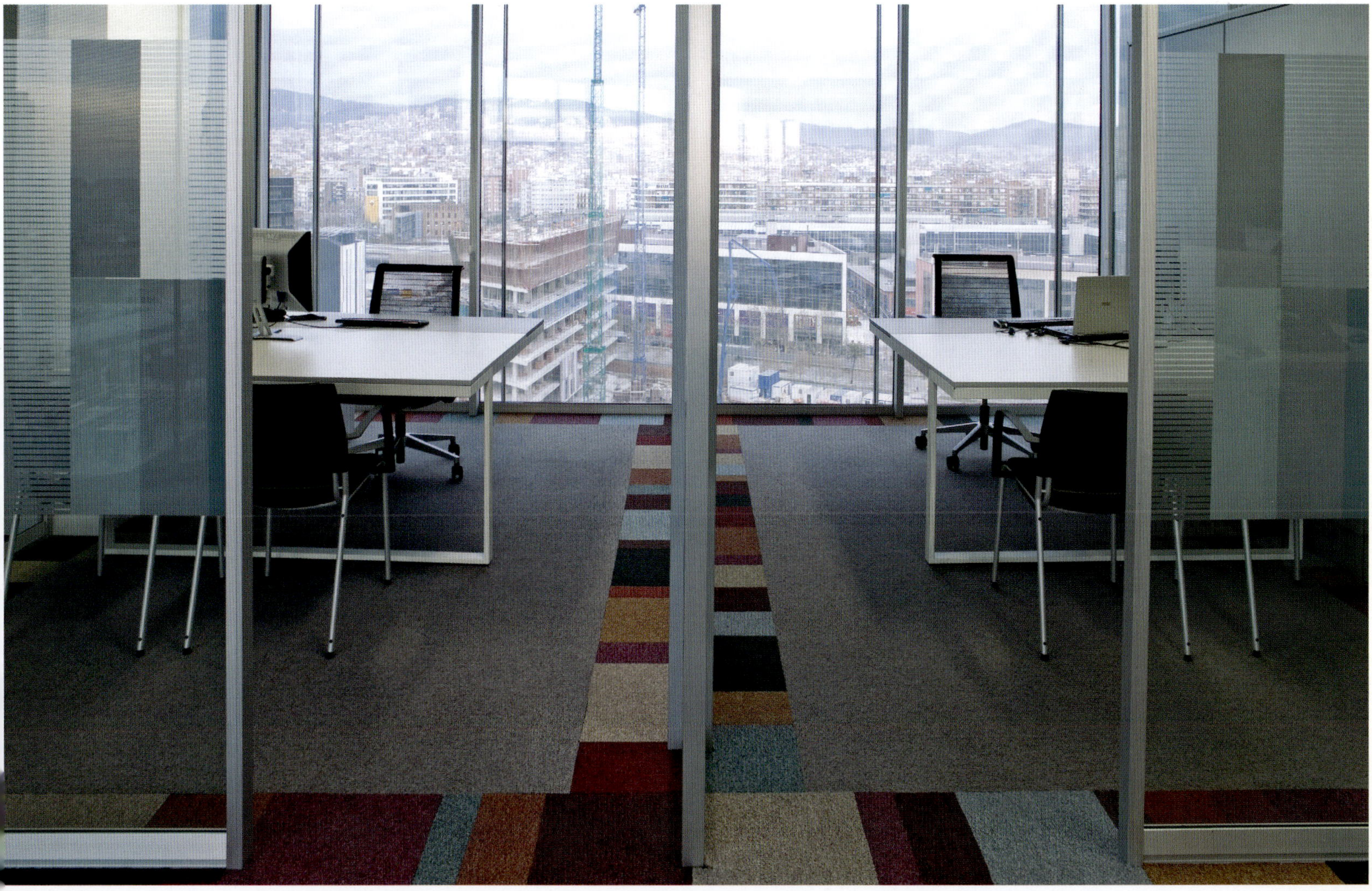

INDRA OFFICES
532

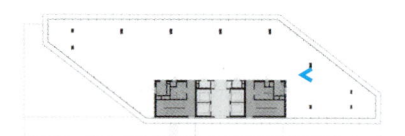

INDRA OFFICES
533

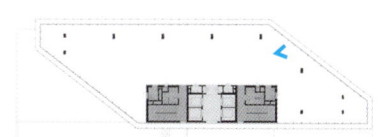

○ The elements that delineate the spaces are glass between the offices, and lacquered cupboards, which separate the work tables within an area. The space allows for future subdivisions.

INDRA OFFICES
534

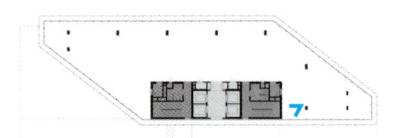

INDRA OFFICES
535

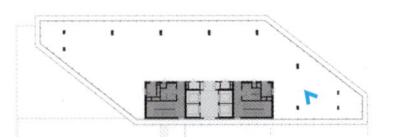

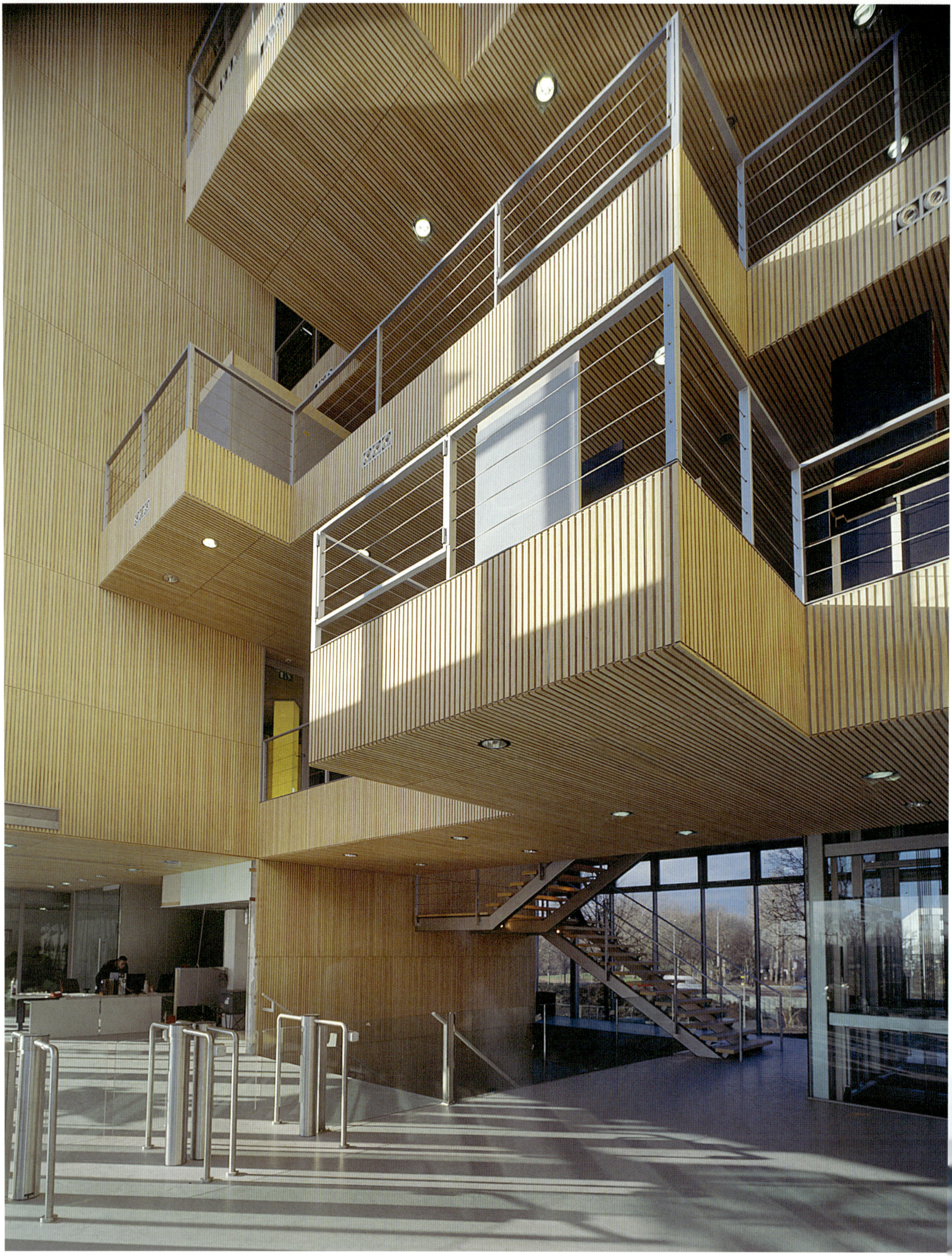

Rijkswaterstaat Zeeland Head Office

ARCHITECT/DESIGNER:

ARCHITECTENBUREAU PAUL DE RUITER

Client: Rijksgebouwendienst (government building agency)
Photographer: Rob't Hart
Location: Middelburg, The Netherlands
Completion date: 2004
Area: 127,585 SF

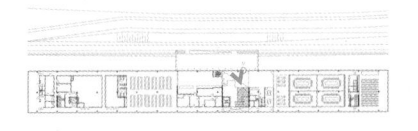

The new central headquarters for the Water and Traffic Management Department of the Dutch government functions as an office building and in 1998 was integrated into an ambitious town planning program for the surrounding district of Middelburg. The client wanted a functional and above all transparent design, both in its visual structure and its accessibility and sustainability. In response to this request, the architects sought to harmonize the design with its surroundings. With this in mind, the building sought horizontal proportions, due to its location parallel to the canal. The interior offers views of the surroundings, and from outside the interior installations can be appreciated, a characteristic that responds to the client's desires to show that important decisions are taken in an informed and clear way.

The interior rooms, with a capacity for 450 employees, include various rooms for filing, a restaurant, a conference center, a fitness room, and a computer center. The ground floor is completely open to the public, although it belongs to the Dutch government. Highly flexible construction methods have been used to create modules, in which the volumes that house the utilities—electricity, telephones, etc.—do not exceed four feet.

This flexible construction allows modifications of the internal divisions when the employees need them. Also, the location of the building in a park, strengthens the connection, integration, and communication among the workers. The new office is a clear example of sustainable building, since it uses innovative materials and techniques, which generate increased energy reductions. The use of materials like wood and stainless steel for the design affords the desired atmosphere of harmony and comfort. The active concrete, which forms part of the 12-inch- thick prefabricated floor, generates a considerable reduction in costs and energy.

RIJKSWATERSTAAT ZEELAND HEAD OFFICE

● Wood, stainless steel, and glass are used throughout and have connotations of functionality and comfort. The active concrete, an innovative material, affords energy efficiency since it absorbs heat from the atmosphere.

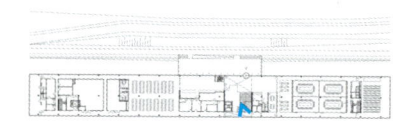

RIJKSWATERSTAAT ZEELAND HEAD OFFICE

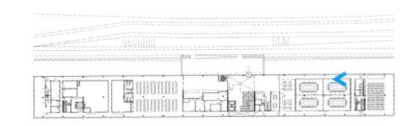

RIJKSWATERSTAAT ZEELAND HEAD OFFICE

RIJKSWATERSTAAT ZEELAND HEAD OFFICE

● The building's façade and the interior divisions are glass, which allows the entry of natural light and improves visibility in the interior. This responds to the client's desire to express their corporate openness.

RIJKSWATERSTAAT ZEELAND HEAD OFFICE

○ Sections

○ Floor plan

○ Office floors

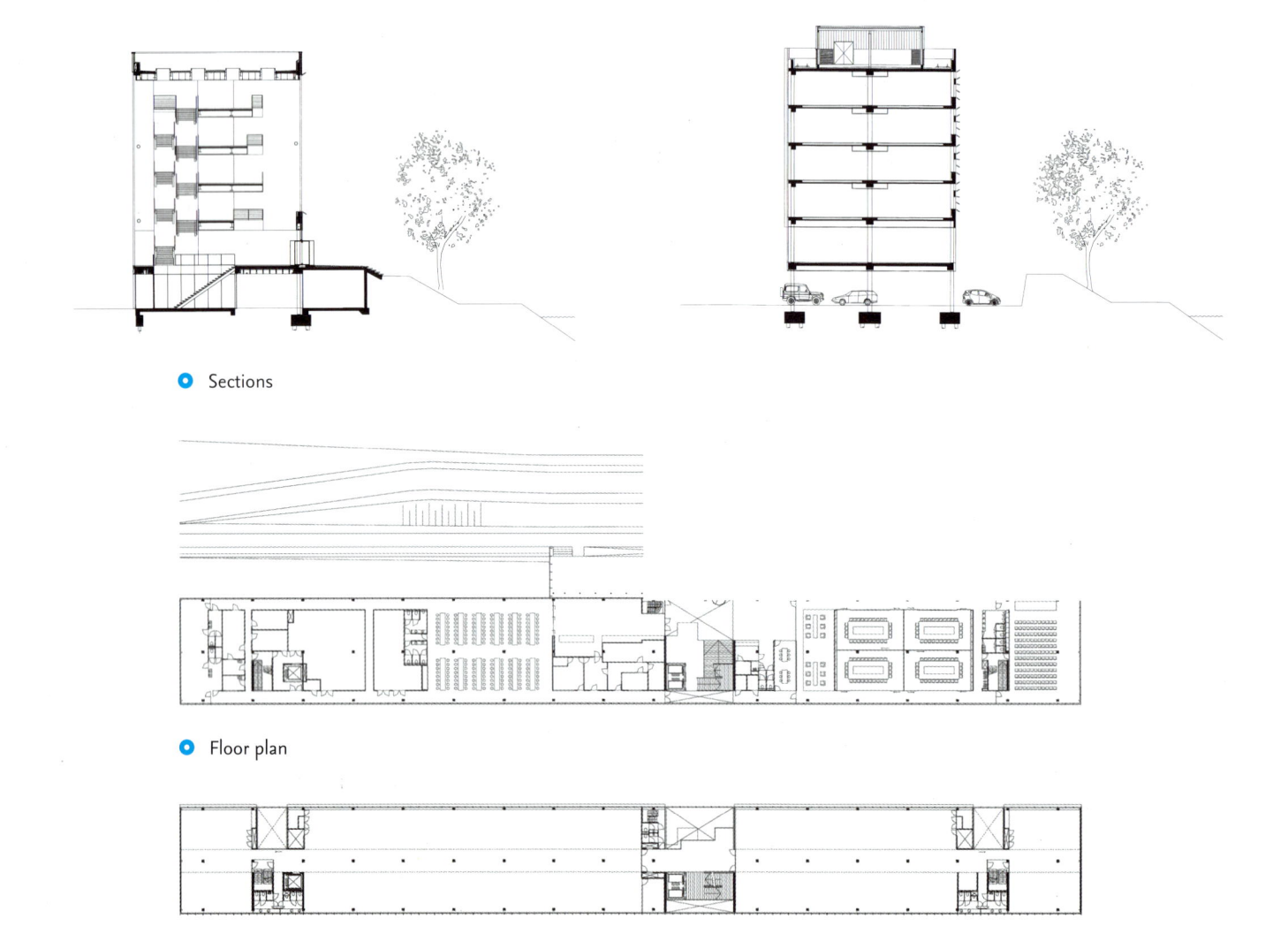

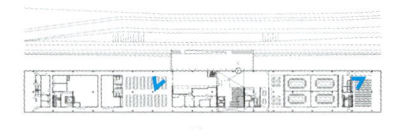

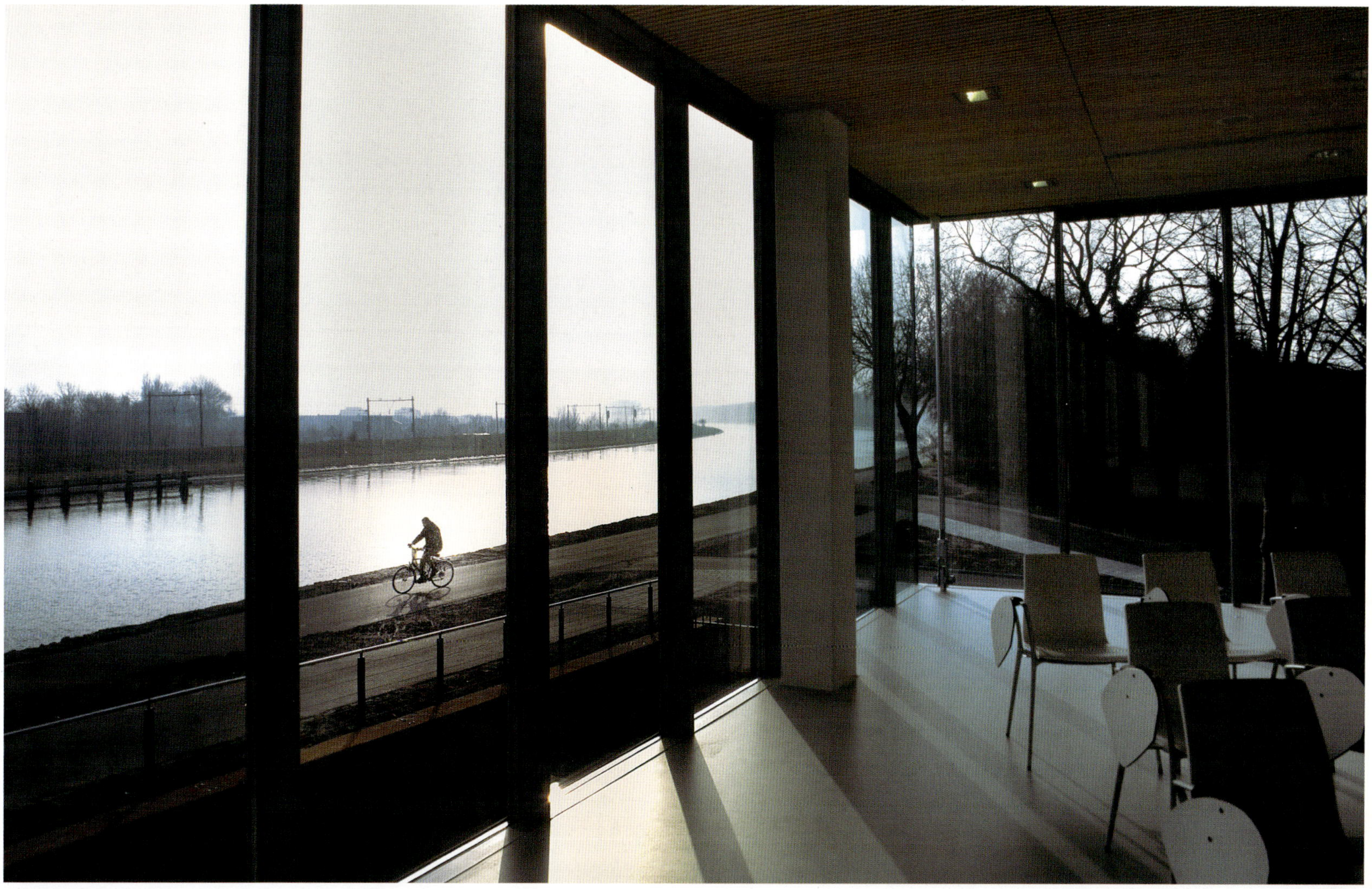

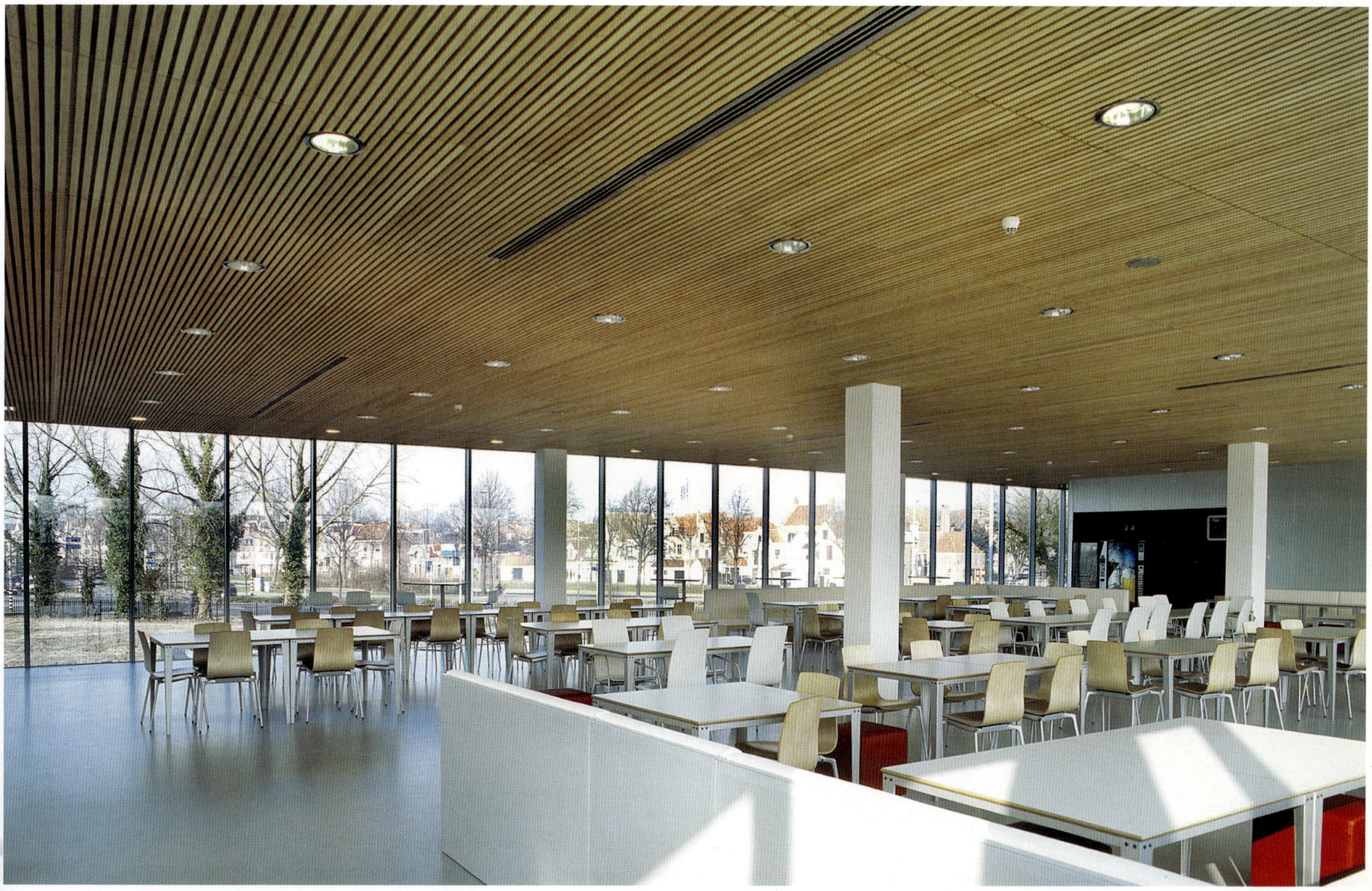

Ermenegildo

Ermenegildo Zegna

Architect/Designer:

Alfredo Arribas Arquitectos Asociados

Client: ITALCO
Photographer: Rafael Vargas
Location: Sant Quirze del Vallès, Spain
Completion date: 2005
Area: 129,167 SF

The building for this fashion design firm had already been planned previously, so the design developed alongside its construction. The pillars are arranged in a 30 x 30 ft square with a height on the ground floor of 26 ft, and 16 ft on the first floor, a typical structure in industrial construction.

The building is divided into two floors and adjoins the neighboring factory, owned by the same company. The façade, like that of the factory, is brickwork, into which large horizontally proportioned windows, measuring 23 ft across, have been inserted, framed with corten steel. Together they form an enormous Venetian blind in the brickwork, making it impossible to make out the distribution across two floors. Around the lobby and the courtyards on the bottom floor a perforated corten steel sheet has been inserted to allow natural light to enter and diffuse through the space.

The communal spaces and reception area are located on the bottom floor, while the 43,000 sqft top floor accommodates the showroom and the offices. The priority when dividing the zones was to maintain spatial continuity and fluidity. The division has been done using the furniture and various half-height metal structures, which frame large sheets of transparent glass.

The slightly sloping roofs manage to destroy the original box by ending at two opposite corners, where the main entrance and the loading bay are located respectively.

A lighting system made up of a network of lights has been chosen that responds to the goal of maintaining the industrial character of the original construction. Some of them are embedded in the ceiling and the floor, others hang from the ceiling distributed in several rows. And in different places fluorescent lights have been installed.

The original metal ceilings have been left exposed, except in the access area, where they are hidden by a false ceiling. In other areas, like the meeting room, the double ceiling also leaves the original ceiling visible.

● The long horizontal windows in the façade, framed in corten steel, form a large-scale Venetian blind on the façade, which harmonizes with the industrial aesthetic of the composition.

ERMENEGILDO ZEGNA
547

ERMENEGILDO ZEGNA

ERMENEGILDO ZEGNA

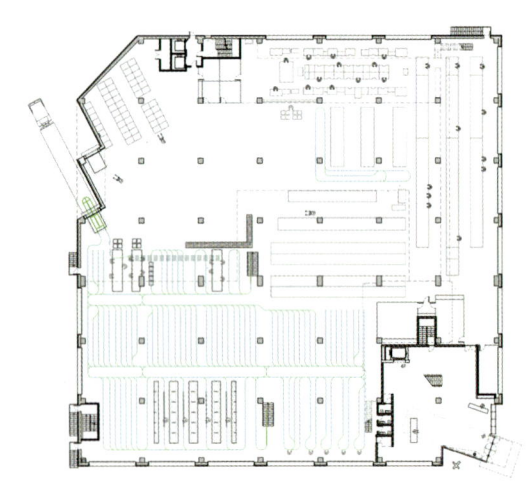

ERMENEGILDO ZEGNA

- Grand floor plan 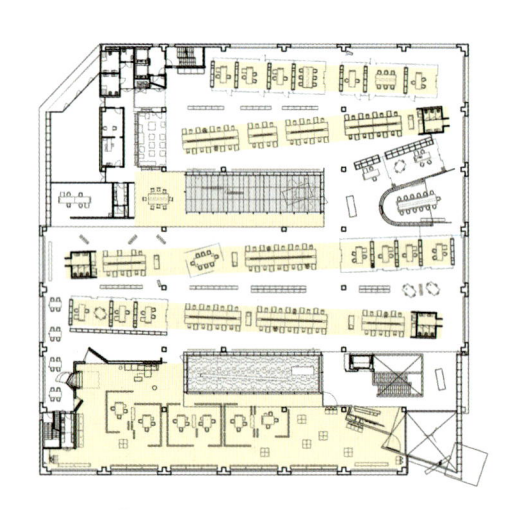
- First floor plan
- Sections

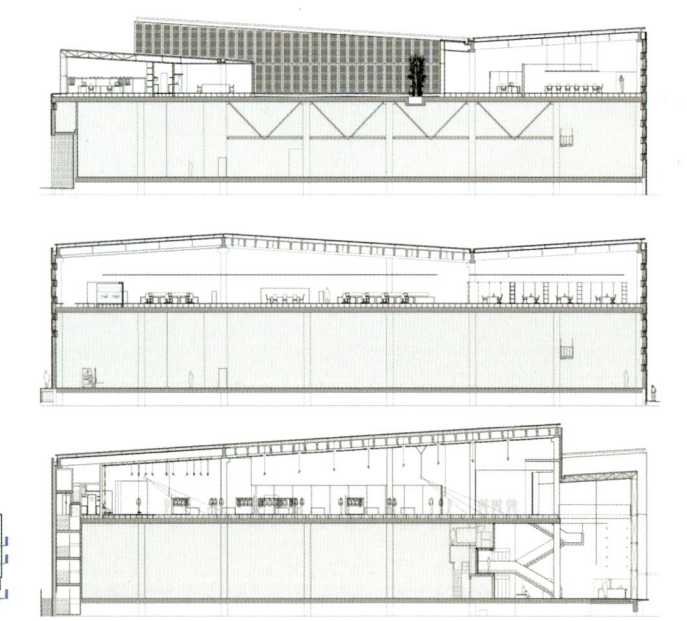

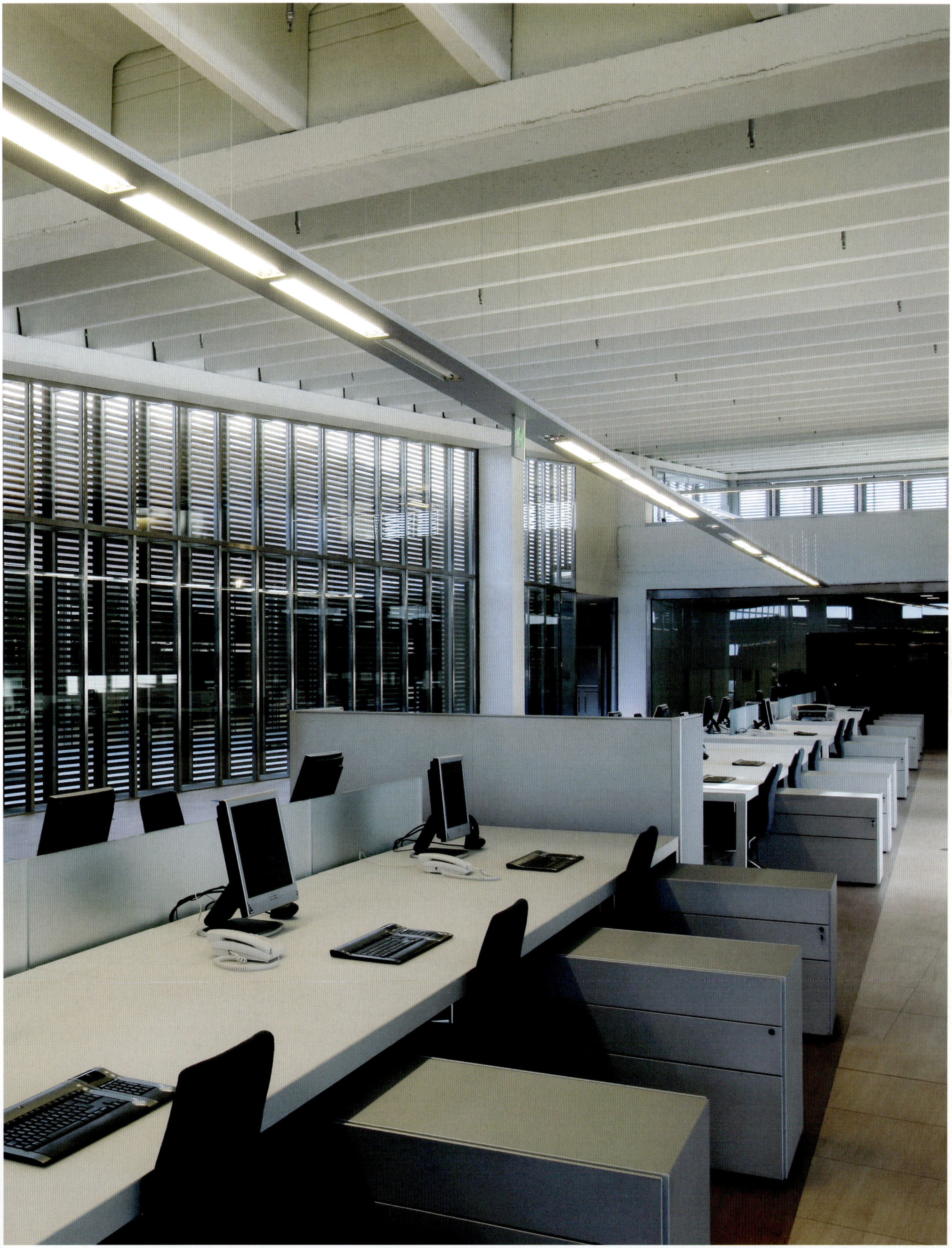

ERMENEGILDO ZEGNA
552

ERMENEGILDO ZEGNA
553

ERMENEGILDO ZEGNA

● Openness and fluidity was the objective when dividing the interior. At no point on the two floors is the visual communication broken between the spaces, which are delineated using furniture and glass partitions.

ERMENEGILDO ZEGNA

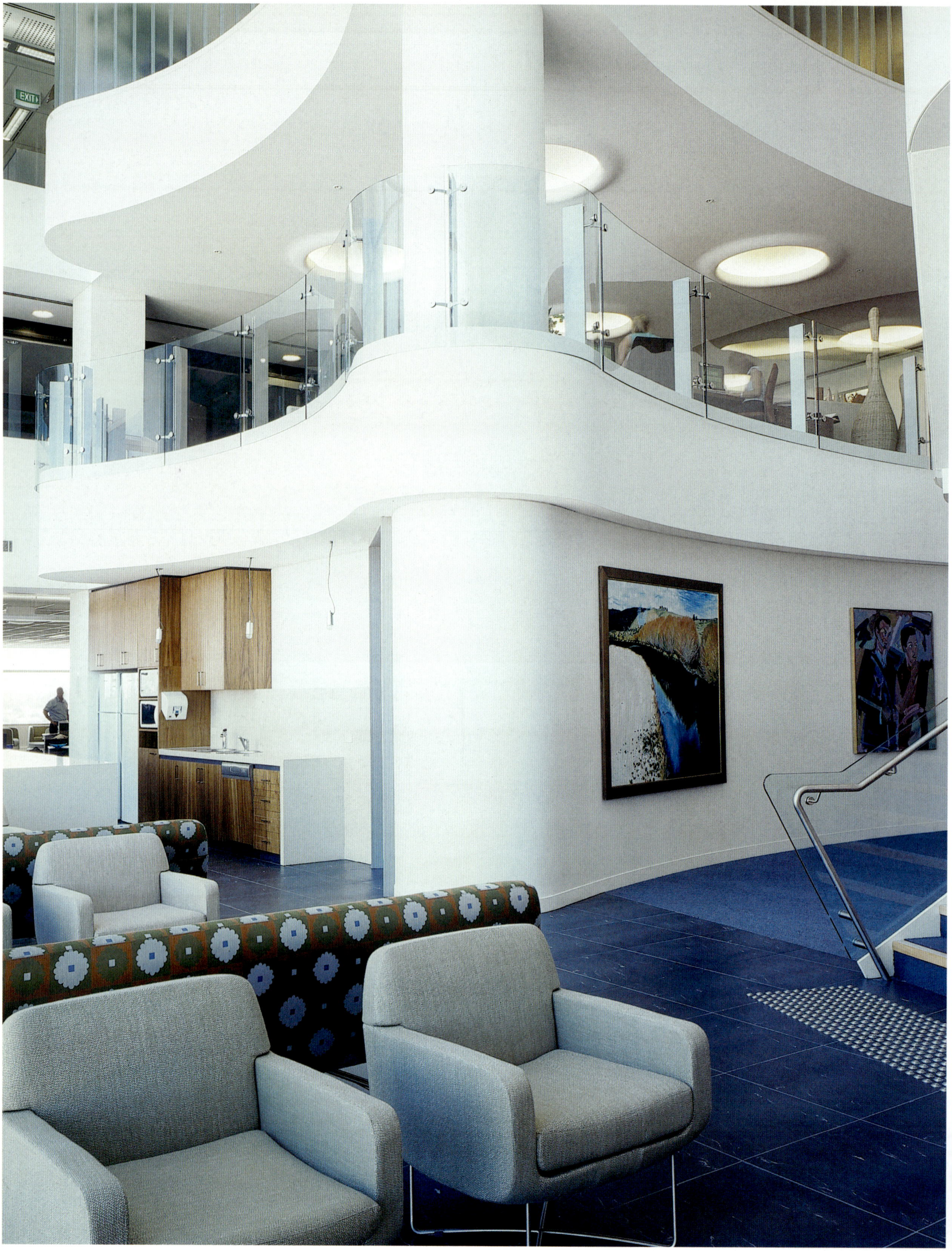
EXIT

Mediabank Private

A six-story building, previously used for apartments, is the site for this project for the headquarters of a bank.

The space distribution is similar on all floors; each one contains meeting rooms, private offices, communal work areas, and service areas.

The architect intended to offer the interior originality through a combination of straight and curved lines. The partitions have been carried out using custom-designed plaster panels, with smooth outlines.

Glass is the other material that characterizes this project. It has been used for the access doors to the different offices and for the banisters of the staircase that joins the building's six floors, where it serves to integrate this circulation space with the rest of the office.

The project is also characterized by its landscaped spaces, located at the eastern and western ends of the building. Almost the entire surface area of both atriums is occupied by spaces for both informal meetings between staff members and for relaxation. In the western atrium, a winding staircase connects to the floors above. Medibank Private has used these atriums to personalize their headquarters and architecturally portray their organizational culture, by creating a place for individual work and development, instead of a corporate building.

Sustainability has been one of the main criteria in the design of the interiors. This is why the computer installations and furnishings are modular, made to last, and can respond flexibly to the changing needs of the company. Furthermore, the artificial lighting is movement sensitive and linoleum has been used for the floor, which is more sustainable than PVC.

The reoccuring theme of creating a contemporary space has been the guiding principle for the design of the interior spaces. These respond to the individual needs of employees—both their work and relaxation—and facilitate communication among the staff.

ARCHITECT/DESIGNER:
GRAY PUKSAND

Client: Mediabank Private
Photographer: Shania Shegedyn
Location: Melbourne, Australia
Completion date: 2004
Area: 134,549 SF

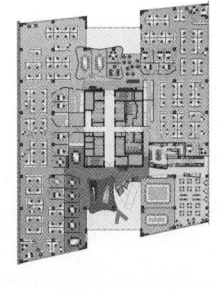

MEDIABANK PRIVATE

● Natural light reaches the interior thanks to the open plan floors and the Linit glass used for the curved interior partitions, which are few and far between, as well as throughout the interior design.

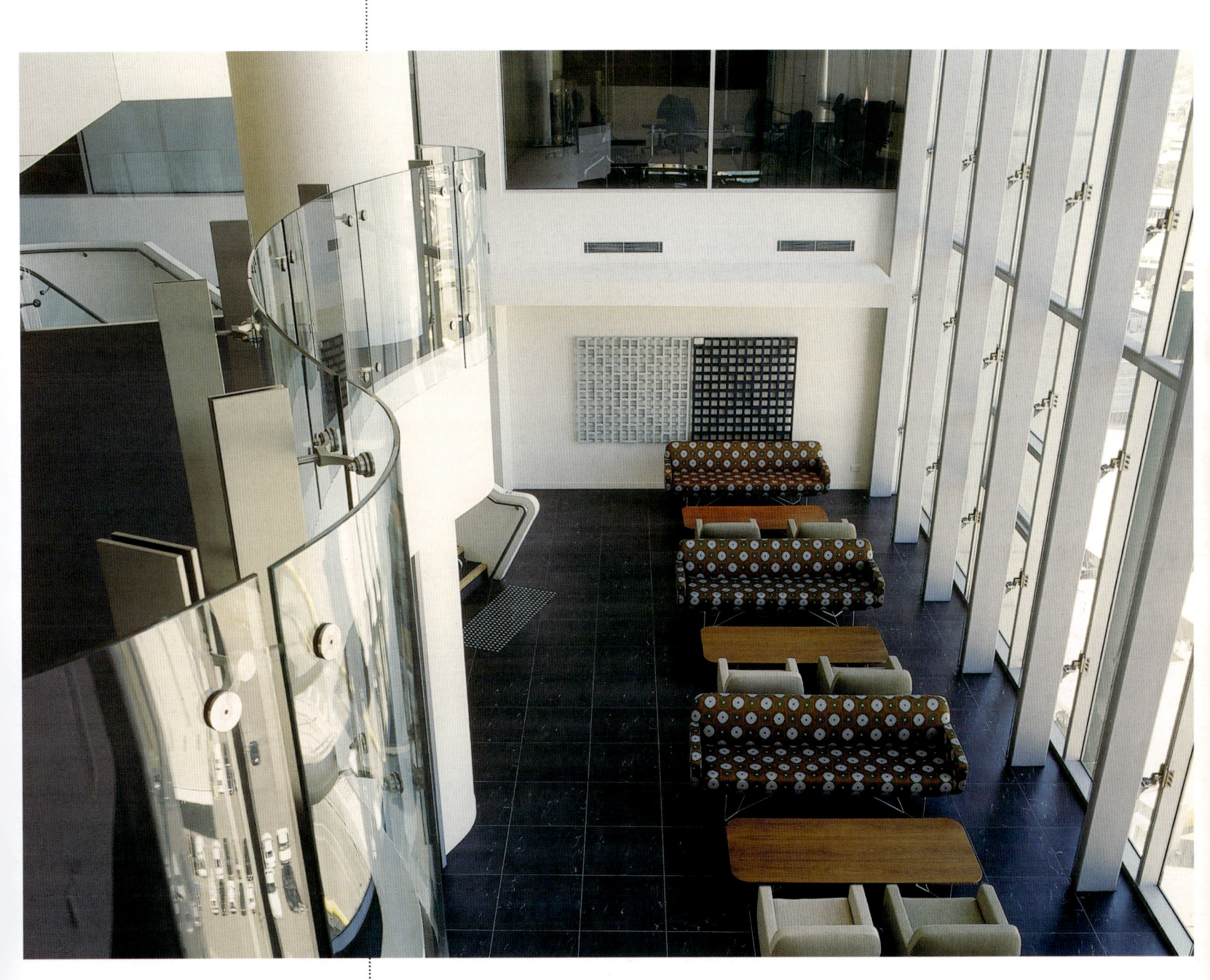

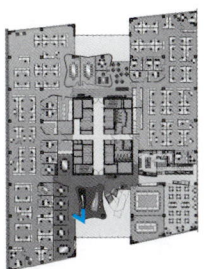

MEDIABANK PRIVATE
559

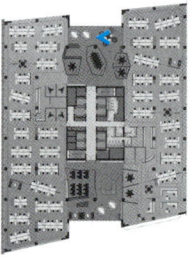

MEDIABANK PRIVATE
560

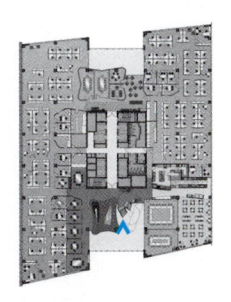

MEDIABANK PRIVATE
561

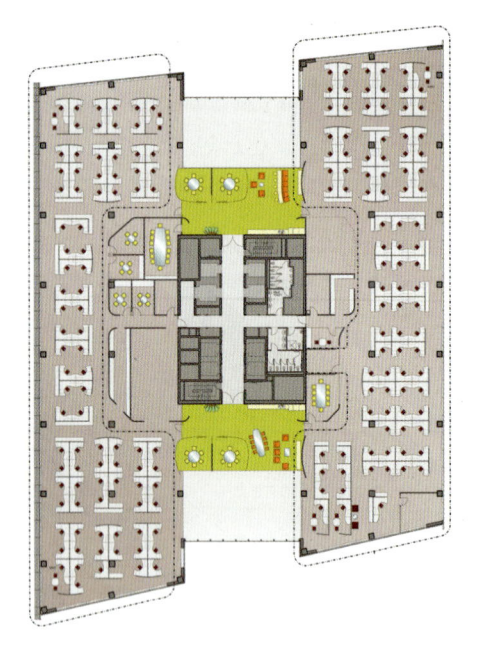

MEDIABANK PRIVATE

○ 13 th floor plan

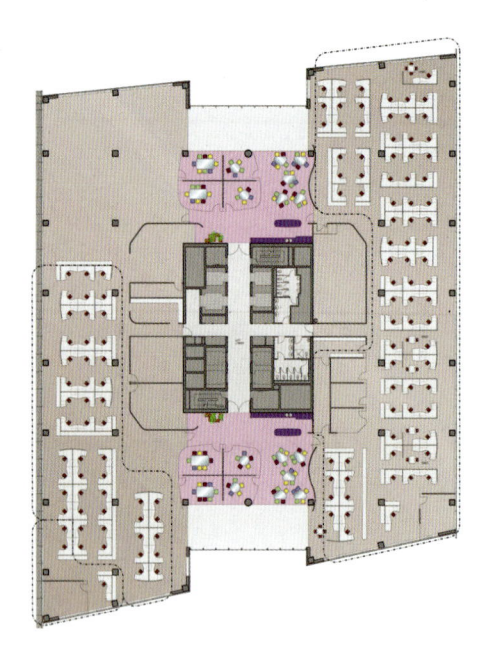

○ 14 th floor plan

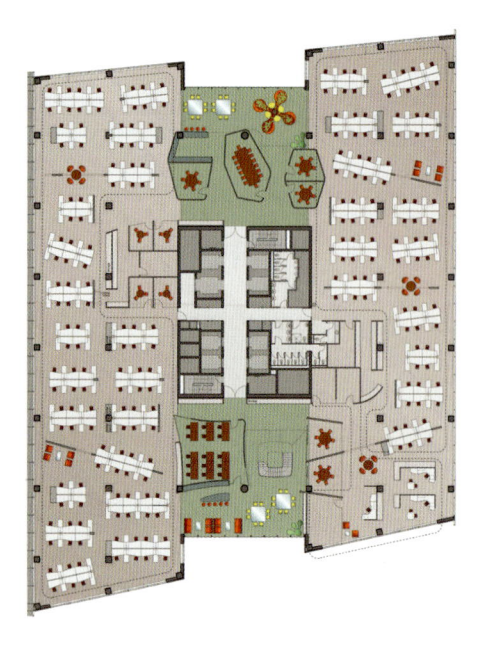

○ 15th floor plan

○ 16th floor plan

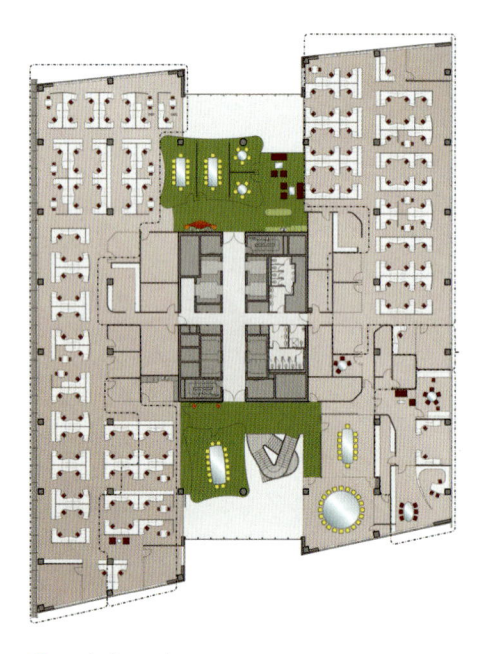

○ 17th floor plan

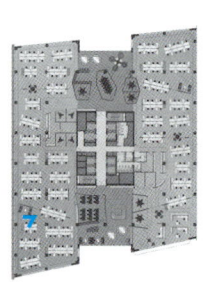

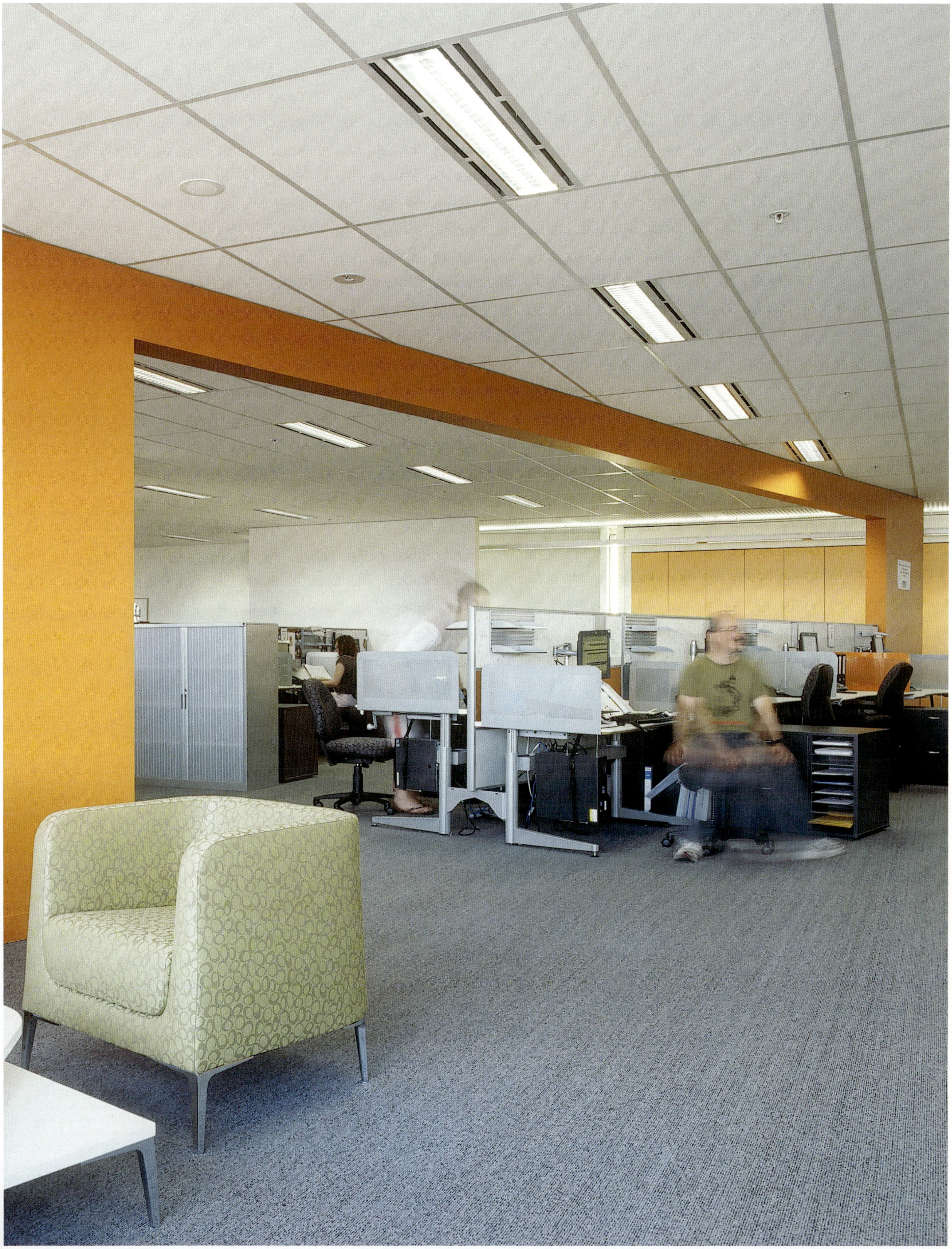

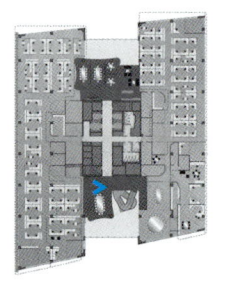

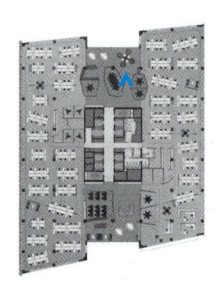

MEDIABANK PRIVATE

MEDIABANK PRIVATE

○ The furniture follows the same modern aesthetic as the building. The curves of each piece are biomorphic and strengthen the design strategy chosen for the interior spaces.

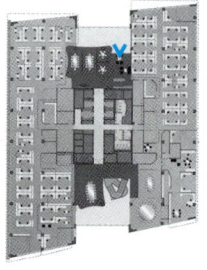

MEDIABANK PRIVATE

MEDIABANK PRIVATE
567

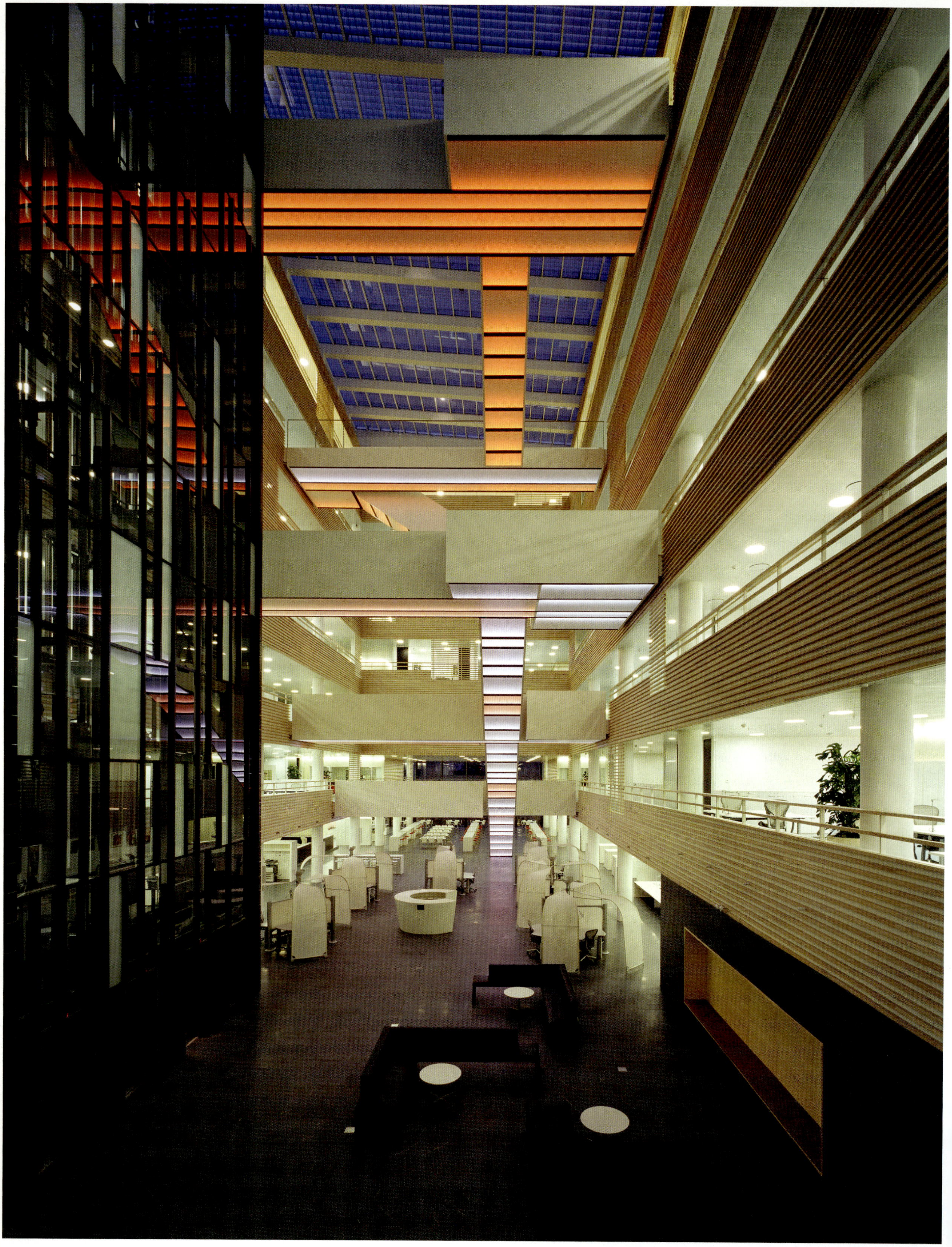

Deloitte Head Offices

The central headquarters of Deloitte in Denmark is an enormous office building, the biggest of a set of three designed as part of the urban development for the area where they are located. The three appear as solitary volumes on the limit between land and water.

Green hanging gardens have been distributed throughout the building with the aim of providing spaces to house work corners and to allow natural light to enter. These openings bring open space into the interior and vice versa; the interior space extends toward the exterior, since the offices are located next to the façades. This allows them to enjoy the panoramic views over the landscape, as well as providing abundant natural light and natural ventilation. The façades are entirely double glazed.

The offices and the central atrium form a long space, allowing the organization of the interior to appear totally transparent and encouraging informal exchanges relating to the work.

In the center of the atrium there is an artistic installation by Steven Scott, whose key element is light. Above this atrium, the stairs and the bridges are illuminated by lights whose beams are different lengths and change color. These have been programmed to prevent repetition in the combination of beams and color, or as the creators said, "so that in a lifetime a single combination is not repeated."

In the areas furthest from the façades are the closed offices soundproofed like cells, and meeting rooms, which are also closed and are soundproofed for working in or holding meetings.

The layout is completed with various installations designed to improve the quality of life of those who work here, such as a fitness room, a bar-lounge, and large circular terrace on the top floor. This set of services is completed with an indoor garage located in the two basement floors of the building.

Architect/Designer:
3XN A/S

Client: Deloitte
Photographer: Adam Mørk
Location: Copenhagen, Denmark
Completion date: 2005
Area: 279,862 SF

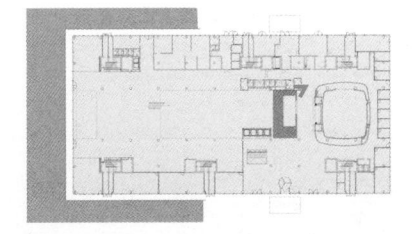

DELOITTE HEAD OFFICES

◉ In the atrium, the artificial lighting has been designed with an artistic dimension, as well as a utilitarian one, with infinite combinations of beams and colors that fall on the stairs and bridges.

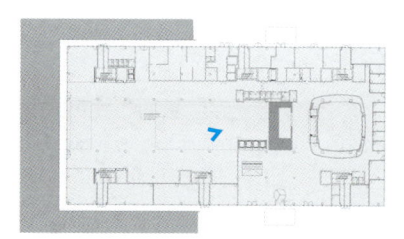

DELOITTE HEAD OFFICES
571

DELOITTE HEAD OFFICES
572

DELOITTE HEAD OFFICES
573

DELOITTE HEAD OFFICES
574

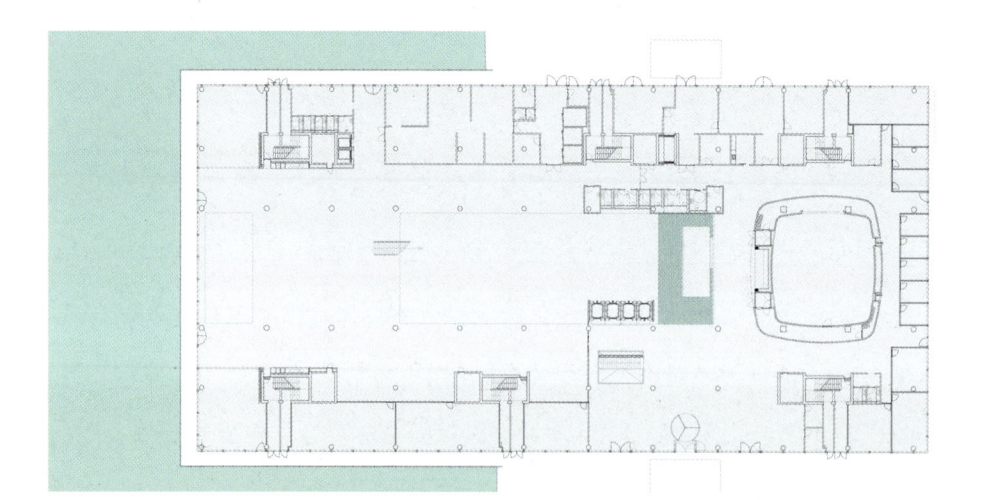

● Second floor plan

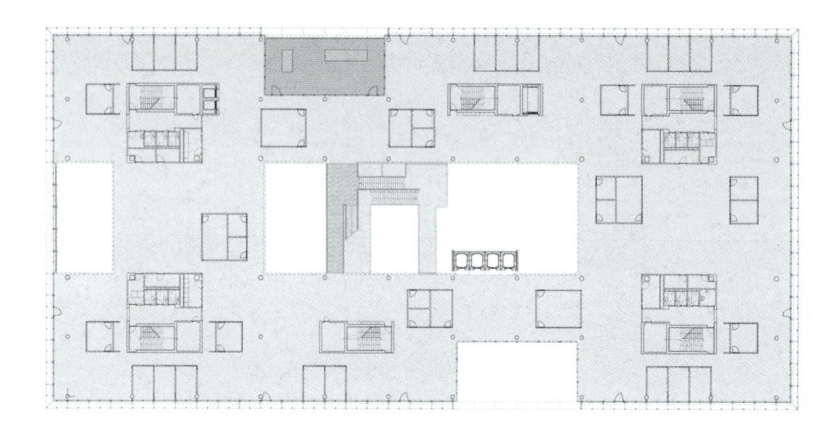

● First floor plan

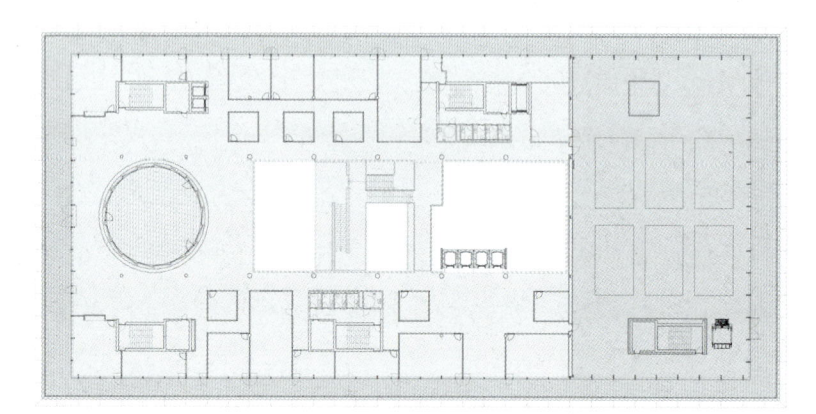

● Gound floor plan

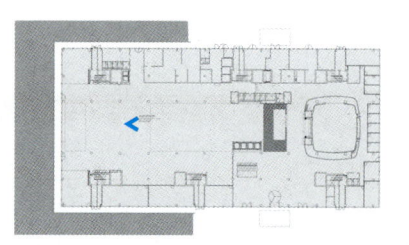

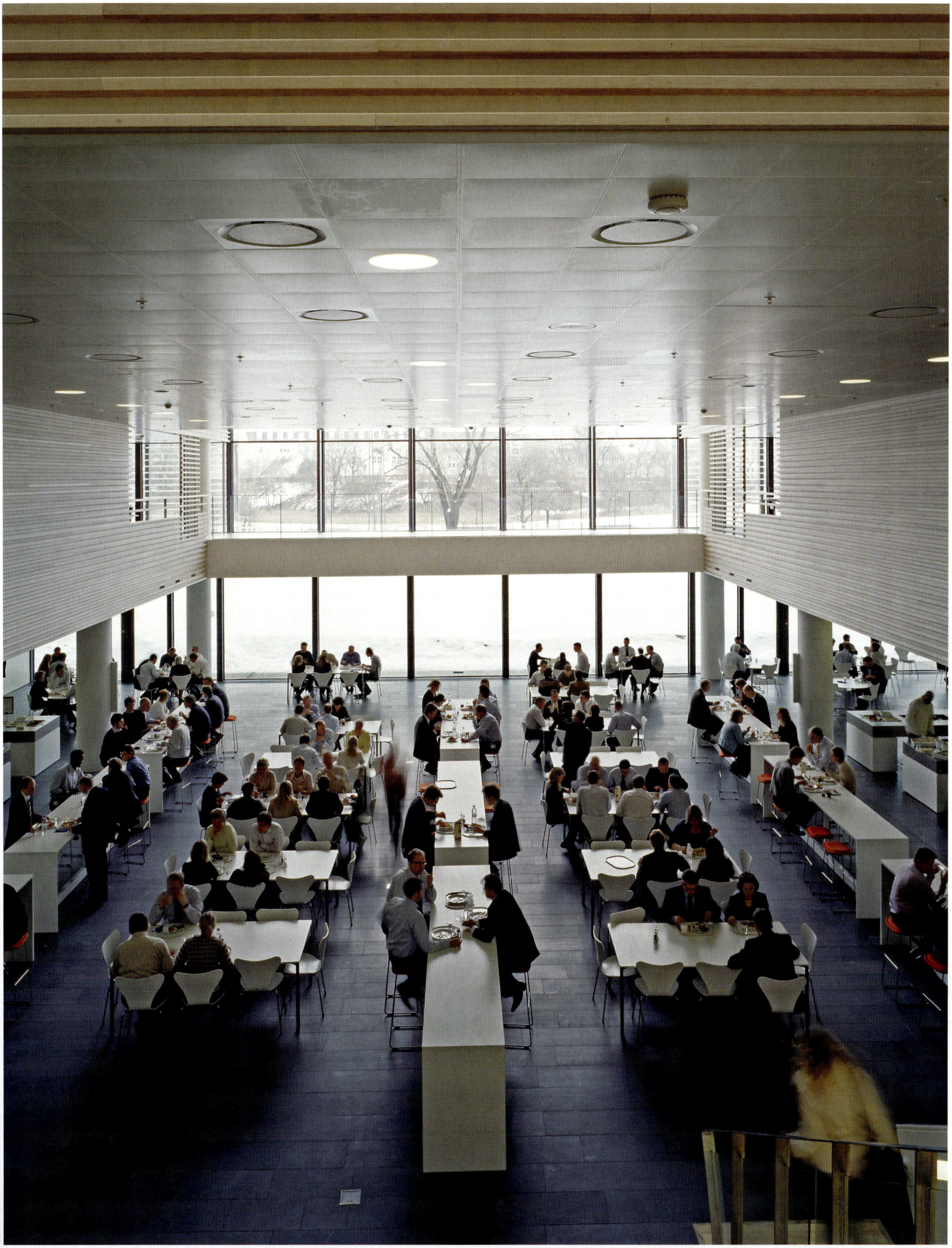

○ The interior is organized in such a way as to enhance access, distribution, and communication. The main entrance hall, large circular terrace, and glass façades allow the inhabitants to enjoy panoramic views and plenty of sunlight.

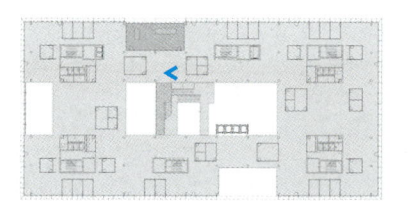

DELOITTE HEAD OFFICES

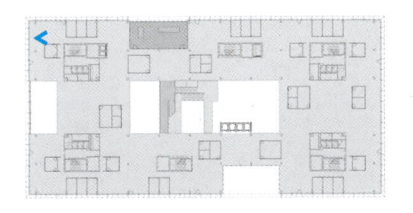

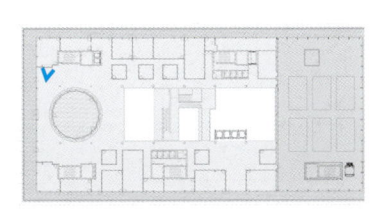

DELOITTE HEAD OFFICES

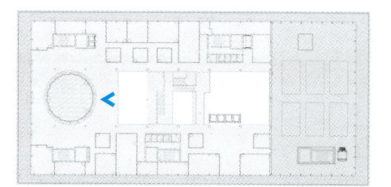

DELOITTE HEAD OFFICES
579

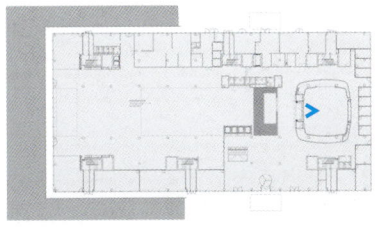

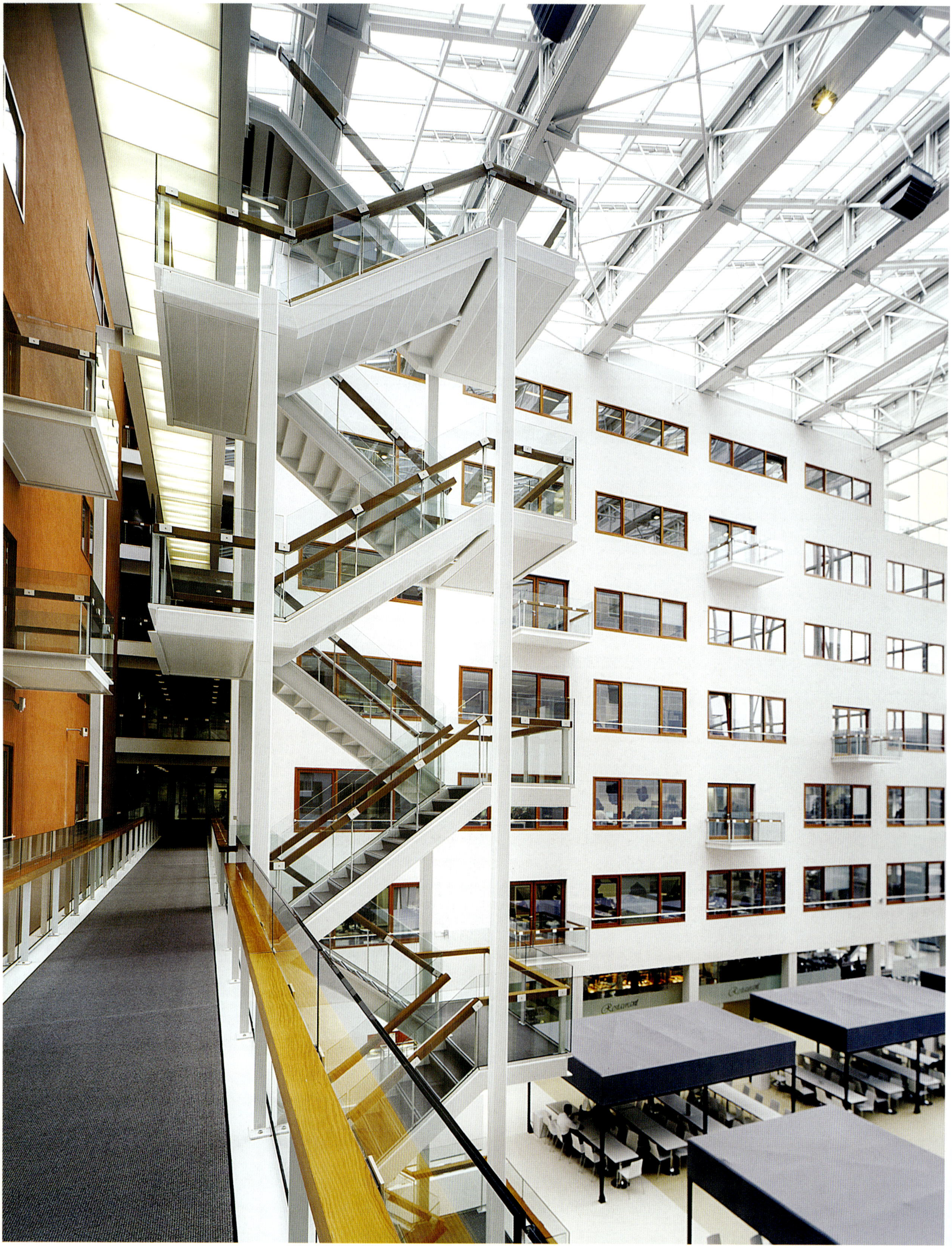

Laakhaven den Haag Complex

ARCHITECT/DESIGNER:
DICK VAN GAMEREN, BJARNE MASTENBROEK/DE ARCHITECTENGROEP

Client: Fortis Vastgoed Ontwikkeling NV Centacon
Photographer: Rob't Hart
Location: The Hague, The Netherlands
Completion date: 2004
Area: 376,737 SF

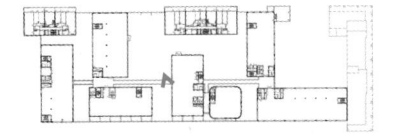

The urban complex of Laakhaven accommodates offices, single-family apartments and several commercial areas. These structures are located in a former industrial area, which has been remodeled to include homes and offices.

The complex's envelope is dominated by glass, both on the roofs and the façades. This marks out the limits of the complex and establishes a connection between the interior spaces. The offices are located in the different architectural blocks, which vary in height, orientation, and façade design. These offices connect with the other constructions through public spaces, such as, for example, a large atrium, shops, restaurants, etc.

The interior design is based on horizontal lines, as the complex is located near to a lake, and the design sought to focus on enjoying the views offered by the landscape and on its total integration into this setting. The linear distribution of the constructions generates a rectangular reoccuring theme for the composition. All the façades respond to the same distribution in groups of three windows. This order is occasionally altered to make way for small balconies.

Together with glass, also used as a decorative element, steel plays a major role, which has been left exposed. Wood was used for the door and window frames, banisters and stairs, and the furnishings. All these materials facilitate the entry of natural light and its distribution throughout the different spaces, allowing the natural light to afford the interior the comfort and serenity needed during working hours. The simplification of forms and the horizontal and vertical straight lines, together with the use of primary colors like white, yellow, blue, and red, demonstrate how abstract art has clearly influenced and inspired this project.

LAAKHAVEN DEN HAAG COMPLEX

● Both interior and exterior are based on horizontal lines, right angles, and primary colors, used by the architects to afford tranquility and balance to the composition.

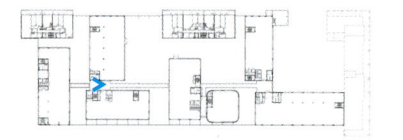

LAAKHAVEN DEN HAAG COMPLEX
583

LAAKHAVEN DEN HAAG COMPLEX

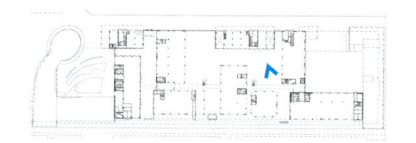

LAAKHAVEN DEN HAAG COMPLEX

○ The glazed structure acts as an envelope that divides the complex and is supported by a visible framework of steel beams. It also connects the offices with their domestic and commercial surroundings.

LAAKHAVEN DEN HAAG COMPLEX

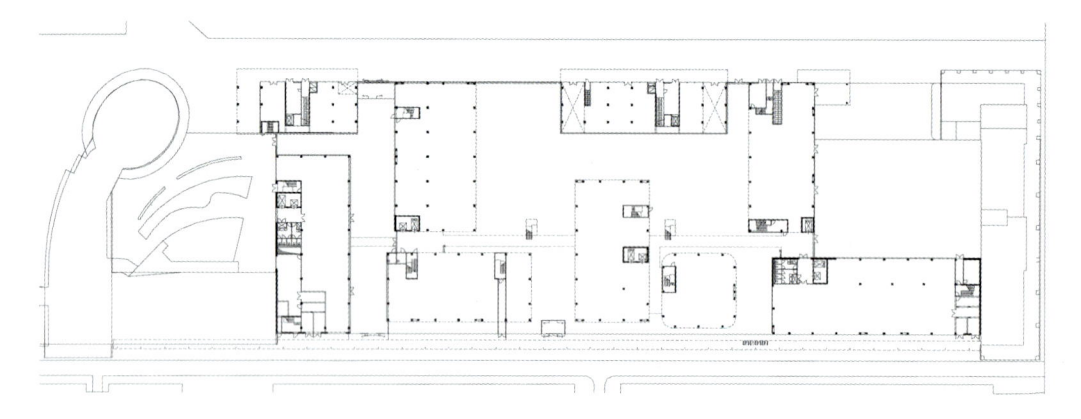

● Ground floor

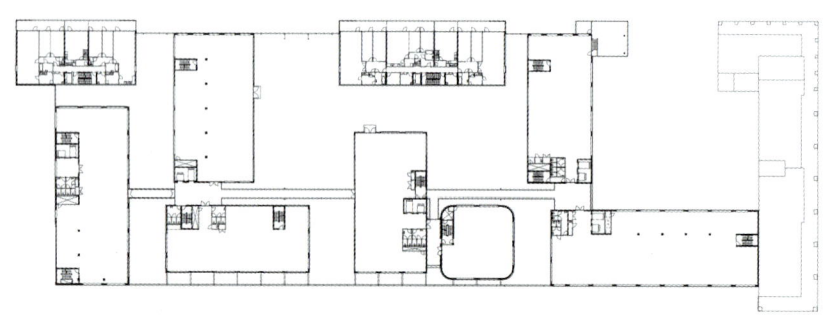

● Second floor

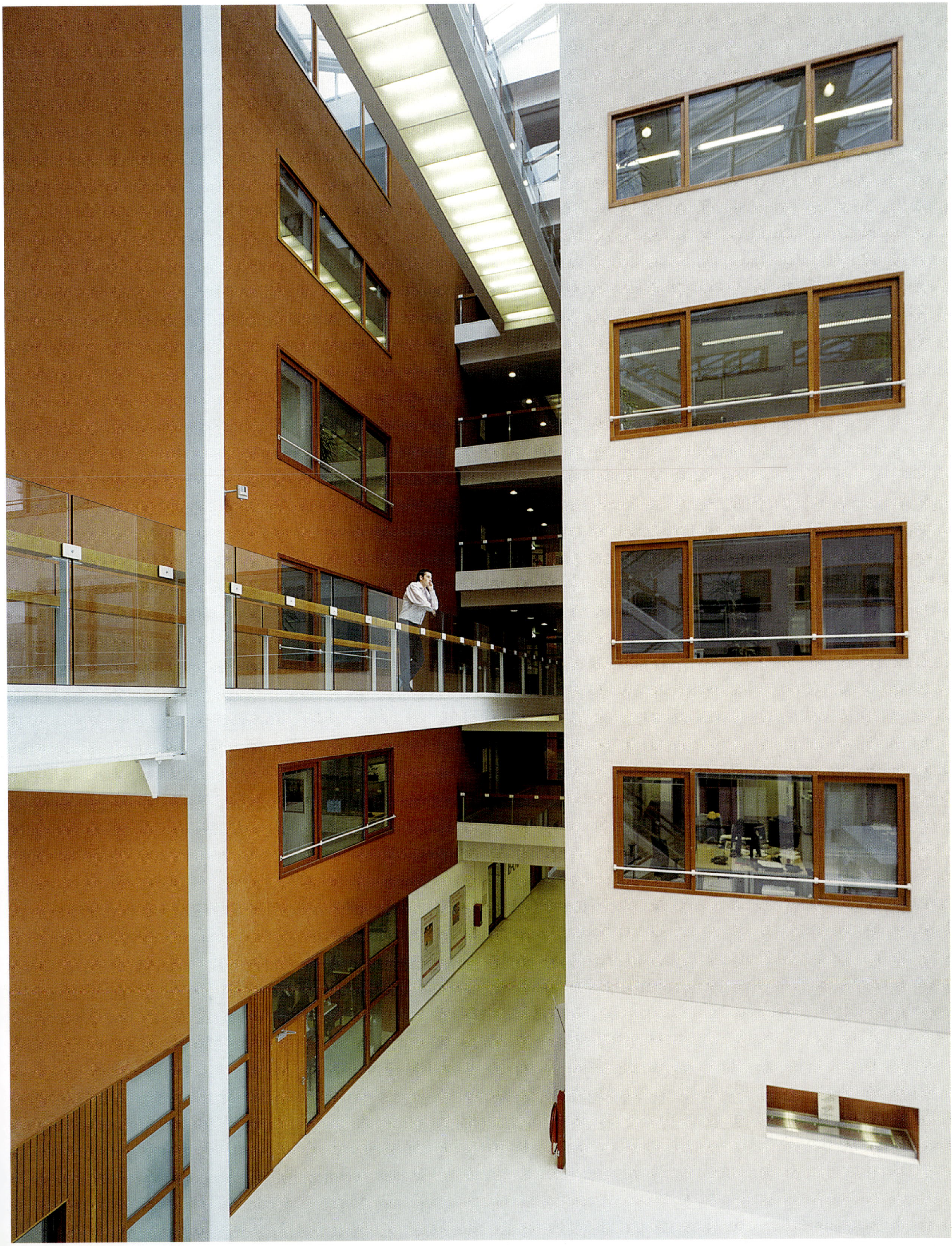

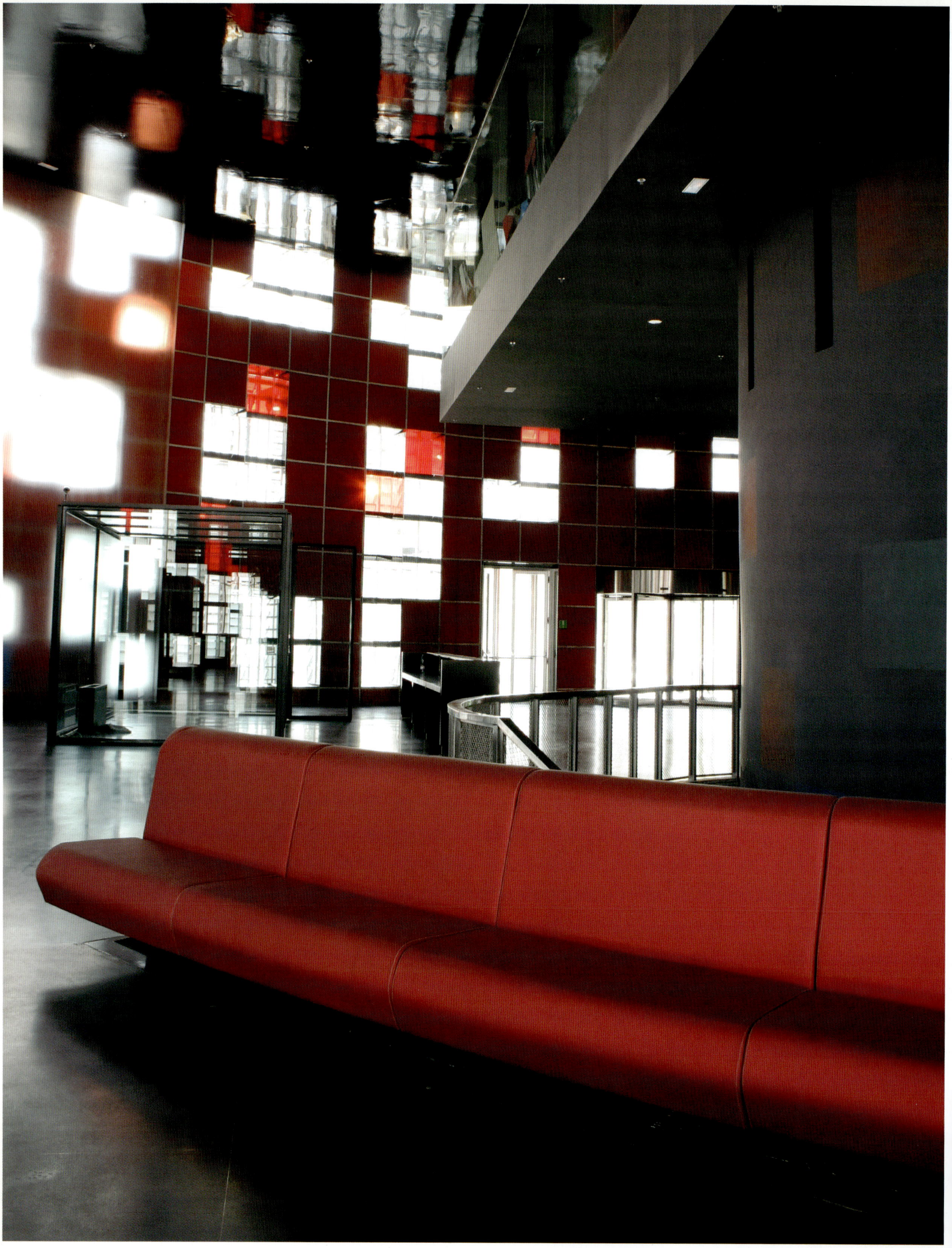

Agbar Tower Offices

Architect/Designer:

Ateliers Jean Nouvel, Fermín Vázquez/B720 Arquitectos

Client: Aguas de Barcelona
Photographer: Òscar Garcia.
Location: Barcelona, Spain
Completion date: 2005
Area: 511,286 SF

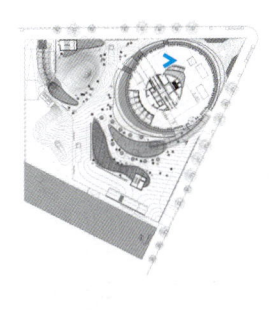

The Agbar Group commissioned this architectural and aesthetical project, which was intended to strengthen their image as well as make their headquarters an architectural landmark within Barcelona.

The building contains thirty-five floors of open-plan surface area, four of which are below ground, where the controls of the management systems are located. Throughout the construction there are no columns that divide the spaces. The main components of the project are the offices, technical installation zones, services, an auditorium, a cafeteria, a large indoor parking garage and a lookout point at the tower's dome.

Two cylinders house, respectively, the area for internal circulation–stairs and elevators–and the different work areas. These are open spaces with a large amount of light thanks to the building's 4,400 windows. For the internal temperature control, the architects have installed large, mobile aluminum panels to the exterior of the tower, which adapt to the movement of the sun to achieve the correct temperature inside the tower.

The floor plan typology has an eccentric nucleus: the free space expands from the elevator area to form the office area. On all floors there is also a rest area for the employees, which includes a kitchen-office.

The top floors have been reserved for management offices. The access to these is made possible through the central circulation zone, composed of stairs and elevators, the only ones that can be used throughout the entire building. Elevators have also been installed on the façade, which comprise most of the circulation up to the twenty-sixth floor, the last one that uses concrete. The flexibility of the offices and their protection against solar radiation has determined the positions of the 4,400 windows, making them appear randomly arranged. The interior privacy is assured by different degrees of transparency of the glass. The building's finish is also exclusively glass, within an aluminum structure.

AGBAR TOWER OFFICES

● As an element that favors communication between the offices of the different floors, a practical, direct lighting has been chosen for the stairs, lobbies, and elevators.

AGBAR TOWER OFFICES
591

AGBAR TOWER OFFICES
592

AGBAR TOWER OFFICES
593

○ Although some of the windows are fixed, operable windows have also been installed to ventilate the work spaces according to their needs. There are more or less 4,400 windows in total, 100 per floor.

AGBAR TOWER OFFICES

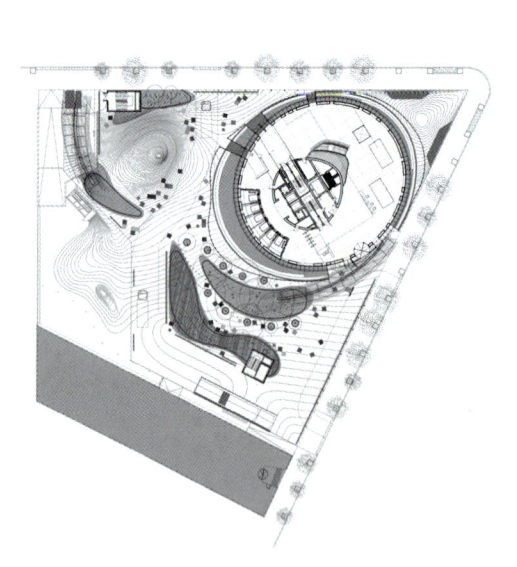

○ Ground floor plan

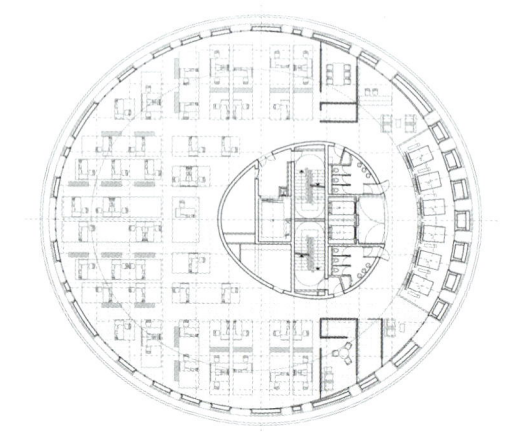

○ Typical floor

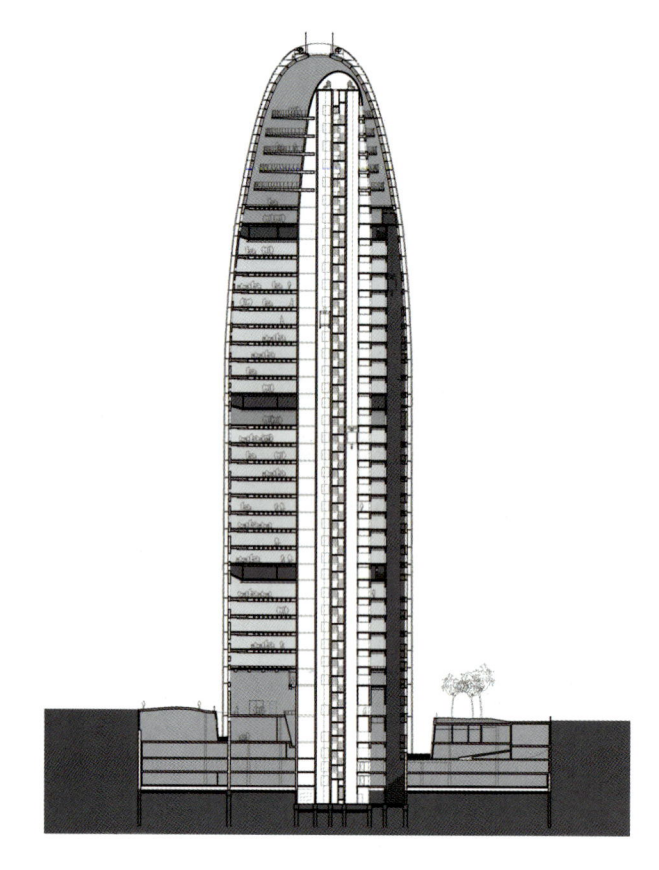

○ Tower section

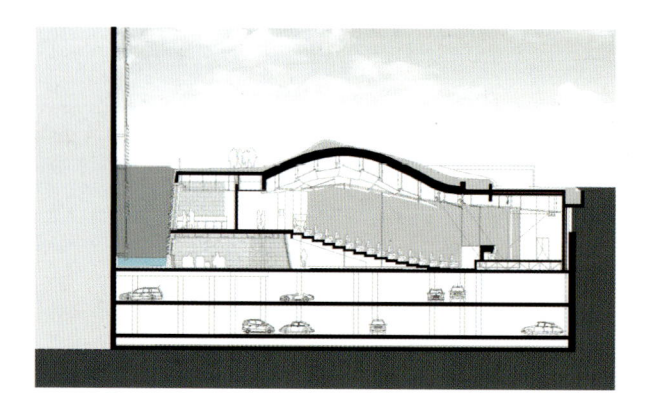

○ Auditorium section

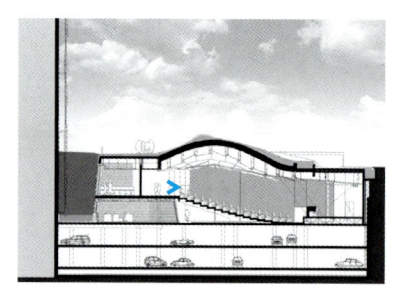

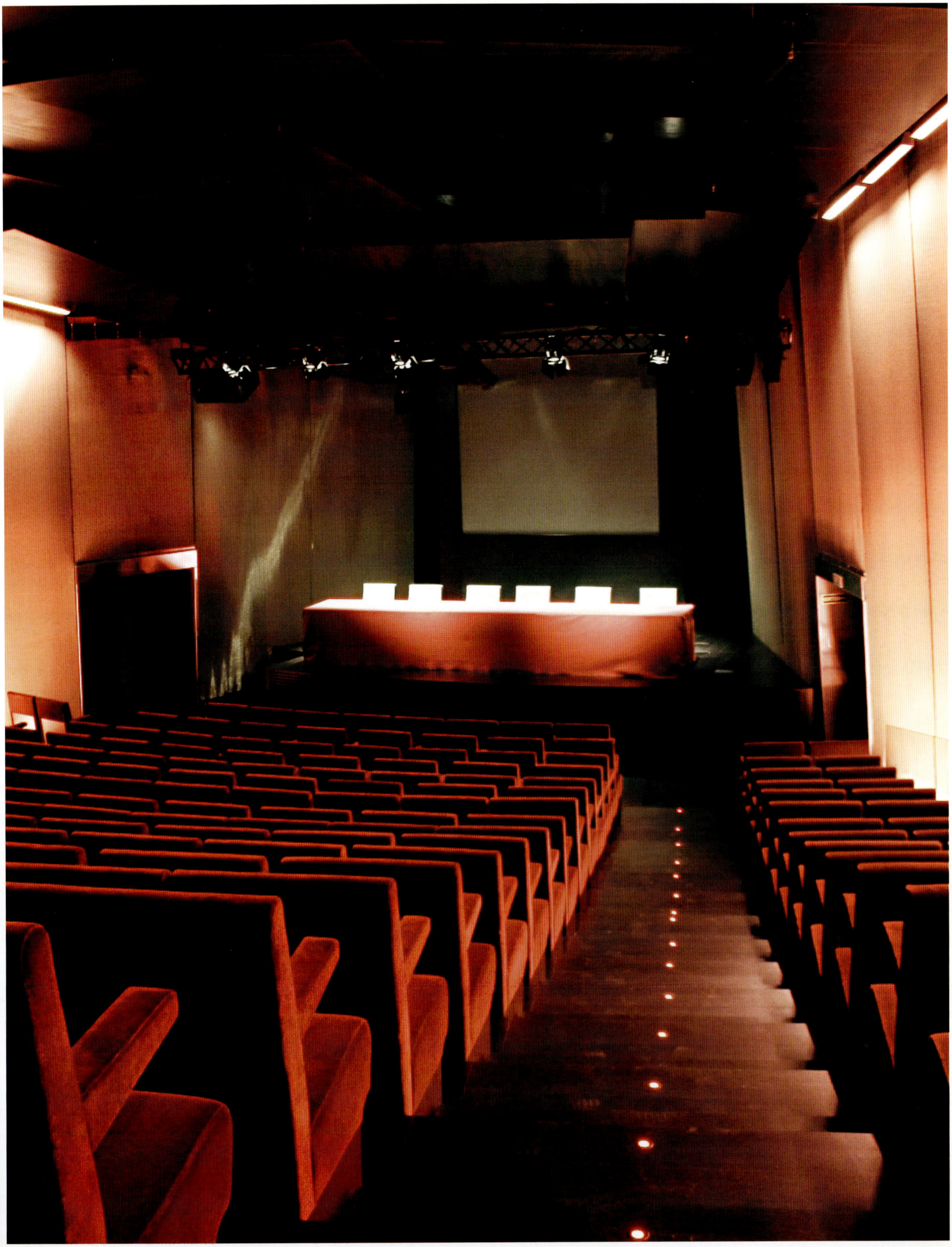

Directory

3XN A/S
Kystvejen 17
DK-8000 Arhus C, Denmark
Tel.: + 45 8731 4848
Fax: + 45 8731 4849
www.3xn.dk
Deloitte Head Offices

Aguirre & Newman
General Lacy 23
28045 Madrid, Spain
Tel.: + 34 913 191 314
Fax: + 34 913 198 757
www.aguirrenewman.es
Affinity Offices

Agustí Costa
Plaça de la Creu 3, 2on. 2a
08600 Berga, Spain
Tel.: + 34 938 211 063
Fax: + 34 938 221 105
www.agusticosta.com
Institut Català de la Dona
Studio in Berga

Alfredo Arribas Arquitectos Asociados
Claravall, 2
08022 Barcelona, Spain
Tel: + 34 932 531 760
Fax: + 34 934 173 591
www.alfredoarribas.com
Ermenegildo Zegna

Angelika Zwingel, Brigitte Feuerer/raum:team92
Gräfestr. 81, 10967 Berlin, Germany
Gotzinger Str. 44, 81371 München, Germany
Mob.: +49(0)170.55 71 783
Mob.: +49(0)151.17 33 0945
www.raumteam92.com
Schröder & Schömbs PR Agency

Architectenbureau Paul de Ruiter bv
Leidsestraat 8 10
NL-1017, Amsterdam, The Netherlands
Tel.: + 31 206 263 244
Fax: + 31 206 237 002
www.paulderuiter.nl
Rijkswaterstaat Zeeland Head Office

Arconiko Architecten
Stationsplein, 45 Postbus 399
3000 AJ Rotterdam, The Netherlands
Tel.: + 31 104 123 181
Fax: + 31 104 047 597
www.arconiko.com
Indes Offices

Architects EAT
Level 2, 227 Commercial Road
3414 South Yarra, Victoria, Australia
Tel.: + 61 3 9824 0813
Fax: + 61 3 9824 0843
www.eatas.com.au
Renegade Film Studio

Ateliers Jean Nouvel
10, cité d'Angoulême
75011 Paris, France
Tel.: + 33 149 238 383
Fax: + 33 143 148 115
www.jeannouvel.fr
Agbar Tower Offices

Bernard Astor/Saguez & Partners
14, Rue Palouzié
93400 Saint Ouen, France
Tel.; + 33 141 666 400
Fax: + 33 141 666 400
www.saguez-and-partners.com
Harrison & Wolf Offices
Mediaedge

Bonetti/Kozerski Studio
270 Lafayette Street, Suite 906
10012 New York, NY, USA
Tel.: + 1 212 343 9898
Fax: + 1 212 343 8042
www.bonettikozerski.com
Ford Models Headquarters
Laird + Partners Offices

Bordonabe
Elena Iglesias
Montejurra, 10
31240 Ayegui, Spain
Tel.: + 34 948 556 271
Fax: + 34 948 556 363
www.bordonabe.com
Bordonabe Barcelona
Indra Offices

Cheeeeese! Happy Designers
6, place Jacques Forment
75081 Paris, France
Tel.: + 33 158 593 030
Fax: + 33 158 590 030
www.cheeeeese.com
Happy Place

Chen Xudong, Shen Yirong,
Gu Jirong/Datrans
1F, Bd 13, 50 MoGranShan Rd.
200060 Shangai, China
Tel.: + 86 (0) 21 629 96 236
www.datrans.cn
Studio DAtrans

CL3 Architects Limited
7/F Hong Kong Arts Centre
2 Harbour Road,
Wanchai, Hong Kong, China
Tel.: + 852 2527 1931
Fax: + 852 2529 8392
www.cl3.com
DDB Office Hong Kong
Vanke Cheugdu Commercial Complex

Conrad-Bercah/W Office
Via Malaga, 4
20143, Italy
Tel.: + 39 0 287 389 399
Fax: + 39 0 287 389 901
www.west-office.it
Glocal Law
W Loft

Cossman_de Bruyn Architecktur
Innenarchitektur Design
Comenlusstrasse, 1
D-40545 Düsseldorf, Germany
Tel.: + 49 (0) 211 559 00 69
Fax: + 49 (0) 211 559 00 68
www.cossmann-debruyn.de
GREY Worldwide
Office Building A. T. Kearney

De Architectengroep
Barentszplein, 7
1013 NJ Amsterdam, The Netherlands
Tel.: + 31 205 304 850
Fax: + 31 205 304 860
www.architectengroep.nl
Laakhaven den Haag Complex

DWP Cityspace
The Dusit Thani Building, Level 11
946 Rama IV Road
10500 Bangkok, Thailand
Tel.: + 66 (0) 2267 3939
Fax: + 66 (0) 2267 3949
www.dwp.com
Krungthai AXA Life Insurance

Eduardo Gascón
Tuset, 8 6è 1a
08006 Barcelona, Spain
Tel.: + 34 932 922 208
Fax: + 34 932 922 708
Affinity Offices

Elisabet Faura, Gerard Veciana/Arteks
Arquitectura
L'Aigüeta, 12 1r. Pis
AD500 - Andorra la Vella, Andorra
Tel.: + 376 823 202
Fax: + 376 823 272
www.arteks.ad
Attic in Andorra La Vella

EQUIPxavierclaramunt
Pellaires, 30-38 Nau. G.01.
08019 Barcelona, Spain
Tel.: + 34 933 034 660
Fax: + 34 933 034 665
www.xclaramunt.com
Laiguana Studio

Eric van Eck/Architectenbureau
van der Broek en Bakema
Van Nelle Ontwerfp Abriek Schiehal G
Van Nelleweg 1
3044 BC Rotterdam, The Netherlands
Tel.: 31 104 134 780
Fax: 31 104 136 454
www.broekbakema.nl
Kropman

Estudio Joaquín Gallego
Lagasca, 125
28006 Madrid, Spain
Tel.: + 34 91 369 20 50
Fax: + 34 91 369 20 50
www.joaquingallego.com
Joaquín Gallego Studio

Fermín Vázquez/b720 Arquitectos
Josep Tarradellas, 123
08029 Barcelona, Spain
Tel.: + 34 933 637 979
Fax: + 34 933 630 139
www.b720.com
Agbar Tower Offices
Indra Offices
Offices on Mestre Nicolau Street

Forteza Carbonell Associates
Passeig Picasso, núm. 10, 4art 3ª
08003 Barcelona, Spain
Tel.: + 34 93 315 24 43
Fax: + 34 93 315 24 43
www.fortezacarbonell.com
Graphic Design Studio

Francesc Rifé
Escoles Pies, 25 Baixos
08017 Barcelona, Spain
Tel.: + 34 934 141 288
Fax: + 34 932 412 814
www.rife-design.com
Bordonabe Barcelona

GCA Arquitectes Associats
València, 289 Baixos
08009 Barcelona, Spain
Tel.: + 34 934 761 800
Fax.: + 34 934 761 806
www.gcaarq.com
CODECSA Offices
Habitectura Offices
Beauty Lab

Gray Puksand
Bourke Place Studio 577 Lt.
3000 VIC Bourke St. Melbourne, Australia
Tel.: + 03 9221 0999
Fax: + 03 9221 0998
www.graypuksand.com.au
Bendigo Bank Offices
Bourke Place Studio
Mediabank Private

Group A
Pelgrimsstraat, 3
3029 BH Rotterdam, The Netherlands
Tel.: + 31 (0)10 244 01 93
Fax: + 31 (0)10 244 99 90
www.groupa.nl
Caballero Factory

Hangar Design Group
Via Terraglio 89/b
31021 Mogliano Veneto, Treviso, Italy
Tel.: + 39 041 593 6000
Fax: + 39 041 593 6006
www.hangar.it
Hangar Design Group Headquarter

Héctor Restrepo, Cristina Cuberes/Heres Arquitectura
Balmes, 130 Entresol
08008 Barcelona
Tel.: + 34 934 879 989
Fax: + 34 934 879 989
www.heresarquitectura.es
Zonabarcelona Office

IADarquitectos
Emilio Muñoz, 3
28037 Madrid, Spain
Tel.: + 34 915 758 760
Fax: + 34 915 759 059
www.groupiad.com
Amec Spie Offices

Ian Ayers
Ronda de Sant Pere, 31 3er 1a A
08010 Barcelona, Spain
Tel.: + 34 934 124 736
ianayers@gmail.com
FTVentures Offices

INNOCAD Planung und Projektmanagement
Grazbachgasse 65a
A-8010 Graz, Austria
Tel.: + 43 1 990 8805
Fax: + 43 1 990 8944
www.innocad.at
Golden Nugget

Joel Hendler/Hendler Design
300 Kansas Street, Suite 206
94103 San Francisco, CA, USA
Tel.: + 1 415 255 7979
Fax: + 1 415 255 7963
www.hendler.com
FTVentures Offices

John Lee/Workshop For Architecture
195 Chrystie Street Suite 603 F
10002 New York, NY, USA
Tel.: + 1 212 674 3400
Fax: + 1 212 674 6097
www.wfora.com
Maritime Intelligence Group Offices

Jordi Torres
Joan d'Àustria 95, 6è. 4a
Tel.: + 34 933 096 253
Fax: + 34 933 096 237
www.jorditorres.com
Signes Offices

José Abeijón Vela, Miguel Fernández Carreiras/Abeijón-Fernández Arquitectos
Juan Flórez, nº 18 Planta Primera
15005 A Coruña, Spain
Tel: + 34 981 153 544
Fax: + 34 981 925 229
www.abeijon-fernandez.com
Afeijón-Fernández Architecture Office
Construcciones Mon Offices

Juan Ignacio Morasso/Morasso Tucker Arquitectos
Centro Profesional Santa Paula
Torre A, Piso 1, Oficina 13.
Urbanización Santa Paula,
El Cafetal, Venezuela
Tel.: + 58 212 986 9589
Fax: + 58 212 986 0709
www.morasso-arquitectos.com
Amazon Air Offices

Lehrer Architects
2140 Hyperion Avenue
90027-4708 Los Angeles, CA, USA
Tel.: + 1 323 644 4747
Fax: + 1 323 664 3566
www.lehrerarchitects.com
Lehrer Architects' Office

Leven Betts Studio
511 West 25 ST #808
10001 New York, NY, USA
Tel.: + 1 212 620 9792
Fax: + 1 212 620 3235
www.levenbetts.com
Mixed Greens Gallery

Lichtblau.Wagner Architekten
Diehlgasse 50/1718
a-1050 Wien, Austria
Tel.: + 43 1 54 518 54 0
Fax: + 43 1 54 518 54 4
www.lichtblauwagner.com
Hidm. Office Vienna
Klangforum House
Solar roof Vienna 5

Lola Lago Interiores
Balmes 5, Bellaterra
08193 Cerdanyola del Valles, Spain
Tel.: + 34 935 807 968
Fax: + 34 935 807 968
www.lolalagointeriores.com
Amalgama 7
Studio in Sant Cugat

Marta González
Blanquerna, 29
07003 Palma de Mallorca, Spain
Tel.: + 34 636 450 655
www.industriaszero.org
9MAR Offices

Marta Torelló Raventós/Marta Torelló Interiors
Terol, 11 Àtic 2
08012 Barcelona, Spain
Tel.: + 34 609 163 840
www.martatorello.com
9MAR Offices

Massimo Mariani Architetto
Via Don Minzoni, 27
51016 Montecatini Terme, Pistoia, Italy
Tel.: + 39 0572 766 324
Fax: + 39 0572 912 742
www.massimomariani.net
Bank in Cerreto Guidi, Mill with Bank
Bank in La Fontina, Still Life with Bank 1
Bank in Pontedera, Bank with Eyes

Mercedes Isasa Seco/ Estudio TBC
Endrinas, 22
28016 Madrid
Tel.: + 34 914 165 786
Indra Offices

Murray O'Laoire Architects
Merriman House,
Brian Merriman Place
Lock Quay, Limerick, Ireland
Tel.: + 35 3(0)61 316 400
Fax: + 35 3(0)61 316 853
www.murrayolaoire.com
Mayo Institute of Technology

Rios Clementi Hale Studios
6824 Melrose Avenue
90038 Los Angeles, CA, USA
Tel.: + 1 323 634 9220
Fax: + 1 323 634 9221
www.rchstudios.com
Rios Clementi Hale Studios Office

Sarah Bitter/Metek Architecture
3, Villa de l'Adour
75019 Paris, France
Tel.: + 33 0 142 411 910
Fax.: + 33 0 142 411 910
www.metek-architecture.com
MK/3-VA

Shubin + Donaldson Architects
3834 Willat Avenue
90232 Culver City, CA, USA
Tel.: + 1 310 204 0688
Fax: + 1 310 559 0219
www.shubinanddonaldson.com

Hydraulx
Slade Architecture
150 Broadway Suite 807
10038, New York, NY, USA
Tel.: + 1 212 677 6380
Fax: + 1 212 677 6330
www.sladearch.com
Thirdpoint Offices

Takashi Yamaguchi & ASSOCIATES
5F Fusui Bldg. 1-3-4 Ebisunishi,
556-0003 Naniwa-ku, Osaka, Japan
Tel.: + 81 666 333 775
Fax: + 81 666 335 175
www.yamaguchi-a.jp
Metal Office

The Lawrence Group Architects
307 West 38th, Suite 1618
1008 New York, NY, USA
Tel.: + 1 212 764 2424
Fax: + 1 212 354 6909
www.thelawrencegroup.com
Momentum St. Louis

Wirth + Wirth Architekten
Leimenstrasse 47
4051 Basel, Switzerland
Tel.: + 41 612 701 219
Fax: + 41 612 701 210
www.wirth-wirth.ch
Clariant Flexible Office

Wolff Ollins
10 Regents Wharf, All Sanits Street
London N1 9 RL, United Kingdom
Tel.: + 44 207 713 7733
Fax: + 44 207 713 0217
www.wolff-olins.com
Affinity Offices